Measured Constructs

A history of Cambridge English language examinations 1913–2012

For a complete list of titles please visit: http://www.cambridge.org/elt/silt

Also in this series:

Measured Constructs

A history of Cambridge English language examinations 1913–2012

Nescire autem quid antequam natus sis acciderit, id est semper esse puerum.
Marcus Tullius Cicero, De Oratore (XXXIV)

Cyril J Weir
Powdrill Professor in English Language Acquisition, University of Bedfordshire
Director, Centre for Research in English Language Learning and Assessment
(CRELLA)

Ivana Vidaković
Senior Research and Validation Manager, Cambridge English Language
Assessment

and

Evelina D Galaczi
Principal Research and Validation Manager, Cambridge English Language
Assessment

CAMBRIDGE UNIVERSITY PRESS
Cambridge, New York, Melbourne, Madrid, Cape Town,
Singapore, São Paulo, Delhi, Mexico City

Cambridge University Press
The Edinburgh Building, Cambridge CB2 8RU, UK

www.cambridge.org
Information on this title: www.cambridge.org/9781107677692

© UCLES 2013

First published 2013

Printed and bound in the United Kingdom by the MPG Books Group

A catalogue record for this publication is available from the British Library

Library of Congress Cataloging-in-Publication Data

Weir, Cyril J.
   Measured constructs : a History of Cambridge English Language
Examinations 1913–2012 / Cyril J Weir, Powdrill Professor in English
Language Acquisition, University of Bedfordshire, Director, Centre for
Research in English Language Learning and Assessment (CRELLA);
Ivana Vidaković, Senior Research and Validation Manager, University
of Cambridge ESOL Examinations, and Evelina Galaczi, Principal Research
and Validation Manager, University of Cambridge ESOL Examinations.
      pages cm. -- (Studies in Language Testing ; 37)
   Includes bibliographical references and index.
   ISBN 978-1-107-67769-2
   1. Language and languages--Ability testing. 2. Language and languages--
Examinations. 3. University of Cambridge. ESOL Examinations. I. Title.

   P53.4.W54 2013
   428.0076--dc23
2012046200

ISBN 978-1-107-67769-2

In memoriam
Gladys May Weir 1927–2009
and
Cyril Weir 1919–2010

Contents

Abbreviations

ACT	American College Test
ACTFL	American Council on the Teaching of Foreign Languages
AERA	American Educational Research Association
ALTE	Association of Language Testers in Europe
ANOVA	Analysis of Variance
APA	American Psychological Association
ARELS	Association of Recognised English Language Schools
ASTP	Army Specialised Training Programme
AWL	Academic Word List
BEC	Business English Certificate
BNC	British National Corpus
BULATS	Business Language Testing Service
CAE	Certificate in Advanced English (Cambridge English: Advanced)
CASE	Cambridge Assessment of Spoken English
CBT	Computer-Based Testing
CCSE	Certificates in Communicative Skills in English
CEF	Common European Framework
CEFR	Common European Framework of Reference for Languages
CEIC	Certificate in English for International Communication
CELS	Certificates in English Language Skills
CET	College English Test
CFA	Confirmatory Factor Analysis
CIS	Candidate Information Sheet
CLA	Communicative Language Ability
CLB	Canadian Language Benchmarks
CLT	Communicative Language Teaching
CoE	Council of Europe
C.O.L.E	Colgate University Oral Languages Examination
CPE	Certificate of Proficiency in English (Cambridge English: Proficiency)
CRELLA	Centre for Research in English Language Learning and Assessment
CRTEC	Centre for Research in Testing Evaluation and Curriculum

CSE	Certificate in Secondary Education
CT	Correlated-trait model
CUEFL	Communicative Use of English as a Foreign Language
DIF	Differential Item Functioning
EAL	English as an Additional Language
EAP	English for Academic Purposes
EFA	Exploratory Factor Analysis
EFL	English as a Foreign Language
ELBA	English Language Battery
ELT	English Language Teaching
ELTS	English Language Testing Service
EPS	Examination Processing System
EPTB	English Proficiency Test Battery
ERIC	Education Resources Information Centre
ESM	Electronic Script Management
ESOL	English for Speakers of Other Languages
ESP	English for Specific Purposes
ETS	Educational Testing Service
FCE	First Certificate in English (Cambridge English: First)
FSI	Foreign Service Institute (USA)
GCE	General Certificate of Education
GCSE	General Certificate of Secondary Education
GEPT	General English Proficiency Test
GF	Gap-Filling
GLP	General Language Proficiency
GMC PLAB	General Medical Council's Professional and Linguistic Assessments Board
GPC	Grapheme-phoneme correspondence
iBT TOEFL	Internet Based Test of English as a Foreign Language
ICFE	International Certificate in Financial English
IDis	Item difficulty and discrimination
IELTS	International English Language Testing System
IF	Item Facility
IIS	IELTS Impact Study
ILEC	International Legal English Certificate
ILR	Inter-Agency Language Round Table (USA)
ILTA	International Language Testing Association
IP	Interactive Performance
IPA	International Phonetics Association
IQ	Intelligence Quotient
IRT	Item Response Theory
IW	Item Writer
JMB	Northern Universities Joint Matriculation Board

KET	Key English Test (Cambridge English: Key)
KR-20	Kuder-Richardson 20
L1	First Language
L2	Second Language
LCE	Lower Certificate in English
LIBS	Local Item Banking System
LMS	Lower Main Suite
LT	Language Teaching
LTRC	Language Testing Research Colloquium
LTTC	Language Training and Testing Centre
MC	Multiple Choice
MCQ	Multiple Choice Questions
MFR	Multi-faceted Rasch Analysis
Michigan ECPE	Michigan Examination for the Certificate of Proficiency in English
MLA	Modern Language Association
MLAT	Modern Language Aptitude Test
MM	Multiple Matching
MMMT	Multi-method Multi-trait
MQC	Marking-Quality Controller
NEAB	Northern Examinations and Assessment Board
OE	Oral Examiner
OMR	Optical Mark Reader
OPI	Oral Proficiency Interview
PET	Preliminary English Test (Cambridge English: Preliminary)
PLAB	Pimsleur Language Aptitude Battery
PTE	Preliminary Test in English
QCA	Qualifications and Curriculum Authority
QMS	Quality Management System
QPP	Question Paper Production
RAF	Royal Air Force
RITCME	Recruitment, Induction, Training, Coordination, Monitoring, Evaluation
RL	Real Life
RM	Reform Movement
RSA	Royal Society of Arts
SAQ	Short Answer Questions
SAT	Scholastic Aptitude Test
SD	Standard Deviation
SE	Standard Error
SEM	Standard Error of Measurement
SeqM	Structural Equation Modelling

SiLT	Studies in Language Testing
SLA	Second Language Acquisition
SOPI	Simulated Oral Proficiency Interview
SPEAK	Institutional version of TSE
TEAP	Test in English for Academic Purposes
TEEP	Test in English for Educational Purposes
TEFL	Teaching English as a Foreign Language
TEM	Test for English Majors
TESOL	Teaching English to Speakers of Other Languages
TL	Team Leader
TOEFL	Test of English as a Foreign Language
TOEIC	Test of English for International Communication
TSE	Test of Spoken English
TWE	Test of Written English
TTR	Type Token Ratio
UCL	University College London
UCLES	University of Cambridge Local Examinations Syndicate
UETESOL	University Entrance Test in English for Speakers of Other Languages
UK	United Kingdom
UMS	Upper Main Suite
UODLE	University of Oxford Delegacy of Local Examinations
UoE	Use of English
US	United States
VP	Vocabulary Profiler
VRIP	Validity, Reliability, Impact, Practicality

Acknowledgements

This diachronic account of the constructs being measured by Cambridge English examinations 1913–2012 follows a series of academic volumes published at two-yearly intervals since 2007 which focused on the testing of the four main language skills from a synchronic perspective: *Examining Writing, Examining Reading, Examining Speaking* and *Examining Listening*.

There exists a long list of friends and colleagues to whom we are indebted for their contribution in bringing this volume to publication. Special thanks must go to Tony Howatt (University of Edinburgh), Richard Smith (University of Warwick) who reviewed Chapter 1, Bill Grabe (Northern Arizona University) who commented on Chapter 2, Liz Hamp-Lyons (CRELLA University of Bedfordshire) for examining Chapter 3, Glenn Fulcher (University of Leicester) for reviewing Chapter 4, Dr John Field (CRELLA, University of Bedfordshire) who reviewed Chapter 5 and also commented on several versions of Chapter 1, and Professor Barry O'Sullivan (British Council) who provided comments on Chapter 6. Bernard Spolsky (Professor emeritus, Bar-Ilan University) served as external reviewer once the complete manuscript had been assembled. The insightful comments and constructive criticism of all these reviewers enabled us to revise and refine the manuscript at various points before it went into production. Thus their expertise, sound advice and collaboration have contributed significantly to the quality of this volume.

Gillian Cooke, Group Archivist in the Cambridge Assessment Archives Service, and her colleagues deserve a special vote of thanks. Their helpfulness, patience and diligence in securing access to appropriate materials in the archives were invaluable for the successful completion of this volume. The copious references in the book relating to materials from the archives is testimony to their endeavour.

We are extremely grateful to a large number of other people from both academic and practitioner communities within and beyond ESOL who also provided valuable input to or feedback on the individual chapters. Lynda Taylor (CRELLA, University of Bedfordshire and consultant to Cambridge ESOL) carefully reviewed all the draft chapters offering, as ever, valuable constructive criticism. Her guidance and advisory feedback have been invaluable and a source of constant encouragement. Fumiyo Nakatsuhara (CRELLA, University of Bedfordshire) reviewed Chapters 4 and 5 of the manuscript, and helped gather together much of the secondary materials we have drawn on. Shigeko Weir and Sathena Chan were a great help in tracking down information electronically and in compiling the rather extensive set of references. John Savage copyedited the manuscript. We also acknowledge the support and encouragement of Dr Nick Saville (Director of the Research and Validation Group, Cambridge ESOL) who has been involved with the volume throughout its development. Finally, we would like to acknowledge Dr Michael Milanovic (Cambridge ESOL Chief Executive and Series Editor for *Studies in Language Testing*) whose vision made the publication of this and of the other construct-focused volumes in the SiLT series a reality.

To all of the above and to any others we have failed to mention, we extend our sincere thanks and appreciation.

Cyril J Weir
Ivana Vidaković
Evelina D Galaczi

Series Editors' note

Measured Constructs provides an engaging and comprehensive account of the evolution over the last century of the Cambridge English exams and their underlying constructs. It does so in the context of the significant, theoretical, and practical advances in pedagogy and socio-political developments which have shaped language testing in the last 100 years. The authors take us back to the 19th century as they document developments in language teaching and testing, which provide the backdrop for the emergence in 1913 of the first Cambridge English exam, the Certificate of Proficiency in English (CPE). The CPE at the time was a hybrid of legacies in language teaching from the previous century and was taken by 3 candidates. The volume traces its development alongside the introduction of other exams to the present day, when the tests are taken by hundreds of thousands of candidates and are based on a theoretical construct of communicative language ability, influenced by a number of earlier models which include Bachman's (1990) Communicative Language Ability, Canale and Swain's (1980) and Canale's (1983) Communicative Competence, and conceptualisations of Interactional Competence, as seen in the work of Kramsch (1986) and McNamara (1997).

The authors also document the change in the exams from highly integrated and unspecified constructs to modern-day conceptualisations of constructs based on the interactions between a targeted cognitive ability and a highly specified context of use. The volume takes the reader through the emergence of a system targeting distinct proficiency levels documenting the evolution from the 1913 CPE exam, which started as a loosely specified proficiency level to the current Cambridge exams, whose multi-level system includes explicit and appropriate proficiency-level definitions and is closely aligned with the *Common European Framework of Reference for Teaching, Learning and Assessment* (CEFR), published by the Council of Europe in 2001. The authors base their analysis and description of the tests on Weir's (2005a) socio-cognitive framework, which provides a useful lens for the description and discussion of the exams with its explicit focus on constructs as comprising both aspects of cognition, related to the mental processes the individual needs to engage in order to address a task, and features of language use in context that affect the way in which the task is addressed.

An examination board does not exist in a vacuum. It is part of a network of stakeholders and partners, who both influence and are influenced by the evolution of the exams. This volume is as much about the development of the Cambridge exams as it is about the people and organisations behind them. Key among those individuals is Jack Roach, Assistant Secretary at the University of Cambridge Local Examinations Syndicate (UCLES) from 1925 to 1945, who was an influential figure in the early history of the Cambridge English examinations. Fortunately, Roach left a wealth of papers and other documents he had written at his time at Cambridge which provide invaluable insights into central themes in the first half of the 20th century. The volume also highlights the important alliance between UCLES and the British Council. The British Council/UCLES alliance is brought to life, documented and discussed in the book, alongside the role of the British Council-UCLES Joint Committee, a powerful committee which existed between 1941 and 1993. The volume also sheds light on the professionalisation of UCLES, as seen in the appointment of language testing specialists from the 1970s onwards and the influence of Peter Hargreaves, who joined UCLES in 1989, and was followed by Neil Jones, Mike Milanovic, Nick Saville and Lynda Taylor. These individuals were instrumental in establishing the EFL Evaluation Unit (now the Cambridge ESOL Research and Validation Group).

In addition to the people and organisations that have been influential in the development of the Cambridge exams, the authors also focus on important milestones which have made a mark in Cambridge history. Key among them is the Cambridge-TOEFL Comparability Study commissioned in 1987 and conducted by Professor Lyle Bachman and his team at the University of California Los Angeles (UCLA). At its simplest level, this study sought to establish proficiency level relationships between the Cambridge First Certificate in English exam and the Test of English as a Foreign Language produced by Educational Testing Services (ETS). This comparative study revealed a wealth of information about the approaches to language testing prevalent at ETS and Cambridge in the 1980s and before, and was instrumental in initiating some changes at Cambridge (for more information, see SiLT 1 *An Investigation into the Comparability of Two Tests of English as a Foreign Language* by Bachman, Davidson, Ryan and Choi (1995)).

The historical account in this volume also offers food for thought in terms of theoretical concepts. As the authors discuss the evolution of the Cambridge exams, they trace the intricate relationship between teaching practice and testing and their effect on one another. Their discussion raises the interesting question of washback and its two-way influence, with testing affecting teaching, but teaching theory and practice also making their mark on testing. This is especially strongly seen in the United Kingdom, where the relationship between teaching and testing historically has been a strong one.

This volume joins a number of volumes in the SiLT series which have taken a historical angle and have documented the diachronic development of a range of Cambridge English exams. The first among them was SiLT 15

Continuity and Innovation: Revising the Cambridge Proficiency in English Examination 1913–2002 by Professor Cyril Weir and myself (published in 2003). I have always been struck by the ephemeral nature of many aspects of language testing, in particular that when a test ceases to operate or goes through a major revision, the reasoning supporting these changes frequently disappears from all but the memory of a few of the people who worked on it, and then finally altogether. I was keen that this should not be the case and began the process of documenting the Cambridge history with SiLT 15. Other volumes have continued this historical exploration and documentation. Among them are SiLT 17 *Issues in Testing Business English: The revision of the Cambridge Business English certificates* by Barry O'Sullivan (published in 2006), which traced the development of exams for the business context, SiLT 23 *Assessing Academic English: Testing English Proficiency 1950–1989 – the IELTS solution* by Alan Davies (published in 2008), which focused on the evolution of the IELTS exam and SiLT 28 *Examining FCE and CAE: Key Issues and Recurring Themes in Developing the First Certificate in English and Certificate in Advanced English Exams* by Roger Hawkey (published in 2009). All these volumes situate the Cambridge approach in a historical context and examine the development of the exams as influenced by theoretical and socio-economic influences.

Measured Constructs completes a set of 'constructs' volumes, which have provided comprehensive discussions and descriptions of the state-of-the-art of the Cambridge English exams. Four SiLT volumes address the assessment of writing, reading, speaking and listening at Cambridge (*Examining Writing* by Shaw and Weir (2007), *Examining Reading* by Khalifa and Weir (2009), *Examining Speaking*, edited by Taylor (2011) and *Examining Listening*, edited by Geranpayeh and Taylor (2013)). These volumes define the Cambridge approach to the assessment of language skills. Their synchronic here-and-now focus is complemented by the diachronic approach of this volume. As a set these five volumes provide a comprehensive and in-depth contribution to the language testing field.

This volume takes the reader from an introductory chapter which sets the scene and provides a detailed and comprehensive account and discussion of the historical development of English language testing in the United Kingdom. Where relevant those developments are compared and contrasted with developments in language assessment theory and practice in the United States. Four chapters follow, each focussing on one of the four skills: reading, writing, speaking and listening. The authors chronicle the operationalisation of the reading, writing, listening and speaking constructs at Cambridge at various points in the last century. The relevant examinations are situated in a broad social, educational and political context and exam-external developments are clearly and carefully traced as they have shaped the measurement of the constructs underlying the four skills. At all times the evolution of the exams is illustrated with past exam papers and archive materials. The authors' careful study of the Cambridge ESOL archives helps the reader understand the thinking that supported the introduction of the Cambridge English exams and their subsequent development. The Conclusion provides a synthesis of the main themes from the volume and also provides a useful look to the future.

The volume has traced the first 100 years of Cambridge English exams, but the development of those exams does not end here. Test evolution is a cyclical and iterative process, rather like a spiral where each subsequent stage is at a higher level from the one below both in terms of theory and practice. In this volume the authors have reflected changing times, conditions and expectations and have managed to capture not only where the Cambridge exams have come from, where they are, but also where we can expect them to go in the future years. That future will most likely be affected by the greater advances of technology. Technology has already made its mark in language testing and is set to play an even more significant role in various aspects of the exams, including the way they are delivered and scored, the way organisations are able to interact with their stakeholders, the various aspects of the administration of the examination, quality assurance issues, examiner training and monitoring. Crucially, technology is also making its mark on the definition and operationalisation of the constructs of computer-based exams. The chapter discussing the evolution of the speaking construct makes this point especially salient, as it shows that the changes in construct coverage are quite significant in oral computer-based tests.

The future of the Cambridge exams will also likely be affected by the changing role of English and its role as world lingua franca and by the advances in mobility which have allowed people to move freely about the world. A further influence on the future of the exams will come from research endeavours and findings. One such potential influence will be the English Profile Programme, a long-term collaborative programme of inter-disciplinary research, which is designed to enhance the learning, teaching and assessment of English worldwide. The English Profile Programme has the potential to provide uniquely detailed and objective analysis of what levels of achievement in language learning actually mean in terms of the grammar, vocabulary and discourse features that learners can be expected to have mastered at each level. Such comprehensive empirical findings will surely make their mark on future exams.

Measured Constructs is a rich source of information on the educational, linguistic and socio-economic factors which have shaped the development of EFL tests over the last century. This volume represents a comprehensive endeavour on the part of the organisation and the SiLT series editors to ensure that the development of the English language examinations at Cambridge are not only fully documented, but also explained and contextualised within theory and practice at the time. I hope that it will be of considerable interest to both researchers and practitioners in the field of language assessment.

Michael Milanovic
Cambridge
November 2012

1 An overview of the influences on English language testing in the United Kingdom 1913–2012

Cyril J Weir
University of Bedfordshire

> . . . who will write the more general, more fluid, but also more determinant history of the 'examination' – its rituals, its methods, its characters and their roles, its play of questions and answers, its systems of marking and classification? For in this slender technique are to be found a whole domain of knowledge, a whole type of power.
> *Discipline and Punish: The Birth of the Prison* (Foucault 1979: 185)

Introduction

In recent years assessment issues have assumed an increased importance in the economic, educational and socio-political affairs of society. Spolsky (2008a: 297) argues that by the 21st century 'testing has become big business', and Shohamy (2008:xiv) points to 'the societal role that language tests perform, the power that they hold, and their central functions in education, politics and society'. A significant role for testing language proficiency can be seen *inter alia* in migration and citizenship policy and practice, the professional registration of those involved in the provision of health care, appointment and promotion in business, industry and commerce, the certification of air traffic and maritime personnel, and entry to tertiary level education. Such uses testify to the critical gatekeeping function that language assessment fulfils in contemporary society.

As the power of tests and the potential for their misuse/abuse grows, assessment literacy in our society seems more important than ever. Taylor (2009:29) argues that narrative accounts which chronicle testing developments over time may have an important role to play in fostering this:

> They contextualize the practice of language testing as a socially constructed and interpreted phenomenon, rather than treating it primarily as a pseudoscientific endeavour that is removed and isolated from human individuals and social values. It may well be that popular adaptations of this narrative, storytelling approach will prove a more effective means of developing assessment literacy among the wider stakeholder community in the future.

Despite the importance of language assessment in the United Kingdom, we still lack a satisfactory account of its historical development in this country. In *A History of English Language Teaching*, Howatt and Widdowson (2004:332) acknowledged that they had not given English language testing 'the prominence it deserves'. Spolsky's (1995a) authoritative work on language testing, *Measured Words*, for the most part covered the development of English language testing in the United States with only partial reference to events on this side of the Atlantic. In this volume we seek to make good this discrepancy by adopting a mainly British perspective which focuses on Cambridge English language examinations over the course of the last century. This takes us from a small cottage industry in 1913, with the Certificate of Proficiency in English (CPE) administered to three students in one London centre, to the big business of a leading international examining board in 2012. Cambridge now offers multiple English language examinations at different levels, across different domains, to over 4 million candidates per annum, in 2,700 authorised centres across 130 countries.

In delimiting our study to Cambridge English language examinations we are mindful of the advice of Stern (1983:83) that: 'by selecting a restricted field historians have a better chance of discovering and analyzing a manageable body of data'. Accordingly the centre of attention in our survey 1913–2012 is on English language testing developments in one examining board in the United Kingdom. This will enable us in Stern's terms to examine English language testing more rigorously, both synchronically at a given stage in history in a social and educational context, and diachronically over a 100-year period.

We will for the most part further limit our study to those general English examinations for non-native speakers developed in Cambridge from 1913–2012. We will concentrate on the Certificate of Proficiency in English (CPE) 1913–2012 and the Lower Certificate in English (LCE) 1939–1975, rebranded as the First Certificate in English (FCE) 1975–2012. The history of these particular examinations offers us an accessible and manageable perspective and critically it enables us to make comparisons in relation to the same examinations over an extended period of time. Such a focus will enable us to trace *continuity* and *innovation* in the measurement of language constructs in one examination board over an entire century.

Initially these were known as English as a Foreign Language (EFL) examinations but more recently as examinations in English for Speakers of Other Languages (ESOL). For ease of reference, especially when talking about them collectively, we will use the generic term Cambridge English examinations throughout. The body responsible for running the English language examinations was initially the University of Cambridge Local Examinations Syndicate (UCLES), then UCLES EFL and more recently Cambridge ESOL. We will maintain these distinctions when referring specifically to the examination board itself.

At various points in our history we will compare what was happening in the United Kingdom with developments in the United States, the two world leaders in the field of language testing in the last century as in this. Although English Language testing is now similarly informed by most aspects of construct validity in both countries, this was not always the case and the path testing was to take differed markedly in each. The reasons behind these contrasting journeys can be found in the prevailing, socio-economic contexts in the two countries, but the differing approach in the United Kingdom also reflects European legacies from the past in both theoretical and practical approaches to language teaching and assessment. A comparison of the two traditions in the United States and United Kingdom is informative and helps us understand some of the differing, if less clear-cut, emphases that are still present in approaches to theory and practice in language assessment in these two countries.

Our historical approach signifies the importance of establishing a 'big picture' to serve as a holistic frame of reference into which present phenomena can be fitted. For the language testing community to fully understand its present practice, we feel it needs to appreciate how its past has been shaped.

We first establish the main themes of our study viz *language constructs*, and the impact of *external forces* and *language teaching practice* on how these constructs were measured in Cambridge English examinations over the period 1913–2012.

Language constructs

Alan Davies (1984:68) wrote in the first issue of the journal *Language Testing*:

> . . .in the end no empirical study can improve a test's validity. . . What is most important is the preliminary thinking and the preliminary analysis as to the nature of the language learning we aim to capture.

The construct(s) Cambridge sought to measure in English language test tasks are the focal point of our story. From a 21st century testing perspective, we consider a construct as not just the underlying, latent trait of a particular ability measured by a test task but a combination of the trait, the context in which the task is performed and the criteria used for scoring performance on that task, together with the interpretation of the resulting scores. This approach is effectively an *interactionalist* position, which sees the construct as residing in the interactions between an underlying cognitive ability, a context of use and a process of scoring. Cambridge ESOL's current approach to construct validation might thus be labelled *socio-cognitive* in that the abilities to be tested are demonstrated by the cognitive processing of the candidate; equally, the use of language in performing tasks is viewed as a social rather than a purely linguistic phenomenon.

The socio-cognitive framework utilised to describe the measurement of constructs in this volume builds on Weir (2005a) and represents a unified approach to establishing the overall validity of a test (see also Field 2013). It addresses the three central aspects of construct validity:

1. *Cognitive validity*. Do the cognitive processes required to complete test tasks sufficiently resemble the cognitive processes a candidate would normally employ in non-test conditions, i.e. are they *construct relevant* (Messick 1989)? Are the range of processes elicited by test items sufficiently comprehensive to be considered representative of real-world behaviour i.e., not just a small subset of those which might then give rise to fears about construct *under-representation*? Are the processes appropriately calibrated to the level of proficiency of the learner being evaluated?

2. *Context validity*. Are the characteristics of the test task an adequate and comprehensive representation of those that would be normally encountered in the real life context? Are they appropriately calibrated to the level of proficiency of the learner being evaluated?

3. *Scoring validity*. How appropriate and comprehensive are the criteria employed in evaluating test output? How well calibrated are they to the level of proficiency of the learner being evaluated? Also included here is the traditional concern with *reliability*: how far can we depend on the scores which result from applying these criteria to test output?

Scoring validity is used as the superordinate term here in preference to the traditional term reliability as it embraces more than just the statistical consistency of the scores themselves. In particular, the *criteria* used in the assessment of test output are seen as a critical and integral part of the construct being measured. The term scoring validity emphasises its part in a unified conception of validity as compared to the narrower term reliability, the frequent use of which in conjunction with the term validity (as in 'validity and reliability') risks conveying the idea of separateness.

Language test constructs were never as explicitly or comprehensively specified in the early tests of the 'pre-scientific period' (Spolsky 1978), the 'Garden of Eden' as it was termed by Morrow (1979), when the University of Cambridge Local Examinations Syndicate (UCLES) examinations started back in 1913. As Taylor (2011a: 21) points out: 'We cannot be definitive about what was in the minds of the original CPE test developers and it is probably unlikely that the test developers of a century ago worked with the terms and definitions that are familiar to language testers today.'

While language examinations under UCLES, UCLES EFL and later Cambridge ESOL must have been intended to measure a trait or 'construct' (Saville 2003), for much of the period under review we have no direct evidence as to what test developers thought the underlying language construct(s) they intended to measure were. In the first half of our history, there is little documented evidence available on the underlying basis for test construction, no suggestion of systematic post hoc analysis of test outcomes, nor any evident concern with the use made of test results in society. The language constructs underlying examinations in these early days have to be interpreted largely from the test papers themselves and what little supporting documentation is still available. Examination revisions in recent times are better documented, as Hawkey (2005, 2009), and Weir and Milanovic (2003) bear testimony to. The early period thus presents a greater challenge for the historian as it requires more interpretation as to what the test developers intended to test than is necessary for recent practice.

An explicit definition of test construct in Cambridge ESOL is in fact a relatively recent phenomenon. The influence of the *Cambridge-TOEFL Comparability Study* in the late 1980s (see Bachman, Davidson, Ryan and Choi 1995) was a catalyst for this, with its promotion of a broad construct of communicative language ability, first proposed by Canale and Swain (1980) in their seminal paper *Theoretical bases of communicative approaches to second language teaching and testing* and later more fully specified by Bachman (1990) and Bachman and Palmer (1996).

Socio-economic factors such as the move towards European standardisation, occasioned by the growth of the European Community from the 1970s onwards, required a more explicit, transparent specification of linguistic performance at differing levels of ability from beginner to advanced, and together with the Comparability Study served to encourage greater attention to test constructs and construct validation at Cambridge ESOL.

A noticeable exception to this general lack of attention to construct was a concern with rater reliability (an important element of scoring validity) which taxed examination providers much earlier in our history than either context or cognitive validity. The issue of reliability was aired at an early stage by Edgeworth (1888), Burt (1921) and Hartog, Rhodes, and Burt (1936) in the United Kingdom, and by Thorndike (1904, 1911 and 1912) and Wood (1927) amongst others in the United States. The reliability aspect of scoring validity was to be the dominant validity paradigm for testing in the United States, but it was not to be of particular concern to those testing English language at Cambridge for most of the 20th century, until the establishment of a professional English language testing cadre there from 1988 onwards.

With an increased public expectation of transparent and explicit test specification in the late 20th century, a broader conceptualisation of construct validity (i.e. qualitative as well as quantitative) was seen as necessary. The current demand from stakeholders in high-stakes examinations, for example learners, employers, receiving institutions, professional bodies (see Khalifa and Weir 2009:177 for a full listing of all potential test stakeholders), is for transparent, comprehensive, evidence-based answers to questions on the language construct(s) being measured in the tests they use. Test providers need to satisfy stakeholders' expectations concerning the comparability of the constructs measured by each test version in terms of both cognitive and contextual, as well as scoring validity (Weir and Wu 2006).

The publication of four 'constructs' volumes in the *Studies in Language Testing* (SiLT) series in the early 21st century, almost 100 years after the first CPE examination, was one response to this modern day imperative for comprehensive specification and transparency (see Shaw and Weir 2007, Khalifa and Weir 2009, Taylor (Ed.) 2011 and Geranpayeh and Taylor (Eds) 2013). These volumes, building on the earlier work of Weir (2005a), further developed and elaborated socio-cognitive frameworks for specifying the various elements of construct validity in each of the broad skills areas of writing, reading, speaking and listening and then applied the parameters within these frameworks to an analysis of current Cambridge English examinations.

In Chapters 2–5 of this volume we first provide a general overview of how new ideas in teaching, applied linguistics and testing, as well as external societal forces, acted as drivers for change in the way each construct (reading, writing, speaking and listening) was conceived and measured at various points in the last century. We then look more closely at any surviving evidence from the Cambridge archives relating to the measurement of these constructs in its English language examinations and describe in greater detail how approaches changed along the way from 1913–2012. To analyse accurately and precisely the nature of these specific changes in Cambridge's approach we needed a conceptual framework to help us understand how each construct was viewed at a given point in time.

The socio-cognitive frameworks in the four 'constructs' volumes offer a useful heuristic for analysing the key features of the constructs underlying test tasks (Weir and O'Sullivan 2011). They enable us to draw on workable categories of description for informing our understanding of the changing nature of the constructs being measured by Cambridge tests during the 100 years under review in this volume. These 21st century frameworks will not be used to critique and criticise tests developed in earlier times, rather, their function is to provide a useful lens through which features of specific tests – present or past – can be discussed. Additionally they will serve as consistent frames of reference for tracking and discussing the changes to constructs in these tests over time. We are not intent on privileging one test format over another but on establishing the ways in which the measurement of a particular construct changed as test formats came into and went out of fashion.

As well as analysing the nature of the constructs being measured at various stages, we also need to consider the effects upon test design of the wider social context and of shifts in pedagogical practice, if we are to understand fully why any specific changes came about.

The impact of external forces on language testing

Spolsky (1990a:159) rightly reminds us of the important connection of developments in testing with:

> . . .external, non theoretical, institutional social forces, that on deeper analysis, often turn out to be a much more powerful explanation of actual practice. . . A clearer view of the history of the field will emerge once we are willing to look carefully at not just the ideas that underlie it, but also the institutional, social and economic situations in which they are realized.

Individuals and ideas certainly have an impact on test development as we will see but so too do institutions, government national and regional, and social and economic forces. As far as possible in this volume, we will try to locate English Language Teaching and associated testing developments in their wider social and economic contexts. By doing so, we hope to identify the influence of both the prevailing socio-economic conditions as well as the human ideas, experiences and practices that influenced both testing at Cambridge and teaching in the United Kingdom in the period under review 1913–2012.

For example, we will examine how English developed into a global language after World War Two (Brutt-Griffler 2002, Crystal 1997 and Graddol 1997, 2006). This was to promote a shift in focus in examining English at Cambridge away from a number of earlier tasks which had a distinctly academic stance and treated English principally as an object of study (e.g. translation, literature and grammar), to tasks which reflected a social view of English as a means of international communication.

This globalisation of English was not universally acclaimed and a number of writers saw it as a result of ulterior economic and political motives on the part of government, and expressed reservations concerning the limited cultural, political or social awareness in the way it was reported (see Pennycook 1994:Chapter 5, Phillipson 1992:Chapter 8). Whilst sometimes one-sided, these views nevertheless encourage us to think carefully about our tendency to attribute causality solely to individuals and ideas in developments in language testing and teaching.

It is clear that the British Council and Cambridge shared a mutual interest in propagating the English language. By virtue of its global mission in spreading English language and culture around the world, the British Council was able to acquire considerable knowledge and expertise in teaching English as a Foreign Language and for over 50 years (1941–1993), it would be an informed partner in the development of Cambridge English language tests and their availability overseas. The brief of the *Joint Committee of the British Council and Cambridge Local Examinations Syndicate*, established in 1941, was *inter alia* to collaborate in the actual development and conduct of UCLES EFL exams, make decisions on policy and regulations, prepare examination syllabuses and the general plan of the examination, and cooperate in publicity and finance. The knowledge, professional expertise in English language pedagogy, and the standing of the high ranking academics who served as British Council representatives on the Joint Committee would make a significant contribution to the development of Cambridge English examinations. The Joint Committee would continue until 1993 and was testimony to a close and mutually beneficial working relationship between the British Council and Cambridge in promoting the spread of English and Cambridge English examinations abroad. We will make reference to the influence and work of the powerful Joint Committee throughout this volume.

As we noted earlier progress towards a European Economic Community from the 1970s onwards, with its focus on standardisation across national boundaries, was accompanied by a felt need on the part of governmental agencies to define language teaching and learning goals more precisely at *different levels of proficiency*. This was also to have a marked effect on the work of examination boards in the United Kingdom not least in the way they had to conceptualise language constructs in a more granular fashion, in order to accommodate multilevel tests, than was necessary for tests in the United States which for the most part targeted examinations at a particular level of proficiency.

The influence of language teaching on language testing

A second critical influence on the development of Cambridge English language examinations was the teaching that took place in the English as a Foreign Language classroom and in each chapter we investigate the connection between prevailing approaches to testing and contemporaneous pedagogical practice.

Saville (2009) observes that a close relationship between assessment and the content of learning was an important consideration when UCLES started to administer English language examinations for actual or intending teachers of English in 1913. It was felt that assessment should be relevant to their teaching/learning contexts as well as addressing societal demands for accountability, including maintenance of standards of achievement and impartiality. The assumption that public examinations can help define a teaching syllabus and help to determine learning objectives was to remain a foundational principle in the subsequent development and revision of the Cambridge English examinations right up to the present day.

As far back as the 1920s Jack Roach (Assistant Secretary 1925–45), an influential figure in the early history of Cambridge English examinations, was arguing (against others in UCLES it must be said) for the involvement of teachers in informing the design and development of Cambridge examinations. Roach felt that the voting power of teachers was negligible and that, as experts in educational needs, teachers should have more influence:

> In the Examining Body of the future the teachers must have a permanent pride of place. . . but the net must be flung wider yet to include professional bodies (who can speak for the country's professional needs), the man in the street, the parents. . . (Roach 1929 'Memorandum of Reform', JOR 1/1d ii).

During his European visits in the late 1930s, as well as gathering political information to be passed on to the French and British governments, Roach promoted CPE and the teaching of English, and he discussed issues in relation to CPE with teachers in UCLES centres on the continent. In this way, he initiated the idea of co-operation with teachers on English language examinations that would continue over the decades (see Hawkey and Milanovic 2013 for comprehensive detail of these relationships). The years that followed saw many further developments in the relations between UCLES and teachers. For example, the minutes of the 1947 meeting of the main committee for the management of Cambridge English Examinations, the *Joint Committee of the British Council and Cambridge Local Examinations Syndicate*, reported that suggestions for modifications of the CPE syllabus would be discussed at a conference with teachers (the annual British Council-Cambridge conference held in London in the post-war years); the representatives of the Syndicate who visited centres in Holland, Belgium and France in 1952 to discuss question papers and syllabuses with teachers reported that 'much useful knowledge was exchanged and some proposals were made for the modification of syllabuses' (Joint Committee Minutes May 1952). In 1971, visits to centres abroad (in most cases individual overseas schools) were seen as valuable by the Syndicate's officers because of 'the opportunities they gave for meetings with teachers. . .' (Joint Committee Minutes July 1971). The minutes of the Joint Committee indicate that they took these opinions seriously. This concern for the voices of a wide range of stakeholders to be heard would be a permanent feature of Cambridge English test innovation and change as can be seen in the accounts of the major developments reported below and in the following chapters.

The impact of developments in approaches to language teaching upon testing at Cambridge will be a major theme in our 100-year survey. We will examine the salient conceptualisations of language constructs with reference to the development of language pedagogy in the United Kingdom over the period 1913 to 2012 and compare these with the prevailing methods employed in English language testing by Cambridge over the same period. Changing priorities in the methods and content of language teaching obtaining at various stages over this period in the United Kingdom included: the Grammar-Translation or Traditional Method, well established in 1913 as the system of Modern Foreign Language education in schools based upon the method used for the teaching of classical languages (with origins in the work of Fick 1793); the direct method promoted in continental Europe for the formal education system, not necessarily involving exclusive use of the target language (Passy 1899); the oral method, Harold Palmer's attempt to systematise direct method teaching procedures and align them with emerging ideas on structural and lexical progression (Palmer 1921a, 1921b); improved reading materials with graded texts (West 1926a, 1926b); standard wordlists for pedagogical purposes (Faucett, Palmer, Thorndike and West 1936, West 1953); the audio-lingual method (Brooks 1960, Fries 1945); the situational approach (Billows 1961, Hornby 1950); and finally the communicative approach (Brumfit and Johnson 1979, Candlin 1986, Morrow 1977, Wilkins 1976, Widdowson 1978) with its focus on the needs of learners to use language for real-life communication accompanied by a sub-skills approach to teaching the four macro skills (Munby 1978).

The consequential aspect of language testing

The area of test impact will not loom large in our history as it only really came into prominence in the 21st century. Prior to the late 20th century there is little evidence of any attention being paid in Cambridge to the macro issues of social impact and test use, the consequential aspects of test validity. Nor to be fair, is there much evidence of any such concern in the wider testing community prior to Messick's (1989) seminal publication on validity. It was not until the 1990s that it came onto the radar of most language testers (Alderson and Wall 1996, Bachman and Palmer 1996, Shohamy 2001, Wall 1997, Wall and Alderson 1993). Milanovic and Saville (1996) appears to be the earliest attempt at Cambridge to address the wider impact issues of Cambridge English examinations. There was, however, an interest in the washback on teaching and learning of its English language tests (impact but at the micro level) from the very beginning in 1913 (see Green 2007).

Spolsky (2004:305) describes how:

> from its beginning UCLES accepted the key role to be played in test development by the 'stakeholders', in particular those schools in various countries of the world that wished to establish examination centres, mainly for their own students. From the earliest years, the Cambridge test writers and their various committees saw themselves as sharing with the schools not so much an examination as the culmination of a teaching process. Before the word 'backwash' had been coined, they regularly asked whether modifications being proposed in the form of the examination would be accepted by the schools.

In the 21st century Certificate of Proficiency in English (CPE) revision and First Certificate in English (FCE) / Certificate in Advanced English (CAE) modifications, strenuous efforts were made to elicit feedback on the existing test from test takers. A wide variety of stakeholders contributed to the decisions that were taken concerning changes in the examinations (see Weir and Milanovic 2003 for a full account of the CPE revision, Hawkey 2005 for a description of the Certificates in English Language Skills (CELS) examination change process and Hawkey 2009 for that in FCE and CAE).

It seems to have always been taken for granted at Cambridge that once you had a reliable score, it would be used appropriately. The only ethical issue appears to have been in the words of Jack Roach, that exams were 'felt to be fair' (Spolsky 2004). There is no reported discussion of ethical issues in the minutes of the UCLES British Council Joint Committee apart from an occasional expression of a desire to satisfy the centres, as Cambridge's main customers, with regard to the appropriateness to the curriculum of what was being measured.

In the 21st century this is no longer the case, and, post-Messick (1989), the increased interest in impact exemplifies the growing importance of evidence-based approaches to education and assessment. Measuring the impact of Cambridge English examinations is addressed in a number of recent volumes in the SiLT series, e.g., Hawkey (2006, 2011:234–258, 2013:273–302), Khalifa and Weir (2009:169–189) Shaw and Weir (2007:218–228), various articles in the Cambridge ESOL publication *Research Notes* (see for example articles on ethics in *Research Notes* 22 published in November 2005 and articles on test impact in *Research Notes* 50 published in January 2013), and most recently in the doctoral thesis of Nick Saville (2009), the Director of Cambridge ESOL Research and Validation, on *Developing a model for investigating the impact of language assessment within educational contexts by a public examination provider*. They all attest to the increasing attention paid to test impact in the 21st century by Cambridge ESOL, and detail how this is built into the organisation's test development and validation systems.

Overview of events 1913–2012

Having introduced the main themes of this study, in the rest of this chapter we will provide a synopsis of the powerful influence that language teaching had on the constructs being measured in English language examinations from 1913–2012, as well as considering external, institutional, social and economic forces which influenced the general shifts in practice in pedagogy and assessment during this one hundred year period. For example we will identify:

- the influences of pedagogic legacies from the past that affected the first CPE in 1913

- the changes in assessment arising from the oral–structural–situational approaches to teaching that emerged in the United Kingdom from 1921–1970
- the effects on Cambridge English language examinations of English becoming a global language after World War Two
- the socio-economic factors that led to the acceptance of psychometrics and objective testing at a much earlier date in the USA than the United Kingdom
- the effects of the communicative movement 1971–2012
- the pressure for clearer, more transparent and explicit specification of test content in approaches to assessment at Cambridge from the 1980s onwards
- the development of examinations at different proficiency levels in Cambridge from 1980 onwards
- the professionalisation of English language testing at Cambridge from 1988 onwards and the increased attention paid to scoring validity
- a nascent recognition of the importance of cognitive validity for language testing in the 21st century.

This synopsis will provide the backdrop for a more detailed analysis of the specific changes to the way each of the language constructs was measured in English language examinations in Chapters 2–5.

To help frame the relationships between the teaching and the testing of English language in the United Kingdom from 1913–2012, we include in Table 1.1 below an outline of key events in the period, building on an original suggestion by Tony Howatt (personal communication). It offers a useful set of pegs on which to hang elements of 'a big picture' of the historical pattern of language teaching and assessment, as well as of specific events in language testing at Cambridge, 1913–2012. Phrases like 'onwards' are employed (a) to stress the fact that change is not immediate but takes some time to establish itself in classroom pedagogy and assessment, and (b) to act as a reminder of the fact that successful new approaches do not mean the end of existing ones. They exist side by side for as long as they are felt to be useful. Three broad stages will be considered in the discussion that follows:

- Stage 1 (1780–1913) The Beginnings of Theory
- Stage 2 (1921–c1970) Oral–Structural–Situational Approaches to Language Teaching and Testing
- Stage 3 (c1971–) Communicative Approaches to Language Teaching and Testing.

Table 1.1 Key events affecting the historical development of English language teaching in the United Kingdom and English language testing at Cambridge

<u>Stage 1 (1780–1913)</u>	**The Beginnings of Theory**
1780s onwards	The Grammar-Translation Method (Meidinger 1783; Fick 1793)
1858	**The University of Cambridge Local Examinations Syndicate founded**
1870s onwards	The Direct Method (Berlitz schools 1878-)
1882 onwards	The Reform Movement: *'Quousque tandem?'* (Viëtor 1882); *The Practical Study of Languages. A Guide for Teachers and Learners* (Sweet 1899); Passy's essay on the direct method (1899) and Jespersen (1904)
1886	Foundation of the International Phonetic Association (IPA)
1888	Edgeworth's paper on reliability (1888)
1892	Foundation of the Modern Language Association of Great Britain
1913	**The Certificate of Proficiency in English (CPE)**
<u>Stage 2 (1921 – c1970)</u>	<u>Oral–Structural–Situational Approaches to Language Teaching and Testing</u>
1920s onwards	The Oral Method (Palmer 1921a) aligned with systematic, graded structural progression; *The Oxford English Course* Parts I–IV. London (Faucett 1933–1934); *Essential English for Foreign Students* (Eckersley 1938–42); The Structural approach (Bloomfield 1926, 1933, Fries 1945)
1925	**J.O. Roach joins UCLES as Assistant Secretary (until 1945)**
1932	**CPE: Phonetics paper and grammar knowledge questions disappear**
1936	*Interim Report on Vocabulary Selection for the Teaching of English as a Foreign Language* (Faucett, Palmer, Thorndike and West 1936)
1939	**The Lower Certificate in English (LCE)**
1941	**The UCLES-British Council Joint Committee**
1950s onwards	The Situational Approach (Hornby 1950); *The Oxford Progressive English Course* (Hornby 1954–56)
1956	**CPE: Use of English Paper included as an option**
1957	**UCLES Executive Committee for the Syndicate's Examinations in English for Foreign Students**
1960s onwards	The audio-lingual approach (Brooks 1960); *English Sentence Patterns, Understanding and Producing Grammatical Structures* (Fries and Lado 1962)
1960	**Lado's visit to UCLES 1960,** *Language Testing: The Construction and Use of Foreign Language Tests* (Lado 1961)
1966	**Wyatt (Secretary of the Syndicate 1961–72) visits ETS Princeton;** **CPE revision: availability of a language only pathway;** **CPE: Use of English Paper, 3-option multiple choice items introduced**
1970	**LCE: Structure and Usage Paper**
<u>Stage 3 (c1971–)</u>	<u>Communicative Approaches to Language Teaching and Testing</u>
1971 onwards	Ruschlikon Symposium 1971; Council of Europe initiative on European Language Curriculum; *The Threshold Level* (Van Ek 1975); *Notional Syllabuses* (Wilkins 1976); The notional-functional syllabus; English for Specific Purposes (ESP) (Munby 1978)

Table 1.1 continued

Stage 3 (c1971–)	Communicative Approaches to Language Teaching and Testing
1975	The First Certificate in English (FCE); Dedicated Reading and Listening Papers in FCE and CPE; *Teaching Language as Communication* (Widdowson (1978)
1980	Preliminary English Test (PET); ELTS Test
1987–9	The Cambridge–TOEFL Comparability Study
1988	Peter Hargreaves appointed Head of the EFL Division arrives from the British Council
1989	IELTS Test
1989	Creation of the EFL Evaluation Unit (later the ESOL Research and Validation Group)
1990	*Fundamental Considerations in Language Testing* (Bachman 1990)
1991	Certificate in Advanced English (CAE)
1993	Business English Certificate (BEC)
1994	Key English Test (KET)
2001	*The Common European Framework of Reference for Languages: Learning, Teaching, Assessment* (CEFR) (Council of Europe 2001)
2003 onwards	Studies in Language Testing (SiLT) 'Constructs' Project: a socio-cognitive approach

The Certificate of Proficiency in English (CPE) 1913: A hybrid creation from legacies of the past

Origins of the examination

Little evidence remains as to the genesis of the CPE on the eve of World War One. A Cambridge University Council of the Senate Minute (1910) makes reference to the appointment of a committee in connection with the establishment of a Modern Language Certificate for teachers. The committee was duly convened and the *Report of the Committee on the Proposed Teaching Certificate in Modern Languages* was submitted to the Council of the Senate on 30 January 1911 (copy held in Flather, the Secretary of the Syndicate's papers). The report included a 'memorandum from the Modern Language Association setting forth reasons in favour of the establishment of the Certificate and indicating the desired scope of the Examination'. The advice from the Modern Language Association was well received and a decision to proceed was advised by the Committee:

> The Committee incline to the view that, provided that the Local Examinations and Lectures Syndicate are willing, it would be well to put the Examination under their charge [rather than use an existing internal University examination under the control of the Special

Board of Medieval and Modern languages]. There are advantages in concentrating as far as possible under one management that part of the work of the University which is concerned mainly with external candidates; and the experience which the Syndics have had in the control and conduct of examinations renders them very suitable for the present purpose.

This decision was taken and a request from the Council of the Senate was subsequently sent to UCLES on 8 March 1911 which asked the Syndicate to set up a Teaching Certificate in Modern Languages. Later, on 1 February 1912, the General Purposes Committee of UCLES recommended setting up Certificates of Proficiency in French and German, English for Foreign Students and Religious Knowledge.

Jack Roach was the Assistant Secretary at UCLES from 1925 to 1945. His papers in the Cambridge Assessment Archives offer little additional explanation for the introduction of CPE beyond the fact that rival examinations had such on offer:

And now at last for the Take-over bid. Why the Syndicate started the examination in 1913, no one knows. It must, I think, have been a break away by Exeter University College from the London University Examinations. Both were based on a course for foreigners, both were heavily academic, with a paper on Phonetics. I think both had the same examiner in this, Professor Daniel Jones, leading British phonetician (Roach undated page 5).

Richard Smith (personal communication) suggests that the inclusion of English at all is interesting and that it perhaps reflects a demand from non-native English speaker teachers who were visiting the United Kingdom to improve their English prior to World War One (an aspect of the growing professionalisation / oral focus in several countries which stemmed from the Reform Movement). Perhaps James Flather, the Secretary of the Syndicate (1910–21), foresaw an untapped, potential examination candidature amongst these overseas nationals teaching English as a Foreign Language as a career; as a result he might have decided to support an examination for this purpose to keep up with the competition.

Support for such conjecture can be found in several letters to Flather in his papers in the Cambridge Assessment Archive. For example, encouragement from the Modern Language Association for the decision to initiate a Certificate in English, can be seen in a letter from G F Bridge, its secretary, to Flather. On 1 April 1912 Bridges wrote: 'My committee heard with great satisfaction that it had been decided to establish the certificates. It may interest you to know that the University of London is doing the same thing.' On 6 June 1912 Bridges also wrote:

> . . .I think it quite likely that you will get a good many applications for the English Certificate. I get letters from foreigners asking how such a certificate can be obtained. . . Would it not be well to officially inform the French and Prussian Ministries of Education about the Certificate in English? & the Swiss?

The conceptual basis for CPE in 1913

Having explored the manner of its birth, we now turn to the conceptual basis for the first CPE. CPE appeared in 1913 at the end of a period in language teaching which began back in the late 18th century with the limited introduction of modern foreign languages into the curriculum in a few schools. Howatt (personal communication) notes that the Grammar-Translation Method for language teaching (as it would later be known) was developed in the late 1700s. He describes how with its development the structure of language teaching started to resemble a kind of 'double helix' – with one dimension devoted to the linguistics of the syllabus ('what is to be taught?') and the other to the methodology ('how is it to be taught?'). He argues (op. cit.) that:

> The Grammar-Translation Method, (as realized in the textbooks which gave it birth: Meidinger 1783 for French and Fick 1793 for English), replaced existing grammar manuals, which had offered no pedagogical guidance at all, with an organised sequence of lessons in which a selection of specific grammar rules were taught and exemplified in a step-by-step manner. From a psychological perspective, it introduced the use of practice exercises for the first time, consisting of sentences for translation which displayed the new grammar points.

Richards and Rogers (2001:5) describe how Grammar-Translation Method proponents argued that it enabled pupils to learn a language to access its literature and benefit from the mental discipline and intellectual development such an approach involved. They itemised a number of the Grammar-Translation Method's key features:

- approach the language first through detailed analysis of its grammatical rules
- apply this knowledge to the task of translating sentences and texts into and out of the target language
- focus on reading and writing
- pay little or no systematic attention to speaking or listening
- give high priority to meticulous standards of accuracy.

Hillocks (2008:311) argues that grammar was seen in English 'public schools' as the:

. . .gateway to all of knowledge, it was thought to discipline the mind and
the soul at the same time, honing the intellectual and spiritual abilities
that would enable reading and speaking with discernment (Huntsman
1983: 50).

Kelly (1969:382) similarly places the Grammar-Translation Method in a
scholarly context:

> In deliberately laying aside the oral aim for grammatical exactness and
> translating ability, the eighteenth and nineteenth centuries merely fol-
> lowed the intellectual tendencies of the time. The Cartesian approach to
> knowledge places analysis above all else. Hence the practice of language
> was not rated highly.

The Grammar-Translation Method was originally an attempt to adapt
the scholastic study of foreign languages for a reading knowledge of their
culture and history 'to the circumstances and requirements of school students' (Howatt 1984:131). Throughout the 19th century proponents of the
Grammar-Translation Method tried to carve out a role for it in teaching
modern languages in the schools by modeling their classroom procedures on
the teaching of Latin and Greek with translation of (literary) texts being seen
as the main activity in language learning. Gilbert (1953:2–3) describes how
the approach was still alive and well in both teaching and testing at the end of
the 19th century:

> The methods in general use in Public Schools were in fact. . .: a study of
> formal grammar with some philology, much translation from English
> into the foreign language, and some translation of fairly difficult foreign
> texts into English. . . The recently instituted examinations for Army
> and Civil Service entrance, the Oxford and Cambridge Locals and the
> London Matriculation contained many questions on grammar and
> philology.

The Grammar-Translation Method was not popular with some teachers,
however, and in the 1880s a number of language teachers and academics in
Europe instigated a Reform Movement which, with the assistance of modern
ideas from phonetics, allowed for a new pedagogical approach rooted in the
spoken language.

Howatt and Widdowson (2004:187–198) argue that the Reform
Movement had an important influence in changing perspectives on teaching
language. The Reform Movement stressed the role of the spoken language
informed by the science of speech physiology, which flourished in the second
half of the 19th century. Its founding father, Sweet, was the older, important
influence on the movement; Viëtor, Passy and Jespersen were the 'younger

generation' who led it. Viëtor and Passy were practising teachers (of English) at the time, as well as being phoneticians at the beginning of their respective academic careers. The new science of phonetics embraced by the Reform Movement was to contribute in no small part to the success and scientific prestige it came to enjoy.

English was a 'modern language' in the eyes of European secondary school teachers involved in the Reform Movement, for which the first conference on modern language teaching, held at Cheltenham College in 1890 (Gilbert 1953:1), was significant in the United Kingdom context. The conference passed a resolution that 'phonetics should form the basis of all modern language teaching'. Phonetics was seen by the Reform Movement as at the core of practical language teaching and was closely associated with the view of oral language as primary. The 'phonetic start' for language programmes is described in the 1886 Article 2 of the International Phonetic Association (IPA):

> The teacher's first aim should be to thoroughly familiarize his pupils with the sounds of the foreign language. Towards this end he should use a phonetic transcription which will be employed exclusively in the early stages of the course without reference to conventional spelling.

A number of heirs of the Reform Movement, such as Harold Palmer and Daniel Jones, were phoneticians; they advocated the value of descriptive phonetics in teaching and teacher training (see also Sweet 1899: Chapters 2–7). Sweet (1899:4) argued that phonetics 'is equally necessary in the theoretic and in the practical study of languages'.

From the outset, the Reform Movement was a professional movement by foreign language teachers, including teachers of English, which started in Germany in 1882 and spread throughout Europe in the last decades of the 19th century. The teachers were not native speakers of the languages they taught – hence their enthusiasm for phonetics (cf. this with the Berlitz Method described below where phonetics was proscribed and the teachers employing his Direct Method were usually native speakers). The principal arguments of the Reform Movement were (Howatt and Widdowson 2004:189):

1. Reject the traditional grammar-translation technique of starting each lesson unit with decontextualised grammar rules. Start the lesson with a coherent and interesting text (usually printed in phonetic transcription).
2. Ban the use of disconnected sentences for translation.
3. In presenting the text, try to use as little of the pupils' mother tongue as possible and stress the need for correct pronunciation.
4. The heart of the method was the oral question-and-answer work with a new text.
5. Grammar should only be taught after the work on the text, i.e. inductively. The mother tongue could be used for this lesson.

6. Follow-up written work should avoid translation and consist of exercises which allowed pupils to 'stay inside' the foreign language – re-telling the story, for instance, writing free compositions, and so on.

The Reform Movement, perhaps not surprisingly, was subject to criticism from those traditionalists who believed in teaching a foreign language with the help of the mother tongue and favoured the use of translation and the teaching of explicit grammar rules. Critics were also concerned about what would happen to the intellectual and cultural aspects of learning foreign languages, if learning 'colloquial' speech became a primary aim of Modern Language Teaching.

The structure of the first CPE in the event did not favour one approach over the other, and closely resembled the comprehensive, national, modern language assessments in use at the start of World War One which contained activities derived from both the Reform Movement and the Grammar-Translation Method, as in the French examination in the School Leaving Certificate:

They will be required to answer certain questions on French grammar. . .Moreover they will be required to do two pieces of translation, into and out of French respectively, and a piece of free composition in French, and finally to submit to a short oral test of their ability to read aloud, write dictation and converse in French (Palmer and Redman 1932:80).

Given CPE was introduced as part of a suite of certificates for teachers including French and German, similarities with existing Cambridge examinations in modern languages were perhaps to be expected.

Coverage in the first CPE examination also stands comparison with the contents of Sweet's (1899) *The Practical Study of Languages. A Guide for Teachers and Learners* regarded by Howatt (1984:202) as one of the best Language Teaching methodology books ever written: 'Unsurpassed in the history of linguistic pedagogy'. As well as the importance of phonetics and its practical application in teaching pronunciation (Chapters 2–7), Sweet advocated that practical language learning should be arranged in terms of grammar, vocabulary, the study of texts, translation and conversation (Chapters 8–14).

So CPE in 1913 can be seen as a hybrid creation which drew on a number of legacies from the past:

1. The **Grammar-Translation Method** reflected in the inclusion of translation tasks and questions on English grammar.

2. The **Reform Movement** (Viëtor 1882, Passy 1899, Jespersen 1904) reflected in the inclusion of a phonetics paper, an Oral paper and an English essay.

3. The **Examinations in Modern Languages** approach reflected in the more or less standardised structure of the papers set (see quote from Palmer and Redman 1932 above).

1913 Examination

(i) Written:	(a)	Translation from English into French or German 2 hours
	(b)	Translation from French or German into English, and questions on English Grammar 2 ½ hours
	(c)	English Essay 2 hours
	(d)	English Literature (The paper on English Language and Literature [Group A, Subject 1] in the Higher Local Examination) 3 hours
	(e)	English Phonetics 1 ½ hours
(ii) Oral:		Dictation ½ hour
		Reading and Conversation ½ hour

As the exam outline above shows, the written part of the examination included an English Literature paper and an English Essay, but it also contained a compulsory English Phonetics paper, a translation task from and into French or German (perhaps indicative of the potential target population as Bridges was suggesting to Flather in the letter quoted above), and an English grammar section. There was also an oral component with dictation, reading aloud and conversation. There was a focus on form in the grammar and phonetics sections in the first CPE but attention was clearly paid to active language use as well. In all, a demanding 12 hours of testing against the less than 5 hours required at CPE today (see Appendix A for a copy of the examination).

Marks for the certificates in French, German and English were distributed according to the weightings recorded in the extract below (from a note discovered in Flather's papers in the Cambridge Assessment Archives):

Certificates of Proficiency Paper Weightings

At the Examiners' Meeting held in February 1913 it was proposed that the full marks for each certificate should be 600 to be distributed as follows:
Phonetics Paper   75
Oral Examination   125 (namely, Dictation 50, Reading & Conversation 75)
Other Papers   100 each

The minimum for passing to be 30% in the Essays, 40% each in Translation, Composition, Phonetics, and Oral; and further that candidates be required to get 200 out of 400 in the whole of the written work except Phonetics taken together, and 100 out of 200 in Phonetics and Oral taken together.

An examination for teachers

The CPE was instituted by the Local Examinations Syndicate in 1913 along-side Certificates in Proficiency for teachers in other languages, i.e. French and German. Its stated purpose (Wyatt and Roach 1947:126) was 'to meet the needs of foreign students who wished to furnish evidence of their knowledge of English with a view to teaching it in foreign schools' and this is clearly stated in the accompanying Regulations. The 1913 *Regulations for the Examinations for Certificates of Proficiency in Modern Languages and Religious Knowledge* noted:

> The Certificate of Proficiency in English is designed for Foreign Students who desire a satisfactory proof of their knowledge of the language with a view to teaching it in foreign schools. The Certificate is not, however, limited to Foreign Students (UCLES 1913:5).

Entry for CPE was restricted to candidates aged twenty or over, as the examination at this time was intended primarily for teachers, though interestingly Flather was already receiving a number of letters from younger students requesting a reduction in the age limit. The Regulations in 1923 still state: 'Examinations for the Certificate of Proficiency, designed for teachers, will be held in July 1923 in Religious Knowledge and (primarily for foreign Students) in English' (UCLES 1923).

Further proof of the suitability of the examination for practising or prospective teachers of English can be found in some of the CPE Essay titles (usually Question 4):

1920 The 'direct method' in the teaching of languages
1921 The value and importance of dialect
1922 The art of reading
1923 Intonation in speech as a mark of nationality

This narrowly defined target audience would disappear from the regulations by 1933 and we find that by 1947 CPE was 'open to all candidates whose mother tongue is not English and it is designed not only for prospective teachers but also for other students with a wide range of interest within the field of English studies' (UCLES 1947).

We will now briefly describe the 1913 papers. A comprehensive discussion of all these 1913 CPE tasks can be found in Chapters 2–5.

Translation and grammar

In 1913 candidates had two hours to translate literary passages of just over 200 words from English into French or German, and also a further two hours to translate a passage from French or German into English with an extra 30 minutes for a set of grammar questions. (See Appendix A for copies of the original papers and Appendix D for a statistical analysis of various contextual parameters of texts used for translation out of English into the foreign language.)

The languages available for translation in 1913 were presumably related to the two countries that the three candidates presented themselves from. Initially the languages available were French and German with Italian and Spanish being added in 1926. By the eve of World War Two, as the number of centres offering the examinations round the world expanded, translations into and out of 29 languages were possible (see Hawkey and Milanovic 2013, Weir 2003:56 for details).

A government committee on the state of Modern Languages in the British educational system in 1918 was initially sceptical about translation as a testing device but its final report (Committee GB 1918) fully endorsed the value of translation having received considerable expert testimony in its favour. Translation would be a part of the Cambridge English language examinations until the communicative reforms in 1975. Translation tasks in Cambridge English language examinations are discussed in detail in Chapter 2.

As well as translation tasks, the 1913 CPE included items testing knowledge of grammar in the same paper. Examples of grammar items from the CPE 1913 translation paper included:

1913 CPE translation paper

- Give the past tense and past participle of each of the following verbs, dividing them into strong and weak; add explanations: *tell, wake, buy, eat, lay, lie.*
- Write down the abstract nouns connected with the following adjectives and verbs: *precise, adhere, apt, predominate, optimistic, crystallise, negligent, hate, attain, detain, betray, ingenious, seize, charitable, zealous.*

In addition there were a number of items requiring productive lexico-grammatical knowledge:

- Embody each of the following words in a sentence, in such a way as to shew that you clearly apprehend its meaning: *commence, comment, recommend; incredible, incredulous* (Weir and Milanovic 2003: 482–483).

These items testing knowledge of the linguistic code would disappear along with pronunciation in the early 1930s.

The English Essay and English Literature

A number of tasks in the written part of the CPE examination in 1913 were taken directly from the existing British native speaker English syllabus including the English Literature paper and the English Essay paper. The 3-hour 1913 CPE English Literature paper contained the same essay questions as those for first-language speakers of English taking the University's matriculation exams at the time.

Given the special place accorded to the essay in society and education at the start of the 20th century in Britain, and strong support for its use in the classroom from the Reform Movement in Europe (see Howatt and Widdowson 2004:189 and above), it is perhaps not surprising that there was a two-hour English Essay test featuring prominently in CPE in 1913 as well as an English Literature paper. Direct writing tasks were a permanent feature of CPE from the outset and as new tests were added to the Cambridge suite over the years, composition would continue to be a component of the Cambridge English examinations right up until the present day, though a dedicated, separate English Literature paper would disappear by 1975 (see Chapter 3 for details of these two tasks).

Phonetics

The compulsory 90-minute written phonetics paper in CPE 1913 (see Appendix A for a copy and Chapter 4 for discussion of this paper) was an indication of Cambridge's interest in ensuring that the content of their tests was in line with current approaches to language teaching and it reflected the influence of phoneticians like Daniel Jones, who was an examiner for the contemporary London English examinations for foreign students. Jones' influence can be seen in the Regulations for CPE (1923:3) which suggest only one prior preparatory text for CPE candidates: 'In Phonetics candidates may consult D. Jones *The Pronunciation of English*.' An expertise in phonetics was seen as being a valuable tool for intending teachers who were indicated as the primary audience for the examination according to the Regulations at this time.

The Phonetics paper was to disappear from the CPE in 1932 in what appears to have been part of a concerted effort to increase the number of candidates to ensure the examination's survival. However, the influence of phonetics was to survive in the United Kingdom until the 1960s in other tests such as the English Language Battery (ELBA) and the English Proficiency Test Battery (EPTB) used in university admissions and even later in the Professional and Linguistic Assessments Board (PLAB) test for overseas doctors wishing to practise in Britain (see Davies (2008a, 2008b) for a detailed account of EPTB and ELBA, and Chapters 4 and 5 for a discussion of the place of phonetics in language tests in Cambridge). It was also to endure in parts of the world covered by British, English as a Foreign Language teachers, as a result of imperial and missionary influence. Courses with phonetics practice at the outset were still common in China in the late 1980s. It influenced the teaching of Modern Foreign Languages in British schools and remains important in the teaching of reading in the primary stage to this day.

The Oral Paper: Conversation, reading aloud and dictation

Attitudes to the teaching of spoken language were changing in the United Kingdom by 1913, aided by both the Direct Method and Reform Movement advocates. The inclusion of a thirty-minute conversation with an examiner and a reading aloud task in the 1913 CPE was an early indicator of the important role spoken language would have in English language pedagogy and assessment in the 20th century (see the next section on *1921–70: Oral–structural–situational approaches* for details). Educators were beginning to recognise that the earlier needs of the scholar were being superseded by the needs of the non-scholar for practical everyday use of the language in a spoken form. Shortly after the launch of CPE the *Report of the Committee appointed by the Prime Minister to enquire into the position of modern languages in the educational system of Great Britain* would strongly recommend that oral examinations should be included wherever possible to test a candidate's 'speaking power' (Committee GB 1918:57). The oral test at Cambridge *mutatis mutandis* would continue from 1913 until the present day as a paper in its own right (see Chapter 4 for detail).

Kelly describes how reading aloud was viewed as a means of teaching and testing pronunciation, sentence rhythm and intonation, as well as being traditionally seen as a test of comprehension (1969:98): 'reading itself is generally a sufficient test. Neither Latin nor any other language can be properly read aloud, with due emphasis, unless it is understood.' This task was to remain part of the oral examination until 1986 in LCE and in CPE (see Chapter 2 for full details of this technique and also Chapter 4). To this day reading aloud and dictation both appear in the Pearson Test of English – Academic (PTE-A) launched in 2010 and the current Versant English Placement Test.

Dictation was also a traditional activity in the language classroom (see Chapter 5 for a full discussion and history of this technique). Kelly (1969:94) notes: '... dictation was one of the few exercises consistently employed throughout the history of language teaching'. Dictation was to feature in Cambridge oral examinations until 1975.

1921–70: The oral–structural–situational era

Language teaching in the early 20th century

Kelly (1969) argued that conflicts in method should be seen as a 'function of the social role of the languages taught and the objectives pursued in teaching them'. He emphasised that where social objectives were dominant there would be an emphasis on communication, especially oral. Where aims were scholarly there would be an emphasis on written and analytical skills.

Schools in England were certainly being encouraged to include modern languages with an oral component by the end of the 19th century but headmasters, according to Gilbert (1953:3), 'consented only because they thereby satisfied utilitarian parents and because the Modern Side enabled them to "shunt the empties" or transfer the dullards from classics to modern languages'. Gilbert (1953:4) provides a revealing backdrop on some of the thinking current in the late 19th century on the place of spoken language in language learning:

> During the [eighteen] eighties, therefore, modern languages, although more generally accepted as a worthwhile discipline, were still taught very much by the grammar-translation method, oral French being despised as "nursery," "tea-party", "courier" or "bagman" French. Some voices were raised in protest . . . but the general opinion was admirably expressed by Dr. R.W. Hiley in 1887 (Journal of Education vol IX 308): "The prime object of scholastic education is the training of the mental faculties. Hence a youth is put to hard and dry studies, often confessedly distasteful, though the whole of them may be forgotten when he enters practical life. The mental training is never forgotten; on the contrary, the powers so developed increase in grasp and tenacity. Training by the ear will never do this: it simply cultivates one faculty, memory, and that only for a short time. It is always found that children so trained are the most volatile, have not power of application, and in after life seldom settle to any definite pursuit."

Attitudes were to change though (see Committee GB 1918).

Mackey (1965:148) draws our attention to the rapid growth of Berlitz commercial language schools in the 19th century, with their dedicated use of intensive oral interaction in the target language as a hallmark. Howatt (personal communication) described the ideas originated by Berlitz in the 1870s, as:

a) Learning a foreign language is the same as learning your mother tongue.

b) Speech was seen as primary by advocates of this approach. The basic aim is to acquire fluency in the spoken language. Written language is of secondary importance. There is no place for phonetic transcription, either.

c) The mother tongue was banned in the classroom, only the foreign language is permitted. Meaning is to be taught initially by ostensive techniques and later by definitions using known vocabulary.

d) Grammar is not taught at all. It is absorbed by the learner in the same way as it is by the infant.

e) Translation is forbidden.

The growth in number of the Berlitz schools – and indeed the proliferation of other language schools for adults – contributed to a growing interest in speaking foreign languages. However, Smith (personal communication) cautions that Berlitz was important in the development of Teaching English as a Foreign Language in the United Kingdom mainly due to his influence on Harold Palmer and Palmer's reworking of Berlitz. As we saw above, the 1913 CPE was part of the 'modern languages' culture and the Reform Movement. The associated direct method as promoted in France was more influential than the Berlitz Direct Method.

Harold E Palmer's work founded what came to be known as the *Oral Method* (see Smith 2004 for an authoritative account of his life, works and contribution to ELT). He was a direct method teacher who became interested in phonetics and started work under Daniel Jones at University College London in 1915. His basic aim was to turn the direct method into a linguistically systematic course in spoken English based on his 1921 *The Principles of Language Study*. He emphasised the primacy of speech over the written form and the priority of an oral methodology (Darian 1969). Sweet (1899:49) had succinctly advocated in a similar vein: 'Begin with the spoken language'.

Palmer's work was to give English teachers a theoretical base and, according to Howatt (foreword to Smith 1999:vii), his most influential, practical, teaching manual *English through Actions* (1925) gave English teachers 'workable activities and exercises to develop their pupils oral proficiency'. Palmer (1921a:iv) felt his book would encourage conversation: 'the systematic and graduated dialogue work to be carried on between teacher and pupil'. Daniel Jones worked closely with Palmer at University College London 1915–22 until the latter left for Tokyo and they produced, according to Howatt and Widdowson (2004:234–235), the founding classics of ELT. Jones wrote the *English Pronouncing Dictionary* in 1917 and the *Outline of English Phonetics* in 1922. Palmer published *The Scientific Study and Teaching of Languages* based on his lectures to modern language teachers at University College London in 1917, *The Oral Method of Teaching Languages* and *The Principles of Language Study* in 1921, *A Grammar of Spoken English* in 1924 and *English through Actions* in 1925, which contributed substantially to both the general principles of English Language Teaching and to a methodology with practical detailed programmes for teaching.

Howatt (personal communication) argues that Palmer's work was to be the basis for the development of ELT in the United Kingdom until the 1960s. Smith (2004:269) views his work as the 'major methodological influence on what became British English Language Teaching'. Lawrence Faucett, the author of the *Oxford English Course* (1933–36) came to Tokyo to consult him, Michael West worked closely with him on vocabulary control in the 1930s and his successor in Tokyo, A S Hornby, took his ideas into the second half of the century with *A Learner's Dictionary of Current English* (Hornby, Gatenby and Wakefield 1948) and his *Oxford Progressive English Course* (1954–56). Smith (2004:249) in his evaluation of the work of Harold Palmer argues:

> . . .it is in the overall emphases of Palmer's approach to language teach-
> ing that his most enduring influence is to be found, and in which we can
> identify most clearly the Reform Movement legacy to ELT. Regardless
> of 'surface' changes in methodological fashion over the last forty or so
> years, three of the four major Reform Movement principles have con-
> tinued to hold sway over mainstream ELT, namely (1) a theoretical and
> practical emphasis on the 'primacy of speech', (2) discouragement of
> translation and other uses of the mother tongue, and (3) a preference
> for inductive learning over explicit, deductive grammar teaching. The
> particular emphasis on principled course design (involving selection and
> grading according to various linguistic and pedagogical criteria) which
> can, perhaps, be seen as Palmer's major original contribution within the
> Reform Movement tradition has also maintained its salience. . .

The growing interest in teaching and testing spoken language in the United Kingdom contrasts sharply with concurrent developments in the USA. Barnwell (1996:18–19) paints a different picture for language testing in the United States and notes that there was more scepticism about oral testing (a view shared even as late as Lado 1961 and 1964 because of reliability issues). Few American tests assessed spoken language at this time. In the case of TOEFL, it did not feature until considerably later, with the Test of Spoken English only appearing in 1979 and then only as an optional component. Spolsky (2008b:449) even interprets the latter change as 'a prime example of an industrial test, open to market forces rather than changing theory'.

The early hegemony of objective testing (see below) contributed to a lack of interest in tests measuring speaking in the United States because of the per-ceived 'subjectivity' of this endeavour. Spolsky (personal communication) notes that there were attempts in the United States in the 1920s and 1930s to develop oral and aural tests, but it proved too hard to put into general practice. Large class sizes at that time, typically around 40 in the school system (Barnwell 1996:89) was a further factor militating against a focus on spoken language ability in the United States. (See Chapter 4 for further discussion.) Following the Coleman Report in 1929, which proposed reading as the primary goal of foreign language education (Barnwell 1996:60–62), language teaching was to be dominated by the 'Reading Method' in the 1930s in the United States (see Bond 1953). Conant (1934) argued that as there was not enough time to teach everything, the focus should be on reading, which was often used simply as a vehicle for teaching the elements of the language, namely lexis and structure.

The 1920s witnessed the birth of 'structural linguistics' which was to have a powerful and long-lasting influence on the theory and practice of language teaching for the next 50 years. In the USA, the structuralist approaches to linguistics of Bloomfield (1926, 1933) and Fries (1945) encouraged a primary focus on linguistic form in the language classroom (and on discrete language constituents in assessment). The British structural approach, as epitomised in the work of Palmer, differed in that although it was similarly characterised by attention to graded grammatical structures and systematic word lists, it was usually combined with the direct method with an emphasis on the spoken language (as in Palmer's work discussed above). This would be complemented later on in this period by the situational approach in the United Kingdom, which sought to locate the teaching of structural items in simple, interesting and relevant situations which made their meaning clear.

This period of English language teaching in the United Kingdom (1921–1970) would witnesses a judicious blend of complementary methodologies (oral, structural and situational) rather than a monotheistic approach. Smith (2004:239–240), drawing on Widdowson (1968) and Prabhu (1987), provides a valuable summary of the pre-communicative British orthodoxy in language teaching. He identifies the following principal characteristics of British English Language Teaching that emerged in the period 1920–1971:

(i)   rejection of 'traditional' procedures of explicit grammar teaching, translation and explication of written texts, and reading aloud and memorisation of texts (i.e. modern);

(ii)   emphasis on the need for structurally and lexically graded syllabuses; sentence patterns form the basic content of teaching (i.e. structural);

(iii)   stress on the primacy of speaking among the language skills; new language is presented and practised initially with no reference to written forms (although balanced attention is to be paid to all skills overall) (i.e. oral);

(iv)   presentation of new language items through meaningful classroom situations; pictures, objects and classroom situations are used to maintain a focus on the meaning of what is being presented and practised; much controlled practice using techniques such as use of substitution tables and choral repetition, often in meaningful classroom situations (i.e. situational).

The early demise of phonetics

By the 1930s some important earlier influences on assessment were on the wane. By 1932, the CPE paper on Phonetics had disappeared as a formal test. According to Howatt (personal communication) this probably was connected with the general falling from favour of phonetics as part of the teacher's practical tool-kit. Reasons for the fall from favour were undoubtedly related to the 'academic' / 'difficult' image of phonetics and the need to attract more candidates to the examination.

A typically thoughtful rationale for the rejection of phonetics from CPE was provided by Roach in an internal memo:

> I suggest that the paper on English Phonetics and the requirement of a knowledge of Phonetics be eliminated from this examination.
>
> (1) Neither the Syndicate in the Higher School Certificate Examination nor the University in the Modern Languages and English Triposes require a knowledge of Phonetics.
> (2) Phonetics are no doubt a great aid in learning pronunciation –we can adequately test the results in the oral examination.
> (3) Our Certificate is not one of aptitude for teaching English. Were it so, there might be more point in examining on Phonetics. Some countries may require modern language teachers to be proficient in Phonetics, but even so they may not accept our test as sufficient evidence, while at the same time we may be imposing this test on candidates who have no need of it.
> (4) With many candidates Phonetics are probably a thing to be "got up" for this examination and to be forgotten thereafter. They may deter some possible candidates from ever entering at all and, to be successful, they almost certainly require a teacher. The rest of the syllabus does not – any "mademoiselle" living au pair in a girls' school could readily get such guidance as she needs for the literature paper. The elimination of Phonetics should therefore make the syllabus more possible for a wider public – I do not believe that it need lower the standard (Roach 1931).

An attempt was made to revive a test of phonetics in CPE by W R Lee in 1960 (an ELT specialist on the Executive Committee as a representative of the British Council from 1958) but a lack of demand for it in test centres led to the idea being postponed (according to Executive Committee Minutes 1960 and 1961). The optional paper in Phonetics (three hours) in the later Diploma of English Studies Examination (an advanced, specialist examination in English Literature and background studies at post-Proficiency level), first offered in December 1945 with 16 candidates (Joint Committee July 1943), was to survive until 1967 when the Executive Committee (1967) recommended it be disbanded because of the small entry and 'dispropor-tionate administrative problems' (see Falvey 2008:146–147 for details of the Diploma examination and Hawkey and Milanovic 2013).

The contribution of Jack Roach, Assistant Secretary 1925–1945, to the development of Cambridge English language examinations

Probably Roach's final economic argument (no. 4 in the quote above) was the most telling behind UCLES dropping the phonetics paper in 1932, for as Spolsky (1995a:63–64) commented: 'The examination remaining so small, there may well have been discussions, Roach recollected, of closing it.' In 1929 CPE was about to be discontinued but Roach took over the running of it and stated in a rather self-congratulatory tone that he would spread it around the world: 'I saved it from the scrapheap and was given a free hand to make what I could of it' (Roach 1956b). The need to widen the candidate base (only 14 in 1928 and 33 in 1932) was obvious to Roach:

> It teetered along with 14 or 15 candidates a year, at a loss, though no one was vulgar enough to cost things until I came along and had found my feet (Roach undated :5).

Spolsky (2004:305) provides the following interpretation of Roach's activities:

> The Cambridge examination . . . was seized on by Roach when he joined the Syndicate after the First World War for both ideological and per-sonal reasons. He thought an international test would realize his 'modest ambition of making English the world language' (Roach 1956: 2) and he saw a role for his own activities . . . Roach, in 1929, hoped for 'the reaf-firmation and spread of British influence'.

The revival of CPE is often portrayed by Roach as a one-man job, but, in a few of his papers which survive in the Cambridge Assessment archives, he does acknowledge the librarian at the Foreign Office, Stephen Gaselee's help in expanding the number of candidates taking the examination. From the 1930s this relationship between Roach and Gaselee (and in all probability with the Foreign Office) reflected a shared goal of both Roach and the British government in developing cultural relations with foreign countries in general and expanding the role of English in the world in particular. The changes driven by Roach included: targeting CPE candidature more widely to attract non-teachers as well as teachers (from 1932 onwards, the CPE candidates were more widely defined as 'foreign students who desire to obtain evidence of their practical knowledge of the language, both written and spoken, and of their ability to read with comprehension standard works of English literature' (Exam Regulations 1932:1)); modifying the CPE syllabus to make it more attractive by dropping the difficult Phonetics paper and introducing alternatives to the Literature paper (the 1935 Economic and Commercial Knowledge paper and the 1938 English Life and Institutions); establishing additional test centres in Europe, eventually reaching 30 countries by 1939; and an increase in the number of sessions per year to two, in July and December.

Roach was interested in spreading English ideals and influence and considered English language testing a means for doing this. The personal promotion of the teaching of English and of CPE abroad by Roach, who took grace leave to do this in 1937 and 1939, together with the building of closer relationship with centres, all played their part and numbers were to rise to 752 by the outbreak of World War Two (see Figure 1.1 below).

Figure 1.1 Candidates taking CPE 1913–1939

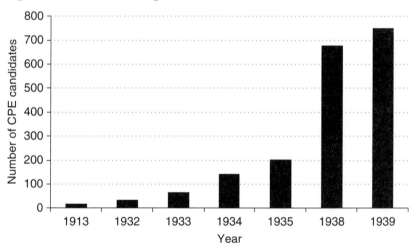

Attention was paid by Roach to the status of the examination in the United Kingdom as well. CPE was recognised by Cambridge University in 1937 and by Oxford in 1938 as the equivalent of the standard in English required of all students before entrance to the University (Roach 1944b). Such recognition added considerably to the credibility and the perceived value of the CPE examination, important factors for both teachers and students. Roach thus played a small but significant part in getting English to where it is today as an international language and without his efforts it is unlikely CPE or Cambridge English examinations would have survived.

The Introduction of a Lower Certificate in English (LCE) in 1939

Smith (2004:229–231) identifies a politically motivated focus on *simplified lexical content* in British ELT from the 1930s until the end of World War Two. He describes how:

> Discussions in the emerging United Kingdom 'centre' from the mid-1930s until the end of World War II had focused quite explicitly and narrowly on needs to propagate English as a world language via simplification of the lexical contents of instruction (in the case of Basic English, especially, but with a consensus emerging among those closer to practice than Ogden and his supporters that vocabulary control should be promoted only as a stepping-stone to 'real English'). Along with Basic, the other main 'systems' considered by the British Council Advisory Committee in the wartime years — West's 'New Method' series, Eckersley's *Essential English* and the *Oxford English Course*, with Palmer and Hornby's *Thousand-Word English* being increasingly seen as a major rival — were essentially all sets of materials and/or proposals for limited vocabularies.

Smith's insightful analysis of the developments in ELT in the 1930s sheds light on the introduction of the Cambridge Lower Certificate in English (LCE) in 1939, with 144 candidates at the first sitting. Developing a test at a lower level than CPE with a large potential candidature seems to fit well with the expansionist rationale for the English language that Smith described and was consonant with the personal agenda of Roach.

Hawkey (2009:Chapter 1) notes how in 1939 'a preparatory examination, the Lower Certificate in English (LCE), was introduced in response to a demand for an examination at a more elementary level'. The UCLES Regulations for the 1939 LCE examination papers (December 1938), as reproduced here, reveal a lot about LCE constructs, in the early years. Note in particular the references to 'simplified' texts, 'simple English' and 'relatively limited vocabulary'.

Description of the 1939 LCE exam

1. The examination will be held on 21 June and 6 December (1939), and only at centres outside Great Britain.
2. The subjects of Examination will be: Oral: Dictation, Reading and Conversation. Written: (a) Prescribed texts: 2 hours. (b) English Composition and Language: 2 hours. There will be no translation from and into English.
3 Paper (a) will contain a choice of straightforward questions on the following texts, which will also be set for 1940: Dickens, *A Tale of Two Cities* (dramatized and simplified, Oxford Univ. Press, 1s.); *Oxford*

English Course, Reading Book IV (Oxford U.P. 1s.); Swift, *Gulliver in Lilliput* (in Basic English, Evans, London, 1s.: Bernard Shaw, *Arms and the Man* (in Basic English, Evans, 1.s.).

Candidates will choose any *two* of the four books for study and will answer the questions dealing with those two. These texts, which are based on one form or another of simplified English, are intended to provide reading matter of a suitable standard of difficulty and to form the basis of the relatively limited vocabulary which, it is recognized, is all that can be expected at this stage. The object of the question paper will not be to test literary appreciation but to give candidates the opportunity of expressing themselves easily and correctly when handling a familiar subject-matter.

3. With the same object in view, Paper (*b*) will provide a choice of subjects for a free composition, such as a letter or an essay on a given subject. It will also include various tests in the correct use of simple English. A specimen paper will be sent from Syndicate Buildings on request.

4. The FEE will be 10*s*. and the local fee will be fixed according to local circumstances. The dates for entry will be 5 May and 8 October, or 24 May and 31 October with a late entry fee of 3*s*. 6*d*. Candidates cannot be accepted for the oral test alone.

The attempt in LCE to control vocabulary through use of Basic English and simplified texts fitted well with the limited vocabulary approach in the ELT materials emerging at the time. Roach was keen to promote research to establish the level of LCE in terms of vocabulary. He wanted to aim for a vocabulary level of 2,500–3,000 words and for this to provide a guide to teachers – the standard to be reached, as well as being useful to publishers in the standardisation of text books and to examiners in their selection of texts. Roach pushed for what is nowadays known as a wordlist (Roach 1944a). However, as we discuss below, this attempt to control vocabulary initially raised some hackles in the British Council.

The introduction of 'Cambridge Lower' in 1939 was to be an important development for many learners. While Proficiency was certainly a suitable examination for a small, university-level elite, Lower was a realistic objective and highly motivating for many adult learners at upper-intermediate level, who had probably spent a lot of time and money attending General English courses. The decision may have been influenced by the sudden influx of refugees in the 1930s who needed help with their English (Smith 2004:67, 237) and included many who were nowhere near the CPE level. The same events probably motivated publishing projects like Eckersley's *Essential English Course* (1938–42) which incorporated controlled and graded vocabulary and the planned recycling of new words. With the growth in the number of new centres in 30 countries worldwide for CPE candidates by 1939 (Weir 2003:6–7), more learners may also have pressed for the opportunity to take Cambridge EFL exams at a lower level than CPE (see Hawkey and Milanovic 2013 for a comprehensive and detailed picture of the origins and work of these centres).

The selection of prescribed texts for the 1939 LCE examination followed the format of the more advanced CPE exam. It also mirrored the form of examinations taken by British and other students then studying 'modern languages' in the United Kingdom (mainly, then, French, German or Spanish) under UCLES and other examination boards. Prescribed texts or 'literature papers' were then a routine element in modern languages exams, and are still to be found to this day. The presence of a literature component in the Cambridge English examinations can be seen as taking account of those stakeholders who held a more academic as against a utilitarian view of language learning.

The new examination thus shared a literary ethos with CPE. However, the Regulations for 1943 say quite clearly that the main aim of the prescribed texts paper was 'not to test literary appreciation' but 'to give candidates the opportunity of expressing themselves easily and correctly when handling a familiar subject-matter'. It was assumed this would be facilitated by literary subject-matter albeit 'dramatized and simplified'.

Hawkey (2009:21) argues that the construct of the study of literature as part of the study of language, like the construct of translation, was part of the LCE heritage. One contemporary 'academic' viewpoint provides some insight into why literature was to play an important part for so long in language testing in the UK:

> The value in use of a language is its literature, and if it has no value in use it has essentially no value at all, except for purely utilitarian purposes. . . The language of any people is embodied and enshrined in its literature. The literature represents the best use to which a people have been able to put its language. Moreover the literature is the representation of the finest and the most valuable thought that a people has been able to evolve. . .it is this which should be taught to the vast number of persons who wish to learn a language simply as a means of culture and education. The educative value of learning a language purely as language is comparable to the educative value of learning shorthand. Thought is not enriched at all in the process (Palmer and Redman 1932:18).

The LCE did not initially assess candidates' translation ability (allegedly for administrative rather than construct reasons), but this was introduced in 1944 when 18 languages were catered for in the LCE translation paper.

At first sight it might seem odd that the first LCE examination was only offered 'at centres outside Great Britain'. According to Roach (1984:6), it was because the British Council opposed the introduction of the LCE that 'I seem to have given way then to the extent of not introducing the examination at home [UK] centres'. The British Council had dissuaded Roach from the idea because in their view LCE texts would not be 'current English throughout' (Roach 1944a:xxviii). According to Hawkey (2009:8–9,17–19), it was likely that the British Council's objections stemmed from a perception that an English examination at a level below that of the CPE might suggest an acceptance of lower target standards in the language.

An interesting minute from an UCLES British Council Joint Committee meeting (Joint Committee 1942:8) confirms continuing concern about this:

> Professor Daniel Jones drew attention to the fact that books in Basic English are among those prescribed for the Lower Certificate in English and suggested that the British Council could not associate themselves with an examination in something which might not be English.

By 1943, however, the Syndicate and the British Council were to agree on the need for the LCE examination in the light of the growing demand for it to be offered at United Kingdom centres as well as overseas. In 1943 Roach introduced LCE in the United Kingdom for the Allied Forces. Roach (1944b:37) described how the war brought a 'growing keenness of Service authorities to promote the study of English among Allied forces on British soil'. His paper on oral examinations (see Appendix C) describes how the examinations were taken for example by Polish airmen. In addition there were 'allied civilians and friendly aliens who were learning English while working in war factories, as teachers and nurses, in commerce, or in the offices of allied governments in London' (1944b:37). Socio-political considerations appear to have won out over cultural sensitivities.

The British Council and Cambridge: An important alliance

The origins of, and the rationale for, the British Council can be found in the Records in the National Archives:

> On the initiative of the Foreign Office, a British Committee for Relations with Other Countries was established in 1934. In January 1935, the word 'Committee' was replaced by 'Council', and in 1936 the title was shortened to 'British Council'. Its primary purpose was to counter cultural propaganda by the Axis powers; more generally its functions were to promote wider appreciation of Great Britain and the English language abroad and develop closer cultural and commercial links with other countries. (http://www.nationalarchives.gov.uk/catalogue/displaycataloguedetails. asp?CATID=40&CATLN=1&accessmethod=5)

The British Council was to become one of the main drivers behind spreading English and Cambridge English Examinations abroad. From 1941 it would be a close partner in the development of these examinations for over 50 years, providing important advice to Cambridge based on its growing experience and expertise in English Language Teaching around the world.

The influence of the British Council on Cambridge English language examinations from the 1940s right through to the early 1990s should not be underestimated. Hawkey and Milanovic (2013) record how for most of the period there were:

> ... relatively few permanent UCLES home staff to grapple with the growing complexity of English language assessment issues ... 'the organisation essentially resembled a cottage industry until the great expansion of the 1980s' (Raban 2008:7).

The 1941 agreement between the British Council and UCLES (see below for a copy discovered by the author in the Cambridge Assessment Archives) makes clear how close the working relationship was to be between the two organisations in running the Cambridge English examinations until their formal parting of ways in 1993. For almost 50 years the British Council, by virtue of its global mission, possessed considerable knowledge and expertise in the area of Teaching English as a Foreign Language, and as a result would play a major role in the development of English language tests at Cambridge. In addition it would promote and deliver Cambridge examinations around the world through its network of offices overseas. By the late 1980s the situation would change and as the British Council dismantled its own professional cadre of experts in English language teaching and testing, Cambridge was heavily investing in building a professional EFL Evaluation Unit of its own. The balance of influence through professional expertise would shift.

The 1941 agreement, British Council and The University of Cambridge Local Examinations Syndicate

Agreement to collaborate in the conduct of examinations in English, drafted at a Conference of representatives of the British Council and the University of Cambridge Local Examination Syndicate held on Saturday, 29th March 1941, for submission to the Council and the Syndicate.

1. A joint committee of the British Council and the Cambridge Local Examinations Syndicate, three members to be appointed by each, shall be set up for the general supervision of these examinations.

2. This committee shall make recommendations as to the syllabus and the conduct of the examinations, subject to the understanding that the ultimate responsibility for the appointment of Examiners, the marking of papers, the assessment of standards, and the issue of certificate shall rest with the Syndicate.

3. Where the establishment of new centres for the examinations is proposed the Syndicate shall act, through the committee, on the advice of the British Council, who will consult, where necessary, with the Foreign

Office, with His Majesty's Missions, and with the local Representative of the British Council.

4. It is understood that in the conduct of the examination the Syndicate will co-operate in every possible way with the Institutes of the British Council and with other centres in which the Council are interested.

5. The regulations issued by the Syndicate for these examinations shall state that they are conducted by the Syndicate in conjunction with the British Council.

6. The British Council shall consider with the Syndicate year by year what grant, if any, should be made by the British Council towards the cost of conducting and advertising these examinations.

7. Nothing in this agreement shall be regarded as restricting individual Institutes of the British Council, or other centres in which they are interested, from conducting their own examinations.

8. This agreement may be terminated at two years' notice on either side and may be reviewed at any time at the request of the Syndicate or of the British Council (Joint Committee 1941:55–56).

Sir Stephen Gaselee KCMG, the librarian of the Foreign Office, acted as Chairman of the Joint Committee of the British Council and Cambridge Local Examinations Syndicate at its inaugural meeting on the 29 March 1941. Roach also served on this powerful committee along with a number of high level academic representatives of the British Council: Professor F Clarke the Director of the Institute of Education of the University of London and member of the British Council Committee on the Overseas Teaching Service, Professor Ifor Evans, Educational Advisor to the British Council and Provost at University College London (UCL) 1951–1966, and S H Wood representative of the Board of Education of the British Council who was involved in helping refugees from Germany in particular in the 1930s and helped set up the Resident Foreigners Committee, later the Home Division of the British Council. Professor Daniel Jones, Head of the Department of Phonetics at University College London, was a further addition to the British Council representation in the July 1941 committee meeting. A S Hornby an English grammarian, lexicographer, and pioneer in the field of English language learning and teaching, the founder and first editor of the *English Language Teaching* journal (published by the British Council from 1946 onwards) and the linguistic adviser to the British Council joined in July 1946. The Syndicate was represented at the first meeting by S W Grose a Fellow and Tutor of Christ's College, Cambridge, J O Roach an assistant secretary at the Syndicate (1925–45), H S Bennet and W Nalder Williams, Secretary of the Syndicate (1921–45). There was additional representation from the Foreign Office at these committee meetings for example Mr Gurney at the October 1943 meeting, a member until January 1945 when he was replaced by Montagu Pollock until 1946 when A H Ballantyne representing the Cultural Relations Department of the Foreign Office took over.

This Joint Committee was to continue in this form until 1993 and evidences a close and mutually beneficial working relationship between the British Council and Cambridge in promoting the spread of English and Cambridge English examinations abroad. The knowledge, professional expertise and academic standing of these high-ranking British Council representatives resulted in a significant contribution to the development of Cambridge English examinations, and the need to report annually to such a committee containing leading experts in the field would have been salutary for the very small group of Syndicate officers involved in the Cambridge English examinations.

English as a world language

This close connection with the British Council was not unrelated to the powerful, external forces that were beginning to impact on the direction of English language teaching and assessment. In the years following World War Two it was less the traditional attitudes to language and language learning, less the new insights from linguistics or developments in modern language pedagogy that influenced assessment practice at Cambridge, but rather the economic and social forces that were at work in making English a dominant language around the globe. Traditional approaches such as the Grammar-Translation Method and teaching English as an access route to great literature were to succumb to pressing utilitarian needs for English as a means of communication between people rather than as a rarefied object of academic study. Changes in Cambridge English language examinations in this period reflect this mind shift. In Stern's words the interest in language became 'social' rather than 'scholarly' (Stern 1983:81). Palmer (in Palmer and Redman 1932:22–23) had insightfully argued at a very early stage that language should be seen: 'In its essence as a means of communication . . . teachers generally miss this fundamental point. They look upon the language as a code or as a subject or as a literature – in short as something to be learned or studied, whereas a language is rather something to be used.' The latter view was to become more widespread after World War Two.

The growth of English as a world language is explained by Crystal (1997) as the result of British military and political imperialism and economic strength in the 19th century as well as it being the best means at the time for societies and individuals to access new knowledge (see also Phillipson 1992:6 et seq. for a detailed discussion of the dominance of English and chapter 5 for a discussion of British linguistic imperialism). Its survival as a global language in the 20th century Crystal puts down to American economic supremacy (Crystal 1997) and Phillipson (1992:7) to United States military and technological leadership. Phillipson also points to the availability of massive government and private foundation funds in 1950–70, for example to the British Council in the United Kingdom to support the propagation of the language: 'the ultimate purpose being to achieve the foreign policy goals set out in the Drogheda report. . .little effort is made to legitimate the expansion of English in terms of anything other than British self interest' (Phillipson 1992:150–152).

Pennycook (1994:134) similarly links the growth of applied linguistics to the need felt for cultural and linguistic expansion rather than material exploitation by the United States after World War Two. A 'search for new means of social and political control in the world' saw 'the prodigious spread' of English in the post-war era. Phillipson's and Pennycook's perspectives and comments both reflect a particular philosophical position and a 'conspiracy' view of the world.

De Swaan (2001:27) provides an alternative explanation:

> A language is a 'hyper collective' good: the more speakers it has, the higher its communication value for each one of them. Thus, when people think that a language is gaining new speakers, that in itself is a reason for them to want to learn it too. That is why, in an age of globalization, only a few languages remain for transnational communication and these often prevail even in national societies.

Howatt's and Crystal's pragmatic view of the world and how things come about is equally plausible. Howatt (personal communication) points out that in fact English only became a world auxiliary language after colonialism came to an end. One reason for this perhaps was that the newly independent nations no longer needed to see the language as emblematic of the distrusted colonial power, but as a useful asset which had been left behind – a bit like a railway system, perhaps? The conventions of British materials and pedagogy were well entrenched in many newly independent countries (partly thanks to some of the more enlightened colonial educators) and provided a well defined (if sometimes fossilised) basis for future teacher training and syllabus design.

Howatt and Widdowson (2004:242) reflecting on the growth of ELT in the United Kingdom in this period refer us to the effects of economic prosperity and growing air travel which brought an increasing number of students to the United Kingdom and led to the development of English for Academic Purposes tests such as English Proficiency Test Battery (EPTB) in the 1960s and later in the 1970s English Language Testing Service (ELTS) (see Davies 2008b for a detailed history of both examinations). This together with a substantial rise in the number of immigrant workers arriving from former colonies in the 1960s led to a marked rise in those requiring language courses. People no longer tended to stay in one place as had been the case earlier in the century (Howatt 1997).

Crystal (1997) expands in detail on a variety of other factors which led to the increasing dominance of English as a world language: access to knowledge, and its use in international relations, the press, advertising, broadcasting, motion pictures, popular music, international travel, international safety, education, and communications. English was the *lingua franca* needed 'to meet the needs of international communication' (Howatt 1997: 263).

Concomitantly there was a tenfold increase in those taking LCE from 1946 with an increase from 3,656 candidates to 34,046 by 1966. In the same period CPE numbers rose from 1,379 to 10,422. Total English language candidates (LCE, CPE and Diploma) rose from 6,283 in 1947 to 66,061 by 1976. Spolsky observes (2008b:450): 'The market forces in the period after the Second World War with growing demand for English Language teaching and testing persuaded the Syndics to take the field seriously'. These changes were to influence what was tested and also eventually how it was tested.

Language in use as against language as an object of study

These post-war developments impacted on Cambridge English language examinations in a number of ways. There had been discussion of the possibility of providing a language alternative to literature as early as 1941 as the minutes for the Joint Committee meeting of that year record (Joint Committee December 1941). However this was seen largely as an emergency measure for those centres who could not lay their hands on the set books (e.g. those in prisoner-of-war camps). Rebuilding these texts from the collective memories of other prisoners, though admirable in itself, was not seen as adequate preparation. The Joint Conference minutes (July 1950) record discussion of the possibility of a general language paper for those who could not access literature texts or for whom it was not possible to offer translation papers. Probably for practical and logistic reasons this was not approved at the next Joint Committee meeting (Minutes of Joint Committee meeting November 1950).

A real shift in the balance of 'academic' versus instrumental activities in CPE occurred in 1956 (see Regulations 1956:5, 9) when it became possible to take a 'Use of English' paper containing a variety of formats as an alternative to 'Translation'. This new paper has remained albeit with changed formats until this day. It started with a reading passage with Short Answer Questions, then a sentence reformulation task, a task requiring recombining sentences into a more coherent paragraph, a task involving knowledge of how punctuation can change meaning, an editing task, a descriptive writing task and finally a task testing knowledge of affixes. The long history of the Use of English paper in this form partially explains why the current equivalent is apparently so diverse.

A number of discrete item formats in the Use of English paper illustrate the influence of the structural approach namely the concern with habit formation and pattern practice (see Fries 1945). This aspect of methodology can be traced back to the earlier work of Palmer whose work on habit formation dates from the 1920s (Palmer 1921b). It took hold again in the early 1960s under the influence of structural linguistics and the 'structure drill' or 'pattern practice' in the audio-lingual language laboratory (Brooks 1960). Item 4B from the 1971 Use of English paper is a good example of this:

1971 Use of English Paper

4(*b*). Rewrite each of the following sentences so as to refer to present instead of past time. Give one answer only in each case.

    Example He thought of coming tomorrow,
    Answer   He is thinking of coming tomorrow,
    Example He thought it was untrue.
    Answer   He thinks it is untrue.
    (i)   He seemed to be quite content
    (ii)   I considered giving a party.
    (iii)   The children resembled their father.
    (iv)   She believed him to be a doctor.
    (v)   It struck me he was probably a sailor.

The downgrading of literature

Further important shifts in the balance of activities in the examination were about to happen. Smith (2004:241) again provides us with insightful background that helps us to understand the changes that were to take place at UCLES in the 1960s:

> In 1960, at the beginning of a new era of 'intense cultivation of ELT' (Phillipson 1992: 113), Pattison reported somewhat regretfully that 'Literature had tended to be pushed into the background in recent years by the rapid development of language teaching' (Minutes, British Council English Studies Advisory Committee, 9 November 1960, BW 138/1, in Public Records Office, Kew). The clearest (and most paradoxical) sign of this was the transformation in the views of Arthur King . . ., who between 1959 and 1969 exerted considerable influence as the Controller of the Education Division of the British Council (Donaldson 1984: 218):
>
>> Largely through him, the old system of the British Council Institute and the direct teaching of English as a preliminary to knowledge of the British culture and people fell out of favour [. . .]. [H]e believed, as one of his colleagues put it, that 'it was a mistake to carry the luggage of literature' into the sphere of language teaching. He recognised correctly that not everybody wants to learn literature and that it is not necessarily the best methodological approach to what has become known as English for Special Purposes (ESP) (Donaldson 1984: 218).

Smith argues that King (paradoxically a poet, a writer and an expert in literary stylistics) was the man most responsible for the British Council's shift *away* from literature and 'cultural propaganda' *towards* language in the 1960s. The presence of King as one of the British Council representatives on the powerful UCLES/British Council Joint Committee from June 1960 through to 1969 would appear to be significant given the similar direction Cambridge English examinations were to take in this period.

In the 1960s, we can discern the beginnings of a significant shift in Cambridge's approach to its English examinations, namely that language might be divorced from testing literary or cultural knowledge. The UCLES/ British Council Joint Committee in 1962 discussed recent developments in the field of English teaching and their relevance to the Syndicate's examinations. It was felt that:

> . . .the policy at present followed in the Certificate of Proficiency exami-
> nation, whereby candidates are expected to have some familiarity with
> English background and culture, should not be altered, but that enquiry
> should be made about the extent of the demand for a more purely lin-
> guistic type of examination. Mr. Cartledge [a British Council representa-
> tive] was asked to obtain information from Teheran about proposals
> which have been made there, and it was agreed that the Secretary, in con-
> sultation with the British Council, should send out an exploratory circu-
> lar to Local Education Authorities in this country (Joint Committee of
> the Local Examinations Syndicate and the British Council 1962).

It is possible in this period to date the start of a gradual but critical change in the focus of UCLES English examinations to one of language rather than language, literature and culture. As a result of widespread consultation, a new syllabus was proposed which reflected a shift towards a primarily language-based examination (UCLES 1982:1):

> Change in the Regulations for the Certificate of Proficiency exami-
> nation. After considering detailed recommendations made by the
> Executive Committee, it was agreed that the Regulations for the 1966
> examination should require a candidate to take a compulsory English
> Language paper and two of the following:
> • English Literature (or one of the alternatives);
> • Use of English;
> • Translation from and into English.

Thus a new form of the examination was introduced in 1966: 'The develop-ment of a semi-objective paper at Proficiency level, systematically testing usage and vocabulary, made it possible from 1966 to take Proficiency, by appropriate choice of alternative papers, as a purely language examination' (UCLES 1982:1). As in 1953, candidates still had to take two other papers in addition to the compulsory 'English Language' paper. However, unlike 1953, candidates could choose both 'Use of English' and 'Translation from and into English' as two additional papers, which meant they did not have to take anything from 'English Literature' or its alternatives.

The decision in CPE to contemplate a more language-focused route divorced from literature from 1966 onwards was groundbreaking, and reflected a developing interest in the use of English among the language teaching profession and applied linguists. It signifies the increased importance accorded to English as a global means of communication rather than an object for study.

A *General report on the Use of English paper in CPE* 1971 comments on the widespread popularity of this new paper:

> The Use of English paper was introduced as part of the Certificate of Proficiency in English examination in 1953, as an alternative to the compulsory translation test for candidates in whose languages there were difficulties in arranging an examination. Its popularity as a straight alternative to Translation grew steadily until 1966. In that year a change in the form of examination made it possible to take, with the compulsory English Language paper, both Use of English and Translation, instead of one of these in conjunction with the Literature paper or one of its alternatives. By 1968 the paper had the largest entry of all the optional Proficiency papers, and in 1970 over 65% of the total entry. The paper under detailed report, that for June 1971, was taken by 5,808 candidates, or 73% of the total entry.

Following the increasing popularity of the Use of English paper in the Proficiency examination, a similar paper was introduced in 1970, under the title of Structure and Usage, for the Lower Certificate (UCLES 1973:4).

The presence of Arthur King and other highly respected British Council representatives on the two major committees responsible for overseeing English language examinations at Cambridge was significant.

The British Council and Cambridge English Examinations

The authority and global standing of the British Council in English Language Teaching circles was on the rise in the 1960s. Its influence on the development of Cambridge English language examinations can be seen in its strong presence on the two main committees overseeing the running of Cambridge English examinations at this time: The Joint Committee of the Local Examinations Syndicate and the British Council and The Executive Committee for the Syndicate's Examinations in English for Foreign Students.

The Joint Committee was an influential body in the 1960s and it is revealing to see leading lights in the United Kingdom ELT / Applied Linguistics field, serving as the representatives of the British Council on that Committee, including Professor Bruce Pattison (the first Chair in the Teaching of English as a Foreign Language, University of London 1948), H A Cartledge (a prolific English Language Teaching author) and G E Perren (Director of the British Council, English teaching information centre (ETIC) London, one of the first specialists in English language testing and training of teachers of English as a second language in the United Kingdom and author of *Linguistic Problems of Overseas Students in Britain* 1963). Later representatives of the British Council were to include Dr W R Lee (editor of the *English Language Teaching Journal* 1958–1981 and chairman of the International Association of Teachers of English as a Foreign Language (IATEFL) 1970–1984), B M Lott, Controller of the British Council English Language Teaching Division, Roland Hindmarsh (author of the *Cambridge English Lexicon: a graded word list for materials writers and course-designers*), Brendan Carroll (lead developer of the ELTS test), Arthur H King (Controller of the Education Division of the British Council, a poet and an English literature specialist), R A Cavaliero (to be Deputy Director General of the British Council), and Peter Hargreaves (Senior Consultant to the Testing and Evaluation Unit).

The Syndicate was represented at this time by J M Y Andrew, J Winny, J M Burchnall (the first woman appointee at officer level in 1954), J O Roach (Assistant Secretary 1925–45), T S Wyatt (Secretary of the Syndicate 1961–72), M E Overton (Assistant to the Secretaries from 1946 and later subject officer for English) and W G Shepherd (Assistant to the Secretaries 1962–88). Only later would there be staff with specialised expertise in English language testing and/or Applied Linguistics such as E F Chaplen from 1971–75, John Trim from 1972 and Peter Hargreaves from 1988.

Sir Fred Clarke, a representative of the British Council, was the chair 1941–46, Dr G B Jeffrey, again a representative the British Council, from November 1946–50, S W Grose, a representative of the Syndicate from 1951 –54 (a member since 1941), the Master of Christ's College 1955–57, B W Downs, a representative of the British Council was the chairman 1959–65, followed by Bruce Pattison a representative of the British Council June 1966– 86. Finally, it was chaired by Sir John Lyons an eminent applied linguist 1986–93 after which the committee was dissolved, the minutes of its meeting of 8 July 1992 explaining that 'many of the functions formerly undertaken by the Joint Committee could be performed in other more efficient ways'.

The disbanding of the committee marked the end of an era in another sense. For almost 50 years the British Council was an invaluable source of support and professional advice on ELT matters for the Syndicate and its English language examinations. With the development of the Syndicate's own in-house professional English language teaching and testing cadre from the late 1980s (see below), and the radical downsizing by the British Council of its own at the same time, the central role played by the British Council in the development of Cambridge English examinations began to dissipate. But this is further on in our history. In the 1950s and 1960s the British Council was a very powerful voice in the Cambridge English language testing story. Close co-operation between the British Council and UCLES can be seen in the annual Joint Conference of the Cambridge Syndicate and the British Council which appears to have been held annually in London from July 1947–52 (according to the minutes of the conference surviving in the Cambridge Assessment archives). It was attended by representatives of the British Council from it offices around the world, a small number of representatives from the Syndicate, and representatives of the examiners. Topics ranged from administrative issues such as dates of Cambridge examinations, entries, safeguards against impersonation by candidates, to professional issues – for example of syllabus, test content, time allowed for question papers, allocation of marks within and between papers, possibility of examining candidates in pairs in the oral (rejected at 1950 meeting), dictation of punctuation in the dictation part of the oral test and other method-related issues. It provided a formal opportunity for Cambridge to listen to various stakeholders from the field and build upon input from a wide range of professionals from the British Council's professional ELT cadre. Given the small number of Syndicate staff working on the three papers (CPE, LCE and the Diploma), and their relative lack of professional expertise in ELT, this was clearly beneficial for the development of the Cambridge examinations.

It is interesting to note that Roach, despite his resignation in high dudgeon in 1945 on not being awarded the Secretaryship, was to continue to make a contribution to Cambridge English Language examinations on the Joint Committee until 1971. The strength of Roach's influence and of the Syndicate's appreciation of it had been evidenced in the minute of the Joint Committee for 17 July 1945: 'It was further agreed that, in view of his unique experience and the high value of his services, Mr J O Roach should continue to receive an invitation to attend the meetings of the Committee and should also receive copies of all Committee papers'. Perhaps his continued, authoritative presence is not surprising in the light of the limited number and expertise of personnel working on the Cambridge English examinations within the organisation itself. Hawkey and Milanovic (2013) interviewed Bill Shepherd, Assistant to the Secretaries at UCLES from 1962 to 1988, and much involved with the English as a Foreign Language exams. Shepherd provided the following portrait of UCLES staffing in the early 1960s:

> I find it now hard to conceive how this whole range of highly responsible activity was left to one "Secretary" and one admin Chief Clerk, the latter with, however, up-and-coming younger specialised staff, something not available to the Secretary. My recollection now is of something analogous to the old variety artiste controlling for laughs, the simultaneous spinning on long sticks of large dinner plates.

The UCLES Executive Committee for the Syndicate's examinations in English for foreign students was set up in November 1957 as a sub-committee of the Joint Committee. Hawkey and Milanovic (2013) detail how:

> This committee was expected to do business as well as direct it, 'to conduct under the general direction of the Joint Committee, the detailed business arising out of the examinations'. The Executive Committee would be supported by a new Syllabus Sub-committee 'responsible for drafting syllabuses and considering suggestions for modifications' (both citations from UCLES Cambridge Examinations in English Survey for 1957, p.7). The committees were often influential in their own right because their decisions took account of the academic and professional views and actions of members from outside the Examinations Syndicate.

It was served by a small number of Syndicate members (up to four), initially including S W Grose as Chairman, D Daiches, F C Powell, and Syndicate secretarial staff, two representatives of the British Council to be nominated by the Controller, Education Division for each meeting, two representatives of Local Education Authority schools, one Local Education Authority official, one university teacher of English to foreign students, one or two examiners, occasional centre representatives, plus the chair of the Joint Committee (normally a British Council representative) as an ex-officio member.

The Committee provided a useful forum for eliciting external professional advice on syllabus and examination content as well as administrative practices. John Sinclair, later Chair of Modern Languages and Professor of Corpus Linguistics at Birmingham University, joined the Executive Committee at the October meeting in 1963 and was invited to set the CPE Use of English paper with a team at the Applied Linguistics Department of Edinburgh University. British applied linguists and English Language Teaching specialists on the committee such as J Sinclair, H A Cartledge, K Cripwell, G. E Perren, M Swan, E F Candlin, B Pattison, R Hindmarsh, J Eckersley, Pitt Corder and P Strevens, all played an important part in the 1960/1970s developments in Cambridge English examination history as it moved towards the structure of the tests as we know them today.

Outside UCLES changes were also taking place in language teaching in the United Kingdom from the 1950s onwards. A further indicator of the growing importance attached to language in use can be seen in the development of the *situational approach* in language teaching.

The Situational Approach

The Situational Approach to teaching English as a Foreign Language (see Hornby 1950 for an early variant of this) in the early 1950s and 1960s sought to locate the teaching of paradigmatic grammatical items in simple interesting and relevant situations which made their meaning clear and which were carefully graded. Examples of this can be found post-war in C E Eckersley's *Essential English for Foreign Students* (the course was first published between 1938 and 1942; 1955 was a new edition) and A S Hornby's *Oxford Progressive English for Adult Learners* (1954–56) which were the only full-scale courses available from British publishers. The approach grew out of the preference in parts of the world influenced by the UK in favour of inductive teaching, in which the L1 played a minimal part. Howatt (personal communication) provides the following insightful sketches of these two influential books:

> Eckersley (1938–42) was one of the first to notice that there was an increasing demand for English from foreign students in London, many of whom were refugees from the growing political turmoil on the continent. The background for this course is London in the 1930s. He devised a set of dialogues purporting to be conversations about the problems of learning English grammar and related comments from the 'students' to the difficulties of different mother tongues. The lessons were set in the sitting-room of their teacher Mr Priestley who lived in a 'typical' middle-class home in suburban London. In this way he combined the language of everyday conversation and the grammar the students needed to know.
>
> Hornby's course owes a lot to Palmer, but he added a new dimension of his own which he called 'the situational approach' (Hornby 1950) but he used the term 'situation' in a special and rather unfamiliar sense. For Hornby, a 'situation' was a context that a teacher could invent in the classroom which would help to teach the meaning of new words and sentence patterns without having to translate them. So, for example, the teacher would walk to the door while saying "I am walking to the door", open it while saying "I am opening the door" and close it while saying "I am closing the door". These 'situations' are intended to display the meaning of the teacher's utterances and they have nothing to do with social interaction.
>
> By contrast, there are also 'situations' which are essentially social events like a visit to a café, for instance (the situation is typically illustrated with a picture in the textbook) and the characters involved say things like: "Can I help you? Yes, I'd like a cup of coffee, please," . . . etc. Hornby never used dialogues in this way but they became popular in the 1960s aided by new audio-visual technologies, and they were of course the first choice for teaching materials designed to implement notional-functional syllabuses in the 1970s and beyond.

Howatt notes that almost every candidate for LCE at the time would have 'done' one or the other of the two books in preparation for the LCE (from 1975 FCE) examination.

Later textbooks for adults such as *English in Situations* (O'Neil 1970) used social, interactional situations to teach new grammatical patterns. In *New Concept English: First Things First; Practice and Progress; Developing Skills; Fluency in English* (Alexander 1967) situations were used as events with real-life language use. In *First Things First* Alexander used recorded dialogues to introduce new points of grammar orally, at other levels he relied on short reading passages, mainly based on jokey anecdotes. Howatt (1997:264) notes: 'One of the characteristics of English Language Teaching in the 1960s and 1970s was a concern with practical communication at a relatively low level which lead to a stress on situational teaching'.

The influence of the situational approach is mirrored in the increasing use of dialogues in the reading aloud task in the CPE oral paper. By 1970 there were no more passages of continuous prose set for this task and they were almost entirely dialogic.

Year: 1945 June
Passage: 2
Page: 2

"And you know, Ernest always had a soft spot in his heart for me."

"Yes," said Lilla, "Ernest's soft spots are often highly inconvenient. Today, for instance, when I wanted the car to take me home after a busy afternoon, he chooses to lend it to someone else. I have to be at the chapel this evening for the Literary Society Meeting and I should be worn out if I made two journeys across the Downs beforehand."

"Good for your figure," Hannah said. "The time may come when your tailor won't be able to cope with it. So that's why you're dining out. I should like to see you at the Literary Meeting, trying not to yawn. What's the subject?"

"Charles Lamb."

"Hardy annual," Hannah muttered, twitching her nose.

"It's a duty," Mrs Spenser Smith said patiently, yet with a touch of grandeur. "I'd much rather stay at home with a nice book, but these things have to be supported, for the sake of the young people."

"Ah yes, but it isn't the young people who go to them. It's the old girls, like myself, who have nothing else to do. I've seen them, sitting on the hard benches, half asleep, like fowls gone to roost."

"They'll go to sleep to night," Lilla admitted, "though", she added, as she remembered to keep Hannah in her place, "I don't see why you should try to be funny at their expense. Trying to be funny is one of your failings."

In 1975 in the June Oral FCE Paper 5 has a component entitled Situations, where the candidate has to cope with extended response situations such as:

1975 FCE Oral paper

2 You are in a shop waiting to buy some sweets. A lady comes into the shop and says to you "Do you sell large envelopes?" What do you say to her?

17 You are in a station in your own country. An English tourist asks if you would tell him how to use the public telephone. What do you say?

These items were reminiscent of the *Association of Recognised English Language Schools (ARELS)* taped oral tests at the Certificate and Diploma levels which were popular in language schools in the United Kingdom in the 1970s and tested social responses to recorded remarks (see Hawkey 2004: 40–56 for a comprehensive discussion of the ARELS oral test).

The tasks in the Paper 1 Composition are similarly contextualised in meaningful situations:

Paper 1 Composition

1 You and a friend have quarrelled. You feel that you are at fault. Write a letter to apologise and arrange another meeting.

2 Write an account of an occasion when you and a friend were caught in a heavy storm and had to find shelter.

The concern with meaning in the situational approach and its relation to context was perhaps not surprising given the presence of a strong socio-linguistic tradition in the United Kingdom. This was evidenced in the work on the context of situation by Malinowski 1923 who was based at the London School of Economics 1922–42 and perhaps more so in the career of the prominent social anthropologist J R Firth. Firth pioneered academic research into the relationship between meaning and context first at University College London and later the School of Oriental and African Studies.

However, although the contextualisation of language with the arrival of the situational approach in teaching and testing was welcome, it would become apparent that situations on their own did not form a sound basis for developing language syllabuses. Far too many uses of language could not readily be encapsulated in a limited number of situational scenarios with the danger that the learner might be left 'unprepared for anything out of the ordinary' (Wilkins 1976:18). We will return to a discussion of the more sustainable 'communicative' developments in English Language Teaching in the final part of this chapter (*1971–2012: The communicative era*).

The issue of scoring validity 1913–1970: Different gods, different mountain tops

Two very different traditions

The concern for contextualising language in pedagogy and testing in the United Kingdom was in stark contrast to the situation in the United States, where the structuralist linguistics of Bloomfield (1926, 1933) and his followers, with an emphasis on the study of language as a decontextualised system, dominated approaches to language teaching and testing. The presentation and practice of new language in classroom situations was not a defining feature of American versions of the structural approach in contrast to the British Orthodoxy of the Oral–Structural–Situational approach. Smith (2004:226–7) cites the following differentiation provided by Tickoo (1964:177):

> ... whereas (American) structural linguistics 'contributes usefully towards one important aspect of foreign-language teaching, i.e. what to teach' (pp. 176–77), 'It has little to offer us as to the "why" and "how" of teaching English' (p. 176). On the other hand, British orthodoxy 'is as much pedagogic as linguistic. [. . .] [A] very distinctive feature [. . .] is its emphasis on meaning. Simplified and graded patterns are therefore associated with situations'.

This decontextualised structural approach in the United States formed an ideal bedfellow for the psychometric predilection that was to dominate educational testing in the United States for most of the 20th century (see below). The concern with psychometrics, so pronounced in the United States, was not to be so influential in the United Kingdom, though as we shall see it was not entirely absent.

In order to complete the review of our early history of the years leading up until 1970, we need to look at approaches to *scoring validity* in testing practice. The scoring validity of a test is a matter of the appropriateness of the criteria employed in evaluating the output of test tasks and how far can we depend on the scores this assessment produces in terms of the consistency of the results obtained from the procedures employed. Along with cognitive and context validities it forms an important aspect of defining the language construct(s) being measured in a test (Weir 2005a).

We have focused so far on the influence of the content and methods of language teaching and the wider socio-economic context on the language abilities tested at Cambridge 1913–1970. However, as well as the content of tests, '*what*' is to be tested, we must address the '*how*' This involves consideration of the appropriateness of various test task types e.g. constructed response versus objective formats, the aptness of the criteria employed in marking candidate performance, and the consistency of their application. This takes us into the technical field of psychometrics: a branch of psychology dealing with the measurement of mental traits, capacities, and processes.

Psychometrics, an important technical component of professional expertise in language testing, was to dominate education in the United States, but was to have less influence in the United Kingdom at a national and an institutional level. However, in the late 19th and early 20th century in the United Kingdom there were individual contributions to the field, for example Edgeworth (1888, 1890), Hartog (1918), Burt (1921), Valentine and Emmett (1932) and Hartog, Rhodes, and Burt (1936) (see also Chapter 3 for additional detail on psychometric concerns in assessing writing in British Examining Boards and Chapter 4 for consideration of psychometric concerns in assessing speaking). These contributions notwithstanding, language testing was not yet a profession in the United Kingdom in this early period. In contrast Danziger (1990) and Brown (1992) provide intriguing accounts of the early development of psychology as a professional discipline in the United States, which was to add intellectual weight to the psychometric approach.

Substantive differences grew between the United Kingdom and the United States in their approaches to language testing from 1913–1970. In the United States the predominant focus was to be on the *reliability* aspect of scoring validity, the psychometric qualities of a test whereas, as we saw above, in the United Kingdom we find a far greater concern with *context validity*: a concern with the *how* in the United States as against the *what* in the United Kingdom. In this section we examine the genesis of these transatlantic differences, which in turn helps shed light on the growth of two very different testing traditions.

Spolsky is critical of the United Kingdom (Cambridge) position with regard to reliability in this period:

> . . . the issue of reliability that Edgeworth had raised in 1888 continued to be of only marginal interest, and the examinations remained untouched by psychometric notions. One can see this by comparing the 1931 College Board's examination, with its true-false questions, its concentration on language, and its lack of curricular concern, with the forms of the Cambridge papers . . ., with their emphasis on curriculum, their inclusion of literature, and their absolute reliance on subjective grading. The Cambridge examiners continued until quite recently to be more concerned about what to test (i.e. about curriculum) than about how to test it (1995a:65).

Valentine and Emmett (1932:9–10) were initially fairly circumspect in their criticism of United Kingdom examinations at the time. Valentine, who was the chairman of the Joint Northern Matriculation Examining Board and later Professor of Education at Birmingham, and Emmett, took pains to stress that 'the majority of examining boards are facing their difficult tasks . . . with the utmost desire to use every kind of examination technique, every device, statistical and psychological, which may improve the reliability and fairness of their examinations'.

Nevertheless they then go on to catalogue a range of reliability issues that remained: variability in the relative difficulty of alternative questions (1932: 20), the adventitious nature of some pass/fail decisions (1932:21), examiners' varying standards (1932:23), variability and unreliability of marking in the examiners themselves especially in essays (1932:26–27), and compared this instability in the marking of examination papers with the 'remarkable constancy of the marking of mental tests' (1932:30) and their 'freedom from subjective variations in marking, and the possibility of exact comparisons' (1932:31).

Barnwell (1996:56), though, is in turn equally critical of language testing in the United States at the time. He reverses the argument: 'They never noticed the lack of fit between the new measurement instruments and the kind of instruction pupils were actually receiving in foreign languages . . . there is very little . . . debate about what it is that is being tested'.

Socio-economic pressure: The catalyst for objective approaches to language testing in the US

An important reason for the diverging cross-Atlantic approaches can be found in the differing socio-economic climates prevailing in Britain and the United States in the early 20th century. The compelling need to produce tests on an industrial scale in the United States was to strongly influence testing organisations in the direction of objective, multiple choice methods at a very early stage in our narrative. Monahan (1998) provides the following explanation with an emphasis on faith in measurement and a crisis in the school system:

> The history of standardized educational testing in the United States finds its roots in the interstices of the rise of progressive reform, the emergence of psychology as a profession, the bureaucratization . . . of education . . . and the increasing dependency upon scientific expertise and quantification . . . the context they created provided educators and policy makers with a mechanism for dealing with overwhelming numbers of students in the face of mass immigration and compulsory schooling.

Resnick (1982:177,187) provides telling detail on how in the US:

> . . . the need to identify those who had the least probability of being able to carry on normal work for their age, was stimulated by the demographic explosion, which enlarged very quickly the rolls of schools . . .

immigration and natural population growth in the period 1880–1910 were the main contributors to this expansion . . . In 1870 there were about 500 high schools . . . in 1910 there were 10000. In 1870 there were about 80000 students . . . by 1910 there were 900,000.

Venezky (1984) points out that at the turn of the century with money, time and space in short supply, especially in large cities, school efficiency became a critical driver. Brown (1992:133), with reference to the early history of achievement testing in the United States school system similarly highlights the growing cult of accountability, the presence of school efficiency engineers and the appearance of bureaus of educational research in most major cities in the United States. She shows how in the interests of 'efficiency' achievement tests gave way to objectively scored intelligence tests in the school system and how the existing framework of the school survey was used to institutionalise testing practices in the schools. Brown notes that by the mid-1920s about 4 million children were being tested annually (1992:136).

Fulcher (1999:390) draws our attention to the role played by politics and war in establishing the objective approach to assessment in the United States. He argues that the logistical demands faced by the army in World War One and later in World War Two contributed to the spread in use of objective test formats. Resnick (1982:182) records the 'successful' placement in appropriate jobs of 1.7 million army recruits who were mobilised in 1917–18.

In short, the pressure of numbers and business pushed United States testing in the direction of psychometrically driven tests and the move was by no means unwelcome to school authorities as standardised tests provided them with the serendipitous means of enforcing accountability in schools. The influence of publications such as *Introduction to the Theory of Mental and Social Measurements* by Thorndike in 1904, the mindset of applied psychologists, and the interests of the publishing industry, who took over most of the psychological testing units, encouraged testing to move in this psychometric direction.

Brown (1992) observed that by 1922 mental testing was no longer a diagnostic tool used by psychologists on individuals for small-scale research but a powerful commercial enterprise. She cites the example of the close involvement of textbook companies with the school system and describes how many individuals and institutions had a stake in the testing enterprise with the commercial test industry alone employing thousands of experts in measurement psychology. She concludes: 'the psychologists' work justified itself and the quantitative and metaphorical language by which the first generation defined their professional authority became the received wisdom of the next' (1992:139). These developments contributed to an assessment context in the United States in which the psychometric qualities of a measuring instrument were paramount.

The birth of multiple-choice tests

The new paradigm required appropriate tools for delivering quantifiable data with appropriate psychometric qualities. The multiple-choice question was to be its handmaiden. Samelson in Sokal (1987:115–16) describes the invention and impact of multiple-choice question objective tests in the United States as follows:

> The humble yet all pervasive multiple choice question and its variants – an invention ingenious in its simplicity – was the indispensable vehicle for the dramatic growth of mass testing in this country in the span of a few years. It had not existed before 1914: by 1921 it had spawned a dozen group intelligence tests and provided close to two million soldiers and over three million school children with a numerical index of their intelligence: it was also about to transform achievement testing in the classroom.

He credits (1987:118–119) the take up of multiple-choice questions to Arthur Otis and Robert Yerkes in their work for the Army Alpha test but the original use was linked to the Kansas Silent Reading Test in 1914–15 produced by Frederick J Kelly, Dean of Education at the University of Kansas, who had completed a doctorate a few years' earlier on the unreliability of teachers' marks (Kelly 1916). The first item in his test read:

> Below are given the names of four animals. Draw a line around the name of each animal that is useful on the farm: cow, tiger, rat, and wolf (Samelson 119).

Samelson's research indicated this to be the first published multiple-choice item.

Fulcher (2000:486) argues that the use of such objective tests was perpetuated by 'the development of new automated marking machines that were designed especially to process multiple choice items' in particular the IBM model 805 test scoring machine introduced after earlier encouragement from Ben Wood in 1935. With the introduction of such machinery, the costs of marking plummeted (Resnick 1982:190). The optical scanner introduced in the 1950s would have similar effects. Samelson (op. cit.:123) concludes:

> The multiple choice test – efficient quantitative, objective, capable of sampling wide areas of subject matter and easily generating data for complicated statistical analysis – had become the symbol or synonym of American Education.

A rationale for the objective approach

The work of Wood (1927) in using 5-option multiple-choice question objective tests of reading, grammar and vocabulary to assess French and Spanish ability was an early harbinger of the importance of the psychometric movement in the United States language testing tradition. In the United States such tests were viewed as a major improvement on translation and composition and demonstrated high levels of split half reliability, Spearman Brown whole test reliability, suitable discrimination indices and lower standard errors of measurement (Barnwell 1996:29, Wood 1927:113–128).

A quote from Wood (1927:4) sheds some light on the wholesale American acceptance of objective testing and its psychometric qualities in this early period:

> Each test thus consists of 220–225 elements, which constitute a sampling of modern language materials much broader and more varied than is possible in the old type subjective examinations . . . The broad sampling is made possible by the fact that little time is lost in irrelevant activities, such as writing out translations of whole sentences and paragraphs. . . . When we consider the complete objectivity of the scoring of responses to this large number of carefully graded questions, it is not surprising that we achieve with examinations of this type results which are two or three times as reliable as those obtained with old type tests.

Wood (1927:96) in a section on the limitations of the new type modern language tests is aware of the opportunity cost of the psychometric approach but considers it the only acceptable option:

> These tests do not pretend to measure the oral and aural skills or cultural content. They are designed to measure only knowledge of the written language . . . Moreover pencil and paper tests of oral and aural skills do not seem practicable at the present time. The best way to measure these is by means of conversation with students one at a time using carefully prepared sets of questions and conversational materials. Such measures, however, would be subjective, would be mixtures of many relevant and irrelevant qualities in both student and teacher and would not be comparable from place to place and from year to year.

Porter (1995:209–210) describes the multiple-choice question with the promise of mechanical objectivity as a uniquely American phenomenon that emerged from military and industrial environments. He describes how it became a staple of American schooling but was almost unknown in Europe until the latter half of the 20th century.

The standing of objective measurement in the United Kingdom

In the United Kingdom it was the 'subjective' elements such as oral ability and the essay (tested in the CPE since 1913) that were highly regarded in the curriculum and in testing. There was not the pronounced faith in psychometric measurement there was in the United States and no crisis of numbers in the educational system. Cambridge CPE was only taken by 752 candidates in 1939, a cottage industry rather than an industrial behemoth.

According to Spolsky (1995a), compared to the United States, the 'scientific' issue of test reliability attracted relatively little attention in the United Kingdom. Relatively, perhaps, when compared with the enthusiasm for a psychometrically driven approach and multiple-choice questions in the United States, but there is nevertheless evidence of a growing interest in the United Kingdom particularly in examination boards (albeit mainly outside Cambridge initially).

Ballard's book *The New Examiner* (1923), published in London, built on his work in intelligence testing and suggests that these concepts were not totally unknown in the United Kingdom (see also Crofts and Caradog Jones (1928), Hartog (1918), Hartog and Rhodes (1935), Roach (1936), Valentine and Emmet (1932) and Chapter 3 in this volume for an extended discussion of United Kingdom Examination Boards' early work in this area). Ballard's book was intended to help language teachers improve reliability in their classroom tests by moving from 'the subjective to the objective, from the precarious and personal to the independent and impersonal – in a word from guesswork to measurement' (1923:9–10).

Ballard makes reference to similar concerns for reliability at the start of the 20th century in the work of Burt (1921) and in Hartog (1918). Burt, a psychologist for the education department of the London County Council, advocated the use of objective intelligence tests which were to be introduced after World War Two for selection to secondary schools in England and Wales. Hartog (1918) in *Examinations and their Relation to Culture and Efficiency* discusses in detail such issues as setting pass scores, oral methods of assessment, parallel forms from year to year, problems of marking, content sampling and includes a section containing three memoirs by F Y Edgeworth investigating the results of examinations statistically (Hartog 1918:102–135) and their deficiencies in terms of reliability. Valentine and Emmett (1932) looked closely at the issue of reliability in examinations in the United Kingdom both at the school and the university level. Hartog and Rhodes (1935) criticised the systems used by examining boards in particularly as they affected the reliability of the examinations claiming results were unsafe given the 'large irregularities'.

In Cambridge English Language examinations there was generally less concern with objective measurement, less concern with the internal consistency or the marker reliability aspects of scoring validity. That said, Jack Roach had started innovative work on enhancing marker reliability in the subjective assessment of speaking from an early date (see Roach 1936, 1945a and Chapter 4 of this volume).

Spolsky (1990a:158) was one of the first admirers of Roach's work and argues that Roach (1945a; see Appendix C):

> Appears to have been one of the first discussions in print of the problems of reliability and validity in the testing of oral proficiency in a second language . . . pride of place for a direct measure of oral language proficiency is usually granted to the oral interview created by the Foreign Service Institute (FSI) of the US State Department developed originally between 1952–56 . . . It turns out to be the case, however, that many of the important issues the FSI linguists had to struggle with, especially those concerning reliability, had been anticipated and intelligently ventilated in a paper written some years before the FSI activity started, printed and circulated internally among examiners of the University of Cambridge Local Examinations Syndicate (UCLES).

Jack Roach (1936) shows he was well aware of the work of Hartog and Rhodes, including their critical *An Examination of Examinations*, but he questioned some of their conclusions concerning the reliability of the marking carried out by examination boards. Roach (1936) first raises concern about the methodology they employed in their marker reliability study bearing little relationship to how scripts are normally marked by examination boards. He emphasises that Cambridge markers are rigorously standardised and scripts cover a wide range of ability in contrast to the Hartog and Rhodes (1935) study where the authors selected a very small number of scripts (15) on different essays that had been previously adjudged to be of the same standard, and then set up a group of raters to establish differences between the scripts (failure, pass or credit) without a common marking scheme, any exemplars of levels or any preliminary discussion of standards.

Roach (1936:114–116) sought to justify the Syndicate's way of doing things. He argued that at Cambridge mark schemes were drawn up and discussed in advance of the examination, specimen marked scripts were exchanged and discussed, and the chief examiner was present to advise and adjudicate. He argues that a substantial degree of uniformity was achieved in the marking before the marks were sent to an awards committee. Roach does concede, however, the mark schemes were in their own way subjective and possible improvements might be raised well into the marking process when it was too late to make changes.

He was also concerned with the grade boundaries which were often dependant on the chief examiner and statistical comparison with previous years. His concern with fairness is shown in his consideration of the plight of the borderline fail candidates who may have been exposed to a paper more difficult than the previous year's (a similar cause for concern in Valentine and Emmett 1932). In terms of setting a general standard he argued strongly for use of the overall aggregate of marks in an examination rather than its component parts, which apparently had been received well by the schools. Scaling was also employed to equalise the subjects and 'give them the right emphasis' in the School Certificate examinations (Roach 1936).

Roach's seminal paper on testing oral language (1945a) (see Appendix C) further demonstrates a conviction that subjective assessments could be made more reliable and enable examination boards to test something of value that reflected the activities that were taking place in the English language classroom and real life i.e. speaking and writing.

However, Roach adds a rather tongue in cheek caveat at the end of his 1936 paper: if there was to be 'a change of attitude going far beyond the examining board' (1936:118), he was not averse to:

> ... some reasonably exact test of general intelligence ... though it need not, perhaps, cause rejection in the examination. If such a test could be devised and applied, we might on occasion have the pleasant duty of issuing certificates to candidates who had satisfactorily demonstrated their lack of intelligence. Or perhaps not, for it might be found that the two tests – school certificate and general intelligence, usually agreed and, where they differed, we might be left arguing which test was to blame. But a little fresh argument and a little fresh thought would scarcely be a disadvantage.

A cautiously sceptical response to the new objective tests perhaps, but a hint of wider, societal constraints that were bound to affect the adoption of a novel but 'alien' approach to assessment by an organisation charged by government with administering the School Certificate examinations. It also suggests he is still convinced of the value of the existing assessment tasks used by Cambridge and saw no real reason to change. The Cambridge papers would continue with an emphasis on curriculum, with questions requiring essay length rather than brief, discrete, objective answers, and with the use of subjective judgements of examiners to arrive at scores. The professional *judgement* of fellow academics at Cambridge was preferred to *counting* by pyschometricians. Spolsky (personal communication) sums the situation up succinctly: 'a faith in experts in suits and ties as against white coats'. Watts (2008a:66–67) provides further detail on how such psychometric notions were viewed in the Syndicate:

> In 1944 Joseph Brereton, the other Assistant Secretary at the time [Secretary of the Syndicate 1945–61], published a book entitled *The Case*

for Examinations, which sought to answer the critics of the system. He addressed the issues raised by what he described as 'the attempt to reduce examinations to mere measuring devices'. His main point was that examinations were a 'mobilizing force in education', and their purpose was to stimulate teachers and students. They were thus intimately linked to the courses of study leading to them and in this respect they differed from intelligence and aptitude tests. The latter 'have no concern with a previous course, and in fact presuppose that there had been no such course'.

However, the scoring validity of Cambridge examinations was not totally neglected. The Joint Committee minutes in 1944 provide evidence of the commitment to ensuring the examinations were as fair as possible as the following reference to an experiment in double marking showed:

> We found time to make a preliminary survey of certain problems, to conduct some interesting experiments, and to prepare a first report. This has had an immediate influence in causing certain modifications of the oral tests to be held in 1945, and we hope that it will stimulate discussion wherever the examinations are taken. The chief experiments in joint examining took place at the Polish Initial Training Wing, R.A.F., and at the Polytechnic, Regent Street, London (Joint Committee of the Local Examinations Syndicate and the British Council 1944).

There is other evidence of the development of sound examination practice in these early years that was critical for establishing test reliability. For example, piloting of tests appears at an early stage:

> Mr. Burton reported that questions from the specimen 'Use of English' paper had been worked by a small number of students in Portugal and London, and were also being worked by a group of students in Paris. The results of the first two sets appeared to be satisfactory (quoted in Weir and Milanovic 2003:13).

These practices notwithstanding, in the general absence of a national culture supportive of psychometrically driven, objective testing, an interest in using objective methods for testing skills or language at Cambridge was largely absent for the first half of the 20th century.

The first 'green shoots'

One of the first expressions of interest in objective testing at UCLES appears in this internal discussion at a 1951 meeting at which Roach was present:

> Mr. Butlin suggested the 'necessity for a more objective method of examining reading . . .' (Joint Committee July 1951: 7).

R T Butlin (in 1950 the new editor of *ELT* after Hornby) 'undertook to inform the Committee of the results of experiments to be made in "objective" methods of testing [for reading]' (Joint Committee October 1951). At these Joint Committee meetings, in addition to Roach, the syndicate was also represented by T S Wyatt (later to become UCLES Secretary 1961–72 and in 1966 to visit the USA to look at objective testing there). The topic appears not to have been addressed again in this committee until 1959 when the following lukewarm response to using objective tests is recorded (Joint Committee June 1959:7):

> Objective Tests. The possibility of using objective tests was briefly discussed and it was agreed that this should be borne in mind in future. The possibility might well be a limited one, however, since examining bodies using such tests in English language use a test in composition of the type set by the Syndicate, and some of the Syndicates questions (e.g. on the meaning of words and phrases) resemble 'objective' questions to some extent.

Public opinion was to change, however, and in fact as early as the 1940s articles had begun to appear in the United Kingdom expressing similar concerns to Ballard's about the reliability of constructed answers in tests and supporting research into the use of standardised, objective tests to provide: 'a more accurate assessment of the linguistic ability of children taught by different methods in different schools ... our present examination techniques are often imperfect and allow of subjective bias' (Ewing 1949:141–2).

Hawkey (2009:28–29) records how:

> It was in the 1960s, too, that the minutes of the Joint Committee record professional contacts between UCLES and the Educational Testing Service (ETS) in the USA. Robert Lado himself visited UCLES in 1960, the year before publication of his *Language Testing: the Construction and Use of Foreign Language Tests*, seen by many as epitomising Lado's pioneering role in the development of foreign language tests based on the psychometric model ... his tests matched a view of language. For him, this was a structuralist language theory and a view of language learning as behaviorist stimulus and response/habit formation. Lado supported techniques developed in psychological measurement because they suited a model where each item of a test was independent and seen as measuring a single language element or skill.

However, it is also clear that for Lado language knowledge consisted of skills (reading, writing, listening and speaking, with an emphasis on the receptive skills) as well as elements (e.g. grammatical structure, lexis, pronunciation). Lado (1964) provides a succinct summary of his views on language teaching with a clear statement that spoken and written communication with native speakers are important goals, though, as in his book on testing, he expresses strong reservations concerning the practicality and reliability of attempts to measure language ability through testing these directly (1964:161–163).

By the 1960s candidate numbers for Cambridge examinations were increasing rapidly and the Syndicate was actively considering psychometric/ structuralist tasks in its exams and seriously contemplating the inclusion of some objective formats to enhance test reliability:

> Research into methods of testing
> It was noted that the Executive Committee had recommended 'as a matter of urgency' that research into tests of an objective type be undertaken, with a view (i) to finding out the linguistic skills which can most satisfactorily be tested objectively, and (ii) to building up a bank of pre-tested items which could be used for the C.P.E. Use of English paper. After discussion, it was agreed to refer the matter to the syndicate. . . (Joint Committee July 1964: 5).

Around this time the Committee of Vice Chancellors in the United Kingdom had initiated a project for the study of the objective multiple choice Scholastic Aptitude Test (SAT) which they thought might be helpful for selection for entrance to universities. In this climate Wyatt, the UCLES Secretary (1961– 72), paid a visit with Harold Otter to both the College Entrance Examination Board and the Educational Testing Service in the United States in October/ November 1966 and on his return wrote a comprehensive and positive report on the use of objective items by these two American examining boards (Wyatt 1966).

In this 1966 publication Wyatt detailed the beginnings of the use of objective formats in school examinations both at ordinary and advanced levels in England at the time and provided a considered summary of the advantages and disadvantages of these suggesting (1966: 8–9): 'Both the traditional English system and the current American one have their merits and defects. I consider that the opportunity should be taken to utilise the advantages of both, while minimising the disadvantages.' He suggested that where appropriate in the English exams for foreign students the Syndicate should make use of objective testing.

In 1966, in Section (b) of the CPE Use of English paper, 3-option multiple-choice items were introduced. The Regulations for 1969 (13) indicated that in the English Composition and Language Paper some of the comprehension questions 'may include multiple choice questions'.

Elsewhere in the United Kingdom Hamp-Lyons (2000:585) describes how:

> The British Council for many years used the 'subjective test' which was an informal interview with the in-country English language Officer to

determine whether a particular promising young person had the English necessary to succeed at university in United Kingdom. During the 1960s the 'subjective test' was gradually replaced with carefully developed, objective tests such as the Davies test (the English Proficiency Test Battery) and the English Language Battery, and these tests continued until the end of the 1970s.

An English language testing specialist arrives in Cambridge

A critical development for Cambridge English language examinations occurred at the 21st meeting of the UCLES Executive Committee in May 1968 where the report of the *Sub Committee on Research and Development* was received. It contained an innovative proposal for the appointment of a research officer for the language exams. The aims of the research would 'not be confined to testing techniques, but concern the needs of candidates and the content and range of the examinations' (Executive Committee 1968). The minutes for the October 1969 meeting discussed the draft of the announcement: 'Applicants should have appropriate linguistic training and knowledge of testing techniques and experience of teaching English as a foreign language'. Here was the first tentative step to recruiting professionals in English language teaching and testing into the organisation.

The appointment of E F Chaplen was confirmed in the Executive Committee minutes of May 1970. Chaplen was based in the English Examinations Section of the Syndicate and the Test Development and Research Unit, established in 1968 under David Shoesmith. A consultative committee was formed to direct the programme of research and Dr B Lott was appointed to serve on it as the nominee of the British Council. The committee included John Trim of the Department of General Linguistics, Cambridge University, Dr D Shoesmith of the Development and Research Unit, Mr Bruce Willis and officers of the Syndicate. The Executive Committee minutes record (1969):

> The terms of reference of the consultative committee were discussed and It was felt that attention should be given to work on existing tests . . . and questions of validity, reliability and comparability in the various parts of the three examinations. Research will include participation by examiners and consultation with teaching centres as necessary.

Support for a move towards the use of more reliable item types in Cambridge English language examinations followed in the wake of Chaplen's appointment. Chaplen had completed his doctoral studies in language testing at Manchester University (Chaplen 1970) and had produced an objectively scored multiple-choice question discrete point test: *The Chaplen Speeded Grammar and Vocabulary Test*, which has remained in use there for international student placement purposes to this day. He was the first full-time, professional, English language tester to be appointed by UCLES but was only to remain at Cambridge until 1975 when, after completing work on the 1975 syllabus, he left for a university appointment in Kuwait.

The executive committee in fact contained few specialists in testing in the early 1970s apart from G E Perren representing the British Council. J B Heaton was to become a member in 1976 followed by Brendan Carroll of the British Council in the same year and then Doug Picket in 1977. Allan Moller became a member in 1979 and Peter Hargreaves (also from the British Council) in 1984. Their professional experience provided a welcome injection of English language testing expertise.

With the arrival of Chaplen it had seemed like a new dawn for Cambridge English language examinations but after his departure in 1975 there were to be no more such internal appointments of 'professional testers' until the arrival of Peter Hargreaves from the British Council and Mike Milanovic from Hong Kong in the late 1980s. The financial situation at UCLES was certainly a cause for concern in the 1970s and this may have restricted further appointments, but through careful management of resources under the Secretaryship of Frank Wild (1972–83) and the escalating profits from its English language examinations, the situation had eased by the 1980s. Hawkey and Milanovic (2013) record:

> Leedham-Green recalls UCLES Secretary Dr Frank Wild informing staff of a £180,000 loss for the financial year 1972–73 and Wild introduced an era of what Leedham-Green calls 'careful husbandry', leading to a 'swift and sustained recovery'. Over his eleven years in office Wild succeeded in rebuilding the Syndicate.

Under the influence of Chaplen, UCLES made a considered attempt to work on the marking reliability side of its examinations whilst retaining a clear view of the need for other aspects of validity as shown in his June 1971 report, *An Appraisal of the Syndicate's Written Examinations in English as a Foreign Language together with Some Suggested Modifications*. Chaplen raised issues reflecting the Syndicate's key concerns including the need to modernise the Cambridge English exams in the direction of a clearer focus on objectivity and reliability. The 1975 modifications to the CPE and FCE exams (see below) would be clearly driven by these concerns e.g., the new Reading Comprehension Paper 2 in FCE and CPE has 60 multiple-choice questions and the Listening Comprehension Paper 4 has 20. The Executive Committee minutes of 1971:1 discussed Chaplen's report and drew attention to: 'the reliability gained by using the complementary effects of objective testing, with its wide but standardised coverage of the testing area and its effective distribution of candidates'.

Chaplen was also concerned with parallel forms reliability (the equivalence of an examination from administration to administration or between different alternatives of a test that were available to candidates in the same sitting) as well as inter-marker reliability and internal consistency. The Joint Committee minutes (July 1971) record his criticism of:

(1) the absence of a substantial compulsory element of objective testing as a yardstick for the assessment of candidates
(2) The incompatibility, in terms of measurement of attainment, of the present range of optional tests.

Chaplen felt that the system of optional papers, for example the alternatives of Translation, Structure and Usage or Prescribed Texts in the 1970 LCE exam, made it 'impossible properly to equate the performances of different candidates who elected to complete different optional papers' (1971). Chaplen's solution to this problem was to impose common standards on the marks awarded for an open-ended task such as a composition by scaling the marks awarded by examiners against a common reference test, with objective items and computerised scoring, to determine the relative positions of the batches of scripts scored by different markers.

Scoring versus consequential validity?

It is clear that historically the starting point for UCLES had always been the context and how the examination might encourage best practice in teaching towards this context. The positive washback of its examinations on what was taught in the classroom was critical for UCLES. The examinations had always been characterised by a close relationship with pedagogy, i.e. curriculum, syllabus, classroom practice and the teaching profession. The Executive Committee in 1965 noted: 'The need for more precise information on the function of the examinations and their relationship with the curriculum and teaching they encourage' and the Joint Committee (July 1968) 'underlined the need for research and progressive development in the English examinations with due consideration of the sort of teaching which is to be encouraged.' As Bachman et al (1995:131) observed:

... the British examinations system is particularly concerned with promoting positive effects of examinations on curricula and instruction, and thus is sensitive to including features in its examinations that are consistent with those found in instructional programs.

In these early days UCLES had felt it essential to base CPE on the needs of the teachers and their students and best classroom practice. In addition, it probably felt the need to satisfy the various felt needs of its client base by providing a variety of attractive options for papers that would best match their developing performance abilities. A broad range of pathways through the examination was therefore possible, e.g. the alternative options to English literature:

> Future arrangements. . . . .Arrangements are contemplated for the
> provision in 1946 of complete alternative papers, including English
> Language and translation passages, for candidates of a commercial
> bent. These papers will go some way to recognize their particular inter-
> est, but will not be merely tests of 'commercial English'. A further pro-
> ficiency paper, alternative to Literature, will be provided in 1946. It will
> offer a choice of texts of a scientific rather than a literary character. . .
> (UCLES 1945:4).

Such choice was in all likelihood a response to the varying curriculum content
of diverse educational systems in existing and former colonies as well as an
attempt to maximise candidate numbers. This wide range of options, though
addressing context and consequential validity demands, has obvious shortcomings in terms of parallel forms reliability (see Chapter 3 for extended discussion of this issue in relation to the large choice available in the writing
paper).

The conflicting demands of a broad choice of options and parallel form
reliability are undeniable; they reflect the sometimes diverse pulls of different
aspects of validity. The guiding principle for UCLES in this period was to
work for context and consequential validity followed closely by utility. This
does not mean they did not seek to achieve scoring validity but this was not
the overriding determinant of what went into the examination in this period.
The approach was to aim for consequential and context validity and work
on the reliability aspects of scoring validity rather than through the single-
minded pursuit of objectivity seriously curtail what CPE would be able to
measure. A valid test that might not present perfect psychometric qualities
was preferred to an objective test which though always reliable might not
measure that much of value, e.g.,not test speaking or writing.

We have seen in our middle period 1921–1970 how, under the influence of
developments in the United States, there was some concession in Cambridge
with regard to the potential relevance of a more objective approach to test
formats but this was nibbled at rather than being swallowed whole. Test
developers at Cambridge were mindful of the enhanced statistical reliability
the approach could offer to the results of their examinations, but they were
also aware of its limitations in terms of construct validity. They regarded the
adoption of objective formats as a matter of strategic assimilation, as in the
introduction of some objective items the Use of English paper in Main Suite
examinations from the 1960s onwards, and in the Reading and Listening
papers from 1975, rather than a wholesale acceptance of the psychometrically driven approach which had marked the United States experience.

In the next period under review, *the communicative era*, UCLES was to
continue in its receptiveness to new ideas in terms of enhancing contextual
validity. More critically, as the numbers of test takers increased exponentially, as international standards for language testing were codified and

accepted, as testing professionals occupied leading positions in the organisation and as transatlantic testing links and co-operation improved, it was also to pay greater heed to the demands of scoring validity.

Finally, in the early 21st century attention was to be paid to cognitive validity spurred on by research that underpinned the production of the 'construct volumes' in the SiLT series (see Shaw and Weir (2007:Chapter 6), Khalifa and Weir (2009:Chapter 6), Taylor (Ed.) (2011:Chapter 6) and Geranpayeh and Taylor (Eds) (2013:Chapter 6)).

1971–2012: The communicative era

This period witnessed major change in both the teaching and testing of the English language. As well as the powerful influence of the communicative approach, with all the transformation this occasioned in theory and its application to pedagogy and assessment, it was a time of intense activity, growth and diversity in a progressively more professional, global, language testing community. In tracing the gradual ascendancy of the communicative approach in detail, it is instructive to examine the diverse and often contending approaches to the measurement of language constructs through the voices of language testing specialists at the time.

Approaches to language testing

Davies (1978) argued that by the mid-1970s, approaches to language testing seemed to fall along a continuum stretching from 'discrete' item tests at one end, to integrative tests at the other. He took the view that in testing, as in teaching, there was a tension between the analytical on the one hand and the integrative on the other, and considered that 'the most satisfactory view of language testing and the most useful kinds of language tests are a combination of these two views, the analytical and the integrative' (1978:149).

The analytic had always been well represented in Cambridge examinations, e.g. the Part II Grammar section of the 1913 CPE contained items such as:

1913 CPE Grammar section

Give the past tense and past participle of each of the following verbs, dividing them into strong and weak; add explanations: *tell, wake, buy, eat, lay, lie.*

The Phonetics paper had contained a large number of discrete focus items such as:

1913 CPE Phonetics paper

3. Explain the terms: 'glide,' 'narrow vowel,' 'semi-vowel,' and give two examples of each in both phonetic and ordinary spelling.
4. How would you teach a pupil the correct pronunciation of the vowel sounds in *fare, fate, fat, fall, far*?

At the integrative end of the spectrum, the writing and speaking papers had been there since 1913 in one form or another including such tasks as summary, conversation, reading aloud, dictation and translation. Cambridge had always taken a fairly balanced approach to language test design, if erring slightly on the side of the integrative. This was altered slightly in the 1950s with the deliberate inclusion of an additional Use of English paper at the analytic end of the spectrum to enhance scoring validity.

Oller (1979) felt that testing should focus on the integrative end of the continuum (see also Carroll 1961) as against the analytical. He made a strong case for following the swing of the testing pendulum away from what Spolsky (1978) had described as the 'psychometric-structuralist era', the so-called 'discrete point' approach to testing, to what Spolsky termed 'the integrative-sociolinguistic era': the age of the integrative test. In the description of these approaches below, they are treated as if they were 'distinct' or 'pure' types. It is recognised that, in practice, most tests contain elements of the discrete and the integrative, either in the test format or the assessment procedures adopted, but, while the distinction between the two is neither real nor absolute, approaches to testing can be usefully described in terms of the particular focus they represent.

The psychometric-structuralist approach

The clear advantages of testing 'discrete' linguistic points are that they yield data which are easily quantifiable, as well as allowing a wide coverage of items. Tests which focus on items testing specific language elements also tend to be the most efficient and reliable sections of a test. They are less susceptible to measurement error than other test sections which focus more generally on the transmission of meaning, and so provide more consistent scores.

The research evidence suggests that discrete point tests of lexico-grammatical knowledge can provide a useful indication of a learner's general language abilities and of their performance on skills-based test components – particularly reading and writing (Alderson 1993, Hughes 2003, Purpura 2004, Read 2000, Shiotsu and Weir 2007, Weir 1983). Where tests include components addressing grammar and vocabulary as well as the broader macro-skills, the highest correlations between individual test parts and the overall scores are generally those for lexico-grammatical components such as the Use of English papers found in Cambridge examinations or the Structure and Written Expression component of the earlier paper-based TOEFL test (see for example Educational Testing Service 1997). In fact, the relationship between lexico-grammatical measures and overall ratings of language abilities is so strong that grammar tests are often used by researchers as indicators of general language proficiency (see, for example, Purpura 1999).

Indeed, after a comprehensive, 4-year, multi-faceted, test development programme, the high correlations found between the 60-item grammar section of the Test in English for Academic Purposes (TEAP, now Test in English for Educational Purposes TEEP) led Weir (1983:521) to conclude that 'the test of grammar might be a sufficient indicator on its own of a student's ability to cope with the language demands made on students by English medium study'. In the TEEP development the grammar test was eventually abandoned because it offered no additional information to that provided by the skills-based components. Similarly, Alderson (1993) found the pilot grammar component of IELTS correlated so highly with other components of the test that a distinct grammar component was felt to be unnecessary in the operational test. For both TEEP and IELTS the use of skills-based components was in the event favoured over grammar because the test developers wanted to encourage learners to develop their academic study skills in preparing for the test (as did teachers), and end users of the test results were generally convinced by more direct tests of academic language ability.

However, in the eyes of many critics the 'discrete point' approach and the various formats employed in it suffered from the defects of the construct they sought to measure. They argued that the problem with this approach to the measurement of proficiency was that it depended on proficiency being neatly quantifiable in this fashion. Oller (1979:212) outlined the deficiencies in terms of the construct validity of a hypothetically pure form of this approach:

> Discrete point analysis necessarily breaks the elements of language apart and tries to teach them (or test them) separately with little or no attention to the way those elements interact in a larger context of communication. What makes it ineffective as a basis for teaching or testing languages is that crucial properties of language are lost when its elements are separated. The fact is that in any system where the parts interact to produce properties and qualities that do not exist in the part separately, the whole is greater than the sum of its parts, organizational constraints themselves become crucial properties of the system which simply cannot be found in the parts separately.

Spolsky (1968) argued at an early date that instead of attempting to establish a person's knowledge of a language in terms of a percentage mastery of grammar and lexis, we would be better employed in testing that person's ability to perform in a specified sociolinguistic setting. Rea (1978:1) later makes the point more vehemently:

. . . although we would agree that language is a complex behaviour and that we would generally accept a definition of overall language proficiency as the ability to function in a natural language situation, we still insist on, or let others impose on us, testing measures which assess language as an abstract array of discrete items, to be manipulated only in a mechanistic way. Such tests yield artificial, sterile and irrelevant types of items which have no relationship to the use of language in real life situations.

Morrow (1979:145) argued that if we are to assess proficiency, i.e. potential success in the use of the language in some general sense:

. . . it would be more valuable to test for a knowledge of and an ability to apply the rules and processes by which these discrete elements are synthesized into an infinite number of grammatical sentences and then selected as being appropriate for a particular context, rather than simply to test knowledge of the elements alone . . . knowledge of the elements of a language in fact counts for nothing unless the user is able to combine them in new and appropriate ways to meet the linguistic demands of the situation in which he wishes to use the language.

The integrative-sociolinguistic approach

In response to a feeling that 'discrete point' tests were insufficient indicators of language proficiency, the testing pendulum on the whole swung in favour of global tests in the 1970s, into what Spolsky (1978) termed the integrative-sociolinguistic era, an approach to measurement that was in many ways contrary to the supposedly atomistic assumptions of the 'discrete point' tests (see Davies 1978).

It was claimed by Oller (1979) that global integrative tests such as cloze and dictation went beyond the measurement of a limited part of language competence achieved by 'discrete point' tests and could measure the ability to integrate disparate language skills in ways which more closely approximated the actual process of language use. Oller's view (1979:37) was that:

The concept of an integrative test was born in contrast with the definition of a discrete point tests. If discrete items take language skill apart, integrative tests put it back together. Whereas discrete items attempt to test knowledge of language one bit at a time, integrative tests attempt to assess a learner's capacity to use many bits all at the same time and possibly while exercising several presumed components of a grammatical system, and perhaps more than one of the traditionally recognized skills or aspects of skills.

Oller's work was an important, innovative attempt to link construct theory with test method. It displayed an interest in the psychological and linguistic processes behind language use albeit in a restricted context with little concern for the social and interpersonal aspects.

The integrative approach, in the form of summary, translation, reading aloud and dictation, had been present in Cambridge examinations since 1913. Cloze, a flagship test format of the 'new' integrative approach which came to the fore in testing in the 1970s and early 1980s, in particular with the work of John Oller (1971, 1973, 1976, 1979), was to have little impact on Cambridge examinations as such. Cloze in Oller's sense of an nth rate mechanical deletion of items in a passage was never taken up as a format for testing by Cambridge, though selective deletion gap-filling ('modified cloze' as it is inaccurately described in FCE terminology) was present in the Use of English papers and in the reading test at CPE. Dictation had been used since the 1913 CPE but would be dropped for more communicative activities in listening in 1970 in LCE and CPE in 1975.

A major cause of concern arose with the assumption made by Oller (1979) that General Language Proficiency, the grammar of expectancy his integrative tests were aimed at, was a single principal factor underlying all language skills. His concept of 'overall proficiency' inevitably merged into a hypothesis of an underlying unitary competence. This was a view implicit in Oller's concept of the internalised expectancy grammar and, though it is one which is seductive for the purposes of those having to take administrative decisions, as Davies (1981) pointed out, it conflicted with substantial evidence in favour of at least two competences, namely reception and production (see Vollmer 1981). The differences between knowing how to analyse input and knowing how to construct output would seem to outweigh the correspondence between the two processes as the gradual development of cognitive models in the 1970s and 1980s was to show.

Davies (1981) emphasised that although Oller claimed that his integrative tests represented total language proficiency better than any other single test or combination of tests, this was not in itself an argument in favour of the unitary competence hypothesis, as measures such as cloze and dictation are so integrative that they necessarily draw upon both receptive and productive processes. High correlations between cloze and other measures may only reflect that they are measuring different skills which are highly correlated among individuals; however, this does not mean that there will be no individuals whose performances in the various skills differ considerably.

The empirical evidence in favor of the 'unitary competence hypothesis' came under scrutiny and a growing body of evidence emerged favoring a divisibility hypothesis (see Bachman and Palmer 1981, Geranpayeh 2007, Hughes 1981, Porter 1983, Vollmer 1979, 1981). The statistical tool of principal component analysis was often used to substantiate the 'unitary competence hypothesis' but this method was essentially designed to simplify data, and might be expected to produce one factor from a battery of seemingly different language tests (see Porter 1983). More crucially, this general language proficiency factor did not necessarily explain all the variance in the results, and the percentage of variance explained differed from study to study (see Vollmer 1981). Because of the existence of factors other than the principal component, which explained reasonable proportions of the remaining variance, it was often possible by pursuing further factor analysis, for example Varimax rotation of the factor structure, to obtain a number of independent factors each of which made a sizeable contribution to the total variance.

Critics also argued that integrative tests such as cloze only told us about a candidate's linguistic competence (see Kelly 1978, Moller 1981, Morrow 1979, Rea 1978). They did not tell us anything directly about their performance ability, and their main value in their unmodified form was in designating competence levels rather than relating candidates' performance to any external criteria. They were perhaps only of limited use where the interest was in what the individual student could or could not do in terms of the various language tasks he may have to face in real-life situations.

Though the integrative tests Oller advocated had been global in that they required examinees to exhibit simultaneous control over different aspects of the language system, they were nevertheless indirect. Although they might integrate disparate language skills in ways which more closely approximated actual language use, critics argued that their claim to the mantle of communicative validity remained suspect, as only direct tests which simulated relevant authentic communication tasks could claim to mirror actual communicative interaction (see Kelly 1978, Morrow 1979). As Moller (1982:25) pointed out, the indirect tests Oller had advocated did not: 'require subjects to perform tasks considered to be relevant in the light of their known future use of the language'.

Advocates of testing communicative language ability argued that Oller's view paid insufficient regard to the importance of the productive and receptive processing of discourse, arising out of the actual use of language in a social context with all the attendant performance constraints, e.g. the interaction-based nature of discourse (see Moller 1981, Morrow 1979). Both Rea (1978) and Morrow (1979) emphasised that although indirect measures of language abilities claimed extremely high standards of reliability and concurrent validity as established by statistical techniques, their claim to other types of validity remained suspect. Morrow (1979) cited as evidence for this the fact that neither testing procedure offered the possibility for oral or non-controlled written production, and since the oral and written skills are generally held to be highly important, some means of assessing them reliably in communicative situations should be found. Although such integrative measures appeared to correlate highly with other similar measures of general language proficiency, there was empirical evidence that cloze correlated only moderately with tests of written production and with spoken production (see Vollmer 1981). Given that the tests concerned were reliable, this would suggest the possibility that proficiency in these areas cannot be adequately predicted by a test of overall proficiency.

Concerns about the type of information provided by the 'discrete point' items in the psychometric-structuralist approach and by the 'new' integrative approaches of cloze and dictation led practising testers in the United Kingdom in particular to look to the 'communicative paradigm' to see whether this approach might prove more satisfactory.

The communicative paradigm: 'The promised land?'

In the 1970s and 1980s we can determine a gradual shift in the United Kingdom away from structural approaches to language teaching to approaches which involved using language as a means of communication. This takes us into Stage 3 of our historical survey: *Communicative Approaches to Language Teaching and Testing* (see Table 1.1 above).

In the classroom there was a growing interest in the functional and communicative potential of language, communicative ability rather than knowledge of structures *per se* (see Richards and Rogers 2001:153–177). The spread of Communicative Language Teaching (CLT) in the classroom would be supported by the work of a growing number of Applied Linguists in British Universities.

The growth in English language teaching (ELT) and testing as a worldwide 'commodity' from the 1960s onwards (see Pennycook 1994: Chapter 5) coincided with the appearance in the English-speaking world of Applied Linguistics departments concerned with the empirical and theoretical investigation of real-world problems in which language is a central issue. Spolsky (personal communication) notes:

> The development of applied linguistics and the growth of demand for ELT were not unconnected. With the development of applied linguistics in the United Kingdom and US, the two groups became closely connected and a good number of the applied linguists in both countries took an interest in testing, and started to add psychometric skills and knowledge to their professional capability.

A School of Applied Linguistics was set up in Edinburgh with the help of the British Council in 1957 to service English Language Teaching, and another was established at Birkbeck in 1965 (see Mackey 1966 for an account of the development of Applied Linguistics). Developments in English language teaching theory and practice, especially in the Linguistics Department and Centre for Applied Language Studies (CALS) at the University of Reading in the 1970s, early 1980s, and at the University of Lancaster and the Institute of Education, London, contributed to the theoretical base of the communicative approach.

The work of Chris Brumfit (Brumfit and Johnson 1979), Chris Candlin (1981, 1986), Keith Johnson (1982), Keith Morrow (1977, 1979) (leading to the RSA Communicative Use of English as a Foreign Language Examination (CUEFL)), John Trim (1970, 1980), Henry Widdowson (1972, 1978, 1983) and David Wilkins (1973a, 1973b, 1976) was notable in this respect. Their work contributed substantially to a theoretical base for the growing interest in the Communicative Teaching of English that subsequently led and influenced the modern language teaching and testing fields in the United Kingdom.

The developing communicative approach a) signalled the importance of meaningful activity (i.e. a reaction against mindless drilling); b) gave birth to the notional-functional syllabus; c) built on developments in the growing field of sociolinguistics; and d) promoted an interest in authentic materials. Additionally, it was to provide a conceptual framework for a more comprehensive, richer and transparent specification of content for learning and assessment (see below).

By the late 1970s and early 1980s this communicative perspective could be found in the work of language testers generally supportive of a broadly-based model of communicative language ability, where there is a marked shift in emphasis from the linguistic to the communicative dimension. The emphasis was no longer on linguistic accuracy, but on the ability to function effectively through language in particular contexts of situation. As Rea (1978:4) succinctly put it, the focus shifted to: 'the ability to communicate with ease and effect in specified sociolinguistic settings'. Kelly (1978:350) argued:

> To take part in a communicative event is to produce and / or comprehend discourse in the context of situation and under the performance conditions that obtain. It is the purpose of a proficiency test to assess whether or not candidates are indeed capable of participating in typical communication events from the specified communication situation(s).

In the United Kingdom the spread of communicative language testing was facilitated by a small number of testing specialists including Brendan Carroll (1980), Arthur Hughes (1989), Alan Moller (1982), Keith Morrow (1977, 1979), Pauline Rea (1978), and Cyril Weir (1983, 1990, 1993). The 'new' communicative approach to language testing was extensively discussed and critically evaluated at the inaugural meeting of the United Kingdom Language Testing Forum (LTF) in Lancaster in 1980. The discussion was recorded and written up along with the discussion papers and accompanying critiques in Alderson and Hughes (1981). Changes had also been taking place at Cambridge.

Cambridge Examinations: The 1975 and 1984 revisions

A number of major revisions took place in both FCE and CPE in the 1970s. They illustrate the start of a mind shift in Cambridge towards communicative language testing as well as a growing awareness of the need to address the demands of scoring validity. *The Cambridge Examinations in English: Changes of Syllabus in 1975* describes how

> ... the CPE and the new FCE exams now have a parallel structure consisting of free writing exercises, objective tests of comprehension, controlled practical tests in the use of structures and vocabulary, and a series of oral tests separately assessing specific skills and aspects of performance.

The handbook for the 1975 exams claims:

> ... a significant gain in the validity and reliability of assessment through the use of a common range of tests for all candidates, and the combination of objective techniques with the testing of active command of the language.

The 1975 revisions saw CPE taking a shape that in its broad outline is familiar to the candidate of today (see Chapters 2, 3, 4 and 5 for full details of changes in individual papers). The listening and speaking tests in particular represented major developments on the 1966 revision and echoed the burgeoning interest in communicative language teaching in the 1970s. The five papers (Composition, Reading Comprehension, Use of English, Listening Comprehension and Interview) replaced the old division of Oral and Written.

In the newly added Listening Comprehension paper candidates listened to four passages and answered a total of 20 multiple-choice questions. There were changes to the former Oral paper. 'Reading and conversation' had become the new 'Interview' paper which still included 'conversation' and 'reading aloud', but now also comprised such tasks as 'prepared talk' and 'providing appropriate responses in given situations'. Under the influence of functionalism the writing tasks now often had a focused slant, e.g. requiring comparison, argument or narrative description:

> Either (a) Discuss whether it is possible to solve the problem of pollution without losing too many of the advantages of the modern life.
> Or (b) Compare the position of woman today with their way of life in your grandparents' times, and comment on the difference.

These contrasted sharply with the open-ended essay format of earlier pre-scientific times:

> Fascism
> Good companions
> Any English writer of the twentieth century

In addition there was a new multiple-choice questions Reading Comprehension paper (1 hour and 15 minutes) albeit testing knowledge of vocabulary and usage in the first part but with a second section designed to test meaning construction. Again, note the balance between linguistic and communicative competence tasks. The increased reliance on multiple-choice formats acknowledged the attention international examinations felt they now had to pay to the demands of scoring validity.

In the 1984 FCE revision, texts and tasks were to be further improved in the direction of improved authenticity and realism. There would be increased weighting for the sub-tests of listening and speaking to bring them in line with the other skills. It is in Paper 4 (Listening Comprehension) that the most significant modification was made (see Chapter 5). Recorded material was now to be used in place of 'live' voices (the examiner reading aloud) at each examination centre. This was seen as a move towards 'authentic spoken English in a variety of realistic contexts' (Changes of Syllabus booklet 1982:28). Radio news or features, situational dialogues or announcements were to be used to 'provide a fair test of aural understanding as a basic skill'.

Establishing operationaliseable features for use in communicative language testing

Agreement on what components should be included in a model of communicative language ability was by no means unanimous (see Courchene and de Bagheera 1985:49). Indeed, in the 1980s relatively little was known about the wider communicative paradigm in comparison with linguistic competence per se and adequately developed theories of communicative language use remained works in progress. However, testers could not wait for completion of such theories before appropriate testing procedures could be developed. Rather they had to investigate systematically some of the available hypotheses about language use and try to operationalise these for testing purposes. In this way the constructs and processes emerging from linguistic and applied linguistic research could be examined empirically and their status evaluated.

Work by linguists such as Halliday (1970) (discourse – language functions), Van Dijk (1977) (discourse – text/context relationships) and Hymes (1972) (situation – sociocultural factors) in the 1970s had led to an expanded concept of language proficiency which recognised the importance of context beyond the sentence level (see Chapter 2 for discussion of the increased interest in text rather than sentence, and meaning construction as against decoding, in reading research in this period). The focus was now on language beyond the level of the sentence and the concern was with how an understanding of the organisation of larger units was critical for successful communication.

For Hymes (1972), communicative competence included the ability to *use* the language in specified contexts, as well as having the knowledge which underlay the actual performance. Following Hymes's two-dimensional model of communicative competence, comprising a 'linguistic' and a 'sociolinguistic' element, most subsequent models have included consideration of a sociolinguistic dimension which recognises the importance of context to the appropriate use of language and the dynamic interaction that occurs between that context and the discourse itself.

An awareness of the dynamic interaction between context and discourse was expressed in Canale and Swain's (1980) framework of 'language competence' which has been seminal in subsequent research on communicative ability and has impacted on language teaching and testing in recent decades. Canale and Swain (1980) provided a useful starting point for a clarification of the terminology necessary for forming a more definite picture of the ability to use language communicatively. They extended the definition of the L2 construct to include pragmatic knowledge as well as linguistic knowledge as important components. These authors took communicative competence to include grammatical competence (knowledge of the rules of grammar), sociolinguistic competence (the ability to use language to fulfill communicative functions in social contexts) and strategic competence (knowledge of verbal and non-verbal communication strategies learners might use to compensate for their shortcomings in other areas of competence and to maintain or repair communication). The model was subsequently updated by Canale (1983), who proposed a four-dimensional model comprising linguistic, sociolinguistic, discoursal and strategic competences; the additional distinction being made between sociolinguistic (sociocultural rules) competence and discoursal competence (cohesion and coherence: the combination of utterances in forming a coherent text or interaction).

An important distinction was also made between communicative competence and communicative performance, the distinguishing feature of the latter being the fact that performance is the realisation of these competences and their interaction in the actual production and comprehension of utterances in a meaningful communicative situation (Canale and Swain 1980:34, Morrow 1979).

These views of leading language testers/applied linguists illustrate how, by the 1980s in language teaching and subsequently testing, emphasis was now placed on use and a concern with communicative functions rather than with the formal language patterns of usage (Campbell and Wales 1970, Widdowson 1978, 1983). Such theoretical descriptions were used to describe the broad parameters within which testing communicative language should fall but practitioners needed more tangible specific attributes to ascertain the nature of the communicative language ability that was being assessed within the constraints obtaining.

In the event, building on the work of Canale and Swain, it was an

American Lyle Bachman (1990) who collected these elements into a seminal framework of Communicative Language Ability (CLA) in an attempt to provide a sound basis for assessment activity. The framework proposed by Bachman (1990) was consistent with these earlier definitions of communicative language ability. Bachman saw performance on language tests as the product of both an individual's language ability and the facets of the test method employed. He proposed an approach that involved two separable frameworks, one for CLA and another for test method facets.

For Bachman, CLA consisted of language competence, strategic competence, and psycho-physiological mechanisms. Language competence included organisational competence, which consisted of grammatical and textual competence, and pragmatic competence, which consisted of illocutionary and sociolinguistic competence. Language competence is composed of the specific knowledge and skills required for operating the language system, for establishing the meanings of utterances, for employing language appropriate to the context and for operating through language beyond the level of the sentence. Strategic competence consists of the more general knowledge and skills involved in assessing, planning and executing communicative acts efficiently. Psycho-physiological mechanisms involved in language use characterise the channel (auditory, visual) and mode (receptive, productive) in which competence is implemented. However in Bachman's model there is a lack of any cognitive dimensions in the form of procedural linguistic competence.

The other part of Bachman's model dealt with skill and test method factors which were meant to handle the actual operation of language in real situations and so locate competence in a wider performance framework. Bachman and Palmer (1996) attempted to make the model more suitable for practical test development and the two parts were relabelled language ability and task characteristics.

Bachman's CLA model provided test developers with useful theoretical questions to ask in the design of language tests, but the existence of the components of the CLA model even as separate entities was never clearly established. The relationship between the various competences was not established, nor was the way they are integrated into overall communicative competence.

Taylor (quoted in Shaw and Weir 2007:242) argues that Bachman's 1990 framework was: 'helpful in provoking us to think about key issues from a theoretical perspective but generally proved very difficult for practitioners to operationalise in a manageable and meaningful way'. The model proved to be extremely difficult to use, not least because of its breadth and depth but also its lack of clear prioritisation as to what might constitute criterial parameters for language testing purposes (Chalhoub-Deville 2003, McNamara 2003) especially where there was a need to differentiate different levels of language proficiency. As such Bachman's model has contributed less than might have been hoped to empirical test validation. This point is highlighted by McNamara (2003:468) who argued that: 'Those who have used the test method facets approach have found it to be difficult to use, and it has in fact been implemented in relatively few test development projects'.

McNamara also questions the value of the model in so far as it lacks an interactional/social dimension (see also Chalhoub-Deville 1997, 2003, Chalhoub-Deville and Deville 2005, Kramsch 1986, 1998, and Chapter 4 of this volume) arguing that it needs to take into account social theories of language use, and directs the reader to O'Sullivan (2000) for an example of how this might be done in speaking tests. To be fair, Bachman is well aware of this shortcoming and comments in reference to his approach (2007:55): 'It does not solve the issue of how abilities and contexts interact, and the degree to which these may mutually affect each other'. As we will note below this is hardly surprising as we are only beginning to address this issue and it may take language testing some considerable time to resolve.

The present writer broadly shares the above reservations concerning Bachman's CLA model but would add that the inadequacy of the treatment of the cognitive processing dimensions of the various language macro-skills is also a considerable disadvantage when considering its use for test development purposes, especially where it is necessary to define and test at *different levels of language proficiency*. No consideration was given to how phases of cognitive processing employed in each of the four skills might be calibrated to various levels of proficiency, Bachman explaining that: 'the realm of general cognitive abilities . . . is beyond the scope of this book' (2007:106).

British Examination Boards needed to know what cognitive demands should be made upon test takers at each proficiency level and what contributory processes each level taps into. Without such an account it is difficult to decide what the cognitive parameters of tasks should be across the language proficiency spectrum (see Shaw and Weir (2007: Chapter 3) for an initial attempt to do this in relation to writing, Khalifa and Weir (2009: Chapter 3) in relation to reading, Taylor (Ed) (2011: Chapter 3) for speaking and Geranpayeh and Taylor (Eds) (2013: Chapter 3) for listening). How to examine different levels of ability has been an important consideration for Cambridge since 1939 and this was to encourage Cambridge in its attempts at a more granular approach to construct definition in its cognitive dimension than the rather broad brush strokes contained in Bachman's account.

Bachman's model offered the first cogent, theoretical model of CLA, albeit with limitations in its cognitive processing and contextual dimensions. It was potentially useful for academics in testing research, but despite its valuable description of test method facets it suffered in terms of its suitability for use as an operational framework by language testing practitioners. At the same time, work was being carried out on the Common European Framework of Reference for languages (CEFR) which *claimed* to be directly useful to both testers and teachers as a descriptive framework of language ability over a series of distinct levels (Council of Europe 2001). This framework was certainly more usable than Bachman's but it was to fall a long way short in terms of its underlying theory and descriptive adequacy (see Weir 2005b). As with Bachman, the CEFR itself was of little help in identifying the suitability of various types of cognitive processing demand or specific, criterial distinctions between contextual parameters at its six proficiency levels (A1–C2) in each of the language skills areas (see, for example, Khalifa and Weir (2009: 34–142) for a later attempt to meet this deficit for reading).

Test constructors in the United Kingdom, who committed to the communicative approach in the 1980s and 1990s (Brendan Carroll, Caroline Clapham, Tony Green, Peter Hargreaves, Roger Hawkey, Ian Hill, Mike Milanovic, Allan Moller, Keith Morrow, Barry O'Sullivan, Don Porter, Pauline Rea, Nick Saville, Lynda Taylor, Cyril Weir and Richard West), sought to identify those abilities (operations/activities) and performance conditions that seemed to be important components of language use in particular contexts (see Alderson and Hughes 1981, Carroll 1980, Hawkey 1982, Moller 1982, Morrow 1977, 1979, Porter 1983, Rea 1978, Weir 1983, 1990, 1993 for details of these). As well as keeping pace with developing theory in applied linguistics, as outlined above, these language testers drew on developments in skills based approaches in teaching and syllabus design (e.g. Munby 1978, and for reading Grellet 1981, Nuttall 1982). They felt that test tasks should involve appropriate use of activities/skills (the surface level manifestations of what in the 21st century would be better understood in terms of cognitive processing). Additionally, test tasks were to be situated within appropriate and criterial conditions of that real-life context as far as was practically possible. So, for example they took those textual parameters from Bachman's earlier theoretical framework which lent themselves most readily to operationalisation in actual tests.

Comprehensive, explicit and practical specifications were to take some time to emerge though (see section *Additional level tests and enhanced specification in the communicative era* below). However from the 1970s onwards we can chart real progress in attempts to include relevant activities and appropriate performance conditions in Cambridge examinations, under the influence of language teaching developments and those in applied linguistics where language testers themselves began to have a much more influential voice.

As well as increased attention to a communicative orientation in all its examinations new and old, the 1980s were also destined to see Cambridge make a substantial investment in enhancing the scoring validity of measurement in their examinations and it is to this we now turn. The catalyst for this latter development was the landmark *1987–1989 Cambridge TOEFL Comparability Study* which was later written up as Volume 1 of the SiLT series (Bachman et al 1995).

The Cambridge–TOEFL Comparability Study 1987–89 and the birth of a profession at Cambridge

The Cambridge–TOEFL Comparability Study of the FCE and TOEFL examinations, as well as encouraging a more explicit focus on the constructs underlying Cambridge examinations, was to provide further encouragement for the continued pursuit of scoring validity and the embedding of systematic test development and validation procedures in the organisation (see Bachman et al 1995 for a full discussion of the study and below for further details). The study took place from 1987–89 and was commissioned by John Reddaway (Secretary 1983–1993) for UCLES EFL and led by Lyle Bachman as Principal Investigator. Its stated purpose was to investigate the construct validity of each examination through content analysis and a comparison of performances on each test.

The choice of the high volume Cambridge FCE examination for the comparability study, rather than IELTS (a comparable test of academic English, like TOEFL used for university admissions purposes but unlike FCE jointly owned with other partners and so at the time less economically important), suggests that other reasons in addition to academic research may have had a part to play in the decision. Spolsky (personal communication) hints at an additional agenda on the part of Cambridge and a spin-off benefit:

> ... the search for comparability was to deal with the threat of CITO developing a European version of TOEFL and so competing with the UCLES tests, a business motivation. The shock was that Bachman and colleagues could not find enough reliability to do a comparison. The good effect was the rapid professionalization of Cambridge.

The Comparability Study took place about the same time as the arrival of a group of newly appointed key professional staff in Cambridge (Michael Milanovic, Nick Saville, Neil Jones and Lynda Taylor) appropriately qualified in applied linguistics and testing and ably led by Peter Hargreaves a former British Council officer. Hargreaves' arrival in 1988 coincided with a fourfold increase in the EFL department's staffing according to the August 1989 *UCLES Newsletter* which provides the first organogram of UCLES EFL. Following on from the earlier, rather isolated contribution of Chaplen in the 1970s, professionalism would now make itself felt in an organisation which had previously somewhat neglected to address directly the requirements for establishing construct validity and the ongoing need for systemic validation of tests especially in the area of scoring validity. The creation in 1989 of the EFL Evaluation Unit (now the ESOL Research and Validation Group) would be a key legacy of Cambridge's response to Bachman – its growth providing evidence of the increasing recognition of the importance of psychometric respectability and growing professionalism in an organisation during a period in which language testing, in the words of Alan Davies, was to become 'the cutting edge of Applied Linguistics'. Spolsky (2004:306) looking back on the leading testing organisations in this period commented:

> ... by reinvesting its [Cambridge's] proceeds to build a solid staff of highly qualified language testers, it has produced a team capable of the highly professional and demanding work of test revision. ETS, after years of minimal tinkering with a profitable test and reluctant addition of speaking and writing tests, was finally persuaded to start designing a new form, 'TOEFL 2000', but after a rather messy computerization experiment, this is still some time away; the managers rather than the testers seem to be still in charge.

It is interesting to recall why these changes in the direction of a psychometrically more sophisticated approach had taken so long. As we noted above, examinations in the United Kingdom and United States had been largely informed by different epistemology. Bachman et al (1995:131) commented on the Cambridge approach:

> ... one feature that distinguishes the FCE from the ETS tests of EFL is its relative complexity, in both design and procedures. This complexity is not fortuitous, but is a direct consequence of the positive value that is attached to a test design that includes a wide variety of test tasks and scoring procedures that include expert human judgment. That is, the British examinations system is particularly concerned with promoting positive effects of examinations on curricula and instruction, and thus is sensitive to including features in its examinations that are consistent with those found in instructional programs. At the same time, the extent to which this introduces variation in test performance that is unrelated to differences in levels of language ability has been made clear by this study and needs to be continuously evaluated.

One clear implication from the results of the comparability study was the need to investigate the effect of test method on test performance especially with the Communicative Language Teaching approach being operationalised more and more through tasks which were 'authentic' in the sense that they were: 'related to non-test language use. The effects of such tasks on test scores ... are less well understood than those of more traditional testing methods' (Bachman et al 1995:127).

Bachman et al explained:

> ... we believe our results suggest that the very features that are seen to be the strengths of the Cambridge exams are also potential sources of unreliability that need to be investigated in further studies. Specifically,

> we believe that the complexities of test design, test administration and marking procedures provide numerous sources of variation in test scores, whose effects need to be empirically examined to demonstrate that Cambridge examination scores are reliable indicators of the abilities they are intended to measure (1995:131).

As a result, they advocated a systematic, iterative programme of test validation research.

Spolsky (1995a) also makes reference to a number of outstanding points of concern in the area of reliability raised by Bachman et al in the Comparability Study (1995). Bachman et al (1995:121) had noted: 'the intra-and inter-rater reliabilities of ratings for Paper 2 [composition] and 5 [interview] are essentially unknown'. Spolsky takes this up:

> A second source of measurement error was the subjective marking of items by different examiners. As a result of the administrative procedures followed it proved impossible to establish the intra- and inter-rater consistency of the subjective papers. . . The interesting point to note here is not the lack of reliability, but the complete lack of concern for it evidenced by the Cambridge method of administration (1995a: 62–3).

The subsequent work on standardising the formats used in the oral test and the development of the *interlocutor frame* would be of major importance and instrumental in improving the scoring validity of the Speaking tests across the Main Suite (see ffrench 2003:367–472 and Taylor and Galaczi 2011:171–233 for details of revisions in CPE 2002, and Chapter 4 in this volume). The Team Leader system introduced by Peter Hargreaves in 1994 would contribute to examiner standardisation and management. Scoring validity in Speaking was further enhanced by the introduction of the pair format (two candidates: two examiners – Interlocutor and Assessor) for all Main Suite Speaking exams. The paired format was introduced as mandatory for CAE Speaking (rather than optional, as in PET, FCE and CPE at that time) when CAE was first launched in 1991; it was adopted as standard in FCE in 1996 and it has since spread to the other exams (see Taylor and Galaczi 2011:171–233 for a full description of the current approach to rating Speaking). It became routine practice to collect data in order to estimate rater agreement and to investigate the possibility of differential performance as a result of other features of the procedure, such as the tasks used (Calver and Bell 2010 and Malarkey, Bell and Somers 2010).

CAE was also innovative in that it saw the introduction of double-marking for the Writing test and with the possibilities of electronic script management this is now under review for other Cambridge examinations (see Chapter 3 for further discussion on the pressing need for this).

Spolsky (1995a) also returned to the criticism raised by Bachman and noted earlier by Chaplen (later revisited by Chalhoub-Deville and Turner 2000):

> A further source of measurement error was introduced by the multiple topics offered in the composition and the multiple forms used in the listening comprehension paper and in the interview. (ibid.:66). . . a study of the variance introduced by using different forms of the listening comprehension test suggested that their use introduced a considerable degree of measurement error (ibid.: 67). Variations in examiners and methods (individual versus group) masked the variance introduced by having alternative forms for the interview (ibid.: 68).

At the time of the Comparability Study there were sometimes up to 14 versions of the Listening paper for operational and security reasons but now there are never more than four. More importantly procedures were subsequently introduced to help obviate such criticism. Pretesting, standards fixing and item banking using Rasch modelling all helped achieve the same distribution of difficulty across item-based papers 1, 3 and 4 (Reading, Use of English and Listening) from administration to administration. Post-examination checks and scaling are also employed to guard against this potential threat to reliability.

By the 1990s the processes used by Cambridge ESOL to produce examination papers had been greatly enhanced through employing item-banking as the method for storing the test materials and constructing test papers with known measurement characteristics. In Cambridge ESOL Reading, Listening and Use of English papers, question paper production is now based on the Local Item Banking System (LIBS), which is a computer-based management and analysis tool developed by Cambridge ESOL to handle the entire production cycle. LIBS contains a large bank of materials for use in the examinations which have all been fully edited and pretested according to the procedures described below.

Item banking is an application of item response theory (IRT) (Bond and Fox 2001, Wright and Stone 1979). It involves assembling a bank of calibrated items – that is, items of known difficulty. Designs employed for collecting response data ensure a link across items at all levels. Items are pretested in specially constructed papers which include anchor items. Because the anchor items are of known difficulty, the analysis that is carried out on the pretest responses allows the new items to be calibrated on a logit scale. This scale, produced using Winsteps, is re-scaled to produce a conventional ESOL scale, which is used for examination construction purposes. It is this scale which underpins the Local Item Banking System (LIBS).

The Cambridge ESOL Common Scale, a single measurement scale covering all Cambridge ESOL levels, was constructed with reference to these objective items. The Cambridge ESOL Common Scale relates different testing events within a single frame of reference, greatly facilitating the development and consistent application of standards. Examinations are constructed from the calibrated tasks in the item bank. Each task, therefore, consists of items of measured (Rasch) difficulty, which are selected from within a specified range to determine the mean difficulty of the task.

The standard operating procedures for test construction ensure that tasks selected for Main Suite objective papers fall within the specified range of difficulty and achieve the targeted average for the paper as a whole. They help to ensure comparability of difficulty and maintenance of standards across different forms of the paper and between sessions (June to December etc). This applies to the Reading, Listening and Use of English components and takes place before the exams are administered.

Papers are also analysed after each 'live' administration prior to the grading. This allows for additional checks to be made on comparability where alternative forms of a component may have been used, e.g. for the Listening test. If necessary, further adjustments can be made at this time, for example, by scaling both versions of the paper to the same mean and standard deviation.

Although statistical comparability is clearly important, the cognitive and contextual aspects of validity should never be forgotten and it must be stressed that high indices of alternate-form reliability alone do not necessarily yield a significant meaning unless supported by evidence of comparability in other aspects of validity as well. For example, inconsistent context validity across examination forms may influence examination scores, resulting in bias against particular cohorts as a consequence and affecting examination fairness. There is a clear need for all items in the bank to be tagged with criterial information relating to their contextual and cognitive validity properties as well as their Rasch logit values. As more and more examinations are provided on demand per year, this makes it even more imperative that information on the constructs being measured by the items is available to test constructors.

For the Writing component the issue of multiple topics raises different concerns and other procedures have been developed to deal with this threat to scoring validity. The candidates complete two writing tasks, the first of which is obligatory, the second is chosen from four other possibilities representing a fixed set of 'genres'. The element of choice has been retained in the Writing paper and is seen as an important consideration in relation to the validity and impact of the examination. However, the choice is carefully controlled and efforts are made to ensure that the tasks are of comparable difficulty, administered under standardised conditions and can be marked effectively by trained raters using task specific and general rating criteria. The obligatory task acts as an anchor and helps to ensure that the positive feature of choice does not impact negatively on scoring validity.

In Speaking, precise instructions in the internal Item Writer Guidelines now help control various task characteristics (e.g. topic, nature of information, length of rubric). Piloting of Speaking materials helps maintain the difficulty level and ensures historically comparable tasks (see Galaczi and ffrench 2011). In order to monitor the relative difficulty of the task-based materials used in each administration of the Speaking tests, data are routinely analysed and experimental studies have also been carried out using G-theory and multi-faceted Rasch studies. These techniques allow the researchers to investigate the influence of tasks compared with other facets of the testing procedure, such as the rater and the rating scale. The evidence suggests that the tasks used randomly on large number of candidates are of comparable difficulty (e.g. in terms of the mean and standard deviation of ratings).

So, substantial steps were taken to improve all aspects of scoring validity in this period and it is perhaps not surprising that Taylor and Jones (2006:3) refer to the Cambridge –TOEFL Comparability Study as a milestone for the Syndicate's English language examinations:

> . . . for Cambridge ESOL this established an empirical imperative and we invested heavily in approaches and systems to address measurement issues such as test reliability and version comparability.

The study helped reinforce a direction Cambridge was contemplating with a new professional team at the helm, and encouraged them to develop efficient and effective systems which would enhance both scoring validity as well as its traditional concern with context validity

Weir (2005a) observed that from the 1980s there was a degree of convergence of views on testing internationally, helped in no small part by the growing influence of the Language Testing Research Colloquium which annually brought together researchers and scholars interested in language testing from around the world. The birth of the journal *Language Testing* as a result of a weekend meeting of a small group of six British testers (Charles Alderson, Clive Criper, Alan Davies, Arthur Hughes, Alan Moller and Cyril Weir) organised at Lancaster University, United Kingdom in 1980 (see Alderson and Hughes 1981) was to further promote the exchange of views across the Atlantic. The advent of the Language Testing list-serve, a web-based discussion forum in the 1990s, similarly promoted the exchange of views and an understanding of different traditions. Hamp-Lyons (2000:585) similarly notes evidence of convergence:

> The tendencies seen in American and British testing, the two epistemologies which Spolsky (1995a, p.357) has called "the plural scepticism of the humanities and the search for unique certainty of the rationalism of the modern sciences" can be seen to be moving closer to each other . . . The tension between epistemologies still exists, but there is much less disagreement about goals and values.

The growing acceptance of international standards for language testing in part spawned by the drawing up of the AERA/APA/NCME (1985) standards made an equally positive contribution. It gradually became clear to the leading international examination boards that all aspects of validity had to be addressed to satisfy potential public and governmental demands for accountability and to meet increasingly explicit and codified professional norms.

A further important requirement for UCLES, made clear by the Comparability Study, was the pressing need to define the communicative competence construct 'precisely enough to permit its assessment' (Bachman et al 1995:127). We will see below how, with the development of CAE, it became a matter of some urgency to specify more closely the exams either side of it, namely FCE and CPE. The growth in the provision of examinations at different proficiency levels in the latter part of the 20th century, encouraged by European governmental pressure for standardisation, took place alongside the growing availability of descriptive language frameworks based on developments in applied linguistics. Both were to encourage British examination boards to specify more closely the various constructs they were attempting to measure.

Enhanced specification and new level examinations in the communicative era

Explicit specification of the language constructs measured in Cambridge examinations was to occur relatively late in the history of the suite. Earlier in the century Roach, the Assistant Secretary at UCLES, had obviously been troubled by the absence of any specifications of performance levels, described in terms of agreed criterion descriptors. 'The Syndicate did not define standards of attainment to the examiners for the LCE when the examination was started in 1939', notes Roach (1944b:8). 'Candidates', Roach worried, 'tend to set the standard in any test which has no absolute criterion'(1944b:8). 'Public confidence in the tests is likely to depend for a long time on the extent to which they are felt to be directly controlled by the University and to represent worldwide standards' (Roach 1944b:24, 1945a). The importance of standards of attainment was clearly understood, but the conceptual framework and criteria for their definition were not yet established. In 1944 the standards of attainment were those based on candidate performance without any recourse to external levels other than the remembered performances of candidates in previous years.

It was to be some time after Roach's early concern before examination boards began to take seriously the idea of attempting comprehensive definitions of proficiency levels. Stern (1983:109) identifies the start of this process:

One of the most powerful trends of development of the decade (1970s) was the shift from a concern with teaching methods to one with language teaching objectives, language content and curriculum (or syllabus) design.

In the early 1970s there was an attempt at an Executive Committee meeting in Cambridge to define for the first time 'the basic aims of the examinations', and 'to assess the content and balance of the suggested form of examination in terms of these basic aims' (Executive Committee Minutes October 1971). It considered how to achieve a more precise description of the language abilities the examinations set out to test. Importantly, this discussion took place within a wider external context of Council of Europe (CoE) activities, where defining language competence in general was assuming a greater importance than hitherto (Executive Committee Minutes October 1971):

> Mr. Trim reported that further progress regarding a unit-credit system for language learners in Europe, a subject of discussion at the Zurich conference in May 1971, had been made, with the publication of several attempts to delimit the elements in a common core of language competence. In addition, the investigation behind a European unit-credit system for adult language learning started the same year. The idea was to create a system which would:
> – Be learner-centred and needs-oriented
> – Cover all stages of language development
> – Contain specification of learning objectives: knowledge and skills
> – Allow assessment of the extent to which the objective had been reached.

It was hoped that these Council of Europe activities would lead to the publication of 'attempts to delimit the elements in a common core of language competence' (Executive Committee Minutes October 1971). However, this system was to be short-lived as it soon became clear that it was not possible to divide up language learning so neatly into a set of discrete modules that could be learned in any arrangement.

The notional-functional syllabus associated with the work of David Wilkins at Reading University (e.g. 1973a, 1973b, 1976) was to prove more generative. Wilkins (1976) turned the traditional structural syllabus on its head. Instead of starting with grammatical structures as the basis for syllabus design (an organising principle for English language learning since Fick (1793)), he recommended that the meanings that learners might want to express should be the organising principle, with grammatical structures relegated to the role of exponents for realising meanings. Semantico-grammatical categories (later termed notions) and functions would provide a generic base, providing a clear rationale for selecting 'the language to which the learner will be exposed and which we will expect him to acquire' (Wilkins 1976:1).

Such specification of language competence was to be made with reference to the communicative needs of European target language users. Research into distinguishing various basic functions of language and identifying these with minimum vocabulary and structure ranges resulted for example in the development of the *Threshold* level specifications (later version available in the public domain as Van Ek and Trim1998a) and the *Waystage* level (later version available in the public domain as Van Ek and Trim 1998b). The Council of Europe sponsored such research in order to provide learning objectives for teaching the various European languages for social, work related, and academic purposes, and they were intended to reflect meaningful levels of language competence at the lower range of proficiency. In many other publications emanating from the Council of Europe from the 1970s onward, we can see indicators of this agenda (Bung 1973, Munby 1978, Richterich 1973a, 1973b, Richterich and Chancerel 1978, Trim 1970, 1980, Van Ek 1975, Van Ek and Trim 2001, Wilkins 1973a, 1973b, 1976).

The desirability of specifying levels of performance more closely had also been evident at an early date to one of the few professional language testers associated with the English examinations at Cambridge in the 1970s. Frank Chaplen's June 1971 report, *An Appraisal of the Syndicate's Written Examinations in English as a Foreign Language together with Some Suggested Modifications*, as well as stressing the need to modernise the Cambridge English exams with a clearer focus on objectivity and consistency in scoring, had also pointed out a need for a clearer focus on the constructs they sought to measure. He reported how LCE was increasingly used as a qualification for employment and felt the examination needed to provide evidence of the language skills that employers would require. He also expressed concern about blurred distinctions between the constructs measured by the LCE Composition and Comprehension, Structure and Usage and Translation papers.

In May 1972, John Trim, Director of the Council of Europe's Modern Languages Project from 1971 to 1997, became the Chairman of the Syndicate's powerful Executive Committee (Executive Committee Minutes May 1972) which he was to chair from 1972 to 1979. Hawkey and Milanovic (2013) describe how:

> ... Trim had also set up the Department of Linguistics at Cambridge University, lectured and conducted seminars in some 40 countries, and been Director of CILT (Centre for Information on Language Teaching and Research) in the United Kingdom ... as Director of the Council of Europe's Modern Languages Projects Trim oversaw developments ranging from the Threshold Level to the Common European Framework of Reference.

Trim, with his CoE background was clearly a positive influence on the Syndicate's move towards more clearly specified language proficiency levels from elementary to advanced. By May 1973, the Syndicate was seriously considering a 'preliminary testing service': a series of tests as 'a progress measurement at the early stage of a teaching course, or as a qualifying test for entry to the First Certificate examination' (Executive Committee minutes May 1973).

At the UCLES EFL Executive Committee meeting of November 1975, the target of Council of Europe research into Threshold level was noted, namely 'for examination syllabuses in various languages to be prepared by 1978, for possible independent implementation by interested examining bodies in 1980'. The Executive meeting of November 1977 noted:

> It was agreed that although the Syndicate's policy has been to examine only at recognizable and significant levels of achievement, further consideration should now be given to appropriate ways in which the demand for some form of progress testing might be met within the framework of the administrative structure developed for the Cambridge examinations.

LCE, subsequently rebranded as the First Certificate in English (FCE) in 1975, had become a well-established examination by the mid-1970s, and a demand for a test at a more elementary level was growing. The Executive meeting of May 1978 received a sub-committee report on 'Examining at Elementary Levels' (78/2). It noted the viability of a proficiency examination level below FCE closely related to the Council of Europe Waystage, which would equate with approximately 300 hours of teaching. The minutes of the executive committee meeting of November 1978 (78/19) noted that a new Preliminary English Test (PET), had been approved by the Syndicate and it eventually appeared in 1980 (2094 candidates) on a restricted basis to monitor administrative aspects. The Syndicate was apparently so confident of the potential demand that they had decided on designing the examination as a large-scale operation from the start, rather than a pilot scheme (Executive Committee Minutes May 1978:1). Steps were being taken towards a set of general English exams linked to a common frame of reference.

PET was 'an achievement test which should be an encouragement in the early stages of learning' (PET information for centres and candidates, n.d:1). Its specifications were developed in the context of the Threshold specifications and the focus was on basic communication needs. PET was designed 'to test written and spoken communicative competence in a social survival context as achieved from complete beginner level' (Cambridge ESOL 1987:5). The level was more precisely described as elementary, being two-thirds of the way towards FCE or about 350 study hours from complete beginner level (Cambridge ESOL 1984:10). PET was a 4-skills test without a Use of English paper and was billed as a test rather than a certificate as in the FCE and CPE and available only on demand rather than at fixed dates.

By 1980 there were also soundings on a further new level of examination at a level between FCE and CPE. There was a widespread view among teachers that the gap between these two examinations was too wide. There was evidence of quite large numbers of students going on to study for CPE after FCE and failing the examination in some cases on multiple occasions. An examination between these levels, as an achievable staging post, was seen as desirable especially in key markets such as Greece. This would entail further clarification of the level of FCE itself, of course, which was not best served by inappropriate scales of recognition making comparisons between CPE and FCE with A and O levels (Executive Committee Minutes 1980). Here was the beginning of the Certificate of Advanced English exam, CAE, initially labelled the Certificate in English for International Communication (CEIC).

Hawkey (2009:94) describes how in 1986, an internal UCLES EFL memorandum notes:

> The Syndicate has announced its intention to develop an examination tentatively called the Second Certificate in English [one of several names for what is now the Certificate in Advanced English (CAE)], "to be at a level between FCE and Proficiency (CPE)." Neither of these exams, it was admitted, however, had 'a clearly defined syllabus', since 'both examinations were developed long before the existence of models for syllabus description such as the Council of Europe's Threshold.

Hawkey (2009:64) cuts to the chase and singles out some telling quotations from this memorandum:

> Then the rub: '. . . we cannot introduce an examination which claims to be between two other levels, without defining these levels!' A Working Party would thus analyze past papers in order to produce a 'retrospective syllabus which will serve as a basis for the syllabus in the new exam'. The vexed problem of the systematic definition of proficiency levels was raising its head again.

Hawkey (2009:98, citing the *UCLES International Examination EFL General Handbook* (1987)) explains that the initial designation of the new Cambridge examination at the C1 level, the Certificate in English for International Communication (to be renamed later as CAE), was clearly chosen to reflect its communicative construct and target candidature and 'in its development integrated skills tests were seen as particularly relevant to "those with professional and vocational needs as well as for those who wish to further their education through the medium of English"'. CAE was and still is an accepted language qualification for entry purposes to most United Kingdom universities. He records how:

... the CEIC specifications in the 1987 Handbook included detailed criteria and syllabus analysis. The performance criteria were in the form of 'Can Do' statements, clearly showing the influence of work on the Council of Europe project. A further significant feature of the CEIC was an attempt to specify an examination syllabus across the main linguistic and communicative elements [see Hawkey 2009: 98–101 for full details].

The 1991 CAE general specifications document describes it as 'an examination in reading, writing, the structure of the language, listening and speaking at post-First Certificate level'. The aim of the CAE was to 'offer a high-level final qualification in the language to those wishing to use English in their jobs' and 'to encourage the development of the skills required by students progressing towards CPE, with the emphasis very much on real-world tasks'. In many ways CAE in its earliest manifestation exhibited one of the fullest realisations of the communicative approach in the Cambridge family of tests (see Chapters, 2, 3, 4 and 5, and Appendices A and D for details and examples of the CAE examination papers). Later developments to bring it in line with the 'Main Suite family', however, were to dilute its earlier faithfulness to this approach.

Much of the available evidence on the proficiency levels of the Cambridge English examinations at this time was conceptual and theoretical, and derived from the historical context, in terms of linguistics and pedagogy, in which the examinations developed (Taylor and Jones 2006). During the 1980s, Cambridge ESOL (among other stakeholders) helped fund and provided professional input to the revision of the linguistic and functional level descriptions contained in the *Threshold* (van Ek and Trim 1998a) and *Waystage* levels (van Ek and Trim 1998b). Threshold 1990 and Waystage 1990 had underpinned the revised test specifications for PET, strongly defining its lexico-grammatical and functional/notional content, as well as the selection of texts and tasks for language ability assessment. Work to develop the *Vantage* level specifications (Van Ek and Trim 2001) drew heavily on the existing FCE-level examination and received financial and professional support from both Cambridge and the Association of Language Testers in Europe (ALTE) partners.

The combination of functional and general notional categories and their linguistic exponents in the early COE publications (for example Richterich and Chancerel 1978, Trim 1980, van Ek and Trim 1998a, 1998b, Wilkins 1976) were to be finally brought together in the Common European Framework of Reference for Languages (CEFR) brought out by the Council of Europe in 2001. Together with the Can Do project of the ALTE they provided a clearer definition of what the 'general' proficiency levels meant. As a result of attempts to link UCLES examinations to the five ALTE levels and subsequently to the six Council of Europe levels (see Khalifa and Weir (2009:190–216) for details of the linking with regard to reading comprehension tests), the UCLES Main Suite (UMS) proficiency levels were to become clearer and more explicit (see Council of Europe (2001), Jones (2000, 2001, 2002), Jones and Hirtzel (2001) for details of the ALTE framework; see Alderson (2002) Council of Europe (2001), North (2000, 2002) for details of the CEFR).

These external developments encouraged examination boards to look more closely at what they were trying to test and provided useful external reference points for distinguishing between proficiency levels albeit at a rather underspecified level of description (see Weir (2005b) for discussion of some of their limitations). By relating examinations to a single common framework, the interpretation of levels by end users of certificates, such as employers, was facilitated, making qualifications more usable and increasing people's potential mobility within the European Community. The Can Do statements offered a useful description of how language users use the language: what they can typically do with it at different levels, in the various language skills and in a range of contexts (Social and Tourist, Work, Study).

An increasing concern with the construct being measured

Hawkey (2009) describes how the FCE Revision Project began in 1991 with the benefits deriving from the work done on CAE, and the recommendations and change arising out of the Comparability Study (1987–89). He notes that the *Revised FCE Internal Specifications* (1994) were a far more comprehensive document than the equivalent material accompanying previous FCE revisions. It was testimony to an increasingly professional attitude to testing at Cambridge, informed by developments in applied linguistics theory and research and in communicative pedagogy. The document makes clear that the Revision Project was theory-based and had addressed the 'possibility of designing tests based on models of language rather than on or in addition to analyses of students' linguistic needs'.

The Bachman model is reproduced wholesale as a figure in the internal specifications and its role is made clear:

> It is important to define the general target language use situations within which FCE candidates are expected to operate so as to be able to pinpoint relevant abilities, make use of contexts that are appropriate to candidates' affective schemata and world knowledge and to be able to define certain categories of test method characteristics (1994:8).

Hawkey (2009) describes how Bachman (1990) was a useful source for insights into metacognitive processes (as potential test constructs), test authenticity and test method facets. The 1994 FCE Specifications section for the Writing test sums up the usefulness and limitations of Bachman's model:

> . . . current models of language ability are extremely valuable as they are able to help define the construct being tested and can also provide some insight into the general features that a writing task should exhibit. The more specific features of writing tasks are suggested by current research into the writing process . . .

The published specifications for FCE 1996 were structured to take account of both theoretical considerations and feedback from stakeholders. The Specifications were critical of the 1984 version of the examination because it was 'not accompanied by an explicitly stated construct'. It was felt that the construct of the 1984 examination 'had to be pieced together by study of documents such as item-writer guidelines, item descriptions and UCLES EFL Regulations' (1996:13).

In the Specifications for the 1996 FCE, there are 'theoretical consideration' sub-sections for each of the five papers in which the construct being measured in each is discussed. Hawkey (2009) points out that what was particularly striking was the attention paid to recent theory and research to ground decisions made on the modifications of the papers. He makes the important point that it is often the actual exam-related research, feedback, discussion, trial and error, within a consciousness of developments in applied linguistics that actually operationalises changes to exams. Thus, in addition to the Bachman model of communicative language ability, there were references to writing processes (e.g. Elbow 1973, Hayes and Flower 1983, Raimes 1985, Spack 1984, Zamel 1983); listening (Bhatia 1993, Brindley and Nunan 1992, Buck 1995); grammar (Hudson 1991); genre and discourse analysis (Ede and Lunsford 1985, Hinds 1987); study skills (Wallace 1980); reader–writer relationships (Carrell, Devine and Eskey 1988); group interaction (Bygate 1987); teaching of language as communication (Widdowson 1978); communicative approaches to language testing (Alderson and Hughes 1981, Morrow 1979, Oller 1979, Porter 1983 and Weir 1988).

Hawkey (2004), in research externally commissioned by the Research and Validation Group, drew attention to:

> . . . increasing high-stakes examination stakeholder demand for information on test theory, construct and evidence-based test validation. It is more common nowadays for people to ask 'What is/are the construct(s) of FCE?' or 'Are you changing the construct(s) of CAE?' Reference to constructs remained mainly implicit, despite pressures in the late 1960s and into the 1970s for more rigorous definition and validation of test constructs. Then, as key constructs changed in the 1980s towards the communicative language ability macro-construct and pressures increased, through the Comparability Study and the restructuring of UCLES EFL for a higher priority to test validity and test development

systems we noted a rather clearer, more explicit focus on test constructs and construct validation.

He describes how in the FCE update from 2004 onwards, the *Modifications to Examinations Working Group* (Anne Gutch, Angela ffrench, Richard Hall, Ardeshir Geranpayeh, Janet Bojan, Jason Hurren, Meredyth Rodgers and Helen Coward) was originally tasked to produce a 'model for Cambridge ESOL construct-based examination specifications, to be accessible to test users and amenable to adaptation, streamlining and rationalization'. A progress update paper in November 2004 notes that in late 2003 Research and Validation began intensive work towards 'a more clearly articulated theoretical position for each skill area underpinning our tests: Reading, Writing, Listening, Speaking and Use of English'.

Hawkey details how the *Research and Validation Constructs-focused Working Group* (Lynda Taylor, Hanan Khalifa, Tony Green, Ardeshir Geranpayeh, Fiona Barker, Neil Jones and Evelina Galaczi) co-ordinated theoretical and practical research into the constructs to be measured across the four language macro-skills using insights from a socio-cognitive validation framework. This was based on collaborative work, beginning between Cambridge ESOL and Cyril Weir in 2002. The internal draft paper *Defining the construct(s) underpinning the CE UMS tests: a socio-cognitive perspective on overall language and individual language skills* (Taylor, Barker, Geranpayeh, Green, Khalifa and Shaw 2006) represents an important contribution to the constructs debate and to the modifications project.

For the FCE/CAE modifications project Weir's framework was used as a check on the validity of the updated exams. The report *FCE/CAE Modifications: Building the Validity Argument: Application of Weir's Socio-Cognitive framework to FCE & CAE* (ffrench and Gutch 2006) tabulates the framework for validity evidence on each area and sub-area within Weir's model.

The updated 2008 FCE and CAE Specifications would appear to be a further development on those issued in 1994, now reflecting in particular Weir's validation framework with its socio-cognitive focus.

A socio-cognitive approach to test construct definition

A broad concern with making test materials as 'authentic' as possible had been a dominant theme for adherents of the communicative approach from the 1970s onwards as they attempted to develop test activities that *approximated* to the 'reality' of non-test language use (real-life performance) (see Bachman 1990, Bachman and Palmer 1996, Canale and Swain 1980, Hawkey 2005, Morrow 1979, Weigle 2002, Weir 1983, 1990, 2005a).This 'real-life' approach, though initially the subject of much criticism in the United States, proved a useful heuristic for guiding practical test development (Bachman 1990:41). It proved particularly helpful in situations in which the domain of language use was relatively homogeneous and identifiable (see O'Sullivan (2006) on the development of Cambridge Business English Examinations and Davies (2008b) on the development of English for Academic Purpose examinations).

Considerable progress had been made by the end of 20th century in characterising communicative language ability and, after a minor hiccough occasioned by the debate concerning Oller's unitary competence hypothesis, Kunnan (1998) felt able to assert there was now a consensus that English as an L2 was a multi-componential construct. However, despite a widespread acceptance of the partial divisibility of the macro skills (listening, reading, writing and speaking), and a general agreement on the need for test tasks to resemble real life as far as was feasible, the precise nature (cognitive and contextual) of each of the component macro skills had not yet been fully revealed by research (see Douglas 2000:25). For example there were still major sub-skills issues: a) whether the surmised sub-skills were psychologically real; b) whether it was reasonable to consider targeting them separately; and c) how they were co-ordinated and interacted in real-world language use.

A review of approaches to validation in the language testing literature invariably attests to the importance attached to the theoretical dimension of the language ability being measured in tests (see Davies 1984). However, in much language test development, little attempt was made to establish what this theoretical dimension was at the *a priori* stage before the test was administered to candidates. There was a tendency to rely on *a posteriori* statistical analyses to establish what has been tested and to determine whether different abilities could be distinguished through such procedures (see Bachman and Palmer (1981) for a specific example of such an approach in speaking tests and Khalifa and Weir (2009:35–38) for an historical account of such *post hoc* approaches in reading).

While this might have offered insight into the psychometric qualities of a test, it did not take us very far in trying to establish the processing that had taken place to complete the test task(s) in the first place. Building on the earlier work of Weir (2005a), and in collaboration with external, applied linguists in the United Kingdom such as John Field, Anthony Green, Liz Hamp-Lyons, Barry O'Sullivan, Norbert Schmitt, Lynda Taylor and Eddie Williams, Cambridge ESOL embarked on further development of its own conceptual frameworks for developing and analysing tests of second language ability. These frameworks sought to articulate the Cambridge ESOL approach to construct validity in English language test construction: in writing Shaw and Weir (2007), in reading Khalifa and Weir (2009), in speaking Taylor (Ed.) (2011) and in listening Geranpayeh and Taylor (Eds) (2013).

The starting point was to examine how the socio-cognitive validity framework first described in Weir's *Language Testing and Validation: An Evidence-based Approach* (2005a) might contribute to an enhanced validation framework for use with Cambridge examinations. In this approach each of the macro skills, reading, writing, listening and speaking was viewed as not just the underlying latent trait of ability but as the result of the constructed triangle of trait, context and score (including its interpretation).

This approach to construct definition, based on Weir (2005a), is represented pictorially in Figure 1.2 below. The graphic representation is intended to depict how the various validity components might fit together both temporally and conceptually. 'The arrows indicate the principal direction(s) of any hypothesised relationships: what has an effect on what, and the timeline runs from top to bottom: before the test is finalised, then administered and finally what happens after the test event' (Weir 2005a:43). Conceptualising validity in terms of temporal sequencing is of value as it offers test developers a plan of what should be happening in relation to validation and when it should be happening. The test-taker characteristics box in Figure 1.2 below connects directly to the cognitive and context validity boxes because:

> ... these individual characteristics will directly impact on the way the individuals process the test task set up by the context validity box. Obviously, the tasks themselves will also be constructed with the overall test population and the target use situation clearly in mind as well as with a concern for their cognitive validity (Weir 2005a:51).

Figure 1.2 A socio-cognitive framework (based on Weir 2005a)

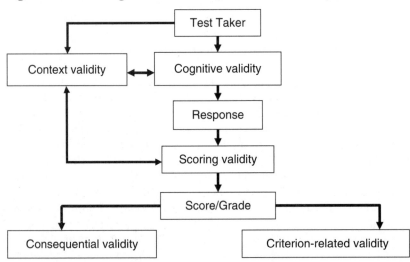

A concern with interactional authenticity (Bachman 1990:315–323) in a test requires that the cognitive processes candidates engage in while completing the test task are representative of, and offer an adequate coverage of, the cognitive processes which would prevail in a natural (i.e. non-test) context. Language test constructors need to be aware of the currently available theory relating to the cognitive processing that underpins equivalent operations in real-life language use beyond the test; and in any test task we need to establish that what is taking place during task completion in the test reflects this.

We are obviously restricted in our diachronic survey to making pooled *subjective* judgements of the cognitive processing that is likely to have taken place in the various test tasks employed in Cambridge English language examinations over the 100-year period. The stronger empirical base that employing student recall protocols during or after individual test taking experiences would provide (Plakans 2008, Smagorinsky 1994), along with the possibilities opened up in reading by technological innovations such as eye tracking (Eger, Ball, Stevens and Dodd 2007, Bax and Weir 2012), and in writing by screen capture software programmes and keystroke logging (Severinson-Eklundh and Kollberg 2003), is unfortunately not a feasible option for this present study.

We do, however, have recourse to work in the general area of cognitive psychology (e.g. Anderson 2000, Ericsson, Charness, Feltovich and Hoffman (Eds) 2006, Gernsbacher 1990, Glaser 1991) and more specifically to established theory relating to the cognitive processing that underpins equivalent operations in real-life language use (e.g. Field (2013) for listening, Kellogg (1996) for writing, Levelt (1989) for speaking, and Rayner and Pollatsek (1989) for reading) as informing sources. Through well-researched theoretical models of the real-life processing of expert users, we can start to identify which processing aspects of the constructs are likely to have been activated by the tasks under review in this volume. We would, though, accept the criticism that using the framework in this way for the most part offers only a heuristic rather than the grounded empirical proof some readers might wish for.

A concern with situational authenticity (Bachman 1990:303–315) requires test takers to respond to contexts which simulate 'real life' in terms of criterial parameters without necessarily replicating it exactly. The term content validity was traditionally used to refer to such content coverage of the task. Context validity is preferred in this volume as a more inclusive superordinate as it signals the need to consider not just linguistic content parameters, but also the social and cultural contexts in which the task is performed. The contextual dimensions for a test task are often fairly well understood by language testers and address the particular performance conditions, the setting under which it is to be performed (such as response method, time available, text length, order of items as well as the linguistic demands inherent in the successful performance of the task), together with the actual examination conditions resulting from the administrative setting (Weir 2005a). Empirical evidence is of course often more readily available with regard to the quantifiable contextual parameters in test tasks, as Appendix B illustrates with reference to reading.

Scoring validity is linked directly to both context and cognitive validity. It accounts for the extent to which test scores are arrived at through the use of appropriate criteria in constructed response tasks and exhibit consensual agreement in their marking, are as free as possible from measurement error, stable over time, appropriate in terms of their content sampling and engender confidence as reliable decision-making indicators.

Messick (1989) argued the case for also considering consequential validity in judging the validity of scores on a test. From this point of view it is necessary in validity studies to ascertain whether the social consequences of test interpretation support the intended testing purpose(s) and are consistent with other social values. There is a concern here with the washback of the test on the learning and teaching that precedes it as well as with its impact on institutions and society more broadly.

Consequential validity also takes account of test bias. This issue takes us back to the test-taker characteristics box. The evidence collected on the test taker should be used to check that no unfair bias has occurred for individuals as a result of decisions taken earlier with regard to the contextual and cognitive features of the test. This raises the issue of whether consideration of (potential) consequential validity should in fact take place right from the start of the test development process. Saville's (2009) exploration of the idea of *impact by design* would support such a theoretical modification to our model above (see also Weir and O'Sullivan 2011) linking the consequential validity box to the context validity box, thus demonstrating the importance of impact throughout the testing cycle.

Messick authorised the growing interest in test use as a critical feature, and opened the way to the ethical concerns that now dominate much language testing debate. As we noted above in the Introduction, this area was largely ignored at Cambridge, and elsewhere, prior to the 21st century, but the work of for example Hawkey (2006), Geranpayeh and Kunnan (2007) and Saville (2009) illustrate the importance it is now given in Cambridge ESOL.

Criterion-related validity is a predominantly quantitative and *a posteriori* concept, concerned with the extent to which test scores correlate with a suitable external criterion of performance with established properties (see Anastasi (1988:145), Messick (1989:16) for details).

Test task performance needs to be generalisable to the wider domain of real-world tasks that candidates may be exposed to and it is, therefore, important to be able to specify target activities in terms of their criterial validity parameters (context, cognitive and scoring) and to operational-ise as representative a sample of these parameters as possible in the test task(s). As a general principle in the socio-cognitive approach, language tests should, as far as is practicable, place requirements on test takers similar to those involved in communicative settings in non-test 'real-life' situations.

This approach requires attention to both the cognitive and social dimen-sions of communication, i.e. a focus on both ability and task. The symbiotic relationship between the contextual parameters laid out in the task and the cognitive processing involved in task performance is crucial. Lynda Taylor (personal communication) believes it is important in language testing that we give both the socio and the cognitive elements:

> ... an appropriate place and emphasis within the whole, and do not privilege one over another. The framework reminds us of language use – and also language assessment – as both a socially situated and a cogni-tively processed phenomenon. The socio-cognitive framework seeks to marry up the individual psycholinguistic perspective with the individual and group sociolinguistic perspective.

Although for descriptive purposes the various elements of the model in Figure 1.2 are presented as being separate from each other, undoubtedly a close relationship exists between these components, for example between context validity and cognitive validity, which together with scoring criteria constitute for us what is frequently referred to as construct validity. Decisions taken with regard to parameters in terms of task context will impact on the processing that takes place in task completion (see Appendix B for a spe-cific investigation of this in relation to CPE reading texts 1913–2012). The interactions between, and within, these aspects of validity may well *eventu-ally* offer further insights into a closer definition of different levels of task difficulty and the nature of the constructs themselves.

The metaphor of a journey is an important, albeit overused one, and it is salutary to remember in 2012 we are still on it and in *interactionalist* terms just beginning it (Chalhoub-Deville 2003, 2005, Weir and O'Sullivan 2011). Widdowson (2003:169–170) reminds us of the lack of a dynamic interface between components in existing models:

> The essential problem with these different models of communicative competence is that they analyse a complex process into a static set of components, and as such cannot account for the dynamic interrelation-ships which are engaged in communication itself. As a consequence,

> when you make such models operational in language teaching and
> testing, you can only deal with the separate parts as discrete features,
> since the essential interrelationships that make the whole are missing.

Testing researchers in the future will need to explore these interrelationships
further and determine more closely if and how individual ability and contextual facets interact, and whether and how the ability changes as a result of
that interaction.

Endnote

The greater importance now attached to defining and validating the constructs of the Cambridge ESOL examinations is clear as we come to the
end of our 100-year survey. In addition to the extensive qualitative research
that was brought together in the SiLT 'constructs' volumes project from
2007–2012, recent empirical work by Geranpayeh in statistically exploring
the constructs underlying Cambridge examinations provided Cambridge
ESOL with an additional layer of evidence for its multidimensional view
of the L2 language construct. Geranpayeh's research (see Geranpayeh and
Somers 2006a, 2006b, 2006c) provided empirical evidence for an overall
communicative language ability divisible into skills and language elements as represented by the Reading, Writing, Listening, and Speaking and
Use of English papers in Cambridge English examinations. Each of these
papers, as Geranpayeh (2007:12) puts it, 'can claim to make a unique contribution to the assessment of the overall proficiency (pass/fail), i.e. they
are all necessary for arriving at the composite score'. The historical view
of the test developers, teachers and other stakeholders of the constructs to
be measured in Cambridge English language exams was at last supported
empirically.

In the 2007 *Specifications* document for FCE, as in the 2007 *Handbook for
Teachers*, we are reminded of the Cambridge ESOL 'skills and components'
model:

> Cambridge ESOL examinations reflect a view of language proficiency
> in terms of a language user's overall communicative ability; at the same
> time, for the purposes of practical language assessment, the notion of
> overall ability is subdivided into different skills and sub skills.

The four target skills for assessment in FCE are then defined:

> Reading and Listening are multi-dimensional skills involving the interaction of the reader/listener's mental processing capacities with their language and content knowledge; further interaction takes place between

the reader/listener and the external features of the text and task. Purpose and context for reading/listening shape these interactions and this is reflected in the FCE Reading and Listening components through the use of different text and task types which link to a relevant target language use context beyond the test.

Writing ability is also regarded as a linguistic, cognitive, social and cultural phenomenon that takes place in a specific context and for a particular purpose. Like Reading and Listening, FCE Writing involves a series of complex interactions between the task and the writer, who needs to draw on different aspects of their (sic) knowledge and experience to produce a written performance for evaluation.

Like Writing, Speaking involves multiple competences including phonological control, vocabulary and grammatical knowledge, knowledge of discourse and pragmatic awareness which are partially distinct from their equivalents in the written language. Since speaking generally involves reciprocal oral interaction with others, Speaking in FCE is assessed directly, through a face-to-face encounter between candidates and examiners.

A fifth test component in FCE (Use of English) focuses on the language knowledge structures or system(s) that underpin a user's communicative language ability in the written medium; these are sometimes referred to as 'enabling (sub)skills' or language knowledge base and include knowledge of vocabulary, morphology, syntax, punctuation, and discourse structure.

In the final chapter of Weir and Milanovic (Eds) (2003), the SiLT volume on the CPE 2002 revision, Weir emphasised the need for Cambridge ESOL to continue to keep abreast of and initiate research into the complex cognitive processes and performance conditions involved in the four macro-skills tested by its exams. This was to be one of the core aims of the 'constructs' volumes in the SiLT series (see Shaw and Weir (2007) *Examining Writing*, Khalifa and Weir (2009) *Examining Reading*, Taylor (Ed.) (2011) - *Examining Speaking* and Geranpayeh and Taylor (Eds) (2013) *Examining Listening*), which provided a synchronic analysis of Cambridge English language examinations as they are at this point in time. This volume will differ in that it takes a diachronic approach and provides a different perspective on constructs through examining how the testing of each skill has evolved over the last 100 years.

Informed by the descriptive frameworks for analysing test tasks detailed in the 'constructs' volumes in the SiLT series, and supported by Geranpayeh's empirical *a posteriori* evidence concerning multidimensionality in Cambridge Main Suite examinations, we will now revisit the development of Cambridge examinations 1913–2012. This time each chapter will focus on a particular macro skill and how it was conceptualised at various stages in its 100-year evolution, first in a wider testing context and then more specifically in Cambridge English examinations. In this way we hope to understand the nature of each construct and reflect on how it has been operationalised in English language examinations at various points along the way. We first consider the measurement of reading 1913–2012.

2 The measurement of reading ability 1913–2012

Cyril J Weir
University of Bedfordshire

There is nothing new under the sun.
Is there a thing of which it is said,
'See, this is new'?
It has already been
in the ages before us.
[Ecclesiastes, Chapter 1, verses 9–10]

Introduction

The professional standards of the International Reading Association (2004: 9) include the foundational knowledge requirement that educators: 'recognise historical antecedents to contemporary reading matters and materials'. Language testers might be similarly well served by an appreciation of past approaches to the testing of reading. A familiarity with how the reading construct was measured in the past provides us with a valuable perspective when developing 'new' reading tests or critiquing existing ones.

In this chapter we first describe the long history of oral reading in the United Kingdom in the years leading up to the 20th century. This helps to contextualise the presence of oral reading in the reading aloud task, one of the *integrated* methods by which reading ability (together with pronunciation) was assessed in the first CPE administered in 1913.

We then turn to a general overview of the predominantly silent approaches to testing reading in the 20th century. We chart a changing focus in English language reading tests from an initial concern with lower level decoding processes to a more comprehensive approach in the 1970s that embraced higher level meaning construction processes as well. All of these developments took place within a mainly *careful* as against an *expeditious* reading paradigm (Urquhart and Weir 1998).

Having established a general background for the assessment of reading in the 20th century, we then establish the parameters of a socio-cognitive, conceptual framework applicable specifically to the assessment of reading. These parameters are used in the second half of the chapter to inform a detailed analysis of how Cambridge measured reading ability in English from 1913 to 2012.

We note how reading was never tested in a separate paper by Cambridge until 1975, but was rather a component of a number of integrated tasks that were favoured at the time. In the early period testers were concerned with whether students could write a good summary (a shortened version of a written text, containing the main points and omitting minor details), or translate a passage from a work of literature, or read a literary prose passage out aloud. Such integrated tasks would *involve* rather than uniquely *focus* on reading ability. Most probably testers did not think of themselves as measuring a reading construct *per se* in this early period.

The emergence of a dedicated, multiple choice examination paper, testing reading in its own right from 1975 onwards marked a watershed. It indicated an increased awareness of, as well as a receptiveness to, new developments in cognitive psychology, applied linguistics and classroom pedagogy on the part of Cambridge staff and their British Council partners on the Joint Committee. As an understanding of *comprehension* as against lower level *decoding* developed in the communicative era (Urquhart and Weir 1998); as classroom reading materials and teaching began to focus on higher level reading skills and strategies from the 1970s onwards, test developers at UCLES abandoned tasks which had involved reading merely in an integrated mode, such as translation, reading aloud and summary, and focused more specifically on the testing of reading in its own right. Post-1975 dedicated reading tests would cover a range of reading types as appropriate to level.

Reading aloud and reading silently

Reading aloud

Urquhart and Weir (1998) suggest that reading is now viewed as the silent, internal process of receiving and interpreting information encoded in language form via the medium of print. Manguel (1997) describes how in earlier times this was not always so, and oral reading, i.e. reading aloud, was often the preferred, if not the requisite medium, with silent reading regarded as a departure from the norm (see Chaytor (1945) for an informed account of this). It had been common, indeed often necessary, for texts to be read out aloud where there was widespread illiteracy.

Littau (2006:14–15) describes how it was usual until the 11th century for texts to be written without spacing between words as the nature of writing surfaces (tablets, parchment etc.) encouraged writers 'to cram together letters and words so as to fill up the available space economically'. It was easier to read such unpunctuated text out aloud to determine where the breaks between words might be. She also notes that, despite silent reading becoming widespread among educated readers, the tradition of reciting literature persisted and she cites as an example the numerous references to the listening audience in Cervantes' *The Ingenious Hidalgo Don Quixote of La Mancha*, the first part of which was published in 1605.

Despite the general demise of a shared oral literary culture by the 20th century (Mathieson 1975), reading aloud would continue in a variety of specific contexts. Tinajero (2010) provides a fascinating history of the ongoing tradition of reading aloud in the workplace in the Americas and Spain with special reference to the work of lectors in the cigar factories in Cuba (1870–2010) whose job was to relieve the monotony of the workshop and at the same time educate and enrich the lives of the often already literate workers (2010:xvi) and create the habit of reading (2010:222). He also provides historical detail (2010:8) of this tradition in England and describes how often one of the duties of servants was to read aloud to their masters during or after evening meals. In the monastic tradition, of course, the practice of reading aloud from the scriptures during communal mealtimes has continued right up to the present day.

Reading aloud featured in a number of early language tests. Following the murder of the Archbishop of Canterbury, Thomas Becket, in 1170, the king sought a a way of placating an important, religious power elite. Clergymen were accordingly allowed to claim that they were outside the jurisdiction of the secular courts and could only be tried for a felony in an ecclesiastical court, with the expectation of being treated with far greater leniency than in a secular court, e.g. a penance rather than hanging in a number of cases. Initially, being tonsured and wearing ecclesiastical dress were taken as sufficient proof of being a cleric but after 1351 a literacy test was required. As most of the people who could read at this time were clerics, so the ability to read aloud a verse from the bible was taken as proof of clericity. This reading test for benefit of clergy was not abolished in England until 1706.

The reliability of the test was open to question, however, as often it was reportedly the same verse of Psalm 51 that was used (Cranney and Miller 1987:391).

Psalm 51: 1   Miserere mei, Deus: secundum magnam misericordiam tuam et secundum multitudinem miserationum tuarum: dele iniquitatem meam.

(Have mercy upon me, O God,
according to thy loving-kindness:
according unto the multitude of thy tender mercies
blot out my transgressions.)
(King James version equivalent)

The 'benefit of clergy' law in 14th century England meant that successful performance on this high stakes reading test was often the difference between life and death. For this reason Psalm 51 became known as the *neck verse* as through its successful rendition hanging could thereby be avoided. In those cases where defendants were deserving of death for particularly heinous crimes, a different part of the bible might be chosen to identify any illiterates who had rote learned Psalm 51 verse 1 in the Latin of the time in the hope of cheating the hangman.

The role of reading aloud in language assessment persisted. Venezky (1996:52) argues that in the United States 'Reading aloud, generally from a religious text or school reader, was the most common direct assessment technique for reading ability until the end of the 19th century'. Allington (1984) provides detail of Gray's *Standardized Oral Reading Paragraphs* (1915), and cites it as the first formal assessment of oral reading performance in the United States. The examiner recorded oral reading errors such as mispronunciations, omission, additions and repetition as well as self-corrections (the latter was rightly excluded by later researchers more cognizant of the important monitoring operation in reading – see Figure 2.1 below).

It is still well regarded in the 21st century as a pedagogical device for learning to read in primary schools and is also frequently advocated for the testing of reading ability at this level in the United Kingdom. The following news item appeared in the Daily Telegraph on 6 December 2011:

> Primary school pupils should be given an oral reading test at the age of 11 to assess whether they can read properly, according to one of the Government's most senior education advisers . . . "If a child cannot read fluently at age 11 they are going to have a problem at secondary school," Sir Cyril [Taylor] told The Sunday Telegraph. In some cases, the English results in the Key Stage 2 tests are overstating what a child is capable of. Any teacher will tell you, if a child cannot read, they can't learn. What we need is a test where they read out loud — then you can tell in seconds."

A view strikingly close to that behind the introduction of the benefit of clergy test in the 14th century detailed above.

It was perhaps hardly surprising, given this tradition, that a reading aloud task figured in the first CPE examination in 1913. An ability to read aloud was clearly seen as a key integrated skill (involving reading and pronunciation) for the classroom teacher of English as a foreign language, the initial target audience for CPE at the time

Reading aloud would be retained as a test component in CPE from 1913 until 1985 and is still in use in different parts of the world; for example, as part of the Taiwanese General English Proficiency Test (GEPT), in the oral examination. The recent Pearson Test in English (PTE Academic) features a reading aloud task in its speaking paper as does the Versant Aviation English

Test, the Versant English Placement Test, the United States Army Aviation Medical Standards Reading Aloud Test and the Stanford English Language Proficiency Test.

Reading silently

An early stimulus for the growth of silent as against oral reading came with the Reformation in the first quarter of the 16th century as dependence on interpretation of the written text by the village priest gave way, in Protestantism at least, to individual responsibility for interaction with the Scriptures; hence encouraging the silent reading of the word of God (Venezky 1996:48).

Spufford (1981:xviii) provides evidence of the continuing spread of silent reading in her research into the United Kingdom small book trade in the 17th century:

> There had already been direct access by the relatively humble to religious ideas expressed not only in the bible, but also in a multiplicity of printed tracts, from at least the beginning of the C17th . . . (45) we can state the existence of the school teachers in the dioceses . . . the firm figures of differing ability to sign amongst different social groups in East Anglia, and say from the number of signatories to the Protestation Returns of 1642 that there was at the very least a reading public of 30% of men in the second half of the seventeenth century . . . We can start from the other end of the argument, and produce firm evidence of the fortunes made by the specialist ballad and chapbook publishers catering specifically for the cheap end of the market . . . We can add evidence on the volume of these publications.

The practice of silent reading gathered momentum thereafter. The need for communication linked to the spread of trade in response to the development of the market economy, the expansion of schooling in the late 19th century with elementary education compulsory in the United Kingdom from 1880 onwards, and increasing political awareness as the nation moved from feudalism to modern industrial society, all drove the spread of literacy, thereby increasing the number of people who were able to interact with text personally and silently (see Spufford 1981). Venezky (1996) offers this insight: 'These and other changes expanded continually the mental and physical space within which the ordinary person lived, making communication beyond the immediately observable world both necessary and desirable.'

Cipolla (1969), Pugh (1978) and Manguel (1997) argue that silent reading began to supplant the long tradition of oral reading in the 19th century as the growth of literacy reduced the numbers of those needing to listen to texts read aloud by others This increased literacy led to a marked increase in the volume of printed works made available to the public often in the form of periodicals and newspapers or 'penny dreadfuls' rather than expensive books of substantial literary merit (Altick 1957:373). By the mid-19th century popular papers such as the *Family Herald* and the *London Journal* had circulations numbering six figures (Altick 1957:3).

The breakthrough in using readily available wood for making pulp after 1860 facilitated an explosion in publishing especially at the lower end of the fiction chain. Weedon (2003) examined the growth of the mass book market in Britain, and describes how between 1846 and 1916 the number of books published increased fourfold, while prices halved.

Altick (1957) chronicles a cultural concern that grew in England in the 19th century as a mass semi-literate reading public were increasingly exposed to print of a less than serious kind, often brief, and usually 'easy to digest' capsule literature. Initially this gave rise to paranoia in some circles that once the masses read, this might lead to widespread social disruption. This was replaced by fears in mid-Victorian times of the potential threat to morality caused by exposing the public to salacious tales, especially in the case of those readers rather uncharitably classed as 'fiction vampires' (Altick 1957:239).

Venezky (1984:21) in a seminal article on the history of reading research dates a change in instructional emphasis from oral to silent reading in the United States at around the end of the first decade of the twentieth century. He points to the emergence of a social need for literacy in occupations and daily life due to a change 'from a rural, cottage-industry society to an urban, mass production society'. This was matched by an increased availability of inexpensive reading material thanks to cheap paper and high volume printing techniques. With wealth there also came an increase in cultural activities including reading.

Barry (2008) argues that, in education in the United States, the move to silent reading away from elocutionary texts 'began late in the 1800s and was reinforced by experimental evidence, which found that children understood text more easily when they read it silently rather than aloud (Gray 1917)' and quotes the studies of Kelly (1916), Courtis (1917) and Monroe (1918) in support of silent reading. Schools increasingly felt the need to emphasise silent reading for reasons of efficiency, practicality and authenticity, and the dominance of oral reading in the curriculum found in the United States in the 19th century and early 20th century disappeared. Slow silent reading not surprisingly features in many of the second language tests produced in the United States in the earlier part of the 20th century (Spolsky 1995a:41, Venezky 1984:13).

Pugh (1978) makes an important link with wider societal developments at the time when he points out that silent reading was more appropriate to certain of the types of reading that began to occupy a large number of the population in the United Kingdom in second half of the 19th century. The growth of mass media (see Altick (1957) for a history of this development in the 19th century) was accompanied by a tendency to expeditious reading (Urquhart and Weir 1998 describe this as quick, efficient, selective reading); 'skipping and skimming' was in fact advocated for these expeditious purposes at an early date by the prominent Scottish politician, later prime minister, Arthur Balfour, in his essay *The pleasures of reading* (1905:32): 'He has only half learnt the art of reading who has not added to it the even more refined accomplishments of skipping and of skimming.'

For reasons of efficiency there was often no need to faithfully render every word incrementally from the beginning of a text to its end as in the oral tradition or in the careful, incremental reading aloud of 'great fiction'.

Reading tests in the 20th century

Testing reading in the United States and United Kingdom in the early 20th century

There appeared to be a different perception of the place of reading in the modern language curriculum in the United Kingdom as compared to the United States in the first part of the 20th century. We saw in Chapter 1 how, under the influence of the Reform Movement and the work of leading figures such as Harold Palmer and Henry Sweet, the emphasis was placed on spoken language in the modern language classroom in the United Kingdom at this time. Barnwell (1996:60–62) in contrast draws our attention to the impact of the Coleman Report in 1929 in the United States which proposed reading as the primary goal of foreign language education (see also Conant 1934).

The importance of reading as a separate skill for accessing and comprehending information (see West 1926b, Ewing 1949:152–153) appears to have been slow to emerge in mainstream language teaching or testing in the United Kingdom (perhaps with the notable exceptions of reading to access the great works of literature in CPE in 1913, or in reading as part of the summary task from the 1930s onwards). The first signs of viewing language as a gateway to non-literary knowledge appear late in Cambridge English examinations with an option to take a paper in General Economic and Commercial Knowledge in 1935 and one on English Life and Institutions in 1938 as alternatives to the English Literature paper. Directly testing the ability to read and understand ESP texts in Science is first found in the 1955 Cambridge CPE. Testing reading as a language skill in its own right would not happen in CPE until 1975.

Further evidence of differences in approach between the United States and the United Kingdom can also be seen in the use of statistically normed, reading tests in school systems in the former. Such standardised tests were employed by government for accountability purposes from a very early date in the United States (see Chapter 1). Venezky (1984:19) traces the development of these standardised silent reading tests in the United States back to the start of the

20th century and details how they became 'an indispensable component of the schooling ritual, a position they still hold today'. Johnston (1984:149 et seq) points out that the support for testing reading came largely from administrators because of its accountability, gate keeping function and met considerable opposition from teachers. The standardised, group, silent, product-oriented model for testing reading became institutionalised in the United States and an individualised, descriptive, process-oriented model did not emerge (Johnston 1984:168 et seq). A concern for summative assessment 'externally mandated for policy guidance' (Calfee and Hiebert 1991:301), as against formative assessment 'internally driven for instructional direction' (1991:301), maintained its dominance at least until the later years of the 20th century.

Pugh (1978:74) confirms that this interest in testing reading was far less noticeable in the United Kingdom as compared to the United States until the 1970s. He cites as evidence the plethora of reading tests in the United States, mainly objective in format, listed in the Buros (1978) *Mental Measurements Handbook*, which contrasts sharply with the very limited selection available in the United Kingdom as listed by Pumfrey (1976), which included Black's Comprehension Tests for College of Education Students (Black 1954) and the Manchester Reading Comprehension Test (Senior) I (Wiseman and Wrigley 1959).

From decoding to meaning construction

For a considerable part of the 20th century the focus in both the teaching and testing of reading was on decoding at the clause and sentence level rather than comprehension at the text or intertextual levels (Venezky 1984:14). This may partially explain a focus on lexis in the limited number of specifically reading items set on passages that one finds in the early Cambridge English examinations prior to World War Two. Attention to careful local reading at the clause and sentence level rather than careful global reading (beyond the sentence right up to the level of the complete text or texts) was the norm with no concern either for expeditious, quick selective forms of reading (search reading, skimming or scanning) that might be useful for study or leisure purposes. (See Khalifa and Weir (2009:34–80), Moore, Morton and Price (2010), Urquhart and Weir (1998) for discussion of these reading types and related cognitive processes. They are summarised in Figure 2.1 below.)

Venezky (1984:13) makes the important link with what was happening in reading research at this time. He argues that in the period 1885–1960:

> ... the investigation of cognition in reading comprehension was never pursued as systematically as word recognition was ... the present day importance given to comprehension in reading research is a phenomenon of the last two or three decades.

Venezky (1984:13) argues that in the US, with notable exceptions such as Thorndike (1914, 1917a, 1917b), research on comprehension processes was sparse until the 1950s and even the phrase 'reading comprehension' was seldom found in the psychology literature although references did occur occasionally in relation to methods of teaching and testing. In contrast great emphasis was put on vocabulary which was seen as the determining factor in the difficulty of understanding reading materials and was the major concern in intelligence testing.

By the 1970s this focus was to change. In an editorial in the *Reading Research Quarterly* in 1980, under the heading *Why Comprehension?*, the editors noted that the earlier emphasis on decoding was attracting much less attention by the 1970s, being replaced by a new emphasis on comprehension. Urquhart and Weir (1998) argued that this view could be substantiated statistically; they provided data from the Education Resources Information Centre showing the number of articles and other publications, published between 1966 and 1996, which mentioned 'comprehension' in their title (1998:21). The graph they presented shows a massive increase in such papers by the 1970s, presumably reflecting a major increase in interest in reading. They provided related data (1998:89) detailing how the rapid rise in reading and comprehension studies after 1966 was paralleled by a rise in interest in *reading skills and strategies*. With the move towards research in 'comprehension' and skills and strategies, covering all the cognitive processes involved in meaning construction, reading attracted wider interest than it had when decoding was the main preoccupation. It was now attracting the attention of cognitive psychologists and psycholinguists, as well as educationalists and applied linguists (Urquhart and Weir 1998).

A bias towards careful reading

Pugh (1978:20) notes that from about 1910 in the United Kingdom there was an increased pedagogical interest in exercises on texts requiring close, careful, often iterative textual study rather than any interest in teaching silent reading *per se* as a skill. Texts were viewed largely as vehicles for teaching language (lexis and syntax) rather than reading skills. This is apparent in the first Short Answer Questions (SAQ) reading items one finds in the Cambridge English examinations in the early Literature, and Composition papers (see below).

Pugh (1978:20) contrasts this with an emphasis on the *speed* of silent reading in research in the US, which he argues was noticeable by its absence in the British research literature and pedagogy for most of the 20th century. He cites its almost complete absence from the influential Bullock report, a United Kingdom government report published in 1975 by an independent committee, to consider the teaching of language (1978:32). The pioneering early American work on the speed of reading would seem to have had little influence in the United Kingdom and there was no sign of it in United Kingdom teaching practice 1900–1970 according to Shayer (1972) though Vernon (1931) was obviously well aware of the research in the United States whilst dismissing its value. Pugh notes of United Kingdom reading researchers up to the 1970s (1978:74): 'They tended not to examine very closely the phenomenon of reading in various ways to achieve various purposes'. Farr, Carey and Tone (1986:62) noted in a similar vein: 'The passage was seen simply as a stretch of prose providing language for comprehension. . . the concept that readers read in different ways according to their purpose and the type of text was as yet unrecognised.'

So whilst attention was paid to the assessment of slow, careful, incremental reading, expeditious reading (fast, efficient, selective reading) has not been explicitly tested in many high stakes examinations in the United Kingdom to this day, despite its inclusion in CEFR reading descriptors for academic purposes at the C1 levels (Council of Europe 2001). The British Council's first test for overseas students coming to study in Britain in use from 1965–1982, the English Proficiency Test Battery (EPTB) devised by Alan Davies, did address this part of the reading construct albeit indirectly in its Test 6 Reading Speed (see Davies 2008b: 19–20). The 1991 CAE reading paper (see Appendix A) contained more direct examples of expeditious reading items, as did the later multiple matching tasks in the PET and FCE reading papers (see below). The Higher Intermediate General English Proficiency Test (GEPT) in Taiwan has had a separate expeditious reading paper since its inception in 2000 (Weir 2005a) but apart from GEPT and the Test for English Majors (TEM) in China (see Zhou, Weir and Green 1998) these appear to be the only high stakes English language examination papers dedicated to expeditious reading. One might speculate that the lack of research interest in the speed of reading in the United Kingdom that we noted above may partially explain why there have been few attempts to develop models for expeditious reading or to include such reading types in research, tests or teaching as compared to the focus on careful reading particularly at the local level (Khalifa and Weir 2009, Urquhart and Weir 1998, Zhou, Weir and Green 1998, Weir, Yang and Jin 2000). These different types of reading from Urquhart and Weir's 1998 typology are discussed in more detail in *A framework for reading test task analysis* below.

Examining reading: An analysis of Cambridge English Reading test tasks 1913–2012

In the previous section we provided a brief overview of the way the reading construct was measured at various points in our survey period. We will now examine in more detail how Cambridge assessed various types of reading ability, indirectly or directly, in its English language examinations in the last one hundred years. We will look closely at evidence from the Cambridge archives relating to the measurement of reading ability in the past century and examine how the testing of reading changed along the way from 1913–2012. To analyse accurately and precisely the nature of the specific changes in Cambridge's approach to measuring reading we need a detailed conceptual framework to help us account for the various elements of the reading construct.

A framework for reading test task analysis

As we argued in Chapter 1, to fully explain what is being tested, account needs to be taken of the *cognitive* as well as the *contextual* dimensions of task performance. We will base our analysis of Cambridge English language reading tasks on the processing model suggested initially by Weir (2005a) and elaborated in Khalifa and Weir (2009) which draws on the external evidence from cognitive psychology concerning the nature of the expertise that examining boards should aim to sample through test tasks. The principal concern is with the mental processes readers actually use in comprehending texts when engaging in different types of real-life reading. We start by looking more closely at types of reading and the cognitive processes they give rise to.

Careful reading is intended to extract meaning from presented material at a local or a global level, i.e. within or beyond the sentence right up to the level of the complete text or texts. The approach to reading is based on slow, careful, linear, incremental reading for comprehension. Models of reading have usually been developed with careful reading in mind. Hoover and Tunmer (1993), for example, considered that their notion of reading: 'assumes careful comprehension: comprehension that is intended to extract complete meanings from presented material as opposed to comprehension aimed at only extracting main ideas, skimming, or searching for particular details'(1993:8). Rayner and Pollatsek (1989:439) state that for most of their account of the reading process they are focusing on the skilled, adult reader reading carefully material of the textbook variety. They admit that careful reading models have little to tell us about how skilled readers can cope with other reading behaviours such as skimming for gist (Rayner and Pollatsek 1989:477–478).

There is, as Carver (1992) found, a case for taking account of the speed of reading as well as comprehension (see discussion of early American research on this above). This is in line with Beard (1972), Weir (1983) and Weir et al (2000), whose studies into students' reading abilities indicated that 'for many readers reading quickly, selectively and efficiently posed greater problems than reading carefully and efficiently'. Urquhart and Weir (1998) refer to the former type as expeditious reading. Expeditious reading of continuous prose to access desired information in a text is difficult because it demands rapid recognition which is contingent upon sufficient practice in reading in the target language.

Expeditious reading includes skimming, search reading, and scanning. Skimming is generally defined (e.g. Munby 1978, Urquhart and Weir 1998, Weir 2005a) as reading to obtain the gist, general impression and/or superordinate main idea of a text. For Urquhart and Weir (1998) search reading involves locating information on predetermined topics. The reader only wants information necessary to answer set questions or to extract data for example in order to complete written assignments. Search reading differs from skimming in that the search for information is guided by predetermined topics so the reader does not necessarily have to establish a macro-propositional structure for the whole of the text. Search reading can take place at both the local and global level. Where the desired information can be located within a single sentence it would be classified as local and where information has to be put together across sentences it would be seen as global. In both cases the search is for words in the same semantic field as the target information unlike scanning where exact word matches are sought. Scanning draws on perceptual abilities and word recognition, to achieve very specific reading goals, e.g. looking quickly for specific words/phrases, figures/ percentages, names, dates of particular events or specific items in an index, at the local word level. The overriding attention paid to careful reading in the theoretical literature has meant that we have somewhat ignored expeditious reading strategies such as skimming, search reading and scanning (Hudson 1996 and Urquhart and Weir 1998) in both L1 and L2 teaching and testing of reading (see however Weir et al (2000) for a description of the Advanced English Reading Test in China; Zhou, Weir and Green (1998) for an account of the validation of the Test for English Majors, again in China; and Weir (2005a) for an account of the GEPT test in Taiwan).

The various types of reading and the cognitive processes they may give rise to are represented in diagrammatic form in Figure 2.1 below. In the left hand column we have the metacognitive activity of a *goal setter* because, in deciding what type(s) of reading to employ when faced with a text or texts, critical decisions are taken which affect the *level(s) of processing* to be activated in the central core of our framework. The *monitor* can be applied to each of the levels of processing that is activated in response to the goal setter's instructions. The *knowledge base* required for text comprehension constitutes the right hand column (a full discussion of this framework is provided in Khalifa and Weir 2009:34–80).

In our analysis of Cambridge examinations below, as well considering the cognitive dimensions of a task, we will make reference to the contextual parameters that are likely to influence test task performance in the reading tasks under review. The context for reading activity is sometimes understood in a wider sense to refer to the situation that surrounds reading acts in real world contexts: who reads what kinds of materials for what reasons, where, when, how, and why? Under such an interpretation, the 'context' relates

Figure 2.1 Types of reading and the cognitive processes they give rise to (Khalifa and Weir 2009)

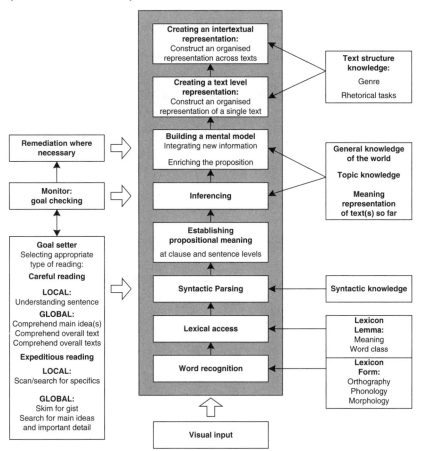

to the wider context (pragmatic, social, linguistic) surrounding the reading activity. Such full situational authenticity is not normally attainable within the constraints of the testing situation. For example, the time that would normally be available for careful reading (and rereading) in real life has to be constrained in a test for reasons of practicality. In our analysis context validity only addresses the particular performance conditions that impact on actual test task completion (see Khalifa and Weir (2009: Chapter 4) for full details of these test task related contextual parameters).

In Figure 2.2 below, we draw on the contextual parameters suggested by Weir (2005a) as being most likely to have an impact on reading test performance. Using this framework as our informing source, we will explore the task parameters of context validity in terms of *Task Setting* and *Linguistic*

Demands (Task Input and Output). In Appendix B we provide an additional perspective drawing on recent quantitative approaches to establishing context validity that can be used as well as the pooled subjective judgements we make below to analyse Cambridge reading tests 1913–2012.

Figure 2.2 Some criterial aspects of context validity for reading test tasks

CONTEXT VALIDITY	
Task Setting	**Linguistic Demands:** **Task Input & Output**
• Response method • Text length • Time constraints	• Discourse mode (genre/rhetorical task(s) • Grammatical resources • Lexical resources • Abstractness/concreteness • Content knowledge (subject and culture)

We will consider some of these key parameters of context validity in our analysis of the Cambridge English language reading tasks below.

The way examinations were scored prior to 1970s has been largely lost in the mists of time and little evidence remains as to how this was carried out except for a small number of occasional examiner reports produced by UCLES which have been preserved in the Cambridge Assessment Archives, and the detailed discussion on the reading aloud task which can be found in Roach (1945a) reprinted in Appendix C in this volume.

This is perhaps not surprising in the early part of our history as the number of candidates was small (only 3 for CPE in 1913 rising to 675 by 1938) and only a small group of trusted, experienced Cambridge academic staff were responsible for the subjectively assessed parts of the examination. Roach (1984:5) describes the procedure for awarding when he became involved in the CPE examination in 1925 with 14/15 candidates a year: 'My chief, Nalder Williams [Secretary of the Syndicate 1921–45] and I did the Award, a hole-in-corner affair of fifteen minutes', testifying to the limited scale of the assessment operation at this early stage. We will refer to any surviving evidence in the discussion below but we will have to rely mainly on conjecture for the gaps remaining.

Examining Reading at Cambridge 1913–2012

Cambridge ESOL has been involved in the assessment of reading skills ever since it launched its first English language examination in 1913. Since that time there have been significant developments in the testing of the reading construct from its early conceptualisation as an integrated skill, assessed largely by translation, written responses to questions on great works of literature, and reading aloud tasks, through to a focus on specific 'communicative' reading skills and strategies in the present day.

In the light of the prevailing educational context, the lack of a research base on reading comprehension before the 1970s (Urquhart and Weir 1998), and the relative absence of any real tradition in developing reading tests in the United Kingdom, it is perhaps not surprising that a separate paper on reading was not to appear in Cambridge examinations until 1975. This is not to say that reading was not measured before this but it will be necessary to examine closely the formats employed in the various papers in the early Cambridge examinations to identify the elements of the reading construct being measured and the methods for doing this.

It would not be until the 'communicative revolution' in approaches to ELT in the 1970s (see Chapter 1) that teachers and testers in the United Kingdom began to focus on the skills and strategies involved in reading as worthy of attention in their own right. In the early period in the United Kingdom there was no focus on reading *per se* and reading was tested only in so far as it was part of an 'academically' credible, or professionally useful, reading into writing summary task or as prior reading for a content based English for special purposes paper such as English literature or English Life and Institutions, or for translating a work of literature into a foreign language, or as the means of accessing the input for the reading aloud of a prose extract.

1913 Certificate of Proficiency in English (CPE)

CPE Reading-related components

* Translation into French and German
* Reading aloud
* Accessing English Literature

When the CPE was introduced in 1913, reading as a skill in its own right did not feature explicitly among those to be tested. While various reading skills were required throughout the 12-hour examination, the skill itself was not singled out for particular attention in a separate paper as it would be today, nor in the way that phonetics, grammar, translation, conversation and the English essay were tested individually in the 1913 examination.

At this time texts were usually seen as vehicles for teaching and testing language. There was some attention to *lexical search* in Part 1 of the English Language and Literature paper shared with the Higher Local Examination, and to *syntax* e.g.:

> Comment with illustrations on the distinction between the prose style of Milton and Dryden with respect to a) structures of sentences b) phraseology.'

Reading comprehension was tested indirectly in a number of the papers albeit in an integrated fashion through translation, reading aloud, and literary appreciation/content knowledge.

Translation: The academic tradition

We saw in Chapter 1 how translation was a well-regarded testing and teaching device at the start of the 20th century embodying as it did the centuries old tradition of approaching language as a form of academic study which facilitated access to important works of literature in the target language.

This paper from the 1914 CPE examination illustrates the perceived value of translation as the access route to great literature.

Name of paper: Translation (into German)
Year: 1914
Passage: b
Page: 123–124

It is a truth universally acknowledged that a single man in possession of a good fortune must be in want of a wife. "My dear Mr Bennet," said his lady to him one day, "have you heard that Netherfield Park is let at last?" Mr Bennet replied that he had not. "But it is," returned she; "for Mrs Long has just been here, and she told me all about it." Mr Bennet made no answer. "Do you want to know who has taken it?" cried his wife impatiently. "You want to tell me, and I have no objection to hearing it." This was invitation enough. "Why, my dear, you must know, Mrs Long says that Netherfield Park is taken by a young man of large fortune from the North of England. . ." "What is his name?" "Bingley." "Is he married or single?" "O! single, my dear, to be sure! A single man of large fortune – four or five thousand a year. What a fine thing for our girls!" "How so? how can it affect them?" "My dear Mr Bennet," replied his wife, "you can be so tiresome! you must know that I am thinking of his marrying one of them."

JANE AUSTEN.

Translation into and out of various L1's was to be part of the Cambridge CPE from 1913 until 1975 and an optional paper thereafter until 1989. One of the few surviving documents on its use in the Cambridge Assessment archives is the LCE June 1961 report on the French translation paper which has been saved in the Cambridge Assessment Archives. The report provides us with some insight into how examiners perceived the construct being measured by translation. It makes an interesting statement in point 3 about the importance of reading for success in the paper and also the demands on a candidate's vocabulary knowledge. Faithfulness to the content and style of the original is seen as important in point 4.

3. In the opinion of the examiners, it is a mistake to regard translation as a 'soft option' to the Prescribed Books paper or as a last-minute substitute for it. Translation demands, if anything, a wider range of reading than the Prescribed Books paper. It also calls for the ability both to comprehend and to write quickly and accurately. The range of vocabulary and phrase of the prescribed books is determined by the content of the books themselves; but the candidate for translation is faced with something unprepared, 'unseen', to use the technical term for it. Even if he has met with all the words and phrases in a passage before, these words are most likely used in new combinations to express new thoughts or to describe new incidents. The only valid preparation is the widest possible reading, reinforced by specific training in accurate comprehension and precise rendering.

4. The examiners expect that a candidate shall, within the limits set by the level of the examination, do his best
    (a) to reproduce in the other language, as accurately as possible, the content of the original;
    (b) to render as closely as possible the phraseology and style of the original;
    (c) to produce as his translation a passage of French or English which in itself is correct French or English.

It is interesting to note the advice on the need for candidates to *plan* and *monitor* their own work in the writing stage of this task in point 5 (see Chapter 3 for discussion of these critical metacognitive strategies in writing). These reports were available to teachers so one might assume some of this advice filtered down to students in the classroom.

5. Candidates should be trained to do two things as a matter of routine:
    (a) read completely through the original and satisfy themselves that they have done their best to comprehend both the content in general and the actual phrases in particular, before they begin to write their translation;
    (b) read over what they have written when they have finished, and ask themselves whether it really means something. If it does, it may be right or wrong, though more than likely right. If it does not, then it can only be wrong.

6. One of the most disconcerting features of many papers was the failure of candidates to write their own language correctly. An examiner is placed in an awkward position when confronted, in a passage of French written by a French-speaking candidate, with mistakes in such elementary matters as accentuation, agreement of subject and verb, or spelling, for which English-speaking candidates would be penalized in any parallel examination. It is impossible to over-emphasize the necessity of making sure that a translation, in addition to giving an accurate

statement of the content of the original, should itself be correct linguistically. To fulfil this requirement in his own language should not be beyond the competence of any candidate. Otherwise he should not be taking this examination at all.

7. There are two other points, which concern examination technique in general:
    (a) The conventions of English punctuation, which differ in some respects from those of French, should always be observed when a passage of English is being written. The constant tendency of candidates to head their efforts 'Translation into english' is an example of carelessness in this respect.

Items 6 and 7 reinforce the importance of accuracy in this task and signal the need for the candidates to monitor their work.

Limited additional evidence remains as to how precisely it was marked in the early days but a rare mark scheme, this one from 1980, can be found in the Cambridge Assessment archives (filed with Roach's papers) which shows what was taken into account in the translation from English into the foreign language and the weighting it was given and thus offers rare insight into perceptions of the construct being measured:

CPE 1 Guidelines for Marking Translation Papers 1980

1 The allocation of marks is as follows

Accuracy of translation (General impression)	10
Handling of target language (General impression)	10
Selected marking points	20 (10x2)

2 The marks for accuracy of translation should reward ability to render the meaning of the original with strict accuracy and an appropriate degree of sensitivity to style and expression.

3 The marks for the handling of the target language should reward ability to write naturally, idiomatically and correctly, avoiding over literal translation.

4 The marking points for special consideration should be assigned to words or phrases which constitute a balanced and effective test of translation skill. A range of 0–1–2 marks can be awarded for each point in such a way that the ability to appreciate special translation problems, whether involving comprehension or expression, syntax or vocabulary is tested.

Alderson (2001) expands on some of the difficulties in employing translation as a testing device: the issue of the reliability of an instrument where so many solutions are acceptable; difficulties in constructing scales for its assessment; the dangers of muddied measurement: students may understand but are not able to translate accurately; the complexity of translation as a skill, and the difficulty of objectively comparing translations and deciding that one is better than another.

Buck (1992a:124) initially concludes from the literature that it is not clear what translation is meant to measure but after careful empirical research he admits that (1992a:132): 'translations are not measuring anything so very different from more commonly used measures of passage comprehension'. They in fact proved as reliable as other measures used in his Multiple Method Multiple Trait (MMMT) study, viz gap-filling, multiple-choice and Short Answer Questions on a variety of written texts, showed adequate convergent and discriminant validity and (1992a:138) '. . . were providing as good a measure as any of the testing methods'. His findings corroborate the results of an earlier study on reading tests including translation by Bachman and Palmer (1981).

Nearly a century after the introduction of translation into CPE, translation does not merit a single mention in Alderson's (2000) volume on *Assessing Reading* or in Khalifa and Weir's (2009) *Examining Reading*. This might be seen by some readers as an unfortunate oversight on both parts in the light of the multi-method multi-trait study carried out by Bachman and Palmer (1981) where translation proved to be the purest measure of the trait of reading ability.

The potential value of translation as a reading test was not disproven by Alderson's (2001) rhetoric against its continued use in Hungary or proven by the limited empirical findings available in its favour (Bachman and Palmer 1981, Buck 1992a). However, in the era of washback the impact of a test on the teaching that preceded it was seen as critical. Testers were worried about the negative washback effects of such a test on teaching, and similar concerns were eventually to lead to its demise in the communicative era in most countries around the world. As we saw in Chapter 1, from the 1970s onwards tests designed to measure communicative language use were in the ascendancy and there was increasing pressure for teachers and testers to shift to more communicative methods because of the perceived, positive benefits for learners. Berggren (1966) makes such a case against the limitations of the sole use of translation as the method of choice in the Finnish school leaving test in English.

The fact that at any given time 20–30 different languages could be the target for translation in Cambridge English examinations must have led to some concern about the equivalence of the translation test between languages (see Spolsky's concerns with parallel form reliability discussed in Chapter 1).

Apart from the problems posed for the reliability of the marking, construct irrelevant variance may have been introduced by the different L1's of those taking part. Candidates translating into languages most similar in structure and orthography to English may have been advantaged (e.g. French and Spanish versus Arabic, Chinese, Hebrew or Russian). The practical difficulties of organising such an exercise may well have contributed the most to its demise especially when faced with competition from more communicative reading tasks which could be sat in common by the growing number of candidates taking the examination in the second half of the 20th century.

Reading aloud

In dealing with the reading aloud component we faced the dilemma of whether this integrated task would fit best in a chapter on speaking or one on reading. As we noted above reading aloud had a long-established tradition as a test of reading and a means of teaching it in the classroom in the United Kingdom. Grabe (2009:449) also refers to its contemporary use in the form of miscue analysis in the classroom assessment of student reading ability in the United States. Since elements of both the reading and speaking constructs are invariably activated through this integrated task, we thought it sensible to treat it briefly both in this chapter and in Chapter 4 on speaking.

Reading aloud was introduced into CPE in 1913 as part of the Oral test but was seen by Cambridge, according to the early instructions to candidates, as 'both a test of good reading and of the candidate's ability to make him readily understood'. The later 1970 Instructions to Oral Examiners explain that the reading of a prepared passage is a test 'of general fluency and understanding, giving the examiner the opportunity to assess the candidate's pronunciation in a more concentrated way than in the conversation' (UCLES 1970). It was very much viewed as an integrated task rather than a testing of reading *per se*, but the limited evidence we have on how it was marked suggests that, in the early days at least, examiner perceptions of the candidate's comprehension of the passage played some part in the mark received.

Its appearance in the oral paper may merely be an indication that this was the easiest, most practical place to assess it, especially given the need to pronounce the words aloud. It had to be examined individually as, for logistical and scoring validity reasons, it could not be applied to whole groups at the same time as was the case in later silent reading tests.

The CPE example below from 1936 uses mostly continuous prose. It is written language not spoken, with all the textual characteristics of the former. By the 1970s most of the passages to be read aloud would be more conversation-like in an attempt to bring the experience closer, albeit in a restricted manner, to a more authentic spoken communicative interaction.

UNIVERSITY OF CAMBRIDGE
LOCAL EXAMINATIONS SYNDICATE

CERTIFICATE OF PROFICIENCY IN ENGLISH
READING PASSAGE

July 1936 2 hours

Depression

Here and there a ship showed itself through the light mist that covered the docks, but the great basins, faintly shining, dream-like, seemed sadly vacant. Not long ago, I was told, all those docks were crowded with shipping, were a maze of derricks and smoke-stacks, but now not only was there room enough and to spare, but there was desolating vacancy. The rails were empty of trains, and we could stroll at ease over all the bridges, there "Keep to the Left" notices being now simply farcical. There was no traffic over them. No lorries came clattering through, no crowds of men rushed over them towards the town or the waiting boats. The great cranes were all motionless, as if they forlornly sniffed the raw, empty air, monsters awaiting a prey that never came. We left the docks, passed once more through the little square where the Board of Trade and the idlers stared at one another, and came at last to a great block of shipping offices, the tallest building in the neighbourhood. "I'll take you up to the roof," my companion said, pointing the way to the lift. "You get a good view up there."

Evidence on how reading aloud was marked in Cambridge examinations before 1945 is sketchy. Roach (1945a:7) (see Appendix C) clarifies that the marks for reading aloud were split evenly at the time with 10 marks going to fluency of reading and 10 for pronunciation and intonation. It was presumably difficult to score well on fluency of reading if one did not understand the meaning of the passage in the first place. In 1958 the Instructions to Oral Examiners (UCLES:4) note 'a Proficiency candidate should be fluent in his reading (which does not necessarily mean he will speak rapidly), that he should know the pronunciation of any ordinary English word and should not have grossly foreign habits of speech'.

In the initial years 1913–1930 no trace remains in the archives of the passages used for reading aloud and it seems likely that it was left to oral examiners to select their own two passages. Oral examiners were instructed to select a passage from the two offered and advised: 'Please use one till you tire of it and then change to the other' (Roach 1945a). Scoring validity was, however, a concern (though never an obsession) for Cambridge in the early period of our history.

No evidence is offered on the parallelness of test forms but Spolsky (1995a:205–207) quotes extensively from Roach (1945a) to illustrate how UCLES attempted to ensure fairness to candidates in the reading aloud test:

> . . . Oral examiners received copies of Roach's (1945) study, revised mark sheets and instructions. They were invited to describe 1) the general conditions of the examination (Was it better to give the reading first? Was it possible to prevent communication between candidates? What was the average time? Would more time be an advantage?) . . . (2) the reading test (Did two separate reading tests help? What did the examiner listen for in each? How would the examiner define the degree of proficiency expected at the different levels? Were any of the early candidates retested?)

In this landmark report (see Appendix C) Roach describes in detail how attempts were made to standardise raters in the reading aloud task. The raters and observers awarded a score out of 20 with 8 as a passing grade, 12 for good and 16 for very good. The standardisation procedures included:

- using experienced raters who brought internalised standards with them
- telling examiners what they should be listening for and what they should leave out of account: in the reading aloud test comprehensibility was the bottom line
- using gramophone recordings made by the post office to set permanent standards
- moderation of a rater's consistency by a chief examiner
- particular care with borderline cases
- having a second marker to check reliability (if cost permitted), if not a teacher who had been standardised.

However, despite such efforts to be fair to candidates, professional concerns about the reading aloud task never really went away. A number of reviewers of oral reading tests in Buros (1978) question the reliability of oral reading assessments and Allington (1984:839) cites a number of other studies which found low levels of inter-rater reliability and widespread subjectivity in the identification of error. These studies suggest that the reliability of marking in this particular test task may not have been as well grounded as we have come to expect in examinations today.

A further problem lies in the fact that oral and silent reading place different demands on cognitive processing. Because of the additional oral production component, oral reading presents different task demands to silent interaction with a written text (see Field (2011:65–111) for an account of cognitive processing in speaking and Khalifa and Weir (2009:34–80) for cognitive processing in reading). Furthermore, there are different contextual constraints: it is a public not a private performance, the expectation is accuracy of production as against successful meaning construction, the implication being that performance on one type might not serve as a useful indicator of performance on the other. A number of writers felt that the chief complaint against oral reading is that it did not deal with understanding and that it was not the most important kind of reading (Johnston 1984:152).

Reading aloud was to last in Cambridge examinations until 1986, when, as with translation, it was sacrificed in the interest of more 'communicatively satisfying' tasks.

Content based papers: Accessing great literature and English for special purposes

Literature

Extensive reading was required to provide a knowledge base for writing essays on literature in many language examinations in the United Kingdom in this early period. One of the rare early reports available on this area is the June 1958 CPE *Report on the work of candidates in the English Literature paper* which points clearly to the importance of the prior reading to performance and the focus on content in marking answers to questions in the Literature paper. Note the clear indication that mechanical accuracy, an important criterion in the Essay paper, is specifically downgraded in marking this paper; an early appreciation of the danger of construct irrelevant variance perhaps.

Aims of the Question Paper

The questions in Part I of the paper are primarily intended to enable the candidates to show that they have studied the prescribed books of their choice. They also, however, call for some capacity to select and discriminate between main and secondary issues and for some personal judgment. They are worded to allow for as elastic an approach as possible; thus the more interested and mentally mature candidates have a chance to show their ability, but the diligent student of the text also has full scope.

The General Literature section of the paper (Part II) assumes that the candidates have read more than the three books required for Part I, and gives them a chance to show and discuss their knowledge and their views. The passages for summary and comment (Part III) are to some extent comprehension tests but also ask for some appreciation of the style and content of the passages as literature.

Since this is a literature and not a language paper, candidates are not penalized, point by point, for linguistic mistakes. They must, of course, show reasonable fluency and not make elementary errors; but even faultless command of English will not enable them to reach the pass standard if the substance of their answers is inadequate.

There has traditionally been much support for the use of literature in the language classroom and, as we saw in Chapter 1, access to the host culture's literature was often seen as the primary reason for learning a foreign language in the early part of our study. Horner (1990:336) describes how in the 19th century literature was introduced into the rhetoric course at Scottish Universities and later the University of London 'as models for good oratory and writing'.

Many contemporary writers still advocate the inclusion of literature in the language learning classroom arguing that it provides useful authentic material, develops personal involvement, broadens learners' horizons and helps contribute to their cultural as well as language enrichment especially in terms of vocabulary range and the relationship between form and meaning (Carter and Long 1991, Collie and Slater 1987, Hall 2005). Khalifa and Weir (2009) note the use of literary texts at FCE level in the Main Suite examinations to cater for the wider vocabulary knowledge required from the candidates at this level (B2) and they comment on their value as one criterial contextual parameter for helping distinguish between FCE (B2) and PET (B1) reading examinations.

The prominent place of English literature in Cambridge's early approach to assessing English Language in CPE and FCE was noted in Chapter 1 and also its apparent downgrading by the time of the 1975 major revisions. A general assumption took hold in the communicative era that the study of literary English had little bearing on EFL learners' needs to promote a functional command of English (see Boyle (1986), Moody (1983) and Littlewood (1986) for discussion of its demise). Boyle (1986:199) notes: 'this tendency is reinforced when English for Specific Purpose (ESP) becomes fashionable and the generalities of literature are considered less relevant to the students' needs than the more purpose-specific language of other disciplines'.

Thus the first (1975) FCE had no Prescribed Books paper, which might have been taken as heralding the end of the literature construct in foreign language testing at the FCE level. At CPE level the study of prescribed literary texts was examined only in an optional paper after 1975.

Even after it was excised from the main suite in the 1970s in the wake of the communicative, utilitarian approach, lobbying for its inclusion, particularly from representatives of the British Council, continued and the issue of language and literature resurfaced once more in the 1980s. Hawkey (2009:52–53) notes that by the early 1980s, the British Council in its direct teaching operations abroad were met by a perceived need in some countries for courses containing an English literature component. At the November 1981 meeting of the Executive Committee, therefore, British Council representatives suggested the inclusion of literature questions in the Cambridge exams to address this demand for instruction linking language and literature skills.

Hawkey reports (2009:59) how:

... Paper 2 of the revised 1984 FCE examination tested Composition. The range of genres included, as in the predecessor exam, letters, descriptive, narrative and discursive topics, two from a choice of five. The new task, in response to the wish of the British Council and its direct teaching of English operations, was an item (choice of one from three) based on a candidate's reading of prescribed texts. The carefully worded note on this in the 1982 booklet suggests interesting discussions between UCLES, the Council and others on the re-entry of 'literature' following its exclusion from the FCE examination since 1975.

He is referring to the following note:

> The introduction of prescribed texts as an alternative stimulus for free composition has been decided on in response less to specific recommendations of teaching centres, during the general syllabus consultation than to later lobbying by the British Council on behalf of overseas teaching operations and a wish to encourage work on extended texts as a basis for the enrichment of language studies (UCLES 1982a:15).

Hawkey (2009:60) muses:

> The British Council, true to its mission remains concerned with the study and use of the English language and to extending knowledge of British literature. UCLES, as a major international provider of tests for the certification of language proficiency levels of users needing them, is required to match the constructs of its examinations with these needs. This at a time where, as we have seen, it is the communicative competence construct, that is the use of the language system 'for normal communication purposes' (Widdowson 1978:18) that is being tested by most proficiency exams. Literary texts (such as for the 1984 FCE examination Dickens' Nicholas Nickleby, The Card (Arnold Bennett) and even, perhaps, the more 'modern' Rebecca (Daphne du Maurier) might not have been considered reading or writing 'for normal communication purposes'.

English for Special Purposes (ESP)

Roach was personally concerned with the role of language in international relations in the 1930s. In 1935 he commented:

> We had slipped back into academic seclusion . . . pupils of to-day would either be the victims of the next war or live to make closer contacts with European nations. The ideals of the modern language teacher must be revised; he must not give way to a snobbery of literature. Language & literature students should be expected to study history and economy, too – to understand other nations (Roach 1935).

In line with his views, alternatives to English Literature appeared in Cambridge English Language Examinations in the 1930s.The questions in 1935 *Economic and Commercial Knowledge*, 1938 *English Life and Institutions* and 1955 *Science* optional papers all involved the candidate in reading extensively beforehand. Though for the most part these were initially indirect measures of reading comprehension, a deep understanding of extensive specialised texts was likely to have been an essential prerequisite to successful performance in writing on these papers.

Candidates had to read extensively in order to engage with these papers but did so outside the context of the examination room, clearly extremely powerful with regard to the washback of the test on learning/teaching.

1930s CPE: The inclusion of summary tasks

Summary tasks, which by necessity involved reading comprehension at the global text level, were included as test formats in Cambridge examinations from early in the period under review. Such tasks had a long historical pedigree in the UK. Beak, in *Indexing and Précis Writing* (1908), identifies one of the earliest examples of an occupation-oriented need for précis writing:

> The appointment of Precis Writer, which today is virtually equivalent to that of Private Secretary, was first officially recognised during the reign of Queen Anne [1665–1714], by which time it was probably realised that the Secretary of State for Foreign Affairs could not possibly himself wade through all the original documents with which he was called upon to deal . . .

Its currency in affairs of state continued as is attested to in 1856 when Florence Nightingale was invited to meet with Queen Victoria and Lord Panmure to discuss the establishment of the *Royal Commission to Enquire into the Sanitary Condition of the Army*. Panmure and the Queen assigned Nightingale the task of writing a précis on her experience at Scutari in the Crimean war (Aravind and Chung 2010).

By the beginning of the 20th century précis featured widely in many ESP and educationally-oriented tests. Robeson (1913), a Master at Eton, describes its use in Civil Service, Army and Navy qualifying examinations, in the Royal Society of Arts and the London Chamber of Commerce examinations in their commercial and teacher awards, and by the Oxford and Cambridge Schools Examination Board in its Examination for School or Leaving Certificates. Its value was perceived in terms of its fit with the academic approach to language learning: 'Adopted originally as a time-saving device, it is only recently that the value of précis writing as a means of mental training has come to be recognised' (Robeson 1913). Pocock (1917:3) in the introduction to *Précis writing for beginners* supports its academic value: 'Incidentally, there is no better training than précis writing for concentration of thought and expression.'

Robeson (1913:9) offers some useful insights into the qualities looked for in successful précis at this time:

> A precis in the strict sense of the term means a summary of some document or documents, but this definition is insufficient as an explanation of what is now commonly required of anyone who is instructed to draw up a precis. A document or series of documents is given him, and he is expected to write in the form of a consecutive narrative an abbreviated account of what occurred as shown by the document or documents before him. The narrative, while including all that is important with regard to the matter in hand, must rigidly exclude all that is unimportant. The object of the precis is to present to anyone who has not time to read the original document or documents the leading features of what is there described, and to present them in a readable form and as concisely as is compatible with clearness. The writer of a precis should constantly put himself in the position of a person who has not seen the original documents and yet wishes to have a clear knowledge of all that is essential in them. He must try to imagine what such a person would need to know and what would be useless to him.
>
> It is not easy to fulfill these requirements. The attempt to include nothing but the important, and to express this concisely, must not be allowed to obscure the natural sequence of events and to result in a jerky agglomeration of items of information. Without being longwinded the narrative must be continuous; it must, so to speak, read like a story; the connecting link between one event and another must be obvious. One of the great difficulties of precis writing is the combination of such a clear consecutive statement with terseness of expression.

He quotes from the London Chamber of Commerce Regulations (1913:15):

> The object of the precis is to enable any one reading it to be put into possession, in the smallest space of time, of the essential points of the subject to which the documents refer. The characteristics of a good precis accordingly are (a) the inclusion of all that is important and the exclusion of all that is unimportant in the correspondence ; (b) the expression of this in a consecutive story as clearly as possible, and as briefly as is compatible with distinctness.

The intention of a summary in this early period was to provide the reader with a condensed and objective account of the main ideas and features of a text; no place for postmodernist interpretation here.

In 1931 a précis of a passage or a poem was introduced into the *English Literature* paper in Part B. Typically, candidates had to choose between summarising a passage, which included defining the meaning of words and phrases in the text, and explaining a poem in detail including a focus on style and diction (see examples below from the 1936 paper).

UNIVERSITY OF CAMBRIDGE
LOCAL EXAMINATIONS SYNDICATE

CERTIFICATE OF PROFICIENCY IN ENGLISH
ENGLISH LITERATURE

December 1936 3 hours

B.

9. Give the meaning of the following passage *concisely* in your words, explaining particularly the words printed in italics:

> The nature of man, considered in his simple *capacity*, and with respect only to the present world, is *adapted* and leads him to attain the greatest happiness he can for himself in the present world. The nature of man considered in his public or *social* capacity leads him to a right *behaviour* in society, to that course of life which we call virtue. Men follow or obey their nature in both those capacities and respects to a certain degree but not entirely: their actions do not come up to the whole of what their nature leads them to in either of these capacities or respects; and they often violate their nature in both, *i.e.* as they neglect the *duties* they owe to their fellow-creatures, to which their nature leads them; and are *injurious*, to which their nature is *abhorrent*: so there is *manifest* negligence in men of their real happiness or interest in the present world, when that interest is *inconsistent* with a present gratification, for the sake of which they negligently, nay, even knowingly are the authors and *instruments* of their own misery and ruin. Thus they are as often unjust to themselves as to others, and for the most part are equally so to both by the same actions.
>
> JOSEPH BUTLER (1692–1752)

10. Explain in your own words the meaning of the following poem, and add brief critical notes on its form and style:

> I heard a thousand blended notes,
> While in a grove I sate reclined,
> In that sweet mood when pleasant thoughts
> Bring sad thoughts to the mind.

To her fair works did Nature link
The human soul that through me ran;
And much it grieved my heart to think
What man has made of man.

Through primrose tufts, in that green bower,
The periwinkle trailed its wreaths;
And 'tis my faith that every flower
Enjoys the air it breathes.

The birds around me hopped and played,
Their thoughts I cannot measure: –
But the least motion that they made,
It seemed a thrill of pleasure.

The budding twigs spread out their fan,
To catch the breezy air;
And I must think, do all I can,
That there is pleasure there.

If this belief from heaven be sent,
If such be Nature's holy plan,
Have I not reason to lament
What man has made of man?
                WILLIAM WORDSWORTH (1770–1850)

In addition, by 1936 there was a further summary task in the English Essay paper as in the example below (in 1938 rebranded as the English Composition paper, presumably because candidates by then had to write more than just an essay). Summaries were viewed in the school system as valuable, integrated tasks and an appreciation of the validity of the task took precedence over any concern with difficulties of marking. The tasks were intended to test comprehension of a whole passage (careful reading at the global as well as the local level – see Figure 2.1 above) as well as writing ability and this stands in stark contrast to the emphasis on decoding in many tests of reading (see above) and in the research literature in the first half of the 20th century

---

UNIVERSITY OF CAMBRIDGE
LOCAL EXAMINATIONS SYNDICATE

CERTIFICATE OF PROFICIENCY IN ENGLISH
ENGLISH ESSAY

July 1936 2 hours

9. Give the meaning of the following passage in your own words, explaining particularly the words printed in italics.

> There is nothing that more betrays a base ungenerous spirit, than the giving of secret *stabs* to a man's *reputation*. *Lampoons* and satires, that are written with spirit, are like poisoned *darts*, which not only inflict a wound, but make it *incurable*. For this reason I am very much troubled when I see the talents of humour and ridicule in the possession of an ill-natured man. There cannot be a greater gratification to a barbarous and inhuman *wit*, than to stir up sorrow in the heart of a private person, to raise *uneasiness* among near relations, and to expose whole families to *derision*, at the same time that he remains unseen and undiscovered. If, besides the *accomplishments* of being witty and ill-natured, a man is *vicious* into the bargain, he is one of the most *mischievous* creatures that can enter into a civil society. His satire will then chiefly fall upon those who ought to be the most *exempt* from it. Virtue, merit, and everything that is praiseworthy, will be made the subject of ridicule and *buffoonery*. It is impossible to enumerate the evils which arise from these arrows that fly in the dark, and I know no other excuse that is or can be made for them than that the wounds they give are only imaginary, and produce nothing more than a secret shame or sorrow in the mind of the suffering person.
>
> JOSEPH ADDISON (1672–1719)

By 1938 we can see a number of reading based tasks at CPE with a summary task appearing in the Composition paper and in English literature Part B.

1938 CPE Reading Related Components

- Translation into French and German
- Reading aloud
- English composition Question 2: read passage 525 words in length and summarise into 185
- English Literature Part B summary: give meaning of passage or poem in own words:

    A question on an unprepared English passage which candidates will be asked to explain in such a way as to shew that they have a proper appreciation both of the meaning and of the form of the passage

- General Economic and Commercial Knowledge

The instructions for the 1938 English Composition paper are more specific and for the first time we are given contextual parameters that need to be observed (for example text length) and alerted to the criteria that would be employed in the marking: main ideas covered, attention to the general effect of the passage (presumably on the reader), carefully worded (presumably appropriateness of vocabulary) and consecutive statement (presumably cohesion and coherence). No time is specified however for the individual tasks in this paper.

**UNIVERSITY OF CAMBRIDGE
LOCAL EXAMINATIONS SYNDICATE**

**CERTIFICATE OF PROFICIENCY IN ENGLISH
ENGLISH COMPOSITION**

July 1938 2 hours 30 minutes

2. When you have finished your Composition, write a summary of the following passage, being careful to give not only its main points but also the general effect of the passage. Your answer should be in the form of a carefully worded consecutive statement not exceeding 185 words in length. Failure to keep within this limit will be penalized. The passage itself contains 525 words.

In writing a clear condensed paragraph the words and phrasing of the original will not usually prove appropriate, and your own words are more likely to be suitable.

I suppose there is no man to whom the education of the people in this country – and very largely adult education – is nearer the heart than it was to a great Englishman who has just died, I mean Lord Morley. Lord Morley spoke on this subject nearly fifty years ago, and he came back to it again and again; so recently as just before the war, speaking to the Manchester students, he used these words, which I feel I must read to you:

"Generous aspiration, exalted enthusiasm, is made to do duty for renewed scrutiny. The ardent spirits see every fact or circumstance that makes their way and are blind to every other. Inflexible preconceptions holding the helm, they exaggerate. Their sense of proportion is bad."

There can be no greater object of true education than to teach and to preserve a sense of proportion, and it seems to me that the great advantage you have here over what I may call the definitely propagandist schools is that you have every opportunity of learning to exercise a trained sense of proportion, because the teachers here are chosen in exactly the same way as the teachers are chosen in the free and open universities. They are chosen because they are masters of their subjects. They are chosen not to give propaganda; they are chosen to speak the truth, and those who are responsible for the conduct of this college know that it is only by giving students the opportunity of exercising to the full the ability that is in them that they will be able to choose the truth honestly and freely, and will exercise their minds to the solution of the problems to which they have to devote themselves, without bias and without preconceived notions. They will clear their minds of cant, and try to see things as they are.

We all of us want understanding – understanding of ourselves and understanding of our brothers and sisters – and that true understanding is the salt that savours the whole life of the community. It was never more needed than it is today, and those who understand will realise that there is no greater need in the world, abroad and at home, than peace, peace from the warfare of arms and peace of spirit . . .

Do not let yourselves be dispirited when you get into the world again, but hold fast to what you believe to be true and what you believe to be right wherever it leads you, and whatever difficulties you may encounter. Whatever troubles you may have, you will, at all events, always have the comfort of a conscience which will tell you that you have tried to act up to the highest lights that are in you, and you will feel that you are playing your part in helping to bring your country, your fellow-men and women, through one of the most difficult times that she has ever had to face in her history, and that you are laying, or trying to lay, the foundations of a happier, healthier and saner life for those with us now and for those who will come after us.

STANLEY BALDWIN, 1923.

The research literature attests to the value of summary in testing the higher level cognitive processes in our model of reading outlined in Figure 2.1 above. According to Bensoussan and Kreindler (1990:57), summary writing is 'a whole-text, super-macro-level skill'. Nuttall (1996:206) favours summarisation as a reading task because it 'demands full understanding of the text'. Cognitive psychologists working at the discourse level from the 1970s onwards argued that comprehension naturally involves summarisation (Kintsch and van Dijk 1978, van Dijk and Kintsch 1983). The student has to establish the main ideas in a text, extract them and reduce to note form, and then rewrite the notes in a coherent manner in their own words. Brown and Day (1983) identified a number of rules for summarising which match those of Kintsch and van Dijk (1978) for establishing macro propositions:

- delete trivial information
- delete redundant information

- provide a superordinate term for members of a category
- find and use any main ideas you can.

In terms of our model of reading laid out above in Figure 2.1, the summarisation of main ideas at the text level is one of more demanding levels of processing activity in real-life language use and thereby appropriate for advanced level candidates such as those entering for CPE. Yu (2008:522–23) offers an impressive list of references in support of the use of summary in teaching and testing reading and provides empirical support for the use of summary as a test of reading comprehension:

> Reading comprehension was the only statistically significant predictor for both English and Chinese summarization performances. Students with better reading comprehension produced better summaries (Yu 2008:544).

Urquhart and Weir (1998:121), and more recently Weir (2005a:101), whilst recognizing the authenticity of the summary task, had some reservations concerning the danger of 'muddied measurement' in terms of the effects of writing abilities on summarisation performance as, in addition to comprehension, knowledge transformation was usually required for successful rendering as this was the hallmark of a skilled writer at the C2 level (see Shaw and Weir 2007). Taylor (1986) expressed similar concerns that writing ability may feature strongly in performance on summary tasks. Most recently Yu (2008:547) in his doctoral research on summarisation in English and Chinese concluded that 'complexities in judging the quality of summarization performance resonate with Weir's (1993:154) concern regarding the subjectivity of marking written summaries'. Weir might argue now of course that if we can mark essays reliably, this must be possible for summary too.

As to how précis/summary was marked in the early days after its introduction into Cambridge CPE examinations in 1931 in the Literature paper and in 1936 in the Essay paper, there is little evidence remaining (apart from that in the rubric discussed above). There may, however, be some clues in Robeson's description (1913:15) of the instructions in the earlier Oxford and Cambridge Schools Examination Board précis:

> The object of the précis (which should proceed not paragraph by paragraph, but in the form of a narrative without marginal references) is that anyone who had not time to read the original correspondence might, by reading the précis, be put in possession of all the leading features of what passed. The merits of such a précis (which should not exceed two pages in length) are (a) to include all that is important in the correspondence, (b) to present this in a consecutive and readable shape, expressed as distinctly as possible, and as briefly as is compatible with distinctness. Attention should be paid to Spelling, Handwriting, Grammar, and Style.

However, we do have the 1957 Occasional Report on the Work of Candidates in the English Language Paper which gives us some insight into the criteria that were actually applied to the summary task at Cambridge:

Part I

Question 1 Summary. There was a general feeling that the passage was not found difficult and that its understanding was well within the capacity of the candidates: Some examiners reported that at many centres the exercise was well handled and that a number of the candidates constructed well written new paragraphs which contained most of the points of the original. Others reported that while there was evidence that the candidates knew how to do a summary and showed little tendency to introduce extraneous material or to make irrelevant comment (faults which often do occur in this exercise) yet there was failure to reflect adequately the points made in the original, that there was a good deal of carelessness and inaccuracy in syntax, and that answers were written as a string of sentences which were not linked together by appropriate conjunctions so as to make the answer really coherent in thought and language. Most of the examiners found evidence in at least some of their centres of good training and preparation for summary writing and of careful thought in its treatment.

In addition the examiners drew attention to a number of candidates who lost marks 'by writing greatly in excess of the number of words allowed'.

A General Report on the work of candidates in the English Language Paper December 1969 (8–9) adds:

material must now be arranged into a logical argument and re-expressed in the form of a well-constructed paragraph, the ordered structure of which, with properly-linked phrases, is the first quality looked for. For this reason, answers offered in note form, though correct in subject matter, incur a penalty . . .

In re-expressing the ideas in sequence a good candidate will necessarily employ words and phrases of his own choice. The paper asks the candidate to express the answer in his own words as far as possible, but candidates should realize that they need not find elaborate alternatives for technical or specialized words which the original passage employs. An answer made up of a series of quotations, however, lifted without comment or explanation from the passage (and sometimes even given in inverted commas) is marked down accordingly . . . The word limit given to each question is based on trial working and consideration of possible answers . . . short answers, it is found are possible but likely to be deficient , while long answers are likely to lead the candidate into diffuseness and irrelevance.

Summary was to last as a task in CPE right through to 1975 and, given the critical use of CPE for university entrance in the 21st century, the demise of such an authentic academic reading into writing task might, with the advantage of hindsight, be regretted (note however its return to favour in 2003 albeit in a reduced intertextual form in the Use of English paper). Cambridge were not alone in abandoning summary and the well regarded Schools Council Research Studies Monograph *The Development of Writing Abilities (11–18)* (Britton, Burgess, Martin, McLeod and Rosen 1975) contains only one brief and fairly disparaging reference to summary on page 47.

From a present day perspective we would argue that (albeit in an integrated format) summary effectively tests the important advanced level reading skill of *creating a text level representation* (see Figure 2.1 above), a vital element of academic study, in an authentic manner. No other task type has filled this vacuum and the recommendation that summary should be reintroduced in CPE made in Khalifa and Weir (2009:220) will take place in the 2012 version of the writing paper in this examination (the intertextual summary from the Use of English paper is being moved there).

Up until the eve of World War Two there had been no questions that specifically focused on the other types of reading we identified in our Framework in Figure 2.1. With the birth of LCE in 1939 (see Chapter 1 for details) this began to change.

1939 LCE: The emergence of dedicated reading items

Though the ability to create a text level representation was tested in the summary/précis sections of various papers at both CPE and LCE, it was only as part of an integrated test of reading into writing ability rather than a test of reading ability *per se* in these early days. Given the paucity of research studies on comprehension until the 1970s that we noted above, and a lack of any real understanding of the cognitive processes that contributed to reading comprehension at the time, it is perhaps hardly surprising that reading was not yet a dedicated focus of interest for language testing at Cambridge except in an integrated sense.

However, in the presence of a small number of reading items in the LCE examination of 1939 and CPE in 1940 (note the questions on *lexical access* especially 7b in the LCE English Composition and Language paper below but also items that appear to be concerned with *establishing propositional meaning at the sentence level* (7d), *building a mental model* (7c) and even *establishing a representation at the text level* (7a)) we can trace the beginnings of an interest in posing specific questions to test a candidate's processing ability (see central column in Figure 2.1 above) as well as various elements of a candidate's knowledge base (see right-hand column in Figure 2.1 above) in relation to a text; even so reading was not to become a dedicated paper in its own right until 1975 when the communicative era ushered in an interest in skills and strategies relating to spoken and written comprehension.

The Lower Certificate in English, introduced in 1939, began this process particularly in items such as 7a and 7c in this part of the *English Composition and Language* paper:

Sample from LCE English Composition and Language 21 June 1939

Read the following passage carefully:

Many years ago in Australia three young children went out into the dark and <u>desolate</u> wood to gather broom.[1] The eldest was a boy of nine years old; Jane, his sister, was seven, and little Frank was five. When they did not come back, their parents became very alarmed, as once lost in this wood it is very difficult <u>to find one's way</u> out again and there was little chance of discovering food or water. The father and his <u>neighbours</u> looked for the children, and searched the wood day by day until a week had passed. Finally he got the help of some natives, who have a wonderful power of following the slightest <u>trail</u> in their woods. They soon saw signs where the children had been from the bent twigs or the <u>trampling</u> of the grass. "Here little one tired," they said, "sit down. Big one kneel down; carry him along. Here travel all night; dark – not see that bush; her fall on him."

On the next day the natives led the father to a <u>clump</u> of broom, where lay three little figures, the smallest one in the middle with his sister's frock over his own clothes. <u>To their amazement</u> the elder boy roused himself, sat up, and said: "Father!" and then fell back <u>from sheer weakness</u>. Little Frank awoke as if from a quiet sleep and Jane had just the strength to <u>murmur</u> "Cold – cold." When the elder brother was carried past the places that the natives had pointed out, his <u>account</u> of their wanderings and adventures exactly agreed with what the natives had suggested from the signs they had <u>noticed</u>. He said that <u>the whole time</u> they had been without food and had only had one drink of water – from a special plant with a deep cup, which keeps water for many weeks. (About 310 words.)

[1] A shrub or plant with yellow flower.

. . . .

7. Now answer all the following:

(a) Give a short name to the story, using not more than six words.

(b) Twelve words and phrases in the passage are underlined. Take **six** of these and show in a few words that you are clear about their sense.

(c) What in your opinion are the four chief points in the story? Write a complete sentence about each point so that you have the story in a shortened form.

(d) Say in good English what the natives said in their bad English to the father. Put what they said in complete English sentences. Do not use more than 50 words.

In the paper entitled *Prescribed Texts* (see extract below), candidates had to read up to four prescribed texts typically taken from what today would be seen as the classics of English literature but what would then have been closer to contemporary fiction. In the examination candidates had to answer questions on two of the texts. A short excerpt from each was presented and candidates were asked a number of open-ended questions, mainly at the level of lexical access, sometimes requiring close inspection of the text itself and sometimes a broader interpretation. These were followed by more broadly based questions on the prescribed text itself.

Sample from LCE Prescribed Texts 21 June 1939

THE OXFORD ENGLISH COURSE: READING BOOK FOUR.

*Do **all** of Question 1 and then give as complete an answer as you are able to **one** other Question.*

1. "The problem is clear: How can such villages be made clean and bright, and how can the lives of the villagers be made happier and more interesting? The answer is equally clear: The responsibility for village improvement rests on the village leaders. Until these leaders study the facts about modern progress in health, communication, building, scientific farming, and other related subjects, we can not expect great changes. Even after they have learned the power of science and modern industry to improve village life, the changes may not come. Almost any well-informed leader can tell what should be done, but leaders of great patience, tact, wisdom, and determination are needed before such plans become realities."

(a) What kind of village is here being talked about?
(b) "The responsibility rests on the village leaders." What does this mean?
(c) Give some examples of improvements in communication and in scientific farming.
(d) Say in other words what patience and tact are.

2. How should a cottage in a village be built?
3. How can farmers cooperate?
4. How do moving pictures make life more interesting?
5. What was Sir Thomas More's answer when he was charged with having received gifts from persons on trial?

1940–45 CPE: The inclusion of reading items at the decoding level

The pattern established by the introduction of LCE was partially taken up in CPE by 1940 when for the first time reading items focusing on decoding were set in Part II of the English Language Paper.

1940/45 CPE Reading Related Components

CPE English Language Paper Part II

- Précis 120 from 350 words
- Paraphrase 2 sentences
- Explain the meaning of any of the five following words and phrases

English Literature Paper

give a summary of the argument of this passage and explain the meaning in their context of the words printed in *italics*

Part II of the English Language paper was mandatory and required candidates among other things to summarise a passage and to answer some short questions focusing on the meaning of vocabulary and sentences in a text (see items 2 and 3 in the example below from 1945). Some of these activities would be familiar in reading tests today.

**UNIVERSITY OF CAMBRIDGE
LOCAL EXAMINATIONS SYNDICATE**

**CERTIFICATE OF PROFICIENCY IN ENGLISH
ENGLISH LANGUAGE**

July 1945 3 hours

Read the following passage carefully and answer the three questions set on it:

> News comes from abroad which should strengthen the fibre and determination of all those whose ambition it is to see their verses acquire the dignity and status of print. Even a person 3 who knows how seriously a conscientious artist regards the making of poems can hardly have supposed that anyone would go to "the heroic lengths of Lance-Corporal James Horton. 6 Lance-Corporal Horton had, it appears, decided to have some of his poems published, but for some reason it was necessary for him to get from his station to Algiers to make the arrangements. There were obvious difficulties in the way, but it so happened

that an inter-regimental boxing competition was to take place in Algiers and Lance-Corporal Horton, who, does not seem to have had any pretensions as a boxer, entered for it. He underwent, in the brutal phrasing of the report, "ten minutes' bashing in the boxing ring", and the slang description of his ordeal enhances the glory of the gallant soldier's comment: 'It was worth it, for I got some of my poems published.'" The trumpets have sounded on Parnassus for less devotion than that, and midnight oil seems a poor thing to sacrifice compared with the blood that flowed from the lance-corporal's nose.

The Muses, as a body, are perhaps inclined to be sadistic in 21 their behaviour, and others besides those who woo them of their own free will may justifiably complain of them. The majority, indeed, of those, who have suffered most in mind and body from association with poetry have not been so much concerned with the production of the plaguy thing as with the learning of it. It is greatly to be hoped that Lance-Corporal Horton's resource 27 in getting his poems published, will result in a suitable financial reward; but his devotion was clearly untouched by such sordid, 29 considerations, and the cheque received—as much the outcome of his heroism in the ring as of his poetic talent—will, alas, in all probability be too insignificant to compromise his amateur 32 status as a boxer.

1. Make a précis or summary of the passage in not more than 120 words, taking care to give a continuous connexion of ideas. The passage contains about 350 words.
2. Paraphrase (i.e. rewrite in your own words), or otherwise explain fully, the meaning of the following sentences:
   (*a*) The slang description of his ordeal enhances the glory of the gallant soldier's comment.
   (*b*) The trumpets have sounded on Parnassus for less devotion than that, and midnight oil seems a poor thing to sacrifice compared with the blood that flowed from the lance-corporal's nose.
3. Explain the meaning of any **five** of the following words and phrases:
   (*a*) dignity and status of print (1. 3),
   (*b*) conscientious (1. 4),
   (*c*) go to heroic lengths (1.6),
   (*d*) sadistic (1. 21),
   (*e*) resource (1. 27),
   (*f*) sordid considerations (1. 29),
   (*g*) compromise (1. 32).

Where individual elements of the comprehension process were tested in these papers, the focus was mainly on *lexical access* in a specified context or on *establishing propositional meaning* at the sentence level. However there were clearly a few items that required *inferencing*. No documentation remains to indicate whether these questions were marked solely on content or whether mechanical accuracy features were considered.

In terms of format there is a reliance on traditional, open-ended, constructed responses which had to be subjectively assessed. Spolsky (1995a:206), whilst appreciating the UCLES concern for the felt fairness of tests, wonders why the lessons from Edgeworth and Hartog on marker reliability were not taken (see Roach (1936), Brereton (1944) and discussion in Chapter 1 for some answers to this). Spolsky's point is that there was no evidence yet of any concern with objectively scored items in the reading and writing papers (see Chapter 1 for an account of Cambridge's lack of any real interest in objective testing prior to the 1960s).

We have examined in detail a number of the integrated tasks used for assessing reading ability in the discussion above: viz précis/summary, translation, and reading aloud. We have not yet examined closely the specific assessment of lexical knowledge where, though the focus was admittedly discrete, the constructed responses required to answer the questions on lexis introduced an element of writing ability into the processing equation.

Testing lexical knowledge

Earlier in this chapter we noted the interest in and attention given to decoding in the psychology literature in the first six to seven decades of the 20th. Shiotsu and Weir (2007), in a study which examined the relative contribution of knowledge of syntax and knowledge of vocabulary to L2 reading, describe how in advance of their study the prevailing view in second language learning and assessment was that vocabulary knowledge was one of the most important, if not the most important, component in reading ability. They describe how Barnett's (1986) data led her to conclude that both syntactic and vocabulary knowledge affect reading comprehension, as increases in the levels of syntactic and vocabulary knowledge of her students seemed almost symmetrical in their effects on reading recall performance. Haynes and Carr (1990) found their students' reading comprehension performance correlated better with vocabulary than grammar. In his study of the reading performance of L2 learners of Dutch, Bossers's data (1992) indicated that vocabulary and grammar were both significant predictors of reading ability, with vocabulary achieving a slightly stronger prediction. On the other hand, Yamashita (1999) claimed on the basis of her regression results that the contribution of vocabulary was much larger than that of grammar. Pike (1979) in one of the first TOEFL research studies found that the 'words in context' items correlated highly with the reading comprehension items and as a result these lexical items were subsequently integrated into one section with reading.

Despite the reservations Shiotsu and Weir (2007) express about the methodological shortcomings of some of the studies suggesting a substantive role for lexis in reading comprehension, they do agree on its importance and its value as a predictor of reading ability. In their own study vocabulary proved to be a significant indicator of reading ability albeit slightly surpassed in its predictive power by syntax.

In terms of the cognitive processing model we outlined above (see Figure 2.1) this is perhaps not surprising as efficient lexical access is necessary before any of the higher level integration of meaning activities are possible. Lexical access and syntactic parsing constitute the critical building blocks of processing in reading and it is not surprising that in numerous studies they have been shown to account for a considerable proportion of the variance in reading tests. Purpura's (1999) research employing Structural Equation Modeling (SEM) showed his lexico-grammatical ability variable to almost perfectly predict his latent reading ability variable (beta = .985*).

Given the importance of lexis in both the teaching and assessment of reading, and its suitability for enhancing the psychometric qualities of a test (e.g. large number of items can be tested in an efficient and reliable fashion thereby enhancing reliability coefficients), one can understand why it assumed a position of importance in the testing of reading at Cambridge from 1939 (LCE) and 1940 (CPE) until the present day. In the TOEFL, launched in 1964, vocabulary had its own section (see Read 1997).

In the earlier examples above from the 1945 CPE papers, the vocabulary items seemed to target knowledge of the particular meaning sense used in the reading passage. Schmitt (1999) in a later study on similar TOEFL items found (208):

> As might be expected, the TOEFL vocabulary items were able to give only a limited amount of information about the wider range of word knowledge necessary to master a word. The items were not particularly strong in indicating the subjects' association, word-class and collocation knowledge of the target words.

However, later Cambridge items, as in our example from the June 2005 CPE reading paper below, come closer to satisfying Schmitt's desire (1999) to see depth as well as breadth of knowledge tested. Schmitt (1999:190) is concerned with what lexical items are actually testing and questions the prevailing assumption that many existing vocabulary items fully address the underlying lexical construct. He points out that many vocabulary items test only breadth of knowledge, i.e. provide an index of how many words the candidate might know. The focus is on single meanings and not how well each word is known and he questions whether vocabulary size on its own is a sufficient indicator of vocabulary knowledge. He argues for depth of knowledge to be tested as well: i.e. how well words are known.

Sample from CPE Reading Part 1 June 2005

For questions **1–18**, read the three texts below and decide which answer (**A, B, C** or **D**) best fits each gap. Mark your answers **on the separate answer sheet**.

Listing

In Britain the badge of distinction awarded to historic buildings is unheroically called 'listing'. When a building is listed it is **(1)** . . . for preservation and it is expected to stand more or less indefinitely – nobody expects it to be demolished, ever. But what is the **(2)** . . . expectancy of, **(3)** . . . , a nineteenth-century terraced house? A few years ago most people assumed that such houses would eventually wear out and be replaced – and millions were demolished in slum **(4)** . . . . But about 2.5 million of these terraces survive, and in some towns they are being given 'conservation area' **(5)** . . . , so don't expect the bulldozers there. The very low rates of demolition and construction in the United Kingdom **(6)** . . . that the building stock as a whole is ageing, and this has enormous implications for the long-term sustainability of housing.

1	A	branded	B	earmarked	C	minted	D	tagged
2	A	time	B	age	C	strength	D	life
3	A	say	B	imagine	C	Think	D	look
4	A	removal	B	riddance	C	clearance	D	dispatch
5	A	quality	B	class	C	Rank	D	status
6	A	mean	B	convey	C	explain	D	determine

These CPE reading test items focus on collocation i.e. depth of knowledge as well as breadth. However, in the wider scheme of things, the appropriateness of including lexical items testing lower level cognitive processing at the expense of including items testing higher level processing at the text level in a CPE CEFR C2 level test is debatable.

1953: The introduction of reading comprehension items in CPE

In Chapter 1 we described a move towards a more language oriented examination at CPE in the 1950s and early 1960s. We saw how the 1953 variant of CPE introduced a *Use of English* paper and reading was tested both in this paper and in the *English Language* paper (introduced in the place of the Composition paper in 1955) though it was not referred to as reading in either. The Use of English paper for 1955 contained a number of *short answer questions* (see Items a, b and c below) requiring constructed responses on items requiring the comprehension of both local and global information.

**UNIVERSITY OF CAMBRIDGE
LOCAL EXAMINATIONS SYNDICATE**

CERTIFICATE OF PROFICIENCY IN ENGLISH

USE OF ENGLISH

22 June 1955 3 hours

1. The following passage, adapted from a book on the growth of the English language, deals with the effect of the Renaissance in the 15th and 16th centuries. Read through the passage carefully and then answer the questions which follow it.

> Just at the time when the boundaries of knowledge were being widely extended, and language was being developed to cope with the new ideas being introduced, there was invented a means of spreading this knowledge and these ideas more extensively than had ever been dreamed possible, and, moreover, of 5 making more enduring records of them than the hand-written scrolls so industriously filled by toiling clerks and devoted clergy. One may safely say that the results of the adventurous voyages of the people of those times, both physically into uncharted seas and unexplored continents and mentally into the treasure-houses 10 of Greek and Latin literature, would not have been so great or so permanent had there been no invention of printing. Works which before had been laboriously, and often inaccurately, copied by hand could now be reproduced in great numbers and with something more closely approaching fidelity to the words and 15 ideas of their original authors.
> The two processes were complementary: the wider dissemination of printed books gave more general currency to new ideas, and the rapid growth of ideas stimulated the production of more and more books. Nothing could have been more favourable to 20 the enrichment of the English vocabulary and the development of the English language.

> > (*a*) What, according to the writer, was the chief event which made it possible for the Renaissance to influence the development of the English language?
> > (*b*) To what two aspects of the Renaissance does the writer refer in lines 8 to 11?

(*c*) Give a word or phrase which means approximately the same as each of the following, as they arc used in the passage:
- (i) Just at the time when (I. 1);
- (ii) cope with (I. 3)
- (iii) enduring (I. 6);
- (iv) industriously (I. 7);
- (v) uncharted (I. 9);
- (vi) with something more closely approaching fidelity (II. 14–15);
- (vii) were complementary (I. 17);
- (viii) dissemination (II. 17–18).

(*d*) Suppose that the author had written, instead of the last sentence in the passage as it stands, a sentence beginning:

Nothing could have been more favourable to the enrichment of the English vocabulary and the development of the English language than . . . .

Complete this sentence in its new form, in not more than 40 words, using only ideas contained in the passage.

In 1955 short answer reading comprehension questions were also used for the first time in the *English Science Texts* paper available as an alternative to English Literature. Apart from the summary (i), the focus in (ii) and (iii) still appears to be on careful reading at the local level.

UNIVERSITY OF CAMBRIDGE
LOCAL EXAMINATIONS SYNDICATE

CERTIFICATE OF PROFICIENCY IN ENGLISH
English Science Texts

22 June 1955 3 hours

SECTION 1
Read the following passage carefully, and answer questions (i), (ii) and (iii):

It has become a commonplace of biology that the function of the nervous system is conduction, and that all the activities of the body are integrated by messages sent within it from place to place. But the notion of conduction is really very inadequate to describe the function of the brain, which is far more than a mere 5 relay station or even than a switchboard. It is an organ whose activities literally control and dominate our life and well-being. The systems of telegraphic and telephonic communication provide a too-ready analogy for the nervous system, and the comparison is responsible for the fact that most people still think of all 10 nervous activity as consisting fundamentally of the transmission of messages in something like a telegraph system. The essentials of such a system are a set of connections in which when a particular impetus (stimulus) is applied at one end, a propagation of some sort takes place, which, if suitably routed, sets up a response 15 somewhere else.

This gives quite a good picture of some parts of nervous activity; certainly there are sensory and motor nerve fibres, and messages are propagated along them. The messages are even of an electrical nature, though fundamentally different from those 20 propagated in metallic conductors, and passing only very slowly. The speed of conduction varies in different nerve fibres from less than 1 to more than 100 m./sec., that is, between about 2 and 200 m.p.h. But evidence makes it necessary to reject the telegraph or telephone analogy, because the system is not simply 25 a passive one which comes to rest when unstimulated.

(i) Summarise the above passage in your own words. Your answer should not exceed 110 words.

(ii) Explain the meaning of the following phrases as they are used in the passage: is responsible for (1. 10); sets up a response (1. 15); makes it necessary to (1. 24).

(iii) Write down six only of the following words, and against each write a word, or short phrase, which could be substituted for it in the passage: function (1. 1); activities (1. 2); inadequate (I. 4); literally (1. 7); provide (1. 8); fundamentally (1. 11); essentials (1. 12); sort (1. 15); parts (1. 17); reject (1. 24).

Further changes in the assessment of reading were afoot. The 1966 CPE 'British Life and Institutions' paper and 'Survey of Industry and Commerce' paper (see example below) now both include a reading passage with questions which are testing reading comprehension. Neither of these papers in 1955 included a reading passage (cf the CPE June 1955 English Science Texts paper above), and simply tested the productive knowledge of the subjects by requiring them to explain, compare, distinguish, and describe things in a written essay. Again this may be taken as part of the shift to measuring language rather than subject competence as well as a move towards a more comprehensive skills based assessment.

UNIVERSITY OF CAMBRIDGE
LOCAL EXAMINATIONS SYNDICATE

CERTIFICATE OF PROFICIENCY IN ENGLISH

15 June 1966 3 hours

SURVEY OF INDUSTRY AND COMMERCE

SECTION 1

1. Read the following passage carefully and then answer questions (a), (b), and (c).

If Mr. Edward Lloyd, "Coffee-Man," who flourished towards the end of the seventeenth century and in the earlier years of the eighteenth, had revisited this planet on May 23rd, 1925, he would have been an astonished coffee-house keeper. He would have seen a vast stand accommodating three thousand persons 5 to witness the laying by the King of the foundation-stone of an enormous building called Lloyd's. Assuming him to lie gifted with the insight sometimes attributed to the immortal, he would know that many ships of all sizes and flags were connected with his name, and that lines of steamers navigating all the oceans 10 also bore the magic name of Lloyd's . . .

If our friend were as conceited as some personages now living, he might perhaps have attributed these astonishing phenomena to some remarkable qualities of his own, whose existence he did not suspect when he carried on his house in Tower Street or 15 Lombard Street. Here he would have been wrong, for his name has been immortalised by generations of traders and by the characteristics and the energies of those who, in the course of two centuries and a half, have built up British commerce and carried the flag to the remotest seas. 20

At no time, so far as we are aware, did any group of men say to each other: "Go to; let us make the greatest centre of insurance in the world." Even association waited for well over a century, and incorporation for nearly two centuries. Certain men took their seats at a coffee-house table, and pledged themselves, 25 individually, for a consideration, to take upon themselves the perils of the seas, men-of-war, fire, enemies, pirates, thieves, etc., with all other perils which might, come, to the hint or detriment of the subject-matter of insurance. The coffee-house was frequented by all and sundry, and the merchants of that day 30 found reliable men at some of the tables who would give them good assurance. Amid all the changes of the centuries, with the growth of banks and limited liability companies, the two great principles of individual trading (each for himself and not one for

another), and unlimited liability, have been maintained. It is a 35
striking example of evolution as distinguished from creation.
Conditions have been made, rules instituted not in preparation
for new factors and developments, but to systematise a practice
which had already been adopted to meet the requirements of
commerce as they arose. 40

The founder of Lloyd's was not Edward Lloyd, but there is
a certain euphony about the name which has been helpful. It had
no old associations and conveyed no meaning. It was not
commonplace like John's, nor half comic like Boodle's. Neither
familiar nor recondite, it was a name well fitted to gather new 45
associations about it. And so the business men who resorted
to the house retained the name throughout the centuries, and
continued it when the coffee-house stage had long passed . . .

Wright and Fayle: *A History of Lloyd's* (1928)

(*a*) Give an account of the passage in your own words. Your
answer should not exceed 150 words.

(*b*) Explain the meaning of three of the following phrases as
they are used in the passage:
(i) the insight sometimes attributed to the immortal
(I.8);
(ii) carried the flag to the remotest seas (I, 20);
(iii) to take upon themselves the perils of the seas (II.
26–27);
(iv) a striking example of evolution as distinguished
from creation (I. 36).

(*c*) Write down six only of the following words or phrases
and against each write a word or phrase which could
be substituted for it in the text to retain the same meaning:

flourished (I. 1);	hurt or detriment (I. 28);
this planet (I. 3);	all and sundry (I. 30);
navigating (I. 10);	systematise (I. 38);
conceited (I. 12);	euphony (I. 42);
astonishing phenomena	associations (I. 43);
(I. 13);	recondite (I. 45).
incorporation (I. 24).	

Again the focus still appears to be mainly on the decoding level (except for
the summary in (a) which is at the whole text level) although a degree of propositional inferencing is required in a number of items.

Before the advent of objective multiple-choice question formats in
Cambridge English examinations in the 1970s, short answer questions were
seen as the most effective way of testing most types of reading. We examine
this response format in more detail next.

Short answer questions (SAQ's)

Short answer questions are generically those which require the candidates to write down answers in the spaces provided on the question paper, which serve to limit the length of the response, even if the number of words required is not specified. The questions set in this format can potentially cover the important information in a text (overall gist, main ideas and important details) as well as an understanding of the structures and lexis that convey this. The guiding principle for this test format is to keep the answers brief and to reduce writing to a minimum to avoid possible contamination from students having to write answers out in full.

Though relatively rare in these early reading papers, activities such as inference, recognition of a sequence, comparison and establishing the main idea of a text, requiring the relating of sentences in a text to other items, which may be some distance away in the text, could also be accommodated in this format. This could be done effectively through short answer questions where the answer has to be sought rather than being one of those provided. Answers are not provided for the student as in multiple choice; therefore, if a student gets the answer right, one can be more certain that this has not occurred for reasons other than comprehension of the text. Answers need to be worked out from the passage and should not be already known through existing knowledge, or easily arrived at by matching wording from question with wording in the text.

It is not clear what criteria were employed in the marking of short answer questions in the 1950s. Current thinking is that the number of acceptable answers to a question should be limited so that it is possible to give fairly precise instructions to the examiners who mark them (Alderson 2000, Khalifa and Weir 2009, Weir 1993). The mark scheme should allow for the range of semantically acceptable answers. Mechanical accuracy criteria (grammar, spelling, punctuation) would not normally feature in the scoring system as this affects the accuracy of the measurement of the reading construct.

The main disadvantage of this technique is that it involves the candidate in writing, and there is some concern, largely anecdotal, that this interferes with the measurement of the intended construct. Care is needed in the setting of items to limit the range of possible acceptable responses and the extent of writing required. For example, ensuring rater reliability may have been problematic in Question d) of the 1955 CPE Use of English paper above (p. 146) without a clear schema for marking.

In those cases where there is more debate over the acceptability of an answer, for example, in questions requiring inferencing skills, there is a possibility that the variability of acceptable answers might lead to marker unreliability. If such concerns are allowed to unduly influence item choice, issues concerning adequate coverage of representative cognitive processing levels may arise. For example in the present day IELTS, item writers are advised to focus short answer questions on factual information as otherwise the items end up too open to be workable. Questions a and b in the 1955 Use of English paper above (p. 146) would seem to have followed this principle. This of course is likely to limit the extent of coverage of the processing stages outlined in our model in Figure 2.1 and raise questions relating to a test's cognitive validity (similar problems occur in the testing of listening; see Chapter 5 and discussion of the gap-filling tasks in reading below). For a test to be considered cognitively valid, the cognitive processes required to complete the language tasks must be an adequate resemblance of the cognitive processes a candidate would normally employ in non-test conditions, and be sufficiently comprehensive to be generalisable to that real-world behaviour.

1966: The first objective items

As we saw in Chapter 1 there was much talk internally in the 1960s that the Cambridge approach lacked objectivity, that it was in some way behind the times, that it needed to focus more explicitly on the four skills and that it was time to start making use of more 'scientific' methods of assessment, i.e. multiple-choice questions, statistical analysis, and, importantly, the demonstration of test reliability.

Consideration was accordingly given at the 1965 Executive Committee meeting to the introduction of objective items. Multiple-choice questions were introduced into the 1966 variant of the Use of English Paper Section 4B. The focus was largely on vocabulary and the meaning caused by punctuation. The extent to which the questions were subjected to pre and post test statistical analysis was almost certainly limited (Chaplen had not yet arrived – see Chapter 1, pages 62–64), but an important statement had been made.

1975 CPE and FCE: Improving both contextual and scoring validity

The 1975 changes to both FCE and CPE made a bold statement in terms of both construct and measurement. Cambridge exams were now to explicitly test the four skills of Reading, Listening, Speaking and Writing through objectively scored multiple-choice questions. Both Listening and Reading would constitute papers in their own right.

Paper 2 Section B Reading Comprehension involved reading a number of short passages and answering 20 multiple-choice questions on them. The focus was on explicit and implicit meaning in both the FCE and CPE items. There were also 40 discrete-point multiple-choice vocabulary questions in CPE Paper 2 Section A and likewise in FCE. The reading construct appeared to reflect a combination of reading skills along with knowledge of vocabulary, sometimes of a somewhat esoteric nature.

1975 FCE: The introduction of multiple-choice items

The 1975 FCE Paper 2 demonstrates a balance between the analytical, discrete, and the communicative ends of the testing spectrum we discussed in Chapter 1. Attention is paid to the need to improve the internal consistency reliability estimate of the test by the inclusion of 40 multiple-choice question items with a micro-linguistic focus in Section A. Section B in contrast focuses on reading comprehension, employing two or more prose passages at an appropriate level of difficulty in terms of lexis as determined by West's *General Service List* and structural frequency counts. This was the first overt sign of an attempt to pin down level to quantifiable contextual parameters outside of the work of Roach on the lexical content of LCE (see Chapter 1 for details of Roach's work on this in the 1930s and 1940s and Appendix B for a modern day automated approach to this challenge).

FCE 1975 Paper 2: Reading Comprehension (1¼h)

A The forty multiple-choice items in this section will each consist of a sentence with a blank which could be filled by one of five words or phrases suggested.
Example:
She quickly washed the milk off the carpet so that it would not leave a

_____

A stain B colour C fault D wound E remark.
B This section will consist of twenty multiple-choice items based on two or three passages each of between 250 and 600 words. The passages will normally be taken from modern British sources and care will be taken that the questions do not unfairly test general knowledge.

In the setting of this paper Michael West's *General Service List* (including the Supplementary Scientific and Technical Vocabulary in the Longman 1953 edition) will be used as a general guide. Current research in the field of word and structure frequency counts will also be taken into account in the development of this paper.

1975 CPE: The introduction of multiple-choice items

The 1975 CPE Reading paper demonstrates similar facets to the FCE paper we have just described. The scoring validity of the paper was improved by the use of multiple-choice questions testing decoding at the micro-linguistic levels as well as testing meaning comprehension at the sentence, inter-sentential and textual levels.

Spolsky (1995a) describes how in this period traditional descriptive-humanitarian tests, usually short answer questions (SAQs) or translation, were largely supplanted by rational-empiricist objective measures, most commonly multiple-choice questions (MCQs), on the basis of the superior reliability and psychometric qualities of the latter.

Reading Components in 1975 CPE

- Paper 1 Composition Section B: passage plus Short Answer questions
- Paper 2 Reading comprehension multiple choice gap filling (40), multiple choice comprehension questions: 2 passages 20 questions,
- Paper 3 Use of English: single word gap filling, single passage with 18 short answer questions, summary, reading into writing
- Paper 5 Reading aloud (dialogue)
- General Economic and Commercial Knowledge, British Life and Institutions or English Science texts
- English Literature Part III

The example of 10 items from Part 5 Section A of the Reading Comprehension Paper 2 below shows a clear focus on lexical access (see also Figure 2.1 above).

1975 CPE Paper 2 section A Reading Comprehension

PAPER 2: READING COMPREHENSION

Answer all questions. Indicate your choice of answer in every case on the separate answer sheet already given out, which should show your name and examination index number. Follow carefully the instructions about how to record your answers.

Section A

In this section you must choose the word or phrase which best completes each sentence. **On your answer sheet** cross through the letter A, B, C, D, or E against the number of each item 1 to 40, for the word or phrase you choose. Give **one answer only** to each question.

1   It was sympathy she was _____ in need of, not advice.
    A considerably   B attentively   C mercifully   D perfectly
    E sore

2   We were fortunate in having a car entirely at our _____
    throughout the holiday.
    A usage   B disposal   C pleasure   D serving   E disposition

3   Customers' money will be _____ if they are not satisfied with
    our product.
    A recovered   B compensated   C settled   D paid
    E refunded

4   The unpleasant taste _____ in his mouth for hours.
    A insisted   B prolonged   C waited   D lingered   E rested

5   She's a very selfish person who doesn't show much _____ for
    others.
    A consternation   B consideration   C complacency
    D estimation   E humanity

6   The lecturer asked whether anyone had any _____ to changing
    the time of the class.
    A conflict   B resistance   C inconvenience   D objection
    E mind

7   Our company has been _____ by an international company.
    A taken over   B taken out   C merged   dealt   E disposed

8   Although the workers' _____ hourly rate was increased by ten
    per cent, they still felt their wages were inadequate.
    A foundation   B bair   C primary   D fundamental   E basic

9   I have only _____ memories of things that happened to me
    before I was five.
    A dim   B dazzling   C unfixed   D loose   E illegible

10 The young man _____ quickly at his watch.
    A glimpsed   B gazed   C spotted   D glanced   E viewed

Section B of the Reading followed this objective trend with five multiple-choice
questions set on each of four passages. Items covered a range of processing
levels in our framework in Figure 2.1 above: from establishing propositional
meaning at the sentence level, through inferencing and building a mental
model with the occasional question requiring a text level representation.

Clear instructions are given to 'read each passage right through before
choosing your answers': a strong indication of the intended careful reading
nature of the task.

1975 CPE Paper 2 section B Reading Comprehension

Section B

In this section you will find after each of the passages a number of
questions or unfinished statements about the passage, each with four
suggested answers or ways of finishing. You must choose the one which

you think fits best. **On your answer sheet**, cross through the letter A, B, C or D against the number of each item 41 to 60, for the answer you choose. Give **one answer only** to each question. Read each passage right through before choosing your answers.

First passage

Flats were almost unknown in Britain until the eighteen-fifties when they were developed, along with other industrial dwellings, for the labouring classes. These vast blocks were plainly a convenient means of easing social conscience by housing large numbers of the ever-present poor on compact city sites. During the eighteen-eighties, however, the idea of living in comfortable "residential chambers" caught on with the affluent upper and upper middle classes, and controversy as to the advantages and disadvantages of flat life was a topic of conversation around many a respectable dinner table. In Paris and other major European cities, the custom whereby the better-off lived in apartments, or flats, was well established. Up to the late nineteenth century in England only bachelor barristers had established the tradition of living in rooms near the Law Courts: any self-respecting head of household would insist upon a West End town house as his London home, the best that his means could provide.

The popularity of flats for the better-off seems to have developed for a number of reasons. First, perhaps, through the introduction of the railways, which had enabled a wide range of people to enjoy a holiday staying in a suite at one of the luxury hotels which had begun to spring up during the previous decade. Hence, no doubt, the fact that many of the early luxury flats were similar to hotel suites, even being provided with communal dining-rooms and central boilers for hot water and heating. Rents tended to be high to cover overheads, but savings were made possible by these communal amenities and by tenants being able to reduce the number of family servants.

One of the earliest substantial London developments of flats for the well-to-do was begun soon after Victoria Railway Station was opened in 1860, as the train service provided an efficient link with both the City and the South of England. Victoria Street, adjacent to both the station and Westminster, had already been formed, and under the direction of the architect, Henry Ashton, was being lined with blocks of residential chambers in the Parisian manner. These flats were commodious indeed, offering between eight and fifteen rooms apiece, including appropriate domestic offices. The idea was an emphatic departure from the tradition of the London house and achieved immediate success.

Perhaps the most notable block in the vicinity was Queen Anne's Mansions, partly designed by E. R. Robson in 1884 and recently demolished. For many years, this was London's loftiest building and had strong claims to be the ugliest. The block was begun as a wild speculation, modelled on the American skyscraper, and was nearly 200 feet high. The cliff-like walls of dingy brick completely overshadowed the modest thoroughfare nearby. Although bleak outside, the mansion flats were palatial within, with sumptuously furnished communal entertaining and dining rooms, and lifts to the uppermost floors. The success of these tall blocks of flats could not have been achieved, of course, without the invention of the lift, or "ascending carriage" as it was called when first used in the Strand Law Courts in the 1870's.

41 Flats first appeared in Britain in the middle of the 19th Century when
   A they were principally built for those with several servants
   B people were not conscious of the crowded housing of the less well-to-do
   C there was increasing concern over the unsatisfactory accommodation for the poorly-off
   D people became conscious of the social needs of the rural population

42 In the 1880's, dinner table discussion of flat dwelling centred mainly on whether it was
   A convenient
   B expensive
   C respectable
   D healthy

43 The passage claims that in London, before the late 19th Century,
   A only unmarried men in the legal profession might have a room near their office
   B ancient tradition obliged lawyers to live near the courts
   C all young bachelors were accustomed to living in flats
   D there had long been a tradition of renting a room for one's bachelor relatives

44 The traditional preference of English upper middle class families was to
   A live mainly outside London, where it was healthier and cheaper
   B live in the West End only if they could afford no better
   C be content with a less imposing house, as long as it was in the West End
   D live in London, but mainly not in the West End

45 The first effect of the coming of the railways to central London was to stimulate the building of
   A large and well-appointed hotels
   B blocks of self-contained flats
   C rows of elegant town houses
   D flats similar to hotel suites

The dedicated Reading paper for both FCE and CPE and a wholesale adoption of the multiple-choice question format to test reading comprehension at a range of processing levels from lexical access up to building a representation of the text were major developments on earlier papers. To date we have not considered what the research literature has to say on these multiple-choice question formats and their effect on the measurement of reading ability and it is to this we now turn.

Multiple-choice question format

Multiple-choice formats are often favoured by examination boards not least for their ease of marking and contribution to overall test reliability (in the form of internal consistency as well as marker reliability). The 1975 multiple-choice dedicated Reading paper was machine-scored so high levels of scoring validity were now possible. If a test consists of selected response items, and is machine scored, we can expect a high degree of reliability of marking. An Optical Mark Reader (OMR) form which is accurately designed and printed, and properly filled out and handled will read with 100% accuracy.

Such items when well constructed tend to be good discriminators between strong and weak candidates and difficulty can be increased or lessened appropriate to level through careful selection of the text (see Appendix B for details of the way this might be done) but less acceptably through the manipulation of the distractors.

Multiple-choice items are acknowledged to be an appropriate vehicle in large-scale assessments for testing detailed understanding of the text. They are thought to allow more sophisticated elements of text content to be tested, e.g. opinion, inference, argument, in a more controlled way than is possible through open-ended formats.

There is some concern, however, about the appropriateness of multiple-choice questions for activating the higher level processing required in constructing an organised representation of the text (one of the top levels of processing in our framework in Figure 2.1 above). For example, an empirical study by Rupp, Ferne and Choi (2006:468–469) questions their value 'as composite measures of higher order reading comprehension'; i.e. their usefulness for assessing comprehension of the macrostructure of a situation model. They conclude (2006:469) that the format may involve the reader in 'response processes that deviate significantly from those predicted by a model of reading comprehension in a non-testing context' and they hypothesise (2006:454) that 'responding to MC reading comprehension questions on many standardised reading comprehension tests is much more a problem-solving process relying heavily on verbal reasoning than a fluid process of integrating propositions to arrive at a connected mental representation of a text'.

There is also concern that the mental model which is normally created while reading a text is affected if candidates try to incorporate all the options provided in an item into an ongoing text representation. The processing that takes place in working out which option fits, and which does not, would bear little resemblance to the way we process texts for information in any of the types of reading we identified in our framework in Figure 2.1 above (see Farr, Pritchard, and Smitten (1990), Nevo (1989), Rupp et al (2006), Wu (1998) for informed research studies on the process of taking multiple-choice tests).

However, in practice, the way the question is phrased and the way in which the candidate approaches the task will make a difference to the creation of the mental model. In the CAE Handbook for Teachers (UCLES 2008:9), candidates are advised to read the question and establish which part of the text contains the answer, and only then go through the multiple-choice options to see which one is correct (as opposed to reading all the options first). The Rupp et al (2006:468) study itself showed that 'test-takers first tended to apply macro-level strategies in order to have an overall idea of what the given text and the related questions were about'.

There is some evidence too from classroom practice which indicates that candidates are trained to read the text first then look at the items. The presence of exercises in published textbooks focusing on Cambridge examinations, which train students to read the text before answering the questions, would support this. Also, the fact that Cambridge ESOL presents the text first in careful reading tasks encourages the student to read the text before the questions and as we noted in the instructions to the 1975 CPE paper above clear instructions are given to this effect. Evidence from test takers themselves, on how they approach the tasks, would be the most convincing evidence and research is needed on this.

1975: The introduction of selective deletion gap filling items

The 1970s also saw the introduction of a new format viz selective deletion gap filling. Selective (as against random) deletion enables the test constructor to determine where deletions are to be made in a text in their attempts to test an appropriate level of reading ability. Items are relatively easy to construct for this format, and texts are selected to satisfy appropriate contextual parameters, e.g. propositional and organisational complexity of passage, text type, size, topic, etc. (see Appendix B for details of what might be done with respect to quantifiable parameters).

In our example below the candidate has to supply the missing word to construct the response. The technique becomes a selected response format if a pool of possible answers is provided as in CPE Part 1 (see example on page 144). Even where answers are not provided, with careful consideration at the moderation stage, marking should be relatively straightforward, and items can be selected which have a restricted number of possible answers. It seems reasonable in this version to accept equivalent responses in marking and not to penalise for spelling unless it cannot be understood or the spelling could be taken as another word.

FCE Paper 3 Use of English June 1975

SECTION A

1. Fill each of the numbered blanks in the following passage. Use only **one** word in each space.

In the summer of 1970 we spent two weeks camping in northern England. It rained every day. The —————————— (1) year we spent two weeks camping in the south west. Again it rained every day. It may not surprise you,—————————— (2), that in 1972 we decided to go —————————— (3) where we would be certain to have good weather for at ——————— —————————— (4) two or three days of our holiday.

We spent many a dark winter evening discussing —————————— — (5) to go to southern Turkey, Jugoslavia or Spain. It was a short newspaper articles which finally decided the matter —————————— (6) us. We —————————— (7) go overland to Turkey by —————————— ———(8) of Holland, Germany, Austria, Jugoslavia and Greece.

I spent —————————— (9) weekend in March, April and May working on our car. Although I —————————— (10) always kept it in first-class condition, it was by —————————— (11) means new, and I wanted to make sure that there was nothing which ——— —————————— (12) threaten the success of our 4000—————————— (13) journey. Meanwhile, my wife took —————————— (14) of all those matters which required letters to be written and forms to be completed. This may sound a comparatively simple job. In fact, it was quite the ——— —————————— . (15)

At last the great day arrived. We had packed the car the evening —————————— (16) so that —————————— (17) we had to do was have a hurried breakfast, lock up the house and set off. We had gone no more —————————— (18) five miles when, as I was waiting for the traffic lights to change from red to green, another car crashed into the back of us. —————————— (19), neither my wife nor I was injured, but our poor car was a complete wreck. Our Turkish adventure had come to sad —————————— (20) with only 3995 miles to go.

Read (2000:106–107) notes 'there has only been a small amount of research that has investigated this "rational cloze" in a systematic way with second language learners'. Such investigation may be difficult to conduct as, apart from the unconscious and interrelated nature of these aspects of processing, individuals may vary in the way they process deleted items. There is thus some debate on what is being tested where only single word items are deleted in gap filling tests which employ 'rational' or selective deletion by the item writer of individual words. Is it testing the ability to recognise which form of the word is required and/or lexical knowledge. i.e. lexical access, or is it testing any of the higher level processes in our model?

Kintsch and Yarbrough (1982) suggest cloze tests are not sensitive to macro processes but related only to micro processes. Markham's (1985) study showed that cloze procedure does not provide an adequate assessment of inter-sentential comprehension (the ability to build an accurate mental model) which led him to conclude that 'cloze procedure may not yield a valid and reliable assessment of global comprehension in second language context' (Markham 1985:423). Kobayashi (1995) provided evidence that cloze tests are likely to measure local comprehension whereas open-ended questions can more easily target global comprehension (see also Alderson 1978). In other words, whereas other constructed formats such as short answer questions can measure the reader's global comprehension of main ideas of the text and text structure, cloze tests or selective deletion gap filling items do not necessarily reflect the reader's ability to comprehend beyond the sentence.

Gap filling would appear to measure only a limited part of what might constitute reading proficiency in terms of the processing model we presented in Figure 2.1 above, namely lexical access, syntactic parsing skills and establishing propositional level meaning. It does not usually require the higher level of processing involved in text level reading or ongoing text representation (see, however, Bensoussan and Ramraz (1984) who proposed the deletion of phrases to try to test understanding of the functions of sentences and the structure of the text as a whole). Anecdotal evidence suggests that after many candidates take single word gap filling tasks they are often unable to say what the passage was about and so the candidate's knowledge of text representation or the integration of information would not seem amenable to investigation by this procedure.

The more restricted tasks are in terms of the level of processing required to complete them in terms of the framework of reading types and cognitive processes outlined in Figure 2.1 above, the more difficult it might be (especially at upper proficiency levels like CAE and CPE) to generalise from scores on the test to statements about students' reading ability in real life. It is difficult to determine what the student would have to score on these lower level processing tests to be deemed to have demonstrated adequate reading ability, and to be deemed a competent reader, since such tests normally only tell us about the processing involved in careful local reading to establish propositions at the sentence level. In addition, we have no evidence concerning the other levels of processing or types of reading on which we might premise a more grounded inference. On its own, therefore, a test of the ability to replace single words is likely to be an insufficient indicator of a candidate's reading ability because of the restricted processing involved. If the purpose of a test is to sample the range of our hypothesised components of reading, including inferencing, mental and situation model building and establishing an overall text level representation, then additional techniques to gap filling are essential.

In Chapter 1 (pages 90–91) we described how a major development in Cambridge English tests occurred in the early 1990s with the introduction of a paper between FCE and CPE at the C1 level of the Common European Framework of Reference viz the Certificate of Advanced English (CAE). The new examination showed clearly the effect of concurrent developments in the communicative teaching of English. Grabe (personal communication) comments:

> . . . the role of the CAE revisions in the 1990s is an important pivot to newer innovations in reading test tasks. It represents a significant change to construct-driven assessment guidelines and task formats that are still central to reading assessment discussions today.

1991: CAE – A communicative examination for the 1990s

Hawkey (2009) provides a definitive account of the development of the innovative CAE examination and we draw heavily on that volume in our description of the conceptualisation of the CAE reading test below (see Appendix A for copy of the first 1991 CAE reading paper). The significant innovations of the CAE are clear, in particular its attempts to achieve greater authenticity of task and to tap into a wider range of cognitive processing levels.

The degree of specification that was provided for the examination contrasts sharply with the almost nonexistent information available on ESOL tests before the 1980s (see Chapter 1 *Enhanced specification and new level examinations in the communicative era* (pages 87–92)). The guidelines for the new CAE Paper 1 Reading, for example, provided information on:

- outline of paper, general approach, nature of texts and rubrics
- list of target abilities (micro-skills)
- texts: specifications, lengths, sources, genres, iconic forms
- authenticity and permissible modification
- examples of (un)acceptable text topics, levels, types
- item and task types, formats
- item difficulty.

Hawkey (2009) describes how the Paper 1 Reading would use texts 'selected to test a wide range of reading skills and strategies with various types of matching and multiple-choice items'. The *Specifications* state that the texts concerned would be authentic 'in form and content', with titles and sources supplied. Texts could be in the format of several shorter pieces, which might be brought together for the purposes of the examination to form a larger text (e.g. a magazine feature). Text types would include:

- informational; opinion/comment; descriptive
- advice/instructional; narrative; imaginative/journalistic
- persuasive; complaint; or
- combined types, e.g. narrative/descriptive; informational/opinion.

'Authenticity' of presentation would be emphasised, for example using actual newspaper extracts in near their original forms, giving details of sources and other contextualisation.

The CAE Reading paper specifications announced possible item types including various forms of multiple-choice, cloze and matching. Task items could come before as well as after the text to encourage the candidate to search the text expeditiously for specified information in the case of the former or carefully in the case of the latter. Questions printed after the text for careful reading items would normally appear in the same order as the information in the text. Items calling for understanding of the text as a whole would tend to come towards the end of the careful reading items. In expeditious items the order would not necessarily correspond to the order of information in the text. Target *reading micro-skills* would include:

- forming an overall impression by skimming the text
- retrieving specific information by scanning the text
- interpreting the text for inference, attitude and style
- demonstrating an understanding of the text as a whole
- selecting relevant information from the text required to perform a task
- demonstrating an understanding of how the text structure operates
- deducing meaning from context.

Two new reading formats, *multiple matching* (Parts 1 and 4) and *matching paragraphs with a gapped text* (Part 3), made their appearance as modifications of the traditional 4-option multiple-choice questions in various reading papers in the Upper Main Suite (UMS). They could lay claim to being less susceptible to guessing than the standard Multiple Choice Questions and to facilitate processing which approximated more closely to real-life processing in various reading types (see Khalifa and Weir 2009 Chapter 3 for a full discussion of this). In the second type of matching they involved candidates in forming a representation of the whole text and required higher level processing for successful completion. We now turn to examples of each.

This introduction of a variety of test formats in the latter part of the 20th century can be seen as an attempt to guard against method effect and the possibility of construct irrelevant variance interfering with the measurement of the reading skill.

Matching

Matching is a variant on multiple-choice tests and it can take a variety of forms, all of which can be scored objectively. A range of different matching methods can be found in the current Cambridge English language examinations.

Multiple-matching

In multiple-matching tasks, candidates are required to locate a section of text where an idea is expressed, discounting ideas in other sections which may appear similar but which do not reflect the whole of the question accurately. Some of the options may be correct for more than one question, and there may be more than one correct answer to some questions. If so, the instructions to the candidates will say this. Multiple-matching tasks conform to one of two basic patterns:

- matching two lists, e.g. people to opinions expressed, companies to services offered
- matching a list to location in the text, e.g. matching statements to sections of text where they appear.

CAE 2008 Sample Paper Part 4

You are going to read an article containing reviews of crime novels. For questions **20–34**, choose from the reviews (**A-F**). The reviews may be chosen more than once.

Mark your answers **on the separate answer sheet**.

In which review are the following mentioned?

a book successfully adapted for another medium	20
characters whose ideal world seems totally secure	21
a gripping book which introduces an impressive main character	22
a character whose intuition is challenged	23
the disturbing similarity between reality and fiction within a novel	24
an original and provocative line in storytelling	25
the main character having a personal connection which brings disturbing revelations	26
the completion of an outstanding series of works	27

the interweaving of current lives and previous acts of wickedness $\quad$ 28 ☐

a deliberately misleading use of the written word $\quad$ 29 ☐

a rather unexpected choice of central character $\quad$ 30 ☐

an abundant amount of inconclusive information about a case $\quad$ 31 ☐

a character seeing through complexity in an attempt to avert disaster $\quad$ 32 ☐

a novel which displays the talent of a new author $\quad$ 33 ☐

the characters' involvement in a crime inevitably leading to a painful conclusion $\quad$ 34 ☐

CHILLING READS TO LOOK OUT FOR

Some recommendations from the latest batch of crime novels

A Zouache may not be the obvious heroine for a crime novel, but November sees her debut in Fidelis Morgan's wonderful Restoration thriller *Unnatural Fire*. From debtor to private eye, this Countess is an aristocrat, fleeing for her life through the streets of 17th-century London. Featuring a colourful cast of misfits and brilliantly researched period detail, *Unnatural Fire* has a base in the mysterious science of alchemy, and will appeal to adherents of both crime and historical fiction.

B Minette Walters is one of the most acclaimed writers in British crime fiction whose books like *The Sculptress* have made successful transitions to our TV screens. Preoccupied with developing strong plots and characterisation rather than with crime itself, she has created some disturbing and innovative psychological narratives. *The Shape of Snakes* is set in the winter of 1978. Once again Walters uses her narrative skills to lead the reader astray (there is a clever use of correspondence between characters), before resolving the mystery in her latest intricately plotted bestseller which is full of suspense. Once again she shows why she is such a star of British crime fiction.

C Elizabeth Woodcraft's feisty barrister heroine in *Good Bad Woman*, Frankie, is a diehard Motown music fan. As the title suggests, despite her job on the right side of the law, she ends up on the wrong side – arrested for murder. No favourite of the police – who are happy to see her go down – in order to prove her innocence she must solve the case, one that involves an old friend and some uncomfortable truths a bit too close to home. *Good Bad Woman* is an enthralling, fast-paced contemporary thriller that presents a great new heroine to the genre.

D *Black Dog* is Stephen Booth's hugely accomplished debut, now published in paperback. It follows the mysterious disappearance of teenager Laura Vernon in the Peak District. Ben Cooper, a young Detective Constable, has known the villagers all his life, but his instinctive feelings about the case are called into question by the arrival of Diane Fry, a ruthlessly ambitious detective from another division. As the investigation twists and turns, Ben and Diane discover that to understand the present, they must also understand the past – and, in a world where none of the suspects is entirely innocent, misery and suffering can be the only outcome.

E Andrew Roth's deservedly celebrated Roth Trilogy has drawn to a close with the paperback publication of the third book, *The Office*, set in a 1950s cathedral city. Janet Byfield has everything that Wendy Appleyard lacks: she's beautiful, she has a handsome husband, and an adorable little daughter, Rosie. At first it seems to Wendy as though nothing can touch the Byfields' perfect existence, but old

sins gradually come back to haunt the present, and new sins are bred in their place. The shadows seep through the neighbourhood and only Wendy, the outsider looking in, is able to glimpse the truth. But can she grasp its twisted logic in time to prevent a tragedy whose roots lie buried deep in the past?

F And finally, Reginald Hill has a brilliant new Dalziel and Pascoe novel, *Dialogues*, released in the spring. The uncanny resemblance between stories entered for a local newspaper competition and the circumstances of two sudden disappearances attracts the attention of Mid-Yorkshire Police. Superintendent Andy Dalziel realises they may have a dangerous criminal on their hands – one the media are soon calling the Wordman. There are enough clues around to weave a tapestry, but it's not clear who's playing with whom. Is it the Wordman versus the police, or the criminal versus his victims? And just how far will the games go?

Matching paragraphs with a gapped text

A gapped-text task consists of one text from which a number of sentences (e.g. at FCE), or paragraphs (e.g. at CAE and CPE), have been removed and placed in jumbled order after the text together with a further sentence or paragraph which does not fit in any of the gaps and functions as an additional distractor. Candidates are required to decide from where in the text each sentence or paragraph has been removed. Each sentence or paragraph may only be used once. An example from CAE is provided below.

CAE sample reading paper 2008 Part 2

You are going to read an extract from a magazine article. Six paragraphs have been removed from the extract. Choose from the paragraphs **A–G** the one which fits each gap (**7–12**). There is one extra paragraph which you do not need to use. Mark your answers **on the separate answer sheet**.

THE HONEY-GUIDE

The message most frequently declared by one species to another is simple and straightforward – 'Go away!'. But inter-species communications can be more complicated than that and can, on occasion, even be co-operative. The honey-guide is a good example of this.

The honey-guide is a lark-sized bird that lives in East Africa. Its diet is insects of all kinds and it has a particular liking for the grubs of honey-bees. Getting them is not easy, however. Wild African bees build their nests in hollow trees or clefts in rocks. The honey-guide's beak is slender and delicate so the bird cannot cut away wood, still less chip stone. If it is to procure its favourite food, it has to recruit a helper, usually a man.

In northern Kenya, where honey-guides still live in some numbers, the men of the semi-nomadic Boran tribe specialise in collecting honey. Indeed, their standing within the tribe will depend on the frequency and quality of their honey collecting.

7	

As soon as the two have registered one another's presence, the bird flies off with a peculiar low swooping flight, spreading its tail widely as it goes so that the white feathers on each side of it are clearly displayed. The man follows, whistling and shouting to reassure the bird that he understands its summons and is following.

8	

It is now up to the man to take the initiative. If the day is hot, a stream of bees may be buzzing in and out of the entrance. Something has to be done to pacify them if the man and the bird are not both to get badly stung. The man lights a fire close to the nest and, if possible, pushes burning sticks into holes beneath it so that smoke swirls up around the nest itself.

9	

The honey-guide can in turn get its share. It flies to the remains of the wrecked nest and pulls out the fat white bee-grubs from the cells of the combs. It also, very remarkably, feeds enthusiastically on the wax. It is one of the very few animals that can digest it. The bird does not find its bees' nests by accident. It has a detailed knowledge of its territory and knows the exact location and state of every bee colony within it.

10	

When the bird starts guiding the man, it does not wander about at random but leads him directly to the nearest nest. And the reason it leaves him for a short period just after their initial meeting is because it makes a quick flight to the nest it has in mind, perhaps to check that it is still flourishing.

11	

There is ample evidence to suggest that the bird has been plundering bees' nests for a very long time and that, therefore, the relationship with man is an ancient one. Human beings have certainly been collecting honey in this part of the world for some twenty thousand years, as is proved by rock paintings that show them doing so. Perhaps the partnership was forming as far back as then.

12

It is a powerful digger with very strong forelegs and it can squeeze into very narrow openings. It can even rival a man in pacifying the bees. Like its cousins, it has a large scent gland below its tail which it rubs all round the nest entrance so that the wood or rock is smeared with scent. The smell is so powerful that the bees are stupefied, and human beings who have peered inside a plundered nest after a visit by one of these animals have said that they were made almost as dizzy as the bees themselves.

A But the bird probably had other honey-hunting helpers even earlier still. The ratel, a badger-sized relative of the skunk, is also a lover of honey. A honey-guide encountering one will behave in just the same way as it does towards the man. When they reach the bees' nest, the ratel tackles it with great efficiency.

B Nomadic tribesmen like this spend most of the year travelling across a vast area in search of a variety of food. Their way of life is clearly illustrated in the rock paintings found in East Africa.

C The bird may now disappear for several minutes. When it comes back, it perches some distance away, calling loudly and waiting for the man. As the two travel together, the bird stops and calls frequently until its song changes into one that is low and less agitated. It then falls silent and flutters to a perch, where it stays. Beside it will be a bees' nest.

D Furthermore, if, having reached the nest, the man for some reason does not open it, the bird, after a pause, will once more give its 'follow-me' call and lead him to another.

E Watchers in camouflaged hides have observed a bird visiting every one of its bees' nests, day after day, as though mapping them out and checking on their condition. On a cold day, when the bees are quiescent, it may hop onto the lip of the entrance and peer inquisitively inside.

F When one of them sets out to do so, he begins by walking into the bush and whistling in a very penetrating way. If he is within the territory of a honey-guide, the bird will appear within minutes, singing a special chattering call that it makes on no other occasion.

G With the bees partially stupefied, he now opens up the tree with his bush knife or pokes out the nest from a rock cleft with a stick and extracts the combs, dripping with rich, deep-brown honey.

There is a strong argument for the use of such gapped texts/tasks as a response method at higher proficiency levels, especially in terms of their placing more demands on cognitive processing of a text, so as to distinguish reading ability at these levels from that at lower levels, where less complex forms of matching may be used. In CAE, for example, the reader needs to understand the whole text in order to be sure of having completed the gapped-text task correctly. The testing focuses of text structure, text cohesion and coherence require the reader to select an option which fits the text both before and after the gap. This means that it should fit not only the immediate co-text but also fit so that the text after the gap follows on smoothly. Readers need to identify not only a wide range of linguistic devices which mark the logical and cohesive development of a text, but also to understand the development of ideas, opinion and events [over the whole text] rather than the recognition of individual words. Finding which paragraph fits into which gap in a given text may require the reader to understand how the text develops from start to finish rather than just the section of text which occurs before and after the particular gap.

To conclude, matching is less subject to guessing than multiple-choice questions as there are a greater number of options to choose from. The questions set in this technique normally try to cover the important information in a text: main ideas, gist and at higher levels text representation in careful reading, and scanning for detail and search reading global for main ideas in expeditious tasks. Matching is a flexible and useful format as it allows the coverage of all the reading types described in our model in Figure 2.1 above and all of the levels of cognitive processing as appropriate to the level of candidates being assessed.

Encouraged by the innovative developments in CAE and the greater attention paid to examining the construct that was being measured in the communicative era, similar improvements can be seen in the Upper Main Suite FCE and CPE Reading examinations in the 1996 FCE and the 2002 CPE revisions (see Weir and Milanovic (2003) for details of the 2002 CPE revision and Hawkey (2009:83–89) for the 1996 FCE revision to their respective reading papers).

Optical scanning of the objective responses on the Reading paper was designed to enhance rating reliability and to economise on marking fees so that more funding was available for the most expensive paper, Speaking. But the marking forms would, despite the additional expense involved, have 10 rather than the usual four spaces to shade in, to accommodate the new multiple-matching tasks.

Reading into writing

With the introduction of CAE we see the return to favour of reading into writing tasks; further testimony to its communicative pedigree. Hawkey (2009) describes how CAE Paper 2 (Writing) consisted of two tasks of approximately 250 words, each carrying the same marks (see Appendix A CAE 1991 for copies of both these tasks). For the first task there would be no choice, making it a useful standardising measure. It acted as an anchor item against the choice from four variable writing tasks in the second section and ensured a degree of similarity of test experience. The CAE Writing tasks were to be as authentic as possible, contextualised in terms of their purpose and intended audience. In both sections of the Writing paper candidates would be completing non-specialist tasks based on materials drawn from sources such as: newspapers/magazines, leaflets, notices, announcements; personal notes and messages; formal and informal letters; invitations; reports, reviews; instructions. The candidate's presentation, register and style would be assessed in terms of their appropriacy to the task.

In the first question writing skills would be integrated with reading in that candidates would be asked to produce pieces of writing in response to a 'substantial reading input'. 'Satisfactory processing of this input would be required to complete the task(s) successfully.' The kinds of responses required would include: applying the information contained in the input to another task; selecting and summarising information from the input; eliciting information on the basis of the input; comparing items of information from the input. In the second question in the Writing paper, candidates would be required to write in response to one task selected from four 'based on a range of writing activities such as: articles; reports; letters; instructions and expanded notes'. Task descriptions would, true to Communicative Language Teaching principles, outline the content required and specify purpose and intended audience. Labels such as 'essay' or 'composition' were avoided in the CAE Writing sub-test rubrics, as suggested in the CEIC review.

The integration of reading and writing was to be one of the hallmarks of the new examination which made reading demands at both the text and intertextual levels as well as appearing to initiate all the cognitive processing activities associated with advanced level writing (planning, organisation, translation, monitoring and revision) as detailed by Shaw and Weir (2007) in Chapter 3 on cognitive validity in their book *Examining Writing* (see also Chapter 3 below for a discussion of the socio cognitive approach to writing test validation).

Reading into writing activities are indeed well supported in the current research literature on writing assessment (Grabe and Stoller 2002:14) and have been used in high stakes writing tests around the world, for example, up to 1995 in IELTS, more recently in iBT TOEFL and since the 1980s in TEEP (see Weir 1983), CAE and CPE Part 5 in the Use of English paper. Pollitt and Taylor (2006) make a convincing argument for this type of task as does Hughes (2003).

There is obviously a good case for providing input in writing tests where provision of stimulus texts reflects the real-life situation (e.g. in response to an informal email from a friend at the lower levels, or the writing of university assignments at the higher levels. (See Moore et al 2010 for a criticism of a serious deficit in IELTS in this respect.) The highest level of processing in our model in Figure 2.1 above is where students have to integrate information across texts to develop a combined representation of the texts they have read (see Weir, Hawkey, Green and Devi (2009) and Weir, Hawkey, Green, Unaldi and Devi (2009) for a detailed study of undergraduate reading habits and the relationship with the IELTS reading test). Summary or an integrated reading into writing activity would seem to be among the most appropriate techniques for doing this. Such an approach also helps ensure equal access to domain knowledge among candidates and reduces the potential bias that such internal knowledge can have.

The impact of background reading as task input on the quality of L2 written production has been investigated by Lewkowicz (1997). Whilst offering students a rich source of ideas, the provision of a background text in her study did not appear to enhance quality of writing. Moreover, there was evidence of significant 'lifting' of the input task material by students (see also Shi (2004) for discussion of this issue) and encouraged reliance on the language of the source text. Lewkowicz found that the provision of an input text in her tasks tended to restrict the development of ideas as compared to the situation where students were not given a text.

Integrating reading with writing activities not surprisingly presents problems for markers in making decisions about what level of borrowing from these texts is permissible and in being confident about what the candidate is capable of actually producing rather than just copying. The extent of borrowing can be reduced by ensuring that the writing task demands a significant level of input language transformation from the candidate, i.e. the candidate has to do something more than simply lift input material. Additionally, it may be necessary to make clear to candidates what is not permissible in terms of borrowing from the text provided, and also limits may have to be set on how much text can be quoted as in real-life rules concerned with plagiarism. Systematic training in preparation for such test tasks and a clear understanding of the ground rules is of course both essential and beneficial.

Integrated reading into writing tasks would go somewhat out of favour by the end of the 20th century disappearing from the IELTS test in 1995 (Charge and Taylor 1997), and the input reading texts were to be scaled down radically in CAE. However, it is revealing that TOEFL iBT has recently incorporated integrated reading/writing tasks. The 'revival' in using integrated reading/writing tasks as a measure of reading and/or writing abilities has been the focus of recent research, in particular in relation to the new TOEFL (e.g. Cumming, Grant, Mulcahy-Ernt and Powers 2004, Cumming, Kantor, Baba, Eedosy, Eouanzoui and James 2005).

An interesting version of the reading into writing task would however be introduced into the Use of English Paper Section 3 in CPE from 2002 (see example below) where candidates have to summarise two texts. It comes closer to creating an intertextual representation than any other previous task at CPE and offers a more demanding task (in terms of processing) than those currently employed in CAE. It is intended that the task should be moved to the CPE writing paper in 2012 following the advice given in Shaw and Weir (2007:246–247).

Sample from CPE Use of English 21 June 2005

Part 5

44 In a paragraph of **50–70** words, summarise **in your own words as far as possible** the reasons given in **both** texts (A and B below) to explain the continuing popularity of the motor car as a form of transport.

Write your summary **on the separate answer sheet**.

Many people in the western world consume half their lives, three quarters of their energy and 99% of their emotions in travelling, without once using their legs and, arguably, without ever really getting anywhere; and no one seems to stop for long enough to ask why. 'The pedestrian remains the largest single obstacle to free traffic movement,' a Los Angeles planning officer reportedly once said. It's an attitude which typifies 20th-century urban planning in the western world and goes a long way towards explaining why so many cities are dominated by cars.

The inevitable result is a world where the motor car rules supreme; one with cities hemmed in by ringroads and flyovers, with sprawling suburbs where nobody walks and residents must drive endless kilometres for work or nourishment. In such an environment, children no longer play outside their houses or walk to school; people no longer stroll along the street or stand outside talking to the neighbours. Pedestrians have all but disappeared from the streets – and walking from the culture.

Moreover, people seem to live in complete awe of the device to which they have surrendered their lives,despite knowing that it denies them the clean air, peace and quiet and a pleasant living environment they claim to value so highly. It must have something to do with the fact that, once inside, they enjoy the unreal sense of power that comes from a complete surrender to mechanism. For although I'm not alone in regarding the car as a fearsome engine of destruction, nobody seems prepared to give it up.

B

Traffic congestion in Britain could be eased if it weren't for the nation's addiction to the absurd cult of the lone driver. But let's face it, sharing cars is something the British just don't do. Next Monday morning the streets will be overflowing with cars once again, most with spare seats front and back, and there will be few lifts on offer for those friends or colleagues who have no choice but to trudge through fumes or jostle in bus queues.

Many drivers, it seems, echo the view of one former transport minister who observed, albeit light-heartedly, that with cars 'you have your own company, your own temperature control and your own choice of music – and you don't have to put up with dreadful human beings sitting alongside you.' Many a true word, it seems, is said in jest. Indeed, sharing would threaten the very independence that makes the car such an attractive option in the first place. Offer a colleague a regular lift and you're locked into a routine as oppressive as any other, with all individual flexibility lost. So, what's in it for the driver?

> But even in a motor-obsessed city such as Los Angeles, drivers have been won over by the idea of car-sharing. It is attractive because cars with more than one occupant are allowed access to fast moving priority lanes. So desirable are these amid the six lanes of jam-packed traffic that, in the early days, Californian students charged motorists several dollars a time to pick them up.

Present day constructs

Building on the work of Bachman (1990) which informed validation activities in the 1990s, as well as the VRIP (Validity, Reliability, Impact, Practicality) approach developed by Cambridge in the same period, skills assessment at Cambridge is now underpinned more formally than ever before by a validation framework based on Weir (2005a). The approach not only allows Cambridge to determine where current examinations are performing satisfactorily in relation to a range of relevant validity parameters, it also provides the basis for improvement and the construction of an ongoing research agenda.

The Main Suite examinations in reading now offer a carefully graded set of stages which cover the progression up the proficiency continuum in reading from KET at A2 in terms of the CEFR up to CPE at the C2 level. Khalifa and Weir (2009:34–142) provide a detailed and comprehensive description of this progression in the Main Suite Reading tests in terms of the specific contextual and cognitive parameters outlined at the start of this chapter. Drawing on Khalifa and Weir we now present a brief overview of the cognitive and contextual validity of the current Cambridge Main Suite examinations concerned with the reading construct

Cognitive validity in the current reading papers

Examinations in the Main Suite would seem to follow the order of difficulty in cognitive processing, lower level to higher level, that is suggested by the model in Figure 2.1 above and the literature (see Khalifa and Weir (2009:34–80) for an extensive explication of the cognitive processing model). The term lower-level is used here, as in other psycholinguistic contexts, to refer to processes that take place when a message is being decoded into language. Higher-level processes are those associated with building meaning.

The attentional resources of a reader are finite and, in the early stages of L2 development (A2 level candidates), one might expect a large part of those resources to be diverted towards lower level considerations concerning the linguistic code. No matter what the L1, decoding processes are reliant upon recognising not only letters but letter clusters, grapheme-phoneme correspondence (GPC) relationships and whole words. Decoding at the level of form is bound to be problematic for the low level L2 reader – only assisted by the extent to which there are cognates in L2. Whereas in L1 word recognition is usually highly automatic for practised readers, new form–meaning relationships need to be set up gradually for L2 and only slowly become automatised.

The effort of decoding makes considerable cognitive demands on the less skilled reader and as a result is likely to become the principal focus of attention for many up to the A2 level and the main focus for tests set at these levels. There is often a failure to employ comprehension processes (e.g. using contextual information to enrich comprehension or higher level meaning building) partly because of the demands of decoding and partly because of the unfamiliar situation of reading a text where there are gaps in understanding and words and phrases are perceptually unfamiliar (see Perfetti 1985).

Textually implicit questions require the reader to combine information across sentences in a text and such questions are generally more difficult than explicit items based on a single sentence given the additional processing that is required (see Davey and Lasasso 1984). Oakhill and Garnham (1988) suggest that the less skilled reader fails to make a range of inferences in comprehension, from local links between sentences, to the way(s) the ideas in the whole text are connected. Hosenfeld (1977) likewise shows that use of inferencing strategy can discriminate between good and poor readers (see also Chamot and El-Dinary 1999).

Inferencing makes an appearance at A2 and B1 level in a few items at the sentence level but it is only at FCE (B2) and above that it begins to be tested widely and across larger areas of text. From FCE onwards, certain question types require the candidate to report not on information contained in the text but upon what that information entails.

Until learners have relatively automatic processes for dealing with word recognition, lexical access and syntactic parsing i.e. lower level processing, meaning-construction beyond dealing with base information in sentence level propositions is restricted. This is usually well established by the B2 level, when there is likely to be more processing capacity available in working memory for making propositional inferences, building a mental model and integrating information.

Tasks requiring understanding of text level representation may be less suitable below a C1 level in the CEFR (CAE in Cambridge Main Suite examinations) because of the more demanding processing required for their successful completion. Thus the ability to cope with questions requiring the candidate to develop an overall text representation of argumentative texts now only takes place on reaching the C1 (CAE) level.

The highest level of processing – that required to construct an intertextual representation of several texts – currently comes into play at the C2 (CPE) level albeit in the Use of English paper. In terms of our model presented in

Figure 2.1 above, we would argue that the ability to engage in such higher level processing activities (i.e. those associated with building meaning) is appropriate at this level of language proficiency whereas a task demanding lower level processing skills only (i.e. Part 1 in CPE; see example above pages 145–146) is not. Given the limited time and space available for testing reading skills and strategies and the necessity to establish clear water between proficiency levels, it might be prudent to ensure that a reading paper at the C2 level is eliciting data on the ability to cope with the higher level cognitive processes required in forming textual or intertextual representations.

Reading types and cognitive processes

In general across the current suite of Cambridge examinations, the range of careful and expeditious reading types we established in our model in Figure 2.1. above are covered appropriately, although there are a few anomalies at CAE and CPE that may merit consideration e.g. the absence of search reading global items critical for academic study (see Khalifa and Weir (2009:62–80) for an extended discussion of this). In general the reading types are roughly calibrated to reflect the demands they are assumed to make upon the candidate in terms of the levels of language processing upon which they draw. The processing necessary for these reading activities can be imagined as a cline from decoding through the various layers of meaning construction as we move upwards through the suite. In grading the specifications for the five levels of the suite, careful thought has been given to the assumed cognitive difficulty both of the tasks and of the texts employed. Text demands are increased only gradually; and the more demanding types of reading, for example reading to comprehend the whole text and integrate information across texts, are reserved for higher levels of the suite (see Appendix B for evidence of increasing text complexity between FCE, CAE and CPE).

This analysis of the Cambridge ESOL Main Suite examinations is based on expert judgement and does not include research evidence from readers' views of their real-life reading, or from how students set about answering these reading questions in examinations. These require the generation of empirical evidence – obtainable through observation (possibly using modern, computerised, eye tracking technology; see Bax and Weir (2012)), survey and protocol analysis. Such research is necessary to provide further support for the relationship between the examination and real-life reading. Weir, Hawkey, Green and Devi (2009) and Weir, Hawkey, Green, Unaldi and Devi (2009) demonstrate some of the ways this might be done in relation to reading at undergraduate level in the United Kingdom and discuss how processing in real-life reading equates with the processing of reading items in IELTS.

Context validity in current reading tests

So far in the discussion of current ESOL reading examinations we have said little about the performance conditions, the contextual parameters under which reading activities take place. Drawing on the findings in Khalifa and Weir (2009:81–142) we can identify how Cambridge has attempted to calibrate test input along a number of dimensions. For example the length of a text and the frequency of vocabulary in a text will affect ease of reading. The complexity of the text is a function of how such contextual parameters are realised within it. Both individually and in combination they are likely to impact on the cognitive demands imposed upon the reader. A text with high frequency lexis is likely to be easier to process than a text of the same length on the same topic with a large number of low frequency lexical items. A shorter text is likely to be easier to process than a significantly longer text *mutatis mutandis*. A calibration of a number of the key parameters affecting cognitive load across Main Suite levels is relevant here and is discussed next. Key contextual parameters in current reading tests are summarised in Table 2.2 below.

KET

The cognitive load imposed by the texts is likely to be relatively low, thanks to short sentence length, simple sentence structure, simple conceptual relationships within and between sentences and the familiar nature of the vocabulary used.

PET

Again lexis is familiar and structures mainly simple and easy to parse. Propositional complexity is quite low and inter-sentence relationships are quite simple.

FCE

The cognitive load is increased by the use of a broader range of vocabulary some of which may be unknown to the candidate or less familiar, sentence structure and propositional content is more complex and text length is greater. The range of patterns from simple to complex at FCE as against mostly simple sentences at PET, and total text lengths amounting to 2,000 words as opposed to around 1,500 at PET add to the increase in cognitive demands between these two adjacent levels in the Main Suite.

CAE

The cognitive load in the parts testing careful reading for main ideas (Parts 1 and 3) is also increased by the use of more complex passages and a broader range of source materials than at FCE. This complexity is evidenced in a broader range of vocabulary including idiomatic expressions

Table 2.2 The cognitive demands imposed by relative text complexity at each stage in our examples of Cambridge ESOL Main Suite Reading Papers (Khalifa and Weir 2009)

	Overall number of words	Time allowed	Lexis	Grammatical structure
KET (A2)	Approximately 740–800 words	35 items with a recommended 40 minutes	Restricted to common items which normally occur in the everyday vocabulary of native speakers.	Mainly simple sentences / single independent clauses, which contain a subject and a verb, and express a complete thought.
PET (B1)	Approximately 1460–1590 words	35 items with a recommended 50 minutes	General vocabulary sufficient for most topics in everyday life.	Mostly simple sentences but some use of relative and other subordinate clauses.
FCE (B2)	Approximately 2000 words	30 items administered in 60 minutes	Good range of vocabulary. Topics are addressed in detail and with precision.	A range of sentence patterns – from the simple to the complex.
CAE (C1)	Approximately 3000 words	34 items administered in 75 minutes	Broad range of vocabulary including idiomatic expressions and colloquialisms as well as language relating to opinion, persuasion and ideas.	This level is typified by: many complex sentences; frequent use of modals; some use of ellipsis; complex approaches to referencing; use of synonymy.
CPE (C2)	Approximately 3000 words	40 items administered in 90 minutes	Very wide range of vocabulary including idiomatic expressions and colloquialisms as well as language relating to opinion, persuasion and abstract ideas.	Most sentences are long and complex. No restriction on the types of structure employed by the text. Many examples of structures typically used for effect in writing – sentences with several subordinate clauses, for example.

and colloquialisms as well as language relating to opinion, persuasion and ideas some of which may be unknown to the candidate or less familiar. There are also a number of quite low frequency words. The prevalence of more complex grammatical structures as opposed to a spread of patterns from simple to complex at FCE. Text lengths amounting to 3,000 words as opposed to 2,000 at FCE. Changes in these parameters add to the increase in cognitive demands between these two adjacent levels in the Main Suite (see Appendix B for details).

CPE

In terms of length both CPE and CAE texts are very similar. Vocabulary range is hard to distinguish between the two except perhaps for the treatment of abstract ideas at CPE, many examples of structures typically used for effect in writing, and occurrence of the language associated with conative purpose (see Khalifa and Weir (2009:81–142) for a more in-depth discussion). Sentence structure may be slightly more sophisticated at CPE and occasionally longer sentences may be used which may occasion slight differences in sentence complexity (see Appendix B for a discussion of these contextual factors and how they link to cognitive processing).

Lexical development across Cambridge ESOL levels

There are a number of points to notice with regard to lexical development throughout the current Cambridge ESOL examinations. Inevitably, as candidates progress up the levels of the Main Suite examinations, the lexical demands that are put upon them are stronger. The amount of less frequent, less well-known vocabulary increases. The number and complexity of the items that they are required to understand increases by level. Lexis at lower levels is restricted to everyday, literal and factual language. As students advance, they are gradually expected to deal with increasingly subtle uses of the language of feelings and ideas. The senses associated with the words are less concrete and issues of polysemy may arise. More abstract texts will not be presented to candidates until levels C1 and C2 (CAE and CPE). Fiction beyond that written especially for L1 children normally requires a broader receptive vocabulary and this is introduced from FCE onwards taking the vocabulary beyond the familiar everyday vocabulary found at KET and PET.

From FCE upwards the extent to which the text deals with or includes content and/or language extending beyond the knowledge or personal experience of the reader increases. By CPE the candidate may be exposed to texts on any subject.

Grammatical structures across Cambridge ESOL levels

The key points which relate to the structural resources used in reading texts in Cambridge ESOL practice are:

- A survey of the papers across the five levels shows a very clear progression in terms of sentence structure from short, simple sentences to long complex sentences. This is mirrored in the length of the texts used as very short texts are used at KET level and increasingly longer ones are employed at higher levels.

- This structural progression does not mean that some short sentences may not pose considerable difficulty and so still have a place in higher level texts. Ellipsis and colloquial use of language may make for short sentences that are hard to process and so only appropriate at more advanced levels.

- An increasing complexity of verb forms is also noticeable in texts as we move up the Cambridge ESOL levels. The use of modals, conditionals, inversion and other structures becomes more common as the texts used in the examinations become more concerned with conveying feelings and opinions, persuading and hypothesising rather than dealing simply with information as they do at lower levels.

- As well as sentence length and verb form, referencing is an aspect of structure that becomes noticeably complex in higher level texts where a reader needs to engage in quite complex anaphoric resolution and be aware of the contribution of synonyms to text coherence. In addition, as one progresses up the levels propositional density and the complexity of relationship between propositions increases and adds to the cognitive load.

A way forward: The automated analysis of contextual validity features

In Appendix B we report on a systematic, quantitative analysis of Cambridge CPE reading texts 1913–2012 using Cohmetrix Version 2, an automated text analysis procedure. This offers a principled and systematic methodology for establishing the complexity of a text in future tests through automated analysis of a range of salient, quantifiable, contextual parameters, in particular lexical and syntactic. It provides detail of the stability of Cambridge CPE examinations in its various reading tasks across the century in terms of a range of contextual indices and identifies where there are large differences which could be addressed in developing reading tests in the future.

Appendix B also attempts the specific linking of each contextual parameter to an associated effect on cognitive processing. So in this Appendix we can perhaps begin to see more clearly the symbiotic relationship between contextual and cognitive parameters. It is probably only at this micro level of description that we will be able to clearly identify the precise interactional relationship between the two.

Endnote

We have now completed our survey of the measurement of the reading construct at Cambridge from 1913 up to 2012. It showed how reading had become one of the core focuses in Cambridge English tests by 1975 rather than being subsumed within more traditional integrated tasks such as translation, essays on English literature or reading aloud.

The chapter illustrated the increased attention paid to testing reading as a macro skill in its own right, as staff responsible for examining English in Cambridge become more professional, and external developments in applied linguistics and cognitive psychology, as well as communicative classroom practice from the 1970s onwards, helped clarify and broaden the potential focuses and methods for assessing the reading ability construct in Cambridge English language examinations.

We now turn in Chapter 3 to a closer inspection of the writing tasks which had been a central part of English language examinations since the first CPE in 1913. These range from the original 2-hour essay task in 1913 to an intertextual representation of the summary of two reading texts in 2012.

3 The measurement of writing ability 1913–2012

Cyril J. Weir

University of Bedfordshire

Introduction: Direct versus indirect tests of writing

> The writing of Essays shews two things; what a man has to say, and how he can say it.
> *On the Action of Examinations Considered as a Means of Selection* (Latham 1877:261)

> The best way to test people's writing ability is to get them to write.
> *Language Testing for Teachers* (Hughes 1989:75)

The concern in this chapter is with the *direct* testing of written language performance which, along with the direct testing of spoken language, has been a stable feature of Cambridge English examinations since 1913. By a 'direct' test of writing we mean one which measures writing ability through involving candidates in the actual construction of extended, continuous, written text (see Hamp-Lyons (1991:5–6) and Weigle (2002:58) for further definition) in contrast to 'indirect' or 'objective' tests of writing which principally focus on a receptive knowledge of the micro linguistic elements of writing through completion of multiple-choice, cloze, gap filling or error recognition response formats (Hyland 2002:8–9).

In indirect tests the overall skill of writing is subdivided into more specific 'discrete' elements, e.g., of grammar, vocabulary, spelling, punctuation and orthography, and attempts are made to test these formal features of text typically by the use of selective response, objective test formats. Such indirect 'objective' tests seriously under-represent writing skills as they are only measuring parts of what we understand to be the construct of writing ability. While what they test may be related to proficient writing as statistical studies have indicated (Godshalk, Swineford and Coffmann 1966:40), they cannot fully represent what proficient writers can do (Hamp-Lyons 1990). It might nowadays be seen as 'adventurous' to generalise from performances on these types of test to how candidates might perform on productive tasks which require the construction of a complete extended composition or to make direct statements about how good a writer might be in a target situation context. White (1995:34) is convincing on the difference:

> Every essay test shares the artificiality of all tests, but it does require an active response rather than the passive submission called for by multiple-choice examinations. While it is naive to imagine an essay test as a valid measure of all writing, it is disingenuous to ignore the fact that the production of writing for an essay is a wholly different activity than filling in the bubbles on an answer sheet.

Hamp-Lyons (2001:3) also makes a telling case for direct writing tests:

> ... multiple choice tests cannot measure the skills that most writing *teachers* identify as important to effective writing: inventing ideas and arguments; building material into a coherent and effective overall structure to convince, persuade, and teach readers; revising and editing one's own work to more closely approximate conventions of accurate and excellent text and to meet the expectations of a range of audiences ...

This chapter first examines a gradual shift from an oral to a written basis for assessment in the United Kingdom in the years leading up to the 20th century in order to help us better understand why writing ability in English as a foreign language appears as a paper in its own right in the inaugural Cambridge English examination in 1913.

We then turn to a general overview of approaches to assessing writing in the 20th century and examine the role of the essay in the United States as well as the United Kingdom. We describe a shift from the essay, a direct writing task, to multiple-choice indirect formats in the United States and then back again to the essay over that period. In the United Kingdom we note the uninterrupted reliance on the essay as the means of providing evidence on writing ability throughout the 100 years under review and focus on the more pressing iterative concerns of most United Kingdom Examining Boards regarding the *scoring validity* of the essay task (e.g. issues relating to the development of appropriate criteria of assessment and scales, and consistent rating).

Having established the general background for the assessment of writing in the 20th century in the United Kingdom and United States, we then describe the *contextual* and *cognitive* parameters of a socio-cognitive, conceptual framework applicable to the assessment of writing. These parameters are used in the second part of the chapter, together with relevant parameters from the earlier *scoring validity* discussion, to inform a detailed analysis of how Cambridge assessed writing ability in English as a foreign language from 1913 to 2012.

From spoken to written tests in the 19th century

In Chapter 2 we described the gradual transition from oral to silent tests of reading ability by the 20th century. A similar change from oral to written assessment, in particular involving the essay (see Horner 1990), is evident in other examination practice. For example, the traditional *viva voce* in university undergraduate examinations at Oxford and Cambridge had been largely replaced by written examinations by the end of the 19th century (see Stray (2001, 2005) for scholarly accounts of this), although it still survives in the PhD thesis defence to this day. Russell (2002:3) describes a similar situation in academia in the US:

> ...before the 1870s writing was ancillary to speaking. Because the whole curriculum and much of the extra curriculum was based on public speaking (recitation, declamation, oratory, debate), there was little need for systematic writing instruction.

One of the main drivers of a general shift from oral to written assessment practice in the United Kingdom was the need to select people according to capability and to put an end to the long-standing practice of patronage and elitism. Tattersall (2007:44) describes how:

> In 1838 the University of London set a matriculation examination to facilitate objective selection for entry to the two colleges in order to avoid the privilege inherent in the Oxbridge systems.

Sutherland (2001:52) describes a similar situation in the medical profession:

> Examinations were seen as disinterested because they were the sword which had been used to hack at the luxuriant, rank, corrupt growth of patronage. This had been the role assigned to them by the radicals in London medical education as early as the 1830s.

The introduction of an entrance examination for the civil service followed the 1854 *Northcote-Trevelyan Report* in Britain. This Report on the organisation of the permanent Civil Service identified patronage as a source of endemic inefficiency and public disrepute, and recommended open, competitive, written examination based on merit as a way of overcoming this. Up until 1854 the *Patronage Secretary* to the Treasury in the United Kingdom had nominated candidates for appointment to posts in the Civil Service. The first exams were held for the Indian Civil Service in 1858, and the exams for the Home Civil Service followed Gladstone's Order in Council in 1870. These new written examinations ensured that entrance to the civil service was competitive and that promotion was based at least partially on merit even if it did little to alter the social composition of the service.

In 1855 the first Civil Service Commissioners were appointed and set up an office – the Civil Service Commission – to run written examinations and to give approval for the appointment of civil servants. Written examinations gained precedence thereafter and were seen as more likely to achieve appointment by merit than the earlier oral examinations (see Latham (1877) on the value of these new written examinations).

> We are of opinion that this examination should be in all cases a competing literary examination. This ought not to exclude careful previous inquiry into the age, health, and moral fitness of the candidates. Where character and bodily activity are chiefly required, more, comparatively, will depend upon the testimony of those to whom the candidate is well known; but the selection from among the candidates who have satisfied these preliminary inquiries should still be made by a competing examination. This may be so conducted as to test the intelligence, as well as the mere attainments of the candidates. We see no other mode by which (in the case of inferior no less than of superior offices) the double object can be attained of selecting the fittest person, and of avoiding the evils of patronage (Northcote and Trevelyan 1854:11).

The introduction of written examinations in the British Civil Service might be considered rather slow off the mark when compared to the earlier use of competitive written examinations to select officials in China on the basis of merit and knowledge rather than patronage (see Miyazaki (1976) and Cheng (2008) for accounts of these early examinations in China). Hamp-Lyons (2002:6) records how:

> In the Chou period (1111–771 B.C.) writing was one of the "six arts" through which sons of the nobility were prepared for the service of the Imperial Court, using the writing system that had been developed more than a thousand years earlier (and that is basically the same today)...Throughout a thousand-year period, the writing skill was rigorously evaluated as a prerequisite for imperial, governmental or feudal service. The establishment of a national university during the Han period (206 B.C.–220 A.D.) formalised the system of written examinations.

The delay in the introduction of written examinations into the United Kingdom is partially explained by the long tradition of oral examinations in the West (Morris 1961:26–27) but its roots lay deeper in the nature of society. Unlike China, where, because of its size, there was a need to establish and maintain a huge network of public officials, in Britain there was no such pressure for the introduction of mass examining techniques. The absence of a centralised educational system in the United Kingdom similarly precluded the need for national examinations and Morris (1961) argues that up to the 19th century examinations in the West were sporadic.

Gradually in the 19th century the oral examination ceased to be an effective instrument and was generally perceived as being open to abuse, as noted above, or to ridicule. P B Ballard in *The New Examiner* (1923:16) cites the extreme example of the Earl of Eldon's account of his examination for a degree at Oxford in 1776 to cast doubt on the procedure:

> I was examined in Hebrew and History, 'What is the Hebrew for the place of a skull?' I replied 'Golgotha'. 'Who founded University College?' I stated (though, by the way, the point is sometimes doubted) that King Alfred founded it. 'Very well' said the examiner, 'You are competent for your degree.'

Stray (2001, 2005) provides a fascinating and erudite account of the move from oral to written assessment at Oxford and Cambridge from the 18th century onwards, where concerns over patronage, elitism and merit were mounting. He places the rhetorical display involved in the undergraduate *viva voce* examination firmly in the culture of 'gentlemanly orality' and charts its virtual disappearance by the late 19th century (2001:47). He sees this as a shift from 'socio-moral assessments of members of status groups, toward purely cognitive assessments of individuals' (2001:8–9) and provides an insightful summary of the whole social process (2001:113):

> The individual emerges from a social nexus in which social status is a vital determinant of the way he or she is treated, and in which he is to a large extent a known quantity to become a bearer of intellect which is to be assessed on a par with any other. The differential treatment . . . fades away in the face of the examination machine . . . In the oral tradition, individuals were usually interrogated by individuals; when printed papers were introduced, the focus shifted from such one-to-one relationships to the standardized testing of groups. A climate of patronage gave way slowly to a climate of access via examination.

Sutherland (2001:51) chronicles similar motivation behind the spread of public written examinations in the 19th century. She describes

> . . . the increasing use made of formal written examinations by occupational groups aspiring to professional status in nineteenth and early twentieth century England. At first such groups devised their own examinations; subsequently they also came to use the examinations of an expanding education system. In deploying the instrument of the

examination professions were also invoking the challenge to patronage and the appeal to merit which it symbolised.

Stray (2001:47–48) identifies a further driver for change in the pressure of increased numbers of students presenting themselves for examination at Oxford in the 19th century, which overloaded a *viva voce* procedure where there were insufficient examiners to cope with individual oral presentations (Latham (1877:179) refers to the same problem in his appraisal of the *viva voce*). Stray (2005:101) refers to the 1850 Royal Commission on Oxford, which in its historical retrospect stated that after the 1807 reforms:

> . . . the increase in the number of the Candidates had an effect which had not been foreseen. It became necessary that the Examination should be conducted more and more on paper, and therefore knowledge of Philosophy, together with skill in Composition, increased gradually in importance, and perhaps skill in Construing proportionably declined.

Here again we see how social change often affects the nature of examinations (cf the weight of numbers behind the growth of the dominant paradigm of objective testing in the United States in the early 20th century described in Chapter 1) and how yet again practicality impacted on language testing.

Stray (2005:111) provides further detail of how the written examination at Cambridge in the 18th century spread to other British universities in the 1820s and 1830s and to written examinations at the East India Company's college at Haileybury from 1807. The importance of the formal written examination as an instrument of assessment became established in the United Kingdom and it has maintained its dominance to this day.

The teaching and testing of writing in the United Kingdom in the 19th century

Teaching

Ferreira-Buckley and Horner (2001:173–174) describe how the sovereignty of the classical languages was eroded in the 19th century in England and 'writing instruction in English evolved in response to social, political, religious and economic developments'. At the beginning of the 18th century most textbooks and manuals had been written in Latin, the language of the educated classes. Indeed grammar schools were precisely that, a place to study Latin grammar intensively in order to turn out pupils who could read and write in Latin. As Latin declined, English became the language of instruction in education across the curriculum and students wrote in English more and more. By the second half of the 19th century, according to Horner (1990:325), publications were mostly in English, and writing, which had largely been confined to sermons and letter writing in earlier times, increasingly 'became the medium of communication and record'.

However, for large sections of the population, writing literacy in early 19th century England was often discouraged. Gillard (2011) describes how

> Campaigners for reform in England found themselves up against vicious hostility to the very idea of universal education. One Justice of the Peace, for example, opined in 1807 that: 'It is doubtless desirable that the poor should be generally instructed in *reading*, if it were only for the best of purposes – that they may read the Scriptures. As to *writing* and *arithmetic*, it may be apprehended that such a degree of knowledge would produce in them disrelish for the laborious occupations of life' [from Williams 1971:156].

Ferreira-Buckley and Horner (2001:196) identify a similar class anxiety:

> Defying the many who believed that the poor should remain illiterate, the evangelical Hannah More pioneered efforts to teach reading to the poor (typically their aim was to make the bible accessible) but she refused to teach writing on the grounds that such skill might make them ungovernable.

Gillard (2011), drawing on Williams (1961:157) points out that by 1835 the average duration of school attendance was just one year and by 1851 it had only risen to two. As late as 1841, 33% of all Englishmen and 44% of Englishwomen signed marriage certificates with their mark as they were unable to write even at the word level for social purposes. In 1861 an estimated 2.5m children out of 2.75m received some form of schooling, 'though still of very mixed quality and with the majority leaving before they were eleven' (Williams 1961:137). The Elementary schools provided only basic education to poor students who were not going on to higher education. In the main it was students from higher class backgrounds that went to the grammar schools or private tutories which prepared them for university.

Testing

From 1862 the system of payment by results for teachers in Elementary schools included standards for writing as well as for reading and arithmetic (see Armytage (1965:124–125) for discussion of the pros and cons of this system). The 1882 Standards (Midwinter 1970:84) ranged from:

Standard I	Form on blackboard or slate from dictation, letters, capital and small manuscript
Standard II	Copy in manuscript character a line of print
Standard III	A sentence from a short paragraph in an elementary reading book, slowly read once and then dictated in single words
Standard IV	A sentence slowly dictated once, by a few words at a time from the same book
Standard V	A sentence slowly dictated once, by a few words at a time from a reading book used in the first class of the school
Standard VI	Another short ordinary paragraph in a newspaper, or other modern narrative slowly dictated once, by a few words at a time

Dictation was appropriate as a technique given that the low level of ability of the candidates probably precluded them from tasks that required any planning and organising in their writing.

For the educationally advantaged classes, British university examination traditions helped shape the overall approach to public assessment in the development of Locals Examinations in the second half of the 19th century, the forerunners of 'O' and 'A' levels in the United Kingdom (see Montgomery (1965:48–51) and Roach (1971:77–163) for an account of their history and significance for assessment in the school system in the UK). The purpose of these 'Locals' Examinations is indicated by the name they were commonly known as for many years viz. 'the Middle Class Examinations' (Adamson 1919:283). Sanderson (1975:15) sees them as having 'a vivifying effect on the academic standards of the public schools . . . and on the grammar schools' which in turn improved the standards of entrants to the universities.

In order to set up a high, uniform standard for expanding numbers of candidates in disparate centres across the country the use of oral tests would be problematic; the logistical complications and prohibitive costs of utilising individualised oral tests were clear, leaving aside the questionable reliability of judgements across a multitude of examiners and candidates. Written exams were seen as impartial, fair, administratively efficient, searching in scope, and capable of producing a wider sample of candidate performance.

Watts (2008a:37) describes how in 1858 a number of schools approached Cambridge University for a system of examinations that boys could take in centres in provincial town and cities 'local' to where they lived rather than requiring them to undertake costly rail journeys to Cambridge. Girls had to wait longer and were not officially permitted to enter public examinations until 1867. This development of localised, university-administered, public examinations systems brought educational and employment opportunities to a wider cross-section of the British population than hitherto. It was a critical factor in enabling the development of mass public education and provided a recognised national standard of education.

The University of Cambridge Local Examinations Board was officially established on 11 February 1858. Its first examination took place on 14 December 1858. There were two examinations: the Junior (for students under 16 years of age) and the Senior (for students under the age of 18), and they took place in local 'centres' – schools or any suitable venues like church or village halls. The presiding examiners travelled from Cambridge to examination centres, usually by train, wearing academic dress and carrying a locked box containing the question papers.

1858 Essay questions in English for native speakers

Wednesday, Dec. 15. 1858. 101/2–12

II. 2 English Composition
[NB Only *one* of the following Subjects is to be chosen]
(a) Give an account of the late Indian mutiny
(b) Contrast the life of a soldier with that of sailor in both peace and war
(c) Write a letter to a friend in Australia announcing your intention to emigrate and asking for information
(d) Discuss the change produced in the habits of the people by Railways

---

There were serious concerns about the performances of many students on these new examinations (over one third failed the Cambridge Locals according to Roach (1971:96) as against two thirds who failed the Oxford Locals). The Cambridge Assessment website records how:

> After the very first public examinations were taken by 370 15-year-olds in Birmingham, Brighton, Bristol, Cambridge, Grantham, Norwich, Liverpool and London, one examiner despaired: "Their answers, even when accurate, showed a general uniformity of expression which seemed to imply that meagre handbooks had been placed before the students to be 'got up' and that little attempt had been made by their instructors to excite the interest of their pupils by questionings or remarks of their own".

The Syndicate's first annual report, published in 1859 said:

> The general tone of the Examiners' Report may perhaps to some seem somewhat unfavourable to the performances of the Candidates. But it must be remembered that the greater number of the Candidates were under sixteen years of age, unused probably to written examinations . . .

It also comments on the nature of the content expected from the candidate:

> In the Syndicate's early History, Geography, Science and Scripture papers, question after question asks for the recall of facts, often from set books or periods of history, or sections of the Bible . . . This reflects a view of the educated person as being a collector of knowledge . . . Not surprising at a time when new worlds of knowledge were opening up. Think of Charles Darwin spending five years on 'The Beagle' collecting facts about animals and plants. His 'Origin of Species' was published just the year after the Cambridge local exams began . . .

This focus on facts is perhaps not so surprising when one considers that *Commonplace Thinking* formed part of a long tradition for the literati in society. *Commonplacing* referred to the extracting of information on a topic by borrowing information from books and ordering and recording particular phrases or passages in notebooks of their own (see Kelly (1976:157–58) for an account of its place in the history of written transcription). They identified gobbets of information which could be used later in various discursive contexts. Montaigne's *Essaies* (1575) have their origins in his commonplace book.

The nature of English language writing tests in the 20th century

During the 20th century the nature of written examinations in the United States was to take a different turn from those in the United Kingdom and before considering the latter we will briefly examine the American experience where psychometric concerns were to take assessment away from the direct testing of writing (see Chapter 1 for details). In the United Kingdom the focus was to remain on direct tests of writing throughout the period under review. The method for testing writing was to have a clear impact on the construct being measured.

United States

Hamp-Lyons (2001) describes the first three generations of writing assessment in the United States as: *direct* testing (i.e. essay tests); *multiple-choice* testing; and *portfolio-based* assessment. She points out that it is not normally acknowledged that direct assessment of writing was the first rather than the second generation in writing assessment in the United States, preceding rather than being a reaction against multiple-choice, 'objective', testing (see also Hobbs and Berlin 2001 for a similar breakdown). Russell (2002:158) provides an analogous perspective:

> The history of the essay examination illustrates a central shift in the ways that learning was conceived of from the old curriculum to the mass education system; from communal oral performance in the rhetoricals and oral examinations to an individually written synthesis in an essay examination and finally to an individual performance on an aggregate of discrete objective items.

Haswell (2004) provides evidence of a growing interest in *first generation* written examinations in the United States towards the end of the 19th century. He notes how in 1874 Harvard University added a writing component to their entrance examinations, a short extemporaneous essay rated by teachers. Hobbs and Berlin (2001:251–2) describe it as an essay on 'such works of standard authors as shall be announced from time to time'. They concur with Applebee (1974) that the essay was designed to test writing ability, not knowledge of literature and argue that the new entrance examination was decisive in shaping English courses in secondary education.

Lunsford (1986:1) describes how the Harvard catalogue stated the essay should be: 'correct in spelling, punctuation, grammar and expression'. More than half of the students failed the essay examination, and many had to take 'sub freshman' courses or undergo extra-curricular tutoring. Ten years later the outcomes were still no better, and Harvard moved its sophomore forensic English course to the first year, dubbing it English A (Russell 2002:53), turning it into a remedial writing course required of everyone who did not exempt out of it; this was the birth of 'Bonehead' English as it is quaintly known in some circles today (Stone 1974).

Moore, O'Neill, and Huot (2009) amplify the story behind this development in America echoing a shift from Latin similar to the change in the language of choice experienced in the British education system in the 19th century:

> ... the composition entrance examination and the mandatory composition courses that followed from it were originally designed to foster educational and structural changes at both the secondary and post-secondary levels. As part of his goal to change the language of learning from Latin and Greek to English, Harvard president Charles Eliot added an examination in English composition to the battery of entrance exams in 1874. A key component of the formation of Harvard's writing program—considered to be the first modern composition program—was the testing of incoming students' performance in written English ... Harvard's move to include written English composition in its entrance exams and curriculum quickly spread to other prestigious North-eastern schools and beyond. By 1900, these exams were commonplace features of higher education in America.

So before the psychometric domination of testing in the United States in the 20th century that we described in Chapter 1, the essay was well regarded, at least in some circles, for university admissions.

The College Board (which later joined forces with ETS for its Admissions Testing Program) began testing writing ability with essay tests in 1916 (Godshalk, Swineford and Coffmann 1966). A spokesman for the College Board describes the situation in the early 20th century:

> The "College Boards" were traditional written examinations and so too were the second generation of College Boards, the "Comprehensives." Still using the essay, free response, written examinations, they were based on a much more generalised course content in order that colleges might draw upon students from secondary schools which, because they did not traditionally prepare for college board colleges, were not following the standard carefully prescriptive syllabi.
> (www.education.nic.in/cd50years/g/52/76/52760A01.htm)

However things were to change. As we saw in Chapter 1, a belief in the value of extended writing was to be replaced by an almost unquestioning faith in indirect, objective measures of writing assessment. Raimes (1990: 430) describes the transition:

> It was in 1947 that the College Board first experimented with testing writing objectively without an essay. An objective section was included in the English Composition Test (ECT), one of the subject area Achievement Tests. When the Board compared the essay with the objective section and with course grades and teachers' ratings, the findings were that a 60-minute essay would have "markedly less predictive value [of teachers' ratings of ability to write expository prose, and course grades in English] than a full length test composed entirely of objective material" . . . Objective approaches then replaced the essay in the ECT.

Spolsky (1995a:65) was positive about the College Board's adoption of objective true/false questions and questioned the continued reliance on a choice from a wide range of options in the subjectively scored essays in Cambridge English examinations. However, the switch to an objective format as against written composition by the College Board in the United States was not entirely the result of psychometric enlightenment but more one of war-time exigency. In a talk given by a speaker from the Board in the late 1960s the following reasons were given:

> These were the circumstances in 1941 when history in the more usual sense intervened and the United States became directly involved in the Second World War. Travel restrictions made it impossible to assemble readers to grade centrally; as was the custom for written comprehensives

and so the template-scoreable Objective Tests became the "College Boards." (op. cit.)
(www.education.nic.in/cd50years/g/52/76/52760A01.htm)

More crucially, the speaker took pains to point out:

> ... as one studies our large-scale use of objective testing for university entrance, one must remember that the ultimate battle between the respective proponents of essay examinations and objective tests was never joined; that the ultimate definitive debate over the relative merits of hand-written, people-graded examinations and hand-stroked, machine scored tests was never held. It was the fortunes of a real war, so to speak, that swept S.A.T. and the Achievement Tests through our cross roads of decision in the United States without a murmur of dissent and that some of the continuing controversy over the use of objective tests in our country reflects the fact that – the debate never took place, that the issues were never clearly drawn, the necessary accommodations and compromises never satisfactorily derived. (op. cit.)

Yancey (1999), in her account of developments in the history of writing assessment in the United States, identified the implementation of objective tests as the predominant format used to evaluate learners' composition skills from the 1950s to 1970s. TOEFL was first administered in 1964 following its inception at a meeting organised by the Center for Applied Linguistics. From the outset it followed the prevailing orthodoxy and employed indirect objective measures to assess writing. The decision against direct testing of writing apparently was also influenced by the cost of sending examination books by air mail (Spolsky, personal communication). It was to take TOEFL a long time to offer the Test in Written English in place of indirect measures. It was not until the 1986–87 testing year that the Test of Written English (TWE) was added to the TOEFL on an experimental basis in direct response to the widely-felt criticism that the TOEFL only measured writing proficiency indirectly with unfortunate consequences in terms of its negative washback on teaching and student preparation for university study.

Yancey (1999) described how objective assessments of writing were gradually replaced during a subsequent assessment phase (1970–1986) characterised by the use of the holistically scored essay, promoted by increasingly reliable procedures for assessing writing developed from the 1960s onwards (see for example empirical support for this in the work of Godshalk, Swineford and Coffmann (1966)). Hillocks (2008:325) reports how:

> in the 1980s, in the United States certain states began the direct testing of writing, using samples of writing rather than objective tests. At present, nearly all but two or three of the 50 states require such writing exams.

Yancey concluded her overview by describing a third phase in the United States at the end of the 20th century that was largely influenced by the portfolio approach to writing assessment; one instigated by teachers rather than assessment specialists. (See Hamp-Lyons and Condon (2000) for a comprehensive treatment of portfolio assessment.) Portfolio assessment involved the evaluation of a body of texts 'written in non-testing situations over an extended period of time' (Weigle 2002:59). Supporters of this approach were often overly critical of the use of the essay as an assessment tool. White (1995:31) provided a reasoned defence for the use of the essay in assessment in American schools and warned these critics that:

> The time has come for portfolio advocates, among whom I number myself, to recognize the important role essay testing has played in the past – and can still play – and to stop attacking essay testing as an unmitigated evil in order to promote portfolios, which can stand very well on their own. The recent turn against essay testing is a natural result of conversion to a new and more convincing belief system which seems to demand denunciation as well as renunciation of the old one.

He stressed the need to remember that for many in the US, in particular administrators, the alternative to the essay was not the portfolio but objective multiple-choice questions and forcefully reminded its critics (1995:32) that the essay:

> . . . developed as a response by writing teachers to the dominant multiple-choice testing in American education . . . Anyone with a role in writing assessment must keep in mind the multiple-choice spectre that hovers just off stage; no stake has ever been driven through its heart to keep it in its coffin, however much it may be wounded.

White concluded that essays were not an invalid measure of writing but a form of writing which provided useful information about writing ability even if they did not necessarily measure *monitoring, text editing* and *revision (* these key stages in a cognitive processing model of writing are discussed below).

Despite widespread support for the impromptu essay test compared to multiple-choice questions by the late 20th century, the proportion of time and weight allocated to it in examinations remained limited in the United States. It is noticeable that, although contemporary ACT and SAT have a section on writing, only twenty-five minutes are provided for students to write. IbT TOEFL is similarly restricted:

> You have 20 minutes to plan and write your response. Your response will be judged on the basis of the quality of your writing and on how well your response presents the points in the lecture and their relationship to

the reading passage. Typically, an effective response will be 150 to 225 words.
http://www.ets.org/Media/Tests/TOEFL/pdf/ibt_writing_sample_responses.pdf.

In contrast the essay was to assume a more important place in the United Kingdom assessment system throughout the 20th century.

United Kingdom

In comparison to the insightful histories of written assessment in the United States (Hamp-Lyons 2001, 2002, Hobbes and Berlin 2001, Huot, O'Neill and Moore 2010, Raimes 1990, Yancey 1999), there appears to be no comparable monograph that deals comprehensively with changes in the teaching and testing of writing in the United Kingdom. The reason for this may simply lie in the uninterrupted reliance on the essay/composition to provide evidence of student writing ability in the British education system throughout the 20th century. There were to be no major sea changes as there were in the United States with its initial acceptance of direct writing tasks, then after the psychometric tsunami a switch to indirect, reductionist measurements with multiple-choice questions on 'discrete' linguistic features of writing, followed by a return to favour of essays and finally an interest in portfolio assessment in a number of educational sectors (Hamp-Lyons 2001).

The reductionist view of assessing writing objectively through its constituent parts found little favour in the United Kingdom (Hamp-Lyons 2002:10) where, as we saw in Chapter 1, the emphasis was on what was being tested and the effect this had on those preparing for examinations. Wiseman (1949) was an early advocate for the direct approach because of his concern for a positive backwash effect (consequential validity as it is known today) for examinations.

In the later part of the 20th century there was certainly a growth of interest in the process of writing on the ESOL teaching side in the United Kingdom (for example see Hedge 1988 and White and Arndt 1991). However, most examinations in the United Kingdom remained firmly rooted in a focus on product rather than process often at the expense of cognitive validity as a result. The notable exception to this was the continuous assessment models being implemented in some subject based Certificate of Secondary Education/ General certificate of Educations (CSE/GCE) examinations in the United Kingdom beginning in the early 1970s (and maintained in the 1990s under the National Curriculum), which provided a model for the later proponents of portfolio assessment in the United States and Canada. In these Mode 3 examinations the school determined its own syllabus, set its examination and carried out the marking subject to approval and moderation by the board. These ideas were first aired at the Dartmouth Conference in the United States in 1966 (see Sublette 1973) where the 'British growth model' with its emphasis on 'process and personal growth' generated a good deal of interest (Trimbur 2008).

Tattersall (2007:23) added a necessary note of caution:

> The [Joint Matriculation Board] JMB, for example, had introduced an English O level in 1967 based entirely on coursework, which proved to be extremely popular . . .The examination continued until 1994 when the rules governing coursework were tightened and 100% course-assessed examinations were proscribed. The increased use of coursework added to the difficulties of applying comparable standards across schools, regions and nationally.

Concerns with the reliability of assessment in this form of Mode 3 examination never went away though (at least as far as the examination boards were concerned) and with the appearance of the internet, the Qualifications and Curriculum Authority (QCA) in 2006 further restricted coursework to the classroom in order to prevent plagiarism.

The main issue with regard to examining writing in most of the British education system throughout the 20th century would not be with the nature of the tasks themselves, over which there was little debate, but rather with the various parameters of *scoring validity*. Before looking more closely at assessment practice in Cambridge we will examine how scoring validity was addressed in general by United Kingdom examining boards in the past.

Scoring validity in the United Kingdom: The marking of writing in the late 19th and 20th centuries

Scoring validity accounts for the extent to which writing test scores are arrived at through the application of appropriate and representative marking criteria, exhibit consensual agreement in the marking, are as free as possible from measurement error, stable over time, and engender confidence as reliable decision-making indicators. Drawing on Weir (2005a) we outline the parameters we are concerned with in this aspect of validity (see Figure 3.1 below).

The first scoring validity parameter is that of the *criteria* and type of *rating scale*. Weigle (2002:09) quotes McNamara (1996) on the centrality of the rating scale to the valid measurement of the writing construct:

> . . . the scale that is used in assessing performance tasks such as writing tests represents, implicitly or explicitly, the theoretical basis upon which

the test is founded: that is, it embodies the test (or scale) developer's notion of what skills or abilities are being measured by the test. For this reason the development of a scale (or set of scales) and the descriptors for each scale level are of critical importance for the validity of the assessment.

Figure 3.1 Aspects of scoring validity for writing (based on Weir 2005a)

SCORING VALIDITY
• Criteria/rating scale
• Rater characteristics
• Rating process
• Rating conditions
• Rater training
• Post examination adjustment
• Grading

Three discrete and separate sources of variability in the direct assessment of writing were also identified by McNamara (1996:121). Variability associated with: *candidate* (relative abilities of candidate will probably differ unless the task is too easy or too hard); *task* (particularly where the candidate is given a choice of tasks to select from – no two tasks, for example, measure exactly the same thing and so tasks may interact with candidate idiosyncrasies to make them appear slightly more or less difficult to different candidates or groups of candidates); and *rater* (the greater the degree of judgement exercised by a rater, the greater the scope for the rater to exhibit severity or leniency – that quality that causes him or her to systematically under- or over-mark all similar tasks or differ in the marks from those that would have been given by a different rater).

McNamara (1996:123–5) details four ways in which raters may be at variance with one another in the rating process:

1. A pair of raters may differ in terms of their tendency to overall leniency.
2. Raters may exhibit bias towards certain groups of candidates or types of task. Such bias may manifest itself in sub-patterns of either severe or generous marking giving rise to two kinds of interaction: *rater-item interactions* (the tendency for a rater to display consistent severity on one particular item type whilst simultaneously showing consistent generosity on another item type) and *rater-candidate interactions* (the tendency for a rater to over- or under-rate a candidate or a group of candidates).
3. Raters may reveal differences with regard to their consistency of rating behaviour. In other words, the degree of the random error related to their judgements.

4. Raters may display differences in how they interpret and apply the rating scale instrument. In their actual interpretation of the scale, raters do not behave in identical ways. Systematic variations may exist amongst raters in the manner in which they employ the available mark range. For example, some raters may exhibit *central tendency* (when a rater tends to give ratings clustered closely around the mid-point on the scale) whilst others may consciously restrict their use of the scale to its extremities, preferring instead to perceive differences between candidates more 'starkly and hedging their bets less' (McNamara 1996:124) i.e. consistently rating higher or lower than the performance merits, or than other raters.

The *rating conditions* under which marking takes place (e.g. temporal, physical or psychological) are increasingly seen as having a potential impact on scoring and need to be standardised too. As Weir (2005b: 200) noted: 'papers marked in the shady groves of academe may receive more considered treatment than those scored on the 5.30 rush hour tube out of London on a Friday afternoon'.

The importance of *rater training* has been stressed in the literature (Alderson, Clapham and Wall 1995:112, Bachman and Palmer 1996:222, Brown 1995, Lumley 2002, Weigle 1998, Weir 1988:89). Alderson et al (1995:105) argue that it is widely accepted in second language writing assessment circles that the training of examiners is crucial to validity in testing language performance and emphasise the vital role training has to play in the removal (or at least the reduction) of rater variability.

Statistical analysis of examiner performance normally takes place after marking is complete. Scaling of writing is one accepted statistical method for detecting errant writing examiners and this is often used in *post examination adjustment* to alter their marks to bring them in line with the population of markers as a whole. Multi-faceted Rasch analysis is a further possible procedure for ensuring fairness in marking that will be discussed below.

When examination papers have been marked and a series of checks to ensure that all candidates have been assessed accurately and to the same standards have been carried out, *grading* of examinations takes place. A Grading Meeting is held to review the performance of candidates and to set the boundaries for each grade, according to the performance criteria defined for that grade. At this meeting, reports and analyses which have been carried out on the score data, and in relation to various groups of candidates, are reviewed according to an established procedure.

Those responsible for the examination review the item analysis and descriptive statistics and this enables them to confirm whether the examination materials 'performed' as predicted by the pretesting and standards fixing activities which were carried out during the question paper production cycle. They then compare the performance of the entire candidature and large groups of candidates (or cohorts) with performance in previous years. In combination, this ensures that the standards being applied are consistent and fair to all candidates, and that a particular grade 'means' the same thing from year to year and throughout the world (Shaw and Weir 2007, Weir and Milanovic 2003).

This seems to resonate with the description provided by Crofts and Caradog Jones (1928:45–46) on how statistics were used to address grading issues at the Northern Universities Joint Matriculation Board (JMB) in the United Kingdom in the early days:

> Where large numbers of candidates are being dealt with, the variation of standard among them from year to year is small, or, at any rate, small compared with the variations we know take place in the standard of examiners. The candidates are not like a fruit crop, which may suffer blight and produce poor results in any one year; in normal percentage of passes in the important subjects fairly constant from year to year. The Chief Examiners should therefore be asked . . . whether their percentage of passes differs much from previous years, and if so to state what in their opinion is the cause of the difference, and whether there is any reason why the figures should not be altered so that the final figure might be brought into line with the previous one.

Where documentation has been preserved we will refer to these parameters in our discussion of historical approaches to scoring validity in the United Kingdom in the 20th century below. As Shaw and Weir (2007:143–217) point out, scoring validity is critical because, if we cannot depend on the rating of examination scripts, it matters little that the tasks we develop are potentially valid in terms of both cognitive and contextual parameters. Faulty criteria or scales, unsuitable raters or procedures, lack of training and standardisation, poor or variable conditions for rating, inadequate provision for post examination statistical adjustment, and unsystematic or ill-conceived procedures for grading can all lead to a reduction in scoring validity and to the risk of construct irrelevant variance. If scoring validity is compromised this may vitiate all the other work that has gone into creating a valid instrument (Alderson et al 1995:105). Examination boards need to devote attention and resources to each of these aspects of scoring validity.

In the 19th century, Edgeworth (1888) had observed that one-third of scripts marked by different examiners in the British civil service examinations received a different mark and, further, that in a re-examination of scripts by the same examiner one seventh received a different mark. Edgeworth (1890:653) noted:

> I find the element of chance in these public examinations to be such that only a fraction – from a third to two-thirds – of the successful candidates

can be regarded as safe, above the danger of coming out unsuccessfully if a different set of equally competent judges had happened to be appointed.

Much later in our history, Bardell, Forrest and Shoesmith (1978) found a similar degree of marker (un)reliability in cross-moderation studies conducted by the United Kingdom GCE examining boards in the 1950s and 1960s.

Edgeworth had offered two solutions to these problems in scoring validity: increasing the *number* of components in an examination and *multiple-marking*. He argued the more components that were aggregated, the more likely that individual marker errors would be eliminated. He also stressed that the more markers that were involved in examining a script, the more likely it was that a 'true value' would emerge. In the 20th century a great deal of research was also conducted in the United Kingdom into the criteria for assessment themselves to determine whether *analytic* or *impression* based schemes could further enhance marker reliability. These three potential solutions to marking reliability problems in scoring validity viz number of tasks, multiple marking, and analytic versus impression based marking, are now discussed in turn.

Number of writing tasks

Edgeworth's first solution was that the number of samples of a student's work that were taken could help control for the variation in performance that might occur from task to task. Both scoring and context validity have been found to be increased by sampling more than one composition from each candidate. Finlayson (1951:132) found that: 'the performance of a child in one essay is not representative of his ability to write essays in general'. The research of Vernon and Milligan (1954:69) also threw: 'very grave doubt on the common practice . . . of trying to assess English ability in general from a single essay marked by a single examiner'.

Murphy (1978) found that an important factor in determining the varying reliability of the eight GCE examinations under review was the number of marks for individual parts contributing to the final examination marks. This effect of increasing reliability, by having more parts of an examination was clearly demonstrated by the case of English 'A' level. This observation is consistent with the now established principle that combinations of measurements are more reliable than the individual measurements themselves. The more samples of students' writing that are taken the better this will be for reliability and validity purposes, provided each sample gives a reasonable estimate of the ability in question (see Willmott and Nuttal 1975). Godshalk, Swineford and Coffmann's (1966:39–40) landmark study in the United States reached the same conclusion as Edgeworth, namely that:

The reliability of essay scores is primarily a function of the number of different essays and the number of different readings included. The increases which can be achieved by adding topics or readers are dramatically greater than those which can be achieved by lengthening the time per topic or developing special procedures for reading.

Single or multiple marking

Though some doubt had been expressed in the past (see Edgeworth 1888) about the expediency of having more than one marker, research in British examining Boards in the 1960s and 1970s, for example Britton (1963), Britton et al (1966), Head (1966), Wood and Quinn (1976) all found that multiple marking improved the reliability of marking English essays.

Britton, Martin and Rosen (1966), in an experiment designed to devise a more reliable marking apparatus for use by examining boards, compared experimental multiple marking with the single marking carried out by a GCE examining board. They found (1966:21):

> The figures clearly indicate that in this case marking by individual examiners with very careful briefing and elaborate arrangements for moderation was in fact significantly less reliable than a multiple mark.

When the official marking and multiple marking were correlated with external criteria of coursework produced by candidates throughout the year, multiple marking was found to correspond more closely.

Head (1966) conducted an experiment to discover whether the added impression marks of two examiners would be more reliable than individual examiners. He found (1966:71): 'The raising of the coefficient form 0.64 for single mark correlations to 0.84 for paired mark correlations shows clearly that the added marks were more reliable.'

Wood and Quinn (1976) using 'O' level English Language essay and summary questions found that impression marking by pairs of markers was more reliable than a single marking. They suggest, however, that there is no more to be gained in reliability from a single analytic marking than from a single impression marking. The real improvement is in double marking.

In many of the early studies there often seems to be an unquestioning belief that work marked independently by two different markers, with their marks being averaged, is a more reliable estimate than if it were marked by a single marker. This general viewpoint needs qualifying though, for as was noted by Wiseman (1949) and Wood and Wilson (1974), it is dependent on the markers being equally consistent in their own individual assessments for the duration of the marking period.

Edgeworth (1888) provided evidence that marking behaviour does not remain stable during the whole marking period, when a large number of scripts are involved. Wiseman (1949:208) stressed that: 'The efficiency of markers should be judged primarily by their self-consistency'. He pointed out (1949:204) that intra-rater reliability, the consistency coefficient obtained by a pure mark/re-mark correlation using the same marking method on both occasions 'is the one single measure which is quite clearly a true consistency, and one which is closest allied to the normal concept of test reliability'. If both raters are not equally consistent themselves, the reliability of the more consistent marker on his own might in fact be superior to the combined reliability estimate for two markers who exhibit unequal consistencies. These provisos must be borne in mind in considering the potential value of a double marking system. With an adequate marking scheme and sufficient standardisation of examiners, however, a high standard of inter-marker and intra-marker reliability should be feasible and the advantages of a double as against a single marker system would obtain. By using a system of multiple marking based on this principle of self consistency Wiseman was able to achieve very high levels of reliability.

Tattersall (2007:51) in her wide ranging study of British examining board practice concludes that double marking was undoubtedly feasible – provided that there was an adequate supply of reliable examiners; but notes 'this practice was adopted for English examinations by some boards until burgeoning entries for the subject in the early 1980s made it impossible to recruit sufficient examiners'. Logistical considerations (time, money, computing, personnel) affecting multiple marking were used to support reluctance among examining boards to adopt it in large-scale marking operations (see Penfold1956). Additionally one problem in the past with multiple marking was that examiners sometimes found it difficult to avoid annotating a script to help them form their impression. If this script is to be remarked then the second examiner approaches it in a dissimilar state to the first, the marks have to be tediously removed, or multiple copies of the script need to be made.

In this era of scripts electronically-delivered to markers and online scoring; and with the increasingly common use of automated scoring for some aspects of writing e.g. syntax and lexis, 'logistic' constraints are no longer a tenable argument against double rating either by human raters or by human and computer. Furthermore we now have IRT tools such as multifaceted Rasch to help identify 'errant' human raters without full double marking. Nevertheless, despite a growing consensus in the profession on the need for and the value of double marking, albeit with the intra-marker consistency caveat expressed above, practicality is still proffered as an excuse for not utilising this means of improving scoring validity even in the 21st century.

Analytical versus impression based marking

The scoring criteria in assessing direct writing tasks are a critical part of the writing construct as they establish the level of performance that is required. Analytical marking refers to a method whereby each separate criterion in the mark scheme is awarded a separate mark and the final mark is a composite of these individual estimates. The impression method of marking usually entails two or more markers giving a single mark based on their total impression of the composition as a whole. Each paper is scored using an agreed scale and an examinee's score is the average of the combined marks. The notion of impression marking specifically excludes any attempt to separate the discrete features of a composition for scoring purposes.

Hartog et al (1936) conducted one of the earliest studies into the relative effectiveness of analytical and general impression marking for assessing English composition. They were intent on finding out which method produced the superior results in terms of ability to reduce marker error. Their research found (1936:123) that variation between markers was, to some extent, reduced by the analytical method:

> there are greater discrepancies between marks awarded by impression than between marks awarded by details. . . it appears that these discrepancies are entirely due to greater differences in the standards of marking of different examiners when they mark by impression.

Like Hartog et al (1936), Cast (1939) found the analytical method slightly superior in a single marker system. His criticisms of the impression method were that, though it discriminated more widely among individual candidates, it judged them on more superficial characteristics than the analytical method. However, although the analytical method was considered the more suitable, Cast felt that the results did not provide definitive evidence of the superior reliability of analytical marking and, therefore, refused to advocate the exclusive use of either method.

Cast pointed to important characteristics inherent in the two systems. An important feature of the analytical method to which he drew attention (1939: 263–4) was: 'On averaging their marks for all the questions, the range inevitably shrinks . . . The "regression" is the inevitable consequence of all forms of summation of incompletely correlated figures.' In comparison, he noted (1939:263) that impression marking discriminated more widely among individual candidates and that the range of marks awarded by different examiners to the same script tended to be unusually wide. He also noted the tendency of impression marking (1939:264): 'to seize on a few salient or superficial points – errors of spelling, grammar or fact, perhaps – and weight those out of all proportion to the rest; on the other hand, the analytical methods, by dealing with numerous isolated and possible inessential points, may overlook certain general qualities that characterise the essays as a whole'.

Wiseman (1949) investigated the possibilities of improving assessment by summing the multiple marks of four independent, unstandardised markers, using a rapid impression method compared with an analytic scheme whereby each separate criterion in a mark scheme is applied to the essay, awarded a separate mark and the final mark is a composite of these individual estimates. He found that multiple marking by impression method improved reliability and was much quicker than comparable analytic procedures. He (1949:205) estimated that if the average inter-correlation of a group of four impression markers was as low as 0.6 with each other: 'the estimate of the probable correlation of averaged marks with "true" marks is 0.92. This is in all probability higher than we could expect from *one* analytic marker.'

Penfold (1956) compared impression marking with analytic marking and found the latter much more effective in reducing inter-marker variance than the impression scheme. Morrison (1968) found that using impression marking did not produce more reliable marks than the standard analytical marking procedures employed by the Examining Board at the time. Morrison's findings (1968) were confirmed by a similar study he conducted a year later (Morrison 1969).

Francis (1978) also pointed out that a great danger of impression marking a piece of writing is that impression of the quality as a whole will be influenced by just one or two aspects of the work. He argues that the prejudices and biases of the marker may play a greater part in determining the mark than in the analytical scheme.

A further problem with impression based banding system such as can be found in Carroll (1980:136) and Chaplen (1970) is that they do not cater easily for learners whose performance levels vary in terms of different criteria. A candidate may be a band 7 in terms of 'fluency', but a band 5 in terms of 'accuracy' (see Hamp-Lyons (1984, 1987) for further detail of the innovative assessment guide used for marking the ELTS M2 writing task which attempted to deal with these inherent problems).

This problem of collapsing criteria is avoided by a more analytic mark scheme, whereby a level is recorded in respect of each criterion and to a certain extent one of the most integrative of measures is brought back somewhat to a discrete point position. This method had the added advantage in that it would lend itself more readily to full profile reporting and could perform a certain diagnostic role in delineating students' strengths and weaknesses in written production.

Additionally an analytic mark scheme is seen as a far more useful tool for the training and standardisation of new examiners. Francis (1978) working at the Associated Examining Board in the United Kingdom pointed out that by employing an analytic scheme, examining bodies can better train and standardise new markers to the criteria of assessment. A measure of agreement about what each criterion means can be established and subsequently markers can be standardised to what constitutes a different level within each of these criteria. Analytic schemes have been found to be particularly useful with markers who are relatively inexperienced. The data reported by Adams (1981) and Murphy (1982), also working at the Associated Examining Board, are consistent with this view.

Analytic mark schemes are devised in an attempt to make the assessment more objective, insofar as they encourage examiners to be more explicit about their judgements. Although one of these criteria may take account of the relevance and adequacy of the actual content of the essays, they are normally concerned with describing the linguistic qualities which an essay is expected to exhibit.

Brooks (1980) pointed out that the qualities assessed by mark schemes in the past were often extremely elusive. She cited as examples the qualities 'gusto' and 'shapeliness of rhythm' outlined in the Schools Council Working Paper – Monitoring Grade Standards in English, as being particularly nebulous and inaccessible to assessment. Thus, although analytic schemes may facilitate agreement amongst examiners as to the precise range of qualities that are to be evaluated in any essay, the actual amount of subjectivity involved in the assessment in many schemes may be reduced very little because of lack of explicitness with regard to the applicable criteria, or through the use of vague criteria.

Weaknesses of analytic mark schemes in the past were in the choice and delineation of appropriate criteria for a given situation. In the design work for the TEAP test (see Weir 1983) it was felt that the assessment of samples of written performance should be based on appropriate, analytic criteria graded according to different levels of performance. The criteria needed to be comprehensive and based on empirical job sample evidence. The data informing the selection of criteria of assessment came from a survey carried out on language teachers in ARELS schools, and more particularly from the returns to that part of a national questionnaire to academic staff in the United Kingdom which requested an estimation of the relative importance of the different criteria they employed in assessing the written work of their students. Empirical evidence was gathered from 560 academic staff to help decide upon those criteria which could be used for assessing the types of written information transfer exercises that occur in an academic context. From the returns to the staff questionnaire it appeared there was a need for evaluation procedures that would assess students, particularly in relation to their communicative effectiveness and in such a way that a profile containing a coarse diagnosis of candidates' strengths and weaknesses could be made available. *Relevance and adequacy of content* and *organisation* were seen as the critical criteria for evaluating students' work (Weir 1983). As we note below these criteria appear on an early CPE examination paper (1931) and play an important part in today's assessment of writing in CPE.

The most recent work on this area has been done on IELTS. In a case study on IELTS, Shaw and Weir (2007:161–167) conclude that the IELTS Writing Scale Revision Project indicated that an analytic approach to marking had advantages over an impression banded approach for marking IELTS, not least because of the enhanced marker reliability it led to and the possibilities of more detailed profiling.

Cambridge ESOL had employed both holistic and analytic rating scales in its performance assessments, but by the end of 2011 the new Main Suite and Business English Certificate scales for writing became analytic in the Writing test components and the use of analytic marking schemes was increasing in other areas.

Research suggests that an analytic approach, double or targeted double marking and the employment of multi-faceted Rasch analysis and calibration might serve to increase the scoring validity of Cambridge examinations. We will return specifically to the issue of scoring validity in relation to Cambridge English examinations below.

Scoring validity at Cambridge: The marking of writing 1913–2013

Limited concern in the early years

Spolsky (1995a:65) is disappointed by the apparent lack of concern with reliability in the early years of Cambridge English language examinations.

> ... the issue of reliability that Edgeworth had raised in 1888 continued to be of only marginal interest, and the examinations remained untouched by psychometric notions. One can see this by comparing the 1931 College Board's examination, with its true-false questions, its concentration on language, and its lack of curricular concern, with the forms of the Cambridge papers described above, with their emphasis on curriculum, their inclusion of literature, and their absolute reliance on subjective grading. The Cambridge examiners continued until quite recently to be more concerned about what to test (i.e. about curriculum) than about how to test it.

As we saw in Chapter 1, psychometric considerations in assessment assumed a greater importance at a much earlier stage in the United States than was to be the case in Cambridge examinations. As well as the interest in objective testing in the United States, there had been a strong interest in standardising the marking of written performance from very early on in the 20th century, with Thorndike developing a standardised scale for the measurement of quality in the handwriting of children and also one for the handwriting of women in 1908 (Thorndike 1911, 1912). Instead of estimating a scale based simply on *connoisseurship* as was often the case in the United Kingdom, Thorndike took a large sample of student handwritten scripts and used 200 teachers to rank these scripts in order. From the data he created a scale upon which he placed each script. He then provided a set of exemplar scripts at various levels to operationalise a scale from an absolute zero base with scale points defined, and their distances defined (1912:295–299). Teachers were asked to compare their student's scripts with those samples on the scale and identify the closest match to give the level.

Building on Thorndike's work, Hillegas (1912) developed the first standardised scale for written composition and Courtis (1914) compiled the first standardised test of English, in which he combined a number of the above scales with additional measures to come up with a profile of each candidate. Hamp-Lyons (2001:3) makes the important connection between Hillegas's work and how writing was to be assessed in the United States:

> Hillegas (1912) proposed the separation of writing into its form and the content. This content-form split was the lever that pried open the door of so-called "objective" tests for application to writing. From this point on, it could be argued that the skills that multiple choice tests measure, for example, the ability to recognise conventions of grammar, sentence structure, and mechanics, and the ability to make an appropriate stylistic choice among several options, represent the skills that comprise "writing." Form became writing, and writing assessment in the US became the preserve of the statisticians and their supporters.

Spolsky (1998:206), with reference to Cambridge examinations in the 1913–71 period, notes a clear difference in approach:

> It is clear from the kind of questions set that the objective question had no place in the thinking of Cambridge examiners . . . Examinations like these [CPE] were invitations to the candidates to display their linguistic prowess in a variety of formally prescribed situations.

For Spolsky (1995a:63–63) reliability was the problem right from the beginning in Cambridge examinations:

> The notion of reliability was much less influential in Britain. In spite of Cyril Burt's early support for the objective achievement test and the continuing growing acceptance of intelligence testing, traditional examining in Britain remained virtually uncontaminated by psychometric notions.

This may be seen from the contemporary forms of the Cambridge tests in English for foreigners.

In the almost total absence of any archival or published information to the contrary, this judgement appears well founded in the case of Cambridge English written examinations in the early period (pre-1980s) but it does not do justice to the multiple examples of an interest in marking reliability cited in the previous section for the other United Kingdom examination boards.

Despite his general criticism of Cambridge's approach to scoring validity Spolsky nevertheless highlights a number of positive aspects in relation to fairness to be found in Cambridge examinations in this early period (1995a: 205–208):

> The examiner was then expected to apply educated and moderated judgment in order to arrive at a fair and equitable decision on the standard that had been achieved. While we have no detailed account of the concern taken within the system to assure that this moderation worked in written examinations, we can see from his work on the oral examination the kind of care that Roach considered must be taken to make these judgments as fair as humanly possible . . . With regular moderation and constant meetings of examiners . . . some degree of fairness would be possible.

Spolsky (1990a) also paid tribute to the early work of Roach in establishing reliability in Cambridge spoken English examinations in the 1940s. However, with regard to assessing writing, his criticisms of a lack of concern for reliability at Cambridge seem justified in the absence of any real evidence to the contrary. The only exception to this can be found in a few general principles for assessing writing provided by Roach (1936) in a paper, published in a relatively obscure journal (*Overseas Education: a Journal of Educational Experiment and Research in Tropical and Subtropical Areas*), prepared in reaction to criticisms concerning the marking of writing in examination boards made by Hartog et al (1936) (see Chapter 1 for details). What appears to be otherwise totally absent from Roach's papers in the Archives at Cambridge is any indication of systematic attempts to standardise the marking of writing in similar rigorous ways to those employed in connection with speaking (see a copy of Roach (1945a) in Appendix C and Chapter 4 for detail of the latter).

One can only speculate that the small group of his fellow Cambridge dons who marked the written papers in the early days considered they were professionally competent to assess written composition by virtue of their day jobs. They also had the benefit of personal contact, and the availability of the test papers gave them greater confidence. Roach possibly perceived there to be a more serious problem in relation to the oral exams where there was no way to observe that performance; to solve it he brought in post office engineers to record samples to train judges. Unfortunately the apparent lack of such rigorous standardisation in the assessment of written work and an unquestioning acceptance of the connoisseurship of University staff enabling them to mark students' written work reliably on their own pervade academia in the United Kingdom to this day.

Spolsky (1995b:208) was also concerned with the serious problem of a lack of parallel forms at Cambridge and considers this worsened in the 1950s as more choice became available:

> The 1955 examination . . . candidates could choose among a number of papers: English Language (a passage for summarizing and a formal essay-the topics included: 'The ordinary man' and 'The customer is always right'); and English Literature (a wide choice of questions); Survey of Industry and Commerce ('Describe a suitable method of insuring a valuable cargo of radio and television sets to be sent from London to New York'); English life and Institutions ('What are the principal outdoor recreations of the English schoolgirl? How do they compare with those in your own country?'); and English Science Texts (summarizing a passage, paraphrasing another, and writing an essay on a topic such as 'Give an account of poisons produced by animals') . . . With this number of options available, the chance of achieving anything like minimal psychometric equivalence, let alone internal or inter-rater consistency, was obviously nil.

Jacobs, Zinkgraf, Wormuth, Hartfiel and Hughey (1981:1) advised in the case of writing:

> For large-scale evaluations, it is generally advisable for all students to write on the same topics because allowing a choice of topics introduces too much uncontrolled variance into the test – i.e., are observed differences in scores due to real differences in writing proficiency or to the different topics? There is no completely reliable basis for comparison of scores on a test unless all of the students have performed the same writing task(s); moreover, reader consistency or reliability in evaluating the test may be reduced if all of the papers read at a single scoring session are not on the same topic.

There is clear evidence that different topics may elicit different responses which are at different levels of performance thus allowing a degree of uncontrolled variance into the test (Ebel and Frisbie 1986:132–133, Read 1990). Differences in scores may not then be due to real differences in writing proficiency but rather result from choice of different topics. Furthermore rater consistency in scoring may also be affected if the tasks performed by candidates are on different topic(s).

Heaton (1975) suggested that offering a choice means, in addition, that some students may waste time trying to select a topic from several given alternatives. Where tests are to be conducted under timed conditions, forcing all students to write on the same topic might also be an advantage for indecisive candidates. Jacobs et al (1981:17) concluded:

> In view of the problems associated with offering a choice of topics, the best alternative, unless skill in choosing a topic is among the test objectives, would seem to be to require all students to write on the same topic, but to provide them more than one opportunity to write.

Tattersall (2007:63) refers to the work of Wilmot and Nuttall (1975), who detail how GCE and CSE external examinations provided candidates with a large choice of questions which affected the comparability within and between examinations and across the two systems. She notes how research of this kind was to lead in due course to a drastic reduction in the choice of questions within examination papers.

Improved scoring validity in the 1990s

With regard to the Cambridge Writing component, procedures were eventually developed in the 1990s to try and alleviate the threat to reliability posed by choice. The element of choice was retained and was still seen as an important consideration in relation to the other aspects of construct validity and the impact of the examination. However, the choice was carefully controlled and efforts were made to ensure that the tasks were of comparable difficulty, administered under standardised conditions and could be marked effectively by trained raters using task specific and general rating criteria. All tasks for the Writing component were tried out in advance on candidates representing the target range of ability. This allowed for problems with the rubric to be adjusted to ensure that candidates understand what they had to do. Samples of language produced by candidates were analysed and fed into the production of materials used to standardise examiners (see Shaw and Weir 2007).

A range of writing tasks is still offered in an attempt to satisfy a varied candidature, and sometimes a degree of choice in the anticipation that test takers will respond to or select tasks which align, to at least some degree, with their personal interests and motivation. Some tasks will appeal to candidates who want to write about personal experience; others are designed to permit a more objective treatment, for example, a report on a holiday resort. Cambridge ESOL does allow a choice of topic in one part of the Writing test; however, all candidates have to write one task in common which means that it is then possible to calibrate performance on the tasks where there is a choice. Candidates thus complete two writing tasks, the first of which is obligatory, the second is chosen from four other possibilities representing a fixed set of 'genres'. The obligatory task acts as an anchor and helps to ensure that the positive feature of choice does not impact negatively on reliability.

There have been other important changes in Cambridge's approach to marking reliability, albeit late in the day in our history following the nascent professionalisation of staff in Cambridge from the late 1980s (see Chapter 1). The CAE examination in the early 1990s saw the introduction of double marking of the Writing test – Paper 2. CAE on-site double marking proved viable, but it was expensive, mainly because of the higher examiner marking fees, travel and accommodation costs. This was to delay its roll out to other Main Suite papers. Currently Cambridge ESOL uses 'on site' double marking for CAE and targeted second marking for PET to identify questionable marking, the analysis being undertaken between marking weekends to allow re-marking where required the following weekend. The check on discrepant marking in the double-marking approach deals satisfactorily with differences in marker severity (see Shaw and Weir (2007:277–280) for further detail on double-marking procedures at Cambridge ESOL).

In its other Main Suite examinations with larger candidatures statistical analysis of examiner performance takes place after marking is complete. Cambridge uses scaling to correct for certain individual examiner effects and to identify discrepant examiners (see Shaw and Weir 2007:190–195). In broad terms, the approach is to scale each examiner's mark distribution to the global distribution of all examiners. Scaling of Writing is an effective statistical method that is used to detect errant writing examiners and to alter their marks to bring them in line with the population of markers as a whole. The main purpose of such scaling is to transform a distribution of marks to a specific mean and standard deviation. This may result in the addition or subtraction of marks for candidates. The primary intent of scaling is that the influence of variable examiner severity is progressively reduced and the true rank order of candidates thus better represented. Automated scaling through the Examination Processing System (EPS) is already in operation for FCE, CPE and BEC. It scales from a given examiner group's mean and standard deviation to a new mean and new standard deviation, where these include a comparison with Papers 1 and 3.

Cambridge showed an increased awareness of the need to take on board the demands of scoring validity as the organisation became 'professionalised' from the late 1980s onwards. As we saw in Chapter 1 the increased attention paid to all aspects of reliability was encouraged by the Cambridge TOEFL Comparability Study (Bachman et al 1995). Numerous studies, specifically in relation to Cambridge examinations, have all since contributed to a greater understanding of the rating process leading to an enhanced appreciation of writing performance assessment (Falvey and Shaw 2005, Furneaux and Rignall 2000, Jones and Shaw 2003, Milanovic and Saville 1994, Milanovic, Saville and Shen 1996, O'Sullivan 2000, O'Sullivan and Rignall 2002, Pollitt and Murray 1996, 2003a, 2003b, 2003c, 2003d, 2004, 2005a, 2005b, 2005c, Shaw and Falvey 2006, Shaw and Geranpayeh 2005, Shaw and Weir 2007, Weir and Milanovic 2003).

A number of these references are to internal working reports which are not currently available in the public domain. Cambridge ESOL now undertakes a large number of such investigations and routine analyses relating to its examinations on a day-by-day basis. These typically take the form of internal working papers and reports which cannot easily be released into the public domain without extra attention to write them up for external publication. References to some of these are included here because they are relevant to the discussion in hand; in the case of marking reliability they provide evidence that though some of the reports are not in the public domain, research in these areas is now a regular occurrence.

For descriptive purposes we have treated scoring validity separately but we need to remind ourselves that it is linked directly to both context and cognitive validity. Certain performance conditions (contextual parameters) have the potential to affect test reliability (inadequate sampling, too much choice, unclear and ambiguous rubrics, lack of familiarity with test structure or marking criteria, inconsistent administration, and breaches of test security). Where scoring criteria are made known to candidates in advance this will affect cognitive processing in the planning, monitoring and revision stages of essay writing. All of this emphasises the interconnectedness of these components of the validity construct. There is a 'symbiotic' relationship between context validity, cognitive validity and scoring validity, which together constitute what is frequently referred to as *construct* validity.

In the final part of this chapter we will focus on the assessment tasks used by Cambridge for testing writing in English over the course of the 20th century and where documentation is available we discuss the criteria used in the rating process. Our main interest will be with the language constructs underlying these tests. We will need our socio-cognitive framework to guide such an analysis. The socio-cognitive framework (Weir 2005a, Shaw and Weir 2007) provides us with *workable categories of description* for the evaluation of the tests of writing that emerged during the hundred years of Cambridge writing tests reviewed in this chapter.

A framework for analysing writing tasks

A concern with interactional authenticity in writing tests requires that the cognitive processes candidates engage in while completing the test task are similar to, and offer an adequate coverage of, the cognitive processes which would prevail when expert users write in a natural (i.e. non-test) context. The concern is with the way in which the user plans, assembles and executes output; taking into account the cognitive demands imposed upon the writer by the contextual parameters of the task. Shaw and Weir (2007:34–62) provide a model for writing based upon these information-processing principles, thus enabling us to identify specific phases through which an expert language user is likely to proceed whilst engaged in writing. These phases are not necessarily sequential and not all of them are obligatory. They provide a framework for determining in a systematic way how the various processes which make up performance in writing are represented, explicitly or implicitly, in a test task.

A concern with situational authenticity (Bachman 1990) requires writers to respond to contexts which simulate 'real life' in terms of criterial parameters without necessarily replicating it exactly. As far as possible, attempts are made to use situations and tasks which are likely to be familiar and relevant to the intended test taker. In providing contexts, the purpose for carrying out a particular task should be made clear, as well as the intended audience, and the criterion for success in completing the task.

Cognitive considerations in L2 writing

In line with Emig's (1971) *The Composing Process of Twelfth Graders in the US*, which provided empirical support for a cognitive processing approach, Britton, Burgess, Marin, McLeod and Rosen (1975: Chapter 2) also offer an early and fairly unique advocacy of the importance of the cognitive processing dimension in writing, although the authors (1975:32) admit: 'It is not yet possible to present a coherent theory of psychological processes in writing'. We now have a clearer picture of these psychological processes although it is still not yet part of mainstream thinking in approaches to language test design and much work remains to be done to ground the model empirically.

The cognitive processes that expert writers activate according to the research literature are represented in diagrammatic form in Figure 3.2 below. Field (2004:329–331) provides a useful account of information processing which aims to represent the operations a writer is imagined to perform when engaged in the writing process. Field's model attempts to extrapolate a

Figure 3.2 Cognitive validity parameters in writing (Shaw and Weir 2007)

COGNITIVE VALIDITY
COGNITIVE PROCESSES
• Macro-planning
• Organisation
• Micro-planning
• Translation
• Monitoring
• Revising

widely accepted framework from the work of others based upon information-processing principles. Much of the model draws upon the phases of processing proposed by Kellogg (1996) and employs some of Kellogg's terminology. What is important to note here is that the Field/Kellogg model aims to provide a detailed account of the stages (and within them the operations) through which an expert writer proceeds, though the stages are represented as interactive, with multiple possibilities of looping back. Because the Field/Kellogg model clearly identifies levels of processing and the operations which take place at those levels, it provides an accessible, detailed and structured framework; as such it is useful for the analysis of Cambridge English examinations in our study (see Shaw and Weir (2007) for a full explication of these phases). The model contains the following levels of processing:

- **Macro-planning:** *Gathering of ideas and identification of major constraints (genre, readership, goals).*

- **Organisation:** *Ordering the ideas; identifying relationships between them; determining which are central to the goals of the text and which are of secondary importance.*

- **Micro-planning:** *Focusing on the part of the text that is about to be produced. Here, the planning takes place on at least two levels: the goal of the paragraph, itself aligned with the overall goal of the writing activity; within the paragraph, the immediate need to structure an upcoming sentence in terms of information.*

- **Translation:** *Propositional content previously held in abstract form is converted to linguistic form. It covers translation into words – storage of words in a writing buffer – transmission of signals to the fingers – execution of the signals.*

- **Monitoring:** *At a basic level monitoring involves checking the mechanical accuracy of spelling, punctuation and syntax. At a more advanced level, it can involve examining the text to determine whether it reflects the writer's intentions and fits the developing argument structure of the text.*

- **Revising:** *As a result of monitoring activities a writer will return to those aspects of the text considered unsatisfactory and make corrections or adjustments perhaps after each sentence, each paragraph or when the whole text has been written.*

To the extent that any test task does not appear to result in appropriate cognitive processing, it might be considered deficient and raise concern about any attempt to generalise from the test task to the real-life, language use. For example, using a multiple-choice test of structure and written expression as an indirect indicator of writing ability, one of the objective approaches to assessing writing in the USA described above, might be deemed seriously inadequate in terms of cognitive validity because none of the processing levels described above are required. However, direct tests of writing that do not activate the planning, monitoring and revision stages of processing are also overlooking important processing phases (see below for our discussion of these processes in relation to Cambridge examinations over the last century).

As well as the cognitive dimensions of a task we will need to examine the contextual parameters that are likely to influence test task performance in the writing tasks under review below.

Context validity in L2 writing

Cognitive processing in a writing test never occurs in a vacuum but is activated in response to the contextual parameters set out in the wording of the writing task. Context validity for a writing task addresses the particular performance conditions, the setting under which the task is to be performed (such as purpose of the task, time available, length required, specified addressee, known marking criteria as well as the linguistic demands inherent in the successful performance of the task) together with the actual examination conditions resulting from the administrative setting (see Shaw and Weir (2007:63–142) for full details of these contextual parameters).

In Figure 3.3 below, we summarise the contextual parameters suggested by Weir (2005a) as being most likely to have an impact on writing test performance. Using this framework as our informing source, we will explore the task parameters of context validity in terms of *Task Setting* and *Linguistic Demands (Task Input and Output)*.

Figure 3.3 Some criterial aspects of context validity for writing (adapted from Shaw and Weir 2007)

Context Validity	
Setting: Task	Linguistic Demands:
• Response Format	• Task Input & Output
• Purpose	• Lexical resources
• Knowledge of Criteria	• Structural resources
• Text length	• Discourse mode
• Time Constraints	• Functional resources
• Writer-reader relationship	• Content knowledge

We have now considered all three key components of our framework for analysing writing test tasks: scoring, cognitive, contextual parameters. We will make reference to a number of key parameters from each of these in our analysis of Cambridge English Writing examinations 1913–2012 below.

Examining Writing: an analysis of Cambridge English Writing Tasks 1913–2012

1913 CPE

A number of writers have suggested that second language performance assessment dates from the mid-1950s (Lowe 1988, McNamara 1996). Cambridge English examinations included performance assessment components much earlier. For example, a two-hour essay-writing task and an oral component (including conversation) were included in the Certificate of Proficiency in English (CPE) from the outset in 1913, and the Lower Certificate of English (LCE), introduced in 1939, incorporated both a written composition paper and an oral test (see Weir 2003, Hawkey 2009).

As we noted in Chapter 1, the written part of the CPE examination in 1913 was modeled on the existing British native speaker language syllabus including an English literature paper and an essay. A direct writing task was a permanent feature of this Examination from the outset and, as new tests have been added to the Cambridge suite over the years, direct writing tasks have continued to be major components of the Cambridge English examinations. As the essay will dominate our discussion of examining writing in Cambridge in the 20th century, it is worth trying to narrow down its rather amorphous etymology. The relevant definition from the Compact Edition of the Oxford English Dictionary with reference to Montaigne reads:

> A composition of moderate length on any particular subject, or branch of a subject; originally implying want of finish, 'an irregular undigested piece' (J.), but now said of a composition more or less elaborate in style, though limited in range.

Additional definitions refer to: '(1) the action or process of trying or testing, (5) an attempt, endeavor and (7b) a rough copy; a first draft.'

Montaigne was the first author to describe his writings as *Essaies* in 1575, perhaps in order to characterise them as 'attempts' to put his own thoughts into writing or, as Drew (1935:42) prefers it, to denote 'experiments in a new form of writing'. Francis Bacon's more detached essays, published in book form in 1597, 1612, and 1625 (see Drew (1935: 43) for discussion of these), were the first works in English that described themselves as *essays* and these were to be the start of a great tradition of essayists in literature in this country. Drew (1935:47) argues:

> . . . it was the coming of the periodical newspaper which really established the essay in popularity. It created a market for it, which it never lost so it was not only aristocratic dilettantes who could afford to practise it . . .

It is difficult to define the genre into which essays fall. Aldous Huxley (1958: v, vii) suggests that 'Like the novel, the essay is a literary device for saying almost everything about almost anything, usually on a certain topic'. Huxley argues that:

> Essays belong to a literary species whose extreme variability can be studied most effectively within a three-poled frame of reference. There is the pole of the personal and the autobiographical; there is the pole of the objective, the factual, the concrete-particular; and there is the pole of the abstract-universal. Most essayists are at home and at their best in the neighborhood of only one of the essay's three poles, or at the most only in the neighborhood of two of them. There are the predominantly personal essayists, who write fragments of reflective autobiography and who look at the world through the keyhole of anecdote and description. There are the predominantly objective essayists who do not speak directly of themselves, but turn their attention outward to some literary or scientific or political theme. Their art consists in setting forth, passing judgment upon, and drawing general conclusions from, the relevant data. In a third group we find those essayists who do their work in the world of high abstractions, who never condescend to be personal and who hardly deign to take notice of the particular facts, from which their generalizations were originally drawn . . .The most richly satisfying essays are those which make the best not of one, not of two, but of all the three worlds in which it is possible for the essay to exist. Freely, effortlessly, thought and feeling move in these consummate works of art, hither and thither between the essay's three poles—from the personal to the universal, from the abstract back to the concrete, from the objective datum to the inner experience.

Most examination essays fail to reach the acme espoused by Huxley. Few will compare with Milton's 1644 treatise *Areopagitica* in defence of freedom of speech, the essays of Johnson or those of Voltaire. Examination essays are necessarily a form of rough draft as, given the time pressure most writing in examinations takes place under, there is often limited time for the planning or the monitoring and revision phases we noted above as essential processing elements associated with the expert writer. However, for those minded to it, the two hours for a single essay in 1913 (which compares favourably with the 25 minutes in the contemporary American ACT and SAT and even to the 60 minutes available for each writing task in CPE today) should have afforded ample opportunities for the processing levels of *planning, organisation, translation, monitoring* and *revision* we advocated as hallmarks of cognitive validity for advanced writing by expert users in the discussion above.

Exam essays, unlike published academic papers, have not been read and commented on critically by friendly (or even unfriendly) peers, no feedback has been given, and no external tools for editing or proofing are normally allowed. The essay examination is unlikely to represent fairly or accurately the full range of a person's writing ability. However, well-developed, written reasoning is required as candidates will be expected to demonstrate coherent knowledge and understanding in relation to a certain set of content in a relevant and appropriate response to a set task (see Weigle (2002) for an extended discussion of the nature of written composition). Godshalk, Swineford, and Coffmann (1966:41) in their seminal paper on the measurement of writing made a similar point in commenting on the use of timed essays:

> As in all essays written under test conditions, these place a premium on fluency and ability to write correctly and with some style in a first draft. In actual life situations the writer is seldom under such sharp limitations. He can write and revise. He can consult a dictionary or thesaurus . . . And he will often have to spend long hours outlining and developing an extensive treatment of a truly complex topic.

However, they also provided a timely reminder to American educationalists that despite these limitations, timed essays under test conditions had an important role to play at a time when objective testing reigned supreme (1966:41):

> An essay in the English Composition Test says to the student that skill in actual writing is an important outcome of instruction. It says to the teacher that the ability to answer multiple choice questions, unless accompanied by the ability to compose answers to essay questions, is not sufficient evidence of effective teaching.

Latham (1877) had earlier made a long and detailed argument in support of the essay in his *The Function of Examinations and* among its many advantages he saw it as a good way of separating the bright from the intellectually challenged (274, 276):

> The thinness of the soil is often displayed by the English Essay and frequently its prognostication proves correct . . . What a good essay principally shews is a readiness in putting on paper, in a clear and orderly manner, a view that presents itself on applying the mind to a given subject . . . a good essay will also shew some power of seizing on important points.

Russell (2002:78) notes its importance in the US:

> One genre has defined extended student writing in mass secondary and higher education: the documented essay (or research paper or term paper) . . . this genre has come to be ubiquitous, relatively uniform and almost synonymous with extended school writing . . . In an important

sense, the introduction of essay examinations in the 1840s made modern mass education possible. Permanent, portable, standard exams facilitated curricular standardization, system wide teacher evaluation and a defensible means of sorting students – all without face to face contact among individuals.

Given the special place accorded to the essay in society and education by the start of the 20th century in both Britain and the United States, it is perhaps not surprising that there is a two-hour English Essay test featuring prominently in CPE in 1913.

Choice of topic in CPE in the early days offers some insight into the concerns of the time and the candidature. In 1913, the choice was very anglocentric and culture bound:

English Essay (Two hours)

Write an Essay on **one** of the following subjects.
(a) The effect of political movements upon nineteenth century literature in England.
(b) English Pre-Raffaellitism.
(c) Elizabethan travel and discovery.
(d) The Indian Mutiny.
(e) The development of local self-government.
(f) Matthew Arnold.

Knowledge telling or knowledge transforming?

In these particular expository essays it is the way that the title is interpreted by the candidate that determines how it is answered. None of these titles guide the writer to the type of cognitive processing that is expected as they do not ask questions and merely refer to a general content area. The response might in the event turn out to be simply descriptive or, alternatively, discursive and structured; it might largely involve *knowledge telling* or alternatively it might lead to *knowledge transformation* (see Bereiter and Scardamalia 1987a,1987b, Graham 2006, Hyland 2002). There are no explicit guidelines to help the readers make various rhetorical choices in this essay test including choice of appropriate genre or expectations of the reader except previous training in the writing of school essays.

Hyland (2002:28) provides a clear description of the two categories of processing locating them on opposite ends of a cline of writing ability:

> *A **knowledge-telling model** addresses the fact that novice writers plan less often than experts, revise less often and less extensively, and

are primarily concerned with generating content from their internal resources. Their main goal is simply to tell what they can remember based on the assignment, the topic, or the genre.

A knowledge-transforming model suggests how skilled writers use the writing task to analyze problems and set goals. These writers are able to reflect on the complexities of the task and resolve problems of content, form, audience, style, organization; and so on within a content space and a rhetorical space, so that there is a continuous interaction between developing knowledge and text. Knowledge transforming thus involves actively reworking thoughts so that in the process not only the text, but also ideas, may be changed (Bereiter and Scardamalia 1987[a]).

In 'knowledge telling' content is retrieved from long-term memory and shaped to fit the expectations of the writer regarding the writing task requirements. Its success is obviously dependent on pre-existing content and linguistic knowledge and 'given any reasonable specification of topic or genre, the writer can get started in a matter of seconds and speedily produce an essay that will be on topic and that will conform to the type of text that is called for' (Bereiter and Scardamalia 1987a:9). 'Knowledge transforming' involves a controlled, problem-solving approach, in which opinions are formed through the composing process itself (Bereiter and Scardamalia 1987a:10). The terms denote a distinction between a linear writing process, i.e. telling what is known about a topic, and one which entails organising ideas in terms of their relationship to each other, to the goals of the text and to the expectations of the reader. In a transforming approach text content is planned in accordance with rhetorical, communicative and pragmatic constraints.

Having initially developed a mental representation of the assignment as in knowledge telling, Graham (2006) describes how, in tasks requiring knowledge transforming, the writer is involved in problem analysis and goal setting to work out what to write (content planning), how to write it and whom to write it to (rhetorical process planning). Drawing upon concepts taken from Hayes and Flower he argues (2006:460) that this is done by:

> ... analysing the task, setting content and rhetorical goals and deciding on the necessary means to obtain these objectives. [The] two types of planning are carried out in their own space: *content problem space* and *rhetorical problem space*. Within these spaces the writer retrieves and transforms knowledge about what they plan to say (content knowledge), as well as knowledge about their audience and how to say it (discourse knowledge).
>
> These processes are guided by the goals and constraints established during *problem analysis* and *goal setting*. Planning in these two spaces operate in a close interaction through a *problem translation* component which transfers goals and constraints from one space to the other. Thus topic knowledge can be transformed by taking into account content goals as

well theoretical and pragmatic constraints. Likewise theoretical and pragmatic dimensions can be transformed by content constraints. The resulting plans are then elaborated in writing by the knowledge telling process.

Bereiter and Scardamalia (1987a) make the point that any prompt might lead to knowledge telling or to knowledge transforming – it is perfectly possible to regurgitate an already worked out position in an argumentative essay – and possible to knowledge transform to forge a narrative from a set of events – a history. It is a matter of *what is more likely*.

Marking of essays

Limited evidence remains on the way essays were rated in the early years of CPE except for occasional clues in the brief Examiner Reports at the end of each annual bound volume of UCLES papers held in the Cambridge Assessment archives. No copies of marked CPE examination scripts remain from before 1975. Early Examiner Reports focus mainly on the School Certificate Examinations with only separate treatment of CPE for the years 1913–15. This is perhaps not surprising as numbers of candidates were small (only 3 for CPE in 1913 rising to 675 by 1938) and only a small group of trusted, experienced markers (usually fellow Cambridge dons) were responsible for the subjectively assessed parts of this examination testifying to the limited scale of the assessment operation at this early stage.

However, the limited comments that are available on the English Essay in the first few years of CPE are interesting and the importance given to content and style is evident. The following are taken from the Annual Reports on Cambridge Examinations held in the University Archives:

> 1913 (3 candidates) *Only one of the three candidates wrote a satisfactory essay*
> 1914 (18 candidates) *The essays were, on the whole, very satisfactory, and presented a striking contrast to the poor and scanty work sent in last year. The best candidates treated their chosen subjects with some knowledge and power of expression; the chief fault of the remaining papers was an imperfect command of English idiom, which in one or two cases led to the employment of a stilted style out of keeping with the matter in hand.*
> 1915 (4 candidates) *In the case of three candidates the essays shewed (sic) a fair command of clear and straightforward English. The subject chosen was in three instances the same, and was treated intelligently, one candidate writing with a good general knowledge of the facts connected with it.*

Thereafter there do not seem to be any comments addressed specifically on the CPE examination until much later in our history. The early annual Examiners' Reports do however provide information on the essay in other

Cambridge English examinations of this period and given the common Literature paper shared by the Higher School Certificate and CPE, and the possibility that the exams had examiners in common, one might speculate that similar considerations affected the assessment of the Essay paper in CPE. The following thematically arranged extracts are taken from early Annual Reports on Cambridge Examinations held in the University Archives and give an idea of the criteria that might have been employed in CPE at this time:

Punctuation and paragraphing:
1921 report (Junior Local examination). . . *the compositions of the girls were especially weak, and far too many ignored the rules of punctuation and paragraphing.*
1923 report (Junior Local examination) . . . *Punctuation was frequently lacking, even where it was essential to shew the connexion of words and phrases.*
Relevance and adequacy of content:
1924 report (Junior Local examination) . . . *Many candidates as usual lost marks by writing careless and irrelevant stories, instead of essays on such subjects as "Fishing" and "Life in Wild Country".*
1925 report (Junior Local examination). . . *Candidates and teachers alike should realise that the insertion in essays of previously prepared passages is not a means of obtaining high marks. It is the business of the Examiner to satisfy himself that a candidate can write a thoughtful composition in correct English without irrelevance; he will not fail to recognise an inserted passage which is neither composed in the examination room nor exactly to the point , and he cannot assign high marks to what is really an attempted evasion of the English composition test.*
Lexical range and appropriacy:
1924 report (School Certificate) . . . *Many of the Essays which showed a certain sense of style or some width of vocabulary were marred by exaggerated word-painting which was frequently irrelevant to the subject; and many which dealt sensibly with the subject selected were devoid of style or of any precision in the use of words.*
1926 report (School Certificate). *In Composition . . . the chief faults were incoherence, irrelevance, free use of colloquialisms, and a tendency to overwork (and sometimes to misuse) such words as item, factor, disadvantage and asset; the two latter faults were probably due to meagreness of vocabulary and to habits of indefinite thinking . . .*
Grammatical accuracy, spelling and orthography:
1923 (Junior Local examination). *Many candidates were completely ignorant of the nature of a complex sentence.*
1925 report (Junior Local examination) . . . *Much more thorough teaching of English construction is manifestly necessary in many schools, and in answers to the Literature papers there was much careless spelling and bad handwriting.*

Arrangement:
1926 report (Higher School Certificate). *In the Shakespeare paper the style of many of the answers was poor; pages of unedited material were written, lacking in relevance and arrangement, and the introduction of extraneous matter made some answers almost worthless.*
Style:
1927 report (Higher School Certificate). *Although ample choice of subjects was given, many essays were grossly inaccurate in facts, and full of exaggerated Statements. Candidates tended to use stilted language and to write in wild or high-flown style; they would be better advised to set out their ideas simply and naturally and without striving after effect.*

The 1927 report on the School Certificate is fairly damning but makes clear what the construct of writing an essay involved for its examiners at Cambridge in this period:

In July the standard of essay writing was very low, although there was a fair amount of good material out of which essays could have been made if more practice had been given in the subject. As it was, the compositions were childish in thought and expression, and were characterised by lack of coherence, incorrect use of quite common words and a general ignorance of what an essay means. Irrelevant matter was introduced, sometimes to the entire suppression of the real subject, the use of the first personal pronoun was not uncommon, and there was a prevalent idea that short story is a proper form for essay writing.

In December there was a larger proportion of good essays, but there still prevailed a general incapacity to put ideas or knowledge upon any subject in an orderly, coherent and distinctive way. From the work in the two examinations it appears that many boys and girls who leave school after taking this examination are going out into the world without having equipped themselves with an adequate knowledge of how to treat a given theme and how to express themselves in their own language.

In 1931 the provision of some stated criteria for assessment of the Essay on the CPE paper appears on the CPE Essay paper for the first (and only) time and this may well have helped promote monitoring and revision at the discourse level.

The Essay should be of reasonable length; marks will be given for style, subject matter, and arrangement. The title of the Essay must be written as a heading.

Candidates in this particular version of the examination were given these marking criteria on the examination paper itself whereby, if they were so minded, they could *monitor* their work either during or after completion of the task. Interestingly the criteria of *content* and *organisation* were shown by Weir (1983) to be those regarded by University staff in the United Kingdom as being by far the most important for assessing the work of their students and thus entirely appropriate for an examination that became recognised for university entrance in the late 1930s. Unfortunately even these limited criteria disappeared from public view on subsequent papers and it is not possible to ascertain the extent to which candidates were aware of them subsequently. The lack of any clear specification for the examinations until the 1980s suggests they may not have been.

Essay topics

Roach in his report on a promotional visit made to Switzerland and Italy in 1937, made reference to the need for care in choice of essay topics and acknowledged 'the ones designed for candidates in England had often been beyond the scope of those on the Continent', presumably in the area of content. With the growth of the number of international centres offering CPE in the 1930s and given the desire to increase the number of candidates from all walks of life, not just teaching, it was felt that the topics needed to be as accessible to as wide a range of candidates as possible and to offer a reasonable choice of topics. Roach discussed with certain centres the need for a special Literature syllabus (for Italian centres), the choice of essay subjects and a less specialised alternative to commercial syllabus for Italy and Switzerland. The value of this spirit of co-operation was appreciated by centres and British Council representatives: 'Schoolmasters have come to regard examining bodies as being particularly boneheaded and unhelpful; your attitude is a most welcome change' (a British Council representative, Egypt 1939).

Compared to the 1913 English Essay the choice of topics has become more general and suitable for overseas candidates by the 1930s. However they still provide no guidance for the candidate as to the rhetorical stance that is to be adopted and the type of writing (narrative, discoursal etc.) that is expected. Candidates in one year had to write one essay from the following titles:

1. The topic that is most discussed in your country at the present time.
2. Fascism
3. The best month in the year
4. Good companions
5. Any English writer of the twentieth century.
6. Does satire ever effect its purpose, or do any good?

The issue of generalisability

An important issue for all forms of writing assessment is the extent to which one can generalise from test scores to target situation ability. McNamara (2007:280) argued that a test score:

> ... is the basis for a claim, nothing more, about the candidate's standing in relation to a domain of knowledge or skill or capacity to carry out particular sets of communicative tasks and hence his or her readiness for entry into particular communicative contexts.

White (1995:41) questions the use of a single essay task in this respect:

> ... confidence in a single test rating is usually misplaced and overstated. The essence of reliability findings from the last two decades of research is that no single essay test will yield highly reliable results, no matter how careful the testing and scoring apparatus. If the essay test is to be used for important or irreversible decisions about students, a minimum of two separate writing samples must be obtained or some other kind of measurement must be combined with the single writing score.

At first sight there might seem to be a potential problem in the early days where only a single sample of writing ability is required in the Cambridge CPE Essay paper. We need to remember of course that candidates also had to complete a three-hour English Literature paper (the paper on English Language and Literature [Group A, Subject 1] in the Higher Local Examination). Examples from the July 1938 paper illustrate the nature of writing required as a response in this paper:

- Write a short account of Milton's use of the sonnet
- Examine the part played by the common people of Rome in Julius Caesar

Candidates had to answer three questions from a choice of eleven as well as summarising the meaning of a prose passage or poem in their own words (see Chapter 2 for discussion of these tasks). Performance on five tasks that involved extended writing contributed to the total score in CPE in this period. As the pass in the examination was an aggregate of marks across papers then this considerably increased the basis for any claims about CPE providing an adequate and representative measure of the writing construct.

1938 CPE

In the 1932 English Essay examination paper candidates had to write one essay choosing a subject from 6 options. In the 1938 English Composition paper, there is an additional task which may explain the change in the title of the paper: 'read a passage of 525 words and write a summary not exceeding 185 words' (see Chapter 2 for full details of the integrated reading into writing summary task and sample papers). More time is allocated and the timing for the paper is increased from 2 hours to 2.5 hours. By adding the additional summary task this broadened the base for evaluating the candidate's competence in writing and addressed a number of the concerns we raised above about the single essay format for writing. It also meant the process of writing was, through the summary task, more likely to have involved knowledge transformation as well as knowledge telling (see above for brief discussion of this processing continuum).

1939 LCE

The first Lower Certificate in English (LCE) examination in 1939 required candidates to write about a prescribed text and complete an impromptu essay:

Lower Certificate in English 1939

Subjects:

Oral: Dictation, Reading, Conversation.

Written: (a) Prescribed texts: 2 hours.

(b) English Composition and Language: 2 hours.

No translation from and to English.

The *Regulations* for 1939 claim the object of the prescribed texts paper was 'to give candidates the opportunity of expressing themselves easily and correctly when handling familiar subject-matter' and not to 'test literary appreciation'. Paper (b) in the written part, English Composition and Language, according to the Regulations had 'the same object in view as the prescribed texts', through 'a choice of subjects for a free composition, such as a letter or an essay on a given subject' and 'various tests in the correct use of simple English'.

The tasks in the 1939 English Composition and Language paper, exhibited many of the characteristics of tasks that were later to typify the 'communicative' era from the 1975 FCE paper onwards (see Chapter 1 for details of this period); candidates were required to a) write a letter of 80–100 words and b) a composition of 250–300 words in length. The letter task in Part A appears realistic and well specified in terms of purpose and role relationships. Some of the LCE tasks are indeed strikingly similar to items in recent Cambridge English exams. Here is a June 1939 LCE Section A sample task:

1939 LCE Writing Section A

Write a letter on one of these subjects. It should be between 80 and 100 words long. Give your address at the top and make the ending like that of a real letter.

. . .

2 . A letter to a friend who is ill in hospital. Tell him any news which you think will interest him, and try to be as helpful and cheerful as you can.

By providing candidates with an addressee and context candidates were required to make rhetorical choices in terms of genre, structure and vocabulary. The need to bear in mind the situation of the addressee was also likely to have involved the candidate in knowledge transforming as decisions were taken on what might be interesting content and the effect it would have on the reader.

In Part B of the June 1939 paper the candidates again had three choices to choose from. In each they were expected to write a descriptive account:

> 5. Give a detailed account of a picture which you have hanging in your house or school. Your description should be very clear so that anyone reading your description can see the picture in his mind's eye.

Such descriptive tasks are more likely to elicit knowledge telling which is seen as appropriate at an intermediate (CEFR B2) level to this day.

1945 CPE

In 1945, the CPE 'English Composition' paper (2½ hours in 1938) is changed to an 'English Language' paper (3 hours) with basically the same content as the 1938 paper but with some additional language questions.

For candidates who were unable to access set literary texts owing to wartime conditions (see Chapter 1) there was an alternative to English Literature called English Language with Literature paper. The English Language with Literature paper contained a compulsory first question and thereafter candidates could choose any four out of an eclectic range of thirteen questions that quite clearly made different demands and were hardly comparable. These included:

- a letter or composition on a suggestion from the passage in Question 1
- a paraphrase of the full meaning of a passage of blank verse from Shakespeare

- a description of a man on the basis of a description of his house
- the correction and explanation of errors in five ungrammatical sentences
- the recommendation of two books of English literature a friend would enjoy and one which would present problems to nationals of your country and the reasons for your choice
- an essay on romantic novels in English
- an essay on Shakespeare's view of tragedy or comedy
- a consideration of Wordsworth's view of the aim of poetry in relation to English poetry familiar to you
- an essay on what is characteristically English about English literature, or about English people always acting on principle, or what English cookery reveals about the English character, or about the English taking their pleasures sadly.

This wide choice was to raise doubts in the eyes of some critics (Bachman et 1995 and Spolsky 1995a) about the lack of equivalence between tasks and the consequent threats to reliability (see our earlier discussion of this in the section on *Scoring validity at Cambridge* above).

1953 CPE

Further significant changes had taken place in CPE by 1953 when it became possible to take a 'Use of English' paper as an alternative to 'Translation'. This new paper has remained albeit with changed formats until this day. It starts with a reading passage with Short Answer Questions (SAQ's), then a sentence reformulation task, a task requiring recombining sentences into a more coherent paragraph, a task involving knowledge of how punctuation can change meaning, an editing task (correcting wrong use of words, use of wrong words, illogicalities due to faulty expression, and grammatical errors), a descriptive writing task and finally a task testing knowledge of affixes.

The paper further improved the base for making judgements on writing abilities by adding additional direct and indirect writing tasks to those already in the 3-hour English Language Paper (100-word summary of a passage, lexical and main idea tasks in Part I, and a single Essay from choice of nine in Part II) and the English Literature paper (four extended writing tasks from a choice of nine).

Not many examiner reports are available for the early period in our history but the Cambridge Assessment Archives do have a copy of the 1957 Report on the English Language Paper. This what it says about the Essay:

Part II—The essay

No examiner reported that the essays were in any way distinguished. The best that was said was that some were quite good, with the subjects competently treated. The general feeling seemed to be that there were very few well planned essays showing good control of English idiom, that many were too short and patchy, and others, discursive and rambling. It may be remarked that the very short essays are usually among those which have the greatest number of errors in grammar and syntax.

Some examiners came to the conclusion that large numbers of candidates who entered for this examination had had insufficient preparation and had, therefore, little hope of success. Insufficient time given to preparation would, indeed, seem to account for the baffling inconsistency sometimes found between the wide vocabulary which had been acquired and the way in which the words were strung together so as to produce little meaning in the whole effort. It would also account for the rare instances when a candidate made no attempt at an essay. It may be that many candidates entered without a clear idea of the standard required (CPE 1957 Examiners' Report).

In addition the examiners provided detailed comments on the weaknesses of some essays and make reference to:

a) Lack of paragraphing and poor punctuation were contributory factors to poor results and there was the usual crop of mis-spellings. There were also many cases of the confusion of words of similar appearance. Excessive use of colloquial and slang expressions was also in evidence at some centres.

b) Special weaknesses over and above the poor powers of expression and poor command of English idiom which are noted by the examiners include the following:
- Poor sentence construction . . .
- Inconsistent use of tenses e.g. *I am born in this town* . . .
- Misuse of auxiliary verbs . . .
- Confusion over gerund and infinitives e.g. *the possibility to not suffer* . . .
- Poor word order: *there were only a few gallons left of petrol* . . .
- Concord e.g. *young people has less thoughts* . . .
- Articles wrongly used . . .
- Incorrect prepositional usage . . .
- Vocabulary mistakes e.g. *upholstery for holdup* . . .

So it appears that relevance and adequacy of content, coherence and cohesion, grammatical range and accuracy, lexical range and appropriateness, and spelling all featured in the measurement of the construct of writing at this time. Diederich, French and Carlton (1961) in a landmark study used factor analysis to determine categories that were used to rate effective writing in responses from a very large number of judges, and established that these were: *ideas, form, flavour (style), wording* and *mechanics*; these categories were used to develop a generic scoring system that was to become the basis for analytic scoring (Huot, O'Neill and Moore 2010:503). They bear a close resemblance to those discussed by the Cambridge examiners in 1957 and perhaps not too surprisingly these features, with the addition of the effect on the intended reader, are mirrored in the writing assessment criteria in today's CPE General Mark Scheme (see extract below).

Example extract from 2010 mark scheme: (https://www.teachers. cambridgeesol.org/ts/exams/generalenglish/cpe/writing?tab=marked)

CPE 2010 Writing paper

Good realisation of the task set: BAND 4
For a Band 4 to be awarded, the candidate's writing has a positive effect on the target reader. The content is relevant and the topic is developed. Information and ideas are clearly organised through the use of a variety of cohesive devices. A good range of complex structures and vocabulary is used. Some errors may occur with vocabulary and when complex language is attempted, but these do not cause difficulty for the reader. Register and format are usually appropriate to the purpose of the task and the audience.

A 1969 report provides more detail of the standard required at CPE in this earlier period in response to the following essay prompts which seem to provide a mixture of potential knowledge telling and knowledge transformation tasks:

1969 CPE Report

Write an essay on any one of the following:
1. The purpose of protest.
2. Preparing for the next Olympic Games.
3. Sun-worshippers.
4. Newspapers in today's world.
5. An old man looks back over his life.
6. Compare life in a large block of flats with living in a detached house of your own.
7. "Her voice was ever soft,
   Gentle, and low—an excellent thing in woman."
8. Can the computer replace the human brain in industry and commerce?

The criteria employed for assessment of these essays were described as follows (1969):

> Proficiency, rather than bare adequacy, in the use of the English language is the quality the examiners are required to look for in this paper. It follows that the best general advice that can be given to teachers and candidates is that the latter should aim at doing well rather than at a bare pass, and should not be considered ready to take the Proficiency examination until they are clearly able to produce under examination conditions a sufficient quantity of written English which is natural, correct and expressive.
>
> At the pass level itself, a candidate must submit a script which is free from gross errors and which communicates successfully on a mature level. These two factors are not always found together: a good script containing a number of errors could still pass on its positive merits, whereas a script free of mechanical faults could nevertheless fail for lack of suitable real quality.

And on pages 10–11 more specific detail of the marking criteria were provided and these are reproduced below in full as so little information survives on how writing was assessed in this early period:

> The first criterion in marking is the quality of the English employed; the range of vocabulary, the choice of words and the spelling of them, the appropriateness of idiom, the correctness of grammatical constructions and punctuation, and the soundness of sentence structure. These are assessed and balanced against what an English-speaking employer or a university or similar body might regard as a satisfactory working use of the English language.
>
> Attention is also given to the total structure of the composition; the logical sequence of ideas, the arrangement in paragraphs of related material with appropriate link words or sentences, and the general competence and confidence with which the subject is seen through to a successful conclusion. These architectonic qualities can never make up for poor English and elementary mistakes of language, but without them even a piece of writing free from grammatical errors will rarely go far above the bare pass standard.
>
> Other positive qualities hopefully looked for, and given marks reflecting real proficiency in the language, are: a vocabulary that is not only correct but shows real discrimination in selecting the word or phrase appropriate to the tone or mood of the writing; a complexity of sentence structure sufficient for the ideas it conveys, yet remaining unobtrusive and economical; a real sense of ease in forwarding the argument and a use of English idiom which is modest and unforced; general success in taking the subject through its various natural stages of introduction, exposition and development to an effective conclusion.

The way the examiners are asked to consider which broad category a particular essay falls into, before making their final closer assessment, is shown in the scale below:

Free from errors, of substantial length, sees the subject in terms of a well-constructed pattern. The writer exercises complete control over the choice and arrangement of his words and ideas.

....

Free from errors, good length, good structure but without the absolute ease and command of the first category.

....

Free from elementary errors. Maintains his theme with some assurance and without letting the language run him into difficulties. Good but short.

OR Some errors but none serious, reasonable length (bearing in mind varying ideas about length, particularly on the Continent), competent but not distinguished expression.

....

Some length and substance but with errors which distort or obscure the ideas attempted.

OR Few errors but of too elementary a standard,

....

Errors which distort a good deal of the writing. Un-English-ness pervades the piece.

....

No question of passing, ideas communicated only by an act of translation by the examiner. At the bottom of the scale, writing which can be understood only with greatest difficulty. Candidates who are still in the early stages of learning, or have at most only a conversational phrase-book English.

....

This scale was to stand the test of time and with few alterations it appears once again verbatim in the report on the 1979 paper. An important emphasis was placed on:

Relevance and originality

Although a wide variety of interpretations and treatments of the chosen topic is accepted, a reasonable degree of relevance is a necessary condition for fair assessment of one candidate against another. Wandering away from the subject, disregard for the basic requirements of the topic or the deliberate inclusion of irrelevant, often obviously memorized material are considered as serious composition faults. The deliberate digression within a well-ordered structure is recognized as such and treated accordingly as of course is the inevitable and legitimate use made in all original writing, especially in a foreign language, of appropriate formulations and terminology taken from current usage.

But mechanical accuracy is still required:

Punctuation

Many candidates seem unaware of the fundamental role of punctuation in achieving clarity and right emphasis, where the effective interlocking of units of thought into clause and phrase is concerned. Sometimes no systematic punctuation at all is attempted; pages of discussion are offered written in blurred statements punctuated only by spacing or vague dashes, with no recognisable sentence structure. Many candidates have obviously had too little experience of written English in a continuous form.

Exemplar scripts are provided to illustrate further particular problems with:

* shorter essays
* lack of organisation
* clash between ideas and expression (ambitious ideas beyond candidates power of expression)
* use of prepared material
* irrelevance.

By the 1970s the criteria for assessing written examinations were explicit, well founded and stood comparison with the results of the major research studies designed to establish the important factors in effective writing (e.g. Diederich et al 1961, Lewis and Massad 1975).

However, as is clear from the discussion earlier in this chapter, the *rating procedures* for actually applying these *criteria* in a consistent fashion and checking on this were less well developed. Bachman et al (1995) were to note in the later FCE/TOEFL Comparability Study: the intra- and inter-rater reliabilities of ratings for Paper 2 [composition] . . . are essentially unknown. Spolsky (1995a:62–63) also made reference to this:

A second source of measurement error was the subjective marking of items by different examiners. As a result of the administrative procedures followed it proved impossible to establish the intra- and inter-rater consistency of the subjective papers. Some compositions were re-marked, but the second marker knew the first mark, with the result that reliability could not be estimated. The interesting point to note here is not the lack of reliability, but the complete lack of concern for it evidenced by the Cambridge method of administration.

We noted in Chapter 1 and above how attitudes to this aspect of scoring validity, viz reliability, were to change substantially after the 1987–89 comparability study between FCE and TOEFL as language testing was professionalised at Cambridge in the late 20th century. We now turn to developments in the other aspects of the construct validity of the writing components of Cambridge Examinations in our final period 1971–2012.

The communicative era (c.1971–)

As we saw in Chapter 1, Cambridge responded to the growing demand from teachers and to wider societal pressure for a more communicative approach in the 1970s as the pendulum in pedagogy swung sharply towards the actual *use* of language. A major revision took place in both CPE and FCE in 1975 which brought the examinations in line with external developments in communicative English language teaching for overseas students in the UK.

1975 CPE Composition Paper

> The candidate is required to write on one descriptive or descriptive/narrative topic and on one argument/discussion topic. A choice of topic is given within each category.

The addition of an argumentative task was an important step towards requiring knowledge transformation from the candidate as against the knowledge telling required in a descriptive task. A number of these essays had a focused functional slant, e.g. requiring comparison, argument or narrative description, for example:

- Discuss whether it is possible to solve the problem of pollution without losing too many of the advantages of the modern life.
- Compare the position of woman today with their way of life in your grandparents' times, and comment on the difference.
- The arguments for or against the abolition of marriage.

In marking composition examiners (as in FCE) were instructed to pay particular attention to:

(a) The quality of the language employed: the range and appropriateness of vocabulary and sentence structure; the correctness of grammatical construction, punctuation, and spelling.
(b) The relevance and organisation of the composition as a whole and where appropriate, the individual paragraphs.

The report on the work of candidates on the June and December 1975 CPE describes Paper 1 of the new examination as follows:

> This paper combines the free composition exercise formerly in the compulsory English Language paper, though with two essays to be

attempted instead of one, and the comment and appreciation questions formerly in the optional Use of English paper. The marking of the essays follows a carefully-maintained tradition, in which the examiner's criteria for assessment are closely identified with the general notion of standards for Proficiency and the recognition given to it in Britain and overseas as an indication of competence for purposes of higher education or teaching. The testing of awareness and control of the means of communication as well as comprehension of the matter communicated, something which presupposes varied and extended reading as part of the candidate's preparation, is a feature on which particular stress was laid during the preparation of the new syllabus. There was satisfactory evidence from the papers submitted that many teachers had understood the purpose of the changes and were preparing candidates for these requirements.

The examiners commented on the effects of including an argumentative essay as a compulsory task in the new examination and summarised where problems tended to occur in the various criteria:

Section A
There seemed to be a slight improvement in the overall quality of the language used in the essays, as compared with the standard under the old syllabus. Candidates were obliged to marshal their thoughts and write on a discussion topic, which under the previous syllabus they might have preferred to leave alone. Weaker candidates are generally weaker in argument than in description. Conversely very good candidates are at least as good at close reasoning as they are at narrative.

Problems of length and time affected candidates variously. Some candidates managed to write two essays each as long as the single one submitted formerly, and yet leave enough time to finish Section B. Others showed evident haste over the completion of or one or both essays, but very few indeed failed to finish the paper completely.

The 1979 examiners' report noted the tasks in the argumentative part of the paper proved more difficult for candidates as the marshalling of arguments was often 'very imperfect and ideas limited'. These tasks contrast sharply with the essays for 1913 and 1930 that we discussed above. They are now unequivocally discursive and clearly direct the candidate to knowledge transformation. The need to formulate arguments seems to provide clear water between FCE at a B2 CEFR level and CAE/CPE Cambridge Examinations at C1 and C2 levels (see Shaw and Weir 2007: Chapter 4).

Further writing tasks could be found in the Use of English paper (see Chapter 1 for details of its introduction in the CPE examination).

1975 CPE Use of English

In this section the candidate was required to write in an appropriate style a composition in a given form based on information provided. The exercise might have been in the form of, for example, a letter to which the candidate must compose a reply; a table of figures of which the candidate must provide a written interpretation; an extract from a report, or a list of notes, to be used as the bases of an article; a newspaper article or an extract from a radio or television broadcast to be used as the basis of a formal letter to a newspaper. Note also the attention now paid to the real-world genre.

The integrated nature of these tasks was one of the hallmarks of the communicative approach (Chamot and O'Malley 1994, O'Malley and Valdez Pierce 1996) but, as we noted in our extended discussion of *reading into writing* in Chapter 2, the gain in construct validity was partially offset by the possibility of muddied measurement due to reading interfering with the writing scores. As this situation also obtained in the reality of the future target situation for many candidates, they were perhaps not unduly concerned about this possibility.

1975 FCE

In the 1975 FCE, as in CPE, Composition is now a paper in its own right (Paper 1). Candidates had to write three 120–180 word composition exercises from a choice of five in two hours. The topics included opportunities for descriptive writing or a mixture of description and narrative, together with topics showing ability to organise a relatively simple discussion. Some topics were to be treated, as directed, in letter or dialogue form.

We begin to see a number of the options having an overtly functional purpose although others remain purely descriptive:

> 1. You and a friend have quarrelled. You feel that you are at fault. Write a letter to apologise and arrange another meeting. You should make the beginning and ending like those of an ordinary letter, but the address is not to be counted in the number of words.

Further innovative writing tasks occur in the FCE Use of English paper, Paper 3 Section B which predate the later 1991 reading into writing tasks we examined when looking at the innovative CAE examination in Chapter 2 (see also discussion of CAE below). Here we find a compulsory writing task intended to test the candidate's ability to extract specified information from a passage and to present it in a well-organised fashion. It tries to reproduce the final steps in the writing of a composition when, having assembled a variety of facts, the writer proceeds to select those that are directly relevant to the theme, then to organise them coherently, and finally to write the composition on the basis of these organised notes. This exercise also tests knowledge of and ability to use linking words and phrases such as: but, therefore, it is clear that, etc., and reference words such as: the following facts show . . ., all these . . ., etc.

1975 June FCE Paper 3 Use of English

SECTION B

Your teacher has asked you to write two paragraphs on the advantages and disadvantages of having a television in the family. You have no ideas on the subject at all. Then you hear the following conversation between an old man and his married daughter.

Using only the information given in the conversation, write the two paragraphs in the spaces provided. In the first paragraph write about advantages. In the second write about disadvantages. You will probably need between 80 and 100 words for each paragraph. The beginning of each paragraph has been written for you.

Grandfather: Can't you turn that thing off? I know television is a wonderful invention, but it seems to me you have it on all the time in this house. I never get a moment's peace.

His daughter: Just a moment, father. The children's programme will be on in a minute, then we'll both have some peace. The boys are as good as gold when that's on.

Grandfather: When I was young, children had to make their own amusements, and we did our homework, too. Nowadays I can't see how they can do half of what we did, they stay up so late watching television.

His daughter: But my children usually manage to finish most of their homework. Anyway, some of the programmes are very interesting. I really believe my children know more about the world than we ever did at their age.

Grandfather: And what a world, too! I suppose you let them watch this violence on television. It worries me to see children watching all those westerns. Half the cowboys get killed, and at least ninety per cent of the Indians. That's why some children get so violent when they are older.

His daughter: They don't just watch westerns. They watch educational programmes, and they can see what other countries look like when there's a travel programme on.

Grandfather:	So they learn geography from the TV, do they? Why can't they read a book?
His daughter:	And the news items on television are informative, and they're certainly presented fairly. I mean, there are very few newspapers which give you both sides of the argument the way television does.
Grandfather:	Perhaps. But all a child has to do these days to get in contact with all the horror in the world is switch on the television. At least in the old days he had to wait until he had learned to read before he could find it all in the newspapers.
His daughter:	You may be right there, but don't forget we can stop the children watching anything unsuitable. Anyway, at least they stay at home, and I don't have to worry about them playing in the streets.
Grandfather:	What's the point of having your family at home if you haven't time to talk to each other because you're all watching your favourite programmes? Most people can't hold a good conversation these days.
His daughter:	Well, mother says yon didn't talk much. You were always out with your friends. I can really say that my husband spends far more time at home since we bought a television. I can at least talk to him about his favourite programmes.
Grandfather:	His favourite programmes? What do you know about football or boxing? Anyway, it's only armchair sport. Too many people stay indoors watching, and too few actually get out and take proper exercise.
His daughter:	Well, I certainly agree with you, father. It's time for your afternoon walk. When you get back, I'll make you a nice cup of tea.

Again note the functional slant and the provision of an addressee. As we noted above these discursive essays are likely to involve knowledge transformation on the part of the candidate as they address both rhetorical and content issues. What is particularly innovative is the provision of input to the task making it much more akin to a knowledge transforming task than ever before (though some help is obviously given with regard to overall organisation). In a number of ways this follows in the tradition of the earlier precis/ summary we discussed in Chapter 2 and in a much diluted form pays some heed to the early blue-sky suggestion of Latham (1877: 282):

> But besides affording very ample time, I would also allow candi-
> dates while writing their essay in the examination room to have
> access to some standard authorities on their subject . . . there is now
> no object in forcing men to carry a number of details in their heads
> . . . the range of subjects which can be given for essays is very much
> extended.

Although Latham did come back to earth:

> It may be said that practical inconvenience would be found in supply-
> ing access to books of reference if the number of candidates were large
> and suggests this real world task is best saved for the few distinguished
> candidates.

A novel and sweeping proposal, as Latham admits, but illustrative of a
very early interest in authenticity in written examinations. The reading into
writing tasks in the post-1975 Cambridge examinations were a practical
method for achieving the same purpose. Not real life exactly, but a welcome
approximation to it, especially in the knowledge transformation it was likely
to encourage.

1991 CAE

With the introduction of CAE, additional communicative assessment criteria were taken into consideration (Appendix A contains a copy of the first
CAE Writing paper). The candidate's presentation, register and style would
be assessed in terms of their appropriacy to the task. 'Satisfactory processing
of the input provided would be required to complete the task(s) successfully'
(Specifications 1989:3).

Criteria would include: accuracy of grammar, spelling, punctuation, precision of vocabulary use, vocabulary and grammar range, task organisation
in terms of effective use of cohesive devices, relevance and appropriacy of
register. Raters would also be looking for the likely effect on 'someone receiving the piece of writing in an authentic situation' (Specifications 1989:12).
Additionally 'task-specific assessment guidelines for each paper were added
to the general criteria in order to define the type of organisation, the register
and the content required for each of the five questions' (Specifications 1989).
The clear specification of criteria in the CAE handbook and the addition of
the effect of the writing on the reader were all likely to result in knowledge
transforming processes.

In Writing tasks, the kinds of responses required would include: applying
the information contained in the input to another task; selecting and summarising information from the input; eliciting information on the basis of
the input; comparing items of information from the input (see Chapter 2 for

further discussion of a number of these integrated reading into writing tasks). Such guidance in the tasks meant in all likelihood that knowledge transforming would be a central part of Writing task 1 which all candidates had to take.

In the second question in the Writing paper, candidates would be required to write in response to one task selected from four based on a range of writing activities in broad genres such as: articles; reports; letters; instructions and expanded notes. True to the Communicative Language Teaching approach the rubrics would outline the content required and specify purpose and intended audience.

As we noted in the section above on scoring validity at Cambridge, the 1991 CAE writing was examiner-rated by blind, on-site, double marking with a 10% tolerance level before a Team Leader remarked a script. CAE on-site double marking proved viable, but it was expensive, mainly because of the higher examiner marking fees, travel and accommodation costs. This was to delay its roll out to other Main Suite papers and other procedures (see above) like scaling were the preferred options for dealing with marker reliability issues.

2002 CPE revision

Following a large-scale review of the feedback gathered from the various consultative exercises and the results from the different rounds of trialling, the Paper 2 Revision team drew up the final paper specifications for the 2002 revision (see Weir and Milanovic 2003:175–236). The paper is divided into two parts. In Part 1 there is now one compulsory question. In Part 2 there is a choice of one question from four with one of the choices a set text option. The paper takes two hours.

- Part 1: The compulsory question aims to give all candidates an equal opportunity to produce a representative sample of their written work. The test focus is discursive. The task type and content varies between papers. The discursive task was selected as it was felt that it enabled candidates at this level to demonstrate a high level of proficiency. It was also known from feedback that the discursive focus is familiar to the majority of candidates. It is particularly relevant to students in education. Input for Part 1 is 70 – 110 words and is at a lower level than CPE. Functions which candidates may be expected to produce may include some of the following: present and develop a reasoned argument; defend an argument; attack an argument; express and support opinions; summarise an argument; compare and contrast arguments. The range of task types for Part 1 are: article, essay, letter and proposal.
- Part 2 aims to give candidates a number of topics and task types to choose from. Input for Part 2 questions is a maximum of 70 words. Functions which candidates may be expected to produce may include some of the following: narrating, summarising, comparing and

contrasting, analysing, hypothesising, drawing conclusions, judging priorities, describing, giving/requiring information, giving reasons, persuading and making proposals/ recommendations. The range of task types for Part 2 are: article, proposal (not for set texts), report, review, essay (for set texts only) and letter.

Candidates are expected to produce between 300 and 350 words for each task, so that the overall output across the two tasks is between 600 and 700 words.

The following are brief definitions of the task types which candidates are expected to be able to produce for Paper 2.

- *Article*

  Candidates are asked to produce a piece of writing on a particular topic or theme in a style which would make it suitable for publication in a newspaper, magazine or newsletter. They are given a prompt which they then use to perform the task. The target audience is indicated, as this influences the appropriacy of the register and tone of the article, e.g. how lively or how academic it should be. An article will often include some description and narrative, as both serve to engage the reader. An article will usually be motivated by a central idea which provides a point or purpose to the writing or reading of the article.

- *Essay*

  Candidates are expected to use the prompt material to produce a composition on a relevant topic. The essay should be complete in itself containing an introduction, body and conclusion and be united by a central idea which provides a point and purpose to the writing and reading of the essay.

- *Letter*

  CPE-level formal letters are the most suitable though not business-type letters since they tend to be formulaic and rather short. An example is a letter to a newspaper giving an opinion and making a point, stimulated by the input given and further developed with the candidate's own ideas. The letter may include narrative sections to illustrate a point and interest the reader. A letter in Part 2 could have a narrative focus, e.g. a letter of complaint about an event which has not lived up to the candidate's expectations.

- *Report*

  Candidates are given an appropriate prompt, in response to which they then have to produce a report for a specified audience, which could be a superior, e.g. a boss at work, or a peer group, e.g. colleagues. A report involves the presentation and interpretation in well-organised prose of information in relation to a specified context; this is drawn from the prompt material and from the candidates' own ideas. Candidates are encouraged to use section headings as used in authentic reports.

- *Proposal*

  A proposal has a similar format to the report. Whereas the report is an account of something which has happened, the focus of the proposal is on the future, with the main focus being on making recommendations for discussion. An example of a proposal would be, for example, a bid for funds for a project defined in the rubric, and would entail outlining the way the funds would be spent, the benefits which would accrue, and the way progress would be monitored and evaluated if the bid were to be successful. Proposals should be well structured with clear sections. Candidates are encouraged to use section headings as used in authentic proposals.

- *Review*

  A review should be informative and interesting. It may be about a book, film or play, but it may also be about a restaurant, hotel, etc. The readership is clearly specified in the task outline, so that candidates write in an appropriate register. In addition to providing some information on, for example, plot and characters, candidates should indicate some judgement on the subject of the review. The review may also embody narrative, as well as descriptive and evaluative language, and a range of vocabulary relating, for example, to literature and the media such as cinema or TV.

This change with Part 2 now covering a wide range of text types highlights the increased influence on writing research in the late 20th century of the social aspects of writing (Nystrand 2006:19–21). Nystrand (2006:20) describes how a growing interest in writing across the curriculum 'made problems of text, social context, and genre more salient and interesting to writing researchers'. One result of Cambridge employing tasks covering a range of genres was to make the effect of the writer on the designated audience/reader an important criterion for assessment. This can be seen in the CPE General Mark Scheme below where it is taken into account at every level, e.g. at level 5: Impresses the reader and has a very positive effect. This criterion is noticeably absent from most of the earlier mark schemes discussed above (with the obvious exception at CAE, the most communicative of all the exams at the time). The writer-reader relationship was identified as an important contextual variable by Shaw and Weir (2007:63–142) and is an important parameter in our contextual validity framework in Figure 3.3 above. Nystrand (2006) argues that audience should not be just a relevant constraint on the writer, part of the task environment as in Flower and Hayes (1981), but a central element in the writing process.

However, from another perspective, the increased attention paid to genre in Part 2 may have diverted Cambridge from the earlier attention paid to cognitive processing after the 1975 revision discussed above. In terms of processing, these 2002 CPE tasks do not uniformly guide candidates towards knowledge transformation as was the case in those examples we discussed from the 1975 revision which is perhaps unfortunate at the C2 level. To achieve socio-cognitive validity attention needs to be paid to both the social and the cognitive dimensions (Murphy and Yancey 2008:367).

Sample C2 level paper provided by Cambridge ESOL for bench-marking purposes in *Relating language examinations to the Common European Framework of Reference for Languages: learning, teaching, assessment* (2009)

You have read the extract below as part of a newspaper article on the loss of national and cultural identity. Readers were asked to send in their opinions. You decide to write a **letter** responding to the points raised and expressing your own views

You **must** answer this question. Write your answer in **300–350** words in an appropriate style on the following pages.

> 'We are losing our national and cultural identities. Because of recent advances in technology and the easy availability and speed of air travel, different countries are communicating more often and are therefore becoming more and more alike. The same shopping malls and fast food outlets can be found almost everywhere. So can the same types of office blocks, motorways, TV programmes and even lifestyles. How can we maintain the traditions that make each nation unique?'

Write your **letter**. Do not write any postal addresses.

Part 2

Write an answer to **one** of the questions **2–5** in this part. Write your answer in **300–350** words in an appropriate style on the following pages. Put the question number in the box at the top of the page.

2   You are employed as a researcher by your local tourist office. Your manager has asked you to write a proposal on how to attract more visitors, both from your own country and abroad, to your town or area. Within your proposal you should include ideas on how to improve the amenities in your town or area, and increase income from tourism.
     Write your **proposal**.

3   You have recently seen a film version of a novel you have read. Write a review of the film for a media arts magazine and say what you think are the problems of making films based on books.
     Write your **review**.

4   A monthly travel magazine has invited readers to contribute an article to a special edition entitled *The Best Way to Travel*. Write an article describing a memorable and enjoyable journey you have made and giving reasons for the means of transport used.
     Write your **article**.

5   Based on your reading of **one** of these books, write on **one** of the
following. Write **(a)**, **(b)** or **(c)** as well as the number **5** in the box.

(a)   Anne Tyler: *The Accidental Tourist*
'There was no room in his life for anyone as unpredictable as Muriel.'
Write an essay for your tutor discussing that statement, comparing
the personalities and lifestyles of Macon Leary and Muriel Pritchett
and illustrating the comparison with events from the novel.
Write your **essay**.

(b)   John Wyndham: *The Day of the Triffids*
Your local newspaper has invited readers to send in articles entitled
'It kept me awake. . .' on books they have read. Write an article
about *The Day of the Triffids*, focusing on what makes the book
frightening and how the suspense in the book is maintained.
Write your **article**.

(c)   Graham Greene: *Our Man in Havana*
A library is about to have an exhibition on fathers and daughters
in literature and has asked its readers for some ideas. Write a letter
to the library staff recommending *Our Man in Havana* as a possible
book to appear in the exhibition. You should briefly describe the
characters of Wormold and Milly and discuss their relationship and
its importance to the novel.
Write your **letter**. Do not write any postal addresses.

Marking

As in the earlier CAE, candidates were now assessed according to a general
mark scheme and a task specific mark scheme. An impression mark was
awarded to each piece of writing using the general mark scheme below. The
general mark scheme was used for both parts of the paper. It was used in
conjunction with a task-specific mark scheme, which focused on criteria specific to each task. For examples of task-specific mark schemes see below.
Descriptions of both were available in the CPE handbook (2008) and so
were accessible to the candidate to guide monitoring and revision in the
examination. In fact Shaw and Weir (2007:247–248) advocated including
these on the examination paper itself to proactively encourage the candidate
to engage in these important high-level processing activities.

Each piece of writing was assigned to a band between 0 and 5, as described
on the following page, and could be awarded one of three performance levels
within that band. For example, in Band 4, 4.1 represents weaker performance within Band 4; 4.2 represents typical performance within Band 4; 4.3
represents strong performance within Band 4.

Additional ground rules were provided:

* Length
300 to 350 words are asked for. Candidates producing very short scripts will be
penalised.

* Spelling and Punctuation
These are important aspects of accuracy and must be taken into account.
Consistent use of American spelling and usage is acceptable.

- Paragraphing

  This is a function of organisation and format. The task-specific mark scheme will give an indication to examiners of what is expected.

- Handwriting

  If handwriting interferes with communication without preventing it, the candidate will be penalised. Totally illegible scripts receive 0.

The mark schemes clearly explicate the construct being assessed in Cambridge Writing tasks.

CPE General Mark Scheme (Cambridge ESOL 2008:26)

This mark scheme is interpreted at CPE level and in conjunction with a task specific mark scheme for each question.

	Outstanding realisation of the task set: • Sophisticated use of an extensive range of vocabulary, collocation and expression, entirely appropriate to the task set • Effective use of stylistic devices; register and format wholly appropriate
5	• Impressive use of a wide range of structures • Skilfully organised and coherent • Excellent development of topic • Minimal error Impresses the reader and has a very positive effect.
	Good realisation of the task set: • Fluent and natural use of a wide range of vocabulary, collocation and expression, successfully meeting the requirements of the task set • Good use of stylistic devices; register and format appropriate
4	• Competent use of a wide range of structures • Well organised and coherent • Good development of topic • Minor and unobtrusive errors Has a positive effect on the reader.
	Satisfactory realisation of the task set: • Reasonably fluent and natural use of a range of vocabulary and expression, adequate to the task set • Evidence of stylistic devices; register and format generally appropriate
3	• Adequate range of structures • Clearly organised and generally coherent • Adequate coverage of topic

- Occasional non-impeding errors

Achieves the desired effect on the reader.

2	**Inadequate attempt at the task set:** • Limited and/or inaccurate range of vocabulary and expression • Little evidence of stylistic devices; some attempt at appropriate register and format • Inadequate range of structures • Some attempt at organisation, but lacks coherence • Inadequate development of topic • A number of errors, which sometimes impede communication Has a negative effect on the reader.
1	**Poor attempt at the task set:** • Severely limited and inaccurate range of vocabulary and expression • No evidence of stylistic devices; little or no attempt at appropriate register and format • Lack of structural range • Poorly organised, leading to incoherence • Little relevance to topic, and/or too short • Numerous errors, which distract and often impede communication Has a very negative effect on the reader.
0	**Negligible or no attempt at the task set:** • Totally incomprehensible due to serious error • Totally irrelevant • Insufficient language to assess (fewer than 20% of the required number of words) • Totally illegible

A maximum of 3 points can be awarded within each of Bands 1–5.

CPE Task Specific Mark Schemes: two examples

Question 1

Content

Major points: Letter should cover the points raised in the newspaper article, i.e. that national and cultural identity is being lost and that countries are becoming more and more alike. Candidates should address the question at the end of the input.

Further points: Candidates could expand on the nature of national and cultural identity and whether it is, in fact, desirable to maintain one's own national and cultural identity. Additional ideas of the candidate's own.

Range

Language for expressing and supporting opinions and making recommendations. Candidates may also attack the argument in the article or defend it depending on the point of view they hold.

Appropriacy of Register and Format

Formal letter, with appropriate register, bearing in mind the writer's role as the reader of a newspaper writing in to give his/her opinion(s).

Organisation and Cohesion

Formal letter format, with early reference to why the person is writing. Clear organisation of points and adequate paragraphing.

Target Reader

Would understand the writer's point of view.

Question 2

Content

Proposal should include:
how to attract more visitors to your town or area
how to improve the amenities
how to increase income from tourism.

Range

Language of describing, analysing, making recommendations and perhaps hypothesising.

Appropriacy of Register and Format

Proposal format, probably with clear section headings. Register appropriate to the business relationship between the employee/researcher and the manager who has commissioned the proposal.

Organisation and Cohesion

The proposal should be well structured with clear sections. Ideas should be presented in well organised prose, with appropriate paragraphing and linking.

Target Reader

Would understand what the writer is proposing.

(Cambridge ESOL 2008:28–33)

Further discussion of these criteria can be found in Shaw and Weir (2007: Chapter 5).

FCE and CAE modifications 2008

Similar developments were to take place in the writing tasks in the FCE and CAE modifications in late 2008 (see Hawkey (2009:136–213) for full details of all the changes) where, as with the previous CPE revision, we can see a clear concern with writing purpose, participants and language functions.

An obvious effort was made to improve the connection with real life writing. In FCE a letter or email was now compulsory because writing these was considered an important communicative skill relevant to the candidature; the writing of email messages was added because they were increasingly being used in modern life. Hawkey (2009:232–4) details how in support of the updated FCE Writing paper, the *Handbook for Teachers* (2007) has many pages of useful advice for learners. The appearance of this level of advice compared to its earlier absence from public documentation marks a greater sense of examination board responsibility to test stakeholders and is indicative of an increased synergy between learning, teaching and assessment. It reflects one examination board's growing awareness of stakeholder community and increasing commitment to developing assessment literacy.

Like CPE in 2002 explicit general and task specific mark schemes are provided. The criteria e.g. effect on reader, coverage of content points for task implementation, organisation, language structure and vocabulary accuracy, register and format, are appropriate to the intended FCE and CAE writing construct. They represent a key element in Cambridge ESOL's efforts to combine open-ended test tasks in line with its communicative language ability construct with systematic efforts towards rater and inter-rater reliability through the Team Leader system; the monitoring, advisory and decision-making roles of the Principal Examiner, standardisation to explicit criteria, the co-ordination of examiners, and controls on the distribution of candidate scripts across markers.

Hawkey (2009:173–177) also details the strenuous efforts made in the modifications project to check on the validity of the updated examinations in both FCE/CAE in line with Weir's 2005a construct validity framework. In this FCE/CAE modifications project the framework was used as a check on the construct validity of the updated exams. The report *FCE/CAE Modifications: Building the Validity Argument: Application of Weir's Socio-Cognitive framework to FCE & CAE* (ffrench and Gutch 2006) tabulates the framework for validity evidence on each area and sub-area within Weir's model; timescale for completion of this and reference to activities which support the decisions made (in the Notes column). A clear and explicit concern with construct validity now marked the Board's approach to ESOL's assessment of writing.

Present day constructs

The present day Cambridge Main Suite examinations are arguably the best researched and archived in Cambridge's 100-year history. Weir and Milanovic (2003) and Hawkey (2009) provide full descriptions of the development processes that underpin current CPE, FCE and CAE Writing examinations. In addition Shaw and Weir (2007), provide an in-depth analysis from a socio-cognitive perspective of the current Main Suite examinations in Writing. As in the other chapters on the skills (Chapter 2, 4 and 5) we will conclude our 100-year history by a close inspection of the constructs underlying the current writing tests.

Cognitive validity in the current writing papers

Drawing heavily on Shaw and Weir (2007) we provide below a descriptive analysis of the *cognitive processes* that are assumed to underlie the efforts of candidates currently tackling writing tasks at the different proficiency levels in the Cambridge Main Suite. We will focus on the processing underlying these tasks using those parameters which can be incorporated into test design:

- macro-planning
- organisation
- monitoring and revision.

We are of course aware of the limitations of this subjective approach and would encourage future empirical research in the area where a diversity of methodological procedures e.g. verbal protocols, screen capture software, key stroke logging or eye tracking studies might better ground the discussion below. However, at an operational level examination boards may have to restrict themselves to this type of informed, surface level, focus group exploration where exams appear in multiple forms and on numerous occasions per annum. Despite its limitations, such a surface level exploration nevertheless permits an explicit and intelligent analysis of the ways in which cognitive processing demands of writing tasks are likely to change across the different proficiency levels; such an analysis is likely to enhance our understanding of the developmental progression involved in L2 writing ability as well as make a start on providing the necessary cognitive validity evidence for Cambridge tests.

Planning, organising, monitoring and revision are likely to be employed by most students in writing in their L1 by secondary school (though Purves

(1992:113) argues that in United Kingdom the focus is often only on the first draft). However, the literature does suggest that such editing happens less in L2 especially at lower levels. If we also take into account the limited amount of writing possible at the lower levels (Weigle 2002) and the short history in Cambridge terms of examinations at these levels (PET 1984>, KET 1994>), it seems sensible to exclude them from our survey below and to focus on Upper Main Suite (FCE, CAE and CPE).

The activities of planning, monitoring and revising written work for content and organisation become increasingly relevant in FCE, CAE and CPE, particularly at the CAE and CPE levels. However, in the current writing tests no dedicated time is allocated for these activities and no explicit advice to carry them out is provided in the task rubric, so ways of addressing these limitations will need to be explored in the future.

In skilled writers, provisional organisation of ideas in abstract form both in relation to the overall text and to each other normally takes place in the initial stages of the writing process. The writer evaluates their relative importance, and decides on their relative prominence in the text. Unskilled L2 writers are less likely to engage in such organisation. One reason may be that unskilled L2 writers experience a heavy cognitive load in simply encoding their thoughts in linguistic form so that the resources available for meaning building may be severely limited. Another might be their poor genre competence (see Bax 2011).

In the compulsory task in Part 1 of the FCE Writing paper candidates are provided with an organisational structure through the content organisation in the letter. The points in the task constitute the structure. This means that the requirement for them to demonstrate organisational skill is relatively limited – they simply have to present ideas logically. This partial anomaly at the B2 level needs empirical investigation to ensure that appropriate demands in terms of this level of processing are being made on test takers in the FCE examination.

At CPE, as in CAE, tasks normally lack any direct reference to how candidates should organise their responses. An awareness of the relative importance of topics and the ability to foreground would seem to play a progressively more important part at the organisational level in these examinations. Coherence between ideas and developing a clear overall argument structure are also expected at the upper two Main Suite levels as is a more developed genre performance (Bax 2011:17).

At FCE, some of the writing tasks begin to involve knowledge transformation, albeit at a basic level. Where these FCE tasks seem to represent a step up from PET is in demanding that the writer makes rhetorical decisions related to the purpose of the text and to the reader; that in order to provide coherence, the writer integrates information as new paragraphs are written. Writing tasks at the more advanced levels demand ever more complex language processing, and planning is increasingly required at the CAE and CPE levels. It is reasonable to expect candidates at these advanced levels to demonstrate knowledge transforming as well as knowledge telling.

This is not always required in the current FCE test but ways of building this in more systematically are being explored. The current possibility of candidates being able to choose between tasks in Part 2 of FCE creates something of a dilemma since it allows candidates to potentially avoid demonstrating knowledge transforming skills altogether at this level. In order to determine whether or not all candidates from this B2 level upwards should be required to write a task which entails a degree of knowledge transforming, Cambridge ESOL needs to investigate further the work carried out so far into whether alternative choices (e.g. between knowledge telling versus knowledge transforming tasks) make similar demands on candidates and result in equivalent behaviour.

The knowledge transforming process at the highest C2 level requires the candidate to reflect carefully on the complexity of the task, in order to arrive at the most appropriate method for addressing the problems related to the rhetorical and content demands of the task. Candidates who are likely to be most successful are those who have practised the types of writing tasks which develop knowledge transforming skills. There is an expectation that these test takers will operate in the problem spaces relating to both rhetoric and content and will do so both while writing and post-writing. Less skilled writers may have encountered the need for knowledge transforming – but just can't do it.

As a result of monitoring activities the sensible candidate should return to those aspects of the text considered unsatisfactory and make corrections or adjustments perhaps after each sentence, each paragraph or when the whole text has been written. At a basic level, monitoring involves checking the mechanical accuracy of spelling, punctuation and syntax. At the more advanced levels, it can involve examining the text to determine whether it reflects the writer's intentions and fits the developing argument structure of the text. At these levels evidence from examiners' reports on performance on these tasks would suggest that better candidates were also able to review the appropriateness of the contents and their order and the appropriateness of words while writing.

Context based validity in current Cambridge Writing papers

Drawing on Shaw and Weir (2007) we provide below a descriptive analysis of the contextual validity parameters of current Cambridge UMS Reading tests.

Response format

At FCE, CAE and CPE there is a mixture of semi-controlled tasks where the task is framed by the rubric and/or input texts but candidates are expected to make their own contribution. For example, at FCE, CAE and CPE a number of tasks may involve responding to input provided, usually in the form of a number of short texts. Variation in the length and nature of these input texts might be one way in the future of further differentiating the higher level tests from one another.

A key issue for attention is the role of integrated reading and writing tasks. CAE and CPE are recognised for university entrance purposes in the United Kingdom but in their present format they only include tasks which integrate reading and writing in a limited way; earlier reading into writing tasks such as summary would better reflect reading to learn and writing in that target discourse community and are more likely to activate knowledge transformation which is the hallmark of writing at this level (see Weir 1983, 2005b). From 2012 it is intended to move a short summary of two passages from the Use of English paper into the CPE Writing paper which will help repair the current deficit and ensure that an intertextual representation is included into the highest level examination in the Main Suite.

Task purpose

In terms of task purpose the possibility of having to deal with conative purpose appears from the FCE level upwards. However, within these higher levels (FCE, CAE, CPE) the same broad range of purposes for writing may occur at each of the three levels and there is relatively little differentiation. Only at CPE and CAE is a discursive task compulsory.

The implication of offering a choice of writing tasks emerges once again here. At the moment allowing a choice makes differentiation between levels difficult; and if the tasks are not equivalent in complexity and result in differential performance then this invariably raises issues of fairness

If it was necessary for candidates to complete a conative task as a compulsory requirement at FCE, we might be more certain that an additional criterial distinguishing feature was available for discriminating between the adjacent levels PET and FCE.

Knowledge of criteria

Only at CAE and CPE is there an expectation that an adequate response will have an impact on the reader through the candidate's sophisticated use of language resources. At FCE a positive effect on the reader is expected and although meaning is always communicated, language use is far less sophisticated. The stress on content and organisation at the upper levels is in accord with what we know about processing loads (see also Weir (1983) for an empirical justification for this in terms of academic expectations, and note the earliest criteria reported for CPE above). Below B2 level there simply may not be enough attentional space available for any real planning and organisation as candidates have enough problems in coping with the demands of generating adequate grammar and lexis.

Candidates may need to be reminded of the criteria of assessment before embarking on a writing task as this facilitates not only planning and organisation but also monitoring and revising, which are key processing elements in writing tasks. Attention is drawn to marking criteria elsewhere, particularly in Handbooks, but consideration should be given in future to repeating a synopsis of them on the paper itself. Currently the expectations of the reader in terms of marking criteria are not explicitly spelled out for the candidate on Cambridge Writing papers.

Length and time available

The upper word limit at FCE is substantially greater than that which is expected of Lower Main Suite candidates. There is also a substantial difference between the amount required at FCE and at CAE. There is a significant increase in the amount of time available at CAE and CPE. This increase in time allocation matches the increase in length of writing output. Longer pieces of writing will in themselves add to the cognitive pressures on the writer.

It is important to remember that a symbiotic relationship exists between the various construct validity components of our socio-cognitive framework: context validity, cognitive validity and scoring validity. Clearly, the contextual parameters of the task setting, such as length of output or time allocation, will impact on the actual processing undertaken by the test taker. The linguistic and content knowledge required of the test taker in order to undertake the task, i.e. the executive resources, is initiated by the task setting (the linguistic and content demands intended by the developer of the test are communicated through the task instructions). This means that any decisions which are taken with regard to task context, such as the time available to the candidate, will have potential implications for any subsequent processing and for the executive resources needed for task completion. For example, it might be imprudent to reduce significantly the time available until the potential ramifications of this on performance are investigated not least the knock-on effect of the other parameters discussed in this volume.

If research findings were to suggest that dedicated macro planning and monitoring enhanced performance when proactively encouraged and dedicated time were made available for promoting these critical aspects of cognitive processing, and if such measures were found to be administratively practical, it might in fact be necessary in the future to contemplate even longer writing tests at FCE, CAE and CPE levels.

Writer–reader relationships

There is a gradual progression through the levels from personally known (e.g. friend or teacher) to specified audiences with whom candidates are not personally acquainted (e.g. an editor or magazine readers). Addressing a broader range of audience is required between PET and FCE as candidates only write to people they know personally in PET. By CAE, candidates are no longer writing to people they know personally. A slightly wider range of unacquainted audience distinguishes CAE and CPE. At these two levels candidates must decide what sorts of evidence the reader is likely to find persuasive. The effect of the writing on the reader is taken into account in the marking in Upper Main Suite examinations (see mark schemes for CPE and FCE above).

Lexis

At FCE level, topics need to be addressed in more detail and with greater lexical precision than in Lower Main Suite. For CAE and above, the language expected is more sophisticated and the tasks more lexically challenging than at FCE. Topics, tasks and functions which only require simple language are avoided at the higher levels. At FCE and above there is also an expectation that candidates are able to reformulate input language in their own words. Language associated with conative functions is needed for tasks at CAE and CPE.

Grammatical structure

There is a gradual progression in the complexity of the grammatical constructions required by tasks. This is in line with the structural levels appearing in English Language Teaching course books aimed at language levels corresponding to the Council of Europe levels. At FCE level, candidates should have a good grasp of Vantage level language. They should have mastered the main structures of the language and should not be prevented from communicating by a lack of structural resources. As long as the marker does not have to make an effort to understand the writer's meaning, errors with such aspects of language as gerunds, infinitives or some confusion between the past simple and present perfect will not be unduly penalised. At FCE level, candidates tend to write either simply and accurately or more ambitiously but less accurately. Both types of candidate may achieve adequate performance if other aspects of their writing are satisfactory.

By CAE candidates are expected to use the structures of the language with ease and fluency. There should be some evidence of range; very simple but accurate language is not enough at this level. Candidates must be able to demonstrate some ability to use complex structures even though they are not expected to write error-free prose. CAE candidates must also show that they have a grasp of structures which allow them to express opinions and feelings in an appropriate register. They can, for example, express dissatisfaction in a manner that does not sound aggressive by using appropriately tentative structures.

By CPE level candidates should demonstrate a high degree of range and accuracy with regard to structures. They should have a mastery of the structures needed to present ideas and attitude in a well-organised and sophisticated manner. Some errors will be tolerated if these do not confuse the reader in any way; for example, an inappropriate use of a preposition after a verb or an omitted article will not in themselves cause the writer to lose marks.

Discourse mode

There is a clear distinction between PET and FCE. At FCE the rhetorical task of argument differentiates it from PET and discursive tasks are important throughout FCE, CAE and CPE. CAE is differentiated from FCE by the greater range of genres the candidate might have to address overall and having to deal in the compulsory Part 1 task with varying degrees of persuasion to convince the intended audience of the writer's point of view. The effect of discourse mode on performance in writing is another under-researched area and the ways in which this parameter might contribute to further grounding of distinctions between levels in FCE, CAE and CPE in both the reading and writing papers needs investigating. As previously discussed, the variety of modes which result from the choices available to candidates needs to be looked at to ensure they present candidates with an equally difficult task and lead to equivalent performances.

Functional resources

There is a clear functional progression between PET and FCE in terms of complexity but also in the degree of precision in the structural exponents employed to fulfill the function(s). Functions associated with conative purposes and argumentative tasks for language are necessary at CAE. The functions at CAE and CPE are increasingly diverse and demanding and are intended to produce more complex structures or collocations.

The functional parameter is obviously not a stand-alone element as the structural exponents and the lexis chosen to achieve it will also vary from level to level in those cases where the same functions are being deployed. Research however has indicated a number of functions which seem to occur uniquely for the first time at a particular level (see Shaw and Weir 2007:118–125).

Content

FCE candidates may be expected to deal with a wide range of knowledge areas including any non-specialist topic that has relevance for candidates worldwide (van Ek and Trim 2001). CAE candidates are expected to be able to deal with topics that are more specialised and less personal than those that tend to feature at lower levels. The step up to CAE also involves coping with lexically challenging topic areas (e.g. the environment, the scientific world, traditions). At CPE level more abstract and academic topics appear and the candidate may be expected to be able to write on any non-specialist topic. CPE candidates are expected to be able to operate confidently in a wide variety of social, work-related and study-related situations. At all levels topics that might offend or otherwise unfairly disadvantage any group of candidates are avoided.

Endnote

There was a convergence of two differing traditions in the testing of writing in Britain and the United States over the course of the 20th century. Cambridge had always set great store by the context validity of the direct writing essay tasks included in its examinations since 1913. Since the 1990s additional consideration has been given to the various aspects of scoring validity at Cambridge. More recently increased attention has also been paid to the cognitive validity of the writing activities initiated by the tasks (see Bridges 2010, Shaw and Weir 2007:34–62). In the United States there are now similar concerns with all aspects of validity and the focus is again on the direct testing of writing though contextually and cognitively valid tasks as compared to an earlier preoccupation with scoring validity and indirect methods.

The washback of the test on the teaching that precedes it (see Green 2007) is an important consideration which has militated against the use of indirect measures in Cambridge writing tests since they began in 1913. From our current communicative perspective on testing it makes more sense to be practising activities in advance of a test which are directly relevant to the demands of the candidates' future target situation. In the 21st century it now seems rather perverse to be training students in ways of improving their scores on reductionist, indirect tests of writing, such as multiple-choice tests of written expression, as was necessary for some international high-stakes tests of writing in the not so distant past (notably TOEFL before July 1986). If the purpose is to measure writing ability, examination boards should be employing writing tasks that encourage teachers to prepare students for an examination by equipping them with the writing abilities they will also need in the real-world context.

As a general principle, it is now felt in Cambridge that language tests should, as far as is feasible, place the same requirements on test takers as are involved in writers' responses to communicative tasks and settings in non-test 'real-life' situations. This approach requires attention to both the cognitive and the social dimensions of communication as well as scoring validity. The more features of real-life writing (cognitive, contextual and scoring) that can be built into test tasks, the greater the potential for positive washback on the learning that precedes the test taking experience and the easier it will be to make statements about what students can or cannot do from the test as regards writing in a real-world context. Predictions made on the basis of inferences from test scores are likely to be better grounded if activities in the test reflect those of this future target situation in as many aspects of construct validity as are viable.

As with writing, there was a direct language performance task in the oral paper, viz the interview, right from the start in the first CPE in 1913. However, the history of Cambridge Speaking tests, which we turn to next, demonstrates a far earlier concern with the demands of scoring validity than appears to have been the case with written assessment.

4

The measurement of speaking ability 1913–2012

Ivana Vidaković and Evelina D Galaczi
Cambridge English Language Assessment

> To speak and to speak well are two things. A fool may talk, but a wise man speaks.
>
> Ben Jonson

Introduction

Most language testing professionals would agree that the testing of speaking is not an easy endeavour, since oral assessment brings with it an array of issues which do not fit easily in a dominant psychometric paradigm. Spolsky (1995a) draws a comparison between the measurement of sports achievements and performance assessment: in sports, achievements in some disciplines can be readily measured, e.g. how many seconds an athlete takes to run 100 metres, how high or far he/she can go, while others involve the subjective judgement of expert judges, as in gymnastics or diving, for example. Speaking assessment is clearly in the latter category and even though speaking has been seen as an important component of language proficiency throughout the 20th century, the difficulties involved with speaking tests have either excluded oral assessment from testing batteries or given it a limited presence. When oral assessment has been included in the test batteries, it has presented a whole array of difficult and at times controversial issues which have needed to be addressed and resolved.

The aim of this chapter is to trace the historical developments associated with the assessment of speaking ability over the last 100 years. The focus will be on the constructs underlying speaking tests as reflected in the *test formats* used and associated *scoring parameters*. The discussion will focus on key developments worldwide and on the development of Cambridge English Speaking tests, starting with the Certificate of Proficiency in English (CPE) oral test in 1913. As already noted in Chapter 1 and discussed by Hawkey (2009:8), language test constructs were less explicitly stated in the past than now and so our discussion of construct evolution will be inferential at times, drawing on the test content/format used and scale(s) employed, and not necessarily on explicit institutional statements from test providers.

As in previous chapters, this overview and discussion of the Cambridge English speaking tests will be guided by a framework for test analysis which has been collaboratively developed by Cambridge ESOL and Cyril Weir and is seen as a useful tool which can provide a systematic approach to focusing on different aspects of a test (Weir 2005a). As noted in the introductory chapter, this 21st century framework will be used not to critique and criticise speaking tests developed in the 20th century and before that. Rather, its function is to provide a heuristic through which features of tests – present or past – can be investigated and discussed. It would also serve as a consistent frame of reference for tracking and discussing the changes to the speaking constructs over time.

The chapter, therefore, is divided into three main sections: first, speaking test formats used throughout the late 19th and 20th centuries will be surveyed and discussed, as contextualised by theoretical, pedagogical, socio-political and institutional factors; then, the socio-cognitive framework (Weir 2005a) as applied to speaking assessment will be briefly outlined; finally, the developments of Cambridge English Speaking tests and associated marking criteria/rating procedures will be discussed and analysed through the lens provided by the framework. In this way the evolution of the construct underlying Cambridge English exams will be explored.

In the discussion to come we will draw on key examples which best illustrate significant points in speaking assessment over the last century. For more detailed accounts of the development of speaking tests in the 20th century, the reader is referred to Spolsky (1995a), McNamara (1996) and Fulcher (2003), who provide detailed historical information and insightful discussions. This chapter aims to extend the discussions in the above three sources through its focus not just on the last century, but also on recent developments in oral assessment, such as paired/group test constructs and the constructs underlying computer-based speaking tests, which have seen a growth in use and research in the last decade.

The survey of test formats to follow is categorised according to the three general categories suggested by Clark (1979), which are now widely accepted in discussions of speaking performance: *indirect* (e.g. a paper-and-pen phonetics paper), *direct* (e.g. a face-to-face interview) and *semi-direct* (e.g. responding to computer-delivered prompts). The absence of a speaking test from a test battery will be discussed as well, since that in itself has implications for the construct(s) underlying the examination. In the other chapters in this volume, the discussion of formats has typically followed a historical progression, with more traditional formats giving way to communicatively-driven ones. While this is true to an extent with speaking formats as well, the historical progression in speaking tests does not fit the communicative trends in a simple linear fashion. For example, while indirect speaking tasks are rightly associated with a very limited definition of the speaking construct and hardly survived into the late 20th century, the absence of speaking tests in large-scale test batteries can be seen to cover a large part of the 20th century, and limited communicative tasks such as reading aloud, for example, are used in computer-delivered tests in present times. As will be seen, the forces behind such construct decisions have not been theoretical, but practical, and indicative of a trend of 'feasibility overcoming desirability' (Spolsky 1995a:35). In contrast, direct L2 speaking tests, reflecting a communicative view of language proficiency, can be found as early as 1913 in the CPE exam. So, an important feature of the present overview is that developments in speaking tests have been driven by a whole host of influences, some theoretical, pedagogic and socio-political, and some very practical.

As our survey of different speaking test formats, scoring issues and their historical developments unfolds, it is important to point out what argument will *not* be made: no test format will be presented as better or worse than others, since test validity does not reside with formats *per se*, but rather with the fit between the test, its purpose, the external criterion measured and the evidential argument to support the decisions taken. As Fulcher (2003:19) notes, 'different constructs are useful for different test purposes'. The focus will be, therefore, on tracing how speaking tests and the constructs underlying them have changed in the last century and why, and not on privileging one test format over another.

We start our overview with tests of speaking which contain no speaking component.

Tests with no speaking component

In the 19th century, before the Oxford (1857) and Cambridge (1858) examinations boards were formed, school language examinations were rare in the United Kingdom (James 1988). University language examinations 'were not very serious affairs' and did not test the ability to communicate, being mostly 'infrequent viva voce tests in sight translation, readings aloud, recitations and the constructions of impromptu epigrams in Latin' (James 1988:35). The absence of L2 speaking tests which would test one's ability to communicate is not surprising in view of the fact that the Grammar Translation Method, which placed emphasis on reading and writing, was widespread in language classrooms in the mid-nineteenth century (as discussed in Chapter 1).

Towards the end of the 19th and in the early 20th century, a few tentative steps towards testing speaking were made in the assessment practices of the Cambridge Medieval and Modern Language Tripos (i.e. Cambridge University Bachelor's degrees), which were established in 1886. The speaking component, however, when added was optional:

> Until 1894 there was no oral test; in 1894 a test of pronunciation was
> introduced, not a test of command of the spoken language; and even
> that was optional. In 1909 an optional test of conversation was added
> (Committee GB 1918:4).

The optional status of speaking assessment in testing practices at the beginning of the 20th century is indicative of the limited alignment between
popular pedagogic approaches at the time (the Reform Movement and the
Direct Method) on the one hand, and assessment trends in Britain and the
United States in the late 19th and early 20th century, on the other hand. The
discrepancy between teaching and testing did not go without criticism: a committee which reviewed the modern language teaching and testing practices in
the United Kingdom at the end of the First World War came to the conclusion that 'even now the methods of examining bodies are usually far behind
the practice of the best teachers; they have been improved, but still too often
hamper the teaching and turn it on the wrong lines' (Committee GB 1918:15).
Their recommendation, as a result, was that examination methods 'need
careful and skilful revision' and that oral examinations should be included
wherever possible to test a candidate's 'speaking power' (Committee GB
1918:57). Acknowledging the impact of exams on teaching practices, Smith
(2004:51) also pointed out that the 'dominance of the university-led system of
examinations meant that grammar-translation method was likely to remain
entrenched in schools so long as the exams stayed the same'.

The gap between teaching (and its focus on spoken language) and
testing practices at the beginning of the 20th century was also seen in the
United States. Prokosch's (1922:182) description of the status quo at the
time provides a relevant insight and recognition of the washback of tests on
classroom curricula:

> A survey of examination papers set by colleges . . . reveals a surprising
> fact. Judging from the vast majority of them one would believe that
> translation and tabulated grammar are still holding undisputed sway in
> our modern language instruction, while the direct method has actually
> all but won the day in secondary schools and is steadily forging ahead in
> colleges. Moreover, some colleges state in their catalogs that the courses
> they offer in continuation of the work of the preparatory schools are
> given in the foreign language; thus they urge high school teachers to use
> the direct method in order to prepare their students for those courses,
> yet effactually hinder them from doing so by setting examinations that
> cannot be reconciled with such teaching.

College entrance language examinations in the United States were written,
consisting of translation from German/French/Spanish, etc. into English
and vice versa, as well as questions on grammar. There were no oral and/or

aural tests despite a call by a Committee on Resolutions and Investigations (CORI) appointed in 1913 by the Association of Modern Language Teachers of the Middle States and Maryland for the testing of spoken proficiency (see CORI 1917). The Committee sent out a proposal for an Aural and Oral college admission test in French, German and Spanish to 1,000 public and private secondary schools and Modern Language Departments in the colleges for feedback. In the spirit of the times, the majority of the respondents supported the proposal as a natural extension of classroom practices, reflecting the Direct Method emphasis on speaking the language, encouraging 'the practice of ear and tongue' and 'ensuring real "working vocabulary" and ready use of it' (CORI 1917:257). However, difficulties were also put forward, such as excessive demands on teachers due to large classes, too many classes and too little time available for oral practice due to 'the reading requirement' and the often-cited problem of achieving uniformity in face-to-face oral tests (CORI 1917:258). Despite the great support it enjoyed among teachers, the Committee's proposal was followed up only by two New York State Colleges (Columbia and Cornell) and only partially so (Decker 1925). Decker suggested institutional stasis and the difficulty of administering oral and aural tests over the country as potential reasons behind it. And so we see the limitations imposed by feasibility on oral assessment practices.

So far, we have focused on the state-of-the-art at the end of the 19th and early 20th century. Interestingly, language tests without an oral component continued to exist into the mid-20th century, even though the view of speaking ability as integral to L2 proficiency was by then widespread. In the United States, for example, TOEFL, first administered in 1964 (Kunnan 2008:140), consisted of listening comprehension, English structure, vocabulary and reading comprehension only. Tests of productive skills, writing and speaking, e.g. the Test of Spoken English, were only added two decades later due to public demand (Kunnan 2008, see also Spolsky 1995a). The rationale for not including the speaking construct in the language proficiency construct was mainly 'the cost and administrative complexity of providing an active speaking test capability at the hundreds of TOEFL administration sites worldwide', as well as 'the paucity of relevant research experience and development . . . concerning the direct evaluation of speaking proficiency on a large-scale basis' (Clark and Swinton 1979:1).

We see once again the role played by feasibility in the definition of the second/foreign language construct underlying some oral tests in the United States. In the United Kingdom, the English Proficiency Test Battery (EPTB) or Davies Test (1964–1980), designed for non-native prospective students at British universities, similarly lacked a speaking component and was a discrete-point test consisting of listening, grammar and reading comprehension (Geranpayeh 2000:36). An essay and an interview were optional test components, and their scores were not taken into account in determining the proficiency level of a candidate (Geranpayeh 2000). Similarly, the English Language Battery (ELBA), used by the University of Edinburgh and other British Universities 'as a diagnostic check on the level of English of incoming overseas students' contained no oral production test (Criper and Davies 1988:50).

In hindsight, it is perhaps surprising that in the 1960s and 1970s many tests, whether in the United States or the United Kingdom, produced scores that were used for university entrance that did not include a speaking construct. As mentioned above, practicality and feasibility were important driving forces behind that decision. It is also important to consider the purpose of the tests. In the case of TOEFL, for example, the purpose of the test was to assess L2 proficiency to cope in an American university setting. Spolsky (1995a) notes that when the test was developed it was felt (rightly or wrongly) that university students needed to have adequate reading and listening comprehension skills, as well as writing skills, but not speaking skills.

A further key reason for the exclusion of speaking from language tests was the psychometric concern with reliability and the fact that speaking tests involve uncontrolled variability – both in the delivery of the examination and its scoring (see the discussion on objective tests in Chapter 1). Psychometric reliability concerns had a strong influence on language testing decisions and practices, especially in the United States where the scientific-psychometric approach to assessment shaped the predominant way of thinking in assessment circles at the time. According to Spolsky (1995a:35), considerations of 'technical difficulties in securing absolute uniformity' prevailed over the desirability of an oral test.

Indirect speaking test formats

Indirect speaking tests, where the test taker is not required to speak, belong to the 'pre-communicative era' in language testing (O'Loughlin 2001:4). An indirect method of assessing speaking can be seen in the early CPE test which included, in addition to an oral component, a 90-minute paper on English phonetics focusing on *knowledge* of how words sound and not on the ability to speak. The paper was part of the test battery between 1913 and 1932 and is an example of the strong influence of classroom practices on the CPE construct, and particularly the Reform Movement which attributed primacy to speech and the teaching of accurate pronunciation in the classroom (Howatt and Widdowson 2004). The popularity of phonetics in foreign language teaching was such that 'all modern textbooks in Europe and America begin with a large section on phonetics' (West 1932:123; see Chapter 1 for further detail and exemplification of the CPE Phonetics paper).

Indirect oral assessment also finds an airing in the 1960s with Lado's discrete-point-testing approach and the pronunciation tests of Lado (1961), where a candidate had to read a set of words and indicate which one was pronounced differently. This approach has now famously been criticised by Morrow (1979), but it is worth noting that Lado himself advocated indirect assessment of speaking only if direct assessment was not possible:

> If, however, it is not possible to devise a technique that is direct . . ., we are free under the new view to explore other techniques which, though different from the skill we are testing, will contain the problems we wish to test in essentially valid linguistic situations. We are thus able to break away from having to ask the student to speak when we test his ability to speak, since the process is inaccurate and uneconomical, and we may use instead techniques that test his ability to operate the elements of speaking in indirect but accurate and economical techniques (Lado 1960:160).

Not surprisingly, indirect tests and the elicitation of passive knowledge were generally short-lived, since they were based on a very narrow and atomistic construct defined in terms of knowledge and not performance (but note that some indirect formats such as the test by the Professional and Linguistic Assessment Board for international medical graduates survived well into the communicative era). The limited scope of the construct underlying indirect speaking tests found empirical support in Buck's (1989) investigation, where very low correlations between written pronunciation tests and more direct measures of pronunciation were observed. George (1962:77) presents a common-sense view as he highlights some of the shortcomings of this approach: 'If, to show their ability to write, our students do not have to write, and to show their ability to speak they do not have to speak, we are indeed beginning a new era in foreign-language work' (see also Robinson 1971).

So far, the discussion has focused on testing batteries which did not involve an oral component. We noted in Chapter 1 that as the Reform and Direct Method movements were gaining ground, the assessment circles at the beginning of the 20th century started to take an interest in the development of oral skills, and as a result direct tests of speaking started to gain importance.

Direct speaking test formats

As discussed in detail in Chapter 1, from the 1880s the Grammar-Translation Method started coexisting with the Direct Method (with its focus on oral fluency) and the Reform Movement (with its focus on phonetics and pronunciation in language classrooms). The primary emphasis on speaking in the latter pedagogic approaches paved the way for a change in focus in L2 oral tests at the beginning of the 20th century. This is the context in which the CPE Speaking test – an early exponent of direct L2 oral testing – appeared in 1913. It involved a 1-hour oral paper consisting of a 30-minute dictation, a 30-minute conversation with an examiner and a reading aloud task. While tests of speaking ability were either rare or optional at the time, the CPE Oral was an obligatory part of the examination from the very start, indicating the importance given to speaking ability within the CPE L2 proficiency construct. The CPE did not appear in a vacuum and in its format we see legacies of the past and pedagogic influences of the time. As these early influences are extensively covered in the introductory chapter, we will only deal with them briefly here. One influencing factor was the importance assigned to speaking in the Reform Movement and Direct Method, which was also complemented by the oral tradition in examining in the United Kingdom, e.g. *viva voce* exams and their oral questioning format, and informal interviews in the Civil Service in the 18th and 19th century. As already noted in Chapter 1, the legacy of the Reform Movement was also seen in the strong influence of phonetics and the inclusion of a Phonetics paper in the CPE test. A further example of the influence of phoneticians and the Reform Movement is seen not just in the oral component of the test, but also in the assessment focus on pronunciation only in the CPE Oral. In this very early direct test, the construct was narrowly seen to comprise mostly pronunciation and intonation.

A further legacy from the past can be seen in the inclusion of a reading aloud task in the CPE Oral test (as discussed in more detail in Chapter 2). University language examinations often included a reading aloud task in Latin (James 1988), and it is this tradition which was inherited by CPE. The initial intended candidature of the CPE test, i.e. teachers, and the use of reading aloud in classrooms provided further rationale for the inclusion of this task. Dictation, which was a traditional teaching technique that had stood the test of time and contained an aural/oral element, also found its way in the CPE oral (see Chapter 5 for a more detailed discussion of the dictation task).

In addition to changing pedagogic practices at the beginning of the 20th century, the evolving socio-political climate in the 1930s and 1940s further contributed to the higher prominence given to speaking in language assessment. Tests with an oral component experienced a growth in the United Kingdom and United States post the Second World War, largely due to the effect of the two wars in signalling the low level of L2 proficiency of learners. In the United Kingdom, this could be seen in the addition of another family member to CPE – the Lower Certificate in English (LCE), which was introduced in 1939 to meet increasing demand for an examination at a lower proficiency level than CPE (Roach 1944a; see the extended discussion in Chapter 1 on the origins of LCE). Similarly to its predecessor CPE, the LCE also included a face-to-face interview and so continued the importance assigned to speaking ability in the test construct at Cambridge. It also signalled a vertical cross-level differentiation in the speaking construct in the late 1930s, which now targeted two distinct proficiency levels.

In the United States, the expansion in the constructs underlying second/ foreign exams could be seen in the Army Specialised Training Programme (ASTP), which reasserted the importance of speaking ability, after its neglect in the 1920s and 1930s. The programme was developed due to a shortage of military personnel who could speak, read or understand a foreign language. Launched in 1943, the programme placed speaking proficiency at the core of L2 proficiency, since it was recognised that, as Kaulfers (1944:140) argued, 'it simply cannot be taken for granted that ability to express oneself in writing is correlated with a like ability to speak the language extemporaneously'. This increased interest in developing speaking skills in the classroom and in testing speaking. As a result, in 1944, an oral test was designed at Queen's College (New York) to assess ASTP students' communicative ability. The test elicited descriptive and narrative skills through picture description and a short talk on a topic task, and included responding to prompts administered on a phonograph (Barnwell 1996:86–87). Oral performance was assessed on a three-point rating scale in terms of overall communicative ability. The talk on a topic task was assessed on grammar, fluency, vocabulary and pronunciation (Barnwell 1996). This represented a significant step in language assessment at the time as it indicated an attempt to tackle variability in two areas: administration, by employing a phonograph to standardise the administration of the Conversation task and rating, by using rating scales and assessment criteria as guides for examiners.

The Army Specialised Training Programme is now widely seen as the predecessor of a major American oral test developed in the 1950s for foreign service personnel: the Foreign Service Institute (FSI) Oral Proficiency Interview (OPI) (Fulcher 2003, McNamara 1996, Spolsky 1995a). The FSI oral test was a counter-reaction to multiple-choice and other discrete-item approaches which:

> although capable of discriminating among examinees as to their relative ability to handle the particular questions included in the test, were not able to indicate in any meaningful way how well examinees would be able to carry out the particular language-use tasks they were expected to encounter in the actual assignment abroad (Clark and Clifford 1988:129).

The development of the FSI test is significant in the history of oral assessment since in the United States, the FSI test was at the forefront of the inclusion of the speaking construct in the overall L2 proficiency construct, just like CPE in the United Kingdom in 1913. The FSI Oral Proficiency Interview was developed in 1952, during a period of 'cold war intensification' (Sollenberger 1978:1) to help indicate how well examinees could carry out language tasks they were expected to perform in real life assignments abroad (an apocryphal account records how the validity of the scores was measured by whether the in-field service officers came back or not!). Spolsky (personal communication) notes that an important development which contributed to the quality of the FSI Oral Proficiency Interview was an unpublished review of foreign language testing by John Carroll. Carroll served as a consultant when the test was refined and the original scale revised by the FSI testing unit, which was headed at the time by Frank Rice and Claudia Wilds, his student (see also Herzog 2011).

The oral test was run by an interviewer (a native speaker of the language and a certified examiner) and assessed by a rater (an experienced instructor in that language or a linguist thoroughly familiar with it); the rater had the authority to assign the score, but consultation with the interviewer was encouraged, which would often result in the rating being assigned through consensus (Clark and Clifford 1988). The test lasted between 10 and 40 minutes, depending on the examinee's proficiency level. The interviewer would begin with simple social formulae, after which grammatical structures would be elicited from the candidate. A role-play or a prepared dialogue would follow. For example, one of the testers would play the role of a monolingual speaker of the test language and the other would enact a monolingual speaker of English; the examinee's task was to play the role of an informal interpreter between the two of them (Clark and Clifford 1988).

A further contribution of the FSI oral test is that the raters used a six-band holistic scale which included performance descriptors defining distinct levels of proficiency and signaled a psychometric attempt to define a criterion external to the test candidature itself. Initially, performance was assessed on a six-band holistic scale and, in 1958, a checklist of five 'factors' or criteria (accent, comprehension, fluency, grammar and vocabulary) was added, to be used 'as a check on a single holistic score' (Fulcher 2003:11). The factors were weighted, with pronunciation being awarded less importance (Spolsky, personal communication). The criteria checklist was aimed at addressing potential variation in scores, e.g. different testing teams applying different standards or the tester's familiarity with the test taker, as well as the influence of rank and age of officers (Sollenberger 1978). The test candidates were often higher in rank than the examiners, who were thus constrained to justify their scores (Spolsky, personal communication). Analytic scales were also developed for the above criteria, solely for the purpose of training FSI raters. These scales represent an important step forward in analytic assessment, despite the fact that they have been criticised (with the luxury of hindsight) for insufficiently defined descriptors (e.g. types of errors to expect at each band and the imprecision of modifiers such as 'very', 'frequently'), for apparent lack of concern with the causes of hesitation/pauses in the fluency criterion, and for being based solely on intuitive judgment of developing language proficiency (Fulcher 2003:13).

As Clark and Clifford (1988) testify, the scales descriptors were based on the experience of FSI Washington staff and in-field service officers in relation to language use requirements and degrees of language performance in the field.

The FSI oral test and associated holistic rating scale became influential and were adopted by the Defense Language Institute and the Peace Corps. What followed was an initiative among agencies in 1968 to standardise the speaking tests (in the shape of the Interagency Language Roundtable (ILR) speaking test, see Fulcher (2000:487)) as well as the scale descriptors and to provide a common yardstick. The revised scale is nowadays known as ILR scale, a standardised holistic scale ranging from level 0 ('no proficiency') to level 5 ('functionally native proficiency'). The FSI Oral Proficiency Interview and scale were also adopted in the 1970s by non-government programmes, such as universities, and gave rise to the American Council for the Teaching of Foreign Languages (ACTFL) scale, which included a refinement of the bands at the lower levels. The ILR scale was revised further in 1985 and nowadays this scale is still used to document language proficiency within the American government: 'all U.S. Government agencies adhere to the ILR Definitions as the standard measuring stick of language proficiency' (Herzog 2011). Besides linguistic competence, it is significant to note that the ILR scales also capture aspects of socio-linguistic competence and appropriacy, containing references to the ability to carry out most formal and informal conversations, respond appropriately and use and understand colloquialisms and pertinent cultural references. This was certainly in line with the communicative language teaching and testing approach that was spreading through the 1970s and an important stage in the broadening of the second/foreign language speaking construct to include a consideration of socio-linguistic factors, which in this case were driven by the real-life needs of foreign service officers.

A controversial aspect of the ILR scale, which has been retained until the present day, is that of the native speaker. The concept of the native speaker as a criterion has been extensively discussed by Davies (2003), characterised as vague by Lantolf and Frawley (1985), and criticised as elitist by Savignon (1985). It is worth noting that in addition to such conceptual reservations about the native-speaker criterion, scales based on a native-speaker model are often in effect shortened, since the highest point, an educated native speaker, is seldom used (Spolsky, personal communication). An educated native speaker was also used as the absolute criterion in Cambridge English assessment scales for decades, although scales produced for Cambridge speaking tests from the 1990s onwards did not use the native speaker as the non-test criterion (Taylor 2011b).

In the United Kingdom an attempt at defining rating standards and making sure that examiners were rating to common standards through examiner standardisation were two key developments just after 1945. In contrast, before World War Two much faith was put solely in the expert judgment of experienced examiners (see Roach 1945a and Tattersall 2007).

The 1960s to 1980s, therefore, saw a growth in the explicit description of performance in assessment scales, and by extension, in the explicit definition of the test construct via the scales in the United Kingdom and the United States. The scales at the time, e.g. the ACTFL Oral Proficiency Interview scale, have often been criticised for their intuitive basis and for lack of empirical support (Fulcher 2003:16). Criticising ACTFL guidelines, Lantolf and Frawley (1985:342) point out that the criteria 'measure reality by definition'. It is important to note that the ACTFL scales were not alone in being examples of 'armchair' approaches to scale development which relied on experts' intuition (Fulcher 2003). The Cambridge English scales at the time and the majority of operational scales were also developed drawing on collective expert judgement. Since second language acquisition research provided no description of linguistic ability that could be used for the practical purposes of language assessment, intuitive expert judgment was inevitably relied on. The intuitive development of most scales in the 1950s to 1980s has now evolved into the more widespread use of empirically-derived assessment scales which draw on a range of scale-development approaches, including expert judgement, as well as quantitative and qualitative methodologies (e.g. Fulcher 1996a, Galaczi, ffrench, Hubbard and Green 2011, Upshur and Turner 1995). The move from intuitively-based to empirically-informed scales represents an important development in speaking assessment in the last two decades, since they signal that the construct, as expressed in the scales, started to be based on linguistic behaviours that actually happen in learner speech and not on what experts think happens. It is significant to also note that the CEFR scale (Council of Europe 2001), which is today widely used in Europe and beyond, presents learner profiles and portfolios as part of the assessment framework.

Reliability comes to the forefront

The significance of the FSI oral test lies not just in the inclusion of speaking ability in the L2 proficiency construct in the United States, but in the serious and systematic consideration which was given to psychometric issues in oral assessment. It is necessary, however, to take a step back from the 1950s in the United States to the 1940s in the United Kingdom, when Jack Roach, one of the key figures behind the CPE and LCE exams, was addressing similar issues at Cambridge (see Appendix C for a copy of Roach's 1945a report). As Spolsky (1990a) notes, most historical accounts of the psychometric challenges faced in oral assessment typically take the FSI oral interview as the starting point, but as he points out these issues were previously voiced in the now seminal Roach (1945a) report, which drew on an earlier discussion of reliability in assessment by Edgeworth (1888; see Chapter 3 for discussion of Edgeworth's views on how to improve marker reliability). Roach focused on the reading aloud section of the Cambridge examination and identified a host of relevant issues, which fundamentally addressed two basic questions: 'how closely could the standards of different oral examiners be coordinated by having them examine jointly and . . . could the standards be defined more precisely?' (Spolsky 1990a:161). Roach's report was ahead of its time in that it identified many of the major issues associated with speaking test reliability and 'recognised the fundamental psychometric goals of reliability and validity' (Spolsky 1990a:170). His recommendations included examiner training, joint examining which would help with keeping standard comparable across individuals, and guidance for raters on what exactly to assess. Roach also recommended the use of recorded samples in training examiners and correlating oral marks with more objective parts of the examination. The paper's influence was, unfortunately, limited since the report was published only internally, and no evidence of an American/British synergy in dealing with these issues has been seen in the academic literature. The FSI team faced similar issues which they addressed independently of Roach's recommendations at Cambridge.

Considerations of reliability, therefore, became important in oral assessment, and received empirical attention in the American L2 assessment field in the 1950s. Early examples of attempts to address such issues are numerous conference papers compiled and published in Clark (1978a). As Spolsky notes (personal communication), Clark faced the challenge of adopting the closed institutional test to the needs of the Peace Corps, and worked, for example, on issues of how short the test could be and still reach reasonable reliability and validity. Other researchers investigated the intra-rater reliability and scoring consistency of the FSI interviews (Adams 1978), the severity of third raters; still others provided information on the inter-rater, intra-rater and test-retest reliabilities (Clifford 1978) and relationship of interview scores to other measures of language competence, conducted as part of ETS research (Clark 1978b).

Despite a long tradition of speaking assessment and Roach's work in the 1940s, investigations of speaking test reliability in the United Kingdom generally lagged behind the United States, possibly due to the fact that Roach's work in the 1940s was largely captured in internal reports within a single institution, which Roach left shortly after. Weir (2003:14) further notes that:

> in these early days UCLES felt it essential to base CPE on the needs of the teachers and their students and on best classroom practice . . . The cardinal guiding principle for UCLES was validity, followed closely by

utility. This did not mean they did not seek to achieve reliability, but reliability was not the overriding determinant of what went into the examination.

The delegating of reliability to secondary place was seen by testers across the Atlantic as a serious issue which needed to be addressed. In 1990 Bachman and Davidson reported that 'reliability coefficients [for Cambridge oral tests] were not available for speaking tests because they were never double scored' (1990:34–35). Hamp-Lyons (1987) and Davies (1987) also criticised the lack of publicly available statistical information on Cambridge English examinations.

As we saw in Chapter 1, a significant development which gave impetus to considerations of reliability at Cambridge was the Cambridge–TOEFL Comparability Study (Bachman and Davidson 1990, Bachman et al 1995). This large-scale study was carried out to investigate, among other things, the reliability of the FCE Speaking test and focused on the equivalence of test packs, the reliability of the multiple examiners who administer the test and who rate the test. The study highlighted the threat posed to reliability in terms of 'the large number of individuals whose experience ranges from that of a short training period immediately prior to administering the interview to many years of administering interviews in a number of different countries' (Bachman at al 1995:134) and recommended that 'Cambridge initiate some means of routinely assuring that the marking of . . . oral interviews is consistent across different centres, grouping patterns, information packages and examiners' (1995:135). This large-scale comparability study was influential in encouraging Cambridge to set up means of routine quality assurance monitoring of Oral Examiners. This is seen in Milanovic, Saville and Shen (1991), which can be considered a first example of a speaking test reliability study conducted within Cambridge. The study focused on inter- and intra-rater reliability, as well as examiner performance on the scales for each assessment criterion using descriptive and inferential statistics, in order to ensure that 'the test is a true measure of spoken language ability' (Milanovic et al 1991:7). Importantly, the CAE test which was introduced in 1991 adopted a double-marking model, highlighting the growing importance assigned to score reliability at Cambridge.

The concern with oral test reliability at Cambridge was also seen in the attempts made from the 1990s onwards to standardise the conduct of oral examinations by introducing examiners' scripts to control the content and quantity of the interviewer's contributions. As Taylor and Galaczi (2011) explain, this was largely influenced by the higher importance assigned to reliability concerns with the oral tests and also by empirically-based insights about interviewer variability (Brown 2003, Lazaraton 1992). In addition, again in an attempt to address reliability concerns, from the 1990s onwards

Cambridge implemented a rigorous system of training, co-ordination and monitoring of Oral Examiners which supports the speaking exams to this day (see Taylor and Galaczi 2011), as well as double-scoring in most of its speaking exams.

The authenticity debate

The preceding sections have largely focused on key moments and issues in the development of direct tests of speaking from the beginning of the 20th century until the 1980s. We have also touched on the inherent reliability issues in oral testing, which have implications for the construct underlying the test, since rater variability may lead to construct-irrelevant variance. We now turn to a major body of research from the 1990s which has provided useful insights about the construct underlying speaking tests which adopted an interview format (a format referred to here as a Language Proficiency Interview). As the Oral Proficiency Interview and other direct language proficiency interview tests became more widespread from the 1950s onwards, they became the subject of empirical research which exposed certain caveats associated with this format and brought up the issue of whether a single type of interaction (i.e. an interview) is sufficient to assess oral proficiency and whether it is representative of conversation. The empirical findings mainly related to the authenticity of the test format (which could potentially lead to *construct under-representation* or *mis-representation*) and the variability introduced from the co-construction of interaction in the test (which could potentially introduce *construct-irrelevant variance*). The first issue relates to validity claims about the test, the second is more closely aligned with the reliability of the test. Both issues have relevance for the construct underlying interview speaking tests.

The limited authenticity of the ACTFL Oral Proficiency Interview was first noted by Lado in the 1974 Washington Language Testing Symposium (Jones and Spolsky 1975). In the 1980s, a growing body of research started focusing on the issue of authenticity. The ACTFL Oral Proficiency Interview (which received the brunt of the criticism, although the issues raised applied to other interview oral tests at the time as well, including CPE) was criticised by the American language testing community since the socio-linguistic context of the Oral Proficiency Interview, given as 'polite formal conversation with a relative stranger' (Clark 1983:438), was found to be limited in terms of communicative roles, status between the interlocutors (equal/unequal), and language functions. As Savignon (1985:132) remarked, 'among the many contexts *not* sampled are small group discussion, playing a game, or conducting a survey, contexts requiring very different discourse strategies, strategies that teachers often encourage, or would like to encourage, in their classrooms'. There was also an awareness that information questions which are 'the backbone of OPI testing' may not be the backbone of natural real-life conversation (Lantolf and Frawley 1988:182).

Following the now classic appeal by van Lier (1989) to look *inside* the language proficiency interview, i.e. to analyse the discourse produced, empirical research findings revealed features of both informal conversation and interviews in this test format. Lazaraton (1992) used Conversation Analysis techniques and documented that even though examiner-led language proficiency interview exams shared some features with conversations, the pre-specified system of turn-taking indicated similarities with the interview speech event. Ross and Berwick, in a series of studies (1992, 1996) which focused on the types of accommodations employed by interviewers during the test, concluded that speaking test interviewers adjust their speech in the same manner as native speakers do with non-native speakers in conversation. They suggested that there is a 'greater fit between interview and non-test situations than we think' (Ross and Berwick 1992:170) and proposed that the language proficiency interview is 'a hybrid of interview and conversational interaction' (1992:160). Young and Milanovic (1992) took up the notion of control and contingency in the language proficiency interview, and concluded that oral interviews are asymmetrically contingent and as such bear little resemblance to conversation and the collaborative management of talk by both parties. Johnson and Tyler (1998), perhaps the most strident critics of the ACTFL Oral Proficiency Interview, analysed one representative Oral Proficiency Interview used for interviewer training and focused on the turn-taking behaviour of the participants. The authors suggested that the Oral Proficiency Interview could not be considered a valid example of a typical, real-life conversation since salient features of natural conversation such as turn-taking and topic negotiation were not present. They added: 'Naturally occurring conversation is by its very nature interactive, and . . . a crucial part of this interactiveness is a sense of involvement or reactiveness among interlocutors' (1998:48). This, Johnson and Tyler maintained, is not what happens in the Oral Proficiency Interview, and Johnson further supported this claim in a later study (Johnson 2001).

The available research seemed to indicate, therefore, that the language proficiency interview was not 'natural' conversation. The authenticity debates, however, seemed to disregard a crucial point, i.e. the purpose of the tests and the amorphous meaning of the term 'conversation'. In terms of fitness for purpose between test purpose and test format, clearly a test claiming to test informal conversation would run into problems with its fitness for purpose argument since there will be limited alignment between an oral test and informal conversation as the external criterion. (Stevenson (1985:43) aptly reminded us that 'this is a test, not a tea party'.) Making conversation the only test criterion, therefore, is misguided. At the same time, there are many interactions one engages in on a daily basis which do involve unequal power relations and information question-answer sequences, which form the backbone of the language proficiency interview format (Fulcher, personal communication).

Bachman and Palmer's (1996) discussion of authenticity also has relevance here. The authors have found it useful to discuss authenticity in terms of situational authenticity, i.e. the degree of correspondence between the test task and the non-test domain, and interactional authenticity, i.e. the degree of correspondence between the cognitive processes triggered by a test task and a non-test task from the desired non-test domain. Weir's (2005a) distinction between cognitive validity and context validity is referring to the same dichotomy in conceptualising authenticity. The Oral Proficiency Interview and similar language proficiency interviews, therefore, could be said to have limited situational authenticity, as argued by the studies cited above, but in terms of interactiveness, they could tap into some of the functional resources and cognitive processes found in non-test tasks (Field 2011).

The variability debate

In addition to the body of research focusing on the authenticity of language proficiency interviews, empirical findings in the 1980s and 1990s revealed another fundamental issue in direct oral tests: the variability inherent in jointly constructed interaction, which is potentially present despite attempts to standardise the examination and rating process. Clearly, test variability has implications for a test's reliability and ultimately construct definition, since it creates non-uniform test conditions. If each interview becomes unique, then different tests would be potentially tapping into somewhat different constructs.

In terms of examiner variability, Lazaraton (1996) documented deviations from the Interlocutor frame (i.e. examiner script) for the Cambridge Assessment of Spoken English (CASE). The deviations consisted of different interviewer support and accommodative behaviour, such as repeating questions at a slower rate, echoing and correcting responses, giving evaluative responses and supplying vocabulary. As the author noted, some behaviours were exhibited more by some examiners than others, which 'raised the potential problem of unequal opportunities for candidates to demonstrate ability and to obtain interlocutor support' (Lazarton 1996:166). Brown (2003), in a frequently cited study, also analysed variation across interviewers in the ways they elicited test-taker speech samples and showed that different interviewing techniques could affect a candidate's score. Using a Conversation Analysis methodology in the analysis of two interviews involving different interviewers but the same test taker, the author illustrated 'how intimately the interviewer is implicated in the construction of test taker proficiency' (Brown 2003:1). Brown showed that a candidate was given a higher score and perceived as a 'willing and responsive interlocutor' when interviewed by an interviewer who was more explicit in her questioning technique and topic development, regularly provided feedback and showed interest in what the candidate was saying (Brown 2003:16). The same candidate had a lower score and was perceived as 'unforthcoming or uncooperative' (Brown 2003:16) when interviewed by the interviewer whose technique was different and who used implicit closed questions and echoes which were misinterpreted by the candidate as closures or lack of interest, rather than prompts for more information.

A related body of research highlighted the role of the background variables which interlocutors (both test takers and examiners) bring to the speaking test – the so-called 'interlocutor effect' (O'Sullivan 2002). (Interlocutor effects, it should be noted, are potential threats to the validity of all direct tests, not just one-to-one formats. The effects introduced by test takers will be picked up again when paired and group tests are discussed.) Studies on the jointly constructed nature of interaction highlighted the influence of the interlocutors' background variables in affecting the discourse produced in a speaking test (e.g. Berwick and Ross 1996, Katona 1998, O'Loughlin 2002, Young and Halleck 1998). Such findings are perhaps not altogether surprising, since sociolinguistic research has unequivocally indicated that characteristics such as gender, cultural/L1 background, personality, acquaintanceship and the role of the participants can affect the amount and quality of interaction in a pair or a group (Beebe 1980, Beebe and Zuengler 1983, Wolfson 1989). Who one talks to, in other words, is not unimportant, as the characteristics of the interlocutor affect the way we speak.

The authenticity and variability debates of the 1990s highlighted the growing awareness of constructs and the fact that construct definitions are open to scrutiny and challenge. The available empirical insights at the time revealed an important shift in the construct underlying direct speaking tests and pointed to the need to define it in interactional and socio-cognitive terms. This broadening of the construct is even more pronounced in the case of paired and group oral tests, which we turn to now.

Paired and group speaking tests: Towards a more interactional approach

The models of communicative competence to emerge in the 1980s and 1990s influenced thinking about speaking test constructs. As we noted in Chapter 1, the work of Hymes (1974), Halliday (1975) and van Dijk (1977) led to considerations of performance, in addition to competence, and paved the way for models of communicative competence in the 1980s and 1990s (Bachman and Palmer 1996, Canale and Swain 1980). As a result, that period saw a growth in the use of paired and group oral assessment, partly as a response to the move towards a more communicative approach in language teaching and partly as a reaction to some of the limitations of the language interview test format (discussed above), such as the relatively restricted range of tasks and types of interaction and the unequal distribution of rights and responsibilities between the examiner and candidate. In other types of interactions, such as peer-peer discussions or conversations, the conversational rights and responsibilities of the participants are more balanced and a wider spectrum of functional competence is sampled as a result. The paired/group test format, which creates opportunities for peer-peer interaction, was seen as a viable alternative to the singleton language proficiency interview test format at Cambridge (a format which had in fact been considered as a possibility in the 1950s, but decided against).

The inclusion of a larger range of contextual variables in paired/group tests through a wider variety of tasks has been seen as an opportunity to gather broader evidence about test taker skills, and has led to a tighter alignment between a construct defined in socio-cognitive communicative terms and the test format. Paired/group test formats can be seen in many of the Cambridge English oral tests and the Michigan ECPE oral test. The *Cambridge English: First* test, for example, involves two test takers (and two examiners) and consists of a multi-task format where one task involves an interview, another an uninterrupted candidate long turn, and two tasks involve candidate/candidate interaction and candidate/candidate/interviewer interaction. An example of a group format can be seen in the test developed by the Royal Society of Arts Examinations – the Communicative Use of English as a Foreign Language (CUEFL) test, in which oral interaction is tested in simulated situations (see Hawkey 2009, Simmonds 1985). The group oral test format has also been used in Finland (Folland and Robertson 1976), Israel (Reves 1981), and Italy (Lombardo 1984) in the late 1970s and 1980s. Currently the group format is used by the Hong Kong Examinations and Assessment Authority, as part of its school-based oral assessment component.

As paired and group testing became more widespread, empirical attention turned to this test format and showed that, in contrast to the conventional language proficiency interview test format, paired/group oral tasks result in more symmetrical interaction possibilities (Együd and Glover 2001, Galaczi 2008, Iwashita 1998, Kormos 1999, Lazaraton 2002); elicit a wider sample of learner performance with a bigger range of speech functions (ffrench 2003, Galaczi and ffrench 2011) and provide more opportunities for test takers to display their conversational management skills (Brooks 2009, Gan, Davison and Hamp-Lyons 2008, Kormos 1999, O'Sullivan, Weir and Saville 2002). This body of literature has confirmed Skehan's (2001:169) assertion that such test tasks 'enable a wider range of language functions and roles to be engineered to provide a better basis for oral language sampling with less asymmetry between participants'. Brooks (2009), for example, compared interaction in two tests of oral proficiency – the individual format and paired format, and found more complex interaction between participants in the paired configurations: she observed more prompting, elaboration, finishing sentences, referring to a partner's ideas, and paraphrasing in the paired format. Gan, Davison and Hamp-Lyons (2008) found that equal power distribution and a range of speech functions associated with topic negotiation (initiating, expanding and closing or discarding a topic) were present in the group test performances they analysed. Further features of the group/paired format were cited to be positive washback on classroom teaching in terms of exposure to a wider range of real-life interactions (Együd and Glover 2001, Saville and Hargreaves 1999, Shohamy, Reves and Bejarano 1986) and providing more incentive to speak, especially since the candidate can alter the course of the discussion (Folland and Robertson 1976).

The empirical insights provided by this body of literature have been significant for construct definition purposes, since they have indicated that the construct underlying paired/group oral tests is broader than the language proficiency interview construct, and, in addition to features such as lexico-grammatical accuracy and appropriacy, cohesion, organisation, fluency, intelligibility, it also encompasses interaction management features, such as turn-taking management, topic initiation, negotiation and development, and interactive listening (Ducasse and Brown 2009, Galaczi 2010a, May 2009, Riggenbach 1998, Storch 2002).

Variability in paired/group tests

The positive features of the construct underlying paired/group tests, namely its broader definition and more direct correspondence between the test and the non-test criterion of interaction, also holds a fundamental caveat: the variability associated with co-construction of interaction. Both Swain (2001) and McNamara (1997), in their thought-provoking papers, have raised the issue of interpreting *individual* scores based on *jointly* constructed interaction distributed among participants. Co-construction of interaction and the dynamic two-way influence of the interlocutors have become central to the conceptualisation of the construct underlying paired and group tests. As McNamara, Hill and May (2002:228) have rightly noted, 'the view of oral test performance as interactive, so central to much current work, means that it is difficult to consider the impact of test-taker characteristics in isolation from those of interlocutors'.

As discussed earlier, it is now widely recognised that one of the challenges associated with direct speaking tests is the 'interlocutor effect' (O'Sullivan 2002), and this is especially salient in paired/group oral assessment. (Note that the variability associated with the 'interlocutor effect' is also part of the examiner-led language proficiency interview construct, as discussed earlier, albeit its manifestation is more easily controlled.) The role of the interlocutor effect becomes fundamental in speaking tests which are based on a construct defined in interactional terms, as is the case with paired/group tests. An obvious question is how influential these variables are in paired/group test discourse and what role they play in the underlying construct definition.

The body of literature which has investigated the effect of interlocutor variables in paired/group speaking tests has documented a variety of factors influencing test-taker performance in terms of scores awarded and/or discourse: e.g. test takers' acquaintanceship and gender (O'Sullivan 2002), personality (Ockey 2009), extroversion levels (Nakatsuhara 2009) and language proficiency (Nakatsuhara 2009). Overall, however, the findings are often mixed. For example, Berry (1993) focused on the effect of introversion/extroversion and reported that discourse varied according to personality. In a later study, however, the author findings contradicted the ones from the previous study (Berry 2004). The focus on personality was investigated by Nakatsuhara (2009), who concluded that the extroversion level of test takers had some influence on test performance, but – significantly – was closely related to task type. The author found that introverts preferred structured, highly-prompted tasks, whereas extroverts preferred a higher degree of freedom, which echoed Berry's assertion that the effect of personality could be dominant when 'either extreme is placed in their least favoured situation' (Berry 2004:502). O'Sullivan (2002) focused on the effect of test-taker familiarity on performance of Japanese test takers in paired speaking tasks and found evidence of an acquaintanceship effect, reporting that interviewees achieved higher scores when working with a friend. Importantly, however, the author also found a 'sex-of-interlocutor' effect and further speculated that the effect of interlocutor familiarity and gender may be culturally-specific. In another investigation of the effect of candidate familiarity on test performance in paired tests based on a multi-method approach using quantitative score data, candidate questionnaires and interviews, Chambers, Galaczi and Gilbert (2012) concluded that candidate familiarity did not play a significant role in the Swiss context of the study. As far as test takers' perceptions go, Van Moere (2006:420) reported that the majority of students, regardless of their proficiency level or shyness, felt that they were not prevented from contributing to the group discussion 'due to other group members talking'; the consensus was that being tested in a talkative group would not negatively affect their performance. However, research on group oral tests has suggested that talkative test takers may get higher scores (Van Moere and Kobayashi 2004).

The available empirical research on interlocutor variables in paired/group speaking tests has indicated, therefore, that there does not seem to be a simple linear relationship between interlocutor variables and test discourse/scores. As Brown and McNamara (2004:533) rightly argue in the context of gender-related effects, interlocutor variables 'compete in the context of an individual's social identity' and no linear, clear-cut behaviours based on interlocutor characteristics can be claimed.

The key questions in terms of construct, therefore, shift from the role of interlocutor variables – we know they play a role – to what test developers should do about such factors, whether they should try to eliminate such variability altogether or include it in the construct underlying paired/group tests. In other words, the key question becomes whether such variability should be seen as construct-irrelevant variance or whether the variability is part of the construct. Communicating successfully with different interlocutors is a large part of real-life communicative demands and it can be argued that this should be captured in the construct underlying communicative language tests. In this respect, Swain (cited in Fox 2004:240) has argued that variability related to different characteristics of conversational partners is 'all that happens in the real world. And so they are things we should be interested in testing.' She further contends that eliminating all variability in speaking assessment is 'washing out . . . variability which is what human nature and language is all about' (Swain, cited in Fox 2004:240). As such, coping successfully with such real-life interaction demands becomes part of the construct of interactional competence which underlies paired/group oral tests.

In paired/group tests we see, therefore, a broadening of the speaking construct which is defined not just in communicative terms, but also draws on conceptualisations of interactional competence. Interactional competence – first introduced by Kramsch (1986) – suggests that conceptualisations of communicative language ability have to expand beyond a view of language competence as residing within an individual to a more social view where communicative language ability and the resulting performance reside within a social and jointly-constructed context. Following the same line of thought, McNamara (1997; see also McNamara and Roever 2006) argues that interaction can be defined in two contrastive ways: as a *psychological construct* residing within an individual and as a *social construct* which involves joint construction of interaction. As noted in Chapter 1, models of communicative language ability, such as, for example, Bachman and Palmer (1996), employ the psychological conceptualisation of interaction. However, an interactionist approach to defining the construct underlying some speaking tests would involve recognition of the importance of context and its influence on the performance produced. As such, the interlocutors and the host of variables they bring would become part of the construct. Interestingly, the fundamental interactional dependence of the two test takers in paired/group tests has led to some researchers arguing for the awarding of shared scores for interactional competence in paired tasks (May 2009). Similarly, Taylor and Wigglesworth (2009) contend that we may have to design and use different assessment scales and criteria, some aimed at the assessment of individual performance, and some aimed at joint performance. This is a question which future research endeavours and academic discussions would need to address and shed light on.

Defining the construct in interactional terms, including the inherent variability of co-constructed interaction, has vastly broadened the construct underlying some speaking tests. At the same time, this broadening of the construct has highlighted the responsibility of test providers to acknowledge and address the caveats inherent in paired/group tests to allow for a fair test. This can be done through test design, for example, where different response formats are used. As example can be seen in the *Cambridge English: First* test, which employs a range of tasks, only some of which are paired. Such a range of task formats within a test allows for the speaking test to optimise the benefits of an interactional construct, while minimising some of the associated caveats.

In the next section we continue our overview and explore the influence of technology in oral assessment and its impact on the construct underlying semi-direct tests.

Semi-direct speaking test formats

One of the significant recent developments to impact on oral assessment and the conceptualisation of the speaking construct has been the widespread use of computer-based speaking tests. Computers and related technology have acquired considerable importance in language assessment in the last few decades, and there is no doubt that the use of computer-based tests will become even more predominant in the future. The precursor to the modern-day computer-based speaking tests can be seen in the recorded prompts in the Army Specialised Training Programme oral examinations, which emerged in the 1940s and represent the earliest attempts to standardise the assessment of speaking and to achieve time- and cost-effectiveness (see Barnwell 1996). Since then the use of semi-direct tests has grown. For example, the Test of Spoken English was introduced in 1980 by the Educational Testing Service to meet the need for an efficiently delivered and standardised oral test and was widely used until recently to asses the oral proficiency of international teaching assistants (Clark and Swinton 1979); the Simulated Oral Proficiency Interview (Stansfield and Kenyon 1988) was developed for the oral assessment of less commonly taught languages in the United States, such as Portuguese and Hebrew, followed by its successor, the Computerized Test of Oral Proficiency (Kenyon and Malone 2010); the Test in English for Educational Purposes (James 1988) and the Oxford-ARELS Examinations (ARELS Examinations Trust 1989, Hawkey 2004). More recently, new high-stakes oral semi-direct tests can be seen in the TOEFL iBT speaking test and the Pearson Test of English Academic, both of which aim to assess Academic English. An example from the ESP context can also be found in the Cambridge English Business English online test BULATS which aims to provide an additional, optional estimate of speaking ability for employment purposes.

When they were first introduced, computer-based speaking tests were seen as addressing a variety of problems associated with face-to-face oral testing, such as providing uniformity of administration in terms of instructions and questions asked, speed of delivery and precisely controlled timing, as well as the practical benefit of making the costs manageable. Semi-direct tests were also seen as able to reduce or even eliminate the construct-irrelevant variance associated with the human factor in direct assessment of speaking (computers were not influenced by 'the enthusiastic nod' or a 'bright smile' in a speaking test (Roemmele 1966:54)). They were also seen as holding the potential to reduce examiner and rater fatigue: the oral performances of the Colgate University Oral Languages Examination (C.O.L.E) test test takers were 'recorded on tape for leisurely evaluation after the completion of the entire examination' (Stabb 1955:234), and to facilitate the use of a panel of raters whose averaged ratings are more desirable than a rating of a single rater (Stabb 1955: 235).

A fundamental issue since the advent of computer-based language testing has been whether and how the delivery medium changes the nature of the construct being evaluated. Direct speaking tests espouse a socio-cognitive definition of the construct, as discussed above, where speaking is viewed both as a cognitive trait and a social interactional one. In contrast, semi-direct speaking tests draw on a psycho-linguistic definition of the speaking construct which places emphasis on the cognitive dimension of speaking and on psycholinguistic mechanisms such as automaticity (van Moere 2012). The construct is, as such, defined in relatively narrow terms since it does not tap into the ability to deal with the interactional demands of speech. In other words, one construct is embedded in two-way interaction and the other in one-way production. The difference in constructs is succinctly captured by Xi (2010: 294), who argues that computer-delivered and computer-assessed tests 'intend to *predict* speaking proficiency, but do not *directly measure* communicative competence' (see Galaczi 2010b for a more detailed discussion).

A further narrowing down of the construct is seen with automated speaking tests, which are both *delivered* and *scored* by computer. Natural language processing has provided valuable tools for automated assessment of learner performances, but in the process has limited the construct in automated speaking tests to features of test-taker speech which are elicited through production tasks only and can be measured by machine. Following a similar line of thought, Alderson and Bachman (2006:xi) have cautioned that the use of technology in speaking assessment could introduce a 'conservative element' to the assessment and tasks – and, we may argue, the construct – since such items and tasks are constrained by the machine delivery and scoring.

The issue of domain representation and the threat of under- or mis-representation of the construct is crucial in a discussion of computer-based speaking tests. Research has alerted us, for example, to caveats associated with the automated analysis of lexical features. Schmitt (2009, cited in Galaczi and ffrench 2011) and Iwashita, Brown, McNamara and O'Hagan (2008), for example, have found that the only reliable predictor of lexical progression across proficiency levels is the number of tokens (i.e. words) and types (i.e. different words) used. Such measures could provide an indication of the lexical *range* and *accuracy* found in test-taker speech, but come short of assessing *appropriacy* of lexical use, which as we know comprises an essential element of lexical competence (CEFR 2001).

Semi-direct and automated oral tests, therefore, represent a narrowing down of the speaking construct. In the context of automated oral assessment, Bernstein, van Moere and Cheng (2010:356) have argued that automated speaking tests tap into *core linguistic knowledge* – referred to by the authors as 'facility in L2', i.e. the essential units of knowledge which every speaker of a language has mastery of and which are independent of domain of use. As argued earlier, speaking test formats are not inherently 'good' or 'bad', but depend on the alignment between the test purpose and underlying construct. The relatively narrow construct underlying automated speaking tests, therefore, would have its own appropriate contexts of use. In the words of Bernstein et al (2010: 372):

> . . . we assert that, in many cases, the automated test scores alone should not be the sole basis of decision-making, but rather facility scores are one piece of evidence about a candidate that would contribute to decision-making.

The direct/semi-direct concurrent validity debate

The issue of the comparability of semi-direct and direct speaking tests and their underlying constructs received considerable attention in the academic literature in the 1980s and 1990s. In the first wave of studies statistical correlations between the two test modes were seen as the exclusive evidence needed for score equivalence arguments (e.g. Lowe and Clifford 1980). Importantly, at this stage semi-direct oral tests were seen as second-order substitutes to face-to-face tests, to be used when the latter is not possible. The introduction of the semi-direct Simulated Oral Proficiency Interview (SOPI) in the 1980s by the Center for Applied Linguistics (Washington DC) brought semi-direct oral assessment to the foreground and shifted the debate to the semi-direct test format in its own right and no longer as a second-order substitute. As O'Loughlin (2001:17) notes, the period around the mid-1980s saw a change in the status of semi-direct speaking tests. They 'were no longer necessarily conceived as "second-order substitutes" for direct techniques but as potentially more valid and reliable than their direct counterparts', since they could control for variables which were seen as external to the construct (e.g. interlocutor variability). Stansfield (1991:205), for example, suggested that the Simulated Oral Proficiency Interview may be more appropriate for high-stakes decisions, due to the higher degree of 'quality control' it offers. In another concurrent-validity comparison between the two test modes, Stansfield and Kenyon (1992:363) compared the direct Oral Proficiency Interview and the tape-mediated Simulated Oral Proficiency Interview and concluded that 'both tests are highly comparable as measures of the same construct – oral language proficiency'. Wigglesworth and O'Loughlin's (1993) test comparability study also found that the candidate ability measure strongly correlated (although 12% of the candidates received different overall classifications for the two tests, indicating some test method effect). More recently, Bernstein et al (2010) investigated the concurrent validity of automated speaking tests and also reported high correlations between human administered/human scored tests and automated speaking tests.

The semi-direct/direct concurrent validity studies aimed to address the equivalence of scores between the two modes, but through their sole reliance on statistical evidence, these studies did not directly address the issue of the construct these different formats were attempting to measure. The 1990s saw a body of research which addressed not just the statistical equivalence between direct/semi-direct tests, but extended the focus beyond concurrent validation to qualitative analyses of the language elicited through the two formats. Shohamy (1994), for example, carried out a comparison between the Hebrew Oral Proficiency Interview and Simulated Oral Proficiency Interview and focused on language functions and topics. The author characterised the Oral Proficiency Interview as a 'conversation interview' with the structure question-answer-question and the Simulated Oral Proficiency Interview as a 'reporting monologue' where the structure is performance-new task-performance. Shohamy also observed discourse-level differences between the two formats and reported that when examinees talked to a tape-recorder, their language was more literate; there was less variation in intonation, more unfilled silences, and greater cohesion. Her conclusion was that the two test formats do not appear to measure the same construct. Hoejke and Linnell (1994) compared three speaking tests used to assess international speaking assistants: the semi-direct SPEAK test, the direct Oral Proficiency Interview and Interactive Performance tests, and concluded that the semi-direct test they investigated did not adequately tap into discourse, interactional and sociolinguistic competences. Luoma (1997) used a broad range of methods (audio and video recordings, transcripts of language output, questionnaire feedback and interviews with test takers) to compare direct/

semi-direct tests and also concluded that the underlying constructs are differ-ent, despite the strong correlation observed between them. O'Loughlin, in a multi-method comparative investigation, similarly contended that 'these two kinds of test may tap fundamentally different language abilities' (2001:169).

Recent research by Weigle (2010) in the context of writing assessment has reminded us that computers and humans bring different perspectives to the performance assessment process. Weigle reported that human raters and automated rating systems focus on different features of student perfor-mance, indicating that their evaluations are based on somewhat different constructs. And yet, the author argued, there is enough overlap between the two formats, stemming from reference to the same overarching construct, to provide valuable, albeit differing perspectives. Likewise with speaking tests, computer-delivered/scored tests and human delivered/scored tests bring unique strengths to the assessment process, while tapping into overlapping, but not identical constructs. The former present a consistent but relatively narrow conceptualisation of the construct of speaking, the latter tap into a more complex and broader construct, but at the cost of variability.

Summary

To summarise, this section has discussed developments in the testing of speaking ability throughout the late 19th, 20th and early 21st century. In the early days, the main question faced by testing practitioners was *whether* to test speaking ability at all. As the influence of the Reform Movement and Direct Method gained momentum in second/foreign language classrooms, the L2 test focus shifted to *how* to test speaking ability and how to deal with the fundamental issues of cognitive, context and scoring validity through test format and design, assessment criteria and scales, as well as examiner and rater training. We saw that the speaking construct became firmly embed-ded in the general L2 proficiency construct. It broadened from the relatively narrow conceptualisation of speaking as pronunciation accuracy at the beginning of the 20th century, to a communicative and later interactional definition of the construct, made possible by oral tests which include a range of tasks allowing the display of communicative language ability in a range of contexts. We also saw that the widespread use of computer-delivered and computer-scored oral tests has brought about a narrowing of the construct to core features of speech which are generated in monologic tasks and fea-tures of language which can be computer scored.

Throughout the discussion we have also argued that no test format is inherently superior, but that the question of fitness for purpose drives deci-sions about underlying test constructs. We have seen that throughout the last century language testers have chosen from a range of formats which have been useful in eliciting and assessing speaking skills. All of these formats bring their strengths and caveats and have varied applicability for different contexts and score-user requirements. As Wainer, Dorans, Eignor, Flaugher, Green, Mislevy, Steinberg and Thissen (2000:xxi) emphasised in the context of computer-based tests a decade ago: 'The questions we now must address deal less with "how to use it?" but more often "under what circumstances and for what purposes should we use it?"' A decade later, this key question still informs debates about speaking tests.

A final thought about the two big players on the speaking assessment arena – computer-delivered/marked tests and human-delivered/marked tests. We believe that it is important to view different speaking test formats, and especially the direct/semi-direct formats as *complementary* and not competing possibilities, where technology is seen not as a replacement for other test formats, but a new additional possibility. In a discussion referred to earlier, Bernstein et al (2010) argued that automated assessment of speaking alone should not be used as the sole basis of decision-making, but should be one piece of evidence about a test taker's speaking ability. It is the combination of test formats in terms of delivery and scoring which would optimise their benefits and lead to a symbiotic relationship between technology and humans and enhance the constructs speaking ability is based on. This *symbiotic relationship* between oral test formats, where technology and direct tests are used as elements of the same speaking test would optimise the advantages of the test formats and minimise their limitations. This is perhaps what speaking tests of the future will bring.

Examining speaking: An analysis of Cambridge English Speaking tasks 1913–2012

A socio-cognitive approach to speaking test analysis

We will now move from the general historical account of speaking assessment to a more narrow focus on Cambridge English tests and their evolution throughout the last 100 years. We will do so through the lens of Weir's (2005a) socio-cognitive framework for test analysis. At the heart of Weir's framework are issues related to cognitive, context and scoring validity. Before we proceed with the account of the speaking tests and underlying constructs at Cambridge, a short overview of cognitive, context and scoring validity as conceptualised by Weir (2005a) is in order to set the scene for the discussion to follow.

Cognitive validity in L2 speaking tests

As noted in the preceding chapters in this volume, language test developers need to pay attention not just to the contextual parameters of a given test, but also to established psycholinguistic theories relating to the cognitive processing which underpins language production (e.g. Levelt 1989). Such a cognitive processing approach is concerned with the mental processes that language users go through when they engage in different types of speaking activities. A speaking test can be said to have cognitive validity if its tasks activate cognitive processes in a test-taker's mind similar to those employed in the real-life speaking tasks and situations the test aims to generalise to. Without cognitive validity, one cannot confidently make claims as to what a candidate can do in real life, thus limiting the generalisability and meaning of test scores.

Such an approach would also offer a useful yardstick against which to analyse tasks in terms of the levels of processing they activate. The cognitive processes underlying speaking have been most recently discussed by Field (2011), who has adopted Levelt's (1989) cognitive model to the context of speaking assessment. They can be seen in Figure 4.1.

Figure 4.1 Cognitive processes and processing outputs in speaking (Field 2011:75)

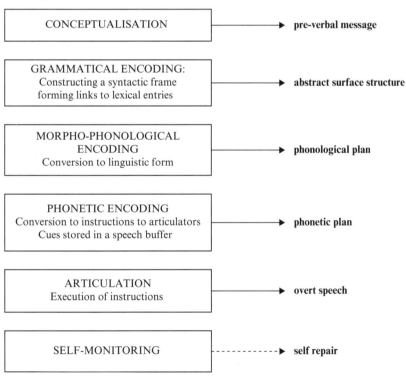

The *conceptualisation* stage involves generating idea(s) on the part of the speaker. Field (2011:88) suggests that conceptualisation is influenced by the following cognitive task demands:

a) *The complexity of ideas*: the nature of information demanded of a test taker can vary from personal to non-personal, from concrete to abstract. The retrieval and expression of personal, everyday and concrete information is normally a simpler task conceptually and linguistically.

b) *The extent to which ideas are supplied* to candidates in a test task, which includes the nature of support, e.g. closed and open-ended questions, the number of prompts and the modality of prompts, e.g. single modality (written only) or multiple modality (written, visual and aural).

c) The extent to which test takers are assessed on their ability to *relate utterances to the wider discourse*.

The *grammatical encoding* stage represents the speaker's construction of a syntactic pattern for the idea to be expressed. This stage in Field's model involves mapping the function one wants to express to the most appropriate syntactic pattern. The following test features, therefore, acquire importance in an investigation of cognitive task demands:

- the number or variety language of functions that a candidate is expected to perform: the cognitive load of a task can increase with increasing the number of functions that need to be expressed

- the accessibility of the required language function(s) in terms of underlying semantic complexity: for example, requesting and providing facts, agreeing and disagreeing are simpler than justifying opinions, comparing and contrasting, evaluating and hypothesising.

Morpho-phonological encoding refers to the retrieval of phonological forms from memory to express what is to be said. This encoding is fast, automatic and accurate in one's mother tongue or at higher L2 proficiency levels. It is manifested in terms of fluency (pausing and hesitation) and length of the spoken output. *Phonetic encoding* and *articulation* involve the (usually) automatic process of mapping phonological representations in the mind to L2 phonemes and articulating them. *Self-monitoring* is the process of the speaker's assessment of whether and how precisely and effectively communication goals have been achieved in terms of rhetorical impact, lexical and grammatical accuracy, pragmatic intentions.

In addition to the cognitive task demands mentioned above, Field (2011:106) also argues that time pressure and the nature of interaction can contribute to the cognitive load of a Speaking task.

Time pressure is typical of real-life spoken communication. It limits the extent to which a speaker can plan what they are going to say or monitor and revise their own utterances. The time pressure of real-life spoken interaction is seen in the amount of planning time provided in a test before and during the speech event, as well as immediately before or during the speaker's turn (Field 2011: 86). It is also reflected in the treatment of pauses in assessment scales.

Various *types of interaction* also contribute to the cognitive load of a task, since they make different cognitive demands on test takers. The cognitive challenge of a solo candidate task, where a candidate performs a monologue, lies in speaking at length, with reduced support on the part of the interviewer. Interviewer-candidate interaction may require rapid responses to interviewer questions, which introduces its own cognitive challenges. Candidate-candidate interaction carries a higher level of unpredictability and involves understanding of the other test taker's L2 variety, as well as decisions about accommodating one's speech to that of their test partner, which imposes additional cognitive demands. Finally, a three-way exchange in which the interviewer and both candidates are involved demands very complex processing since the test taker needs to process input from two interlocutors, and to keep track of different opinions and topics expressed by two other participants in the conversation (Field 2011:101).

To date Field's (2011) conceptualisation of cognitive validity in speaking tests appears to offer the most productive theoretical basis for investigating the construct validity of speaking tests from a cognitive validity perspective. It will be a useful analysis tool for comparison of the cognitive demands made by different tasks as the Cambridge English Speaking tests evolved.

Context validity in L2 speaking tests

The task contextual dimensions outlined in Weir (2005a:46) include the:

a) general non-linguistic task characteristics (task purpose, response format, weighting, knowledge of assessment criteria, time constraints)

b) lexical, structural, functional, discoursal linguistic demands of the task input (i.e. task rubric) and output (candidate's speech)

c) interlocutor demands in terms of status or power relationship (e.g. another candidate or an examiner), number of interlocutors, speech rate and a variety of accent

d) the test administration conditions (see Weir 2005a:46).

These dimensions of context validity are displayed in Figure 4.2 and will be considered in our discussion.

Scoring validity in L2 Speaking tests

Weir (2005a) presents scoring validity as a multi-faceted notion which, in addition to traditional notions of reliability, subsumes other related variables that could influence the assessment process and dependability of test scores. The aspects of scoring validity can be seen in Figure 4.3.

Figure 4.2 Aspects of context validity for speaking (Weir 2005a:46)

CONTEXT VALIDITY	
SETTING: TASK Response format Purpose Weighting Knowledge of criteria Order of items/tasks Time constraints	**DEMANDS: TASK** **Linguistic (Input and Output)** Channel Length Lexical resources Structural resources Functional resources Discourse mode Nature of information Topic familiarity / content knowledge
SETTING: ADMINISTRATION Physical conditions Uniformity of administration Security	**Interlocutor** Speech rate Variety of accent Acquaintanceship Number Gender

Figure 4.3 Aspects of scoring validity for Speaking (Weir 2005a:46)

Scoring validity
Rating Criteria/rating scale Rating process Rating conditions Rater characteristics Rater training Post examination adjustment Grading and awarding

Many parameters of scoring validity intersect with the construct validity of a test, and so the evolution of the Speaking construct underlying Cambridge English exams will be considered with a reference to the evolution of scoring dimensions. Due to space limitations, our account will predominantly focus on the evolution of assessment criteria and scales and rater training and standardisation.

In the remainder of the chapter we will draw on the above-mentioned cognitive, context and scoring parameters in our analysis of the speaking tasks in Cambridge English examinations from 1913 to the present. As in other chapters, the discussion will be exemplified with particular reference to the LCE/FCE and CPE, as the Cambridge exams with the longest history. The

Cambridge English: Advanced (CAE) test will also be included in our overview, since its introduction in 1991 represented a significant change in the test format and tasks, with other speaking tests following suit.

Our discussion will be structured around three main areas:

- the change in importance of the speaking construct within the overall examination construct, as well the increased importance of the communicative aspect of the speaking construct
- the evolution of the contextual and cognitive dimensions of the exam, both diachronically over the last century and synchronically focusing on exams at different proficiency levels at one point in time
- the increased attention paid to scoring validity parameters.

As a reference point for the ensuing discussion, an overview of the CPE and LCE/FCE speaking test tasks and test format over the last 100 years is given in Tables 4.1 and 4.2. Elements of the tables will be referred to in the discussion to follow.

Table 4.1 CPE Speaking test 1913–2012

Year	Test format	Tasks
1913–1945 'ORAL'	1 candidate 1 examiner	• Dictation *30 mins* • Reading aloud (pre-prepared) and Conversation *30 mins*
1945–1975 'ORAL'	1 candidate 1 examiner	• Reading aloud (pre-prepared) *2 mins* • Reading aloud (unseen) and Conversation *10 mins*
1975–1984 'INTERVIEW'	1 candidate 1 examiner	• Conversation based on a photograph *5 mins* • Talk on a pre-prepared topic *2 mins* • Reading aloud (dialogue) *2–3 mins* • Situations *2–3 mins*
1984–1996 'INTERVIEW'	1 candidate 1 examiner Optional paired or group test format Optional 2 examiner format	• Conversation based on a photograph *5 mins solo, 7 mins pair, 10 mins trio* • Reading aloud (short passage), replaced by discussion based on a passage in 1986 *2 mins solo, 3 mins pair, 4 mins trio* • Communicative activity *5 mins solo, 8 mins pair, 12 mins trio*
1996–2012 'SPEAKING'	2 candidates 2 examiners	• Interview based on general questions *3 mins* • Candidate-candidate decision-making task *5 mins* • Individual candidate long turn *4 mins* • Candidate-candidate-examiner interaction *7 mins*

Table 4.2 LCE/FCE Speaking test 1939–2012

Year	Test format	Tasks
1939–1945 'ORAL'	1 candidate 1 examiner	• Dictation *30 mins* • Reading aloud *5 mins* • Conversation based on a photograph or passage *5 mins*
1945–1975 'ORAL'	1 candidate 1 examiner	• Reading aloud *5 mins* • Conversation based on a photograph or passage *5 mins*
1975–1983 'INTERVIEW'	1 candidate 1 examiner	• Conversation based on a photograph *5 mins* • Situations *2–3 mins* • Reading aloud (dialogue) *2–3 mins*
1984–1995 'INTERVIEW'	1 candidate 1 examiner Optional paired or group test format Optional 2 examiner format	• Conversation based on a photograph *4 mins solo, 7 mins pair, 10 mins trio* • Reading aloud (dialogue) *2 mins solo, 3 mins pair, 3 mins trio* • Communicative activity *4 mins solo, 7 mins pair, 10 mins trio*
1996–2012 'SPEAKING'	2 candidates 2 examiners	• Interview based on general questions *3 mins* • Individual candidate long turn *4 mins* • Candidate-candidate decision-making task *3 mins* • Candidate-candidate-examiner interaction *4 mins*

Evolution of the overall importance of the speaking construct

One of the main changes observed with the Cambridge English exams over the last century is the increased importance assigned to the speaking construct in relation to the overall test construct, as reflected in the contribution of speaking scores and length of test to the overall test score and length. Despite the fact that speaking was part of the CPE construct from the very beginning in 1913, tasks involving communication carried relatively little weight in the overall exam, as the speaking mark was shared between performance on the conversation task, as well as the dictation and reading aloud tasks. Unfortunately there are very few archive documents up to 1945 which shed light on the time and importance dedicated to conversation, but we do know that dictation took 30 minutes and reading aloud and conversation shared 30 minutes. In terms of marks awarded, a 1913 mark scheme informs us that in the 1913 oral test, dictation carried 50/125 marks (40%), with reading aloud and conversation sharing the remaining 75 marks (60%).

As the CPE and LCE/FCE exams evolved, more prominence was given to tasks tapping into a language-in-use construct, and non-communicative tasks were discontinued at different revision stages: the dictation marks ceased to contribute to the oral marks in 1945 (although the task continued to be part of the CPE test until the 1970s), and reading aloud had disappeared by 1986 and was replaced by the silent reading of a short passage as a springboard for a discussion between the examiner and test taker.

The year 1945 was a turning point, therefore, as from then until 1975 the result of the oral examination was decided by the candidate's performance on the reading aloud and conversation tasks (Instructions to Oral Examiners 1947:1). Roach (1945a:15–16) rightfully justified the separation of dictation marks from the Oral marks:

> It may well be argued that dictation is a semi-oral test having no rightful place in the oral examiner's personal assessment, particularly as the standard of the passage set is beyond his control and may be a wrong standard, thus vitiating his results.

The change in 1945 served to increase the overall contribution of the conversation task to the final oral score. Conversation was, however, still worth less (40%) than the reading aloud tasks taken together (60%), as shown in Table 4.3.

Table 4.3 CPE marks prior to and post 1945 (Roach 1945a:5)

Oral test parts	Marks prior to 1945	Marks post 1945
Dictation 30 mins	15 (30%)	–
Reading aloud 2 mins	20 (40%)	20 (40%)
Unseen reading 10 mins	–	10 (20%)
Conversation	15 (30%)	20 (40%)
Total	**50 (100%)**	**50 (100%)**

The LCE saw similar changes in 1945, and the contribution of conversation to the overall speaking construct increased to 50%, with the remaining 50% assigned to reading aloud. The increased contribution of conversation to the overall mark on the oral test indicated an important shift in conceptualisation and operationalisation of the speaking construct at Cambridge at the time, with a stronger orientation towards a construct involving communication.

The relative distribution of communicative/non-communicative tasks in the oral examination stayed more or less constant until the 1970s, when it changed with the 1975 examination revisions. At that time several communicative tasks were introduced, and in addition to the traditional reading aloud and conversation tasks, examination time was also now dedicated to tasks involving talk on a prepared topic (at CPE) and responding to prompts based on a variety of scenarios (at FCE and CPE).

The timing of the FCE tasks involving communication increased to 7½ minutes out of 10 minutes for the whole test, and 10 minutes out of 12 at CPE. This was reflected in the marks awarded for communicative tasks: they now constituted 83% and 74% of the overall mark in CPE and FCE oral tests respectively, marking the much larger importance assigned to communication within the speaking construct (see Table 4.4).

Table 4.4 CPE and FCE marks after 1975 revision

Oral test parts	Maximum available mark	
	CPE	FCE
Conversation 5 mins	20 (34%)	20 (51%)
Prepared topic 2 mins	20 (34%)	–
Reading aloud 2–3 mins	10 (17%)	10 (26%)
Situations 2–3 mins	9 (15%)	9 (23%)
Total 10 mins FCE, 12 mins CPE	59 (100%)	39 (100%)

The 1975 revisions represented major developments which, as Weir (2003: 24) notes, 'echoed the burgeoning interest in communicative language teaching' at the time and indicated an increased focus on language as a means of communication.

In 1986 additional changes in terms of relative weight of tasks within the test were introduced, as the reading aloud task was replaced by a discussion based on the silent reading of a short passage. From the mid-1980s, therefore, the CPE and FCE Speaking tests were based exclusively on tasks involving communication, no doubt strongly influenced by the communicative philosophy gaining ground in teaching and assessment (see Widdowson (1978) and Chapter 1 for full discussion of this approach).

In terms of the overall contribution of the speaking construct to the examination as a whole, in 1975 the contribution of the Speaking and Listening tests was merged so that the oral/aural part of the examination carried a shared 25% of the marks for the whole examination (Changes of Syllabus in 1975 1973:5). In contrast, the other papers (Reading, Use of English and Writing) carried 25% each. In the context of FCE Morris (1978:1) criticised the emphasis on reading and writing skills and the relative unbalance in the importance assigned to aural and oral skills, noting that 'any teacher preparing candidates for FCE has to concentrate on those skills awarded more marks'. Her criticism of the bias towards reading and writing was especially significant, as it came at a time 'when many learners wish to develop the skills of listening and speaking' (1978:2). The decision on the part of Cambridge to assign lower weight to Speaking (and Listening) originated, in part, from the fact that Speaking was 'subjectively' assessed. The need to increase the weighting was recognised in 1981, as seen in the Executive Committee minutes (May 1981: 2):

> ... the ... need to give a more functional emphasis to the examinations by a substantial increase in their oral weighting must also be seriously considered, in spite of problems of objectivity and organisation.

As a result, the relative distribution of scores across the examination papers was revised in 1984, with the contribution of Speaking changing to 22% (40/180) of the total weighted mark, in line with the other papers (apart from Listening which contributed 11% (20/180)) (Exam Regulations 1984:4). The substantial increase in the weighting of the oral component in the 1980s was indicative of the growing importance given to a speaking communicative construct.

Context and Cognitive task demands

1913–1945: Proficiency (CPE) and Lower Certificate (LCE)

One of the key contextual features of the CPE and LCE Speaking tests is that from their inception they comprised a range of task types, namely dictation, reading aloud and conversation. As noted earlier in this chapter and in Chapter 1, the CPE oral tasks in 1913 did not appear in a vacuum, but drew on existing pedagogic and assessment practices. As such, the test showed the clear influence of the late 19th century United Kingdom examination and pedagogic practices, such as the emphasis on speaking in the Reform Movement and the Direct Method, which resulted in a conversation task and a view of phonetics as being the primary assessment focus. The dictation and reading aloud tasks were also influenced by traditional teaching techniques which had stood the test of time and so found their way into the CPE Oral. The range of tasks, albeit not all with a communicative element, is an important feature of the tests, since different task types and interactional patterns have been shown to tap into different cognitive processes (Field 2011) and elicit different linguistic resources (Kormos 1999, O'Sullivan, Weir and Saville 2002), thus broadening the construct the test was tapping into.

Another important feature of the initial conceptualisation of the CPE/ LCE speaking construct is its integrative nature which, in addition to speaking skills, also included listening and reading comprehension ability seen in the dictation and reading aloud tasks, respectively. Such integrated tasks had been used in school and university contexts prior to 1913 and therefore had the sanction of tradition, which at the time was reinforced by limited understanding of the nature of the skills. The dictation task (part of the spoken construct until 1945 and of the overall test construct until 1975) focused on comprehending what was being read out by the examiner and the ability to write it down correctly. Even though activating listening comprehension cognitive processes, it was part of the Oral because it tested the 'understanding of the spoken word' (Roach 1945a: 26), the ability to segment the speech stream correctly and one's awareness of phoneme-grapheme correspondences (see Chapter 5 for a more detailed discussion of the dictation task).

Reading aloud was part of the original test specification (and survived until 1986). The reading aloud texts were predominantly dialogues, with the purpose of tapping into both segmental and supra-segmental pronunciation and intonation aspects of language (Examination Regulations 1933:1). Even though interfacing with reading cognitive processes, the purpose of this task was primarily to tap into elements of speaking, as we see from question papers and other relevant documentation, which inform us that reading aloud is a test of 'general fluency and understanding, giving the examiner the opportunity to assess the candidate's pronunciation in a more concentrated way than in the conversation test' (Instructions to Oral Examiners 1970:5). From a cognitive point of view, even though this task involved reading comprehension cognitive processes, it also activated some of the speaking cognitive processes outlined by Field (2011), such as phonological and phonetic encoding, articulation and self-monitoring. It did not activate other cognitive processes, i.e. generation of ideas (conceptualisation stage) on the part of the candidate or constructing syntactic patterns for the generated ideas to be expressed (morpho-grammatical encoding), and had limited relevance for a communicative spoken language construct since it was mostly concerned with pronunciation, intonation and fluency of reading (see Chapter 2 for a more detailed discussion of this task in the context of reading comprehension).

It is, however, worth noting the suitability of such a task for certain score uses and non-test domains. In the case of CPE and LCE, the construct was mainly defined in terms of accuracy of pronunciation and intonation, and such a task could clearly tap into this construct, even if from a 21st century point of view it is seen as excessively narrow. Interestingly, this task type has made a comeback in some computer-based speaking tests of today, e.g. PTE Academic, the Avant English placement test and the BULATS online Speaking test, partly as a result of fitness for purpose between the test construct and its purpose (a reading aloud task may be suitable in certain work contexts, such as call centres where pronunciation is a key aspect of the test construct) and partly due to the influence of practicality taking precedence over desirability (a reading aloud task is more suitable for automated assessment of speech).

The conversation task was the only communicative task in the CPE and LCE/FCE Speaking tests during this period (and, in fact, until 1975). The task consisted of an examiner-led interview with one candidate at a time. Unlike the dictation and reading aloud tasks, this task tapped into a construct which involved communication, even though limited by the interview format.

A distinguishing feature of the CPE examination at its inception was its close alignment to classroom practices at the time. As Spolsky (1995a:339) notes, the emphasis in the Cambridge English tests at the beginning of the 20th century on the importance of listening and speaking shows its sensitivity to the major trends in English language teaching: 'the content of the syllabus and the examinations was completely up-to-date'. The influence of the Reform Movement, which drew on advances in phonetics, and focused on spoken language through the practice of teaching the sounds first, materialised in strong emphasis on pronunciation in the oral paper (and in the separate Phonetics paper). The influence of the Direct Method, which emphasised speech and fluency as primary in language teaching, was reflected in the inclusion of the examiner-led interview. The interview was sometimes partially based on visuals (i.e. drawings), which is also reminiscent of classroom practices inspired by the Direct Method (see Richards 1947 and Travis 1947 on the use of visuals in the classroom).

Difference in levels: CPE and LCE

Our discussion so far has mostly been diachronic in its account of historical development of the CPE. With the emergence of the Lower Certificate in English in 1939, an important synchronic dimension was introduced, since the two exams had to be differentiated according to proficiency levels.

As noted in Chapter 1, LCE was launched in 1939 due to demand for a test of English at a lower proficiency level than CPE. During the Second World War, lower-proficiency candidates included army personnel and prisoners of war 'both ours and theirs' (Roach 1956a:2). We saw how LCE was a controversial examination at its inception, since its acceptance was perceived by the British Council as the acceptance of lower standards in language, partly because the prescribed books and reading aloud passages appearing in the test were written in Basic English (a simplified form of English with minimal syntax, fixed word order and reduced vocabulary; see Hawkey 2009:17 for more detail). Over time, the idea of Basic English was abandoned. Roach (1944a:1) reports that after 1941, the standard of the examinations moved beyond the vocabulary of Basic English and the 1951 Examination Regulations inform us that texts may be adapted and abridged rather than based on simplified English. Incidentally, the controversy which initially accompanied the launch of LCE re-emerged in the 1950s in a different form. At a Joint Committee meeting in 1956, UCLES suggested that:

> it may be possible to envisage a time when it can be considered that in certain areas (e.g. in the United Kingdom and in certain European countries) the first phase of encouraging the study of English is over, and that attention should be centred on consolidation and on the raising of standards. If this time comes, the Lower Certificate might be withdrawn from the areas concerned (Roach 1956b:2).

It seems that LCE was deemed to test and represent a 'below standard' kind of English. Roach was explicitly against such an attitude. In his words:

> "standards" are represented by a mass of individual foreigners, each starting de novo and many not getting beyond the Lower Certificate. It might be a poor service to exclude these German and Scandinavian domestic servants and others in order to raise someone else's standards. It might be a poor service to the Proficiency examination itself, which is at present the natural goal of those who continue beyond the Lower Certificate (Roach 1956b:4).

The Oral LCE test mirrored the structure and the underlying construct of CPE Oral, consisting of dictation, reading aloud, conversation, as shown in Tables 4.1 and 4.2. The differentiation in level was embedded in the differences between the exams in terms of linguistic complexity and the timing of the reading aloud and conversation tasks. As far as linguistic complexity is concerned, Cambridge informed its examiners to bear in mind that:

> candidates for the Lower Certificate may have been learning English for a relatively short time and that they may have read texts chiefly in some form of "simplified" English. Comprehension of what the examiner says is part of the test, but the examiner should use reasonably simple and direct English' (Instructions to Oral Examiners 1947:3).

Other than that, there were no guidelines in terms of linguistic range and complexity to be expected of the examiner or the candidate. In relation to the reading aloud passages, up to 1941 the passages had been written in Basic English, but unfortunately we are not informed what, if any, guidelines were in place for adapting and abridging texts after 1941 when the idea of Basic English was abandoned. In 1944, Roach urged for research with the aim of establishing the level of LCE in terms of vocabulary and proposed a vocabulary level of about 2,500–3,000 words (see Chapter 1). He saw this as a useful guide for teachers in terms of the standard to be reached, to publishers for the purpose of standardising text books and to examiners (Roach 1944a). In essence, Roach was urging for what is nowadays known as a wordlist.

The difference in level was also reflected in the time available for the two speaking tests, with LCE tests lasting 10 mins, compared to 12 minutes for CPE. In addition, the LCE reading aloud passages were shorter and conversation lasted 5 minutes, as compared to 8 or 10 minutes in CPE.

To sum up, in terms of the cognitive and contextual demands of the CPE and LCE tasks, timing and the complexity of language were taken into account for the purposes of designing English language test suitable for candidates at two different proficiency levels. Other than that, no major changes were introduced to the Cambridge English speaking construct with the launch of LCE. The speaking construct in general was primarily defined in terms of pronunciation and intonation, which was based on speech elicited through two tasks involving spoken language: reading aloud and conversation. Interaction was not a major component of the test and underlying construct.

1945–1975: Proficiency (CPE) and Lower Certificate (LCE)

The revised CPE Oral test in 1945 consisted of:

- dictation (30 minutes) (The dictation marks were not part of the overall speaking score, but were counted towards the overall examination score)
- reading aloud of a pre-prepared passage (2 minutes)
- unseen reading and conversation (10 minutes).

The LCE test was similar:

- dictation (The dictation marks were not part of the overall speaking score)
- reading aloud of a pre-prepared passage (5 mins)
- conversation (5 minutes).

One of the reading tasks – pre-prepared reading – involved reading a passage which the candidate was allowed to prepare before reading. The materials for this task consisted of two alternative reading passages. Examiners would use one until 'they tire of it and then change to the other' (Instructions to Oral Examiners 1945:2).

Candidates were advised to 'try to read the conversation as if you were just naturally speaking to someone' (*Fifty Reading Passages* 1944:1). The examiner was instructed to ensure that the candidate is given enough time to prepare the passage and to avoid comment or correction during reading (Instructions to Oral Examiners 1947:3). It seems that the length of preparation time was not standardised, which would have introduced unwelcome variation in the examination conditions. We now know that time constraints is an important parameter both in terms of context and cognitive validity (Field 2011, Weir 2005a). Candidates were also informed of the criteria on which they would be assessed: 'This passage includes conversation and is intended to test your pronunciation and intonation, your "accent" ' (*Fifty Reading Passages* 1944:1).

Examiners were advised to administer this reading task first to all candidates, one at a time, and make an assessment of each candidate after the task (Instructions to Oral Examiners 1945:1). The primary reason for this test order was a concern with achieving 'continuity of standard' by having candidates read aloud 'identical materials under identical conditions' (Roach 1945a:12). This important test feature indicates an early concern with test reliability.

Unseen reading was intended as 'a test of extempore reading of unprepared material and would afford some check on the mark allotted earlier for Reading' (Roach 1945a:12). Passages were four lines in length and were taken from literary sources. The candidate was asked to look silently through the passage once and then read it out loud. Candidates were informed that 'this is a test of good reading and of the ability to make yourself readily understood' (*Fifty Reading Passages* 1944:1). Examiners had several passages to select from and were required to make their choice of passage based on 'some systematic plan', so that they 'do not become familiar with any one passage' (Instructions to Oral Examiners 1945:1). In addition, 'if the examiner has any doubt about his assessment he should try the candidate with a second passage' (Instructions to Oral Examiners 1947:3).

Examiner unfamiliarity with the passage was one of the reasons behind the introduction of unseen reading: listening to the same passage(s) repeatedly would increase familiarity with their content which can then interfere with an examiner's judgement of a candidate's ability to make themselves understood. As Roach (1945a:12) notes, an examiner 'becomes increasingly less able to judge how far he would understand if he did not know the passage'. Candidate unfamiliarity with the passage was another reason for using this task, since it introduced a higher cognitive load: extempore reading is more difficult as it involves decoding, phonetic encoding and articulation under time pressure. The addition of this task in 1945 can be seen as a positive step, since it added to the cognitive and linguistic challenge of the CPE test, even if it did little to add to its communicative nature.

Following unseen reading, the examiner led a conversation with the candidate, based on a passage or picture. The choice of prompt – picture or photo – was down to the examiner. The picture or passage-based part of the interview was followed by a longer general conversation between the examiner and the candidate. A set of 1944/5 gramophone recordings of the Orals used for standardisation of Oral Examiners (Cambridge Assessment Archives) provide useful illustrations of this task.

The conversation task, in line with interview tasks of this nature, was unidirectional: the examiner would ask questions and manage the interaction, while the candidate would respond to the examiner's questions. In hindsight and with the knowledge we now have of the issues related to the correspondence between speaking tests and conversation (discussed in the Authenticity debate section), the task could be more appropriately described as a controlled examination interview rather than conversation.

An example of an interview based on a picture can be seen below (the picture is not included). The examiner would begin by asking a general question eliciting description (e.g. *What is the picture about?*), which would elicit an extended turn from the candidate. Upon the completion of the turn, a series of questions and answers would follow, with the examiner eliciting a more detailed description of the picture. In the following example, the picture used depicted a car accident:

Examiner	Would you tell me what the picture's about?
Candidate	Well, a taxi seems to have run over a butcher boy. And the, the driver of the taxi is talking to a policeman and the butcher boy is talking to another one. And um . . . a fat lady is leaning out of the taxi's window. And is listening to what . . . the driver and the policeman are saying. And er . . . some people have gone over and are looking at these people who are quarrelling. And while the butcher boy is talking to the policeman, a dog has come behind him and is eating the sausages and the, the meat that has fallen out of his basket. And um . . . hmm . . ..
Examiner	Yes?
Candidate	Well . . ., the policeman is writing something on a little book.
Examiner	Yes, eh, how, how many policemen can you see?
Candidate	Two?
Examiner	Two. What's the boy in the centre of the picture doing?
Candidate	He's um, he's fallen down of his bicycle . . . and he's talking.
Examiner	Yes, who is he talking with?
Candidate	With the policeman.
	. . .

(CPE 1945 gramophone recording M-GR-2–1a)

Picture-based tasks are often used in language testing, largely because they can efficiently provide a topic with minimal verbal input and can elicit largely the same vocabulary from test takers, allowing comparison between speech samples. In terms of contextual features, this task tapped into a communicative construct, albeit in a context limited by the Question and Answer task format. Its advantage lies in the elicitation of both long and short turns and in the tapping of informational functional language. This is an important contextual feature of the task, since the different types of candidate contributions translated into different cognitive demands and broadened the underlying speaking construct.

Below we can see an example of a passage-based interview. When this prompt type was used, the candidate would be asked a series of questions by the examiner testing global understanding of the passage (e.g. *What's the story about?*), as well as more detailed comprehension (e.g. *Where did the friends meet? Why was the letter dirty?*). Some questions would explicitly focus on the candidate's lexical knowledge and understanding of a word or phrase in the text (e.g. *What are hypocritical thanks? What are tropical landscapes? "I looked at him sceptically". . . What does it mean?*). The focus of the task was on testing Speaking, even though this was clearly an integrated Reading-into-Speaking task.

Examiner	Can you tell me what the story's about?
Candidate	Er The story's about er . . . ?a/the? boy that er . . . meet er a friend and he er . . . sho, shur, showed him a letter, er that hm . . . his friend er . . . has er ?kept? It was er . . . well writing, well written because er . . . his friend er told him that the, if he writes many letters of that kind, erm he would buy a book, and so er . . . his friend gave him er . . . three er . . . hm . . ., three and sixpence.
Examiner	Right.
Candidate	. . . and with it he er . . . may buy food for his family.
Examiner	Yes, yes. Where did the friends meet?
Candidate	On the street. In the street.
Examiner	Yes. Why was the letter dirty?
Candidate	I beg your pardon?
Examiner	Why was the letter dirty? On the top?
Candidate	Because it was old, I suppose that it was written very, very much time ago. I suppose.
Examiner	Yes. I looked at him sceptically. What does that mean?
Candidate	Um . . . I suppose that er it means er . . .

(CPE 1945, gramophone recording M-GR-2–3b)

Similarly to the picture-based interview, a positive feature of this task was its ability to elicit extended candidate speech, in addition to single utterances. This is important for cognitive processing because the candidate is required to integrate utterances into a wider discourse (see the Cognitive validity in L2 speaking test section).

It is worth noting that at the time the CPE examiners used different prompt types interchangeably. Such interchangeable use of different prompt types in this task is a characteristic feature of the Cambridge English exams at this stage of their evolution in the 1940s. With the benefit of hindsight, we can argue that this variability in task prompts is a shortcoming of the test, since the tests did not have uniform conditions. We now know that the modality of a speaking task prompt, such as, for example picture vs. passage, introduces contextual and cognitive differences in the task (O'Keefe 2006a, 2006b). Similarly, Field (2011) discusses types of prompt (referred to in Weir 2005a as channel of communication) as varying in terms of linguistic and cognitive demands. Picture-based interviews may be more linguistically demanding because the candidate receives no relevant verbal input and has to generate all vocabulary and phrases. A passage-based interview, even though providing the test taker with some relevant linguistic resources which could be used in the response, presents its own linguistic and cognitive challenges, since its successful completion is dependent on both reading and speaking cognitive processes. As we will see, this variability was addressed during subsequent revisions of the test.

The second part of the conversation task consisted of a general unscripted interview. Most candidate output was at the level of an utterance or two, since the expectation was for the examiner to guide the interaction. This was in contrast with the picture- and passage-based stage of the interview, which elicited longer turns. The two stages of the interview are illustrative of the need seen by the test developers at the time to elicit different types of speech during the task, and therefore, to tap into a broader range of abilities and cognitive processes.

The CPE general interview consisted of a combination of closed (yes/no type) questions and open (what, why) questions. Most questions were about books, hobbies and any activities a candidate may be interested in, including their experience of learning English and plans for the future. The excerpt below provides an example.

Examiner	Tell me what sort of books you like best.
Candidate	Um well . . . Novels and travel books. I like all sort of books, really.
Examiner	Yes. What novels have you read lately?
Candidate	Well, Robert Louis Stevenson's. They are not really novels . . . but they are very nice.
Examiner	Yes. What book of Robert Louis Stevenson have you read lately?
Candidate	Hmm . . . "Travels With a Donkey".
Examiner	Oh yes. Where do the things happen er . . . that are told in "Travels With a Donkey".
Candidate	They happen in . . . in the mountains of the Cevennes, in France.
Examiner	Oh, yes. Was Robert Louis Stevenson a French man?
Candidate	No, he was a Scotch man.
Examiner	Yes. Did he live in Scotland most of his life?
Candidate	No, he travelled a lot because he hm . . ., he was ill.
Examiner	Yes. Where did he travel to? Do you know?
Candidate	Yes. He went to . . . to the islands, didn't he? To the . . . to the East?
Examiner	Yes, the Pacific Islands.
Candidate	Yes.
Examiner	Yes. What other novel have you read lately?
Candidate	Well, I'm reading now one by Hudson.
Examiner	Yeah. What's it about?
Candidate	It's called er . . . 'A Shepherd's life'.
Examiner	Yes?
Candidate	And er . . . it's all about England.
Examiner	Yes?
Candidate	And it's very charming.
Examiner	Is there any dramatic excitement in it?
Candidate	Well, it may come later on. I haven't got to that part yet.

Examiner	Do you do any original writing yourself?
Candidate	No.
Examiner	No?
Candidate	I don't.
Examiner	Have you any hobbies?
Candidate	No, not, not hobbies, except reading.

(1945 CPE gramophone recording M-GR2–1b)

The questions varied in terms of language functions elicited. Some required general factual detail on, for example, books, poems, authors and one's own life; others needed expressing and justifying one's opinion and evaluation, e.g. *Would you call that a sentimental novel?*, *Why do you like it/ Why didn't you like it?*, *In what way do you find that boring?*, or expressing preferences, likes, dislikes, e.g. *What books do you like best?*, *What kind of music are you interested in?*, or explaining one's plans or preferences for the future, e.g. *What would you like to do when you've finished your studies?*, *Why do you want to teach English?* (all examples are taken from the 1945 gramophone recordings). Based on the speech samples in the 1945 gramophone recordings, it can be said that each CPE candidate needed to handle a variety of questions and draw on the associated functional, structural and lexical resources. The nature of information demanded of the test taker was a combination of personal and non-personal, concrete and abstract. Naturally, expressing abstract and non-personal information is a more complex task both conceptually and linguistically, and its inclusion at this proficiency level is a positive feature of CPE at the time.

Similarly to CPE, the LCE conversation was a controlled Interview which was partly based on a reading passage(s) or a picture/series of pictures (Exam Regulations 1951:9). The other part of the test consisted of the general interview. Unlike the CPE Oral, the LCE oral test did not include an unseen reading task, and the oral test was 10 mins long, compared to 12 mins at CPE. As 1945 gramophone recordings for the co-ordination of LCE Oral Examiners do not contain examples of passage- or picture-based interviews, but only the general interview, the latter will be discussed next.

The LCE general interview was broadly similar in structure to its CPE equivalent. In contrast to CPE, the questions in the LCE interview were intended to elicit mostly factual, concrete, familiar and personal information. Language functions were largely limited to expressing factual information as well as likes and dislikes. Linguistically and cognitively, this was less demanding than the CPE Oral, in view of the lower proficiency level of LCE candidates. The topics revolved around everyday objects or institutions (e.g. shops), personal details such as date of birth and country of origin, experience in learning English, etc. Importantly, topics would vary to take into account the candidate's professional or educational background. This is an important feature of the task, since it shows a concern with the type of information candidates were asked to talk about, and an attempt to base the task on topics familiar to candidates.

For example, the 1945 recording of an interview with a Polish R.A.F. officer shows that some questions were associated with his military background:

> How old are you?/ When were you born?/ Where were you born?/ How long have you been learning English?/ Where did you come from?/ Why did you leave France?/ And how did you come over?/ Was it a British boat?/ How many troops were there on board?/ How long did you take on the journey?/ Did you have enough food on the journey?/ Was the crew British or Indian or what?/ What are your duties now?/ How many hours instruction do you give a day?/ Do you work on Sundays?
> (LCE 1945, gramophone recording M-GR-1-36)

In contrast, an Italian female candidate was asked to talk about shops and music:

> Tell me some of the things you see in the street [in the picture]./ Tell me something about a shop. What kind of shop do you like best?/ Do you like hat shops?/ Do you know much about music?/ What kind of music do you like best?/ Can you tell me the names of some instruments?/ You play the piano?
> (LCE 1945, gramophone recording M-GR-4-9b)

The non-scripted nature of the interview made each test different, more individualised and authentic. This positive feature of the interview would have also introduced variability in the test, as the solid body of research on co-construction in face-to-face tests has demonstrated (e.g. Brown 2003, Lazaraton 1996).

Factual lexically-focused questions about qualities and functions of everyday objects were also part of the interview. An example is provided below.

> I am going to ask you to tell me what you do with certain things. What do you do with a pen?/ What do you write?/ What do you do with a knife?/ Can you tell me the names of some things that are soft?. . . hard?/ What's this on the floor there?/ Is that hard?/ What can we do with paper?/ Have you read the newspaper this morning?/ Why haven't you had time?
> (LCE 1945, gramophone recording M-GR-4-9a)

The above example reveals the exclusive focus on lexical knowledge in parts of the interview, instead of on communication. This is not altogether surprising, since such question-answer exchanges focusing on lexis were not atypical of pre-communicative language classrooms at the time. (Incidentally, this Question and Answer format which includes thematically unrelated lexically-focused questions can still be found in current tests, such as the PTE Academic Speaking test).

Due to the caveats associated with such strings of questions, Cambridge started considering topic-based conversations in the late 1960s (1967 Joint Committee minutes). In 1969, a topic-based conversation replaced the more or less disconnected Question and Answer stage. According to the Exam

Regulations (1969) and Instructions to Oral Examiners (1971), a candidate would come to the Oral examination with a written list of previously prepared five topics, chosen from a list of ten: 'Education, Family life, Sport, Travel, Personal hobbies, A national figure, Geography (of the candidate's country), Food, Careers and Newspapers and Magazines' (Exam Regulations 1969:13). Candidates could replace two of these topics with two of their own. The list was presented to the examiner who then randomly chose one for the Interview.

Being familiar with the topic under discussion was an important characteristic of the task at the time. Topic familiarity is an important context validity parameter (Weir 2005a), and its role has been documented in past research. Skehan (1998), for example, contends that topic familiarity can significantly affect the fluency of the test taker's response, and as such should be taken into consideration when developing tasks. Similarly, Alderson (2000:29) argues that 'every attempt should be made to allow background knowledge to facilitate performance rather than allowing its absence to inhibit performance'. Additionally, giving test takers the chance to talk about a subject which they have had some content knowledge of and which they are interested in would have a positive and motivational effect.

A topic-based conversation task and the way it was conducted marks a significant step towards more communicative testing of oral ability at Cambridge. The move towards a more communicative test is also reflected in the guidelines for candidates and Oral Examiners, which stressed the importance of building in more communicative features into the examiner-candidate interaction. For example, the candidates were made aware that the topic provides 'subject matter and interest for the conversation' which 'should not take the form of a passage or talk learned by heart' (Exam Regulations 1969:13). The Instructions to Oral Examiners (1971:12) emphasised that a 'natural conversational atmosphere' should be maintained throughout this task. Examiners were advised to indicate the main topic by a 'casual leading-in remark or factual question, not with a formal announcement' (1971:12). Candidates were advised to be prepared to take part in a discussion and not just to answer questions.

To sum up, the CPE and LCE Orals between 1945 and 1975 are good examples of the partial evolution of the speaking tests towards measuring a more communicative construct. The one communicative task in the test – conversation – was designed to elicit both utterance-level and more extended speech. This task brought about different cognitive challenges and allowed the test to tap into a relatively broader construct. The reading aloud tasks however were still a prominent feature of the speaking test. The evolution of the two exams also illustrates the effort Cambridge made to differentiate between linguistic and cognitive demands at different proficiency levels through the nature of information at each level and the length of tasks.

1975–1984: Proficiency (CPE) and First Certificate (FCE) and the Influence of the Communicative approach

The 1970s saw a critical shift in speaking assessment at Cambridge, seen in the introduction of a stronger communicative element to the speaking tests. The 1975 CPE and FCE revision resulted in the following speaking tests:

Table 4.5 CPE and FCE Interview (1975–1984) (Exam Regulations 1975)

Speaking test component	CPE Timing (min)	FCE Timing (min)	Further description
Conversation with the Examiner	5	5	Conversation based on a photograph representing a scene or action as a stimulus
A talk on a topic	2	n/a	A candidate prepares for 15 min before the interview. A candidate can choose a topic from a given list of three.
Reading aloud	2	2	Candidate and examiner each read a part of a dialogue
Situations	3	3	Providing responses which would be appropriate in three given situations
Total	**12**	**10**	

As can be seen, the oral test was renamed 'Interview' and the FCE mirrored the structure of the CPE test. The difference between the two levels was captured by the additional task at CPE (Talk on a topic) and the different linguistic demands of the tasks.

The major changes introduced to the oral component of the CPE and FCE examinations in 1975 reflected the growing influence of the communicative approach in language teaching, learning and assessment which was gaining momentum at the time. The revised test construct was intended to broaden the range of speech activities tested and also included a more analytic approach to marking (to be discussed in the Scoring Validity section below). These were motivated by the pedagogic climate at the time and also by the suggestions of consulted teachers (Report on the 'Cambridge Workshop' held at the British Institute, Madrid on 22 and 23 October 1975 for the meeting of the Executive Committee, October 1975). It is at this time that the Listening component which was previously embodied in the dictation task was separated from the oral test, and now formed an independent Listening Comprehension paper (see chapter 5 for more detail).

Each task type will now be discussed in turn. Since most task types are shared by CPE and FCE, any differences in the way they were realised in these two examinations will also be considered.

Conversation based on a photograph

While similar to its predecessors, this task now incorporated an important new feature: only one type of prompt was used. Examiners were provided with booklets of photographs which were different for the two (CPE and FCE) exams. A set of specific questions about the photos was provided for the examiner as well, including follow-up questions. Again, this is an important change, since it indicates a growing concern with test uniformity and therefore scoring validity. The object of this exercise was to elicit a description of the photos and encourage a candidate to 'take the initiative and to speak a number of connected sentences without interruption' (Instructions to Oral Examiners 1976:7). The follow-up questions were 'intended to "stretch" the candidate, and particularly in the case of Proficiency the conversation should not be allowed to drop to too mundane a level' (1976:7). CPE candidates were assessed on 'Overall Ability to Communicate' and on 'Vocabulary and Idiom' (1976:8), FCE candidates just on 'Overall ability to Communicate'. The follow-up questions differentiated this section of the CPE and FCE Interview from their pre-1975 counterparts and also signalled a concern with the need to provide CPE candidates with enough opportunity to display a higher-level ability.

The content of the photos in this task differentiated between the two proficiency levels in terms of both cognitive and linguistic demands. The CPE questions tended to include abstract and non-personal information captured in topics such as: what makes stories or plays (un)suitable for children, individual taste in entertainment, the influence of environment on character, the outlook of teenagers, etc. In contrast, FCE topics were more concrete and personal, only sometimes drawing on more abstract ideas, e.g. differences between the train station in the picture and one in the candidate's own country, the pleasures of travelling, the candidate's experience of looking after children.

Talk on a prepared topic

This task was part of the CPE speaking test only. The aim of the task was to provide the candidate with an opportunity 'to demonstrate how successfully he can sustain a theme, and is to the oral part of the examination what the essay is to the written' (Instructions to Oral Examiners 1976:7). The candidate was given 15 minutes before the beginning of the interview to prepare. The examiners were instructed not to interrupt the candidate unless it was time to finish this section or to help the candidate if he/she needed support and prompting. Performance was assessed on 'Overall Ability to Communicate', as well as 'Grammar and Structure'.

The topics were abstract and non-personal, inviting the use of a variety of complex language functions, such as expressing and justifying opinion, discussion, evaluation, hypothesising and suggesting. Here are some examples:

CPE June 1975 Speaking test

The aspects of the education system in your country you would like to change.
Everyone, including children, has a right to some privacy. How far do you agree?
Boys should be brought up differently from girls.
Everyone should earn the same no matter what his job is.
It is better to live in a small village than in a large city.
Large families are preferable to small ones.
What society should do with convicted criminals.
Would the world be a happier place if all governments had more women in them?
The role of the father in the family.
(CPE June 1975 Question paper)

Besides the nature of the topics and complexity of language functions elicited, this task also posed further cognitive and linguistic challenges for candidates with its long-turn task format: a candidate was required to speak at length with no or minimal support on the part of the examiner. Since the topics were argumentative, the candidate had to additionally present and support an opinion. The onus was on the candidate to maintain the monologue and organise it in a coherent way. Such monologic speech, Field (2011) has argued, presents a higher cognitive load. In order to address the added cognitive difficulty, 15 minutes of preparation time were given to candidates before the interview to plan their response. Time constraints are important parameters both in context and cognitive validity and Field argues that tasks requiring a longer turn which involve a lot of work at the conceptualisation stage typically need planning time (Field 2011:106). He further cites Levelt (1989), hypothesising that in this type of task a speaker may need time to 'formulate in advance a set of "sub-goals" or "speech act intentions"' (Field 2011:106). The provision of planning time, therefore, can be seen as a positive feature in this task, as it accommodates the higher cognitive load associated with it.

The introduction of this task was an important step in the development of speaking assessment at Cambridge because it added an additional communicative task to the examiner-led interview. A candidate could now engage in a wider range of speaking activities, which in turn tapped into a wider speaking construct.

Reading aloud

This task involved the reading aloud of a dialogue, with the candidate and the examiner each reading a part. A candidate was given the extract 15 minutes before the interview (and in the case of CPE, along with the topic for the long-turn task). The main emphasis in the assessment of this task was on pronunciation, including stress, intonation and rhythm (*Changes of Syllabus 1975* 1973:10).

It is interesting to see that this task type, which was not in the spirit of the communicative ethos gaining momentum at the time, was still part of the exam. The task was clearly changed from its pre-1975 predecessor and now involved the reading of a dialogue and not a literary passage. It had more face validity and allowed a wider range of pronunciation features to be tapped into in a more controlled context. Nevertheless, it activated the same limited number of cognitive processes as the reading aloud task in pre-1975 CPE and LCE and signals a conservative element in the test and a nod to the past. This task was, not surprisingly, subject to some criticism in the 1970s:

> the dialogue section, with its examiner participation, was not felt to be an advance on the old type of reading passage containing a dialogue, and the testing of reading aloud in the examination was questioned in principle (*Report on the Cambridge Workshop* October 1975: 2).

Exam centres had mixed reactions, pointing out that in general the task should be acceptable 'provided that passages are not stilted, dated or too literary [and that] sufficient allowance is made in the range of passages for female examiners and candidates' (Executive Committee minutes October 1975: 2). They thus signalled the need for careful consideration of examination content in view of test taker characteristics.

Situations

In this section, the candidate was asked to imagine him/herself and the examiner in a certain real-life situation and had to provide an appropriate response to the situation. Two FCE examples, from Hawkey (2009: 43) are given below:

FCE 1975 Speaking test

You are by the crossroads near the George Hotel when you see an accident in which a cyclist is badly hurt. You are the only person on the spot, so you go into a telephone box and phone for an ambulance. What would you say?

(Suitable answer) Please come to the crossroads by the George Hotel at once. There's been an accident. A car's knocked over a cyclist and he seems to be badly hurt.

You are in a "No smoking" compartment of a train. A man takes out a cigarette and starts to light it. Ask him not to smoke.

(Suitable answer) Excuse me. Would you mind not smoking in here, please? The smoke bothers me, and this is a non-smoking compartment. Thank you.

The focus of this task was on the use of socially acceptable and appropriate forms. This task presented the biggest innovation in the examination and showed a clear influence of the situational approach in language teaching which became very popular in British English Language Teaching in the late 1960s (see Chapter 1 for details). The focus of this approach was on presenting language through meaningful situations. As Underhill (1994:60) notes, an important aspect of language proficiency was 'the functional aspect of language – recognising when a situation calls for a particular type of response, and supplying it appropriately'.

The task allowed a more precise focus on and elicitation of a variety of language functions, such as suggesting, complaining, apologising, persuading, making arrangements, enquiring, praising, insisting, many of which had not been amenable to eliciting through classical controlled Interviews so far. It marked an important development in the history of Cambridge examinations by introducing a step towards more communicative and more sociolinguistically embedded testing. It attempted to address the need to embed authenticity in the test. It also brought about a number of caveats associated with the task, such as issues of interactional authenticity, since the candidate was not actually engaging in a conversation as they would in a similar real-life situation, but rather just responding to a prompt. A further issue was the significant difficulty of reliably assessing such situationally embedded tasks due to the relative nature of the sociopragmatic and pragmalinguistic competence they entail. There is now a solid body of literature which attests to the challenges associated with the testing of the realisation of specific pragmatic speech acts. One of the main issues is the variation in speech act realisation among native speakers themselves (provided we can define 'native speaker'). Such variation has been shown to depend on, for example, age (Coupland, Coupland and Giles 1991), gender (Homles 1989), or geographic region (Blum-Kulka and House 1989).

The Situations task was generally welcomed by the examination users, but centres did criticise it for proving difficult to 'launch satisfactorily, even with good candidates, and made a rather diffuse ending to the interview' (Executive Committee minutes October 1975:2). It was used in both CPE and FCE, and the two proficiency levels were differentiated through the types of scenarios included: only extended situations at CPE, compared to situations requiring both short formulaic responses and more extended responses at FCE. The extended situations at CPE often required a greater sensitivity to social-cultural norms and included face-threatening speech acts (Brown and Levinson 1987). Compare the CPE situations below with the ones from FCE:

FCE and CPE 1975 June Speaking Test

FCE	CPE
Someone says that the date is May 10. You know that it is May 11. What do you say? (FCE June 1975 Question paper)	Your friend is wearing a very elaborate dress which she is very proud of. You feel that it is unsuitable for the picnic you are going on together. Without hurting her feelings, try to persuade her to change into something more suitable. (CPE June 1975 Question paper)
A friend of yours is wearing a pair of shoes that you admire so much that you would like to buy a similar pair. What do you say? (FCE June 1975 Question paper)	You walk out of a shop without paying for something that you put in your bag. Just as you realise your mistake and are turning around to go back and pay for it, the manager of the score confronts you. What do you say? (CPE June 1975 Question paper)

To sum up, the revision of the CPE and FCE Oral in 1975 marked a significant change from the way speaking ability at Cambridge had been conceptualised for decades. Task types became more interactive and communicative, and new types of communicative tasks were introduced. This allowed for a wider range of speaking skills to be tested and tapped into a broader and more communicative construct. The talk on a prepared topic in CPE was a new task which allowed candidates to independently maintain a monologue, develop and organise their ideas. The CPE and FCE Situations task was also a significant change in oral testing at Cambridge, and was an example of the now widely accepted close alignment between Cambridge exams and classroom practice (Spolsky 1995a). Its focus on pragmatic and socio-linguistic competence and the variety of language functions which could not have been elicited by the traditional controlled Interview signalled a step towards a more communicative and more socio-linguistically embedded definition of the construct. The more communicative approach to testing was also reflected in the phrasing and focus of assessment criteria (to be discussed in more detail later in the chapter).

1984 Proficiency (CPE) and First Certificate (FCE)

Another wave of revisions took place in the 1980s, drawing on lessons learnt from past tests, on the pedagogic climate at the time and on an extensive consultation with centres and teachers. The *Changes of Syllabus in 1984* inform us that one of the main drivers behind the revision of the speaking test was the need:

... to link the form and content of the examination at both levels, even more closely than with the 1975 changes, with communicative approaches in teaching, particularly with regard to the content and weighting of the oral element (1982:1).

A further requirement underlying the revisions was to base oral test material on 'current spoken English' and move away from literary sources (Executive Committee minutes, November 1980:4). CPE, therefore, was revised

> ... without lowering the standard, to the declared demand for a more functional and less academically-oriented examination. This has involved a less literary and more "everyday" range of vocabulary and cultural reference (Executive Committee minutes, November 1986: 5).

An additional aim was to introduce tests which would have a positive impact on L2 communicative classrooms (English as a Foreign Language: General Handbook 1987:3). A number of test features reflected the communicative ethos of the CPE and FCE Speaking tests, such as the introduction of a new task (Communication activity). The CPE and FCE Speaking test now consisted of:

- conversation task based on a photograph
- reading aloud, changed to conversation based on a passage in 1986
- communicative activity.

The tasks were also characterised by higher authenticity of prompts, and materials originated from a variety of real-life sources, such as magazines, radio features, etc. An optional group test format was also introduced for the whole or only the third part of the test, and the weighting of the Speaking test was increased and made comparable to the weight given to the Reading, Writing and Use of English papers in the overall exam, reflecting the increased prominence of speaking skills in assessment.

The basic difference between FCE and CPE was maintained:

> The First Certificate is an examination testing competence in everyday English for a variety of commercial uses (especially public contact) or as a basis for further study ... The level expected for Proficiency involves a certain maturity of approach, with a more open-ended range of tasks and higher expectations, in line with the traditional association of Proficiency with ability to function in English in the context of an aca-demic course, or to teach the language effectively (Instructions to Oral Examiners 1984:7).

From 1984 onwards, CPE and FCE candidates could be examined either individually, in pairs or trios for the whole or one-third of the speaking test. Group and paired formats in speaking assessment were a reflection of the communicative approach to language teaching in 1980s and the widespread use of group work in L2 classrooms. In the examination context they resulted in an 'increased amount of "candidate talking time" and reduction in "examiner talking time"' (General FCE Handbook 1987:69). Their use at Cambridge reflected a move to broaden the construct underlying the speaking tests and to go beyond the roles and functions elicited in one-to-one interviews. The following information was given in the General FCE Handbook (1987):

> The added realism of a group Interview is something which is being strongly advocated by the Syndicate's language advisors though it is realised that organisational difficulties may make it impracticable for some centres and it is therefore treated as an option (General FCE Handbook 1987:69).

The introduction of this new format marked a critical point in assessing speaking at Cambridge, as it placed the exams firmly within a communicative paradigm.

The 'organisational difficulties' led to the optional use of the group format and allowed for a more complex test construct. The optional use of different test formats also introduced significant variation in the speaking construct within FCE and CPE, which we now know could have a negative impact on the validity of the test. It can also be argued that the different formats – solo vs. group – tapped into somewhat different constructs. It has been shown, for example, that different task types and test formats elicit different functional resources (O'Sullivan, Weir and Saville 2002), and that they are associated with different cognitive loads (Field 2011). As a reaction to the variability introduced by different formats, one standard format – a paired test – became the norm in the *Certificate of Advanced English* (CAE) in 1991, to be followed by FCE in 1996 and CPE in 2002.

We now turn to a more detailed discussion of the tasks, focusing on their contribution to a communicative test construct.

The picture-based conversation task remained the same. In the solo examiner-candidate format, examiners were instructed to initiate a natural discussion, while in a group format, they were asked to encourage each candidate to initiate a discussion and invite other candidates to comment (CPE Interview Examiner's materials 1986). Candidates were assessed on fluency and grammatical accuracy in this task.

The role-playing form of reading aloud introduced in 1975, with the examiner and the candidate each reading a part, was discontinued in 1984 and passages were introduced again. Importantly, the passages were no longer taken from literary sources, but from a variety of real-life sources which varied in genre, including announcements, instructions, descriptions of a situation, etc. (sometimes even going to extremes of authenticity of materials and including passages about, for example, wine making). The passages were considerably shorter than before in both examinations. In order to give the task a purpose beyond simply reading aloud, candidates were also required to briefly identify the purpose or genre of the passage (e.g. description, instruction) and its possible real-life source. This task feature aimed to 'increase the candidate's awareness of the character of the passage and encourage attempts at interpretation rather than mere verbalisation of the printed passage' (Instructions to Oral Examiners 1984:5). Candidates were assessed on pronunciation of individual sounds and prosodic features of their pronunciation.

A new communicative task was introduced in 1984 – Communicative Activity – which was characterised by a higher level of interactiveness than in the other two test tasks, as candidates were given the opportunity to initiate turns and maintain an interaction, thus displaying control of a range of functions, including interaction management ones. In a group format, examiners were advised to establish a good balance of contributions, not allowing over-dominance of a candidate and deliberately bringing out reticent candidates (Instructions to Oral Examiners 1984:5). There was often an information gap between the participants which added structure to the task and provided a real-life purpose. Candidates were assessed on 'Communicative Ability' and 'Vocabulary'. An FCE example of this task is given below:

> The examiner outlines as a situation an airport information desk where a flight has been seriously delayed, and elicits by means of spoken or written prompts, specific questions and comments as follows:
> Ask about
> The next flight.
> Hotel for the night – and who pays for this.
> Contacting waiting relations etc.
> (*Changes of Syllabus 1984* 1982:31)

The communicative activity was, overall, a novel type of activity, which partially drew on older FCE and CPE tasks. It was seen by UCLES as combining 'the positive features of two existing sub-tests, that based on situational responses, and the speech on a briefly prepared topic' (1982:31). The situational responses first introduced in 1975 were limited in terms of generating interaction, since the candidates gave a one-turn response to a prompt. The situations task in 1984 gained a stronger interactional element, which allowed a broader range of functional language to be tapped into.

The available prompts in this part of the test were quite diverse and included role plays, discussions involving opinions, short extended talks followed by a general discussion on an open-ended topic, debates, and discussions based on prescribed literary books (e.g. *Sense and Sensibility* by Jane

Austen or *The Great Gatsby* by Scott Fitzgerald). These prompts elicited a more or less similar range of functional language, e.g. describing, expressing opinions, comparing/contrasting, arguing for and against, exemplifying, justifying opinions. It could be argued, however, that they involved different cognitive demands, since the amount of structure provided (e.g. role play vs. open-ended question), the type of talk elicited (e.g. structured role play vs. interactive discussion vs. brief extended turn followed by interactive discussion) and the type of information transformation required (knowledge telling vs. knowledge transforming, Bereiter and Scardamalia 1987b) impacted on the cognitive difficulty of the task. While at the time this variety was seen as positive on the grounds of the principles of Communicative Language Teaching (Fulcher, personal communication), the impact of this variation on cognitive and contextual aspects of candidate performance is now better understood, and in subsequent revisions this variability in prompts was addressed and controlled.

The proficiency level difference between FCE and CPE was maintained through topic complexity and the type of input provided. For example, an FCE discussion task could include a photo prompt and a list of suggestions to structure the discussion. The equivalent CPE task would bear a higher cognitive load and be based on verbal prompts only with abstract content.

The reactions of teachers and centres to the revised CPE and FCE were largely positive since the test was now seen as a better reflection of classroom practices, and was based on current spoken rather than literary English. The Executive Committee reported the following:

> Comments on question papers were received and considered in detail in the context of the significant changes of syllabus content and emphasis. The change to a more realistic and functional examination at First Certificate and Proficiency level had been generally welcomed . . . particularly the emphasis on realistic interchange in the Activity section, on which the training of examiners is being concentrated (Executive Committee minutes October 1984:2).

1986: Further modifications

The major revisions carried out in 1984 were followed up by further changes to FCE and CPE in 1986, and represented yet another step in the move to 'an integrated, communicative-based test format' (Executive Committee minutes May 1986). The main change was the discontinuation of Reading aloud (Amendment to the Regulations for 1986), and its replacement by a passage-based Interview. A further change involved the introduction of a thematic link between all three tasks in the exam. So, the FCE and CPE Speaking tests now consisted of:

- a conversation based on a photo
- a conversation based on a reading passage
- a communicative activity task.

The passage-based task was not a novelty in itself, since it co-existed with the picture-based conversation task in CPE and FCE from their inception. In the light of the explicit aim to make CPE and FCE more grounded in communicative principles, the 1986 passage-based Interview was quite different from its 1945 equivalent, however. It was still an integrated Reading-into-Speaking task, but instead of being derived from literary materials, the passages were now drawn from a variety of real-life sources (CPE Handbook 1995:75). The passages were used in the same way as the photos in the first part of the speaking test, i.e. as a springboard for discussion. In addition, the discussion usually involved referring to the passages and quoting from them at varying length 'thus meeting the purpose of the earlier use of passages for formal reading aloud but more effectively and naturally, i.e. without the distortion of pronunciation factors arising from a relatively artificial activity, and with fluency and communication factors coming into play' (Instructions to Oral Examiners 1986:5). This integrated task certainly added a more real-life communicative element to the speaking test, making it more situationally and interactionally authentic, as both academic and professional candidates are likely to face reading-into-speaking tasks in their respective settings. It also acquired a communicative element and tapped into all levels of cognitive processing underlying speaking, and allowed a candidate to exhibit and be assessed on a wider range of speaking skills (e.g. pronunciation, intonation, fluency).

In an attempt to make speaking tests as authentic and conversational as possible, the entire speaking test now became more coherent through using thematically related tasks (Instructions to Oral Examiners 1986). This was another significant development in the history of the CPE and FCE tests, as it signalled an ongoing concern with replicating non-test conditions.

To summarise, the CPE and FCE Speaking test revisions in 1984 and 1986 were inspired by the aim to make the tests more communicative, and to become a more faithful reflection of the activities associated with a communicative classroom and non-test domains. The task prompts became more interactional and topical issues and authentic task materials were some of the main contextual task features. The diversity of task types in the communicative activity, which introduced much uncontrolled variation in terms of cognitive and context validity (the nature and amount of task input and targeted language functions) was addressed and revised in 1986. In addition to pronunciation and intonation, the focus of assessment also extended to fluency. With the communicative activity task, a greater variety of contexts and task types was introduced, a higher degree of interaction and more diverse language functions were targeted. The introduction of the optional group format increased the range of interaction types and cognitive processing demands. However, making that test format optional introduced much variation in terms of cognitive processing and task demands, which consequently meant that the different test formats were tapping into somewhat different oral constructs. The exclusion of the reading aloud task and its replacement with a passage-based conversation meant that *all* CPE and FCE Speaking tasks now involved interaction and tapped into all stages of cognitive processing involved in speaking.

The 1990s and present day constructs: Advanced Certificate (CAE), First Certificate (FCE) and Proficiency (CPE)

The 1990s were a turning point in the history of the Cambridge English Speaking tests, mainly because the tests became firmly embedded in an interactional construct. The ground was laid with the introduction of the CAE examination (and subsequent revisions of CPE and FCE) which embodied the continuing drive at Cambridge to develop speaking tests along more communicative lines.

As discussed in detail in Chapter 1, there was a strong demand for an 'intermediate level examination' in the 1980s (Joint Committee minutes December 1985). CAE was proposed as a 'post-FCE examination that was recognisably in the FCE-CPE tradition' (Joint Committee minutes July 1989) and was intended for both students and professionals. It was intended to represent a level at which candidates 'are expected to have a good operational command of the spoken language and are able to handle communication in most situations' (Instructions to Oral Examiners 1999:6). It thus fell between FCE, which presupposed 'a generally effective command of the spoken language and ability to handle communication in familiar situations', and CPE, which required candidates 'to have a fully operational command of the most spoken language and to be able to handle communication in most situations, including those which may be unfamiliar or unexpected' (Instructions to Oral Examiners 1999:6).

CAE was launched in 1991 and its design and content are important examples of the balance which face-to-face tests tapping into an interaction construct have to strike. The CAE Speaking test consisted of four tasks:

- an examiner-led interview
- a candidate extended turn
- a candidate-candidate discussion
- a candidate-candidate-examiner discussion.

The continued emphasis on a communicative construct was seen as important, as reflected in an emphasis on real-world tasks and authenticity.

Bachman's (1990) conceptualisation of authenticity was useful in guiding the CAE test design:

> If Paper 5 [i.e. the Speaking test] were to work only with the notion of situational authenticity it might tap only a limited range of abilities, producing assessments that might not be generalisable to other situations. If it followed only situational authenticity for its choice of contexts it would also risk using contexts that candidates might find it hard to identify with or engage with in examination situation, e.g. role plays such as buying items in a shop. The situation presented by an examination situation can be exploited for its own communicative situational potential, e.g. the fact that the interlocutor and the candidates do not know one another. This consideration has in fact influenced the shape of the first two parts of the paper and the fourth part. The third part of the paper calls more on interactional authenticity (Revised FCE Internal Specifications 1994:58).

Two of the main changes introduced through the CAE speaking test involved a *compulsory* paired format and the use of Interlocutor frames which scripted interviewer language. These new features of the test resulted in a much needed standardisation of the contextual and cognitive task demands of the test. The new paired test format meant that candidates were examined in pairs (or in a trio, in the case of an uneven number of candidates) by two external examiners acting as an Observer/Assessor and Interviewer/Interlocutor. This format was soon to be adopted by other Cambridge examinations and is the current format in many of its tests.

The compulsory paired format also ensured that the test now tapped into a broader interactional construct, as it encouraged and supported a higher degree of interactivity and reciprocity in communication and a wider sampling of contexts and language functions than was previously possible with the one-to-one examiner-candidate format (see, for example, ffrench 2003, Galaczi 2008).

The introduction of the 'Interlocutor frame', which largely drew on empirical work in the 1990s (discussed earlier, e.g. Brown 2003, Lazaraton 1994) was intended to standardise the amount and content of the examiner contributions and as such to ensure equal treatment for all candidates. The interlocutor frames had implications both for the reliability of assessment and the construct of the speaking test since they ensured standardised contextual and cognitive task demands. Interlocutor frames have since then been rolled out to all other Cambridge English examinations and are still in use. A challenge with scripting interviewer language is expressed by Lazaraton (2002:152) who notes that:

> it is unlikely . . . that it would be possible, or even desirable, to eradicate the behaviour entirely, since the "examiner factor" is the most important characteristic that distinguishes face-to-face speaking tests from their tape-mediated counterparts (Lazaraton 2002:152).

In an effort to balance these two opposing demands, the interlocutor frames script examiner language to ensure uniformity, but through follow-up questions also allow examiners freedom to co-construct interaction and preserve the human examiner factor which is a unique feature of face-to-face tests (Galaczi and ffrench 2011).

As discussed in the first section of this chapter, the interactional nature of the construct underlying paired tests meant that interlocutor variability now became part of the construct. This important issue was addressed by Cambridge through task design and the use of different response formats in the speaking test, which elicit different types of talk. The multi-task structure of the speaking tests, where candidate-candidate interaction formed the basis of part of the test only, gave the opportunity for candidates to engage in peer-peer interaction, but limited potential unfairness through using other more controlled tasks as well. The tasks in the test had a different task focus each in terms of the purpose of communication (e.g. social and interactional, transactional) and aspects of interactional competence. The examinations intended to elicit (and did indeed elicit – see Lazaraton 1997, Lazaraton and Frantz 1997) a wide variety of language functions, from more basic and simpler ones, typically clustered in the first task (e.g. exchanging personal information, talking about present circumstances and future plans), to more complex ones (e.g. expressing and justifying opinions, speculating, hypothesising, etc.), which were predominant and focal in the remaining tasks. Candidates also needed to exhibit a variety of interaction management skills, starting with the most basic asking and responding, to maintaining and developing a monologue, turn-taking and developing topics. The discourse types could be short turns (interview task, collaborative task) or long turns (the monologue task). In addition to the above variety, FCE, CAE and CPE candidates also systematically engaged in different interaction types (e.g. examiner-candidate, candidate-candidate, examiner-candidate-candidate).

The tasks introduced in the 1990s will now be overviewed in turn. The primary focus here will be on the task format and its evolution from prior formats. CAE will be used as an illustration, since it led the way with its revised four-task format, but the reader should bear in mind that this format was also adopted by other Cambridge exams. Field (2011) and Galaczi and ffrench (2011) provide a comprehensive discussion of the key cognitive and contextual features distinguishing these proficiency levels.

The first task in the newly launched CAE, the Interview, was based on the traditional CPE and LCE general conversation task which was part of those exams until 1975. This task required CAE candidates to talk about personal, familiar and factual information when answering questions about themselves and allowed CAE candidates to interact with each other and exchange information. However, the interaction in this task was also controlled through a) the examiner asking questions from a given selection of questions rather than through spontaneous conversation (Instructions to Oral Examiners 1999) and b) constraining the content of candidates' questions to each other with the bulleted points provided in the examination, to ensure standardisation of test content. An example is provided below:

CAE June 1999 Speaking test

Interlocutor Good morning (afternoon/evening). My name is . . . and this is my colleague . . . And your names are . . .?
Can I have your mark sheets please? Thank you.
First of all, we'd like to know a little about you.
(Select one or two questions as appropriate.)
Where are you both/all from?
How long have you been in this country?
How long have you been studying English?
Have you been studying English together?

Now I'd like you to ask each other something about:
(Select two or three prompts in any order as appropriate.)
• your interests and leisure activities
• life in each other's country
• your reason's for studying English
• places of interest you have visited in this country
(Ask candidate(s) further questions as necessary.)
• What have you both/all enjoyed/disliked the most about studying English?
• What interesting things have you done since you've been here?
• How would you feel about living abroad permanently?
• Looking back on your life, what do you consider to be the most memorable event?
• What do you hope to achieve in the future?
Thank you.
(Oral Examiners' Materials for CAE June 1999:3)

Spolsky (personal communication) has noted the similarity between this opening task and the warm up in the FSI oral interview. While no evidence exists that CAE was modelled on that exam, it is likely that many direct speaking tests would begin with such a task type, which taps into social-interactional language.

This task involved talking to the Examiner and to another candidate and led to interaction configurations with different cognitive and linguistic demands in the same task. Initially, both CAE and FCE candidates were required to respond to the Examiner and also interact with each other, but from 1999, FCE candidates were no longer expected to interact in this task. FCE candidates were still examined in pairs, but the Interlocutor would communicate with each candidate individually in this task, thus reducing the cognitive load associated with this task, through focusing it on one type of interaction only (interviewer-candidate).

The second CAE task was a long turn in which each candidate described and commented on a visual prompt for 1 minute without interruption. The task appeared in the revised FCE (1996), after which it was also included in CPE in 2002. The ability to sustain a monologue, therefore, became an essential aspect of the underlying construct at all three proficiency levels. The difference between the proficiency levels was achieved through different contextual task parameters, such as the amount of support the prompt provided for the candidates, the type of visuals used, the nature of information, and the time allowed for the task.

In the early CAE years, a range of visuals was used in the long-turn task, including photographs, cartoons, diagrams, maps, set of pictures (only one had to be described). As we have noted earlier, describing different types of visual prompts carries different linguistic demands and elicits different linguistic resources. This task feature was the subject of critique due to the measurement error introduced by the range of topics and prompts (Bachman et al 1995, Chalhoub-Deville and Turner 2000). Cambridge addressed this caveat during later speaking test revisions in 1996 and the visual prompt types per task became standardised (e.g. only photographs depicting people doing something are currently used for the FCE long-turn task). Careful attention to using the same type of visual and trialling of materials in advance of live tests also addresses the concern of comparability of forms (Galaczi and ffrench 2011).

The third task, candidate/candidate interaction, gave control of the interaction to the test takers, who had to jointly maintain the discussion in this task. The task typically took the form of problem solving, decision making, prioritising and speculating and is reminiscent of some of the tasks first introduced through the communicative activity task in 1984 CPE and FCE. Unlike the communicative activity task from the 1980s, which consisted of a wide variety of tasks with different purposes and different kinds of prompts designed to elicit different speaking skills, this task was standardised and now involved a brief verbal prompt alongside a set of visual prompts (e.g. photographs, line drawings, maps, or diagrams). An example of a CAE collaborative task is provided below (CAE Handbook 1991:99):

CAE 1991 Speaking test

Olympic Symbol (Evaluate and rank order)

Interlocutor   In this part of the test I'd like you to discuss something between/among
yourselves but please speak so that we can hear you.
Hand over the pictures of the alternative Olympic Symbols to the pair of candidates.
The International Olympic Committee is considering alternatives to replace the current Olympic Symbol of five circles. Please decide which you think are the best two or three in order of merit. You may, if you prefer, choose something entirely different which you think is more suitable.
You have three to four minutes for this.

The final CAE task was a group discussion involving both candidates and examiner. The task focus was on developing topics raised in the previous candidate/candidate interaction task. For example:

> Which Symbol did you like best? Why?/ Do you think that the Olympic Games have become too commercialised?/ Does your country usually do well? Why do you think that is?/ Do you think enough is being done to prevent the use of drugs in sporting competitions?/ Do you think international sport encourages international friendship?/ Do events like the Olympic Games develop feelings of nationalism?/ Do you think sports people enter competitions for the glory of winning or for the money they can win? Why? (CAE Oral Examiner's Materials 1991:99).

The changes to testing speaking ability introduced through CAE in 1991 and adopted by FCE in 1996 and CPE in 2002 were not a complete novelty. All the task types in the CAE Speaking test were derived from older and recent versions of CPE and FCE/LCE, but they were selected with test purpose in mind. The result was a more interactional test which *systematically* included different *theoretically-driven* types of interaction (e.g. examiner-candidate, candidate-candidate, examiner-candidate-candidate, candidate), and elicited a range of language functions and aspects of interactional competence, thus broadening the construct underlying the test.

Making the 2 candidates:2 examiners test format obligatory had a strong impact on the test construct since it reduced the variation previously observed in terms of the interchangeable use of different formats (solo vs. paired vs. group) and led to the consistent realisation of the speaking construct across test versions and sessions. Conversing with a peer and a non-peer, responding to questions and initiating discussions, broadened the cognitive and contextual parameters associated with the speaking test.

In brief, examination developments and revisions that took place in the mid/late 1990s resulted in more explicitly defined, theoretically and empirically grounded speaking constructs. The introduction of the compulsory paired test format lead to a higher degree of test standardisation and a higher degree of interactivity introduced by the different types of tasks. A higher level of standardisation was achieved with the introduction of Interlocutor scripts. Intentional similarities across the exams signalled similarities in the speaking construct, and cognitive and contextual task demands were graded across different proficiency levels.

The speaking construct underlying the tests since the late 1990s has not changed. What has moved forward is the explicit argument presented to support the cognitive and contextual parameters of the construct underlying the examination and the differentiation between proficiency levels. In terms of cognitive task characteristics, Field (2011) presents evidence of a careful gradation across proficiency levels of the post-2008 examinations, in terms of cognitive difficulty of task demands and the range of interaction types. At the conceptualisation stage (the first stage of cognitive processing), Field found that the availability of information (personal and everyday versus non-personal and abstract), specificity and complexity of prompts (e.g. set questions versus loose/more open questions) differentiated across speaking tests at different proficiency levels. In all cases, the amount of support in the test rubric was found to be detailed, regardless of the level, in order to ensure comparability between the performances at the given level and avoid introducing candidates' imagination as an additional factor that could influence assessment. The stage of grammatical encoding was found to be embodied in the number and complexity of language functions to be performed in the task. Language functions were found to consistently differentiate between levels, with their number and level of complexity rising with proficiency levels.

The phonological encoding stage was reflected in the treatment of hesitation and pausing in the Cambridge ESOL assessment scales. For example, at KET level, 'responses are limited to short phrases or isolated words with frequent hesitation and pauses', while at CAE level a candidate 'maintains a flow of language with only natural hesitation resulting from considerations of appropriacy and expression' (Field 2011:93).

The phonetic encoding and articulation stage are reflected in the assessment criterion of Pronunciation and the primary focus on intelligibility in the assessment scales. Field (20011:108) suggests that the 'tension between the need to hold a phonetic plan in the mind and the need to focus attention upon precise articulation' justifies not putting undue emphasis on the accuracy in pronunciation. Finally, self-monitoring is assessed through the ability for self-repair and the level of support needed by a candidate in Cambridge ESOL, which is also captured in the assessment scales.

Field also argued that different interaction types impose different cognitive loads during speaking. As a result, they are graded across levels in Cambridge ESOL Speaking tests. For example, the complex three-way interaction appears from FCE (B2) onwards; the solo candidate (monologic task) is present from PET (B1) onwards, but is assigned less time at that level than at FCE, CAE and CPE.

In terms of contextual task characteristics, Galaczi and ffrench (2011:170) offer the following summary of the gradation of contextual demands across levels of Cambridge ESOL Main Suite examinations:

> In terms of criterial features across levels, a clear gradation is seen from controlled to semi-controlled to open-ended response formats, which accommodates the need for scaffolding and support at the lower levels, and higher communicative demand at the higher levels. There is also a progression (both within a level and across levels) from relatively structured and supported interaction, under the direct control of the examiner, involving topics of immediate personal relevance to more open-ended discussion with less examiner control involving more general topics. In addition, there is an increase in the amount of time assigned to each task type and to the overall test, as one moves up the levels. Another key distinguishing feature is the gradation from factual to evaluative discourse modes, and the larger presence at the lower levels of persuasion and description, compared with the bigger role of exposition and argumentation at the higher levels. The progression (both within a level and across levels) from personal and concrete information to non-personal and abstract information is also shown to accommodate the need for increased cognitive complexity of the task at the higher levels. Furthermore, this gradation is seen in the visuals for the tasks, which provide more scaffolding and are more content-rich at the lower levels, in contrast with visuals which convey more abstract concepts at the higher levels.

(See Field (2011) and Galaczi and ffrench (2011) for more detailed discussions about the gradation of cognitive and contextual task features across proficiency levels.)

So far we have focused on the context and cognitive validity aspects of the Cambridge speaking examinations from 1913 onwards. We now turn our attention to scoring validity considerations.

Scoring validity parameters: Assessment criteria and scales, marking standards and examiner standardisation

The focus in this section will be on the evolution of assessment scales at Cambridge, as well as rater training and standardisation issues. In our overview, we hope to show that the changes in speaking assessment at Cambridge in the last 100 years illustrate a move towards more careful and systematic attention given to scoring validity parameters.

Assessment criteria and scales

1913–1945: Assessment criteria and scales

The Cambridge Archives contain minimal information about scoring validity issues prior to 1945. The Examination Regulations (1933:1) inform us that 'emphasis will be laid in the oral examination on correctness of pronunciation and intonation. The study of Phonetics is recommended as an aid to the acquisition of a good "accent", but knowledge of them will not be tested in the examination.' It seems, therefore, that the assessment of speaking during this period focused predominantly on accuracy of pronunciation and intonation, in line with the dominant pedagogical influence of the Reform Movement, and on having an appropriate accent. The examiners were not given explicit assessment scales, but relied instead on their (subjective) expert judgement.

1945–1975: Assessment criteria and scales

More information about scoring validity issues became available with the publication of the first *Instructions to Oral Examiners* booklet in 1945. Its purpose was to standardise the process of the oral examination. This document marks an important stage in speaking assessment at Cambridge as it reveals an increased awareness of the need to set common standards in test delivery and marking. It noted that the documentation for oral examiners until then gave 'little help in the definition of standards' (Instructions to Oral Examiners 1945:1). The document focused on a range of scoring issues, such as, for example:

- the order of test tasks – 'you should hear all the candidates right through in the normal reading test before proceeding to the conversation and "unseen" reading' (1945:1)

- the value of a second rater – 'if you can get a second opinion on the normal reading test, so much the better' (1945:2)
- the internal standards for each task – 'Very Good 80%, Good 60%, Pass 40%' (1945:2)
- issues of excessive rater harshness or leniency, giving examiners the possibility to 'recommend mercy' where a candidate is borderline, and cautioning against 'undue leniency' (1945:2)
- the importance of examination security
- detailed guidance about the delivery of task prompts and the pace of conducting the exam.

Another important document to emerge at this time was the *Headings for Reports on Oral Examinations* (1945), which invited oral examiners to capture their examining experience in reports, so that collective wisdom can be pooled and drawn on when establishing standards, and contribute to the Syndicate's 'inquiry into the technique of oral examining'. The document provided a list of questions and issues to be addressed by examiners in their reports, such as:

- the general conditions of the oral examination, e.g. the order of test tasks, the average test time taken by LCE and CPE candidates
- the reading aloud tasks, e.g. defining examiner assessment criteria and standards applied by examiners in terms of degree of proficiency at the Pass, Good and Very Good levels
- the conversation task, e.g. defining degree of fluency and range of vocabulary expected of candidates at the different levels, types of questions asked during the conversation task (closed vs. open, focusing on specific lexical items), describing 'a syllabus to indicate the range of the conversation test'
- the standards in the test as a whole, e.g. the balance between standards recommended by the examiners, externally defined standards and the appropriateness of the current standards
- the dictation task, issues of speed of reading, assessment criteria, and the construct it is based on – 'What it is designed to test'
- general suggestions for the improvement or the oral and aural aspects of the test.

The list provided in this document for oral examiners provides a fascinating historical picture of the issues that Cambridge and Jack Roach (the author of the document) were dealing with. It is not surprising that at the time there were no specific procedures in place for examiner training/standardisation and examination standards, or that no explicit assessment scales were in use – these were developments to come in the next decades. What is striking in this document is the breadth of issues which are covered, including issues of construct, contextual parameters and scoring issues, indicating that the time was ripe for some of these issues to be addressed in a thorough way. It is also interesting to see how much the attempts to address these scoring validity issues drew on the *collective wisdom* of the oral examiners at the time, and not on directives from the Syndicate. This can be seen as an early instance of the concern at Cambridge to involve a range of stakeholders in the decision-making process, which, as discussed in chapter 1, is a prominent characteristic of practices at Cambridge.

The mid-1940s also saw the publication of a comprehensive paper by Roach (1945a, see Appendix C), which attempted to address the issues voiced above through empirical study. The paper strongly argued the need for examiner standardisation and for defining marking standards, and as a result there was an attempt to make assessment criteria more explicit. Roach (1945a:31) gives a clear indication of the assessment criteria which examiners needed to take into consideration in their decision-making process:

> It is also clear that while all marks in this kind of work must in the last resort depend upon an impression, it is desirable to tell examiners what they should chiefly be listening for, and what they should try and leave out of account. Thus, in the new "unseen" reading test, what they will endeavour to assess is comprehensibility. The conversation tests fluency and correctness of speech, not the finer shades of pronunciation and intonation; indeed, errors of pronunciation ought perhaps only to affect the mark in so far as they make the candidate difficult to understand. Whether the examiner will succeed in isolating fluency from pronunciation is another matter. Pronunciation and intonation find their assessment in the mark for reading; yet this mark is inevitably affected by the candidate's skill – and perhaps his amount of practice – in the art of reading aloud.

As can be seen, pronunciation, intonation, comprehensibility and intelligibility, correctness of speech and fluency were the main players in the holistic assessment of oral performance at the time.

From a 21st century perspective, we can easily critique these rudimentary definitions of assessment criteria – for example, 'fluency' is not defined, although it is explicitly separated from 'pronunciation', 'correctness of speech' is ambiguous as it may refer to both grammatical and lexical accuracy or only one of the two. At the same time, however, the attempt at explicitness regarding assessment criteria is a positive step forward in the evolution of the scoring parameters at Cambridge at the time.

It is worth noting that a focus on *communicative success* and not errors – a fundamental criterion of current scales – was also a guiding principle at Cambridge at the time. Roach's advice in the above quotation also suggests that comprehensibility rather than finer shades of pronunciation/intonation was of primary importance, which can be considered a further progressive feature of the assessment criteria applied at the time. It anticipates current Cambridge practice, as captured by Field (2011:108):

> The L2 speaker may also face a tension between the need to hold a phonetic plan in the mind and the need to focus attention upon precise articulation. In these circumstances, it is important that test designers do not unduly emphasise the importance of accuracy in pronunciation. The Cambridge English suite deals with this issue sensitively by adopting intelligibility as its principal criterion.

In the two decades to come, the increased provision of detail in terms of what should and should not be assessed was at the forefront of the speaking assessment agenda at Cambridge and was the fruit of the agreement reached at the first Executive Committee meeting (November 1957) which included UCLES and British Council representatives. Members of the Committee felt that 'more guidance for Oral examiners is needed' (Executive Committee minutes 1957, min. 12). An interesting case study was found in an examination centre in France, when during a visit in 1952 representatives of the Syndicate found out that to supplement the assessment guidance provided for oral examiners, examiners in Paris used their own analytic mark schemes with marks split up under seven headings. These marks were then transposed into a holistic assessment (Wyatt and Hudson 1951). The issue of an analytic rating scale was revisited in 1958 at one of the Joint Committee meetings when under discussion was the request by an examination centre to know if 'Cambridge could suggest a system of deciding exactly how the marking in oral examinations was to be assessed' (Joint Committee minutes July 1958:9). Mr Wyatt, the then UCLES Secretary, pointed out that while this was being investigated, the short period of the oral examination 'prevented the application of a very detailed marking system: there was no time to bear a large number of points of detail in mind, to assess a mark for each and then to work out a fair total' (1958). These early attempts to balance the need for more detailed assessment criteria for raters against the cognitive load imposed on raters and the feasibility and reliability of awarding a range of scores are, in fact, reminiscent of current debates on the same issues see Taylor and Galaczi 2011 for a more detailed discussion).

A notable change in terms of assessment scales and descriptors in 1970 was the move at Cambridge towards conceptualising and describing broad levels of proficiency more explicitly and comprehensively. For example, Pass level performance at CPE was as follows:

> To pass, a candidate should have a reasonably wide though not necessarily technical vocabulary. The rhythm and intonation of his speech as a whole, and his production of individual sounds, will be clear and acceptable, even if slightly foreign. His conversational resource on reasonably mature subjects will be adequate, with reasonably grammatical accuracy, with free use of complex sentences, and with adequate comprehension of an examiner speaking at normal speed and in conversational style (Instructions to Oral Examiners 1970:7).

Above the pass level, we are informed that:

> all these qualities should be present in the appropriate degree. Very good candidates will have full comprehension, complete fluency, a command of idiom, and ease of pronunciation. Candidates gaining maximum marks will normally be indistinguishable from educated native speakers, and are usually bilingual and either educated or long resident in an English-speaking country. It is not necessary to require complete conformity with Southern Standard (B.B.C.) English (as above).

This graded description system of performances at different ability levels is notable because it was the foundation of the rating scales to emerge in the mid-1970s at Cambridge. It also indicates a broadening of the construct, as seen in the reference to the fairly wide range of assessment criteria used to assess a candidates' performance: grammatical and lexical range and accuracy, pronunciation at word and sentence level, as well as listening comprehension skills. The above quotations also reveal that the highest level performance was described with reference to the educated native speaker standard. As mentioned earlier, the concept of the native speaker, which is typical of intuitively developed scales (Fulcher 2003), has been criticised because even the educated native speakers are variable in terms of oral ability and 'may only be "expert" within certain contexts, and not others' (Fulcher 2003:94). The Cambridge scales have now moved to an expert-user model. At the time the native-speaker model was seen as a suitable external criterion to aim for.

1975: Towards explicit criteria and scales

In the early 1970s the Executive Committee felt that holistic general impression marking was not adequate, noting that 'the standard in the oral tests appears to be lenient, even after the scrutiny of individual examiners' marks, and this was felt to be the effect of the subjective general impression marking system' (Executive Committee minutes, November 1972). This led to the introduction of analytic assessment scales for different traits at different levels of ability, in order to provide clearer and better-defined descriptions of performance. The launch of these scales was an important step towards better differentiated, more accurate and fine-tuned marking. The 1975 assessment criteria for CPE and FCE are given in Table 4.6.

Table 4.6 1975 CPE and FCE speaking assessment criteria (Instructions to Oral Examiners 1975)

Task	CPE	FCE
Conversation	Overall ability to communicate (11 bands) Vocabulary (11 bands)	Overall ability to communicate (11 bands) –
Topic	Overall ability to communicate (11 bands) Grammar and structure (11 bands)	– –
Reading aloud (dialogue)	Pronunciation, Stress, Intonation and Rhythm (11 bands)	Pronunciation, Stress, Intonation and Rhythm (11 bands)
Situations	Overall appropriateness (4 bands) Impression mark (6 bands)	Overall appropriateness (3 or 4 bands, depending on type of prompt) Impression mark (8 bands)

The above rating system was a significant move towards systematically focusing raters' attention on different aspects of performance in different test parts. It was designed with a communicative ethos in mind. For example, the 'Overall Ability to Communicate' scale included references to a usable and reliable basic competence in English, capability to converse fluently and flexibly, to communicate and elicit straightforward information, to adequately make points, express thoughts with clarity and precision, etc. The same assessment criterion for CPE had a slightly different slant, focusing on the ability to interact and comprehend in an academic context, with references made to English-medium courses, seminars, tutorials, lectures and discussions. The descriptors referred to participating effectively in seminars and discussions, expressing more complex ideas effectively and conversing freely on abstract topics. For the assessment of grammar and structure, the descriptors guided CPE examiners to focus on the nature of topics, range and accuracy of structures, complexity of sentences and the ease of communication.

These scales also indicate the fact that some constructs, e.g. 'Overall appropriateness' of the responses in the Situations task, were seen as covering a construct which is based on a shorter scale. The assessment of the Situations task attempted to unpack the tricky notion of sociolinguistic appropriateness through performance descriptors such as 'an adequate but not fully idiomatic response' or 'an appropriate response, correctly expressed, taking into account the tone and manner of the response' (Instructions to Oral Examiners 1975:12). We now know how problematic this construct is and it is significant that at the time, the attempt to define it in descriptive terms was not very successful. Tellingly, the assessment category itself was not given a precise name, but was simply referred to as 'Scale C1, C2, C3', in contrast to, for example, 'Scale B – Vocabulary' (1975:15).

Similarly to previous definitions of proficiency, where CPE Oral performances at the highest level were described with reference to 'an educated native speaker', the CPE and FCE 1975 assessment scales also described top level ('Excellent') performances with reference to 'an excellent near-native or native command', 'a native speaker' and 'an educated native speaker of English' (Instructions to Oral Examiners 1975). Note, however, that performance at those levels was couched in the rather vague notion of 'approaching' native-speaker command of the language (Spolsky, personal communication). Performance at lower ability levels at CPE and FCE (from 'weak' to 'not quite adequate' levels) was often negatively described in terms of what one cannot do rather than what one can do, e.g. 'incapable of, too limited in range, gross errors would sometimes fail to understand'.

All rating scales (apart from the one applied to the Situations task) consisted of six levels which were captured in a range of 11 marks and 8 categories: weak, inadequate, not quite adequate, adequate, satisfactory, good, very good and excellent (see Table 4.7 and 4.8). Six sets of descriptors were provided per rating scale. As an illustration, the 'Overall ability' scales for FCE and CPE are given in Tables 4.7 and 4.8. The scales also show the scale developers' attempt to capture the overlap between borderline FCE and CPE candidates – a 'very weak' CPE candidate is equivalent to a 'Not quite adequate' FCE candidate.

The introduction of these rating scales in 1975 was a significant step at Cambridge, as it shows the much stronger focus on explicit assessment criteria and scales. In terms of construct, these scales were the first step to explicitly define the construct in terms of the knowledge tapped into and the contexts of use of that knowledge. Hawkey (2009:46) has provided a useful summary of this stage of scale development, in this case in the context of FCE:

> Published test specifications now give both the criteria for the assessment of performance (vocabulary, grammar and structure, intonation, rhythm, stress and pronunciation and the overall ability to communicate in general terms) and the full scale used by the examiners in assessing candidate communicative performance. The six-level scale, from *very weak* to *excellent* reflects the need . . . for more clearly specified exams and assessment criteria. It may also reflect, in the focus of the descriptors, the growing influence of communicative approaches to language teaching and testing.

Viewed in an international context, it can be argued that Cambridge lagged behind American practices with the late introduction of explicitly worded assessment scales and performance descriptors. The FSI scales, consisting of

Table 4.7 CPE Conversation and Topic section: Scale A – General Impression of Overall Ability (Instructions to Oral Examiners 1975:14)

Category	Mark	Description
Very weak	0 1	Although he may be capable of communicating and eliciting straightforward information, does so in a fashion which would require some patience on the part of the listener. Frequently misunderstands straightforward questions and remarks.
Weak	2 3	His comprehension of and ability to communicate in spoken English are distinctly below the standard that would be required for him to participate in an English-medium course with benefit. Would require frequent explanation due to language difficulties. Finds it difficult to express his ideas adequately enough for native speakers to understand.
Not quite adequate	4	He would not sufficiently be able to understand a lecture nor could he adequately make points in a seminar or tutorial. Gets along well on mundane matters.
Adequate Satisfactory	5 6	Would experience no serious linguistic difficulties if he attended an English-medium course. Could participate usefully in discussions, and would cause listeners few difficulties.
Good Very good	7 8	Although still somewhat foreign, he expresses his thoughts with clarity and precision. Finds it easy to rephrase a sentence he sees does not carry quite clearly enough the message he intended. May occasionally misunderstand a question or comment, but is swift to grasp the point if it is rephrased.
Excellent	9 10	His command of spoken English approaches that of a soundly educated native speaker of English.

Table 4.8 FCE Conversation section: Scale A – General Impression of Overall Ability (Instructions to Oral Examiners 1975:10)

Category	Mark	Description
Very weak	0 1	Incapable of understanding simple vocabulary structures when presented in a slow and careful style of speech, or of producing them himself.
Weak	2 3	Though capable of understanding simple vocabulary and structures in a slow, careful style of speech, and producing them himself, would be incapable of sustaining a conversation on everyday situations likely to be encountered by visitors to Britain.
Not quite adequate	4	Although he may be capable of communicating and eliciting straightforward information, does so in a fashion which would require some patience on the part of the listener. Frequently misunderstands straightforward questions and remarks.
Adequate Satisfactory	5 6	Capable of communicating and eliciting straightforward information on everyday topics in conversation with other speakers of English. Has a usable and reliable basic competence in spoken English.

Table 4.8 (continued)

Category	Mark	Description
Good	7	Though still noticeably foreign in pronunciation, stress, and
Very good	8	intonation, is clearly capable of conversing fluently, within the limits set by the examination tasks.
	9	Has an excellent near-native or native command of
Excellent	10	pronunciation and stress, a competent control of intonation patters, and is clearly capable of conversing fluently and flexibly within the limits set by the examination tasks.

descriptors at different proficiency levels, had been in existence in the United States since the 1950s (see Direct speaking test formats section). The state of assessment scales at Cambridge at the time is indicative of the strong faith which had traditionally been assigned to expert judgement, and the fact that this stasis was still in effect at this time. In the national British examination context, Tattersall (2007:52) notes that the marking of Chief Examiners for School and higher School Certificates was 'assumed to be correct' and was 'the absolute standard against which individual markers were measured' (see also Patrick 2008, Watts 2008b).

1984: The communicative influence on assessment criteria and rating scales

The more communicative approach to testing reflected in the CPE and FCE tasks in the 1980s was also seen in the assessment criteria and scales. The guidelines for Oral Examiners emphasised that both 'linguistic and communicative competence' were the focus of assessment (Instructions for Oral Examiners 1984:6) and Oral Examiners were asked to keep the following general criteria in mind:

> Examiners must put themselves not so much in the role of a teacher with sophisticated awareness of the nature of errors, first language interference, etc., but as someone in communication with the speaker in a general real-life situation, neutrally disposed in the sense of not expecting to exercise more than a normal amount of patience in understanding or being understood (as above).

The assessment criteria for CPE and FCE introduced in 1984 are displayed in Table 4.9.

The revised assessment criteria were based on the 1975 ones, with some notable changes. One of the main changes was the inclusion of Fluency as an independent assessment criterion. Fluency had been referred to as part of the CPE and LCE/FCE assessment criteria since 1945, but it had not been explicitly defined and bore a resemblance to the very general notion of fluency as equated with general language proficiency. In the 1984 scales, it was defined

Table 4.9 1984 assessment criteria for CPE/FCE Interview (Instructions to Oral Examiners 1984:7)

Interview task	Assessment criteria
Picture-based conversation	Fluency
	Grammatical Accuracy
Reading passage	Pronunciation – Prosodic features (stress, rhythm, etc.)
	Pronunciation – Articulation of individual sounds
Structured Activity	Communicative Ability
	Vocabulary

in terms of speed and rhythm, and also in terms of the rather vague notion of 'effective and natural standard of expression' (see Table 4.10). Even though the attempt to achieve transparency of definition was welcome, it seems that the performance descriptors still needed development and improvement in order to unpack more comprehensively the constructs for the score users.

Table 4.10 1984 CPE/FCE Fluency scale (Instructions to Oral Examiners 1984:8)

Fluency	
5	NEAR-NATIVE Speed and rhythm, choice of structures, general standard of expression
3	completely effective and natural.
2	UNACCEPTABLE Unsteady, artificial and unclear delivery.
0	Not capable of connected speech.

An important feature of the assessment criteria and scales in 1984 was that they were the same for CPE and FCE, but Oral Examiners were instructed to interpret the descriptors differently in the context of the examination. Their interpretation was closely embedded within the training they received and relevant examiner documentation, and was not explicitly described. Training and standardisation materials were, therefore, crucial, as they carried the burden of both exemplifying and defining the levels. According to the Instructions to Oral Examiners (1984:7), 'oral performance at First Certificate level should be assessed in terms of completeness of communication at the level of the tasks set' and in the light of the fact that FCE tests 'competence in everyday English for a variety of commercial uses (especially public contact) or as a basis for further study'. When deciding on adequacy of performance in CPE, the examiners are advised to bear in mind 'the traditional association of Proficiency with ability to function in a serious discussion or seminar, and with the kind of readiness and competence needed for direct method teaching' (*Changes of Syllabus 1984* 1982:58). While the concept of native speaker was used in the scales 'for convenience', Cambridge clearly realised that 'indistinguishability from a native speaker is too extreme a requirement for a mark 5 on any scale, but a high level of intelligibility and acceptability in terms of rhythm, articulation, fluency and linguistic resource should be looked for' (Instructions to Oral Examiners 1986:7).

Further modifications in 1986 led to more explicitly developed descriptors for all scales, differentiation between FCE and CPE in the performance descriptors used, as well as the replacement of 'communicative ability' with 'interactive communication' – a change which made an explicit reference to the interactional construct of the test. The 'interactive communication' scale included specific references to development of the interaction and the norms of turn-taking. The interactive communication descriptors were a clear improvement on the 1984 scales for 'communicative ability', which only vaguely referred to the 'ability to elicit and communicate information in a competent manner and to function socially in a foreign language' (Instructions for Oral Examiners 1984:10).

Table 4.11 presents an example of the CPE Fluency descriptors. When compared to their predecessors (given in Table 4.10), we can see a clear development in using performance descriptors which are more descriptive, detailed and therefore more open to reliable use by assessors.

Table 4.11 1986 FCE Fluency scale (Instructions to Oral Examiners 1990:4)

Scale 5 (Fluency) FCE
5 Comfortable and natural speed and rhythm in everyday contexts, though there may be some hesitation when speaking on more abstract topics.
4 In everyday context speaks with minimal hesitation. Hesitation when discussing abstract topics, but does not demand unreasonable patience on the listener.
3 Does not hesitate unreasonably in everyday contexts, though may experience some difficulty with more abstract topics.
2 Unacceptable hesitation, even in everyday contexts.
1 Speech very disconnected.
0 Not capable of connected speech.

The introduction of separate FCE and CPE rating scales resulted in a much clearer distinction between performances at these two levels. As an illustration, the FCE and CPE top bands for Fluency are given in Table 4.12.

Table 4.12 1986 FCE and CPE Fluency descriptors (Instructions to Oral Examiners 1990:4 & 6)

CPE Band 5	Virtually native-speaker speed and rhythm, and coherent presentation of thoughts, in all contexts.
FCE Band 5	Comfortable and natural speed and rhythm in everyday contexts, though there may be some hesitation when speaking on more abstract topics.

A further change introduced was the move to provide analytic marks (based on the six scales) for the entire Speaking examination, rather than for each test part. The available archive material suggests that these changes and the development of scale descriptors followed expert opinion and not statistical studies.

1990s: An empirical approach to scale development

In line with the developments in language testing research in the 1980s and 1990s which resulted in models of communicative competence, and following the calls for empirically derived assessment criteria and scales, more attention was directed at Cambridge to the validation (both *a priori* and *a posteriori*) of assessment scales. The Cambridge Assessment of Spoken English (CASE) examination provides a useful illustration (Milanovic, Saville, Pollitt and Cook 1996).

The guiding principles and methodology behind the CASE assessment scales design (1989–1991) paved the way for future scales revisions of Cambridge English examinations. The approach to the design of speaking assessment scales for CASE was multi-faceted. It was primarily a 'model-based approach' which took theoretical models of communicative competence (Bachman 1990, Canale and Swain 1980) as a point of departure. This was deemed an important first step because the model-based approach provided an explicit conceptual framework and thus the potential for test validation, particularly construct validation. As such, the model components, namely grammatical, discourse, pragmatic and strategic competence, were embedded in the speaking test construct and the assessment criteria (i.e. grammar, discourse competence, strategic competence). *A priori* validation was carried out through qualitative analyses of transcripts of spoken performances which were used to guide the phrasing of the descriptors for the different levels of each scale. Rater feedback also fed into the development and revision of scales. Hence, a theoretical and empirical approach were combined and were followed by a series of statistical analyses of the performance of the new scales (Lazaraton 2002). Until then, empirical validation of rating scales prior to their launch had not been the norm (Milanovic et al 1996:31). The CASE scales are an important development within Cambridge practice, as they marked a belief in empirically and theoretically-grounded practice, which was also being advocated at the time in the L2 assessment field (e.g. Fulcher 1996b, Upshur and Turner 1995) and which is still a topical issue, as seen in Fulcher, Davidson and Kemp's (2011) appeal for scales driven by candidate performance data.

The FCE, CAE and CPE scales inherited and carried on the CASE legacy of the importance of scale validation. The assessment criteria in the early CAE (prior to 1998), were largely similar to the CPE and FCE criteria introduced in 1986 and were used to rate performances on the whole test and not per part. Five analytic criteria were used: 'Fluency', 'Accuracy and Range', 'Pronunciation', 'Interactive Communication' and 'Task Achievement'. 'Fluency' was defined with reference to the naturalness of the speed and rhythm, lack of hesitations and pauses. Importantly, the awareness of different functions of pauses was incorporated in the guidelines in view of recent advances in language testing research: 'pauses to marshal thoughts rather than language should be regarded as natural features of spoken interaction and not penalised' (CAE Instructions to Oral Examiners 1993–1994:12). This was in line with Fulcher's (1987, 1996a) research into various aspects of fluency in native speakers' and learners' speech which revealed that certain features, such as hesitation, are not necessarily attributable to a poorer speaking ability and are frequent in fluent native-speaker speech.

'Accuracy and Range' encompassed the range (quantity) and correctness (quality) of both grammatical structures and vocabulary. Importantly, performance on these criteria became better defined in communicative terms, since getting the message across was deemed more important than total grammatical accuracy. The two Pronunciation scales used previously (covering both individual sounds and prosodic utterance-level features) were subsumed into a single assessment criterion. 'Interactive Communication' was included, with particular references to turn-taking and interaction.

A new criterion was added to the set of scales – Task Achievement (previously introduced in CASE). It captured the extent of a candidate's contributions, appropriacy or relevance of contributions, independence in carrying out the tasks (in terms of the frequency of prompting or redirection by the examiner or the other candidate), organisation (coherence and logical sequencing of utterances), flexibility or resourcefulness and 'the degree to which a candidate contributes to successful task management through the selection of appropriate language functions and vocabulary' (CAE Instructions to Oral Examiners 1993–4:12). Task achievement, therefore, covered sociolinguistic and discourse competence, as defined by Canale and Swain (1980) and Bachman (1990).

The assessment scales had 9 bands (0–8); bands above 0 were clustered and described with a joint descriptor. An example of the descriptors at bands 7 and 8 (the top bands) is given in Table 4.13.

Even though the FCE Speaking test was revised in 1996 to follow the CAE test more closely, FCE was the vehicle used to introduce further changes to the assessment criteria which would then be adopted by CAE in 1998 and CPE in 2002. The new FCE assessment scales comprised 10 bands, with detailed descriptors provided for three bands only. The assessment scales were: 'Grammar and Vocabulary', 'Discourse Management', 'Pronunciation', 'Interactive Communication' and 'Global Achievement'.

The speaking tests, assessment criteria and scales were increasingly reflecting the fact that language is a means of communication, and were

Table 4.13 Top bands of CAE analytic scales (CAE Instructions to Oral Examiners 1993–4: 13)

Fluency	Accuracy & Range	Pronunciation	Task achievement	Interactive communication
7–8	**7–8**	**7–8**	**7–8**	**7–8**
Coherent spoken interaction with speed appropriate to the task and few intrusive hesitations.	Evidence of a wide range of structures and vocabulary in all contexts. Errors minimal in number and gravity.	Little L1 accent/ L1 accent not obtrusive. Competent handling of most English pronunciation features.	Tasks are dealt with fully and effectively, with notable coherence and organisation of salient points. The language is fully appropriate to each task.	Contributes fully and effectively throughout the interaction, with sensitivity to the norms and requirements of turn-taking in each task.

therefore defining speaking performance from the perspective of one's ability to use language meaningfully and in a range of contexts. For example, the Grammar and Vocabulary scales covered the overall effectiveness in the use of structure and lexis, in terms of range, accuracy and appropriateness.

A further change was the replacement of 'Task Achievement' with Discourse Management' as a new analytic criterion. The focus of the new criterion was on coherence, cohesion and relevance *within* a candidate's own contributions. The scale which focused on coherence and relevance across turns was 'Interactive Communication'. It explicitly focused on the norms of turn-taking and interaction, and was the focus of an *a posteriori* validation exercise by Galaczi (2003, 2008). Her findings showed that those interactions in the FCE candidate/candidate discussion task which were most collaborative and followed the conversational norms of mutuality were scored highest. In contrast, the interaction types that violated the norms of mutuality were scored lower.

Another new feature of the scales was the creation of a holistic Global Achievement scale (used by the Interlocutor). This was naturally seen as a more reliable method of arriving at a holistic mark than the reliance on memory of the analytic scales. The four analytic criteria ('Grammar and Vocabulary', 'Discourse Management', 'Pronunciation', 'Interactive Communication') and the holistic Global Achievement remain in FCE until the present day.

Double marking was another important development at this time, which enhanced the reliability of the test. Making the 2:2 test format obligatory enhanced test reliability since it allowed double marking from different, but complementary perspectives. The FCE Assessors and Interlocutors were instructed to award *independent marks* and not to discuss the marks or change their assessment in the light of that made by the co-examiner (Instructions to Oral Examiners 1999).

The CPE assessment scales revision in 2002 drew largely on the FCE scales, as well as the Cambridge English Common Scale of Speaking Ability. Introduced in 1996 (ffrench 2001), the Common Scale was primarily a user-oriented scale (Alderson 1991), helping test users identify typical features of spoken language ability across different proficiency levels targeted by Cambridge tests. 'The description at each level of the Common Scale aimed to provide a brief general description of the nature of spoken language ability in real-world contexts' (Taylor 2011:25). Following in the footsteps of CASE, the CPE scales revision was guided by expert judgment and empirical findings, both quantitative and qualitative (see ffrench (2003) for detail). The phrasing of descriptors was adapted to the CPE level and improved in terms of clarity. Each criterion now had two or three main focuses and these focuses were consistently referred to across bands in the descriptors of each assessment criterion (e.g. range, flexibility and accuracy were the focuses for Grammatical resource).

To sum up, the speaking assessment criteria and scales that were designed and revised in 1990s were informed by theory and empirical research. Various aspects of communicative competence from the Canale and Swain (1980) and Bachman (1990) models were incorporated, resulting in a richer definition of the Interactive Communication criterion and the introduction of the Discourse Management criterion. Significantly, double marking was improved by introducing different sets of scales for the two examiners – a holistic one for the interviewing examiner and a set of analytic scales for the observing examiner – which resulted in the bringing together of different, but complementary perspectives in the awarding of the speaking mark. Scales' descriptors attempted to differentiate in a systematic and comprehensive manner between proficiency levels, indicating what kind of language is expected at each level, in terms of range, complexity, sophistication and frequency and gravity of inaccuracies or inappropriacies. The amount of prompting and other Interlocutor support was also taken into account in the light of the then recent research on interviewer accommodation (see the Variability debate section). The wave of revisions in 2002 further harmonised the scales' descriptors across bands and levels.

In this last historical period of our account – the first decade of the 21st century – a further, significant, revision of the scales took place in 2008. The primary reason for the revision was an attempt to align the scales closely with an external criterion – the Common European Framework of Reference for languages (2001). The scales were revised following guidelines from the CEFR regarding the development of scales and performance descriptors, and underwent a programme of *a priori* validation. One of the main driving principles for the wording of the descriptors was to make them brief, transparent and descriptive, so that they could be interpreted independently and not in the context of supporting documentation. The descriptors were positively worded in terms of what a candidate *can do* at a given level. The positive wording of the descriptors also meant that 'levels of proficiency were to serve as objectives rather than just an instrument for screening candidates' (Galaczi and ffrench 2007:28). The revision of the scales was informed by a mixed-methods approach and qualitative and quantitative methodologies were used alongside expert judgement (see Galaczi et al (2011) for more detail of the scales validation process employed).

The investigation of speaking test reliability within Cambridge ESOL has also gained much in importance in the last decade. Statistical post-exam monitoring of Oral Examiners' performance now complements expert-judgement monitoring. Statistical monitoring involves routinely investigating the level of agreement between the Interlocutor and Assessor at the examination centre level and over/under-marking tendencies at the individual examiner level. These statistical monitoring procedures are carried out on a regular basis and the findings provide insights for re-training or further standardisation of examiners.

Setting marking standards and standardising Oral Examiners

1945–1984: The expert-judgement influence

As discussed earlier, the expert judgement of experienced examiners bore much weight in speaking assessment during this period. This had considerable implications for the operationalisation of the oral test construct, since raters could differently interpret assessment criteria (if any) and pay attention to and rate different aspects of oral performance. The issue of standardising Oral Examiners was brought up within UCLES in the context of EFL examinations in 1941. The lack of a 'scientific apparatus to ensure standardisation' was discussed, but, on a positive note, it was commented that 'examiners with a common background and knowing what they were looking for often reached a surprising measure of agreement' (Joint Committee Oct 1941:2). However, the same minutes caution that some examiners were unknown to the Syndicate at that time. Even in those times, this was considered an unsatisfactory state of affairs, which is why the Joint Committee expressed the need for research into the technique of oral examinations. Besides examiner standardisation, another related problem was that of standards and the realisation that all examiners cannot mark to the same and/or correct standard, regardless of their experience, if the rating standards are not defined (and the examiners not standardised in their rating). Roach (1945a) attempted to address both issues through his investigation of the problems faced by Oral Examiners. Admittedly, Roach's research focused on tests of reading aloud rather than conversation, but the issues he addressed and the solutions proposed were relevant for both.

One of Roach's aims was to define standards 'by some more positive means rather than sketchy and abstract instructions' (Roach 1945a:4). This vagueness of the standards could explain why the examiners in Roach's experiment did not realise they were listening to CPE candidates (24 Polish 'officers and men') taking LCE reading aloud, thinking mistakenly they were examining LCE candidates. This gave them 'a wrong sense of standards: when they thought they were working to Lower Certificate standards they were probably nearer to Proficiency standards' (Roach 1945a:8), which indicated that examiners were norm-referencing rather than examining to an external criterion. Roach specifically suggested that the first candidates set the standard. Owing to the stable candidature, however, the standard was more or less constant, as seen in Roach's (1945a:8) contention that 'the statistics indicate that reasonable continuity has been achieved overseas, perhaps because the candidates in the mass have been of fairly consistent quality from year to year'. However, Roach cautioned that 'there is no guarantee that standards acquired by Examiner X through experience in South America will correspond with those learnt by Examiner Y in the Middle East' (1945a:8).

Realising that individual judgment cannot serve as an absolute measure, Roach emphasised the importance of examiner standardisation. For the purposes of training and standardisation, he suggested using gramophone recordings of candidates whose proficiency level had been agreed on by examiners. He made several during the experiment:

> Two hundred candidates at various levels were presented in September by the R.A.F. Polish Initial Training Wing . . . Advantage was taken of this to conduct certain experiments in the standardization of marking. Four examiners were sent, including a British Council phonetician from Cairo, and the R.A.F. Education Officers also took part. The Engineer-in-Chief of the General Post Office very kindly lent a Mobile Recording Unit and the services of his engineers without charge, and several gramophone records were made (UCLES 1944, minute 8.5),

and concluded that:

> gramophone recordings of candidates at various levels should assist examiners, not only to reach agreement on standards among themselves, but also to assimilate standards officially approved by the central examining body (Roach 1945a:39).

The concept of using recorded performances to standardise examiners was innovative at the time. As Roach (1984:3) retrospectively writes:

> The Engineer-in-Chief of the General Post Office and I pioneered the first recording of conversations and examination tests ever made. I have a whole chapter on Gramophone recordings, as a guide to examiners.

This was before the era of the tape recorder, but I saw the whole field of possibilities, of course when the War should be over.

It is worth noting that the idea of using phonographic recordings for the purpose of examiner training was independently put forward by Kaulfers (1944) in the United States at about the same time. Neither Roach nor Kaulfers refer to each other in their papers, indicating that they developed their ideas independently.

Another solution to increasing scoring validity was seen in joint examining by two examiners. Roach (1945a) proposed two options. An examiner would talk to a candidate and mark his performance, while a 'silent examiner' would just listen and provide an additional mark. Alternatively, only the silent examiner would mark. Interestingly, Kaulfers (1944:143) also points out the desirability of 'having one examiner administer the test, and a concealed scorer rate the responses', if the test is not administered by machine. Even though joint examining was a progressive idea, practical constraints in post-war times meant that the supply of examiners was a problem for many overseas centres, which is why Roach realised that he could only urge that a second opinion be sought for the reading aloud test (Roach 1945a:26). He concludes that 'joint examining would be of greatest value where the examiners, by experimental marking of candidates or of gramophone records, or by collaboration on earlier occasions, had "come together" in the matter of standard' (Roach 1945a:41).

The impact at Cambridge of Roach's (1945a) report was multifold. Firstly, internal standards were introduced for each part of the Oral (reading aloud, unseen reading and conversation), as displayed in Table 4.14.

Table 4.14 1945 Internal standards (UCLES 1958:1)

	Reading	Unseen reading	Conversation	Total
Maximum mark	20 (100%)	10 (100%)	20 (100%)	50 (100%)
Very Good	16 (80%)	8 (80%)	16 (80%)	40 (80%)
Good	12 (60%)	6 (60%)	12 (60%)	30 (60%)
Pass	8 (40%)	4 (40%)	8 (40%)	20 (40%)

The conduct of the Oral examination also changed to maintain continuity of standard during marking. Now the examiner took all the candidates in turn for reading aloud, rather than 'interlarding it with the conversation' (Roach 1945a:30). This change in the test was triggered by Roach's experiment which showed that the standard can be better maintained by 'hearing all the candidates in succession handling identical material under identical conditions' (Roach 1945a:12).

Lastly, standardisation of Oral Examiners was put into practice.

Gramophone recordings of CPE and LCE reading and conversation tests made in 1944 were accompanied by comments made by a small committee of examiners in the United Kingdom (Joint Committee June 1944). The first overseas standardisation of Oral Examiners took place in Egypt a year later and another standardisation test was arranged to take place at the Royal Air Force Station in December 1945 (Joint Committee November 1945). Documents from the 1950s reveal that examiner standardisation was overseen by Wyatt after Roach left the Syndicate, and taken seriously, both by the Syndicate and the Oral Examiners. For example, Parisian examiners reported they:

> would welcome specimen recordings of oral tests in order to check their standards from time to time. Ample recording and play-back equipment (wire), installed by Professor Desseignet is available at the British Institute in Paris. The other centres have no equipment at present, but could arrange to borrow or hire some if necessary (Wyatt 1956:2).

If there was more than one Oral Examiner in a centre, examiners were advised to co-ordinate their standards of marking by testing jointly a number of candidates before they begin to examine separately. It was deemed sufficient to test around four candidates in this way (Instructions to Oral Examiners 1953:1). Over time, other methods of examiner standardisation were discussed so that the best way of standardising was deemed to be live examining of dummy candidates with an experienced examiner, 'the advantage of this being that if the chief examiner felt any doubts about the examiner he would then write to the Syndicate and so offset any variation in marking standards' (Joint Committee minutes July 1958:8). Reel-to-reel tapes were considered to be the second-best way of standardising. There is evidence that an examiner monitoring system was in place in the 1950s. Monitoring included both compliance with test procedures and the quality of rating: representatives of the Syndicate would visit overseas centres and evaluate the technique of Oral Examiners, the types of questions asked, the level of agreement on the overall grading of candidates by the examiner and the monitoring examiner (Appendix B Oral Test in Wyatt and Hudson 1952). The possibility of tape recordings of candidate performances was also considered: 'the Chief Examiner would find these recordings most valuable in maintaining a fair standard of marking' (Extracts from the Reports of Chief Examiners 1954). This was an important development which sought to address standardisation and uniformity in test delivery and ratings.

In the 1970s, Oral Examiner training for inexperienced examiners involved joining an experienced examiner during live testing in order to become familiarised with test format and how the examination was conducted. Oral Examiners were standardised once a year by listening to reel-to-reel standardisation tapes, awarding marks to sample performances and getting the marks reviewed. Each examiner would get official marks and comments (interview with Janet Bojan, Cambridge ESOL Performance Testing Unit 2010). In 1975, after CPE and LCE were revised, standardisation procedures were improved. A set of illustrative recordings, accompanied with 'a detailed descriptive manual covering aspects of procedure and marking' was issued by the Syndicate (Instructions to Oral Examiners 1975:3). This was supplemented by further standardisation of examiners if there was more than one Oral Examiner for the same examination in a centre. The suggestion was to co-ordinate standards further by (i) joint testing of a number of test candidates or with sample recordings, (ii) a short practice session at the beginning of the actual examining, (iii) joint testing of a few candidates by the examiner-in-charge and individual examiners.

1984: A new examiner training, standardisation and monitoring system

In 1984, standardisation materials in colour on video cassettes replaced audio recordings (Instructions to Oral Examiners 1986:3). 1987 saw the introduction of a new system for examiner co-ordination and monitoring, with the appointment of a number of Team Leaders/Coordinator examiners. Their role was to arrange shared examining, conduct separate briefing meetings, and participate in the preparation of examining material in the United Kingdom and overseas. An extended series of briefing meetings for examiners was organised and included discussion of video-recorded and live interviews, as well as general procedure. Checks on the standards applied in individual countries were carried out by visiting co-ordinators and via recordings, as part of the new system (Executive Committee minutes May 1987:5). A year later, we are informed that:

> an intensive programme of examiner training is continuing, with pre-examination meetings and systematic on-assignment co-ordination, as part of the arrangements made from Cambridge in the case of UK centres, and with an increased emphasis on co-ordination also at overseas centres (Executive Committee May 1988:4).

However, quality control over training, co-ordination and monitoring did not seem to be systematic, which was most keenly felt to be the case in overseas centres in early 1990s. In a similar vein, Taylor (1992) noted the lack of systematic co-ordination of PET Oral Examiners up to 1992 as an issue.

It is worth noting that the advance of technology (e.g. using recordings in examiner training) eased logistical pressures and marked an important shift in examiner training and standardisation at the time, as these technological developments made it easier to provide exemplary samples for examiners. The related developments and widespread use of computers in the

21st century was to mark a similar shift as online examiner training became possible, thus provided greater flexibility and opportunity for individualised examiner feedback (Hamilton, Reddel and Spratt 2001).

1990s: Present-day examiner training, standardisation and monitoring practice

A comprehensive Team Leader System and a set of procedures – Recruitment, Induction, Co-ordination, Monitoring, Evaluation (RICME) – were developed under the then CEO Peter Hargreaves in the 1990s. The objective was 'to coordinate the training and work of EFL oral examiners' (Annual Report 1994) and ensure a consistent application of the Speaking test procedures and accurate and consistent rating of spoken performances 'in terms of pre-defined descriptions of performance' (UCLES 2003:6). The introduction of a two-pronged approach based on a network of professionals and a set of procedures was a significant and necessary step in view of the 3500 examiners in 88 countries in the early 1990s (UCLES 1992:3). The number of examiners grew to 7,000 by 1999 (Saville and Hargreaves 1999:49) and then to approximately 16,000 by 2011 (Taylor and Galaczi 2011:215).

Cambridge gradually set up a pyramid system of examiner quality assurance across the world, which consisted of Senior Team Leaders at the top, followed by Team Leaders and Oral Examiners. The Team Leader System in the new form was introduced in 1993 and gradually rolled out around the world, starting with key Cambridge markets such as Spain, Italy, Greece, Turkey, Switzerland and Cyprus (UCLES 1992:3). Each level of the hierarchy involved a distinct set of professional requirements and responsibilities. The Senior Team Leader role included reviewing and monitoring the examiner arrangements in-country/region, providing an annual report (summary statistics, feedback from Oral Examiners), implementing RICME set of procedures for the Team Leaders and ensuring that they are implemented by team leaders for examiners. Team leaders were required to run or collaborate on training sessions for new examiners, co-ordination meetings, rate and approve the co-ordinated examiners and also undertake normal examining assignments (UCLES 1992:2). Examiners needed to satisfy minimal professional requirements related to age, experience teaching EFL (at least 5 years), academic background (a recognised higher education qualification) and needed to provide references providing information on their punctuality, clarity of diction, professional demeanour and willingness to conform to procedure (UCLES 1992:1). The appointment of non-native speaker examiners was also considered, under conditions they could provide additional qualifications such as recognised English language teaching diplomas and evidence of speaking skills equivalent to a CPE grade A.

By 1998, due to the large number of centres and team leaders in certain countries, the role of Regional Team Leader was introduced. As the system evolved further with the increasing number of UCLES centres and examiners, Oral Examiner Trainer/Co-ordinator roles were also added (see Figure 4.4).

Figure 4.4 The Team Leader System (UCLES 2003:6)

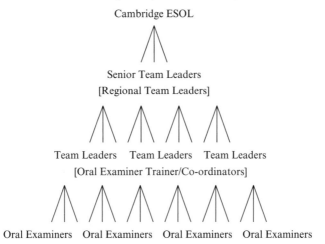

In the next decade the set of procedures evolved into RITCME, adding 'Training' (T) to the set of procedures. This stage involved the familiarisation of examiners with the general issues of test format and assessment procedures, assessment scales and examination materials, which was an essential aspect of examiner knowledge. Recruitment, Training and Induction were typically one-off stages, while Co-ordination, Monitoring and Evaluation are recurrent and cyclical (UCLES 2003; see Figure 4.5).

Figure 4.5 RITCME (UCLES 2003:7)

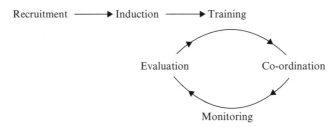

The RITCME system has changed only slightly in the practices currently in use. For a detailed description, the reader is referred to Taylor and Galaczi (2011).

Endnote

We have now completed our survey of the evolution of the speaking construct in a general global context and in the specific context of Cambridge English exams. We have focused on the appearance and use of the different speaking test formats and on the underlying pedagogic, theoretical and practical factors which have played a role in defining the construct(s) underlying them. We have also spent some time on the cognitive, context and scoring parameters underlying Cambridge English speaking tasks in that period. Our overview traced the increased importance of the speaking construct both internationally and at Cambridge and the development of tasks and assessment scales which have acquired more communicative cognitive and context characteristics and more rigorous scoring parameters. The present day assessment of speaking with its range of solo, paired and group direct tests and computer-delivered and scored tests offers an exciting array of possibilities for test developers and test users. Each test format offers its unique advantages and associated caveats. Perhaps the complementary use of direct and semi-direct speaking tests is what we will see in the decades to come.

We now turn to Chapter 5 to investigate the developments in the Listening construct measured by Cambridge English examinations.

5 The measurement of listening ability 1913–2012

Cyril J Weir
University of Bedfordshire
Ivana Vidaković
University of Cambridge ESOL Examinations

Nature gave us one tongue and two ears so we could hear twice as much as we speak.

Epictetus

Who speaks, sows; who listens, reaps.

Argentine Proverb

Listening: The neglected language skill

Introduction

Unlike speaking, listening never had its own powerful advocates, men like Henry Sweet or Harold Palmer in the United Kingdom, who assiduously promulgated the primacy of speaking in language teaching/learning in the early 20th century. In fact, until the late 20th century listening was the skill least practised in the language classroom, the least researched in the literature, and the least understood in the language testing field, and, according to a number of authorities, it remains uniquely undervalued to this day (Brown 1987, Field 2008:1, Mendelsohn 1994, Osada 2002).

Until the mid-1980s, L2 listening was considered to be a passive, internal skill which was regarded as largely inaccessible by teachers and testers alike. Compared to speaking or writing, teachers found it quite demanding to handle the skill in the classroom and perhaps more tellingly to achieve demonstrable results with their students. Practical difficulties and the complexities associated with investigating the aural modality often discouraged language testers from including it in their test batteries let alone researching it. For Buck (2001: 32):

> Testing listening is technically more complicated, more time consuming and far less convenient than testing reading.

L2 listening research was sporadic until the early 1990s and lacked a clear sense of direction. Many of the L2 studies were singularly concerned with the effects of external/top down information upon processing (e.g. Long 1989, 1990, Schmidt-Rinehart 1994). Perceptual processing was almost entirely neglected despite the fact that it clearly forms the foundation upon which meaning has to be constructed. This contrasts markedly with L1 listening where there had been a considerable amount of research into perceptual processing since the mid-1960s, for example in the early work by Liberman and associates in the Haskins laboratories at Yale (Liberman, Cooper, Shankweiler and Studdert-Kennedy 1967).

In Chapter 2 we described the accelerated growth of literacy resulting from widening education and the increased availability of printed material in the 19th century. The landmark events in recording sound had no such effect on teaching and assessing listening in the same century. On 4 December 1877 Thomas Edison was credited as being the first person to record and play back the human voice employing a verse from *Mary had a little lamb*. Ten years later he founded the Edison Phonograph Corporation to market his invention. The basis for a ground-breaking technology which could convey natural speech to a receptive audience was laid, but there was to be no groundswell in listening activity to compare with the developments we noted for reading in Britain in the 19th century.

The relatively late onset of available technology for recording and playing sound might in itself be thought of as a contributory factor to listening's neglected status in the early days but Jones (2008:400) notes the absence of any interest in using emerging technology for the teaching of listening in the period leading up to World War Two:

> . . . precursors of today's technology emerged in the form of wax cylinders and 78 records onto which one could permanently record words and song. Despite the birth of this innovative technology, its use for language learning was out of curiosity at best, limited to the preservation of indigenous languages.

As we noted in Chapter 1, UCLES, through the support of engineers from the Post Office, was able to record the oral part of CPE on wax discs for marker reliability purposes during World War Two (see Roach 1945a included as Appendix C), but there is nothing in the Cambridge Assessment Archives to suggest that the technology was ever considered for use in delivering the dictation test which continued to be read aloud by individual examiners until the 1970s with obvious implications for aspects of scoring validity.

Joyce (2008:4) identified a more serious problem that had kept listening as the poor relation of the language teaching and testing world. He argued that: 'the neglect stemmed from listening having been misconceived as a passive skill mirroring reading . . . That is, it was assumed that the processes involved in both modalities were largely identical.'

Weir (2005a) expressed a similar concern that much of the thinking on the testing of listening comprehension was based on research in reading comprehension because of the assumption amongst some researchers that the comprehension processes required in listening shared many of the same routes (Dunkel 1991a, Brindley and Nunan 1992). Freedle and Kostin (1994, 1999) claimed that reading and listening both required the exercise of a general faculty of language comprehension. This was in line with the views of a number of psycholinguists, who saw parsing as a shared route, independent of modality, once perceptual operations were complete (Gernsbacher 1990).

Frequently reported high correlations between the scores of students in the two modes were often interpreted as construct overlap by language testers (Buck 1992b, Bae and Bachman 1998). However, in considering the high correlations between listening and reading tests, there are of course two possible interpretations: a) that the two skills share a common higher level processing route to achieve comprehension; b) that the extensive use of written items in listening test formats means that much of the score in most traditional listening tests must inevitably load onto reading.

It is now clear that important differences do occur between the two modes for example at the levels of parsing and meaning building, since listeners, unlike readers, have to carry forward information in their minds (including information about intonation and stress patterns) without the opportunity of looking back at a text to check. This imposes a greater cognitive load on processing. Buck (1990) and Rost (2002) argue that, if we are to measure listening ability rather than general comprehension ability, we must ensure we include 'aspects of proficiency and comprehension that are unique to listening' in test input. We return to discussion of critical differences between reading and listening in the section on a socio cognitive approach to listening test task analysis below (see also Buck (2001) for a discussion of these).

During the course of the 20th century the *formats* devised for testing listening were to have serious consequences for the construct being measured. Of all the skills, testing listening was to prove the most problematic. Listening would be tested indirectly through integrated tasks such as dictation (anathema to psychometric structuralists like Lado (1961) who favoured discrete point tests and to those who wanted to measure more than transcription ability); or through phoneme discrimination (unsatisfactory to those who wanted to test meaning construction rather than decoding); through objectively scored comprehension questions like multiple choice (for Field (2008) a rather crude and debatable method of choice for evaluating success in listening in the language classroom given the deleterious effects the written format had on processing), and finally through constructed response items (where the additional need for both reading and writing was likely to further 'muddy the measurement' of the listening construct and the format itself constrained the levels of processing that could be tested).

With this 'impoverished' background in mind, we first consider general trends in the testing of listening in the 20th century. Then in the second half of the chapter we focus in detail on the listening tasks employed in Cambridge English language examinations in this period and analyse the construct being measured at various stages through reference to a socio-cognitive conceptual framework for testing listening (see Geranpayeh and Taylor (Eds) (2013) for a detailed application of the framework to the present day Cambridge English Listening tests).

Listening tests in the 20th century

Despite the low profile accorded to the skill, the assessment of listening features in English language tests from the start of the 20th century, in both the United Kingdom and the United States. We consider the views of testing specialists at different points in the past and examine the way those views changed over time. We describe the main tasks employed for testing listening in the 20th century namely dictation, objective tests (e.g. multiple-choice questions, multiple matching) and finally, in the communicative era we see the addition of a range of constructed response items (e.g. gap filling and note-taking) intended to safeguard against format effect and to enhance meaning construction on the part of the candidate.

Dictation: Listening as language transcription

In Chapter 1 we referred to Kelly's (1969) account of how dictation was used in the classrooms of the early Middle Ages to transmit information to students in their own language given the inaccessibility of printed books at the time. The emphasis was on the content of the text and the students' ability to understand and interpret what they had written down. By the end of the Middle Ages, following its employment in foreign language teaching, the use of dictation altered somewhat and the intention behind it shifted to helping students write and interpret the foreign language. Since then, according to Kelly, it has been 'one of the few exercises consistently employed throughout the history of language teaching'. Under the Grammar Translation approach it was employed for teaching the structure (morphology and syntax) of the target language and in the direct method for practising recognition of sound-symbol correspondence in spellings. Morley (1991) describes its use in the Situational Approach for grammar and pronunciation drills and to help learners imitate dialogues. Modelling in the form of repetition of dialogues was very much used in the audio-lingual approach in the United Kingdom in the late 1960s – under the influence of behaviorism and the ubiquitous language laboratories.

Stansfield (1985) describes the first American attempts at introducing an aural/oral test involving dictation in French, German and Spanish by the Modern Language Association of the Middle States and Maryland in 1913–14 (see also Spolsky 1995a:35–6). He explains (1985:122) how dictation appeared in standardised modern language tests at the start of the 20th century along with the view that oral work had a place in the Modern Language classroom. He provides further detail on the Modern Language Association test:

> The Modern Language Association of the Middle States and Maryland made an effort to accredit oral work done in schools by developing a standardized oral test of Spanish, French, and German which would be administered in addition to the regular written examination on translation and grammar The test, completed in 1915, required examinees to do three things: 1) complete a ten minute dictation, 2) present a written summary in English of an oral passage read by the examiner in the foreign language, and 3) provide written answers to general classroom questions read by the examiner .

These early attempts to introduce dictation in the United States were to fail in the face of practical considerations and the prevailing desire for 'uniformity through objectivity' that we detailed in Chapter 1. Critics regarded the dictation as psychometrically suspect.

Spolsky (1995a:56–7) draws our attention to a later addition of an aural component to the College Entrance Examination Board in 1930 in the form of a 'direct dictation and reproduction from memory of a dictated passage'. However, declining numbers in the 1930s led to the closure of this, the first institutional United States English as a Foreign Language test for assessing the language proficiency of foreigners.

Dictation had a rather unfortunate pedigree in Australia in this early period for political rather than psychometric/assessment reasons (McNamara 2009). The Immigration Restriction Act of 1901 was intended to control immigration into Australia. As part of the entry process it introduced a dictation test. Applicants had to transcribe a passage of fifty words that might be dictated in any European language, not necessarily English, selected at the whim of the person administering the test. Failure to pass the test was used by immigration officials to stop immigrants from entering Australia on the basis of language skills.

The dictation test was in fact a method which enabled immigration officials to exclude individuals on the basis of race without explicitly saying so. Robertson, Hohmann and Stewart (2005:242) record how:

> The dictation test, a key element of the Immigration Restriction Act 1901, has always been associated with the question of race. It was administered to 'coloureds' and 'Asians' in order to have an apparently neutral reason to deport them. The last person to pass the test did so in 1909.

It became 'foolproof', as it was designed to be: the applicant would be given the test in a language that their background firmly indicated they would not know and, upon failing, they would be told that the authorities could go on giving them tests in languages that they did not know, indefinitely . . . Passages used in the Test were selected by the Secretary of the Department of External Affairs, distributed to the State Collectors of Customs, and changed every fortnight to prevent evasion by means of rote knowledge . . . The language is very simple . . . But simple language might contain pronunciation and spelling traps for the less than fluent. . .

Testing listening first appeared in the United Kingdom in the form of an integrated dictation task (see Chapter 1 and Kelly (1969) for details). Its use is recorded in the 19th century in the United Kingdom to evaluate pupils' success in learning, with the results determining teachers' pay (see Chapter 3 for details). As we saw in Chapter 1, dictation was to be an important part of the Oral paper in the first CPE in 1913. There were other test tasks related to listening in the early CPE examinations. Under the influence of the Reform Movement, listening was tested indirectly in the written Phonetics paper of CPE in 1913 where the candidate was expected to demonstrate a detailed knowledge of how words are produced in English and how they sound. An interactional listening ability (involving speaking and listening) was also part of the conversation component of the first CPE Oral test (see Chapter 4 for details). A dedicated paper on listening comprehension was not to appear in Cambridge examinations until 1970 in FCE and 1975 in CPE initially employing listening texts composed of prose passages read out aloud by the examiner. The use of dictation was the closest most United Kingdom examination boards came to testing listening until the communicative revolution of the 1970s albeit as part of an integrated task involving other constructs such as writing and reading.

Stansfield (1985:123–124) traces the use of dictation in the United States from 1915 right through to the 1960s when:

the use of dictation began to decline sharply because of the development and widespread adoption of the audio-lingual method, the historical and theoretical under pinning of which began with the very favourable results obtained by the Army Specialised Training Program (ASTP) in the preparation of interpreters and translators during World War II . . . [This success] caused the inevitable cyclical reaction against all that had been done before. Dictation became a victim of this reaction as leading authors and proponents of the "new-key" audio-lingual method of foreign language teaching either directly attacked it or tacitly rejected it by failing to make any mention of it whatsoever.

In the 1960s testing authorities in the United States such as Lado (1961), and Harris (1969) regarded dictation as an inadequate language testing method and inferior to more objective measures of second or foreign language ability.

> Dictation . . . on critical inspection, appears to measure very little of language. Since the word order is given . . . it does not test word order. Since the words are given . . . it does not test vocabulary. It hardly tests the aural perception of the examiner's pronunciation, because the words can in many cases be identified by context. The student is less likely to hear the sounds incorrectly in the slow reading of the words which is necessary for dictation (Lado 1961:34).

As a testing device, dictation came to be regarded as generally both uneconomical and imprecise (Harris 1969:5).

Dictation's critics saw it chiefly as a test of the ability to identify appropriate phoneme-grapheme correspondences or to employ the accurate spelling of the words. Some, like Lado (1961), inaccurately claimed that it did not test word order or vocabulary because these were provided (ignoring the necessity of segmenting words from a continuous stream of speech) and others felt it did not test low-level listening skills because context and co-text would assist students to infer the words that were present. This perhaps misses the point that if they were unable to recognise the words that were dictated, then they would have no co-text from which to make these guesses (Field 2008:136).

Dictation also fell foul of the pyschometricians in not being a discrete-point test assessing single points of phonology, the lexicon, or syntax, or involving only a single communicative skill at a time (see Brooks 1960, Lado 1961, and Rivers 1968 for extensive criticism of dictation on these points and discussion below). Stansfield concludes (1985:125) 'attitudes toward dictation remained negative throughout the 1960s due to the pervasive influence of the audio-lingual method in language teaching circles'.

Later, Weir (1990, 1993) argued that dictation was restricted in terms of the number of variables associated with spoken input that the tester was able to take into account (see below for a full listing of the distinctive speech based parameters of listening). He felt that there were restrictions on the speaker variables that could be addressed (e.g. speed, pausing, and built-in redundancy). There were also severe limitations on the organisational, propositional and illocutionary features of the text(s) that could be taken account of as even native speakers were restricted in the length of utterances they could handle in this format. In short, the conditions under which this task was conducted did not adequately reflect the normal conditions for natural spoken language reception.

Buck (2001:78) also queried its construct validity as a test of listening *per se*:

> Clearly given the lack of context and no obvious communicative situation, dictation does not seem to require the ability to understand inferred

meanings or to relate the literal meaning to a wider communicative context. Dictation operationalises listening in the narrower of the two level view of listening [decoding level and meaning level]. Dictation also clearly tests more besides listening: it requires good short term memory as well as writing ability, and it seems fair to say that it is far more than a test of listening skills.

On the positive side Buck (2001:74) argued:

> ... advocates of integrative testing argued that it was a good test of expectancy grammar ... Angela Oakeshott-Taylor (1977) examined the errors test takers made when taking dictation tests and found that they related to interpretation of the acoustic signal, phonemic identification, lexical recognition, morphology, syntactic analysis and semantic interpretation. On the basis of this she argued that dictation tests assess performance at all stages of the 'speech perception' process.

A problem remained as to how performance on an indirect test of this type, which appears to measure only a limited part of listening ability, can be translated into a direct statement of proficiency in that skill. The tester cannot easily decide on what would constitute a satisfactory performance. Quantitative indicators of language ability do not easily translate into qualitative descriptors (equally true of course for current approaches based on comprehension questions).

Dictation did, however, stage a comeback in the United States in the 1980s. Its resuscitation was due in no small part to the pioneering empirical work on *integrative* measures including dictation by John Oller (1979) who showed its potential value both as a measure of listening comprehension and overall language proficiency (see Chapter 1 for details and Buck (2001:67–69)). According to Oller's *pragmatic expectancy grammar* (Oller 1979) there are regular and rule-governed relationships between the various elements of the language, and language competence involves understanding how these elements relate to each other. He argued that this knowledge enabled learners to make predictions, or inferences as they were processing the language (see Chapter 1 for further discussion of the integrative approach to testing). Dictation along with written cloze were regarded by Oller as efficient means of tapping into this.

The results of research that showed that integrative tests such as dictation correlated closely with overall language ability (perhaps not surprising as it involved listening, writing and reading) came too late to save its continued use in Cambridge examinations. In the United Kingdom, it was to be swept away by the early manifestations of the communicative approach because it was regarded as a highly artificial form of testing, which confounded listening with accurate writing. As we shall see below, dictation was removed from the FCE Oral test (see Chapter 4) in 1970 and CPE in 1975 and in its stead a dedicated listening comprehension multiple-choice question test appeared as a separate paper in its own right. The introduction of listening tests took place as the communicative approach in teaching in the United Kingdom began to impact on testing practice accompanied by a greater availability of recording technology.

Objective methods for testing listening at the decoding level

Buck (2001:62) describes how:

> During the period when the audio-lingual method was the preferred way of teaching language, structuralism was the dominant linguistic paradigm, and behaviourism the dominant psychological paradigm, discrete point testing was the most common approach to language testing.

In many of the listening tests in the heyday of the audio-lingual method, overall proficiency was seen to equate with recognition of the sounds of the language or other small elements of an utterance such as the meaning of an idiom or expression (Lado 1961). Emphasis was placed on the candidate's ability to discriminate phonemes, to recognise stress and intonation patterns and to record what had been heard through a written (usually multiple-choice questions with 3/4 options or true/false) product. In other words, the recognition of elements of the language in their alternative oral form was used as a test of listening ability.

Advocates of a discrete point approach to testing language sought to identify and isolate the separate elements of the language in their oral form and attempted to test them independently as far as this was possible, though in many cases the candidate had to understand more than just the point being tested (see Examples 3.3 and 3.4 from Buck (2001) below). In the pre-communicative era, the multiple-choice question format, a form of selected-response, discrete point test, was employed with a major focus on the *perceptual* level. In these early listening tests, acoustic-phonetic input was matched by a candidate to his or her knowledge of the phonological system (*input decoding*) and vocabulary repertoire (*lexical search*). Additionally some items focused on the linguistic level which required matching groups of words that had been assembled into syntactic structures (*syntactic parsing*). These lower-level processes take place when a message is being decoded from acoustic cues into language and the output is a context free proposition.

Buck (2001:64–65) provides some helpful illustrative examples of these early discrete point tests:

phoneme discrimination
example 3.1 minimal pairs
Test-takers hear:
I hear they have developed a better vine near here.
They read:
I hear they have developed a better **vine/wine** near here.
. . . .

paraphrase recognition
Example 3.3
Test-takers hear
John ran into a classmate on his way to the library
They read:
a) John exercised with his classmate
b) John ran to the library
c) John injured his classmate with his car
d) John unexpectedly met a classmate

response evaluation
Example 3.4
Test-takers hear:
Male 1: *are sales higher this year*
Male 2: a) *they're about the same as before*
         b) *no, they hired someone last year*
         c) *they're on sale last month*

These discrete point tests did not measure meaning construction, e.g. the ability to integrate information or inference, but focused on the discrete perceptual and linguistic components such as segmental phonemes or small parts of an utterance. In these tests minor components of listening ability were treated as predictors of overall proficiency. This was true not only of audiolingualism in the United States but also of structuralist approaches elsewhere in the world (see Buck (2001) for an informed account of these discrete point tests in Listening and Chapter 1).

Spolsky (1995a:77–78) records the early appearance of a number of these selective response listening tests in the United States in the 1920s and 1930s employing the new-type objective items. These included the *Bryn Mawr Test of Ability to Understand Spoken French* which was first developed in 1926. Questions were read out in French and the candidate marked one of five choices of words in English as the answer thus avoiding involving French reading ability. Spolsky (op. cit. 78–9) also gives details of a study done on the phonetic accuracy section of the *Lundeberg-Tharp Audition Test in French* in 1930 which correlated quite highly with tests using more extensive speech samples. The sum of a candidate's appropriate responses in such 'discrete' sub-tests was often equated with proficiency in listening comprehension.

The exigencies of war hastened the retreat from a focus on reading in modern language teaching in the United States that had prevailed in the 1930s (Spolsky (1995a:100–103) and Chapter 1). The demand for military personnel who could understand and speak foreign languages increased exponentially and this led to far greater interest in the spoken variety of the target languages and in the testing of listening. Spolsky provides a detailed account of a number of objective tests produced for courses set up to support these military language developments.

Spolsky (1995a:181–185) identifies the Brooks/Barnard-Yale Aural listening test appearing in the early 1950s as one of the first listening tests to impact on schools. It involved the reading aloud of a short conversation by two examiners followed by 5 multiple-choice question questions and in 1960 a similar listening comprehension test was to appear in the College Entrance Examinations Board. He also refers to the Modern Language Association-Cooperative Foreign Language Tests administered on tape in 1963 which was indicative of the more advanced state of the technology in the United States at this time as compared to the United Kingdom. Reviewers expressed some concerns with the mixture of reading and listening in multiple-choice question listening tests which was, and still is, regarded as a serious drawback (see Field 2008, 2013).

From the 1940s until the early 1960s, for those subscribing to the audio-lingual approach, listening was mainly used as the presentation part of a language teaching methodology informed by structuralism and behaviourism (see Chapter 1). It was employed to model new items of language for subsequent language practice and production. Field (2008:1) describes how short dialogues on tape provided examples of structures to be heard (Alexander 1967) and this was the principal form that the listening practice took. Its importance as a skill in its own right was largely ignored (Porter and Roberts 1981, Morley 1991,Nunan 1989). Brown and Yule (1983:54) argue that 'this might be due to the assumption that students would just pick it up somehow in the general process of learning the foreign language'. Mendelsohn (1994) talks about the osmosis fallacy in the audio-lingual method whereby teachers believed that just by providing aural input students would necessarily absorb it (see Call 1985). According to Field (2008), even when enlightened teachers began to practise listening as a separate skill in the late 1960s many still saw the function of a listening lesson as demonstrating recently taught grammar in actual use.

In the 1960s we can see a proliferation of these discrete point tests in the United Kingdom. Davies (2008b:12–20) records how, in the English Proficiency Test Battery (EPTB), the precursor of ELTS and IELTS used for University matriculation purposes with overseas students by the British Council from 1965 to 1980, the listening component contained subtests of *phonemic discrimination* (in isolation and in context), *intonation* and *stress* (in conversation), and *comprehension* (science and non-science texts). The listening component of the General Medical Council's Professional and Linguistic Assessment Battery (PLAB) test in the United Kingdom was a further example of a discrete point approach, e.g. using sound discrimination sub-tests. It survived late into the 20th century largely due to its ease of administration and scoring.

The Modern Language Aptitude Test (MLAT) also included phoneme awareness as a critical component of an aptitude for acquiring a language (Carroll and Sapon 1959, 1967). Spolsky (1995a) provides detail of the widespread use of these element focused tests in his comprehensive history of this sister field of language aptitude testing. He also identifies a number of prognosis/aptitude tests employing discrete point formats from the 1920s onwards designed to exclude pupils less likely to succeed from high school foreign language classes.

In the 1950–60s, following government initiatives, a number of new language aptitude tests were developed which are still in use today (Carroll 1981, 1990). These tests included a number of tasks focusing on elements of the language that research had shown to be important for predicting aptitude for learning a foreign language. The Modern Language Aptitude Test (Carroll and Sapon 1959, 1967 and Spolsky 1995a:337–338) contained 5 sections:

- number learning (testing the auditory abilities and memory)
- phonetic script (testing coding and decoding of phonetic symbols)
- spelling cues (testing the ability to associate sounds with symbols)
- words in sentences (testing recognising functions)
- paired associates (testing rote memory).

The Pimsleur Language Aptitude Battery (PLAB) test (Pimsleur 1966) contained tasks which assessed:

- Vocabulary (word knowledge in English)
- Language analysis (similar to grammatical sensitivity)
- Sound discrimination (differentiating between strings of similar sounds)
- Sound-symbol association.

As we noted in Chapter 1, the 'discrete point' approach and the various formats employed to implement it could only provide a partial account of the construct they sought to measure. One problem with this approach to the measurement of proficiency was that it depended on proficiency being neatly quantifiable in this fashion. Oller (1979:212) provided a fairly damning critique:

> Discrete point analysis necessarily breaks the elements of language apart and tries to teach them (or test them) separately with little or no

attention to the way those elements interact in a larger context of communication. What makes it ineffective as a basis for teaching or testing languages is that crucial properties of language are lost when its elements are separated.

Geranpayeh and Taylor (2013) report how by the 1960s other tests such as TOEFL had begun to embrace a wider view of listening ability than these discrete point, micro-linguistically focused tests whilst staying with objectively scored formats:

> ... advances in linguistics and language pedagogy during the 1960s and 1970s, combined with technological developments such as the growing availability of tape recorded material, allowed the assessment of listening skills to assume the more familiar shape that we recognise today. Introduced in 1964, the Test of English as a Foreign Language (TOEFL), offered in the United States by Educational Testing Service (ETS), was designed as a measure to determine 'English proficiency of non-native speakers of the language for academic placement in United States colleges and universities' (Spolsky, 1995[a]:283). TOEFL included a dedicated 'auditory comprehension' component ... Listening input, consisting mainly of short, monologic extracts, was delivered via tape recordings, and test questions were of the objectively-scored, selected response type for quick and reliable marking.

Objective, selected response items (with the rare exception of some items in the Use of English paper) were not to appear in Cambridge tests until the 1970s when the notion of objectivity in assessment received wider recognition in UCLES (see Chapter 1 for background details on the differing testing traditions in the United Kingdom and the United States). In 1970 (LCE) and 1975 (CPE) Cambridge was to adopt objectively scored multiple-choice question tests of listening comprehension in dedicated papers. It has persevered with such objective formats to this day.

How the decisions were originally taken on an appropriate methodology for assessing the listening construct in the pre-communicative period is not clear. The speculative answer, in the United States at least, is that listening tests simply followed the objective formats previously used for assessing reading comprehension and IQ that we discussed in Chapter 1 (with the obvious exception of dictation where previous pedagogical practice certainly had a bearing in the UK). As regards the levels of processing assessed, it is interesting to compare what was happening in listening with what was happening in reading in the pre-communicative period. One striking similarity in both is the widespread focus on decoding and the limited attention paid to comprehension beyond the sentence before the 1970s (see Chapter 2, pages 110–111, for details of this delimited focus in reading tests in this period).

Towards meaning construction: The communicative era

Listening comes in from the cold

By the late 1970s, when language labs were starting to be set up all over, a growing interest in the acquisition of listening skills, and the spread of functional and communicative approaches in language teaching, meant that far greater attention was paid to meaning-based listening comprehension than in the earlier periods discussed above (Richards and Rodgers 1986, and Morley 1991). The work of Brown and Yule (1983), Ur (1984), Rixon (1986), Anderson and Lynch (1988), Underwood (1989), Rost (1990), Brown (1990, 1996), Berne (1998), White (1998), Buck (2001) and Field (1998, 2001, 2008, 2011 and 2013) provided both theoretical and practical bases for a systematic approach to more direct listening comprehension pedagogy. A further influence was the interest in sub-skills following Munby (1978), which resulted in Richard's (1983) taxonomy.

Three distinct movements can be seen here: a) the increase of interest in what was termed 'listening comprehension'; b) the suggestion that listening might be divisible into a set of sub-skills which could be practised (though not tested) individually; c) a move away from an excessive emphasis on the role of context and external information sources and towards a renewed awareness of the important part played by perceptual processing.

This last development was to influence thinking in pedagogy as well as in listening research. It underpinned the second edition of Brown's book *Listening to Spoken English* (1990), and Field (1998). In effect, it marked a swing of the pendulum after years during which the prevailing view had been that top-down information was important and that perceptual information was not because a failure of perception could be compensated by using context. A shift took place in pedagogy and in the general way in which listening was viewed, but there was no support for a return to discrete point phoneme-based testing of the type described in the previous section.

The marked increase in attention paid to listening in doctoral studies was further evidence of a growing awareness of the importance of this previously neglected area (see for example Attia 2002, Buck 1990, Eom 2006, Field 2001, Gruba 1999, Harding 2008, In'nami 2007, Joyce 2008, Kijak, 2009, Liao 2009, Londe 2008, Nguyen 2008, Osada 2002, Pemberton 2003, Perrin 2000, Poelmans 2003, Salisbury 2005, Shin Dong-il 1999, Shin Sun-young 2007, Song 2008, Wagner 2006). Listening was finally receiving the attention it deserved. Dunkel (1991a) was one of the early proponents of the idea that listening was an important skill in society. Hedge (2000:228) emphasised the central role listening plays in communication.

Changes in testing listening

As early as the 1960s there had been signs that some examination boards were moving in the direction of a more communicative approach. Hawkey (2004) provides a valuable history of the Association of Recognised English Language Schools (ARELS) Oral Test which first appeared in the United Kingdom in 1967 and represents one of the first attempts to assess listening comprehension in its own right in the United Kingdom. The ARELS test, in accordance with psychometric-structuralist concerns of the time also reflected a shift to a more objective, and more standardised approach to testing oral English. Hawkey details (2004:42) how:

> . . . The ARELS Test was language-laboratory and tape / cassette based. It used a master tape of the examination script with gaps timed for candidates' responses, and a personal cassette on which a candidate recorded these. The examination tape was played in a language laboratory, with up to 12 candidates examined at a time.

ARELS claimed:

> that the tests were attempting "wherever possible" to base the materials used on "authentic tasks and situations" and to encourage candidates "to see the purpose and relevance of what they are asked to do".

However, the ARELS test content reflects its pre-communicative pedigree, established as it was just before onset of the communicative approach. Hawkey (2004:41) notes: 'the examination did not reflect the communicative approach as defined by Morrow (1979)' and (Hawkey 2004: 47) provides the following example:

> In the 'Social English' sections of the ARELS test, mainly short, fairly standard responses were elicited from the candidate. The mini-dialogues, unconnected with each other and relatively limited in possibility of variation in responses, were probably 'reliable' in marking terms but did not meet many of the CALTe authenticity requirements . . . They might be interaction-based but were hardly authentic in the fullest sense of the term . . . that is, contextualised for purpose, attitude and formality level . . . But the items in this section . . . are probably not intended to be contextualized, the ARELS test seeking high administrability, scorability and reliability among its other aims.

In terms of what was happening in the language classroom, Field (2008:13) describes how by the late 1960s listening practice was a regular occurrence in language schools in the United Kingdom albeit on rather unwieldy reel to reel tape. He cites Abbs, Cook and Underwood (1968) as one of the first listening courses and draws attention to the authentic interviews and oral narratives of Mary Underwood (1971, 1976); real people recounting tales of something that had happened to them. The goals of Abbs, Cook and Underwood in *Realistic English Dialogues* (1968) were rather mixed as between teaching language and practising listening, but it showed the beginnings of a systematic approach to the teaching of the skill.

As we saw in Chapter 1, by the late 1970s, the communicative approach to language teaching was to encourage a more active use of language to perform tasks based on meaning, not form. Taylor and Geranpayeh (2011:90) report how.

> The communicative paradigm of this era acknowledged language as communication, rather than as a system for study, and this view was increasingly reflected in approaches to L2 assessment, including the testing of listening. (See Hawkey, 2004, for comprehensive discussion of the impact of communicative trends on English language testing in the UK.) New testing methods reflected a concern for authenticity, with language testers attempting to create test tasks approximating to the 'reality' of non-test language use (real-life performance). A 1982 document published by Cambridge to communicate the anticipated changes to the CPE Listening Comprehension test highlights this shift: "The use of recorded material makes possible a decisive move away from literature-oriented texts, and towards authentic spoken English in a variety of realistic contexts. The change represents a decisive step towards the alignment with realistic language-learning aims which is so strongly and generally recommended" (UCLES 1982:28).

Buck (2001:83–93) identified a number of features of communicative listening test items that appear to be implicitly agreed as desirable maxims in the literature:

- reasonably authentic/genuine texts from the target language use situation
- language test use takes place for a definite communicative purpose so test tasks should provide a purpose for listening
- tasks should represent target language use tasks as much as possible.

These features started to appear in approaches to the teaching of second language listening in the 1980s but as we will see below they were 'more honor'd in the breach than the observance' in Cambridge ESOL and most other examinations. Brindley (1998:172) asserts that in listening assessment by the end of the 20th century there was:

> a move away from the notion of listening as auditory discrimination and decoding of decontextualised utterances to a much more complex and

interactive model which reflects the ability to understand authentic discourse in context.

There was certainly a clear move away from the former, from the types of selected response tests of perception and lexical access discussed in the previous section, but, as we will see below, the authenticity of the test input and the nature of what was tested in listening in this final stage of our history were to fall short of this idealised communicative picture. A shift along the continuum 'yes', but arrival in the promised communicative land 'no'.

In many situations the testing of listening was handled as part of the testing of spoken interaction (see Chapter 4) and in these cases Buck's communicative maxims (see above) were more clearly adhered to and the measurement of the listening construct was far less affected by the formats selected than in the transactional listening tests we are concerned with in this chapter. Listening and speaking are symbiotic partners in conversation/spoken interaction – with the result that listening plays an important part in any interactive test of speaking involving co-constructed discourse. Nakatsuhara (2012:523) describes how:

> The increasing use of paired and group oral tests has also attracted attention to the relationship between test-takers' listening proficiency and their performance on these formats, and there is clear evidence here that listening ability does play a part in performance.

In her analysis of group oral test discourse, Nakatsuhara (2009) found that communication problems in group tests were attributable in part to limited listening proficiency. Recent studies into paired tests have pointed out the importance of listening as part of successful interaction (e.g. Ducasse and Brown 2009, Galaczi 2010, May 2009). Ducasse and Brown (2009) provided evidence of two outcomes of interactive listening that underpin successful paired interaction: 1) showing evidence of comprehension by the listener (e.g. filling in with a missing word to help the partner) and 2) showing supportive listening by providing audible support with sounds (e.g. back-channelling). Conventionally in speaking tests, listening makes an important contribution but is not, *as yet*, assessed independently.

Coverage of the testing of listening in these interactive situations can be found in Chapter 4. In this chapter we focus on testing transactional language in those non-interactive situations when listening is not the precursor of speech, e.g. listening to lectures, railway announcements, recorded messages or television and radio programmes and 'eavesdropping' material based on listening to everyday conversations. Advocates of a communicative approach (Weir 1990,1993) argued that it was essential in this approach to decide on the contextual and cognitive criteria on which to base decisions on what to include in a dedicated test of listening comprehension. To determine what a satisfactory performance is, he felt we should specify in detail what it is the candidate can do (cognitive operations), under what circumstances (performance conditions) and to what level (scoring considerations).

As regards testing practice in this communicative era, testers were becoming sensitive to the issue of *construct irrelevant variance* (Messick 1989) occasioned by the use of a particular test format, especially objective items as in the multiple-choice question variants discussed above. From the 1980s onwards consideration was given in listening tests to widening the variety of test task formats in order to reduce the possibilities of such a method effect, for example by adding *constructed response* formats. In constructed response format items, candidates respond by completing gaps on the question paper with short answers. These are typically of a specified length, for example one word or up to three words. Whilst overcoming some of the problems of cognitive validity associated with objective formats, as we will see in the next section on Cambridge examinations, constructed response items brought with them their own particular problems not least the limitations in the levels of processing they were able to measure and the need for candidates to write their answers out.

The present day emphasis has certainly moved towards more contextualised tests of listening comprehension using language that exhibits a number of the important facets of spoken language we identify below (for further discussion of the shift see Brindley (1998), Brindley and Nunan (1992), Buck (1991, 2001:83–93), Rost (1990, 2002), Weir (1990:51–54) and Hawkey (2005)). We can identify a growing interest in improving the naturalness of language used as input but again for various reasons (largely practical, and method driven rather than construct focused) the preference has been for rerecording spoken language or using scripted or improvised dialogue rather than using original authentic spoken discourse. Nearly all international examinations still appear to fight shy of using authentic texts and continue to rely heavily on rerecorded ones (see however the account of the RSA Communicative Use of English as a Foreign Language (CUEFL) listening tests in Hawkey (2004:153–157) where some authentic texts were evidently used). Examination boards sometimes claim this is because of the poor sound quality and inadequate contextualisation of much authentic material (Brindley 1998:175); in addition the issue of what playback facilities (e.g. quality of tape recorders or venues for conducting listening tests) are available at the local level in test centres around the world is always something examination boards have to be concerned about as not all centres have high-quality equipment to hand or ideal acoustic environments. This puts a premium on the quality of the recording itself. Once again we have a tension between the pulls of practicality for an examination board working on an industrial scale and those of validity.

The downside to not using truly authentic recordings is that item writers may be tempted to manipulate the text to make it suit their test format (e.g. inserting distractor sentences in the text, adding definitions for low-frequency terms and reducing or increasing the level of redundancy) with all the implications this has for construct validity (see Salisbury 2005 for a fascinating account of the item writing process for listening tests including evidence of such *tinkering,* and Field 2013).

The stated concern is also now with testing the communication of meaning as against low level decoding and transcription. The communicative period is marked by an increased interest in testing meaning construction beyond the utterance level but this often falls short of testing understanding of the overall discourse structure. Examination boards often divide sections of the listening test between sets of short single-issue recordings and longer ones. Short recordings can be used to test for main points in a localised way and longer recordings of 3 to 4 minutes offer the further possibility of activating discourse level comprehension processes. Short single topic recordings are extremely effective in testing the listener's ability to extract information from a spoken passage. Unfortunately the situation so far as the longer passages are concerned is that test setters rarely ask questions which tap into global meaning or ask listeners to interpret the main point of the recording. Instead, what they seem to do is to focus upon discrete pieces of information within the recording, with little regard to the possible links between those pieces of information.

If we wish to make test tasks more like those in real life we need to focus at least some of the test questions on the more global processing skills which enable us to extract meaning from a spoken text. Field provides a useful overview of these processes related to meaning building as against decoding (2008:116–118, 338–339):

- Deriving the bare meaning of an utterance
- Adding to the meaning
- Selecting information
- Integrating information into a discourse structure
- Recognising overall argument structure.

Having provided a general overview of changes in how the listening construct was viewed and measured through tests in the 20th century, we will now examine in more detail how Cambridge assessed listening ability in its English language examinations in that period. We will analyse more specifically the precise nature of the changes made in measuring the listening construct in this particular United Kingdom examining board through the lens of the socio-cognitive framework (Weir 2005a).

Examining Listening: An analysis of Cambridge English Listening test tasks 1913–2012

In the previous section we provided a general overview of how new ideas in teaching, applied linguistics and testing, as well as external societal forces, all acted as drivers for change in the way the listening construct was measured at various points in our survey. In this section we look more closely at evidence from the Cambridge archives relating to the measurement of listening ability in the past century and examine how the testing of listening changed along the way from 1913–2012.

To analyse the nature of the specific changes in Cambridge's approach to measuring listening we need a detailed conceptual framework which can account for the various elements of the listening construct. We first briefly describe a socio-cognitive framework specifically designed for use in analysing listening tests (see Chapter 1 for a fuller account of the socio-cognitive approach in general and Geranpayeh and Taylor (Eds)(2013) for a comprehensive treatment of its application to listening tests in current Cambridge examinations).

A framework for listening test task analysis

Cognitive validity in L2 listening

Based on the theoretical and empirical research literature on the nature of cognitive processing involved in first and second language listening, Field (2013) provides a model against which L2 listening tests can be analysed and described for the purposes of cognitive validation.

In Field's (2013:95–96) model there are five levels of processing:

- Input decoding: when the listener transforms acoustic cues into groups of syllables, some marked for stress and others not;
- Lexical search: when the listener identifies the best word-level matches for what has been heard, based on a combination of perceptual information and word boundary cues;
- Parsing: when the lexical material is related to the co-text in which it occurs in order to a) specify lexical sense more precisely; b) impose a syntactic pattern;
- Meaning construction: when world knowledge and inference are employed to add to the bare meaning of the message;
- Discourse construction: when the listener makes decisions on the relevance of the new information and how congruent it is with what has gone before; and, if appropriate, integrates it into a representation of the larger listening event.

Listening takes place online. This means that the listener has to form a hypothesis about what is being heard at the point at which it reaches his/her ear – despite any possible uncertainty. This first impression will be revised as more evidence comes in either at phoneme, syllable or word level. Field (2013:95) describes this aspect of listening as 'a tentative process, in which provisional hypotheses at word, phrase and clause level constantly have to be updated and revised as acoustic input continues to come in'.

Field (2013) explains how the propositional meaning, the product of parsing is enriched by reference to pragmatic, background and socio-linguistic knowledge and information provided by the ongoing discourse representation. He argues that the raw meaning of the speaker's words is insufficient to convey the significance of what is being said or why it has been said. The listener is therefore responsible for supplying information that enriches what is said in a number of ways. According to Field (2013:100–101) these might be:

- *Pragmatic.* The listener interprets the speaker's illocutionary intentions, using knowledge of the pragmatic forms of the language. . .
- *Contextual.* The listener relates the proposition to the context in which it occurs by making use of a) world knowledge, knowledge of the speaker and knowledge of the situation and b) recall of what has been said to far.
- *Semantic.* The listener draws upon world knowledge of entities and ideas that have been mentioned by the speaker.
- *Inferential.* The listener supplies details that the speaker has not felt it necessary to include.

The main function of the meaning enrichment processes is to embed the bare propositional meaning of what the speaker has said in a specific context and establish meaning representation.

In the final part of his processing model Field (2013) shows how the listener has to make important judgements about the information that has been obtained and to relate it to what has occurred in the listening event so far. He emphasises the distinction between the meaning representation derived from a particular utterance and the ongoing discourse representation (Brown and Yule 1983; the listener's recall of what has occurred so far) relating to the whole of what is being listened to.

Field (2013:102–103) identifies four main processes that are applied as the listener constructs this wider comprehension of a spoken text:

- *Selection.* The listener needs to decide upon the relevance of the new piece of information to the discourse as a whole and can accordingly let the piece of information decay from memory, retain it in an indeterminate form or store it in some detail.
- *Integration.* The listener needs to add the new item of meaning to the developing discourse representation. The process entails recognising

conceptual links between an incoming piece of information and the information that immediately preceded it.

- *Self-monitoring.* Part of integration entails comparing a new piece of information with what has gone before, to ensure that it is consistent.
- *Structure building.* As more and more information is acquired, the listener has to take account of the relative importance of each item. On this basis, he/she constructs a hierarchical pattern of what has been said, consisting of a set of major points with subordinate points attached to them.

A test might be considered deficient and raise concerns about any attempt to generalise from it to real life, language use, if the processes adopted during a test are not sufficiently similar to the cognitive processes a listener would normally employ in a target real-world context. Field (2013) is especially apprehensive where additional processes occasioned by the facets of a particular test (procedure, test method, item) are required other than the normal operations associated with the construct being measured. The inevitable result of this is *construct irrelevant variance* (Messick 1989). Secondly he is worried about the coverage of listening test items. He argues that the range of processes elicited by test items needs to be sufficiently comprehensive to be considered representative of real-world behaviour, i.e. not just a small subset of those which might give rise to fears about construct *under-representation.* A third requirement is that across a suite of tests graded by reference to a scale, the performance features required need to be appropriately calibrated to the level of proficiency of the listeners being evaluated.

With lower-proficiency learners greater attentional resources have to be allocated to the task of decoding language, and so listening tests for lower proficiency candidates would normally have a stronger focus on Field's first three levels: input decoding, lexical search and parsing. This should help reduce the cognitive demands on test takers to an appropriate level. Meaning construction and discourse-level interpretation and evaluation are increasingly appropriate for higher proficiency test takers, i.e. from the B2 FCE level to the C2 CPE level, since by then their decoding skills are much more automatic which leaves more of working memory free. Therefore, cognitive processes involving pragmatic, contextual, semantic and inferential knowledge and establishing a discourse level representation are more appropriate for these higher-proficiency learners (see Field 2013 for a more detailed discussion of the calibration of items appropriate to learner levels in Cambridge English language examinations).

Context validity in L2 listening

Context validity for a listening task addresses the particular performance conditions, the setting under which the task is to be performed and the linguistic demands of task input and output. In Figure 5.1 we draw on the contextual parameters suggested by Weir (2005a) as being most likely to have an impact on listening test performance (see also Geranpayeh and Taylor (Eds) (2013)).

Figure 5.1 Aspects of context validity for listening (adapted from Weir 2005a)

Context Validity	
Task setting	**Linguistic Demands: Task Input & Output**
Rubric	Overall text purpose and
Task purpose	discourse mode
Response method	Functional resources
Knowledge of criteria	Grammatical resources
Order of items	Lexical resources
Channel of presentation	Phonological resources
Text length	Nature of information
Time constraints, including	Content knowledge
number of times heard	**Speakers**
	Delivery
	Familiarity
	Number of speakers
	Gender

There are obviously shared similarities with reading across a number of these contextual dimensions but clearly a number of important differences as well. Rost (2002:31,171–172) lists textual characteristics relevant to listening. They include physical features that are specific to spoken language (see also Carter and McCarthy 1997):

- pause units
- hesitations
- intonation
- stress
- variable speeds
- variable accents.

And linguistic features that are more common in spoken language:

- colloquial vocabulary and expressions
- shorter, practically (additive) organised speech units
- false starts
- frequent use of ellipsis
- frequent use of unstated topics
- more indexical expressions (keyed to visible environmental features)
- more two-party negotiation of meaning (less original clarity).

One of the main differences from reading comprehension is the effect of speaker-related variables on listening, for example, the way speech is delivered (stress, intonation, pausing, rhythm, speed of utterance, degree of sympathetic adjustment, accent and pronunciation), familiarity with the speaker's voice, status, and gender mainly in relation to voice pitch. Field (2008:270) additionally draws our attention to the variability of sounds from one utterance to another as against the standardised spelling system available for the reader. He further argues that readers have blank spaces between the words in a text, while listeners have to work out where one word ends and another begins in connected speech. Decoding involves quite different processing in the two modalities (see also Osada 2004).

The decisions taken with regard to the inclusion of these performance conditions in a listening test are important because of the added load they can place on processing, especially given the serial and transitory nature of the listening experience, where we normally only have an opportunity to listen to something once as we process it under normal time constraints. For example, listening to several interacting voices is likely to increase task difficulty, not only because of the need to distinguish voices from each other, but also because the listener needs to establish 'baseline characteristics' for each voice, such as speech rate, loudness, pitch and articulation; they will be determined by the physiological characteristics of speakers' speech organs as well as by accent (see Field 2008:157–159). The implications of this for teaching and testing are clear: at lower proficiency levels, the range of voices as well as language varieties and accents should be limited and gradually increased with increasing proficiency levels (see Field 2008:160). In addition, since adjusting to the speaker's voice may take some time with L2 learners, listening tasks should allow enough time for it, by ensuring that 'comprehension questions do not target the first 10–15 seconds of a recording' or by playing a text twice (Field 2008:159).

Given the transient nature of spoken language as against the recursive nature of reading, the listener is not normally able to backtrack over what has been said, as a reader can when faced with a permanent written text. Field (2008:27–28) argues that processing has to take place in real time so even though there are some similarities in cognitive processes between the two (extracting ideas, relating the ideas to what has gone before, inferencing and making connections to background knowledge), the resemblance should not be overstated because of the transitory nature of the speech signal.

Buck (2001:112) argues unequivocally that 'listening tests ought to require fast, automatic, on-line processing of texts that have the linguistic characteristics of typical spoken language'. Weir (2005a) feels that if we wish to test listening ability we need to be sure that the input to test takers and the cognitive activities of test takers match real-life speech and listening performance in terms of as many of the construct validity parameters we have identified as are feasible in the testing situation. If we adequately address these cognitive and contextual facets, we can be more comfortable in the construct validity of the listening test than if we do not include them.

These desiderata need to be borne in mind when we survey the texts and the tasks employed to test listening in our historical survey below. They in fact raise serious questions about the use of written texts, often from literary sources, read aloud to assess aural comprehension which was common for much of the period under review in this history. There must also be some concern about the re-recording of authentic original discourse. Further complications arise where additional, extraneous processes occasioned by the facets of a particular *response method* impact on the measurement of the listening construct.

We will draw on some of the key parameters of context and cognitive validity in our analysis of the listening tasks in Cambridge English examinations 1913–2012 below.

Cambridge English examinations 1913–2012

Even though listening comprehension was not separately tested in Cambridge English examinations for the major part of the 20th century (until 1970), it had been a part of the examination's construct(s) since the launch of CPE, through the conversation component of the Oral test and the dictation. Interactive listening is still very much part of the Speaking test construct through the Interview, Collaborative and Discussion tasks (see Chapter 4 in this volume and Galaczi and ffrench (2011:121)).

For an interaction to take place, comprehension of the examiner's questions was always crucial in the CPE oral test, and the ease of comprehension on the part of the candidate was taken into account during the holistic assessment of candidate performance. A CPE candidate was required to 'understand the examiner's questions without difficulty', according to an early version of Instructions to Oral Examiners (Instructions for Oral Examiners 1958:4).

Until 1970, dictation was the closest equivalent to a specific Listening comprehension test in Cambridge English examinations. In 1970, a Listening comprehension test was introduced to LCE, and then slightly later to CPE, after which it spread to other Cambridge English examinations that were launched throughout the 1980s and 1990s. They all consisted of non-interactive, or rather, non-participatory listening tasks, since candidates were required to listen and respond to written questions, instead of answering orally or participating in a conversation.

Developments from 1913 to 2012 in the way in which the comprehension construct was perceived and/or operationalised in Cambridge English examinations, from dictation to the various forms of selected and constructed response Listening comprehension tests, are now examined with particular reference to FCE, CAE and CPE. We also include the Preliminary Test in English in our account since, within UCLES, it represented the very first attempt at testing Listening comprehension that resembles – to a limited extent but more so than dictation – modern-day testing endeavors.

We will discuss developments which represent the major changes in the Cambridge approach to testing listening in the 100 years under review:

- Dictation in CPE 1913–74 and LCE 1939–69
- Preliminary Test in English 1945
- LCE Listening 1970–74
- FCE and CPE Listening 1975–83
- The 1984 revisions to FCE and CPE Listening
- CAE Listening 1991–
- Present day listening constructs.

Dictation in CPE and LCE: 1913–1974

This section discusses the construct of dictation in Cambridge English examinations in terms of cognitive and contextual task demands. Marking and the conduct of the dictation test are also referred to where these procedures impact on the operationalisation of the construct during live examinations.

A dictation, read out loud by the Oral Examiner, formed part of the CPE Oral tests between 1913 and 1974, and the LCE Oral component between 1939 and 1969. The longevity of dictation could be partially attributed to the fact that listening comprehension was seen as less amenable to teaching and testing whereas dictation was fairly undemanding in terms of the time and resources required for its use, e.g. no items had to be developed.

Even though it did not test speaking skills, dictation was part of the Oral paper in Cambridge because it tested 'understanding of the spoken word' (Roach 1945a:26). It was also a test of 'literacy' (ibid) as it required writing down the text that was read aloud by the Oral Examiner. Owing to the dual nature of the dictation construct, Roach looked for a clearer definition of what dictation was intended to measure, i.e. was it more a test of understanding or a test of literacy? This was crucial because decisions needed to be made on 'the relative importance of spelling mistakes and mistakes of understanding' (Roach 1945a:33) for the purposes of marking. Roach (1945a) did not provide an answer or solution to this issue, but invited the experience of overseas colleagues and teachers. This issue was not picked up in any available archived documentation until 1971, when Instructions to Oral Examiners explicitly stated that dictation is a test 'of comprehension of connected spoken English, rather than of the spelling of individual words, whose pronunciation may differ when heard in isolation (that, can, for etc.)' (Instructions to Oral Examiners 1971:6). This was a critical development. Examiners in the later period were required to simulate natural speech, rather than adopting the more traditional read aloud style. They were also required to make use of weak forms rather than (as might occur in some dictation tasks) dictate citation forms for the sake of clarity.

Information on how CPE and LCE Dictation were marked might have revealed more on the way in which the construct measured by the test was perceived but, unfortunately, no available documents between 1913 and 1970 shed any light on this. Annual reports on dictation in the early UCLES national school examinations (Junior Local examinations) highlight punctuation, spelling and handwriting as some of the marking criteria, as does the following commentary:

> More attention to punctuation is still needed. The spelling of the boys in December was generally very poor indeed, and the writing was not as neat as usual (68th Annual Report 1925:21).

All these criteria indicate that dictation in UCLES Junior Local examinations was more a test of literacy, most likely due to the fact that it was for native rather than non-native speakers of English. In contrast to this, punctuation was not assessed in CPE and LCE since it was provided by the examiner (Instructions to Oral Examiners 1945:3). There is no information on how spelling mistakes were treated, but it seems likely that comprehension was more relevant to marking in CPE and LCE than in Junior Locals (even before the above statement in the 1971 Instructions to Oral Examiners), since the former were tests of English as a foreign language.

A better understanding of the listening comprehension aspect of the construct underlying dictation can be arrived at by drawing on Field's cognitive processing model described in the previous section. Judging by the available information on how it had been administered since 1945 and the fact that it consisted of *passages* read out loud, a test of dictation might have resulted in the activation of a range of cognitive processes underlying listening comprehension as identified by Field (2013). Since the first reading aloud of the passage required candidates just to *listen* and *not write* (Instructions to Oral Examiners 1945), the task was likely to activate both decoding (recognition of phonemes, syllables, words, arriving at literal utterance meaning) and meaning building across utterances (i.e. drawing on the text heard so far – co-text).

Clearly dictation is an exercise in which the role of co-text is particularly important. In other words, if particular words had not been recognised, they might sometimes be guessed from the words that surrounded them. However, a questionable aspect of this task is that it forces attention to the word level, with the result that test takers could, in theory at least, score high marks for reproducing the words without necessarily having grasped the overall meaning. This presumably was the point of providing two readings of the text.

The task could have even activated some inferencing, but it certainly could not have encouraged relating the literal meaning to a wider communicative context since dictation passages were neither context-embedded nor a part of communicative situations. The second reading aloud would be accompanied by transcription of the dictated text. This could have predominantly activated more localised processing at the decoding level because utterances, during this second reading, were 'broken down' by an examiner into phrases, words or short segments through pausing (as in the LCE and CPE dictation passages below where bars indicate pauses), thus providing additional cues to word boundaries which would not necessarily be available in normal connected speech. The third reading would allow time for corrections. We can speculate that the third reading could have provided extra time not only for revising one's spelling, but also for monitoring one's comprehension in the sense that candidates could check the coherence of the text as a whole and the consistency of the points made.

Administered in the above fashion, dictation had a potential to elicit a relatively wide range of the cognitive processes underlying real-life listening comprehension. However, this potential should be distinguished from what performance on dictation is actually evidence of. As argued by Anderson (1972, cited in Buck 2001:71), 'texts can be processed on a perceptual or phonological level without actually processing the meaning of words, utterances and the entire text'. Dictation therefore cannot provide definitive evidence of comprehension and is, at best, only a very indirect measure of comprehension. As processing was largely taking place at the level of the word, it tests the ability to segment the speech stream correctly into words and knowledge of word level spellings. Utterances were segmented for candidates by the examiner – who would pause at the end of each segment, as indicated by the guidelines, so that the text could be written down by candidates. Additional indications of word boundaries were given by these pauses and syntactic boundaries were marked more frequently and more reliably than would normally be allowed for in running speech. In cognitive processing terms, performance on CPE and LCE dictation was at best evidence of one's ability to draw on phonological knowledge to decode input (phonemes, syllables and supra-segmental information) and lexical knowledge to enable word recognition.

Dictation passages were of a literary character, normally either narratives or later on discussion. The contextual task demands and the processing challenge such demands would pose for the listener would have originated from the linguistic complexity of written literary language rather than typical features of spoken language, such as ellipsis, false starts, hesitations, colloquial vocabulary, variable speed, pitch and accent of the speakers. Moreover, candidates were not required to listen to a range of speaker voices. They only listened to a single examiner's voice in any one session. This meant that there was no need to adjust to different baseline features of more than one voice, which made the task less cognitively demanding. Finally, dictation did not encourage interpreting meaning in a range of communicative contexts as this was not a communicative exercise and there were no communicative contexts to speak of. Overall, in terms of cognitive and contextual demands, and therefore, situational and interactional authenticity, dictation tasks were quite unlike real-life listening comprehension tasks.

To accommodate for different proficiency levels of CPE and LCE candidates, CPE passages were intended to be linguistically and conceptually more complex. Table 5.1 compares the June 1945 LCE and March 1938 CPE dictation passages that are included in the text below in terms of a number of contextual complexity parameters (see Appendix B for a similar but more comprehensive analysis of Cambridge reading tests using Coh-Metrix Version 2 and Lexical tutor analysis together with explanations of the individual parameters). Clearly in terms of these complexity parameters which affect cognitive load, the dictation passage in CPE is more difficult than that in LCE. Unfortunately without the tools now available for such analysis, this differentiation was not always achieved in the past (see below).

Table 5.1 Comparison of 1938 CPE and 1945 LCE dictation passages

Cohmetrix V2 and lexical tutor indices *	Listening Passages		
	LCE 1945	CPE 1938	Difference
37 Average words per sentence	11.909	33.000	−21.091
39 Flesch Reading Ease Score (0–100)	84.344	38.149	46.195
47 Celex, raw, minimum in sentence for content words (0–1,000,000)'	58.545	12.000	46.545
49 Concreteness, mean for content words	437.170	331.024	106.146
AWL level	0.76	3.03	−2.270

*glosses on the meaning of each of these in indices and their relationship to levels of cognitive processing are provided in Appendix B.

Lower Certificate

DICTATION
JUNE 1945

UNIVERSITY OF CAMBRIDGE

LOCAL EXAMINATIONS

Lower Certificate in English

(*Time to be taken for the first reading*: 65 *seconds.*)

Dictation

An hour later, | the young Russian boy | reached the forest. | He was hungry | and thirsty | and the sun was very hot. | Fear seized him | in the woods. | At one moment | it seemed to him | that enemy soldiers | were watching him | from behind the trees, | crawling out | of the bushes. | He ran blindly, | paying no attention | to the path | until he was out of breath. | Suddenly he saw a man | among the trees. | The man had a gun | and was standing there | and looking | towards the spot | where the boy had hidden. | Evidently | he had heard | the sound of footsteps. | The boy stared hard, | but a heavy shadow | prevented him | from getting a clear sight | of the man. | Suddenly he gave a joyful cry. | He had seen | that it was a friend.   [131 words]

(LCE question paper, Dictation, June 1945)

The pace of reading was also somewhat slower in LCE than in CPE: 'The first reading of the Proficiency passage for June 1945 (128 words) was supposed to take approximately 56 seconds, and of the Lower Certificate passage (131 words) approximately 65 seconds' (Instructions to Oral Examiners 1945: 3). Both speech rates are markedly below the rate of natural speech. It may well be that slower speech allows more processing time, but that is extremely difficult to demonstrate. What would help is an increase in the frequency of pausing in a dictation test for lower proficiency candidates, but it is not clear if this was done in LCE.

Another important issue to consider in terms of context validity is the administration of the dictation test. To ensure that everyone can hear without difficulty, and thereby avoid what is nowadays known as construct-irrelevant variance, examiners were advised to divide candidates into two or more sets of no more than 30 candidates each (Instructions to Oral Examiners 1947).

One very important aspect of test administration, crucial for context and cognitive validity, was neglected until 1945. Since a passage was read out by an Oral Examiner rather than being administered through gramophone recordings (in the early years) or reel-to-reel tapes (in the 1960s), there was much room for variation in certain phonetic features of the text. The fact that students are not being exposed to a unique and single version of the text is a major weakness of this version of the dictation exercise.

The lack of strict guidelines could have resulted in variation in speech rate, in the degree of elision and assimilation, in the placement of stress and intonation, and even in extreme cases the number of times a passage was read out to candidates. All this has implications for the construct validity of the assessment, and affects the realisation of a test construct in live examination conditions. Despite these threats to construct validity, it seems that the guidelines on how to read a passage before 1945 were rather sparse: there were no Instructions to Oral Examiners before 1945 and no instructions appear in question papers before 1949, either. The only guidelines concerned the location of pauses, which were marked by vertical lines in a dictation passage, as in the example below:

UNIVERSITY OF CAMBRIDGE

LOCAL EXAMINATIONS SYNDICATE

Certificate of Proficiency in English

Dictation Passage

Edmund Burke's view of the American Colonies in the Eighteenth Century,

There is still | a third consideration | which serves to determine my opinion | on the sort of policy | which ought to be pursued | in the management of America, | even more than its population | and its commerce. | I mean its temper and character, |

In this character of the Americans, | a love of freedom | is the predominating feature | which marks and distinguishes the whole: | and as an ardent affection | is always jealous, | your colonies become suspicious, | restive, | and untractable, | whenever they see the least attempt | to wrest from them by force, | or snatch from them by trickery, | what they think | the only advantage worth living for. | This fierce spirit of liberty | is stronger in the English colonies | probably | than in any other people of the earth, | and this | from a great variety of powerful causes.   E. BURKE.
(CPE question paper, Dictation passage, March 1938)

It is perhaps not surprising that Roach (1945a:18) discovered no uniformity between examiners, either in England or abroad, in the amount of time they took to read CPE or LCE dictation passages. This is why Roach's concern with standardisation of Oral Examiners' rating and achieving continuity of standard across reading aloud examinations (see Chapter 4) also extended to the conduct of dictation. As a consequence, the first detailed instructions on how to conduct dictation appeared in the 1945 Instructions to Oral Examiners, right after the completion of Roach's 1945 report on *Some*

Problems of Oral Examinations in Modern Languages. The instructions are quoted in full below:

> The passage will be read three times. During the first reading, the candidates will write nothing down. It will be read a second time by groups of words, as divided by bars on the printed copy. These will be read as 'sound-groups', not as a succession of isolated words, and without repetition. After each group, a pause will be made to allow the candidates to write it down. All essential punctuation will be given by the Examiner. An interval of two minutes will be allowed after the second reading. The passage will then be read a third time, and after a further interval of two minutes the exercises will be collected. During this third reading a substantial pause will be made, to allow of corrections, at full stops or at convenient points every two lines or so. No assistance or explanation of any kind will be given, and groups of words will only be repeated as an exceptional matter on the score of inaudibility (owing to sudden traffic noise, etc.); no repetition will be allowed where candidates have merely failed to grasp the sense (Instructions to Oral Examiners 1945:3).

Besides the guidelines on the number and manner of readings, the pace of reading was also specified in the 1945 Instructions. The pace was defined by the time taken to read out sample CPE and LCE passages as provided in Roach (1945a). Timings of other passages could vary somewhat, to accommodate slight variations in text length across question papers. Importantly, the pace of the second and third readings should be the same as the first reading, but timing would be slightly longer to accommodate longer pauses which would allow candidates to write the text down or correct it (Roach 1945a:33). To further standardise the administration of dictation, stress-marks and exact timing for each passage were provided in CPE and LCE question papers from 1949 onwards (see the example below). The reading pace was 'ordinary', as explicated in Instructions to Oral Examiners since 1958.

Proficiency   UNIVERSITY OF CAMBRIDGE
DICTATIONS
PASSAGES   LOCAL EXAMINATIONS SYNDICATE
June 1949

Certificate of Proficiency in English

DICTATION PASSAGES

The stress-marks, which are printed **before** *the stressed syllables, are given as a guide for the first and third readings. The approximate time to be taken for the* **first** *reading is shown at the end of each passage.*

PASSAGE I.

'When I was a 'child | I 'wanted to 'see | if it were 'true, | as 'mother had 'said 'carelessly, | that the 'stars 'shone 'all the 'time, | 'un 'noticeable in the 'daylight, | 'instead of 'springing 'suddenly to 'life | at 'nights | as I had 'hitherto be'lieved. | It was pre'posterous | to sup'pose 'otherwise. | 'In my incre'dulity | I ap'pealed to 'father | who 'backed 'up 'mother's 'statement | in an 'equally 'off-'hand way. | 'Fortunately, I thought, | it would be 'easy to 'check | by 'personal obser'vation. | One had' only to 'watch the 'sky | at 'dusk, | If the 'stars ap'peared 'gradually, | 'their theory was 'right. | I had al'ready 'passed the 'stage | in a 'child's relation-ship with its 'parents, | when they are auto'matically as'sumed | to be 'right, | but I 'still 'hated | the dis'covery | of their falli'bility. [63 seconds] (CPE question paper, Dictation passage, June 1949)

Using gramophone records to capture model readings of dictation, in terms of manner and style, was also suggested by Roach (1945a). However, this was not put into practice. The explicit guidelines for test administration discussed above most likely helped achieve some level of standardisation in contextual task parameters, and to the extent that this was the case it would have helped standardise contextual and cognitive task demands across tests and sessions.

Maintaining a relatively constant level of passage difficulty across sessions of a single examination also seemed to have posed a challenge. A discussion between UCLES and examination centre representatives (i.e. British Institute officials, teachers, oral examiners and supervisors) revealed that some 'dictation passages were found to be significantly easier or more difficult than others set at the same examination, and it was said that the most difficult Lower Certificate passage of December 1955 had been found harder than one of the Proficiency passages by a group of students who had worked both as a test after the examination' (Wyatt 1956:3). This was not uncommon in view of the fact that, to prevent leakage of information, alternative dictation passages were provided in cases where there was more than one examination centre in the same town and the dictation was not given simultaneously at each (Instructions to Oral Examiners 1947) giving rise to a variability issue caused by the examiner having a choice of passages to select from within any given test administration.

This is one of the reasons why dictations stopped being marked locally and were centrally marked, in Cambridge, by a single examiner, following Roach's (1945a) recommendation (Instructions to Oral Examiners 1947:1). Drawing on the score distribution 'and the report of a single examiner who has reviewed all the exercises' was the basis for adjusting the pass mark as 'no two dictations are exactly equal in difficulty' (Roach 1945a:27). In brief, no guidelines seem to have been in place to ensure less variation in the linguistic and conceptual difficulty of dictation passages, but fairness was sought post-hoc by adjusting pass marks.

Dictation was both a comprehension test and a literacy test, as it involved both listening and writing and also reading if students monitored what they had written down. As a test based on transcribing written literary language read out loud, dictation can be seen as part of the legacy of the literary tradition that played a large part in CPE and LCE examinations until the early 1960s (see Chapter 1) and of a centuries long tradition of classroom use.

Following World War Two, social and economic factors created a different language learning climate, so that the teaching of English ceased to be viewed as 'an access route to great literature' and succumbed to 'pressing utilitarian needs for English as a means of communication' (see Chapter 1, for discussion of this trend). In line with the times, the literary nature of CPE began to fade away from 1956 onwards (see *The downgrading of literature* in Chapter 1). Despite this, dictation with its literary and non-communicative character remained in Cambridge English examinations until 1970. This would change with the communicative approach.

The Preliminary Test in English (1945): An early test of listening

The earliest attempt at a dedicated Listening comprehension test within Cambridge English examinations came in the short-lived appearance of a test which was to re-emerge nearly half a century later in 1980 as the Preliminary English Test (PET). The Preliminary Test in English was developed during World War Two to encourage the learning of English by Allied Service Personnel and Italian prisoners of war whose potential proficiency level was lower than the one targeted by LCE but for whom a working knowledge of everyday English was considered beneficial. This war-time test, which was withdrawn after the end of the war, contained reading aloud, dictation and Oral questions.

Oral questions were read out by the examiner and required written responses as a test of 'comprehension and quickness' (Preliminary Test in English 1945). In Part 1, 10 factual questions were read once only and required short, one or two word, responses, e.g. *When do we have most flowers, in summer or in winter? What are houses made of?* In Part 2, 8 questions were to be answered by a full sentence each. The first four were based on the dictation passage, while the remaining four were, again, factual and common-sense. The questions were thus fairly basic, to suit the low proficiency level of these particular Allied Service personnel and prisoners of war. The Oral questions clearly focused on utterance-level comprehension.

Oral questions were part of an integrated task which also involved writing, and as such, the involvement of the writing skill compromised validity somewhat in terms of the listening construct supposedly being tested. Roach (1945a:27) felt:

> The candidates would write what they would have said; the pronunciation which they would have revealed in the saying of it is tested elsewhere. True, literacy and spelling come into account, but these can nearly always be distinguished, in assessing written answers of this kind, from sheer comprehension and ability to give an intelligible answer.

Owing to a time limit for answering each question, the reported advantages of this test were 'a refreshing sense of alertness' and candidates' enjoyment as they found it 'a pleasurable competition' (Roach 1945a:28). Even so, the time allowed for a response would have made decision-making in terms of content much easier than it would have been in the spontaneous conditions of normal interaction.

This semi-oral/integrated test was a rare example of a Listening comprehension test in the United Kingdom at the time. In the US, as we noted above, there were several tests based on questions or passages read aloud to test takers, e.g. The 1926 Bryn Mawr Test of Ability to Understand Spoken French, and two 'aural listening' tests in the 1950s and 1960s – the Brooks/Barnard-Yale and College Entrance Examinations Board test. Not surprisingly, the main difference between the Preliminary Test in English and the listening tests developed in the United States lies in the test formats employed: the former was a constructed-response (integrated) test, which actually did not involve much subjective judgement in marking due to the shortness of responses and the factual nature of the questions, while the latter were selected-response (multiple-choice) objective tests. As pointed out in Chapter 1, US-based testing readily accepted objective test formats very early in 20th century due to the need to administer tests to large numbers of candidates, in view of mass immigration and compulsory schooling. Owing to different priorities, they were only considered and adopted in the United Kingdom much later on (see Chapter 1).

Roach (1945a:28) viewed this semi-oral test as being close to direct oral examining. In other words, the construct measured by this early Listening comprehension test was seen to overlap with the speaking construct of reading aloud and conversation. This partially comes out in the above quotation as well: 'the candidates would write what they would have said. . .'

In addition, Roach (1945a:27) views semi-oral tests as a means of achieving a higher level of standardisation in the oral examination and the examination as a whole:

> If the identical questions were put to all the candidates simultaneously under identical conditions, the answers being written, we should then

have a test of which the evidence would remain and which could be readily standardized.

Since scores on semi-oral tests were perceived to be more reliable than those on oral tests, it was suggested that they might be used as checks on the examiner's own standards in the course of the examination:

> . . . such tests being marked at Cambridge, the Syndicate might establish the correlation between oral and semi-oral results at various levels, both in the examination as a whole and for each particular oral examiner. The resulting statistics might be of some guide to examiners for future occasions (Roach 1945a:28).

Additionally, the potential of semi-oral tests, even if they were not an integral part of the examination, was also seen in the following:

> Each centre might set the same tests in successive years, in order to discover whether, apart from correlation with the Syndicate's central standards, a shift in average mark for oral results at the centre was accompanied by a corresponding shift in the semi-oral tests (ibid).

In brief, 'Oral questions' in the Preliminary Test of English were a step forward in testing Listening comprehension in the United Kingdom. Even though they were a relatively simple version of Listening comprehension assessment as we know it today, they could provide evidence of a candidate's ability to comprehend albeit at the utterance level.

Roach (1945b:29) saw a range of possibilities as far as integrated tests were concerned, considering 'comprehension of the spoken word, accurate listening and reporting, as well as knowledge of the language – in which the examiner speaks, but not the candidate' as worthy of consideration for inclusion in English language examinations. However, the innovation embodied in this early listening comprehension test was short-lived. The construct, as measured by the Preliminary Test in English Oral questions, was not to spread to and/or be expanded and modified for higher proficiency examinations, such as CPE and LCE until much later. Following the withdrawal of the Preliminary Test in English after the end of World War Two, dictation was to remain the only method employed to test some aspects of non-participatory listening ability in Cambridge English exams until a significant change in approach occurred in 1970.

Listening in the LCE: 1970–1974

The year 1970 was an important landmark in Cambridge English examinations. In 1967, it had been decided that a Listening comprehension test should replace dictation in the LCE (Executive Committee minutes, October 1967), and this was finally put into practice in 1970. This was a major development for three reasons. Firstly, it demonstrated that the Cambridge view of the listening construct had moved on beyond mere transcription of a read aloud passage. Secondly, in response to the wider developments favouring a more psychometrically driven approach to testing discussed in Chapter 1, listening comprehension was to be tested through a selected response multiple-choice task format thus further grounding the spread of objective testing within Cambridge English examinations. This change in format itself served to alter the listening construct from the one previously measured by dictation; as we will see below. Finally, it was a clear indication that Listening comprehension was now recognised as an important skill in its own right; perhaps an early example of *impact by design* on the part of UCLES. The testing of this skill would soon be adopted in CPE and, later on, in all Cambridge English examinations.

The LCE Listening comprehension test was still formally a part of the Oral paper simply replacing the dictation test. The new test was taken by groups of up to 30 candidates (Instructions to Oral Examiners 1971:2), as it had been in dictation in previous years. The examiner was required to read aloud the task instructions and task input, while the candidate's task was to answer 30 printed four-option multiple-choice questions, based on the comprehension of those readings. Candidates were required to indicate their choice from the suggested options on an answer sheet (Exam regulations 1974:13). Even though the new test was a considerable novelty, it 'had given less trouble through its unfamiliarity than had been feared, though there were administrative complications' (Executive Committee minutes October 1970:3). The 'trouble' had probably been avoided or mitigated by the extensive preliminary consultations with examiners and centres while the Listening material was being pretested. That all objective forms of LCE were *pretested* extensively, as reported in May 1969 Executive Committee minutes, additionally demonstrates an increased concern with reliability.

The test, which lasted 30 minutes, consisted of four tasks, with progressively increasing length of task input and different task focuses (see excerpt below). It was clearly based on the audio-lingual approach which focused on sound and word recognition as well as comprehension of read aloud, isolated sentences, to the neglect of other more authentic listening skills (see section on *Objective methods for testing listening at the decoding level* above). Even though communicative language teaching and testing were starting to develop by the 1970s, the new test did not exhibit many of the characteristics of the new approach. Its passages and language, even at the outset of the communicative era, were not authentic, and its non-contextualised tasks gave candidates no specific listening purpose in advance. These issues are discussed in more detail below.

December 1972 LCE Listening Comprehension Paper

UNIVERSITY OF CAMBRIDGE LOCAL EXAMINATIONS SYNDICATE

Lower Certificate in English

DECEMBER 1972   LCE(L)6/1-4

LISTENING COMPREHENSION TEST

Instructions for this test are on the answer sheet which you will be given with this question paper, and the examiner will give you further instructions. You will hear everything at least twice, but if you cannot answer a question you must be ready to pass on to the next.

For each of the first seven questions you will hear a single word, which will be said twice. Choose the answer which best explains this word.

EXAMPLES:

[BIRD]

A a feathered creature which flies
B the cat made a low noise
C killing
D hair on a man's chin

[MURDER]

A a feathered creature which flies
B the cat made a low noise
C killing
D hair on a man's chin

1 A not light
   B harbour
   C animal
   D water bird

2 A not light
   B harbour
   C animal
   D water bird

3 A damage
   B sing with lips shut
   C kind of meat
   D house

4 A damage
   B sing with lips shut
   C kind of meat
   D house

5 A complete rest, usually at night
   B not awake
   C slide and fall
   D indoor shoe

6 A fall through water
   B an object
   C use your mind
   D make music with voice

7 A filled right up
   B small lake
   C stupid person
   D not push

For each of the next four questions you will hear twice a short phrase containing only one of the four words given on your answer sheet. Choose the word which you hear.

8 A heard   10 A suppose
   B hurt   B suppers
   C hot   C suffers
   D hotel   D soup

9 A heard   11 A suppose
   B hurt   B suppers
   C hot   C suffers
   D hotel   D soup

For each of the next four questions you will hear three times a sentence spoken in a particular way. Choose the phrase which best explains why the sentence is spoken like that. (Look up at the examiner and listen to the examples which will be given now.)

12 A I just want to know
    B Make up your mind
    C He knows already
    D The same as you've told her?

13 A I just want to know
    B Make up your mind
    C He knows already
    D The same as you've told her?

14 A He can hardly go back to bed yet!
    B So ten o'clock wasn't so late
    C Much later than usual
    D But Mary got up at eight

15 A He can hardly go back to bed yet!
    B So ten o'clock wasn't so late
    C Much later than usual
    D But Mary got up at eight

The rest of the questions are about a short story, which you will hear three times. **Do not turn over until you are told**; it is better not to look at the questions while you are hearing the story for the first time.

REMEMBER TO MARK YOUR CHOICE OF ANSWER ON THE ANSWER SHEET

№ 17406

The first task (items 1–7) of the new test was based on word recognition and comprehension of individual words (see the example below), it only required phonological and lexical knowledge, activating the first two levels in Field's

NOTE:

(i) It is better not to make a final choice of answer until you have heard the story again.

(ii) You need not answer the questions in number order.

(iii) Show your answers **on the answer sheet,** not on this paper.

16 The writer lived in
A the South of England
B the West of England
C the North East of England
D Wales

17 Jack was
A at home
B going to a wedding
C on holiday with his cousin
D in the South of England

18 Leeks are
A herbs
B wild flowers
C common vegetables
D rare hothouse plants

19 They were going to
A a museum
B someone's garden
C a wedding
D a display of vegetables

20 Leek seeds were obtained from
A the town where they lived
B abroad
C a good seed merchant
D a previous season's leek

21 The seeds were planted
A in the garden
B in a greenhouse
C inside the house
D in a trench

22 The plants were put out in
A January
B February
C September
D none of these

23 What was important to leeks was
A continuous sunshine
B occasional frost
C how they were watered
D the size of the trenches

24 The writer's father
A knew how to feed small babies
B was an expert on nutrition
C knew how to cook leeks
D knew how other people fed leeks

25 In that part of England, beer was sometimes
A given to babies
B poured on to special plants
C thrown over people in quarrels
D drunk in a competition

26 Jack
A didn't believe what they said
B believed everything was ready
C didn't know what to believe
D believed it was worth it

27 Feeding the plants was a
A matter of taste
B waste of time
C cause of heated argument
D matter of no importance

28 The prizes were
A refrigerators
B motor cars
C all kinds of things
D not worth winning

29 The writer's father had
A never won a prize
B won a prize years ago
C never tried for a prize
D won prizes several times

30 The winners really wanted
A the prize itself
B to be admired by their friends
C the pleasure of growing leeks
D the experience of entering the competition

REMEMBER TO MARK YOUR CHOICE OF ANSWER ON THE ANSWER SHEET

cognitive processing model, viz input decoding at phoneme and syllable level and lexical search. This meant that at least 23% of the test items (7/30) in the test did not go beyond word-level processing.

December 1972 LCE Listening comprehension paper

The candidate hears: dark   [5 sec pause]   dark

The candidate sees:
A   not light
B   harbour
C   animal
D water bird

Tasks 2 (items 8 11) and 3 (items 12–15), addressed another process-ing level, focusing on comprehension of individual read aloud phrases or sentences:

December 1972 LCE Listening comprehension paper

The candidate hears:

I heard her telling him   [2 sec pause]   I heard her telling him

The candidate sees:
A   heard
B   hurt
C   hot
D   hotel

The candidate hears:
It's hot all day long   [2 sec pause]   It's hot all day long

The candidate sees:
A   heard
B   hurt
C   hot
D   hotel

The ability to link the literal meaning of a sentence to the speaker's intentions (pragmatic ability) was tested to a very limited extent in the third, sentence-based task (items 12–15), whereby candidates had to resolve the intended meaning of four sentences by drawing on different stress/intonation patterns (e.g. *What shall I tell her?* with stress on *I* versus *What shall I tell her?* normal stress, see Question 12). Meaning representation beyond the sentence was not elicited by these three tasks due to the lack of context and co-text. The passage-based task (Task 4, items 16–30) is the only one which could poten-tially elicit discourse level processes that occur in normal listening compre-hension. Since the passage in the task is fairly long, it provides enough co-text for building up discourse representation and could also allow candidates to draw on pragmatic knowledge and possibly, to a limited extent, external knowledge (of the world). Even though, in theory, the task offers the possibility of more global processing – across read aloud sentences and at the level of the entire text – no questions appear to test comprehension at the level of the whole passage or across paragraphs. Judging by the December 1972 question paper (see above), mostly sentence-level comprehension is required to arrive at the correct response, and only rarely, comprehension across two or three sentences (see questions 24, 29 and 30 above). The passage-based task focused on comprehension of literal meaning and factual detail, and only occasionally required inferencing (for the latter, see questions 17, 19, 23, 29 and 30 above). Comprehension of attitude, feelings, opinion, the reasons behind someone's actions and understanding of the discourse structure were seldom required in the question papers, and none of these feature in our example test.

We next examine a number of contextual and cognitive parameters of these tasks in more detail. We start by establishing the contextual task parameters of the 1970 LCE Listening comprehension test viz task purpose, response format, channel of presentation, speaker characteristics (e.g. speech rate, accent, acquaintanceship and number of speakers), the number of times a task input is heard and linguistic demands of task input.

Purpose

Compared to dictation, this LCE test of Listening comprehension was a step forward for one major reason: it introduced *listening for information* through a *passage-based task* (task 4). Listening for information rather than writing down a text word for word was certainly a more authentic listening purpose (see Weir 2005a). Otherwise the test lacked clear specifications as to the type of listening it was aimed at. The remaining tasks could not boast of a realistic listening purpose, since they involved listening to recognise individual words and determine meaning of individually heard phrases and sentences. The lack of context and a predominance of non-realistic listening purposes make this a test with low situational and interactional authenticity.

Test format effect

While objective tests had been in use in the United States for a number of decades (see above), an interest in employing them only emerged in UCLES as late as the 1960s (see the section on Psychometrics and Cambridge in Chapter 1). The same year (1966) as Wyatt, the then UCLES Secretary, visited the College Entrance Examination Board (New York) and Educational Testing Service (ETS; Princeton) to investigate multiple-choice task types, several multiple-choice questions had been introduced to the CPE Use of English paper (see Chapter 1 and Wyatt (1966)). This was followed by the 1970 LCE Listening comprehension test which was to consist solely of multiple-choice tasks. This objective response format meant greater scoring validity and considerably more efficient post-exam processing. As far as measuring a listening (comprehension) construct was concerned, the new format meant that writing ability no longer formed part of the construct measured by the test, in stark contrast to the UCLES tradition up to that date. What the new response format introduced, however, was an element of reading comprehension, since the questions (stems) and the associated multiple-choice options were printed out for candidates to read and respond to.

Candidates attempting a multiple-choice item where the item stem and options are previewed, typically via reading, may select an answer at least in part by a process of elimination of distractors which they identify as being incorrect. In multiple-choice question comprehension tests they are indeed often trained to make this decision as part of their test preparation (e.g. Gude and Duckworth 2002). Such activities are different from the normal listening experience which requires processing the incoming text and constructing a mental representation. Verbal protocol analysis has suggested that multiple-choice questions 'promote a process of checking information against pre-established cues rather than the more ecological one of receiving, interpreting and organising it' (Field 2009:35). In other words, different cognitive processes are activated by the testing method from those employed in typical listening contexts, placing limits on the cognitive validity of the response method.

Field (2013) is particularly concerned with the effects of employing multiple-choice questions on the cognitive processing that takes place in answering the questions:

> In the multiple choice question format, an extra dimension is added by the presence of distractor options. All options need to be processed in depth well ahead of the location in the listening passage where they are likely to occur. But more than that: identifying the correct option does not necessarily entail the immediate abandonment of the others. Test takers do not simply listen out for positive evidence in an MCQ test; they also seek evidence that might disconfirm any of the options. In other words, at any given point in the test, the test taker is striving to match three or more propositions against two possible outcomes (confirmation or elimination). In cognitive terms, this is a complex operation and, importantly, one that is a by-product of the test method rather than of the construct being targeted.

The problem is then further compounded because the two information sources are in different modalities; the candidate has to read the stem and options and listen to the read aloud passage, both of which may interfere with successful performance of the task (see Hansen and Jensen 1994:250–251, Pashler and Johnston 1998). Due to the necessity of reading and listening simultaneously, the multiple-choice question format places a heavy cognitive load on candidates (Hansen and Jensen 1994). Attention becomes divided between two different tasks, with the results that working memory capacity is potentially exceeded and the candidate has to choose which of the two to focus on. Consequently, an element of construct-irrelevant variance (Messick 1989) may be introduced if the reading load in conjunction with the listening task makes excessive demands on the candidate's attention.

However, a significant virtue of multiple-choice, passage-based tasks was that they were versatile, and amenable to eliciting processing at semantic, syntactic, discourse and pragmatic levels (Nevo 1989). They could test understanding of explicit, literal content, implicit meanings, or require combining information from different parts of the texts (Buck 2001:146). Therefore, their presence in the LCE Listening test introduced a whole new range of possibilities relevant to the listening comprehension construct. Multiple-choice questions provided for the use of items that could tap into the various levels of processing identified in the listening model presented above. Field (2013) argues that multiple-choice questions:

> can focus on input decoding through options that are minimally different phonologically; on lexical search through items that target word-level information, on parsing through items that target discrete sentence-level information units; on meaning construction through items that demand inference, anaphor resolution, pragmatic interpretation etc.; and discourse representation through items that require an understanding of the main point of the recording or the goals of the speaker.

Whether and to what degree these possibilities were harnessed for the LCE listening construct is discussed below.

The multiple-choice question, however, has been shown to be guessing-prone and selection of the correct response can sometimes be made without the need to understand the passage (if the task was passage-based) (Cohen 1984, Nevo 1989). It calls on a very specific type of listening, involving the checking of information and the matching of information against input – one that cannot be said to occur very widely outside test and possibly academic contexts.

In a number of studies on reading comprehension multiple-choice question tests, test takers were shown to resort to test-taking rather than real-life reading strategies by scanning texts for key words which occurred in the stem or options (Cohen 1984, Rupp, Ferne and Choi 2006). This resulted in surface-structure reading rather than careful in-depth reading or inferencing. Something similar could happen in listening comprehension tasks when candidates are allowed to pre-view the questions and multiple-choice options and continue having access to them while listening to a passage, as was the case with LCE Listening test.

Along with these advantages and disadvantages, the multiple-choice response format introduced a potential for a higher incidence of cheating on a test. This and other aspects of test security breaches can affect both context and cognitive validity by changing the circumstances under which a test takes place, which, in turn, affects the way candidates process information in a test-taking situation (Weir 2005a:83). UCLES was aware of the potential issues, which is why a variety of requirements and controls were put in place, such as a sufficient amount of space in between each candidate ('5–6 feet between the centre of a candidate's place and that of the next candidate in any direction', Instructions to Oral Examiners (1971:2)), 'prohibition of any contact between candidates who have taken the tests and those who are about to take them at the same morning, afternoon or evening session', a warning for candidates that 'any attempt at copying or allowing copying will be reported to the Syndicate, and may lead to rejection from the examination', maintenance of 'the strictest security on all examination material' (1971) and stricter supervision (Joint Committee minutes June 1974).

In addition, different forms of the Listening question papers were provided for a single examination session when large numbers of candidates were examined in groups over four weeks (Executive Committee minutes November 1972:9). It is not clear if and how comparability of standard between alternative tests was ensured. In all probability there was simply a continuation of the long-established tradition embodied in the earlier use of multiple dictation passages on offer to the examiner at the front of the class, and a reliance on post hoc statistical procedures to iron out any discrepancies occasioned by differing passage complexity.

Channel of presentation

The channel of presentation is another important factor to consider in relation to testing the listening construct. It is a parameter of context validity which can considerably affect cognitive demands in terms of the mental processes it requires. Although reel-to-reel tapes were available in the United Kingdom at the time and although they were used in UCLES to standardise Oral Examiners (see Chapter 4), it was decided that the examiner's voice would continue to be the 'channel' of presentation in the new test of listening comprehension. The major obstacle to the inclusion of audio technology in test administration lay in widely varying conditions across centres, many of which could not support the use of recordings (Executive Committee minutes October 1967:3). In October 1970, the minutes inform that:

the issue of tape recordings in connection with this test is under active consideration, and it was agreed that it would be better if such recordings were issued for the information of examiners, particularly as pronunciation models for the section testing intonation patterns that had given some difficulty, rather than for actual use in the examinations (Executive Committee minutes, October 1970:3).

Having an examiner read out task input had three disadvantages: 1) variability in examiners' read-aloud performance, 2) familiarity of some candidates with the examiner's voice, and 3) lack of voice variety and other associated features (e.g. accent). Variability in the read-aloud performance within and across live examination sessions could have manifested itself as variations in reading rate, voice pitch and manner of reading. This variability in contextual task demands could affect cognitive processing, as already discussed in relation to dictation. However, this issue was tackled very systematically through extensive instructions provided in Instructions to Oral Examiners and in examiners' materials for live question papers. For example, examiners were required to observe specific guidelines in terms of timing repeats and pauses within the task:

> All repeats and pauses, with other notes for the examiner, are *given in italics in this booklet and are in no case to be read out*. The pauses indicated must not be reduced unless all the candidates in a group are very obviously ready for the next item. Seconds must be counted as three beats or syllables, i.e. "one thousand – two thousand" etc. Minutes are best timed with a suitable watch or clock (Oral Examiners' materials for LCE December 1972 Listening Comprehension Tests:1).

For tasks based on individual read-aloud sentences, examiners were advised on the manner of reading (e.g. 'these items must be given as connected phrases at a normal pace, not as separate words', ibid) and intonation, through the highlighting of words or phrases which are the carriers of sentence stress and/ or the points of rising intonation. For the passage-based task, an examiner was informed that the first reading should take approximately 2.5 minutes and that the passage should be read aloud to candidates three times: once probably for the general understanding of the passage, the second time – so that candidates could select their responses, and the third time – so that candidates could look through their answers and potentially revise some of the choices.

The potential problem of familiarity with the examiner's voice was resolved by the stipulation that 'candidates already known to an examiner, as pupils or privately, should not be examined, but allocated to another examiner' (Instructions to Oral Examiners 1971:3). This meant that the examiner's voice was unfamiliar to each and every candidate, which ensured fairness by making listening comprehension equally demanding in this respect for everyone. This is sound from the cognitive processing perspective since candidates at LCE level should have been able to understand an unfamiliar voice and adjust to its baseline characteristics (e.g. pitch, articulation). Given that all (even L1) listeners need some time to adjust to the baseline features of an unfamiliar voice, and that L2 learners may need more time to do so (Field 2008:160), UCLES highlighted the importance not only of making sure that the examiner can be heard clearly, but also of getting the candidates accustomed to 'the examiner's voice and manner' through 'several prelimi- nary remarks' before reading aloud begins (Instructions to Oral Examiners 1971:11). The preliminary remarks included instructions on how to fill out answer sheets and task instructions for the first section of the test.

The shortcomings of using examiners as the channel of presentation were intended to be overcome through specific guidelines on timing and manner of reading. The guidelines helped standardise test administration, and were a conscientious attempt to ensure fairness and provide a consistent realisation of test construct. However, using the voice of a single examiner has other limitations in terms of context validity. Unlike audio recordings with mul- tiple speakers, it does not allow variability in terms of accent, dialect, rate of speech and voice pitch. This makes this LCE test of Listening compre- hension less situationally authentic and less cognitively demanding because a candidate is not required to adjust to a variety of contextual demands which characterise listening situations in real life.

Number of times heard

Speech in real life is transient and normally heard once. However listening twice to verbal input in a test-taking situation can be deemed acceptable on the grounds that, in real life, listeners are advantaged because they can ask for repetition or clarification, and use the speaker's body language and contextual cues to interpret a message or fill linguistic gaps in their comprehension. Field (2013) argues that hearing input twice helps compensate for the lack of the visual and paralinguistic cues which would be available to an L2 listener in a real world context and partially offsets the increased cognitive load on the candidate occasioned by the written format. In addition, Buck (2001:171) con- cedes that playing a passage the second time 'does not appear such an unnat- ural thing to do' given that 'the testing situation is unnatural in demanding that the listener comprehend with a much greater degree of precision than is normal'.

However, listening three times to a verbal input in a test-taking situa- tion, as was the case in some LCE listening tasks (see the excerpt on page 384–385), is perhaps more difficult to defend, as it makes a task less realis- tic and less cognitively demanding. The third reading provided too many chances to fill the gaps in understanding and could also mask somebody's decoding inefficiency and slowness. This was to change in 1975 with each passage read twice only.

Linguistic demands

As far as linguistic demands are concerned, spoken language is generally characterised by more colloquial vocabulary and looser syntax and discourse structure than written language, as well as by hesitations, pauses, and false starts. Everyday spoken language also varies in terms of formality (e.g. an academic lecture vs. a conversation between students), depending on the social context. In addition, spoken language takes different forms in terms of genre (e.g. interviews, speeches, talks, discussions, announcements, conversations) and discourse type (e.g. narration, argumentation), which affects lexical, grammatical and functional features. Different genres are generally used for different communicative purposes and vary in discourse structure.

Available information on the specification of listening comprehension tests 1970–74 LCE made little reference to any of these contextual parameters. Task inputs possessed little of the variety of real-life listening due to the *size of linguistic units* listened to and the *linguistic nature* of the passages. More specifically, the first three tasks only involved listening to non-contextualised individual words (phonemic discrimination task) and individual read aloud phrases/sentences. These tasks were typical embodiments of the audio-lingual tradition in language testing (Brooks 1960, Fries 1945), which placed emphasis on discrete-point testing and knowledge about language elements, by testing one's awareness of phonemic distinctions, stress, intonation, vocabulary or grammar in isolation. This is in contrast to real life, where linguistic elements rarely appear individually and/or out of a communicative context. The fourth task was based on the comprehension of a written literary passage read out loud. Listening to written literary passages is not such a frequent occurrence in real life either.

The 1970 LCE Listening comprehension test was the first Cambridge English listening comprehension test after the Second World War and was also one of the first tests in the United Kingdom which tested listening comprehension as an individual skill. As such, and also as an objective test, it furthered the importance of testing listening comprehension in its own right and affirmed and furthered the use of objective testing in the United Kingdom context. As much as it was an indicator of change in the United Kingdom testing context, the LCE Listening remained an old-fashioned, pre-communicative test. Mostly influenced by the audio-lingual rather than communicative approach, its context validity was quite limited as it lacked situational authenticity. Limited task demands also lowered the interactional authenticity of the test. It was, overall, a more authentic activity than dictation in that in one of the tasks it required listening for information rather than listening to write down a passage word for word. However, the information listened for was predominantly factual detail, rather than the more complex attitude, opinion, implication, integration of ideas or overall discourse structure. Its literary language and an almost complete absence of features that characterise natural spoken language, make this test old-fashioned in terms of the communicative trends which were already emerging in some teaching materials by the 1970s. It was cognitively valid to an extent in that it elicited a range of cognitive processes characteristic of listening comprehension in real life, but the test was biased in favour of lower level processing skills, such as input decoding, lexical search and parsing and lacked any real attention to meaning construction and discourse level representation.

FCE and CPE Listening: 1975–1983

Further changes were to occur in 1975 following research undertaken by UCLES to reappraise the function of its examinations and to analyse the existing syllabuses, methods and procedures. The research drew on extensive consultation with experienced teachers and working parties established in UCLES (UCLES 1975). LCE became the First Certificate in English (FCE) and the former LCE Listening comprehension test was revised. A test of listening comprehension was also now introduced in CPE to replace dictation (see Appendix D for copies of both FCE and CPE 1975 Listening papers). Listening comprehension tests in both examinations were designed to be similar in nature in order to establish continuity and a 'family resemblance' between FCE and CPE as FCE came to be regarded as a stepping stone, if a distant one, on the way to CPE (see Chapter 4, CPE and FCE Interview 1975–1983).

No longer forming part of the Oral (Interview), Listening comprehension became a separate test component in its own right. However, this did not mean that Listening now wielded more power in terms of contribution to the overall examination score. While each written component (Composition, Reading comprehension and Use of English) contributed 25% to the total score, Listening and interview scores – combined – only constituted 25% of the total score. Morris (1978) criticised this imbalance across skills, arguing that it was likely to affect teaching practices, as 'any teacher preparing candidates for FCE has to concentrate on those skills awarded more marks, namely reading and writing' and that surely 'there must be many among these candidates whose needs are more centered on the development of aural/oral skills' (Morris 1978:1).

Passages continued to be read aloud by the examiner, with each passage now read twice, 'at a normal speed' (Instructions for Oral Examiners 1975: 19). Before the beginning of the test, candidates were given question papers with multiple-choice items and a separate answer sheet (see Appendix D for copies of both FCE and CPE 1975 Listening papers). They were allowed to read questions before the test began. There were 25 items on the sheet, and five passages were provided by UCLES for a single session, but only 4 passages were to be read to each group of candidates to whom the test was given. Candidates were required to answer the items associated with the passages read (20 items in total). This variation in the content of each individual test was for the purpose of providing alternative tests for security reasons. Comparability in standard between passages was clearly a consideration: 'a varying selection of four [passages] might then be used to provide a series of alternative tests which would be sufficiently comparable in standard to make statistical adjustment unnecessary' (Executive Committee minutes November 1972: 9). How this comparability was to be established is not made clear.

Compared to the LCE Listening comprehension launched in 1970, the new FCE and CPE Listening tests underwent a considerable change. Discrete-point items which tested at the level of sounds, word recognition and isolated sentence meaning were dropped. Each 1975-revision task was passage-based, which provided much more co-text for comprehension. The strong presence of co-text was a positive development since listening at this level is a normal occurrence in real life, rather than listening to individual, non-contextualised words and read-aloud sentence(s). It allowed the possibility of testing processing across sentences and integration of the information heard so far with the incoming information. However, this did not mean that the presence of co-text automatically increased the situational and interactional authenticity of the test. What matters for situational authenticity is what kind of co-text (connected speech) is listened to. What matters for interactional authenticity is whether questions actually required processing across larger chunks of co-text (i.e. several read-aloud sentences or more)?

Listening passages offered variety in terms of topic and content, but not in terms of language, style and genre: they continued to be predominantly literary narratives, being excerpts from stories or novels. Occasionally, one excerpt from a newspaper article would appear in a single session but even that would not necessarily be heard by all candidates, since there was always an extra passage to allow different passage combinations for security purposes. This meant that subject-matter, genre, (written and literary) language and style of passages were not nearly as diverse as those candidates (and the rest of the population) would normally listen to in their daily, academic, social or working lives.

In a similar vein, the style of the Listening passages was flagged as a weak spot by a consultant during the revision process:

> Mr. Swan felt that the first specimen listening comprehension passage for Proficiency was not in the characteristically spoken style appropriate for this test. It was agreed that this was a problem which would be kept in mind in the setting (Executive Committee minutes May 1973:5).

Unfortunately, the content of the available question papers reveals that this criticism was not acted upon. The issue of using literary texts was also criticised by Morris (1978), who found that Reading and Listening comprehension tasks shared the same weakness: the presence of more than one text was not exploited to test 'comprehension of different styles and subject matter' (Morris 1978:2). This was even worse in case of Listening since.

> . . . it seems quite inappropriate to test listening ability on the basis of literary texts read aloud. This use of literary texts is particularly disappointing here, given the variety of potential sources as tests of listening ability (ibid).

It could be assumed that a considerable obstacle to introducing more variety and real-life contextual features into listening passages was the fact that they were still read out loud by a single examiner. This severely limited the potential for introducing spoken language involving interaction between two or more speakers and a more diverse content into the test. All this indicates that listening comprehension tasks in Cambridge English examinations still could not be classed as communicative in terms of Buck's maxims (see page 362 above and Buck 2001:83–93).

Tasks still lacked an introductory contextualisation of the passage to be heard, such as information on what the passage was going to be about and/or who the characters were (see the June 1975 FCE and CPE papers in Appendix D). This would have helped to activate schematic information in advance of listening. Enabling candidates to activate schemas is important because it influences the way they interact with the task.

Allowing a preview of questions before hearing a passage is normally deemed necessary in selected response comprehension tasks, such as multiple-choice. The main arguments usually given for pre-set questions are: a) providing a set of goals to enable focused listening b) avoiding reliance on memory and favoring those possessing strong powers of recall. Given that such tasks impose the test designers' view of what information is important/ should be listened for, not previewing questions may lead to getting an incorrect response due to not paying attention to a particular piece of information while listening, rather than lack of comprehension. Moreover, 'if we ask test-takers to listen to a text with no specified purpose, and after listening give them questions that require understanding of anything and everything, we are asking them to do something very unnatural' (Buck 2001:137). In a similar vein, Weir (2005a:58) argues that previewing questions provides a clearer purpose which in turn facilitates goal-setting (e.g. deciding on the listening strategies and 'assessing one's available internal and external resources and the constraints of the situation before engaging in the task' (Buck 2001:104)) and monitoring one's comprehension.

Set against this Field (2013) argues that:

... the availability of question items in advance of listening provides the test taker with a great deal of information about the recording to be heard which would not normally be available in a non-test context. This is particularly of concern in a test of listening because the information is expressed in a different modality from the one that is the target of the assessment ... [processing is] also likely to embrace test-wise strategies which exploit the weakness of the format: they include predicting the content of the recording or seeking out what appear to be key words from the test items. Such strategies pose a serious challenge to cognitive validity, since they would not be available in a comparable real-world listening event.

Sherman (1997:185) sums up the paradox succinctly:

... question preview may affect comprehension positively by focusing the attention or supplying information about the text, or negatively by interfering with subjective comprehension processes, increasing the burden on the attention or imposing shallower processing.

Even though FCE and CPE Listening tasks were still lacking in many communicative features, they were at least in some respects gradually gaining more of a communicative character. This is discussed below against the background of similarities and differences in contextual and cognitive task demands in these two tests.

FCE and CPE Listening tests differed in contextual terms, in the complexity of language employed in the passages at each level. CPE passages were lexically more complex and sophisticated, with the caveat that highly technical words were not the focus of items and passages did not contain specialist vocabulary nor extreme dialect or colloquialism 'unless the meaning can be clearly deduced from the context' (Changes of Syllabus in 1975:12). FCE was somewhat more restricted in terms of vocabulary, to accommodate the lower proficiency levels of FCE candidates. West's General Service List (1953) was used as a general guide, and 'current research in the field of word and structure frequency counts' was also taken into account in the development of FCE Listening (Changes of Syllabus in 1975:10). Even though West's General Service List provided a means of specifying and standardising lexical difficulty across passages, it was also quite limiting. As Morris (1978:1) pointed out:

Although published in 1953, the list is based on the Thorndike-Lorge count carried out in the 1930s. This means that the list is out-of-date, and does not contain words, such as television, which are now of high frequency. It is also a short list, being only 3500 words long, so that only a limited number of vocabulary items are available for inclusion ...

In both tests, task and item focus shifted from sound/word recognition and comprehension of single sentences in the 1970 LCE and from the sound/word recognition and awareness of phoneme-grapheme correspondences of the CPE dictation to comprehension of factual detail (see (1) below) and – to a certain extent – opinion, attitude, intention, mood, reason or cause behind somebody's actions (see (2) below).

FCE December 1977 Listening comprehension question paper

(1) Agreement to pay for the new bus service has been obtained from
    A the school's headmaster
    B the education department
    C̲ the bus company
    D the parents

(2) Black Peter finally admitted that the boxes contained gold because
    A̲ he was so satisfied with what he had done
    B he had decided to trust Martin
    C he saw that he could no longer keep it a secret
    D he knew that Martin could not escape

However, the understanding of factual detail was still the main focus (see Table 5.2 below). The figures in the following Tables were arrived at via the pooled subjective agreement of a group of testing specialists in Research and Validation Cambridge ESOL.

Table 5.2 Item focus in CPE and FCE Listening question papers (1975/1977)

Exam Item focus	CPE 1975	CPE 1977	FCE 1975	FCE 1977
Factual detail	18	15	17	16
Opinion, attitude, feeling/mood	2	4	3	3
Reason/cause	5	1	5	1
Total items	25	20	25	20

FCE and CPE Listening comprehension tests during this period were largely similar in terms of item focus.

From the perspective of cognitive demands, the 1975 FCE and CPE Listening tests (see Appendix D for copies of both) were a clear change from the 1970 LCE with its discrete-point items in the audio-lingual tradition, which had focused solely on sound, word recognition and read aloud sentence meaning. These were now gone and replaced by passage-based comprehension tasks. As we noted above, listening to individual words or read-aloud sentences restricts the measurement to a very limited number of cognitive processes due to the lack of co-text and context. In contrast, passage-based tasks involve listening to a continuous speech stream and provide enough co-text and some context for comprehension, thus offering the potential of mirroring a broader range of the cognitive processes underlying listening comprehension that we identified earlier. So, with the 1975 revision, cognitive processes, such as sound and word recognition, began taking place in a more natural and authentic manner as they became part of the entire range of mental processes which normally *co-occur* in listening activities in real life, rather than appearing in isolation.

A wider range of cognitive processes broadened the listening construct being measured and were required in more than one task, in contrast to 1970 LCE. Passage-based tasks facilitated the enrichment of literal meaning through encouraging the building of a meaning representation of the text (inferencing that draws on pragmatic knowledge to interpret a character's/ author's intention, mood or attitude) and even, potentially, drawing on external knowledge of the world, speaker or situation.

However, as in the 1970 LCE Listening test, the 1975 Listening comprehension tests contained almost no items testing comprehension of gist, the main message or wider meaning. Processing at the level of a read-aloud sentence or sometimes across two, was mostly enough to enable a selection of the correct response in FCE and CPE Listening tests, and only occasionally did processing have to occur across 3 or 4 sentences (see Table 5.3). In the light of the discussion above in the section on Cognitive validity in L2 listening, this does not seem to be a satisfactory state of affairs at proficiency levels as high as FCE and CPE, a problem that continues to this day. Since decoding processes in higher-proficiency learners are fairly or fully automaticised, there is enough working memory capacity for using co-text for meaning building. The ability to extract information from co-text increases at higher proficiency levels and therefore can increasingly be relied upon.

Table 5.3 Amount of co-text that needs to be processed to answer CPE and FCE Listening comprehension questions

	CPE June 1975	CPE June 1977	FCE June 1975	FCE Dec 1977
	Number of items		Number of items	
Processing at sentence level	11	16	21	17
Processing across 2 or 3 sentences	14	4	4	3
Total	25	20	25	20

The table above also shows that there was sometimes a difference between cognitive demands in CPE and FCE listening tasks. CPE tasks would require processing across two or more read-aloud sentences much more frequently than in FCE, but that difference does not seem to have been consistently realised across test forms.

Additionally sentences in CPE passages were, on average, longer than in FCE (see Table 5.4 below). Longer clauses and more complex clauses impose greater demands during parsing (see Appendix B).

Table 5.4 Average read-aloud sentence length (words) in FCE and CPE passages

	CPE 1975	CPE 1977	FCE 1975	FCE Dec 1977
Average sentence length (words)	17.91	24.23	15.13	16.04

Even though the number of items requiring inferencing skills (the ability to understand implication) is overall greater in the two CPE test versions examined than in FCE, there is an evident variability in the number of such items across test versions of an examination (see the Table below).

Table 5.5 Inferencing in FCE and CPE tests

	CPE 1975	CPE 1977	FCE 1975	FCE 1977
Inferencing (no of items)	5/25	5/20	4/25	1/20

Overall, there was a degree of similarity in contextual and cognitive task demands within and across listening comprehension tests at the two levels. All tasks had a similar task focus, language, style and genre, employed multiple-choice questions, processing was at the level of a sentence or two rather than larger chunks of a listening passage, and texts were read out aloud by a single examiner.

In sum, the revised Listening comprehension tests which materialised in FCE and CPE in 1975 were a small step forward towards a more communicative understanding and operationalisation of the listening construct. Discrete-point testing and task focus on processing sounds, words and read-aloud sentences in isolation were abandoned. Being passage-based, the new tasks provided much more co-text and some context for comprehension, which permitted simultaneous activation of a range of cognitive processes across items and in a number of cases involved some pragmatic and world knowledge. This approximated more closely to the cognitive processing underlying real-life listening comprehension and increased the cognitive validity of the tests. However, the revised tests were not without shortcomings. Even though cognitive validity improved in some ways, it was lacking in some others. An introductory contextualisation of the passage to be heard, necessary for forming a listening purpose and goal-setting, was still missing, but candidates were allowed to preview and have access to questions throughout the test. Although reading aloud was likely to be at a normal speaking rate it was not 'authentic' in that intonation was more marked, rhythm was more regular and (above all) the reader marked punctuation.

Similar cognitive and contextual demands across all the tasks of a single examination reduced the generalisability of inferences that could be made on a candidate's ability to participate in listening tasks in real life and the use of a multiple-choice question format introduced a danger of test method effect on candidate performance. Another disadvantage, from the perspective of a communicative approach to language testing, was that comprehension of literary and written, rather than spoken, language was still required. As such, 1975 FCE and CPE Listening tests remained firmly rooted in the past. More authentic passages (e.g. excerpts from radio programmes or simulations of conversations between friends or colleagues) with their diverse contextual and cognitive demands were only to appear later, facilitated by the use of audio technology in test administration. The main, and apparently, the only differences between CPE and FCE Listening lay in the contextual parameters of the linguistic complexity of passages and the sentence/utterance length, which served to make cognitive processing more demanding at the CPE level.

The 1984 revisions to FCE and CPE Listening

The 1984 examination revisions were preceded by consultation with exam-ination centres (teachers and administrators) in 1980–81. A general desire was expressed for examinations which were not so literary. It was felt that oral and aural test materials in particular should be based on 'current spoken English' (Executive Committee minutes November 1980:4). This was in line with a general desire expressed by the centres to make both FCE and CPE more communicative in nature, by aligning them more closely to commu-nicative approaches in teaching and they were perhaps also mindful of the 'communicatively authentic' RSA CUEFL listening texts launched in 1981 (Hawkey 2004:153–159). The consultations resulted in a radical revision of the FCE and CPE Listening comprehension tests (see Table 5.6 below and Appendix D for examples of paper post 1984 revision).

The revised tests sought to achieve a more communicative approach, which drew on real life materials to create listening passages. This develop-ment was facilitated through the use of audio recordings, which were now employed in test administration for the very first time. The range of materials and genres of listening passages indeed broadened, as evidenced in Table 5.6.

Tasks for the most part retained their objective character largely for the benefits this brought in terms of practicality and reliability, but task types were diversified (see Table 5.6 below). This was a positive development because it reduced the potential for test-method effect on candidate perfor-mance. Moreover, some new task types, such as short answer questions and

Table 5.6 1984 FCE and CPE Listening comprehension

1984 FCE and CPE Listening comprehension	
Test parts/listening passages	3 or 4
Number of items	25–30
Timing (min.)	30–40
Marks	20/180
Item weighting	None
Task types	4-option MC, re-ordering, gap-filling, sentence completion, note-taking, short-answer questions, true/false, labelling
Task input	Recorded task instructions, recorded listening passages (a monologue or conversation involving 2 to 4 people) and printed questions; tables and diagrams in CPE tasks, or tables and visuals (e.g. drawings of objects) in FCE tasks
Genre of listening passages	Informal conversations, lectures, talks, public address, radio interviews, radio-type sequences of news of features, announcements, etc.
Number of times passages heard	Twice

note-taking, on the surface appeared to be realistic activities for testing listening comprehension, particularly in an academic context.

Ever since the 1984 revision, one or more constructed response tasks have been part of all Cambridge ESOL Main Suite Listening papers. For these, the candidate completes gaps in sentences or notes, using a word or short phrase from the text, while listening to the recording (see Boroughs 2003 for full details of these and Appendix D; further examples are available in Buck 2001:227–229). Elliott and Wilson (2013) describe how constructed response tasks may involve the completion of notes, sentences, forms, tables, or a summary. They can also involve the labelling of diagrams, maps or plans. However, in Cambridge Main Suite Listening examinations only the first three types are used. Note completion is also a common task in IELTS Listening, particularly in Section 4, where the focus is on testing listening skills in an academic context, and the input is part of a lecture. Here the enforcement of a stated word limit helps to constrain keys.

The specification of a word limit, and how long that word limit should be, is an important consideration. Longer word limits allow a greater variety of possible correct answers, which can often result in unwieldy keys that cause practical problems in marking, and potentially lead to inconsistent marking, particularly if a variety of possible spellings are accepted. Furthermore, the more candidates have to write, the greater the effect of the writing trait on the item. A major disadvantage of constructed response formats is that the element of writing they introduce presents a risk of construct-irrelevant variance. This is most prominently manifested in the area of spelling, and the question of what, if any, incorrect spellings to accept in candidates' answers (see Elliott and Wilson (2013) for an extended discussion of how the problem of spelling in completion items is handled in Cambridge ESOL). The danger of construct-irrelevant variance due to the writing element of constructed response formats is also present at a cognitive level, since writing involves different cognitive processes, which are an additional processing burden on top of the listening load and the reading load present in all items. Therefore, such items suffer from an even greater divided attention situation.

It is also important to point out that the candidate is not involved in constructing their own notes, i.e. constructing their own discourse representation, but in completing an outline of the text in note form by identifying key points from the text. The notes may have subheadings and bullet points to indicate the number and relationship of key ideas, and some key information may already be provided. So while both note completion and sentence completion tasks test the ability to identify and interpret micro propositions, neither type of constructed response tests understanding of the structure of the text as a whole. Because a discourse structure was often provided in advance by the written framework, candidates were exempted from certain meaning-building operations at the discourse level, raising questions about cognitive validity in relation to real-life lecture listening.

Field (2009) further cautions that when an outline framework provided for a note-taking task is detailed, the task taps heavily into the reading skill both before and during the listening activity. Although the gap filling in a set of simulated notes appears to replicate a real-life process, the notes are not written by the listeners themselves and therefore have to be read as new text.

Compared to multiple-choice question and other selected response formats, they have the advantage that they do not supply the candidate with options, and hence do not suffer from this particular complication for the cognitive processes involved – the candidate has to construct meaning in a manner closer to real-life listening, rather than seek evidence to confirm or reject hypotheses. Furthermore, the guessing factor present in selected response formats is greatly reduced, although contextual and linguistic cues such as parts of collocations can sometimes make guessing possible (Field 2009). Various studies (e.g. Brindley and Slatyer 2002, Buck and Tatsuoka 1998) have indeed pointed to the impact of lexical overlap on the difficulty of constructed response tasks. If a candidate can 'lift' the correct answer without processing the surrounding text, this tells us only that they can identify word boundaries and recognise individual words, but not that they can understand the speaker's meaning.

Although these formats usually required limited writing (e.g. a word, a phrase) in an attempt to minimise the effect of this modality on the measurement of listening, Field (2013) concludes:

> This is therefore is a task which divides the test taker's attention (Paschler & Johnston, 1998) between three types of processing: listening, reading and writing. It is consequently very cognitively demanding – much more so than most real-life listening events . . .

The requirement to elicit some kind of 'product' in a listening test had led Brindley (1998) to agree with Buck (1990) and Boyle and Suen (1994) that 'it is extremely difficult – some would say impossible – to construct a "pure" test of listening uncontaminated by some other skill'.

The contribution of the Listening comprehension score to the overall examination score remained the same: Listening comprehension still carried the smallest number of marks (20/180 or c.11%), while all other papers contributed 40/180 (c.22%) marks each. Even though the contribution of Listening and Speaking combined has increased to one third of the total score (60/180), not much had changed for Listening. No argument is provided in the available documentation as to why Listening was not on a par with the rest of test components in this respect. It perhaps testifies to the relatively inferior status of this skill we noted in our earlier survey of the place of listening in testing in the 20th century.

It is evident that a number of the contextual task features had changed significantly. The use of semi-authentic material and recordings greatly increased the potential for situational authenticity in the tests. It meant that spoken language, which exhibited the features that distinguish it from written prose could be used in tests, e.g. grammatically incomplete utterances and colloquial vocabulary (e.g. Quite groggy but . . .), contractions (e.g. it's), shortening (e.g. 'cos), pausing/pause fillers and hesitations (e.g. um, er, erm), as illustrated in the excerpts from sample paper tapescripts below:

Interviewer:	. . . Bleary-eyed and still in her dressing gown Margaret Barry hasn't yet had time for a cup of tea so how is she feeling?
Margaret Barry:	Quite groggy but the house is changing so fast it's almost like watching a film.
Interviewer:	Are you worried about all your things, 'cos all your furniture's being used?
Margaret Barry:	I am very worried about it by they all seem to know what they're doing.

(CPE Handbook for Teachers 1995:68)

. . . The motion isn't nonsense – er, there are real problems that modern agriculture must address but if balance and perspective have anything to do with this argument, er, then it's as near nonsense as it could be without actually being nonsense. Um, just think, please, what you have had for breakfast today. Er, a wide variety of cereals, milk and eggs, erm, wide variety of cheeses, tea, coffee, er, even steak and fried potato . . . (CPE Examination Handbook for Teachers 1998:5).

However, the caveat that less edited authentic material 'may be expected' at CPE rather than FCE level (Changes of Syllabus 1984:56) was a clear warning that especially at the lower level material might be edited rather than purely authentic. The additional fact that natural language was then normally rerecorded was also to prove problematic for the cognitive validity of the measurement of the listening construct.

Candidates were required to listen to different voices (as many as four in some passages) with varying pitch and rate of delivery, a range of accents and also with background noise, which all added to cognitive demands. As stated in the 1995 CPE Handbook (UCLES 1995:59): 'the texts are spoken in standard English, in a range of accents, at a rate of delivery appropriate to the situation'. Situational authenticity obviously assumed an important role in these Cambridge English Listening comprehension tests, utilising a large variety of spoken sources for examination material, which now offered a range of topics, discourse types and genres of listening passages as well as variations on the cline of formality-informality. This wealth of material, contextual demands and a wider sampling of listening situations considerably increased the generalisability of test scores: more confidence could now be placed in the test score as an indication that a candidate could indeed perform a range of listening tasks in real life.

Another important improvement in terms of context validity was task contextualisation. Not only was each listening situation in the listening passages now a part of a realistic context, but candidates were also given a brief introductory contextualisation of the passage, e.g. 'You will hear an interview with a woman who allowed her house to be used as the location for a film' (CPE Handbook 1995:67). This served to enable candidates to activate schemata in advance of listening. It was also thought to compensate for the lack of visual information when audio recordings were used. It mirrored to an extent, real-life listening situations where listeners normally know, either vaguely or more precisely, what the forthcoming talk or conversation is going to be about, and listen with some (general or specific) pre-determined purpose in mind. Candidates were also given time (about 30 seconds) to read the questions before hearing the related passage; a practice continued from the 1975 revision.

The new channel of information, cassette recordings, was beneficial for two reasons. It facilitated the use of 'semi-authentic' and diverse material, and also helped achieve a greater level of standardisation in test administration and in the phonetic input. Nevertheless, in the consultation stage, examination centres were not enthusiastic about using recorded listening material due to potential 'technical troubles, nervousness, etc.' (Executive Committee minutes November 1980). Despite that, and after careful consideration, the Executive Committee agreed that:

> the use of recorded material for listening comprehension will become standard as part of the proposed changes, with printed questions . . . The change to recordings will bring advantages in terms of realism and relevance sufficient to outweigh technical difficulties (Executive Committee minutes May 1981:2).

However, given that most of the input was re-recorded it suffered from the disadvantage we noted above in so far as it differed from recordings made for real life transactional and interactional spoken language.

Since audio recordings in a test-taking situation were a novelty for examination centres, UCLES prepared informational and instructional material for supervisors and test administrators with 'careful instructions on conditions for giving the test in respect of equipment, size of rooms, and security' (Executive Committee minutes November 1981:4).

Yet another positive change was the broadening of task/item focus. In 1970 LCE and 1975 CPE and LCE Listening comprehension tests, task and item focus was predominantly on factual detail, and only occasionally on other, more abstract, information, such as attitude, opinion, reason or cause. There were almost no items which required understanding of the main points of a passage. As the 1980–81 consultations with centres revealed that 'wide uncertainty' was felt 'about ambiguous or trivial test items' (Executive Committee minutes November 1980), UCLES decided to concentrate 'on gist testing instead of vocabulary-based comprehension testing' (1980). This was indeed acted upon, and, the task focuses became more diverse, reducing predominant reliance on understanding factual detail. Task focuses included:

- understanding the gist of a spoken text and its overall function and message
- following significant points, even though a few words may be unknown
- selecting specific information from a spoken text
- recognising tone and attitude when clearly expressed
- interpreting attitude and emotion
- inferring underlying meaning
- understanding points of detail in a spoken text.

However, there was still wide variability in different forms of the test and some were more like the tests of 1975 predominantly relying on comprehension of factual detail, and some more like 1984 exhibiting a more balanced diversity in task focuses (see Table 5.7). This variability in task/item focus could have been due to a non-fixed test format, and more specifically, due to different task types in different test forms, which could make it more challenging to keep demands similar. In FCE, the predominant task focus on factual detail was retained, but there was room for a number of items testing comprehension of more abstract information such as emotion, attitude, opinion, reason or cause and occasionally – gist of the entire passage.

Table 5.7 Item focus in post-1984 revision CPE and FCE Listening comprehension tests

Item focus	1995 sample CPE Listening comprehension test	1998 sample CPE Listening comprehension test	1990 FCE question paper	1993 FCE question paper
		Number of items (%)		
Gist	–	1 (4%)	–	1 (4%)
Factual detail	22 (88%)	8 (31%)	23 (69%)	20 (77%)
Emotion/attitude/ opinion/suggestion	3 (12%)	14 (54%)	10 (31%)	4 (15%)
Reason/cause	–	3 (12%)	–	1 (4%)
Total items	25 (100%)	26 (100%)	33 (100%)	26 (100%)

(As above, these analyses were carried out by a focus group of testing experts in Research and Validation on CPE sample tests which were provided in 1995 and 1998 CPE Handbooks, as well as 1990 and 1993 FCE question papers.)

FCE items were designed to test 'basic absorption of information, and ability to identify objects referred to', while the Proficiency items were based on 'a fuller understanding of processes and attitudes described or expressed in the text'. Moreover, at CPE level use could be made of 'standard situations with more emotive and open-ended elements' (Changes of Syllabus 1984: 56). In other words, the information to be processed in FCE was generally more concrete than in CPE.

Post-1984-revision listening comprehension tests were based on non-literary listening passages. In terms of cognitive validity, passage-based listening meant that there was enough co-text for activating higher-level cognitive processes, such as inferencing and building discourse representation of the text listened to. In contrast to 1975 listening comprehension tests, post-1984 test passages possessed a higher degree of situational authenticity, with varied speakers and realistic situations. With such passages and a task focus on interpreting and recognising tone, attitude, intention, and opinion, the revised tests encouraged drawing on pragmatic knowledge or external knowledge of the world, speaker and situation perhaps even more so than 1975 tests.

Inferencing, one of the higher-level cognitive processes, was required in both CPE and FCE Listening tests (see Table 5.8).

Table 5.8 Inferencing in CPE and FCE Listening comprehension tests

	1995 CPE	1998 CPE	1990 FCE	1993 FCE
Inference (number of items and %)	3/25 (12%)	7/26 (27%)	6/33 (18%)	3/26 (12%)

There was an increase in cognitive load in terms of the amount of co-text that needed to be processed in order to answer a question correctly. The previous discussion on 1970 and 1975 Listening comprehension tests (FCE and CPE) revealed that, to find the correct answer to an item, candidates did not need to process much information: processing at a read-aloud sentence level was mostly sufficient, and only occasionally, processing at the level of two or three sentences in a row was necessary. After the 1984 revisions more items required processing longer chunks of a listening passage (4 utterances and above) to ensure the selection of a correct response (see Table 5.9 below).

Table 5.9 Amount of co-text that needs to be processed to answer CPE and FCE Listening comprehension questions

	1995 CPE	1998 CPE	1990 FCE	1993 FCE
Level of processing	Number of items (%)			
Processing at an utterance level	9 (36%)	6 (23%)	12 (36%)	9 (35%)
Processing across 2 or 3 utterances	13 (52%)	9 (35%)	15 (45%)	12 (46%)
Processing across 4 or more utterances	3 (12%)	10 (38%)	5 (15%)	4 (15%)
Processing across larger chunks of discourse (e.g. 14 utterances)	–	1 (4%)	1 (3%)	1 (4%)
Total items	25 (100%)	26 (100%)	33 (100%)	26 (100%)

The quantity of utterances to be processed in order to answer a question varied by task type and item focus. For example, sentence completion and short-answer question tasks used in FCE and CPE Listening comprehension tests required localised processing of the passage listened to, just at the level of an utterance or two per item (see Appendix D, *CPE Listening comprehension test: post 1984 revision CPE Handbook 1998*, e.g. questions 7, 10, 11, 12, 13 and 15). However, tasks which are based on a conversation between two or more participants, and associated multiple-choice items focusing on gist, opinion, intention, inference, as well as multiple-matching tasks which asked candidates to distinguish between the opinions of two or more participants in a conversation, required processing at more global levels: across four, and quite often, even more utterances (see Appendix D, *CPE Listening comprehension test: post 1984 revision CPE Handbook 1998*, e.g. questions 2, 3, 4, 5, 19, 20 and 23). For example, in order to decide whether Anne or Dave, or both, are of the opinion that 'The father should have been portrayed as a nastier character' (Question 23), a candidate needs to construct an ongoing discourse representation which has to be extended and carried forward throughout the dialogue:

Anne:	Well I don't know about her but . . . well . . . her husband was OK really. That's it – he should have been more – well . . . you know.
Dave:	Mmmm . . .?
Anne:	Well, chauvinistic . . . or just generally unlikeable.
Dave:	It's more acceptable then is it if she leaves him?
Anne:	Oh, you know what I mean . . .
Dave:	Well he was pretty cruel to her when he found out that she hadn't obeyed him . . . he locked her in that dreadful room.
Anne:	Yes, but it's like the daughter – he behaved sort of OK most of the time – and he was quite a nice-looking person – I mean he wasn't ugly and he didn't shout or anything – but then suddenly he became almost irrational . . . he over-reacted . . . or that was how it seemed to me anyway . . .

(CPE Listening tapescript, CPE Handbook 1998: 47)

The changes in the amount of discourse to be processed were a natural result of the use of more natural spoken language and conversation. Spoken language, especially when informal, is by its very nature more redundant than written literary prose and sometimes less immediately precise, as it is interspersed with pauses, hesitations, false starts and unfinished utterances which are finished at a somewhat later stage. This particularly applies to conversation, which is co-constructed (as discussed in Chapter 4), since the message or messages are built through interconnected exchanges among participants. Most of these features can indeed be found in the excerpt presented above. All these factors made processing more global by requiring a candidate to understand the information across quite a few utterances to answer a single question correctly.

Another factor which increased cognitive demands, as well as enhancing situational authenticity, was the number of speakers in a single test task and across tasks. Candidates were now required to process more than one voice, which involved not only adjusting to varied physiological characteristics, pitch, rate and accent of each voice but also processing more than one opinion/ attitude in a single task. Every test had a task with two or more speakers/inter-actants, while the remaining tasks in a test would involve one speaker each.

The 1984 revision was a turning point in the evolution of testing the listening comprehension construct in Cambridge English examinations. Decisively parting with the literary tradition, the new CPE and FCE Listening passages and tasks were embedded in a real-life context, and characterised by realistic situations, interactions and spoken language. Listening passages were given an introductory contextualisation for the first time, which allowed candidates to activate appropriate schemata in advance of listening, and thereby approximate what listeners do in real life. Previewing questions before listening to a passage gave candidates specific listening purposes. Candidates were required to process more voices at the same time; interpret opinion, attitude and feelings much more often than was previously the case; distinguish between opinions and attitudes of different speakers, and also process information across larger parts of discourse in order to get a correct answer. The tests undoubtedly became more communicative in nature. Finally, cassette recordings were used to administer listening passages for the first time in the history of UCLES EFL examinations thus improving the scoring validity of the tests as well.

CAE (1991–)

The newly introduced Certificate of Advance English (CAE) was a strong indication that 'the main suite of Cambridge English examinations had taken more account of the assessment of communicative competence' (Revised FCE Internal Specifications 1994:6), a process which had started with the 1984 revisions of FCE and CPE. CAE was introduced in 1991 as the examination which offered 'a high-level final qualification in the language to those wishing to use English in their jobs' and encouraged development of the skills required by students progressing towards CPE (CAE Specifications 1991:1). The intended population was everyone from adolescents to young professionals (see Appendix D for the CAE Listening comprehension test from the 1998 CAE Handbook and Appendix A for the CAE Listening comprehension test 1991).

With the change to a more balanced mark allocation, listening comprehension was finally accorded the same importance as the rest of the skills (Reading, Writing and Speaking) in a test targeted at a higher proficiency level. Each CAE test component now contributed equally (25%) to the total available mark (200). The test lasts 45 minutes and consists of 32–40 items and four tasks (or test parts). Each passage is heard twice, apart from the Part 2 passage which is heard once only.

The 'authentic' nature of the test and tasks are emphasised throughout the specifications, which is not surprising in view of 1984 FCE and CPE revisions and the general popularity of the communicative approach to language teaching. However, much of the 'authentic' material used, as with FCE and CPE, was not taken direct from source but was re-recorded (see Field (2008) and Weir and Milanovic (2003: Chapter 7)).There were actually four types of origin for the material: scripted, re-recorded, improvised and authentic. Field concluded that they were phonologically distinctive – a view that was supported when, in informal tests, he found that teachers could easily distinguish between them.

Listening passages adapted from authentic sources were recorded in a studio (CAE Handbook 2001), albeit with the appropriateness of genre for the intended candidature in mind. They were as varied as the following:

announcements, broadcasts, telephone messages, speeches, talks, lectures, interviews, meetings, etc.. In addition, 'each text is accompanied by a task that aims to test the communicative point of what is said' (CAE Handbook 2001:40). The expressed aim was to use multiple voices across multiple snippets to broaden the range of listening experiences presented to fairly high-level candidates. The communicative points throughout all four tasks can be specific information, main ideas and gist. Comprehension of concrete information and explicitly stated opinions is reserved for the first two tasks, while understanding attitude and opinion is additionally required in the third task. Task focus becomes the most challenging in the final task which requires identification of five speakers and topics, interpretation of context and the purpose of each passage, recognising attitude, gist and main points (see below for further detail and Appendices A and D).

So far, the contextual features seem to be a natural continuation of what was started with FCE, and CPE revisions in the 1980s. However, two important novelties were introduced through the CAE test of Listening comprehension. The two innovations were: 1) a more fixed and standardised test format and 2) a new, multiple-matching task type which introduced a balance into the test in terms of task focuses and the required listening skills. Both of these affected contextual and cognitive task demands, and thereby changed and improved the listening test construct. They are discussed below, in turn.

CAE was not at first a test with a fully fixed format, as task types and the number of items could vary somewhat across test forms (e.g. possible task types in Part 3 were sentence completion and multiple-choice). However, a higher degree of standardisation was introduced by ensuring that each test part had pre-determined criteria for task input in terms of:

- the number of speakers (a monologue in Parts 1 and 2, a dialogue in Part 3 and five short themed monologues by different speakers in Part 4)
- duration of a passage (~ 2 minutes in Parts 1 and 2, ~ 4 minutes in Part 3 and 10–30 seconds per monologue in Part 4).

This was a positive development as it facilitated the standardisation of a number of contextual parameters, thus contributing to a more consistent operationalisation of test construct across test forms and increased fairness to candidates.

With the intention of helping guard against format effect, further testing methods were developed for used in comprehension. For the first time in CAE 1991 a different type of objective format, multiple matching (MM), was introduced into Cambridge English examinations in both the Reading and Listening papers (see Chapter 2 for discussion of the format in relation to reading). Elliott and Wilson (2013) report that for texts which are more discursive in nature multiple matching is likely to be used in Cambridge English examinations. While these task types are a less direct reflection of a listener's response to a listening text than a constructed response such as note taking, they are considered by Cambridge to be more effective in testing a global understanding of extended texts (see Hawkey (2009: 391) for examples of full tasks and Appendices A and D).

A real benefit of this technique was that it facilitated the assessment of comprehension beyond the level of the single utterance, potentially up to the overall discourse representation level. It helped elicit a different range of listening skills which had been either neglected or not consistently required up until then. We noted above that one of the intentions behind the 1984 revision of CPE and FCE Listening was to broaden task focus and include items which test comprehension of gist or main points. Comprehension of gist and main points were indeed a part of test specifications (e.g. 1995 CPE Handbook), but the number of items testing them were fairly negligible. CAE Listening comprehension was evidently quite different, in that quite a few items tested comprehension of gist (see Table 5.10). Moreover, comprehending factual information no longer predominated over other listening processes, as had been the case so far. This is largely thanks to the multiple-matching (Section D) task which requires listening to five theme-related monologues and doing two tasks at the same time: a) identifying the speakers' roles/professions (or rather: differentiating between the speakers), and b) identifying the speakers' intentions/attitudes or topics of their monologues.

Table 5.10 Item focus in CAE Listening tasks (focus group analysis performed on sample tests in 1991 and 1998 CAE Handbooks)

Item focus	1991	1998
Gist or main point	11 (34%)	10 (29%)
Factual detail	15 (47%)	12 (34%)
Attitude/opinion/intention	6 (19%)	13 (37%)
Total	32 (100%)	35 (100%)

In the example below, one out of five theme-related extracts (monologues) is provided as an illustration:

> You need the freshest apples, mind. You cut them up and put in a few sultanas – they've got some good ones down at the market, they sell them loose. You could always pop in and borrow from me if you haven't time to get out. Then you add in the lemon juice – watch out there's no pips in it and sprinkle on a bit more of the sugar. Leave it to stand for a good bit, I should . . . (CAE Handbook 1991:87)

Candidates are required to identify the speakers of the extract by matching the extracts as they hear them with the professional or other roles listed in the question paper (dietary expert, food manufacturer, chef, customer in a restaurant, parent, neighbour, restaurant critic and guest at dinner) and also to match each extract with the intention behind each speaker's comment (giving advice on cooking, warning, criticising, recommending types of food, praising, trying to persuade, expressing disgust and giving advice on slimming). What is positive about this method is that it challenges the test taker to employ a range of attentional levels in processing the recording.

As far as cognitive demands are concerned, the stronger focus on testing the comprehension of gist or main points also meant that the amount of co-text that needed to be processed to arrive at a correct answer increased considerably. This made the test more cognitively challenging, and appropriate for candidates who were expected to use their listening skills in an academic or work environment.

Compared to standard multiple-choice questions, multiple matching has the advantage that the probability of guessing the correct answer to an item is reduced by the increased number of options (Brown and Hudson 1998). Additionally, the format is more compact in terms of space on the page and has a correspondingly lower reading load (Brindley 1998). This partially reduces the cognitive load arising from coping with dual channels (Wicker 1984) since candidates do not need to read a new set of options for each item thus partially avoiding the propositional overload of multiple-choice questions.

By convention in most listening tests, test items follow the order of the recording. In real life, we might be seeking answers to questions that might occur at any point in the recording and in any order. Multiple matching is not constrained, like multiple-choice questions, or gap filling (see below), to follow the order in which information units are heard. Field (2013) points out that it can test comprehension across a range of levels of detail, from local information to general topic to interpretation of speaker intent, in a way that gap filling does not.

In cases where each option can only be chosen once, however, a degree of interdependence between items is introduced, since incorrectly choosing the key for another item naturally has an effect when the candidate attempts the second item. Introducing distractors to this type of multiple-matching task reduces this effect (Alderson, Clapham and Wall 1995), although it cannot be eliminated entirely.

Elliott and Wilson (2013:67) sound a note of caution:

> . . . multiple matching tasks are often used to test elements of global listening such as identifying main ideas, identifying contexts and identifying attitudes. At C1 level, such global multiple matching tasks (with two tasks to be completed over two hearings of the text) have been shown to work consistently well in terms of an appropriate level of difficulty and

a high level of discrimination in live administrations of the Cambridge CAE Listening Part 4 (Murray 2007), although structural equation modelling of the same task indicated that the task can have a tendency to load strongly on the reading factor, suggesting that this particular two-task multiple matching format is in fact an integrated skills task of both listening and reading (Geranpayeh 2007).

Field (2013) outlines yet another way in which demands are made on the candidate beyond those occasioned by the listening construct itself. He points to the need for the test taker to manipulate information:

> The test taker is not required to link propositions, to build an argument structure or to integrate idea units into a larger discourse representation. Instead, he/she has to hold a series of propositions in the mind which can occur at any point in the recording (or even not occur at all); and to match them as and when supporting evidence becomes available.

Exam boards might argue that there are limited practical testing alternatives to the use of the objective formats we have considered (i.e. multiple-choice questions and multiple matching). Their value in terms of reliability, ease of marking and candidate familiarity has seen their use proliferate worldwide. However, they are less than ideal in terms of their cognitive validity. They are essentially flawed not only by a dependence upon reading proficiency but also by the complex cognitive operations that are entailed when three or four options (or more in the case of multiple matching) have to be carried forward in the mind and matched against possible relevant propositions within the recording.

The CAE test of Listening comprehension was a natural continuation on the path of communicative testing of listening ability at Cambridge ESOL. A fixed test format introduced in 2008 would ensure a more systematic operationalisation of the test construct in terms of contextual task demands across tasks. With the introduction of a new multiple-matching task, comprehension of gist, main points and inferencing, fairly neglected so far, finally became an important part of the test construct.

Present day constructs

Efforts are now made to try and ensure that, as far as the conventional test methods (multiple-choice questions, multiple matching and constructed response) employed in the tests permit, the tasks elicit processes from the test taker which resemble those that would be called on in a real-life context (however, see Field (2013) and below for discussion of the enduring limitations of these tasks in this respect). The context and the cognitive validity of the exams approximate more closely than in the past to *what* is listened to in real life (in terms of contextual demands) and to *how* we interact with that information (in terms of the cognitive processing underlying listening comprehension).

Both situational and interactional authenticities were seen as desirable objectives in listening tests in revisions over the last two decades (within the constraints of the conventional formats in use):

> the language of the texts aims to appear natural [situational authenticity] and will be of a level that candidates would generally wish/be able to interact with [interactional authenticity]; texts will be framed to allow candidates to approach the texts in a similar way to how they would approach them in non-exam situations. Rubrics will be worded so as to attempt to encourage this [interactional authenticity] . . . the choice of text type will reflect candidates' interests and needs [situational and interactional authenticity] (Revised FCE Internal Specifications 1994:49).

Scoring validity was also seen as an important consideration: 'a premise of the FCE revision has been that each paper should provide reliable measures' (Revised FCE Internal Specifications 1994:13). Practicality, ease and speed of marking were additional factors behind the retention of optically marked answer sheets in the FCE Listening comprehension test. There is further evidence of increased attention to scoring validity in the standardising of both test form and test administration conditions in an effort to ensure that the test construct is realised more consistently across test versions and sessions. As far as marking reliability is concerned, the preponderance of objective items makes for a more reliable instrument than the dictation CPE began with in 1913.

The FCE Listening comprehension test was revised in 1996, and this subsequently inspired the CPE revision in 2002 (see Hawkey 2009 for full details of FCE revisions and Weir and Milanovic 2003 for comprehensive details of the CPE revision). From the CAE Listening, both of them took on a clearer specification of task focus for each test part and adopted a multiple-matching task which focused on comprehension of opinion, attitude, inference as well as identification of the speakers and function of listening passages.

The revised FCE and CPE Listening test structure, content and focus remained mostly the same through the 2008 updates, with one major change: a standardisation of formats was followed so that test takers knew exactly what kind of format to expect in each unique part of the test. This meant that each test part had a fixed task type, across test forms and examination sessions. This ensured more consistency in contextual and cognitive task demands. Moreover, all three tests, FCE, CAE and CPE, were made more similar in terms of task type and task focus, in order to achieve a family resemblance for Upper Main Suite. This meant that listening comprehension constructs measured by these three examinations converged, supported by the theoretical models of communicative competence and the professional, academic and daily needs of higher-proficiency (B2, C1 and C2 on the CEFR) candidates.

With these important revisions we can see: a) a clearer and better-defined understanding of situational authenticity within the constraints of the conventional formats employed in these listening tests and b) a growing awareness of the importance of cognitive processing in testing listening comprehension. We can identify systematisation in the way the listening test construct is conceived and operationalised across the higher proficiency examinations (FCE, CAE and CPE) and standardisation of task format to reduce potential within-exam variations in contextual and cognitive demands, and therefore in task difficulty. These improvements occurred largely as a result of the growing professionalisation of testing at UCLES/Cambridge ESOL from 1988 onwards that we identified in Chapter 1.

Levels

In Listening comprehension tests at lower proficiency levels in the Cambridge English examinations, attentional capacity is mainly focused on the more local levels of processing (input decoding, lexical search and parsing), i.e. the first three stages of Field's (2013) model. Field (2008) suggested that it is only as decoding becomes more accurate that a learner can be relied upon to construct sufficient co-text to answer questions requiring comprehension beyond the lexical chunk. He warns teachers not to count upon lower level students being able to infer meaning from co-text in order to compensate for their week decoding skills. In Upper Main Suite greater attention is paid to the higher phases of meaning construction and to a more limited extent discourse construction, the two upper levels of Field's model. As we move up through the Upper Main Suite we would expect increasing automaticity in local level perceptual processing and an increasing capacity for handling complex meaning-related processes such as inference, interpreting speaker's intentions, implied attitude, opinion, purpose, or determining which points of a text are important and their relationship to each other.

One can also see an increasing complexity in the texts employed (see Elliott and Wilson (2013) for a comprehensive account of this). For example, from PET upwards, recordings contain a variety of accents, but at the PET level, they are limited to 'standard variants of native speaker accents' (PET Handbook 2009:25). At CPE level, this variety now includes non-native speaker accents that approximate the norms of native speaker accents' (CPE Handbook 2008:50). Non-familiar voices and accents add to the cognitive load to processing because the listener needs to establish the baseline characteristics of each voice (e.g. articulation, speech rate, loudness, and pitch).

The complexity of the syntax also increases with each proficiency level which indirectly leads to increases in length of clause and number of clauses per utterance. Utterance length increases at the higher levels (utterances tend to be much shorter in listening passages for lower proficiency candidates). The amount of co-text that needs to be processed in order to get a correct answer also rises with level. For example most answers to items at the KET level are provided by processing at the level of single lexical units while at the CPE level (e.g. in the CPE sample paper in 2008 CPE Handbook), some questions require listening to and understanding eight or more connected utterances or the entire lengthy passage. Clearly, nowadays, attention is paid to a more systematic differentiation between proficiency levels with contextual and cognitive parameters in mind (see Elliott and Wilson 2013 and Field 2013 for more detail).

A cautionary note

With this we complete our survey of the testing of listening comprehension at Cambridge from 1913 to 2012. The review of literature showed that for the major part of the last century listening was generally the most neglected language skill in language testing, teaching and research. Nevertheless attempts were made to assess this construct in Cambridge English examinations throughout the period. In the CPE, interactive listening had always been part of the speaking test construct in the *conversation* since 1913, but non-participatory, transactional, listening comprehension tasks only appeared temporarily, in a relatively primitive, old-fashioned form, in 1945 and then re-appeared in 1970 in a multiple-choice question format in LCE. For the major part of the last century, transactional listening ability was tested solely through dictation, which had clear limitations in terms of the evidence such a test could provide on candidates' listening ability.

Ever since a multiple-choice question listening comprehension test was introduced to LCE in 1970 and to other examinations from 1975 onwards, measurement of the listening construct has experienced a steady if limited evolution. The listening tests are marked by increasing sophistication albeit limited by practical consideration. From literary passages read out loud in the examinations, requiring not much more than comprehension of factual detail and utterance-level processing, through the more communicatively-oriented tests from 1984 onwards, the measurement of listening has steadily evolved. Context and cognitive validity have improved, with tasks becoming more situationally and interactionally authentic.

Field (2013:133) concludes, however, that a critical deficiency in the coverage of processing levels in the Cambridge Upper Main Suite examinations still remains:

> These conventional formats provide little opportunity to test *discourse construction* . . .: identifying the relative importance of utterances that have been processed, linking idea units, integrating incoming idea units into a developing discourse representation and building a hierarchical structure representing the speaker's line of argument . . . the ability to target the highest levels of decision making is limited by their design. With longer recordings in particular, formats such as MCQ or gap-filling mainly target discrete points of information. There is no requirement upon the candidate to recognise the logical links that connect these points, or to build them into a discourse-level information structure.

Of equal concern are the deficits with regard to test input. Weir and Milanovic (2003:477) stressed that efforts needed to be made at both the item-writing and recording stages to enhance the authenticity of the recorded texts that were used in CPE tests. They argued that there was ample evidence of the extent to which scripted, improvised and re-recorded texts differed from natural spoken language. What the candidate still hears in present day examinations falls short of natural real-world speech even though it attempts to incorporate many of its features: requiring comprehension of more than one voice, different accents, rates of speech, genres and a variety language functions. The lower levels of the suite are perhaps by necessity largely dependent upon scripted material, while the levels from FCE upwards perhaps less justifiably make use of authentic material that has been professionally re-recorded. The latter may well have involved extensive revision by item writers to the original discourse.

The nature of the recorded material used as input in an examination should place a cognitive load on candidates similar to that they would experience in real-life conditions. Field (2013:110) raises a number of important issues concerning the cognitive validity of scripted speech read out aloud. He identifies three problems:

- . . . actors working from a studio script mark punctuation and sentence boundaries much more clearly than they would in natural speech. This has implications at the level of parsing, in that it demarcates clauses and other syntactic groups more precisely than would normally be the case.
- . . . a greater tendency to rhythmicity, with focal stress more consistently marked. This provides additional support at the level of lexical search, since it assists the test taker in identifying the most critical word of the intonation group and thus in building a set of hypotheses as to the main points which the speaker is making.
- . . . the omission of the kind of planning pauses, hesitations, false starts and speaker overlaps that characterize the types of speech that candidates at higher proficiency levels should be capable of dealing with . . .

It is clear that in recent years the possibilities for direct off-air recording have increased exponentially. If examinations are to be better indicators of ability to cope with real-life listening, they should feature good exemplars of natural connected speech. Such an hypothesis would need to be investigated empirically of course. It would be valuable to research whether the current system is or is not as good a predictor of real-life listening abilities as a test using off-air authentic recordings.

Field (2013:114) ends his analysis of listening tests in Cambridge ESOL Main Suite examinations with the timely warning concerning the tasks themselves:

> The fact is that difficulty is being manipulated by means of the written input that the test taker has to master rather than by means of the demands of the auditory input which is the object of the exercise. This appears to be further evidence of test format driving the thinking of test designers and setters rather than the nature of the construct to be tested.

Innovation in listening task types must be considered as a priority in the future development of Cambridge Listening tests. The current selected and constructed response formats (multiple-choice questions, multiple matching and gap filling) survive because examination boards around the world value their reliability, ease of marking and familiarity to candidates. Their cognitive validity is clearly in doubt, though. We need to continue the search for tasks which more closely represent what candidates with each qualification might be expected to perform in real life.

> We have to acknowledge the progress we made, but understand that we still have a long way to go. That things are better, but still not good enough (Barack Obama, CNN interview aired 19 October 2006).

6 Conclusions and recommendations

Cyril J Weir
University of Bedfordshire

A 100-year journey

In the final chapter of Weir and Milanovic (Eds) (2003), the Studies in Language Testing (SiLT) volume on the CPE 2002 revision, Weir emphasised the need for Cambridge ESOL to continue research into the complex cognitive processes and attendant performance conditions involved in completing the tasks in its English language examinations. This was to be one of the core aims of the 'constructs' volumes in the SiLT series (Shaw and Weir 2007, Khalifa and Weir 2009, Taylor (Ed.) 2011 and Geranpayeh and Taylor (Eds) 2013), which provided a comprehensive, synchronic analysis of contemporary Cambridge examinations. *Measured Constructs* has continued with that endeavour but differs in that it takes a diachronic approach. It provides further insight into the constructs being measured by investigating how the testing of each macro language skill has evolved over the last 100 years.

In Chapter 1 we provided a synopsis of the powerful influences that language teaching had on general English language examinations for non-native speakers developed in Cambridge from 1913–2012. Most attention was paid to the Certificate of Proficiency in English (CPE) 1913–2012 and the Lower Certificate in English (LCE) 1939–1975, rebranded after 1975 as the First Certificate in English (FCE) 1975–2012, as these offered us an accessible and manageable historical perspective on Cambridge ESOL examinations over an extended period of time. Such a focus has allowed us to trace *continuity* and *innovation* in the measurement of language constructs in one examination board over a hundred years of its history.

We identified the pedagogic legacies from the past that affected the first Certificate of Proficiency in English (CPE) examination in 1913; the influence of the oral–structural–situational approaches to English language teaching that emerged in the United Kingdom 1921–1970, and finally we traced the effects on Cambridge English language examinations of the communicative movement 1971–2012. We established the changing priorities in the method and content of language teaching in these various stages, which in turn influenced language assessment in the United Kingdom. These included: the grammar translation or traditional method; the oral method: Harold

Palmer's attempt to systematise direct method teaching procedures (Palmer 1921a,1921b); the audio-lingual method (Brooks 1960 and Fries 1945); the situational approach (Hornby 1950 and Billows 1961); and finally the communicative approach (Brumfit and Johnson 1979, Morrow 1977, Munby 1978, Widdowson 1978 and Wilkins 1976) with its focus on the needs of learners to use the language for real-life communication. All were to have an observable influence on English language testing at Cambridge between 1913 and 2012.

In addition, we looked more widely at external, institutional, social and economic forces to help us understand further the shifts in teaching and testing practice. Following World War Two (1939–1945), for example, we found that it was no longer just the influence of traditional attitudes to language and language learning or the insights from linguistics or developments in modern language pedagogy that influenced examinations; increasingly, influence was exerted by the economic and socio-political forces that were at work in making English a dominant language around the globe. Traditional approaches such as grammar translation and teaching English as an access route to great literature were to succumb to pressing utilitarian needs for English as a means of communication between people rather than as a rarefied object of academic study. Changes in Cambridge English language examinations in the second half of the 20th century reflected this mind shift. As Stern astutely observed, the interest in language became 'social' rather than 'scholarly' (Stern 1983: 81).

We also saw how for over 50 years, 1941–1993, the British Council, by virtue of its global mission in spreading English language and culture around the world, was a valuable source of considerable knowledge and expertise in the area of teaching English as a Foreign Language for Cambridge's main English language test committees and a useful partner in making Cambridge examinations widely accessible through its overseas network. The brief of the powerful UCLES–British Council Joint Committee, established in 1941, was to collaborate in the actual development and conduct of UCLES EFL exams, making decisions on policy, regulations, the preparation of examination syllabuses, the 'general plan of the examination', publicity and finance. The high ranking academics who served as British Council representatives on the committee made a significant contribution to the development and global spread of Cambridge English examinations.

Progress towards a European Economic Community from the 1970s onwards brought with it a felt need on the part of intergovernmental agencies in Europe to define language teaching and learning goals more precisely and to make a start on delineating the stages of progression across the language proficiency spectrum. Emerging insights from research and theory building in applied linguistics, coupled with developments in communicative classroom pedagogy, facilitated the shift on the part of the examination boards towards a more explicit specification of the constructs underlying their English language tests at differing levels of proficiency. These developments encouraged the creation of additional Cambridge English language examinations across the proficiency spectrum from 1980 onwards (PET at the B1 CEFR level in 1980, CAE at the CEFR C1 level in 1991 and KET at the CEFR A2 level in 1994).

At various points we compared what was happening in the United Kingdom with developments in the United States, the two world leaders in the field of English language testing in the 20th century. This was revealing and helped us understand some of the differing, if less clear cut, emphases that remain in approaches to theory and practice in language assessment in these two countries. Although ESOL testing in both countries is now similarly informed by all aspects of construct validity this was not always the case in the 20th century, as outlined in Chapter 1, and the path testing was to take differed markedly in each.

Substantive differences are apparent between the United Kingdom and the United States in their approaches to language testing from 1913–1966. An important reason for this Atlantic split could be found in the differing socioeconomic conditions prevailing in Britain and the United States in the early 20th century. The compelling need to produce tests on an industrial scale in the United States, in order to allocate scarce resources in a system with an exploding school population, and to assess the wartime capabilities of over 1.7 million military personnel in a short time frame, was to strongly influence American testing organisations in the direction of objective multiple-choice methods at a very early stage in our narrative. In the United States the predominant early focus was to be on scoring validity, in particular the psychometric qualities of a test whereas in the United Kingdom we identified a greater concern with context validity and relating examinations to what was going on in the language classroom; this could be characterised as a concern with the *how* in the United States as against the *what* in the United Kingdom. The reasons behind these contrasting journeys were often found in the prevailing, wider socio-economic contexts but the differing approach in the United Kingdom also reflected European theoretical and practical approaches to language teaching and assessment.

Looking back over these 100 years of Cambridge ESOL examinations through the lens of CPE 1913–2012 (see Table 6.1 below) it is possible to discern a number of trends in its various constituent papers.

Stability is one of the twin pillars of public examinations that is essential if exams are to fulfill the purposes for which they are intended. The presence of direct tests of writing and speaking throughout the history of Cambridge examinations is testimony to such constancy, as is the length of time other components of the examination were to last (see Table 6.1 below). Furthermore, our history shows how Cambridge was able to achieve this stability whilst at the same time gradually incorporating test tasks that reflected new developments in language pedagogy, linguistics and applied linguistics, first from the Grammar Translation and Reform Movement approaches in

Table 6.1 CPE 1913–2012

Phonetics	1913–32	
Dictation	1913–75	
Listening Comprehension		1975–
Reading aloud	1913–86	
Conversation/oral	1913–	
Translation	1913–75 (1988)	
Essay/ Composition	1913–	
Literature	1913–75	
Reading Comprehension		1975–
Knowledge of grammar	1913–32	
Use of English	1956–	

Europe, then Oral-Structural-Situational, and finally Communicative. This second pillar, innovation linked to improvement, is just as vital if an examination is to keep up with developments and insights available from research in the field. Thus in the 1950s we see a Use of English paper making an appearance with a number of tasks reflecting the increasing interest in the structural approach to language teaching. In the 1970s, as part of the communicative groundswell, we have the introduction of dedicated papers on listening and reading skills, plus a revamped speaking test. We see the gradual introduction of new technology into the listening test in the 1980s as attempts were made to make both texts and tasks more 'authentic' in line with developments in communicative language teaching The more traditional integrated tests of literature, translation, dictation and reading aloud had disappeared by the 1980s just as phonetics and grammar had in the 1930s.

The Table also shows how Cambridge examinations responded to the socio-economic impact of events in the wider world in particular to the globalisation of English that gathered momentum after World War Two. The growth of English as a world language was reflected in the introduction of a language-only route for CPE examination candidates and the downgrading of the importance of literature and cultural knowledge in the overall language ability construct. The idea of English as an international language was also reflected in the later development of the speaking assessment scales in the 1980s and the downgrading of the native speaker concept as the top of the scale.

There was to be additional improvement to the validity of test scores at UCLES–EFL in the late 1980s when, largely as a result of the Cambridge-TOEFL comparability study, far greater attention was paid to scoring validity to bring Cambridge's procedures more in line with the psychometrically sophisticated approach that had long been part of professional language assessment in the United States. This change process was facilitated by the appointment of a critical mass of professional, English language testers at the

Syndicate starting with the arrival of Peter Hargreaves in 1988, closely followed by Neil Jones, Mike Milanovic, Nick Saville and Lynda Taylor. At the same time a strong commitment to the test task as the vehicle for measuring the underlying construct was maintained; a traditional strength of the British assessment approach.

We began Chapters 2–5 by identifying important events in the teaching and assessment of each particular language ability in the years leading up to the 20th century. Then we turned to the 20th century and examined the main trends in teaching and assessing each of our four language constructs in both the United Kingdom and the United States. As far as possible, we sought to do this through the voices of the leading theorists and practitioners of the time. Finally we employed a framework of well-substantiated theory to inform a more detailed analysis of the particular way a construct had been measured by Cambridge 1913–2012 which allowed us to make meaningful comparisons between versions of the same examination across time. This 21st century socio-cognitive framework proved appropriate for purpose. Its use was not in any sense intended to privilege more recent approaches to testing over earlier ones but to provide a set of contextual, cognitive and scoring parameters whereby we could better understand what was being measured at different periods in our history.

This framework for analysing language examinations first outlined in Weir (2005a) and subsequently refined and elaborated in the 'constructs' volumes in the SiLT series provided the springboard for reflecting upon our understanding and conceptualisation of second language ability constructs for assessment purposes (Shaw and Weir 2007, Khalifa and Weir 2009, Taylor (Ed.) 2011 and Geranpayeh and Taylor (Eds) 2013). The framework enabled an in-depth analysis of a number of key test features (cognitive, contextual and scoring) of Cambridge English language tests at different points in our history, and at the same time was effective in highlighting issues likely to need future attention and meriting further research.

In the 21st century it is hard to see how one can build a convincing validity argument for any assessment practice without assigning cognitive processing a central place within that argument and, unlike some of the more abstract, current approaches, attempt to provide *evidence* of such validity (see Davies 2012). Given our desire to extrapolate from performance on test tasks to real-world behaviour, it is essential to carry out research to establish with greater certainty that the test tasks we employ succeed in eliciting from candidates a set of processes which resemble those employed by a proficient language user in real-world events (see Bax and Weir 2012). To the extent that this is not the case, extrapolation from the test data to language use in the wider world is clearly under threat.

In each of the chapters on the macro skills we were limited to a qualitative comparison of the tasks employed in the Cambridge ESOL suite of exams with close reference to an external model of the cognitive processes which the skill in question required of an expert user. The empirical grounding of such subjective analysis will require a long-term research agenda for the future. In this volume we had, for the most part, to content ourselves with pooled, subjective judgement in our reverse engineering endeavors.

The importance of the relationship between the contextual parameters, the conditions under which a task is performed, and the cognitive processing involved in task performance was taken into account in our analysis of Cambridge tests over the 100-year period (see Appendix B for evidence of the symbiotic relationship between these aspects of validity). We believe it is important in language testing that we give both the contextual and the cognitive elements an appropriate place and emphasis in test development, resisting any temptation to favour one over the other. The framework reminds us that language use – and also language assessment – is both a socially situated and a cognitively processed phenomenon. The socio-cognitive framework aims to ensure a complementary balance of these two fundamental perspectives.

In our view, the socio-cognitive framework allowed for serious theoretical consideration of the issues but it also proved itself capable of being applied practically in critical analyses of test content *across the language proficiency spectrum*; it therefore has direct relevance and value to an operational language testing/assessment context – especially when that testing is taking place on a large, industrial scale such as in Cambridge ESOL with examination being offered at differing levels of proficiency from elementary to advanced. While other frameworks developed during the 1990s (e.g. Bachman's (1990) Communicative Language Ability (CLA) model and the Council of Europe's 2001 Common European Framework of Reference (CEFR)) undoubtedly helped Cambridge ESOL to consider key issues from a theoretical perspective, they generally proved somewhat difficult for the examination board to operationalise in a manageable and meaningful way. The results from operationalising the socio-cognitive framework in this volume with regard to Cambridge Main Suite ESOL examinations 1913–2012 are more encouraging.

Our history took us up to the present day and it is only fitting in this final chapter that we take stock of where we are with respect to the way language constructs are measured in the current versions of these Cambridge examinations. Accordingly, we briefly summarise our findings with respect to the cognitive, contextual and scoring parameters of contemporary Cambridge ESOL examinations and identify where we feel these examinations might be improved in respect of these validity components. In this we will necessarily draw heavily on the work carried out for the constructs volumes (see Shaw and Weir 2007, Khalifa and Weir 2009, Taylor (Ed.) 2011 and Geranpayeh and Taylor (Eds) 2013) as they all involved a comprehensive application of the socio-cognitive framework to current Cambridge ESOL Main Suite examinations.

2012: Construct validity in contemporary Cambridge ESOL examinations

Cognitive validity

Reading

The cognitive demands made on the candidate need to vary between the reading tests set at different levels, what Field (2013) characterises as *calibration*. Khalifa and Weir (2009) describe how the examinations in the current Main Suite appear to follow the ascending order of complexity in cognitive processing in reading that is suggested by the cognitive psychology literature.

The attentional resources of a reader are finite and, in the early stages of second language (L2) development (CEFR A1 and A2 level candidates), one might expect a large part of those resources to be diverted towards more low-level considerations concerning the linguistic code. The effort of decoding makes considerable cognitive demands on the less skilled reader and as a result is likely to become the principal focus of attention for many up to the A2 level and the main focus for tests set at these levels. They are generally unable to cope with higher-level comprehension processes (e.g. using contextual information to enrich comprehension, or higher-level meaning construction at the discourse representation level) because the cognitive demands of decoding takes up most of their available attentional capacity.

Textually implicit questions require the reader to combine information across sentences in a text and such questions are generally more difficult than explicit items based on a single sentence given the additional processing that is required (see Davey and Lasasso 1984). Oakhill and Garnham (1988) suggested that the less skilled reader fails to make a range of inferences in comprehension, from local links between sentences, to the way(s) the ideas in the whole text are connected. Accordingly it is only really at the FCE (B2) level and above that inferencing begins to be tested more frequently and across larger areas of text. From FCE onwards, certain question types require the candidate to report not on information contained in the text but upon what that information entails. Until learners have relatively automatic processes for dealing with word recognition, lexical access and syntactic parsing, meaning construction beyond dealing with sentence level propositions is restricted. This is usually well-established by the B2 level, when there is more processing capacity available in working memory for making propositional inferences, building a mental model and integrating information.

It is likely that a task requiring the formation of a text level representation may be less suitable below a C1 level in the CEFR (CAE in Cambridge Main Suite examinations) because of the more demanding processing required for its successful completion. Thus the ability to cope with questions requiring the candidate to develop an overall discourse representation of argumentative texts is normally tested on reaching the C1 (CAE) level.

The highest level of processing – that required to construct an intertextual representation of several texts – comes into play at the C2 (CPE) level albeit in the Use of English paper. In terms of our model presented in Figure 2.1 in Chapter 2, we would argue that the ability to engage in such higher-level processing activities is entirely appropriate at this level of language proficiency whereas a task demanding lower-level processing skills only (i.e. the current Part 1 in the CPE Reading paper) is not. Given the limited time and space available for testing reading skills and strategies and the necessity to establish clear water between proficiency levels, it might be prudent to ensure that a reading paper at the C2 level is eliciting adequate data on the ability to cope with the higher-level cognitive processes required in forming both a textual and an intertextual representation, i.e. that its coverage is appropriate and comprehensive.

At the advanced level then, thought should be given to including even more tasks at the textual and the intertextual levels. The research necessary to guide this might investigate the value of the summary tasks which were excluded from Upper Main Suite reading tests in the 1970s.

In general, across the current suite of Cambridge examinations, the range of reading types is covered appropriately. However, there are serious anomalies at CAE and CPE that merit consideration especially the absence of items directly testing expeditious reading skills at the global level, an important type of reading at university and in the professions. Text demands, in terms of the relative complexity of the contextual parameters exhibited by a text, are increased gradually (see Appendix B for quantitative analysis which lends support to this). In grading the specifications for the five levels of the Cambridge suite, careful thought has clearly been given to the relative cognitive difficulty both in terms of levels of processing activity required by the tasks and cognitive load of the texts employed.

Writing

There has been relatively limited research to date addressing the cognitive processing dimension in the L2 testing of writing, despite a widespread concern with construct validity in the language testing literature in the last 30 years. Given our desire to extrapolate from test tasks to real-world behaviour, it is sensible to carry out research to establish with greater certainty that the test tasks we employ do indeed activate the types of mental operations that are viewed in the cognitive psychology literature as essential elements of the writing processes exhibited by expert users. To the extent that this is not the case, extrapolation from test results to target situation behaviour is threatened.

Shaw and Weir (2007:34–62) in their retrospective analysis of writing tasks in contemporary Cambridge examinations suggest that the characterisation of unskilled and skilled writers can be seen to broadly fit the types of writing which are implied by the tasks at the different English language levels A2 – C2: narrative or instructional texts at the lower levels clearly demanding skills at the knowledge telling end of the continuum compared to texts involving argument at the higher levels usually necessitating knowledge transforming skills.

The activities of planning, monitoring and revising written work for content and organisation become increasingly relevant in Cambridge Upper Main Suite (UMS), particularly at CAE (C1) and CPE (C2) levels. However, in the current writing tests no dedicated time is allocated for these and no explicit advice to address them is provided in the task rubric, so ways of making greater provision for such operations might profitably be explored in the future to further ground the cognitive validity of English Language writing test tasks.

Recent research by Ellis and Yuan (2004) indicates that the addition of a planning condition can lead to improvements in written performance and much of the research on planning in spoken language also reports similar outcomes (Mehnert 1998, Skehan and Foster 1997, 1999, 2001, Wigglesworth 1997) although in a number of studies the evidence was not so clear cut (Iwashita, McNamara and Elder 2001, Wigglesworth 2000). It might be reasonable to assume that positive benefits for learners would accrue if planning activity was proactively encouraged in English Language tests of writing and the preparation that precedes them. Further research in this area is a priority.

For example, research might focus on the effects of incorporating both a planning stage before candidates start writing and a monitoring and revision phase at the end of each task at FCE and higher levels, with dedicated time made available for these. The associated marking criteria of content and organisation at CAE and CPE levels might also be given stronger weightings, given their importance in the real world (see Weir 1983 for empirical evidence to support this in academia). The potential benefits of making this weighting clear to candidates on the paper itself might also be explored.

If positive outcomes result from such research, then future revisions to the higher-level test components might look into structuring and manipulating tasks so that they activate more systematically these critical planning, monitoring and revision processes. Since these are seen to be the hallmarks of the skilled writer, attempts will need to be made to ensure that successful candidates are carrying out these activities to an appropriate extent.

Control of timing for planning and for monitoring phases in a test event clearly presents logistical challenges in large-scale paper-based (i.e. traditional) assessment contexts, though such developments are already beginning to appear in a number of international examinations. Such differentiated phases of the writing process might be more easily achieved through a computer-based mode where timing for individual phases or processing activities within the testing event can be more easily controlled.

Encouraging appropriate cognitive processing is likely to enhance students' scores as well as improve the validity of a writing task. The impact of such operations on future performance in the target situation(s) should not be underestimated.

Speaking

Field (2011) makes it clear that in grading the specifications for the five levels of the Cambridge ESOL Main Suite English examinations, designers have given careful thought to the relative cognitive difficulty both of the tasks and of the interaction formats. Task demands are increased only gradually; and the more demanding types of interaction (particularly three-way discussion) are reserved for higher levels of the suite. He concludes that the Cambridge ESOL specifications correspond closely to what we know of the cognitive processes involved in the production of speech. It is also apparent that the cognitive requirements have been sufficiently finely graded in relation to the different levels of the suite. Full consideration has been given both to task demands and to the types of processing that can be deemed to be representative of performance at different stages of proficiency.

However, an important issue relating to the relative cognitive difficulty of the tasks is the amount of pre-planning time permitted. Field (2011) argues that pre-planning is not provided for in the Cambridge Main Suite Speaking tests – a decision which (in terms of cognitive validity) might be considered sound in the case of tasks that are designed to measure spontaneous spoken interaction. It is more open to question in relation to the monologic tasks, in that the absence of any pre-planning time means that they may not necessarily replicate the cognitive processes which often accompany the preparation of a formal or semi-formal presentation. However, much depends upon the perceived purpose of those tasks. Field (op. cit.) cautions that the Cambridge ESOL test designers might argue that the monologues are intended to provide an indication of a candidate's ability to produce an extended turn, not of their ability to engage in a markedly different type of speech assembly. Interestingly, however, a short one minute pre-planning phase (prior to a one/two-minute 'mini-presentation') is included in the International English Language Testing System (IELTS), Business English Certificates (BEC), and International Legal English Certificate (ILEC) Speaking tests, presumably with the intention of echoing the formal and semi-formal presentation skills that are typically required in the higher education and professional employment contexts. Given that both CAE and CPE are used for admission to academic and professional domains, a case for this pre-planning feature (with or without pen and paper for making notes) to be mirrored in the higher-level

Cambridge Main Suite Speaking tests merits consideration. This constitutes an area for further research investigation and comparative analysis in the future.

Listening

There is a gradation across the Main Suite examinations in cognitive demands reflecting Field's comprehensive processing model for listening at five levels (see Field 2013). The first three levels are the lower level listening processes that take place when a message is being encoded into language, and the remaining two are higher level processes associated with meaning building. In listening comprehension in the lower proficiency examinations attentional capacity is mainly focused on the more local levels of processing (input decoding, lexical search and parsing), i.e. the first three phases of Field's (2013) model. Low proficiency learners are not efficient and fast decoders of the speech signal which is why much of their working memory is taken up by lower-level cognitive processes. This necessarily restricts their ability to activate higher-level processes which involve processing across larger chunks of discourse and meaning construction based on inferencing and using sources of knowledge external to the text viz pragmatic and socio-linguistic knowledge. As input decoding becomes more automatised, working memory is freed for such higher-level processing.

By Upper Main Suite (FCE, CAE and CPE) the focus shifts to testing higher-level processes. This is reflected in: a) the need to process a number of connected utterances to arrive at the correct answer and b) more numerous questions which require the understanding of a wider meaning, the ability to interpret, evaluate, infer, and use pragmatic and socio-linguistic knowledge. Longer listening passages and longer utterances (see Elliott and Wilson 2013) and increasingly complex linguistic features (lexical and syntactic) from FCE upwards also add to the cognitive load as we move upwards through the suite.

Although by Upper Main Suite greater attention is paid to meaning construction, there is unfortunately little requirement for the candidate to recognise the logical links that connect information points, or to build them into a discourse-level representation (see Field 2013 for a critical discussion of this). Geranpayeh and Taylor conclude (2013:331) that this level of processing appears to be under-represented:

> The conventional test item formats used in the Cambridge listening tests provide little opportunity to assess *discourse construction,* which covers identifying the relative importance of utterances that have been processed, linking idea units, integrating incoming idea units into a developing discourse representation and building a hierarchical structure representing the speaker's line of argument. Testing this high-level

processing is a major challenge for test designers since objectively scored test items, such as MCQ or gap-filling, invariably tend to target discrete points of information which have been pre-selected as worthy of attention by the test writer, rather than by the test taker. It may be that the high-level *discourse construction* type of processing (which is likely to be especially relevant for the high-proficiency, C levels – for tests used for university education or professional employment) is best provoked through the use of integrated listening-into-speaking or listening-into writing tasks. Further research is required.

A number of further problems arise from the test formats used in these examinations. Listening tasks in the Main Suite examinations are mostly selected response or structured note or sentence/summary completion tasks. As such, they do not allow candidates to interact with listening tasks in the way they would in real life. This is because questions and options (in selected response tasks) and frames for notes/summaries (in structured completion tasks) impose specific listening goals on test takers, not allowing them to form their own listening purposes nor select on their own the information they think is useful for understanding the developing discourse (see Field 2008 and 2013). In other words, the goal setting, listening comprehension and comprehension monitoring processes are in great part dictated by the very specific task questions rather than mainly by the candidate's goal-setting and evaluation ability. This is another reason why in the future it would be useful to consider integrated listening-into-speaking or listening-into-writing tasks for FCE, CAE and CPE listening tests in order to address the threats to construct validity current tasks give rise to. The merits of a summary completion task might also be investigated to ensure that discourse representation is adequately covered. Such tasks might better reflect the processing of information in work and study contexts, but would require a careful consideration of test construct; test purpose and a comparative investigation of cognitive processes activated in selected response and integrated tasks.

Field (2013) draws attention to a general failing that that the current listening items are often being manipulated by means of the written input that the test taker has to master rather than by means of the demands of the auditory input which is the object of the exercise. He is right to point out that it should be the nature of the construct to be tested, rather than the test format, that drives test development. The current selected and constructed response formats (Multiple Choice Questions (MCQ), Multiple Matching (MM) and Gap Filling (GF)) survive because examination boards around the world value their reliability, ease of marking and familiarity to candidates. Their cognitive validity is less certain. We need to continue the search for tasks which more closely represent what candidates for each level of qualification might be expected to perform in real life.

Context validity

Reading

Critics may query the predominant use of selected as against constructed response format in the Cambridge Main Suite examinations. However, it should be noted that Cambridge ESOL uses variants of selected response formats at all levels in this suite, and these variants in themselves encourage a different approach to completing the different reading tasks. For example, completing a matching gapped-text task (CAE/CPE) can potentially involve different levels of processing to answering a set of multiple-choice questions that may only require processing information at the sentence or between sentence levels. As an examination board, Cambridge ESOL also uses constructed response types, e.g. in the Business Language Testing Service (BULATS) and IELTS. Where such a response type is used, a rigorous marking system has to be in place: a standardised marking scheme is used together with a rater-training manual, an online help desk to answer rater queries is available and close monitoring takes place throughout the marking process.

Cambridge ESOL's view is that the main advantage of using selected response formats is that they allow a broader range of test focuses than constructed response formats. Multiple-choice items are widely acknowledged to be an appropriate vehicle in large scale assessments for testing detailed understanding of the text. They are thought to allow more sophisticated elements of text content to be tested, e.g. opinion, inference, argument, in a more *controlled* way than is possible through open-ended formats. Furthermore for examination boards like Cambridge ESOL who are engaged in large-scale assessments worldwide, the scoring validity, the practicality of objectively scored formats and the quick turnaround of test results are seen as strong arguments in their favour. An argument can also be made that getting candidates to construct their own responses risks muddying the measurement by involving the skill of writing.

Set against this view are serious concerns, especially at the higher proficiency levels, about the use of multiple-choice questions (Hoffman 1961). There is concern about the appropriateness of MCQ for activating the higher-level processing required in constructing an organised representation of the text. Rupp, Ferne and Choi (2006:469) conclude that the format may involve the reader in 'response processes that deviate significantly from those predicted by a model of reading comprehension in a non-testing context' and they hypothesise (454) that: 'responding to MC reading comprehension questions on many standardised reading comprehension tests is much more a problem-solving process relying heavily on verbal reasoning than a fluid process of integrating propositions to arrive at a connected mental representation of a text'.

There is also concern that the mental model which would normally be created in reading a text is affected if candidates try to incorporate all the options provided in an item into an ongoing text representation. The processing that takes place in working out which option fits and which does not would bear little resemblance to the way we process texts for information in any of the types of reading in the framework we presented in Figure 2.1 in Chapter 2.

In general, the length of the text expands as we move up through the examination levels and thereby the number of propositions that have be understood by the candidate. This is true for the following adjacent levels: KET/PET, PET/FCE, and FCE/CAE. There is no marked distinction between CAE/CPE in terms of text length; however, CPE has a greater number of different texts normally with a wider coverage of genres. This may account for the close similarities between texts at CAE/CPE across a variety of contextual parameters that are discussed in Appendix B. Perhaps, they are too close.

On the examination paper, time is specified for the whole paper rather than the parts. Ideally time constraints should be put on tasks to ensure as far as possible that candidates are using the intended reading strategies whether it is careful or expeditious reading. Practically speaking (except in computer based testing (CBT) mode), an examination board cannot easily force candidates to spend more or less time on a certain task.

What Cambridge ESOL does is provide candidates with guidelines on how they should approach a task and what reading type may be best suited to that task; such guidance is provided through examination reports or information in the handbooks and the websites for teachers and students. Cambridge ESOL practice is to present items in a way that suggests what is intended, e.g. by putting questions intended to test expeditious reading before the text, but this does not control whether students skim, search read, scan or read intensively in practice. The disadvantage of this non-interventionist approach is that items that are intended to test expeditious abilities, such as search reading, may for some candidates become careful reading activities and vice versa if time is running out for the candidate (see Weir et al 2000). With the onset of Computer Based Testing this situation might be reviewed as it is a fairly simple procedure to control the time available for a task in a computerised mode. It would then be interesting to explore how actual cognitive processing in reading is affected by Computer Based delivery and establish the impact of changes in response conditions such as controlling the time available to candidates for task completion.

The extended Case Study in Appendix B provides interesting, empirical data on how well Cambridge is doing, in terms of a number of quantifiable contextual validity parameters, in ensuring the comparability of their tests across versions and maintaining clear water between levels. Overall test developers seem to have done quite a reasonable job through connoisseurship in respect of many of the indices under consideration, but more systematic procedures, as exemplified in this case study, would help reduce variability in others where they have been less successful in selecting and editing comparable texts. Furthermore the analysis suggests that there may not be sufficiently clear water between adjacent levels such as PET/FCE and CAE/CPE in a number of these contextual parameters. This finding is mirrored in Wu's comparison of the analogous General English Proficiency Tests (GEPT) in Taiwan and Cambridge PET and FCE examinations (Wu 2011).

The empirical case study of the context validity of the CPE examination 1913–2012 in Appendix B suggests that Coh-Metrix and Web Vocabprofile should prove useful in the future for English language reading test developers (and reading materials producers in general) in a variety of ways. Although most of the reading test passages investigated here had been positively evaluated through a systematic, editorial process (see Khalifa and Weir 2009: 197–201 for details of this at Cambridge), the study none the less identified certain texts with indices outside the normal range typically found in the examination task.

Use of these automated tools in the future would ensure greater consistency in the characteristics of texts employed in a test. We need to ensure that the texts we use in an examination year on year are comparable in respect of as many of our contextual indices as possible. The case for this is clear. What remains is for examination boards to determine what is an acceptable range for each parameter at each level of proficiency for which they offer examinations. An acceptance of collective responsibility amongst the examination boards for this endeavour would guarantee the most dependable specifications for the different levels of proficiency which are, at best, vaguely and sparsely specified in the current Common European Frame of Reference (Council of Europe 2001, Weir 2005a).

Information derived from text analysis tools should also prove of considerable value in item writer training to help those involved better understand the characteristics of suitable texts and to help them to edit sources in ways that are compatible with the aims of the test, and most crucially which do not impact adversely on the authenticity of the original texts (Green and Hawkey 2011).

Writing

Practicality is often cited by examination boards as a reason for altering the performance conditions under which writing tasks are performed (see Hawkey 2009 for details of such changes in FCE and CAE in recent years). What is often overlooked is that any decisions which are taken with regard to contextual parameters will have potential implications for any subsequent processing and for the executive resources needed for task completion.

For example, it might be imprudent to reduce significantly the time available for a writing test until the potential ramifications of this on performance are investigated. If research findings were to suggest that dedicated macro planning and monitoring enhanced performance when proactively encouraged, and dedicated time is made available for promoting these critical aspects of cognitive processing, and if such measures were found to be administratively practical, it might in fact be necessary in the future to contemplate even longer writing tests at FCE, CAE and CPE levels.

These days, in the computerised world of work and increasingly among students in full-time education, relatively few people write without access to a computer and its support facilities e.g. a spelling and grammar checker (though sometimes a fairly bizarre experience in the case of the latter), nor do they have to edit and revise by rewriting whole scripts. Conventional writing tests, therefore, often ask candidates to perform in a way that is far less typical of the real-world context than it once was. Computerisation of a number of Cambridge ESOL examinations are currently under consideration and a computer-based version of PET is already available. Computerised versions will facilitate the vital processes of editing and revision at all levels and in particular it will be easier to move text around to improve organisation and the foregrounding of key ideas on computer.

Another pressing construct issue is the role of integrated reading and writing tasks. CAE and CPE are recognised for university entrance purposes in the United Kingdom but in their present format only include tasks which integrate reading and writing in a limited way; more integrated tasks such as *summary* of a whole text would better reflect reading to learn and writing in that target discourse community and are more likely to activate knowledge transformation which is a hallmark of writing at this level (see Weir 1983 and Chapter 2).

Integrated tasks are not without their disadvantages however, not least in how to deal with candidates 'lifting' from the input texts provided; ways will have to be sought to eliminate this in preparing candidates for such an examination task (Lewkowicz 1997, Weigle 2004). Punitive sanctions might need to be considered to discourage 'lifting', e.g. candidates will be penalised, if more than X number of continuous words are lifted from the source text(s). Systematic procedures for guarding against plagiarism in written assignments are now commonplace in university settings and automated procedures such as *Turnitin* make its detection relatively simple. The whole area of integrating reading and writing activities is in need of further research but the potential positive washback of such integrated tasks should encourage this.

A number of points can be made regarding the calibration of the contextual parameters in writing examinations. In writing examinations in the Cambridge suite there is a gradual progression through the levels from personally known (e.g. friend or teacher) to specified audiences with whom candidates are not personally acquainted (e.g. an editor or magazine readers). Addressing a broader range of audience is required at FCE as candidates only write to people they know personally in KET and PET. A slightly wider range of unacquainted audience distinguishes CAE and CPE. At these two levels candidates must also decide what sorts of evidence the reader is likely to find persuasive. However, the effect of audience on performance in writing is a seriously under-researched area (see Porter and O'Sullivan 1999) and the ways in which this parameter might help to further ground distinctions between FCE, CAE and CPE is worth investigating further.

There is a clear distinction between PET and FCE in terms of the text types students have to produce. At FCE the rhetorical task of argument differentiates it from PET and discursive tasks are important throughout FCE, CAE and CPE. CAE is differentiated from FCE by the greater range of genres the candidate might have to address overall and having to deal in the compulsory Part 1 task with varying degrees of persuasion to convince the intended audience of the writer's point of view. The effect of discourse mode on performance in writing is another under-researched area and the ways in which this parameter might contribute to further grounding of distinctions between levels in FCE, CAE and CPE in both the reading and writing papers needs investigating. As previously discussed, the variety of modes which result from the choices available to candidates needs to be continually monitored to ensure they present candidates with an equally difficult task and lead to equivalent performances.

Empirical research on the effect of topic on performance across levels is noticeably lacking and almost no guidance is available from research on what topics are appropriate as a student progresses through the proficiency levels. Examination board experience is not to be discounted but Cambridge ESOL could add to this with more empirically-grounded evidence.

Speaking

Galaczi and ffrench (2011) examined the context validity of Cambridge ESOL speaking tasks with reference to a detailed taxonomy of contextual task parameters originally outlined in Weir (2005a). This exercise demonstrated that careful consideration is given to the gradation of difficulty across the Main Suite levels.

A range of response formats is used at each of the Cambridge ESOL Main Suite proficiency levels. Some response formats do not appear until a certain level, and sometimes the same response format is used at multiple levels, but manipulated in different ways. In terms of criterial features across levels, a clear gradation is seen from controlled to semi-controlled to open-ended response formats, which accommodates the need for increased communicative demand at the higher levels (Skehan 1996).

There is also a progression (both within a level and across levels) from relatively structured and supported interaction, under the direct control of the examiner, involving topics of immediate personal relevance to more open-ended discussion with less examiner control involving more general topics. In addition, there is an increase in the amount of time assigned to each task type and to the overall test, as one moves up the levels.

Another key distinguishing feature is the gradation from factual to evaluative discourse modes, and the more common presence at the lower levels of exposition and description, compared with the increased role of exposition/argumentation at the higher levels. The progression from personal and concrete information to non-personal and abstract information is also shown to accommodate the need for increased cognitive complexity of the task at the higher levels. Furthermore, this gradation is seen in the visuals for the tasks, which provide more scaffolding and are more content-rich at the lower levels, in contrast with the visuals which convey concepts at the higher levels.

In terms of future research and practice the potential for harnessing computer-based technology for creating Reading/Listening-into-Speaking tasks is clear. This is a road TOEFL iBT have already ventured down (see also James (1988) for details of how this was done in the Associated Examining Board's TEAP test in the 1980s). Using computer-based technology could certainly be of help with Listening-into-Speaking activities. In other words, computer-based technology could facilitate the administration of integrated tasks, which are commonplace in real-life academic and professional contexts.

Listening

Elliott and Wilson (2013) argue that the contextual task demands of listening tasks vary systematically across the Main Suite examinations to accommodate the different proficiency levels of the candidates and the uses they are expected to put English to in everyday life (e.g. the basic 'survival in day-to-day life' context (KET Handbook 2009:3) or professional and study contexts (see CPE Handbook 2008). Some of the main identified differentiators across the suite are: task focus, nature of information, topic treatment, the nature of language and phonological features of the audio input.

From the FCE level upwards, task focus broadens to incorporate a wider range of more complex testing focuses (e.g. comprehending gist of a passage requires processing across the entire passage; understanding opinion may require inferencing ability or drawing on pragmatic knowledge). The gradation of task focuses in this way normally involves the increasing linguistic and conceptual complexity of passage content as well as the increasing cognitive processing complexity required by a listening task.

The information that needs to be understood in KET and PET listening tasks is mainly personal and concrete, whereas from FCE level upwards it becomes more general and abstract. Topic treatment differentiates between FCE and CAE, on the one hand, and CPE, on the other, in that abstract topics are grounded in the speaker's personal experiences in the former, whereas they are given a more objective treatment in CPE. The complexity and sophistication of language as well as phonological features (e.g. elision, assimilation, linking), stress, rate of speech and a variety of accents also distinguish between Main Suite listening tests intended for different proficiency levels, posing simpler demands on test takers' ability to decode the input in KET and PET Listening tests and more complex ones from FCE level upwards. This gradation provides context validity evidence on listening tests in the Main Suite examinations (see Elliott and Wilson (2013) for more detail). Nevertheless, there is room for improvement, such as relating some of the CAE and CPE passages to academic and professional contexts and themes, in view of CAE and CPE candidature and test use (ibid.).

A more serious problem is that the input heard by the candidate often falls short of natural real-world speech even though attempts are made to incorporate a lot of its features: requiring comprehension of more than one voice, different accents, rates of speech, genres and a variety language functions. The lower levels of the suite are perhaps by necessity largely dependent upon scripted material, while the levels from FCE upwards perhaps less justifiably make use of authentic material that has been professionally re-recorded, or use scripted material. The latter may well have involved extensive revision by item writers to the original discourse (see Salisbury (2005) for an extensive discussion of the item writing process for listening tests at Cambridge). Weir and Milanovic (2003:477) stressed that efforts needed to be made at both the item-writing and recording stages to enhance the authenticity of the recorded texts that were used in CPE tests. They argued that there was ample evidence of the extent to which scripted, improvised and re-recorded texts differed from natural spoken language. If examinations are to be better indicators of ability to cope with natural speech, they should feature good exemplars of it.

As far as harnessing technology in language testing is concerned, the introduction of audio recordings to Cambridge ESOL listening tests in the 1980s opened up the possibility of using authentic and diverse material, to add to the situational authenticity of test tasks. Geranpayeh and Taylor (2013: Chapter 8) however raise concerns about the input authenticity of the current audio-based test including the absence of the sorts of visual support that would typically be available in a real-life context. They contend:

> there is considerable scope for Cambridge ESOL to explore the potential for integrating more visual input into its listening tests in the future, especially for computer-based tests. As technology improves, and as test

takers themselves become more accustomed to taking tests on computer as well as to encountering audio-visual contact with the target language through internet sources, examination boards will need to give careful consideration to the practicality of video-based testing of listening.

Videos could indeed improve the situational and interactional authenticity of listening tests because, in real life, the information listened to is often accompanied by visual information which could affect comprehension and interpretation, as suggested by Buck (2001). The role of videos in performance on listening tests is still being researched. It is a controversial issue since recent research on the impact of visual/video information on listening task performance has produced mixed results (see Wagner 2010 and Suvorov 2011). Regardless of whether the presence of videos improves or lowers scores, or has no effect on scores whatsoever, it is important to consider whether they should be part of the listening test construct, in view of the fact that listeners in real life often draw on non-verbal information while listening.

Scoring validity

Reading

There was some concern about the scoring validity of the early read aloud and the short answer item types that were used up until the 1970s (see Roach 1945a, Appendix C). However, as the test now consists solely of selected response items in Upper Main Suite examinations (FCE, CAE and CPE), and is machine scored, we can expect a high degree of reliability in marking. An Optical Mark Reader (OMR) form which is accurately designed and printed, and properly filled out and handled, will read with 100% accuracy.

Writing

A consensus is developing in our field that all writing paper scripts should be double marked or at least calibrated through Item Response Theory (IRT) methods by for example employing systematic overlap in batches of scripts marked (see Taylor and Falvey (2006) for a balanced discussion of this). Although this has cost implications, test fairness demands it. With the developments in electronic script management reported in Shaw and Weir (2007: Chapter 5), this is easier to operationalise.

Weir (2003) reports on a choice of essays being available to candidates in writing tests as far back as the first CPE examination in 1913. The potential effect on scoring validity of allowing a choice in writing tasks needs to be constantly addressed, however, to determine whether or not task choice is introducing construct-irrelevant variance into the system. Using the common compulsory task already required of candidates and calibrating performance on a second alternative task against this, as is the practice in FCE, CAE and CPE, is a good start at addressing this issue.

Should the future be analytic? The report on the recent IELTS Writing Scale Revision Project (see Shaw and Weir 2007: Chapter 5) indicated that an analytic approach to marking had advantages over an impression banded approach for marking IELTS not least because of the enhanced marker reliability it led to and the possibilities of more detailed profiling.

Research suggests that an analytic approach, double or targeted double marking, and the employment of multi-faceted Rasch analysis and calibration, might serve to further increase the scoring validity of Cambridge examinations.

Speaking

The ability to place confidence in the quality of the information provided by test scores is vital if we are to use these for decision-making purposes, especially high stakes decision-making. Taylor and Galaczi (2011) outlined the multiple factors which can impact on the reliability aspects of the scoring validity of speaking assessments, especially direct speaking tests such as those offered by Cambridge ESOL, and the wide range of measures taken by the examination board to control these factors.

Assessment criteria and rating scales are an important part of the examination construct and the rating process, which is why there need to be valid instruments and processes for measuring spoken performance. In view of this, the development and revision of Cambridge ESOL speaking assessment scales nowadays is empirically informed through expert judgment, qualitative and quantitative analyses as well as being validated prior to live use (see Taylor and Galaczi (2011) for detail). The use of both analytic and holistic assessment scales in Main Suite speaking examinations also enhances scoring validity since it provides two marks per candidate from different, but complementary perspectives. The dual roles of the two examiners during the test – one acting as an interviewer and the other as a rater – introduces the possibility of interlocutor and/or rater effects on candidates performance and scores. To minimise the interlocutor effect, Cambridge ESOL trains and monitors its interlocutors and provides them with an interlocutor frame which standardises test conduct and task input across sessions and candidates and examiners. To minimise rater variability and rater effect on candidate performance, Cambridge ESOL has established a comprehensive system of: a) rater registration, induction, training, certification and performance feedback b) statistical post-exam monitoring of Oral Examiners (see Taylor and Galaczi 2011).

Besides ensuring scoring validity, the reporting of scores to test takers and test users in a meaningful way is also important. Cambridge ESOL test takers are currently provided with a statement of results which includes not only a candidate's overall grade for the examination, but also their standardised score (out of 100) which provides information on how well a candidate performed within a grade boundary (e.g. near the top of the grade, middle or bottom) as well as a profile of a candidate's performance across various components (e.g. Reading, Speaking) of the whole examination (see Taylor and Galaczi 2011). Consideration might also be given in the future to an even more detailed account of candidate performance perhaps even down to the level of detailing performance against individual marking criteria (see discussion on latest developments in score reporting at Cambridge ESOL in Geranpayeh and Taylor 2013).

As far as future research and practice are concerned, a potential avenue to explore would be awarding a shared score for interactive communication, rather than a separate score for each candidate. An argument for it would be that interactional competence is the ability to co-construct interaction in Cambridge ESOL Main Suite examinations. Shared scores have been discussed in the literature (May 2009 and Taylor and Wigglesworth 2009), but the feasibility of awarding them in practice requires more research and serious thought to be given to the implications for the construct definition of interactional competence.

Another issue to investigate is the empirical derivation of speaking assessment criteria and scales from the analysis of spoken learner corpora. Since the 1990s, Cambridge ESOL speaking assessment criteria (and tests) have been informed by models of communicative competence (Bachman 1990, Canale and Swain 1980). However, such models are not theoretical models of spoken second/foreign (L2) language acquisition, and, as such, they cannot provide a view of how spoken ability develops across proficiency levels. This is where empirical lexical, grammatical and discourse analyses of learners' spoken corpora across proficiency levels should come into play, as they can provide vital insights into the nature of spoken language proficiency across levels. The work on building a corpus of spoken learner data using audio-recordings of Cambridge ESOL speaking tests has started (see McCarthy 2010, Tao 2003, Taylor 2003).

Speaking assessment criteria and scales could further be informed by an empirical investigation into what raters pay attention to while rating (see, for example, Ducasse and Brown (2009) for paired orals and Pollitt and Murray (1996) on the role of comprehension and paralinguistic features in raters' decisions). Empirical grounding of assessment criteria and scales in actual learner performance data and a better understanding of raters' decision-making processes would enhance the construct validity of speaking assessment.

Listening

We cannot be sanguine about the scoring validity of all the tasks in the present listening papers. The multiple-matching and the multiple-choice items can obviously be objectively scored in the same way as the reading items. Problems may arise, however, in the constructed response items such as gap filling where candidates have to write their answers out by hand. Issues can arise, for example, as to the acceptability of various spellings of a word provided by candidates in answer to the questions.

A rigorous set of procedures are in place to tackle such eventualities. In mainstream general marking at Cambridge ESOL, all general markers are trained and co-ordinated at each administrative session. Co-ordination means version specific training, where general markers are familiarised with both the generic test (e.g. FCE) and the specific test version (e.g. FCE, Dec 2008) they are going to mark. This includes item types, particular tasks and items and the mark scheme, and is conducted by the Marking-Quality Controller (MQC), a suitably qualified external English Language Teaching professional. Though the behaviour of individual items is to some extent predicted by pretesting, this co-ordination process allows general markers to be warned of items where the key may be more flexible than is normally the case, and where, as a result, extra vigilance is required in order to bring potentially correct candidate responses to the attention of the Marking-Quality Controller. As part of Cambridge ESOL's commitment to quality control, it investigates the degree of general markers' accuracy and consistency and determines follow-up.

Endnote

By the mid-1970s the early influence of the academic, scholarly view of language, which regarded it first and foremost as an object of study, had largely disappeared with increased attention being paid to the way language was used for communication. Gone was the prominence given to a knowledge of phonetics, translation, English literature, and grammatical usage to be replaced by an emphasis on the actual use of all four language skills, including reading and listening as well as writing and speaking.

With an emphasis on communication came the need, and with developments in applied linguistics and language pedagogy perhaps the capacity, to be more explicit not just about the constructs being measured but how the measurement of these might differ according to the learner's level of language proficiency. The idea that only one level of English should be tested began to disappear with external forces encouraging the development of Lower Certificate in English (LCE) in 1939. The establishment of English examinations at multiple levels was given further impetus from the 1970s onwards by forces pushing in the direction of a European Community with its desire for both multi and pluri-lingualism at different levels of ability across member states. These developments led to a granular approach to construct definition at different proficiency levels in Europe which was never a major concern for testers in the United States.

The American psychometric tradition established in the early 20th century was only to make serious inroads at Cambridge in the late 1980s, spurred on by the TOEFL/FCE comparability study led by Bachman, and facilitated by the appointment under Peter Hargreaves of a professional core of research staff receptive to such ideas at the heart of Cambridge English activities. Thus scoring validity finally established itself as a fundamental canon of the examination system in Cambridge ESOL by the end of the 20th century.

An overt concern with the constructs being measured in the Cambridge English examinations and their relationship to real-life language use also apparent by the end of the 20th century. The commitment to transparency and the explicit specification of the communicative content of its examinations was further enhanced by Cambridge's adoption of a socio-cognitive approach to language test design and validation in the first decade of the 21st century; such an approach acknowledges that language use constitutes both a socially situated and a cognitively processed phenomenon and that this must be reflected in language assessment theory and practice.

The attention paid to cognitive validity came about as a result of a 10-year project which saw the publication of the 'construct' volumes in the SiLT series, guided by Mike Milanovic, Nick Saville, Lynda Taylor, Cyril Weir on the editorial steering committee. This ambitious project enabled far greater attention to be paid than previously to the cognitive processing typically activated in test and non-test tasks, and to the importance of an appropriate match between the two. There is now a growing recognition within Cambridge ESOL itself and its partners, and in the wider international testing community, of the importance for any successful assessment system of seeking and assembling validity evidence on each of these three core aspects of validity: cognitive, context and scoring, which together constitute test construct validity.

This volume has sought to shed light on how approaches to measuring language constructs evolved at Cambridge in the one hundred years of its English language examinations. It has taken us from the first form of CPE offered to three candidates in 1913, a serendipitous hybrid of legacies in language teaching from the previous century, up to the current Cambridge approach to language examinations in 2012, where the language construct to be measured in the test is seen as an evidence based product of the interaction between a targeted cognitive ability based on an expert user model, a highly specified context of use, and a performance level based on explicit and appropriate criteria of description.

> *We shall not cease from exploration*
> *And the end of all our exploring*
> *Will be to arrive where we started*
> *And know the place for the first time.*
>
> TS Eliot , "Little Gidding", *Four Quartets*

Appendix A

Past question papers: Certificate of Proficiency in English (1913), Lower Certificate in English (1939) and Certificate in Advanced English (1991)

Certificate of Proficiency in English (1913)

Certificate of Proficiency in English

Translation into French

(Two hours.)

My grandfather's recollections of Culloden were merely those of an observant boy of fourteen, who had witnessed the battle from a distance. The day, he has told me, was drizzly and thick; and on reaching the brow of the Hill of Cromarty, where he found many of his townsfolk already assembled, he could scarce see the opposite land. But the fog gradually cleared away; first one hill-top came into view, and then another; till at length the long range of coast, from the opening of the great Caledonian valley to the promontory of Burghead, was dimly visible through the haze. A little after noon there suddenly rose a round white cloud from the Moor of Culloden, and then a second round white cloud beside it. And then the two clouds mingled together, and went rolling slantways on the wind towards the west; and he could hear the rattle of the smaller fire-arms mingling with the roar of the artillery. And then, in what seemed an exceedingly brief

124.   **Certificate of Proficiency in English**

space of time, the cloud dissipated and disappeared, the boom of the greater guns ceased, and a sharp intermittent patter of musketry passed on towards Inverness. But the battle was presented to the imagination, in these old personal narratives, in many a diverse form. I have been told by an ancient woman, who, on the day of the fight, was engaged in tending some sheep on a solitary common near Munlochy, separated from the Moor of Culloden by the Frith, and screened by a lofty hill, that she sat listening in terror to the boom of the cannon; but that she was even still more scared by the continuous howling of her dog, who sat upright on his haunches all the time the firing lasted, with his neck stretched out towards the battle, and "looking as if he saw a spirit." Such are some of the recollections which link the memories of a man who has lived his half-century to those of the preceding age, and which serve to remind him how one generation of men after another break and disappear on the shores of the eternal world, as wave after wave breaks in foam upon the beach, when storms are rising, and the ground-swell sets in heavily from the sea.

HUGH MILLER.

Translation into German

(Two hours.)

Translate into GERMAN:

(a) The sentiments which animated Schiller's poetry were converted into principles of conduct; his actions were as blameless as his writings were pure. With his simple and high predilections, with his strong devotedness to a noble cause, he contrived to steer through life, unsullied by its meanness, unsaddened by any of its difficulties or allurements. With the world, in fact, he had not much to do; without effort he dwelt apart from it; its prizes were not the wealth which could enrich him. His great, almost his single aim, was to unfold his spiritual faculties, to study and contemplate and

Translation into English and English Grammar

(Two and a half hours.)

PART I. TRANSLATION

A. (For candidates taking French.)

Translate into ENGLISH:

(a) On entre d'abord dans un corridor large et bien éclairé, mais dont la largeur est diminuée par de vastes armoires de noyer sculpté, où les paysans enferment le linge du ménage, et par des sacs de blé ou de farine, déposés là pour les besoins journaliers de la famille. A gauche est la cuisine, dont la porte, toujours ouverte, laisse apercevoir une longue table de bois de chêne entourée de bancs. Il est rare qu'on n'y voie pas des paysans attablés à toute heure de jour; car la nappe y est toujours mise, soit pour les ouvriers, soit pour ces innombrables survenants à qui on offre habituellement le pain, le vin et le fromage, dans des campagnes éloignées des villes et qui n'ont ni auberge ni cabaret. A droite on entre dans la salle à manger. Bien ne la décore qu'une table de sapin, quelques chaises et un de ces vieux buffets à compartiments, à tiroirs et à nombreuses étagères, meuble héréditaire dans toutes les vieilles demeures, et que le goût actuel vient de rajeunir en les recherchant. De la salle à manger on passe dans un salon à deux fenêtres, l'une sur la cour, l'autre au nord, sur un jardin. Un escalier, en bois, mène à l'étage unique et bas où une dizaine de chambres presque sans meubles couvrent sur des corridors obscurs. Elles servaient alors à la famille, aux hôtes et aux domestiques. Voilà tout l'intérieur de cette maison qui nous a si longtemps couvés dans ses murs sombres et chauds; voilà le toit que ma mère appelait avec tant d'amour sa "Jérusalem," sa maison de paix; voilà le nid qui nous abrita tant d'années de la pluie, du froid, de la faim, du souffle du monde.

LAMARTINE.

---

improve their intellectual creations. Bent upon this, with the steadfastness of an apostle, the more sordid temptations of the world passed harmlessly over him. Wishing not to seem, but to be, envy was a feeling of which he knew but little, even before he rose above its level. Wealth or rank he regarded as means, not an end; his own humble fortune supplying him with all the essential conveniences of life, the world had nothing more that he chose to covet, nothing more that it could give him. In fact his real wealth lay in being able to pursue his darling studies, and to live in the sunshine of friendship and domestic love. This he had always longed for; this he at last enjoyed.

THOMAS CARLYLE.

(b) Early this morning we left Aix-la-Chapelle and came on to Cologne. The country, which about Aix is very pretty, soon degenerates into great masses of table-land which at last sink down into a plain, and from the edge of it, as we began to descend, we burst upon the view of the valley of the Rhine, the city of Cologne, with all its towers, the Rhine itself distinctly seen at the distance of seven miles—the Seven Mountains above Bonn on our right, and a boundless sweep of the country beyond the Rhine in front of us. To be sure, it was a striking contrast to the first view of the valley of the Tiber from the mountain of Viterbo; but the Rhine in mighty recollections will vie with anything, and this spot was particularly striking: Cologne was Agrippa's colony (*Colonia Agrippina*), inhabited by Germans brought from beyond the river, to live as the subjects of Rome; the river itself was the frontier of the Empire—the limit as it were of two worlds, that of Roman laws and customs and that of German. Far before us lay the land of our Saxon and Teutonic forefathers—the birthplace of the most moral races of men that the world has yet seen—of the soundest laws—the least violent passions, and the fairest civic and domestic virtues. I thought of that memorable defeat of Varus and his three legions which for ever confined the Teutonic nation—the Western side of the Rhine, and preserved the Teutonic element in modern Europe—safe and free.

THOMAS ARNOLD.

Certificate of Proficiency in English 127

(b) Nous venons de faire un empereur, et pour ma part je n'y ai pas nui. Voici l'histoire. Ce matin, d'Authouard nous assemble, et nous dit de quoi il s'agissait, mais bonnement, sans préambule ni péroraison. Un empereur ou la république, lequel est le plus de votre goût? comme on dit, Rôti ou bouilli, potage ou soupe, que voulez-vous? Sa harangue finie, nous voilà tous à nous regarder, assis en rond. Messieurs, qu'opinez-vous? Pas le mot; personne n'ouvre la bouche. Cela dura un quart d'heure ou plus, et devenait embarrassant pour d'Authouard et pour tout le monde, quand Maire, un jeune homme un lieutenant que tu as pu voir, se lève, et dit: S'il veut être empereur, qu'il le soit; mais pour en dire mon avis, je ne le trouve pas bon du tout. Expliquez-vous, dit le colonel; voulez-vous? ne voulez-vous pas? Je ne le veux pas, répond Maire. A la bonne heure. On recommence à s'observer les uns les autres, comme des gens qui se voient pour la première fois. Nous y serions encore, si je n'eusse pris la parole. Messieurs, dis-je, il me semble, sauf correction, que ceci ne nous regarde pas. La nation vient un empereur, est-ce à nous d'en délibérer? Ce raisonnement parut si fort, si lumineux, si ad rem...que veux-tu? j'entraînai l'assemblée. Jamais orateur n'eut un succès si complet. On se lève, on sigue, on s'en va jouer au billard. Maire me disait: Ma foi, commandant, vous parlez comme Cicéron; mais pourquoi veux-tu donc tant qu'il soit empereur, je vous prie? Pour en finir, et faire notre partie de billard. Fallait-il rester là tout le jour? pourquoi, vous, ne le voulez-vous pas? Je ne sais, me dit-il, mais je le croyais fait pour quelque chose de mieux. Voilà le propos du lieutenant, que je ne trouve point tant sot. En effet, que signifie, dis-moi...un homme comme lui, Bonaparte, soldat, chef d'armée, le premier capitaine du monde, vouloir qu'on l'appelle Majesté? Être Bonaparte, et se faire sire! Il aspire à descendre: mais non, il croit monter en s'égalant aux rois. Il aime mieux un titre qu'un nom. Pauvre homme! ses idées sont au-dessous de sa fortune. Je m'en doutai quand je le vis donner sa petite sœur à Borghèse, et croire que Borghèse lui faisait trop d'honneur. P. L. COURIER.

128 Certificate of Proficiency in English

B. (For candidates taking German.)

Translate into ENGLISH:

(a) Aber der augenfälligste Zug im gesammten Leben des Harzes ist das berg- und hüttenmännische Wesen. Das haben seine Blei- und Silbergruben, veranlaßt der Gegenden von Goslar, Klausthal, Zellerfeld, Andreasberg und Harzgerode, veranlaßt. Daher findet sich dort eine große Zahl Anstalten, die sich auf den Bergbau beziehen; daher nehmen dort nicht bloß sämmtliche Stollenmeiler, Walzarbeiten aller Art und die rein und harmonisch tönenden Glocken der Viehheerden, mit denen die einsamen Hirten weit in die Wälder hineinziehen, sondern weit mehr noch die bunten Erscheinungen bergmännischen Treibens unsere Aufmerksamkeit und Theilnahme in Anspruch. Denn überall schwingt dort der Bergmann den Schlägel, schmilzt der braune Hüttemann die von Gebirgstheile entnommenen Erze; überall sieht man dort Gruben, aufsteigende Rauchwolken, Karren mit Erz in unaufhörlicher Bewegung, und in fröhlicher Stunde vernimmt man in der harten, starken Mundart den Trinkspruch des Oberharzes: "Es grüne die Tanne, es wachse das Erz! Gott schenke uns allen ein fröhliches Herz!" Und so zeigt sich das Harzleben seit einer Reihe von Jahrhunderten. Schon in der zweiten Hälfte des zehnten Jahrhunderts sollen die dortigen Silberbergwerke entdeckt worden sein, mit Gewißheit befanden im elften Jahrhundert geschichtliche Zeugniß eine Fülle des eben Metalls als Mittel zum Verkehr und zu Kunstausprägten. Wie würden aber den Erzreichtum des Gebirges von der Bevölkerung so früh gar manche an sich wenig anstehende Höhen zu Ansiedelungen gewählt werden, aber wie würden noch in unserem Jahrzehnt auf ihren in Gegenden gutliche Stätten entstanden sein, wo sonst kaum ärmliche Hütten zu finden waren und die ringsum auch heute weder Obstbäume noch Saatfelder geben, nur einige Sickengemüse dürftig erzielt werden? J. Krraer.

(b) Besonders machen die Cuacqueri zwar nicht so viel Lärm, doch eben so viel Aufsehen als die Methodisten. Die Masse der Cuacqueri scheint so allgemein geworden zu sein durch die Leichtigkeit, auf dem Erdteil alltägliche Kleidungstücke finden zu können. Die Hauptersterniße dieser Masse sind, daß die Kleidung zwar alterthümlich, aber wohlerhalten und von eben Stoff sei. Man sieht sie die Cuacqueri zwar nicht so viel Lärm...

Certificate of Proficiency in English — 129

(German passage in Fraktur type)

...felten antortt, als mit Sammt oder Seide bekleidet, für tragen bewährte oder gekühlte Wesen, und der Natur nach muß der Cunctator beständig sein; seine Geschicklichkeit ist ganz mit Hausleuten und kleinen Augen; seine Vorräte hat wunderliche Zwischen; sein Hut ist klein und meistens bordirt. Man sieht, daß sich diese Figur sehr dem Buffo caricato der komischen Oper nähert, und wie dieser wesentlich einen läppischen, verliebten, betrogenen Toren vorstellt, so zeigen sich auch diese als abgeschmackte Stutzer. Sie schöpfen mit großer Leichtigkeit auf ten Zehen hin und her, fahren große schwere Ringe ohne Glas statt der Vergnetten, womit sie in alle Wagen hineinguffen, nach allen Fenstern hinaufblicken. Sie machen gewöhnlich einen steifen, tiefen Bückling, und ihre Freude, besonders wenn sie sich einander begegnen, geben sie dadurch zu erkennen, daß sie mit gleichen Füßen mehrmals gerade in die Höhe hüpfen und einen hellen durchdringenden unartikulierten Laut von sich geben, der mit den Konsonanten der verbunten ist. Oft geben sie sich durch diesen Ton das Zeichen, und die nächsten erwidern das Signal, so daß in kurzer Zeit dieses Geschrille den ganzen Corso hin und wieder läuft. Mutwillige Knaben blasen indeß in große gewundene Muscheln das Ohr mit unerträglichen Tönen.

GOETHE.

PART II. GRAMMAR

(For all candidates.)

1. Give the past tense and past participle of each of the following verbs, dividing them into strong and weak; add explanations: *tell, wake, bug, eat, lay, tie.*

2. Mark by an acute accent the accented syllable in each of the following words: *subjected, hyperbole, microscopical, photography, contemplative, confident, confidant, pusillanimity, gangrene, turcen.*

3. Write down the abstract nouns connected with the following adjectives and verbs: *precise, adhere, apt, predominate, optimistic, crystalline, negligent, hate, attain, detain, betray, ingenious, seize, charitable, zealous.*

130 — Certificate of Proficiency in English

4. Embody each of the following words in a sentence, in such a way as to shew that you clearly apprehend its meaning: *commence, commend, command, recommend; incredible, incredulous.*

5. Correct or justify **four** of the following sentences, giving your reasons:

(a) I hope you are determined to seriously improve.

(b) Comparing Shakespeare with Æschylus, the former is by no means inferior to the latter.

(c) I admit that I was willing to have made peace with you.

(d) The statement was incorrect, as any one familiar with the spot, and who was acquainted with the facts, will admit.

(e) It has the largest circulation of any paper in England.

(f) The lyrical gifts of Shakespeare are woven into the actual language of the characters.

English Essay

(Two hours.)

Write an Essay on **one** of the following subjects:

(a) The effect of political movements upon nineteenth century literature in England.

(b) English Pre-Raffaellitism.

(c) Elizabethan travel and discovery.

(d) The Indian Mutiny.

(e) The development of local self-government.

(f) Matthew Arnold.

Certificate of Proficiency in English 131

English Phonetics

(One hour and a half)

Candidates may use any consistent system of phonetic notation, but must state what system they use; and if the system they use is not generally known, they should show by examples what values are to be attached to the symbols they use.

1. Make a phonetic transcription of each of the following passage, illustrating in the case of passage (a) a careful pronunciation, in the case of (b) the pronunciation of educated persons in ordinary conversation:

(a) But, whatever be the profession or trade chosen, the advantages are many and important, compared with the state of a mere literary man, who in any degree depends on the sale of his works for the necessaries and comforts of life. In the former a man lives in sympathy with the world in which he lives. At least he acquires a better and quicker tact for the knowledge of that with which men in general can sympathise. He learns to manage his genius more prudently and efficaciously. His powers and acquirements gain him likewise more real admiration; for they surpass the legitimate expectations of others. He is something besides an author, and is not therefore considered merely as to one of their own class; and whether he exerts himself or not in the conversational circles of his acquaintance, his silence is not attributed to pride, nor his communicativeness to vanity.

(b) "Ah, Mr Holmes. I am delighted to see you."
"Good morning, Lanner. You will not think me an intruder, I am sure. Have you heard of the events which led up to this affair?"
"Yes, I heard something of them."
"Have you formed any opinion?"
"As far as I can see, the man has been driven out of his senses by fright. The bed has been well slept in, you see. There is his impression deep enough."

132 Certificate of Proficiency in English

"Noticed anything peculiar about the room?"
"Found a screwdriver and some screws on the wash-hand stand. Seems to have smoked heavily during the night, too. Here are four cigar ends that I picked out of the fire-place."
"Hum! Have you got his cigar-holder?"
"No, I have seen none."
"His cigar case then?"
"Yes, it was in his coat pocket."

2. Describe fully the articulation of the various vowel sounds in the (ordinary) spelling of which the letter o is used (alone or in combination) in the above passages.

3. Explain the terms: 'glide,' 'narrow vowel,' 'semi-vowel,' and give two examples of each in both phonetic and ordinary spelling.

4. How would you teach a pupil the correct pronunciation of the vowel sounds in *fare, fate, fat, fall, far*?

5. Discuss carefully the articulation of the consonants in *quite, huge, dreary*.

ORAL TEST

Dictation *30 mins*
Reading Aloud and Conversation *30 mins*

(Archived CPE 1913 Oral Test not available.)

Lower Certificate in English (1939)

Lower Certificate
READING
JUNE 1939

UNIVERSITY OF CAMBRIDGE

LOCAL EXAMINATIONS

Lower Certificate in English

Reading Passage

Across the harbour the sloping rays of the late sun were moving softly, falling quietly across the back of a young boy who was seated on the old sea wall, his eyes turned with a far-away look across the stretch of water full of boats. He saw before him great sailing-ships which had come with spices. And there were dark ships from the North. Small, quick vessels with jewels of great value and beautiful linens and silks from the East were resting by the side of strange ships which had been through the dangers of the African seas.

The boy was watching them all. He was happy letting thoughts of ships and journeys and danger go through his head. Marco Polo was his name.

His was a trading family. Even now his father and his brother were in far-off countries trading and looking for things of value to take back to Venice. They had been away for nine long years, and Marco had no idea in what strange land they might be journeying.

(From *Stories of Marco Polo*, in Basic English.)

Lower Certificate in English (1939)

Lower Certificate
DICTATION
JUNE 1939

UNIVERSITY OF CAMBRIDGE

LOCAL EXAMINATIONS

Lower Certificate in English

Dictation

Our way was new | and strange. | We had no map | and no knowledge | of the river. | When our canoes | came to a stretch | of white water, | the Indians | would get on their feet | for one quick look | at the long | wide slope | of sharp rocks | and broken river. | In that one moment | they picked the line | they were to follow | better than we | would have done | in half an hour's study. | Then without hesitation | they shot | their little canoes, | whose sides | are no thicker | than cardboard, | at it. | From that time | we only tried | to keep still | Each Indian | did it all | with his paddle. | He seemed to have | complete control | over our course. | Even in a | rush of water | that took us forward | at almost | railroad speed, | he could stop | for a second, | work directly sideways | or shoot forward | at an angle. | Any mistake | in his judgment, | or in acting upon it, | meant going on a rock, | and that, | in these waters, | meant destruction.

Lower Certificate
(a) PRESCRIBED
TEXTS
Wednesday
21 JUNE 1939
2 *hours*

UNIVERSITY OF CAMBRIDGE
LOCAL EXAMINATIONS SYNDICATE

Lower Certificate in English

PRESCRIBED TEXTS.

(*Two hours.*)

Give answers to questions about **two** *of these four books.*

A TALE OF TWO CITIES.

Do **all** *of Question* 1 *and then give as complete an answer as you are able to* **one** *other Question.*

1. "*Carton.* Have no fear! I shall soon be out of the way of harming you, and the rest will soon be far from here, please God! Now, call your men and take me to the coach.

Barsad. You?

Carton. Him, man, with whom I have changed places. You go out at the gate by which you brought me in?

Barsad. Of course.

Carton. I was weak and faint when you brought me in, and I am fainter now you take me out. The parting has been too much for me. Such a thing has happened here, often, and too often. Your life is in your own hands. Quick! Call your men!"

(a) Who are "the rest" and what are they doing?

(b) Why does Carton say that Barsad's life is in his own hands?

(c) What does Carton mean by "I shall soon be out of the way of harming you"?

(d) "The parting has been too much for me." Say in other words what this means.

2. Why did Gaspard kill the Marquis?

3. Why did the people send Darnay to the guillotine?

4. Why did Barsad let Carton take the place of Darnay?

THE OXFORD ENGLISH COURSE: READING BOOK FOUR.

Do **all** *of Question* 1 *and then give as complete an answer as you are able to* **one** *other Question.*

1. "The problem is clear: How can such villages be made clean and bright, and how can the lives of the villagers be made happier and more interesting?

The answer is equally clear: The responsibility for village improvement rests on the village leaders. Until these leaders study the facts about modern progress in health, communication, building, scientific farming, and other related subjects, we cannot expect great changes. Even after they have learned the power of science and modern industry to improve village life, the changes may not come. Almost any well-informed leader can tell what should be done, but leaders of great patience, tact, wisdom, and determination are needed before such plans become realities."

(a) What kind of village is here being talked about?

(b) "The responsibility rests on the village leaders." What does this mean?

(c) Give some examples of improvements in communication and in scientific farming.

(d) Say in other words what patience and tact are.

2. How should a cottage in a village be built?

3. How can farmers cooperate?

4. How do moving pictures make life more interesting?

5. What was Sir Thomas More's answer when he was charged with having received gifts from persons on trial?

GULLIVER IN LILLIPUT.

Do all of Question 1 and then give as complete an answer as you are able to one other Question.

1. "I was getting ready to go and see the Emperor of Blefuscu, when an important person in the King's circle, to whom I had been of great use when the King was very angry with him, came to my house privately at night in a covered seat, and without sending in his name, made a request to be let in. The servants were sent away, and I put the seat, with the man in it, into my coat pocket. Then, giving the order to a good servant to say I was not well and had gone to sleep, I got the door of my room locked....After the first words of meeting, seeing a look of trouble on the man's face, I put a question as to the reason. Requesting me to give him my complete and quiet attention in connection with something which had to do with my good name and my very existence, he gave me this account, of which I made a note the minute he had gone."

(a) What were these covered seats, and how did men make journeys in them?

(b) Why were the servants sent away?

(c) "Something which had to do with my good name and my very existence." Say in other words what this means.

(d) What was the news which the "important person" gave to Gulliver?

2. In what ways did Gulliver give help to the Lilliputians?

3. What did Gulliver do when six of the Lilliputians were put into his hands as a punishment?

4. How did the Lilliputians get Gulliver from the sea-side to his prison?

ARMS AND THE MAN.

Do all of Question 1 and then give as complete an answer as you are able to one other Question.

1. "*Sergius* [naturally, no longer acting]: Yes: I am a man without fear. My heart gave a jump like a woman's when the first gun went off; but in the attack I made the discovery that I had no fear. Yes: that at least is true of me.

Louka: Did you make the discovery in the attack that the men whose fathers are poor like mine had more fear than the men who are well-off like you?

Sergius [with bitter humour]: Not a bit. They were all waving their blades about, and crying out at the tops of their voices, and using bad language like the best of us. Paha! The power to do violent acts and put men to death is cheap. I have an English dog—a regular fighter—who has as much fire in him as all the men in Bulgaria, with Russia at their backs. But he lets my horse-boy give him a whipping, all the same. That's your military man all over!"

(a) Give an account of the attack they are talking about.

(b) Why does Sergius say, "That *at least* is true of me "?

(c) "*As much fire in him as all the men in Bulgaria, with Russia at their backs.*" What is the sense here of the *italicised* words?

(d) What is the sense here of "cheap " and "well-off "?

2. What, in your opinion, are the signs that the feelings between Sergius and Raina were not those of true love?

3. Why did Bluntschli come back to the Petkoffs' house?

4. Do you take the view, put forward by Sergius, that Bluntschli was "a tradesman to his boots"?

Lower Certificate
ENGLISH
COMP. AND LANG.
Wednesday
21 JUNE 1939
2 hours

UNIVERSITY OF CAMBRIDGE

LOCAL EXAMINATIONS SYNDICATE

Lower Certificate in English

English Composition and Language

(Two hours.)

You must answer three questions, one from A, one from B, and all four parts of the question in C.

A.

Write a letter on **one** of these subjects. It should be between 80 and 100 words long. Give your address at the top and make the ending like that of a real letter:

1. A letter of thanks for a present you have been given on your birthday. Say what other presents you were given and what you did that day.

2. A letter to a friend who is ill in hospital. Tell him any news which you think will interest him, and try to be as helpful and cheerful as you can.

3. A letter to a friend living a long distance away, saying how happy you are to know that he is soon coming to live in a house very near to your own. Say a little about your town and the places you will be able to go to together.

B.

Take **one** of these subjects and write a composition which should be between 250 and 300 words long (that is, about 2 pages):

4. You have been teaching your younger brother or sister to ride a bicycle. Say in as interesting a way as you can how you did it, and give an account of anything which took place which caused you amusement.

5. Give a detailed account of a picture which you have hanging in your house or school. Your description should be very clear so that anyone reading your description can see the picture in his mind's eye.

6. You went to the railway station to make a journey, but you were late for the train and had to be there an hour waiting for the next one. Say what you saw at the station while you were waiting.

C.

Read the following passage carefully:

Many years ago in Australia three young children went out into the dark and desolate wood to gather wood for broom.[1] The eldest was a boy of nine years old; Jane, his sister, was seven, and little Frank was five. When they did not come back, their parents became very alarmed, as once lost in this wood it is very difficult to find one's way out again and there was little chance of discovering food or water. The father and his neighbours looked for the children, and searched the wood day by day until a week had passed. Finally he got the help of some natives, who have a wonderful power of following the slightest trail in their woods. They soon saw signs where the children had been from the bent twigs or the trampling of the grass. "Here little one tired," they said, "sit down. Big one kneel down; carry him along. Here travel all night; dark—not see that bush; her fall on him."

On the next day the natives led the father to a clump of broom, where lay three little figures, the smallest one in the middle with his sister's frock over his own clothes. To their amazement the elder boy roused himself, sat up, and said: "Father!" and then fell back from sheer weakness. Little Frank awoke as if from a quiet sleep and Jane had just the strength to murmur "Cold—cold." When the elder brother was carried past the places that the natives had pointed out, his account of their

[1] A shrub or plant with yellow flower.

Certificate in Advanced English (1991)

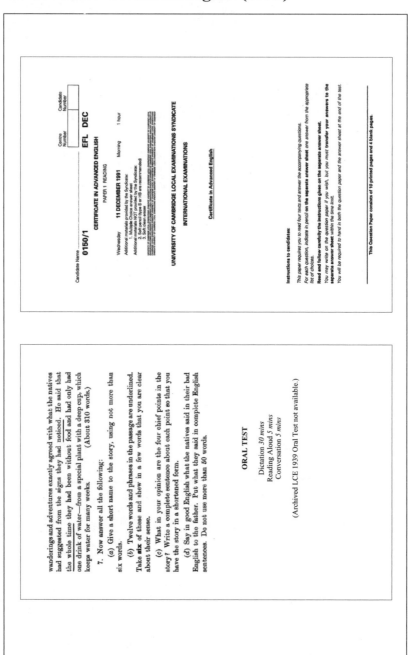

Candidate Name

Centre Number

Candidate Number

0150/1

EFL DEC

CERTIFICATE IN ADVANCED ENGLISH

PAPER 1 READING

Wednesday **11 DECEMBER 1991**   Morning   1 hour

Additional materials provided by the Syndicate:
1. Multiple-Choice answer sheet
Additional materials NOT provided by the Syndicate:
2. Soft pencil (type B or HB are recommended)
3. Soft clean eraser

UNIVERSITY OF CAMBRIDGE LOCAL EXAMINATIONS SYNDICATE

INTERNATIONAL EXAMINATIONS

Certificate in Advanced English

Instructions to candidates:

This paper requires you to read four texts and answer the accompanying questions.

For each question, indicate in pencil on the separate answer sheet one answer from the appropriate list of choices.

Read and follow carefully the instructions given on the separate answer sheet.

You may write on the question paper if you wish, but you must transfer your answers to the separate answer sheet within the time limit.

You will be required to hand in both the question paper and the answer sheet at the end of the test.

This Question Paper consists of 10 printed pages and 4 blank pages.

---

wanderings and adventures exactly agreed with what the natives had suggested from the signs they had noticed. He said that the whole time they had been without food and had only had one drink of water—from a special plant with a deep cup, which keeps water for many weeks.   (About 310 words.)

7. Now answer all the following:

(a) Give a short name to the story, using not more than six words.

(b) Twelve words and phrases in the passage are underlined. Take **six** of these and shew in a few words that you are clear about their sense.

(c) What in your opinion are the four chief points in the story? Write a complete sentence about each point so that you have the story in a shortened form.

(d) Say in good English what the natives said in their bad English to the father. Put what they said in complete English sentences. Do not use more than 50 words.

ORAL TEST

Dictation *30 mins*
Reading Aloud *5 mins*
Conversation *5 mins*

(Archived LCE 1939 Oral Test not available.)

2

FIRST TEXT: QUESTIONS 1–18

Answer questions 1–18 by referring to the magazine's problem page printed on page 3.
Indicate your answers on the separate answer sheet.

For questions 1–6, choose from list A–H the most suitable heading for each of the letters on the problem page.

A A SPOONFUL OF SUGAR
B KEEP UP THE CALCIUM
C NO SMOKE WITHOUT FIRE
D BETTER THAN MEAT

E WHAT'S MISSING?
F KEEP IT CLEAN
G A COMPLETE WASTE OF MONEY
H THE BEE VITAMINS

Questions 6–10. According to the letters and replies, what health problems are associated with the following? Choose your answers from the list of problems A–G. You may choose any of the problems more than once.

6 being a diabetic
7 eating dried fruit
8 being a smoker
9 drinking beyond the recommended limit
10 being a vegetarian

A Diet may be low in iron.
B Chemicals may be present.
C Certain vitamins may be difficult to absorb.
D You must never eat sugar.
E You may be eating too much fibre.
F Be careful about your fat intake.
G You must be careful how much energy you use up.

For questions 11–18, look at the list of statements below (11–18) and choose which of the items from list A–H is referred to in each case. You may choose any of the items more than once.

11 Many doctors now believe that this should make up about half of your diet.
12 This helps you to absorb iron.
13 This is present in both beans and eggs.
14 If you're a diabetic, this won't hurt you provided that you eat fibre at the same time.
15 As a smoker, you might suffer from a lack of this.
16 This is of uncertain benefit.
17 Smokers find this difficult to get into their bloodstreams.
18 The presence of this in soluble form is especially important for diabetics.

A vitamin C
B iron
C calcium
D carbohydrate
E fibre
F protein
G sugar
H vitamin B
I royal jelly

Now transfer your answers to the separate answer sheet.

3

1

After a bad bout of flu left me feeling totally washed out, my mother kindly bought me two months' supply of royal jelly capsules.
I know she meant well, but she can ill afford the £10 they cost. I don't want to hurt her feelings, but I've read that these capsules are useless. I must say I've yet to show any signs of revitalisation! Do you think I should keep on with the course?

It's true that none of the claims for royal jelly have been substantiated, but as you already have a supply there's no harm in going on with the course until it's finished.
Royal jelly contains reasonable amounts of the B vitamins - especially B6 and another one called pantothenic acid. Why not treat your mother for her kindness and explain that, in the future, instead of spending money on this expensive supplement, you would prefer to get vitamins directly from the food you eat?
The main sources of B6 and pantothenic acid are meats, cereals, wholemeal bread and vegetables - plenty of these incorporated into your meals should provide you with a good peptic 'pick-meup' diet. If you're still feeling below par quite some time after flu, you'd be wise to consult your doctor.

2

When going round the supermarket with my daughter, helping to keep an eye on my two-year-old grandson, I was surprised when she opened a packet of apricots and gave him a couple. I always thought that dried fruit should be washed first!
Don't worry, your daughter has hit on a smashing idea. Dried fruit from a packet is ready to eat - and is so much better than sweets or chocolate. A lot of people are concerned about chemicals sprayed on fruit. If you are one of these, by all means wash it, even though it may only be cosmetic as the fruit is often impregnated. Personally, I don't bother.

3

My fiancé smokes about 15 cigarettes a day and enjoys his daily pint or two of beer. He seems to be laid low with any cold or virus that's going around, whereas I stay healthy. I'm sure I've heard that smokers and drinkers need to take extra vitamins, but he just won't take me seriously. Am I right in believing this?

Yes - low levels of vitamin C have been found in smokers, probably because the tobacco components interfere with the availability of vitamin C in the body. Calcium absorption is also adversely affected.

Drinking may also reduce the absorption of some vitamins, if it is above the recommended limit of 21 units a week for a man, 13 for a woman. (A unit being one glass of wine, half a pint of ordinary beer or a single pub measure of spirits). All good reasons for encouraging your fiancé to stop or at least cut down these habits, and eat plenty of fresh food, including fruit and vegetables.

4

My mother is a diabetic and has always followed a strict sugar-free diet. Now she's delighted to hear from a friend that a little sugar will do her no harm. Why the change?

These days, a low-fat, high-fibre diet, with at least 60% of the calories coming from carbohydrate, is recommended by doctors. The presence of fibre, especially the 'soluble' type found in oats and pulses, slows the rate of glucose absorption into the body and this helps diabetics. Sugar, in small amounts, makes such a diet more palatable and, provided that it's combined with fibre, it's not harmful i.e. sugar in tea - no; wholemeal cake - yes). Diabetics also need to make sure that their energy intake matches their output.
But don't let your mother make any major change in her diet without consulting her doctor and/or diabetician first.

5

My 14-year-old daughter has recently decided to become a vegetarian. I'm happy to go along with her decision, but just want to be sure she will be getting everything she needs in her diet.
There's no reason why a meat-free diet shouldn't contain all the essential nutrients, so long as a wide range of foods is eaten. However, your daughter shouldn't simply cut out meat, poultry and fish without giving proper thought to the balance.
Meat contains iron, and dairy products such as cheese and yogurt, which are especially important in growing children, who need calcium for bone development. Some also continue to eat some milk and dairy products such as cheese and yogurt, which are excluded, as in a vegan diet, calcium and vitamin B12 supplements may be necessary.
Your daughter can get all the protein she needs from eating nuts, grains, beans and pulses. Vegetarian diets may be low in iron, which is needed for growth. There's iron in cereal foods such as bread, in eggs and vegetables, particularly peas and beans, though it's not as easily absorbed in this form as it is from meat. The solution is to make sure there's always some vitamin C in a meal on fruit and vegetables to help absorption.

4

Read this extract from a popular science magazine. The text is followed by a number of questions. You must choose the answer which you think fits best. On your answer sheet, indicate the letter A, B, C or D against the number of each question. Give one answer only to each question.

Space Pollution

Is it too early to worry about trashing the moon? Probably not. The US Defense Department already monitors more than 6,000 pieces of junk in orbit - ranging from four-inch bits to rocket bodies. And this litter has caused an upset among astronomers (it interferes with their observational and concern among spacefarers. In 1983 a collision with a paint flake only one hundredth of an inch in diameter left a deep crater in the five-eighths-inch-thick window of the Challenger; a larger object could easily have destroyed the craft.

Small wonder that the side of people treating other celestial bodies as we have our own troubles space environmentalists. A recent initiative calls for mining the lunar surface, for example. A few decades of digging up the moon could cause lunar pollution that would interfere with scientific studies and other types of space utilization. Lucy Stojak, a lecturer on air and space law at McGill University in Montreal, suggests that a harbinger of environmental problems may be seen in the 1967 Space Treaty. "It's deliberately vague. Furthermore, the Liability Convention of 1982 does not directly cover liabilities for damage caused by debris or pollution," she says.

When humankind does move out to space, we will need to mine local resources to survive. The biggest requirement: finding a source of oxygen, which, besides being necessary for life support, is a key rocket propellant.

Unfortunately space mining, when it does exist, will probably make a mess. For that reason, both space scientists and jurists are beginning to consider the environmental ethics of space exploration. Pollution has traditionally taken a back seat to profit here on earth; space offers an opportunity to change that. But the legal aspects of protection - as well as those of exploitation - are murky. Only two international treaties currently regulate space activity, and the

more recent and more restrictive of these, the 1984 Moon Treaty, has few signatories, none of them spacefaring nations. The underlying legal concept of space as the common property of all mankind does not mesh well with the more imperial ambitions of highly developed industrial nations and multi-national corporations.

The delicacy of the space environment adds to the conflict between industrial and scientific interests - and requires that exploitation be well thought out. This may mean making the most of resources as they are rather than making changes to them. For example, the Jet Propulsion Laboratory's James Burke feels that the twilight of the lunar poles is ideal for a scientific camp. The poles lack the extreme temperature swings from high to low found in the equatorial regions, and the permanently shadowed interior of a polar crater would be a perfect site for infrared astronomy. The poles need protection from lunar activity, such as mining, that might interfere with observation.

Proposals to mine water from rocks on Mars' moon Phobos have raised similar environmental concerns. "Water can be more economically delivered from Phobos to the lunar surface and to orbital space stations than from the surface of the earth," author and astronaut Brian O'Leary wrote in a 1987 paper. This brought an impassioned response from three prominent Hungarian astronomers who pleaded that Phobos be left intact "as a natural park for the sake of future generations of explorers".

Today's space environmentalists seem to agree that the past behavior of spacefarers leaves little room for complacency about the issue. Legal specialist Stojak has suggested, somewhat hopefully, that nations might resolve the conflict between exploitation and exploration under the pressure of necessity, as the United States and the Soviet Union are now doing over the growing problem of space debris. Public opinion, she thinks, may ultimately play a decisive role in preventing the reckless despoilment of extraterrestrial territory.

5

19 What problem has litter caused travellers in space?

A It has upset their instruments.
B It has interfered with observations.
C It has already damaged a spaceship.
D It has caused the destruction of a spaceship.

20 How does Lucy Stojak view the law on space litter?

A She thinks it is limited in scope.
B She believes it will prevent future environmental problems.
C She says it is based on outdated information.
D She predicts serious pollution unless it is implemented.

21 What weakness of the 1984 Moon Treaty does the author point out?

A It puts profits before environmental protection.
B Although recent, it is too restrictive.
C Its underlying legal concept is unacceptable.
D Its signatories are not involved in space exploration.

22 Why would a polar crater on the moon be ideal for a scientific camp?

A The light levels and temperature vary only slightly.
B The light level varies but the temperature is constant.
C The light level is constant although the temperature may vary.
D The light levels and temperature vary in the same way as an earth.

23 Why did Brian O'Leary propose mining Phobos?

A to supply water for bases on Mars
B to supply water for the moon
C to replace polluted water on earth
D to obtain water rich in minerals

24 What does Lucy Stojak feel about the future of the space environment?

A She's cautiously optimistic about it.
B She's convinced it will be safeguarded.
C Public complacency will result in conflict.
D Commercial pressures will do great damage.

Now transfer your answers to the separate answer sheet.

6

For questions 25-30, you must choose which of the paragraphs A-G on page 7 match the numbered gaps in the newspaper article below. There is one extra paragraph which does not belong in any of the gaps. Indicate your answer on the separate answer sheet.

The Best of Times

Brian Moore talks to Danny Danziger

Brian Moore, the novelist, born in Belfast, now lives in California. His latest book, 'Lies of Silence', is on the Booker Prize shortlist.

FOR ME, the best of times was the publication of my first novel. I had written and published a few short stories, but was making my living in Montreal as a newspaper reporter. I was 26, and I said to myself: "All my life I've wanted to do some serious writing and if I don't do it now, I'll never do it."

25

And suddenly, I found myself writing as in a trance. I was living a hermit's life, not seeing anyone, and the book was written with great intensity. I would write for several hours, and then fall asleep, wake up, make some food, and go on writing. Days and nights merged into some indiscriminate time.

26

I didn't realise that it was unusual for a young man to start writing a novel from the point of view of a middle-aged woman. But once I had started writing it, I seemed to become my character, an Irish spinster called Judith Hearne.

27

So in the nine months before the book was first published in England I went through a state of nerves and depression about the entire enterprise of writing novels.

28 I was very naive in those days. I didn't realise how lucky I was to get those wonderful reviews. Overnight, in America the same publishers who had rejected the novel were calling me up to ask if they could read it.

29 Although it never became a best-seller in the States or England, the book I had worried about for nine months has been in print for 35 years as The Lonely Passion of Judith Hearne.

30 Another irony. I'd been sending out short stories to The Atlantic Monthly. All were rejected. When my book appeared and got good reviews, I had the idea of sending the stories back to The Atlantic Monthly. I sent them three that they'd rejected - and all were accepted, published and praised by the editor.

I realise now, years later, how incredibly lucky I was. If Diana Athill and André Deutsch had turned the book down, it might never have seen the light of day. That's why I have a special fondness for England, because England took and published my first "too depressing" book.

7

A I remember that Alfred Knopf came to Montreal, took me out to lunch, and in a lordly manner told me he would publish the book. But the day before the visit another publisher had already accepted the novel, and so I was able to tell Mr. Knopf, and all those publishers who wrote to say they were anxious to see the book, that they had already seen it and rejected it, and that I had a publisher. Great fun for me!

B It was the old story; success had many fathers, failure had none. For anyone writing a novel and feeling discouraged, there is a lesson in my experience. What seems to be a failed piece of writing when it is being rejected, can turn on the flip of a coin - in this case a set of reviews - into a book which everyone suddenly acclaims.

C So I saved up enough money to keep myself for six months. I then rented a log cabin on a lake in the Laurentian mountains, north of Montreal, and holed up there all alone.

D And then one day, shortly after publication date, a fat envelope full of newspaper clippings arrived in the post in Montreal. I went to the park, trembling, and sat down to read them - they were all terrific. I remember that same week, Françoise Sagan's Bonjour Tristesse was published in England, and we were reminded of two "new young novelists" for fiction. I remember feeling a fraud. I was 27 while she was only 17.

E I wrote the book in a way that has never happened to me with any of my later novels. I had an idea of the sort of book I wanted to write. I wanted to write a novel about a character losing his or her religious faith. I stood in awe of James Joyce, and didn't want to make my character an intellectual like Stephen Dedalus in A Portrait of the Artist as a Young Man. And then it came to me: "What if I write about an ordinary person, someone - a woman perhaps - my mother might have known?"

F When I had finished I went back to work as a reporter, and sent the novel to American and British publishers. The first British publisher I sent it to was André Deutsch. Diana Athill, one of the editors, read it and sent it to Laurie Lee, who was a reader for the firm. He said that it was "totally depressing" and no one would want to read it. However, Diana Athill said it should be published because I was a good writer, and would, no doubt, write a second novel. In the meantime the American news was terrible. Twelve American publishers rejected it, one after the other, always with the same verdict. "Too depressing".

G He didn't care for it of course but I was determined to make him look at the novel. He didn't use the word "depressing", but I knew what he thought.

For questions **31-33**, choose one answer from the list of statements **A-F**. The answers to these questions are all on page **6**.

What was the writer's state of mind

31 while alone in the log cabin?

32 while waiting for the book to come out in England?

33 after reading the first reviews?

A He was privately amused.

B He took his luck for granted.

C He felt like a great writer.

D He was uncertain about the whole business.

E He became increasingly dissatisfied.

F He was completely absorbed in what he was doing.

Now transfer your answers to the separate answer sheet.

Measured Constructs

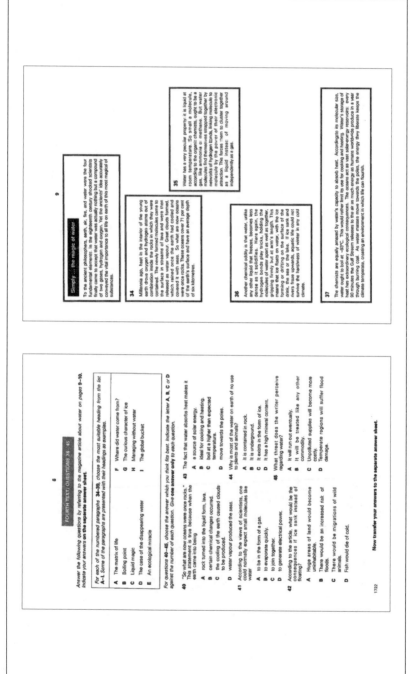

Simply ... the magic of water

To the ancient philosophers, earth, air, fire, and water were the four fundamental elements. In the eighteenth century studious scientists finally came to accept that water was actually nothing but a compound of two gases, hydrogen and oxygen. Yet the ancients' idea accurately conveyed the vital importance to all life on earth of this most magical of substances.

34

Millennia ago, heat in the interior of the young earth drove oxygen and hydrogen atoms out of combination inside the rocks in which they were contained. The newly formed molecules came to the surface in streams of lava and were then released as water vapour. Great clouds formed, which rained once the earth had cooled and covered it with seas. So what are now oceans were once rocks. These oceans cover 71 per cent of the earth's surface and have an average depth of six kilometres.

35

Water has a very peculiar property: it is liquid at room temperature. So small a molecule, according to the organic chemists, ought to be a gas, like ammonia or methane. But water molecules find themselves strapped together by networks of hydrogen bonds, linking molecule to molecule by the power of their electronic attraction. This forces them to cluster together as a liquid instead of moving around independently as a gas.

36

Another chemical oddity is that water, unlike any other liquid that freezes, becomes less dense as it solidifies. Here again, the hydrogen bonds play tricks, holding the molecules of water apart as well as together, gripping firmly but at arm's length. This means that ice floats on water, with the ice forming or drifting on the surface of the drink, the sea or the lake. If ice sank and rivers froze upwards, aquatic life could not survive the harshness of winter in any cold climate.

37

The chemists are equally amazed by water's capacity to absorb heat. Accordingly its molecular size, water ought to boil at -80°C. This would rather limit its use for cooling and heating. Water's storage of heat has extraordinary ecological consequences. The oceans act as vast solar-energy reservoirs: every 90 minutes the Gulf Stream releases to the air as much energy as humans worldwide produce in a year through burning coal. As water masses move towards the poles, the energy they liberate keeps the climate temperate, creating an environment on which life can flourish.

FOURTH TEXT / QUESTIONS 34 - 45

Answer the following questions by referring to the magazine article about water on pages 9–10. Indicate your answers on the separate answer sheet.

For each of the numbered paragraphs **34–39**, choose the most suitable heading from the list **A–I**. Some of the paragraphs are presented with their headings as examples.

A The matrix of life	**F** Where did water come from?
B Boiling point	**G** The curious character of ice
C Liquid magic	**H** Managing without water
D The case of the disappearing water	**I** The global bucket
E An ecological miracle	

For questions **40–45**, choose the answer which you think fits best. Indicate the letter **A**, **B**, **C** or **D** against the number of each question. Give **one answer only** to each question.

40 "So what are now oceans were once rocks." This statement is true because when the earth came into being
- **A** rock turned into the liquid form, lava.
- **B** certain chemical changes occurred.
- **C** the cooling of the earth caused clouds to be produced.
- **D** water vapour produced the seas.

41 According to the views of scientists, one could normally expect small molecules like water
- **A** to be in the form of a gas.
- **B** to evaporate quickly.
- **C** to join together.
- **D** to generate electrical power.

42 According to the article, what would be the consequences if ice sank instead of floating?
- **A** Huge areas of land would become uninhabitable.
- **B** There would be an increased risk of floods.
- **C** Unpolluted supplies will become more costly.
- **D** Fish would die of cold.

43 The fact that water absorbs heat makes it
- **A** a source of solar energy.
- **B** ideal for cooling and heating.
- **C** boil at a higher than expected temperature.
- **D** move towards the poles.

44 Why is most of the water on earth of no use to plants and animals?
- **A** It is contained in rock.
- **B** It is underground.
- **C** It exists in the form of ice.
- **D** It has a high mineral content.

45 What threat does the writer perceive regarding water?
- **A** It will run out eventually.
- **B** It will be treated like any other commodity.
- **C** Temperate regions will become more damage.
- **D** Temperate regions will suffer flood damage.

Now transfer your answers to the separate answer sheet.

0150/2   EFL   DEC

CERTIFICATE IN ADVANCED ENGLISH

PAPER 2 WRITING

Wednesday   **11 DECEMBER 1991**   Morning   2 hours

(No additional materials required)

UNIVERSITY OF CAMBRIDGE LOCAL EXAMINATIONS SYNDICATE

INTERNATIONAL EXAMINATIONS

Certificate in Advanced English

Instructions to candidates:

This paper contains one Section A task and four Section B tasks. You must complete the Section A task and **one** task from Section B.

The two sections carry equal marks.

Read the task instructions and consider the information **carefully** both for Section A and the task which you select for Section B.

Write clearly in pen, not pencil, on the lined paper provided. You may make alterations but make sure that your work is **easy to read**.

Put your name and candidate number at the top of each sheet of paper.

_____

This Question Paper consists of 4 printed pages.

10

Water on the brain

Around 70 per cent of the human body is made up of water. Brain and muscle tissues are water-richest; bone and fat water-poorest. Water also performs the role of solvent and conductor essential to the metabolic performance of the human being. Every day our bodies turn over 2.5 litres of water, losing most of this by respiration, perspiration, and excretion, and replacing the shortfall by the combustion of food and drink. Without the body's natural cooling process - in which water is essential - this combustion would cause a rise in body temperature of 20°C.

38

The vast majority of the water on earth - over 97 per cent - is contained in the oceans. With its high mineral content this is no use for sustaining earth-bound plant or animal life. Most of the fresh water is locked up in the icecaps and glaciers, leaving only 0.6 per cent in lakes, rivers, and under the ground as an accessible resource vital to human activity. Nevertheless there is plenty to go round. 3,000 cubic metres per person per year at present. But pressures from expanding population, irrigated agriculture and thirsty industrial processes are growing.

The hydrological cycle

Every schoolchild is taught the wonders of the rain-and-shine system whereby water is endlessly recycled through the atmosphere from sea to land, fuelling plant and animal fertility in the process. Each year the sun's energy draws 500,000 cubic kilometres of seawater into the air. Around one-fifth of this falls back on land as rain, setting off down rivers and streams towards the sea to repeat the cycle. The amount of water in the cycle is constant and cannot be changed.

The rain in Spain ...

But this constant amount of water in the global bucket pours on some countries and continents much more than others - it favours those who live in the green and pleasant lands of the temperate zones. Many parts of Asia and Africa face grave water shortages. Paradoxically it is also these regions which are most prone to flooding as run-off turns dry seasonal rivers into raging torrents, causing immense damage. Because of population growth, global supplies are heard of this finite resource are dropping, and the sharpest drops are in already water-short countries.

39

We can live without all if we have to; we cannot survive a day on earth without water. Its ready supply is too easily taken for granted, especially in temperate parts of the world. As pressure increases on our supply - pressure from people, industrial processes, pollutants, water is in grave danger of becoming just another commodity in the market place, its supplies are dominated by the rich and powerful. In the traditional world, in religion and even in municipal engineering, water has always been seen as a common resource, indivisible as air. Equity demands that it remains so.

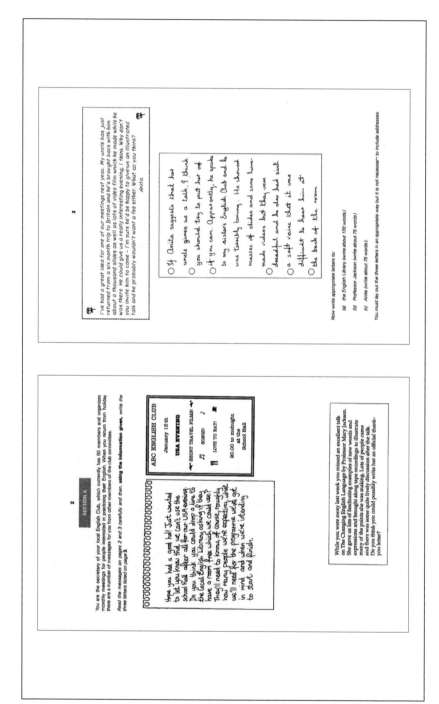

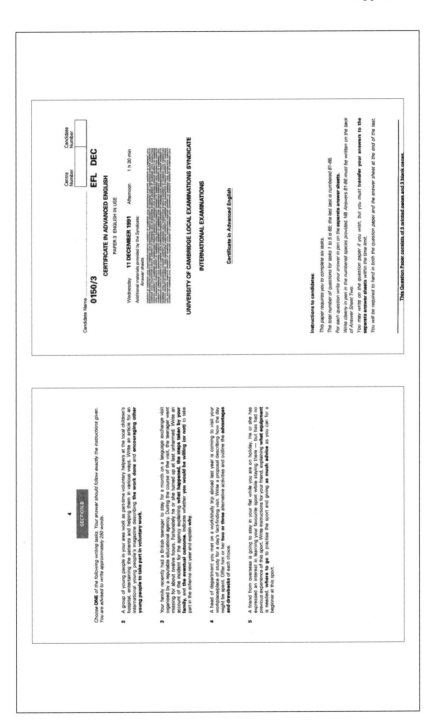

Candidate Name

Centre Number

Candidate Number

0150/3 EFL DEC

CERTIFICATE IN ADVANCED ENGLISH

PAPER 3 ENGLISH IN USE

Wednesday **11 DECEMBER 1991** Afternoon 1 h 30 min

Additional materials provided by the Syndicate:
Answer sheets

UNIVERSITY OF CAMBRIDGE LOCAL EXAMINATIONS SYNDICATE

INTERNATIONAL EXAMINATIONS

Certificate in Advanced English

Instructions to candidates:

This paper requires you to complete six tasks.

The total number of questions for tasks 1 to 5 is 66; the last task is numbered 81–86.

For each question write your answer in pen on the separate answer sheets.

Write clearly in pen in the numbered spaces provided. NB Answers 81–86 must be written on the back of Answer Sheet Two.

You may write on the question paper if you wish, but you must transfer your answers to the separate answer sheets within the time limit.

You will be required to hand in both the question paper and the answer sheet at the end of the test.

This Question Paper consists of 9 printed pages and 3 blank pages.

SECTION B

Choose **ONE** of the following writing tasks. Your answer should follow exactly the instructions given.
You are advised to write approximately 250 words.

2 A group of young people in your area work as part-time voluntary helpers at the local children's hospital, entertaining the patients and helping them in various ways. Write an article for an international young people's magazine describing **the work done and encouraging other young people to take part in voluntary work.**

3 Your family recently had a British teenager to stay for a month on a language exchange visit organised by a reputable educational agency. During the course of the visit, the teenager went missing for about twelve hours. Fortunately he or she turned up at last unharmed. Write an account of the incident for the agency explaining **what happened, the steps taken by your family, and the eventual outcome.** Indicate whether **you would be willing (or not)** to take part in the scheme next year and explain **why.**

4 A head of department you met on a work/study trip abroad last year is coming to visit your workplace/place of study for a day's fact-finding visit. Write a proposal describing how the day might be spent. Offer him or her **two or three** alternative activities and outline the **advantages and drawbacks** of each choice.

5 A friend from overseas is going to stay in your flat while you are on holiday. He or she has expressed an interest in learning your favourite sport while staying there — but has had no previous experience of this sport. Write instructions for your friend, explaining **what equipment** is needed, **where to go** to practise the sport and giving **as much advice** as you can for a beginner at this sport.

2

1 *For questions 1–15, read the text below and then decide which word on page 3 best fits each space. Put the letter you choose for each question in the correct box on your answer sheet. The exercise begins with an example (0).*

SALT

The use of salt has had a long and varied history. For thousands of years it has (0) .... our history and our language as well as our food. Salt was so (1) .... in ancient Rome that it was given out to soldiers as part of their pay called *salarium*, from which our word **salary** comes. In areas where salt was (2) .... it was said to be traded ounce for ounce for gold. In ancient Greece it was even (3) .... to exchange salt for slaves, which (4) .... in the phrase "not worth his salt".

In recent years, however, salt has been firmly (5) .... Salt is bad for you. Everyone would (6) .... by dramatically cutting down on salt intake. Some experts have, for example, pointed to a (7) .... link between salt intake and heart disease.

Many doctors and medical researchers are now beginning to (8) .... this scare talk. A recent report from the Royal Society of Medicine found that there was (9) .... not enough evidence to justify a policy of mass salt restriction. Experts who met at the RSM to (10) .... the problem said that, while some studies showed that patients could (11) .... high blood pressure by cutting down on salt intake, little effect was (12) .... on most patients. Let us give the last (13) .... on salt to the British Heart Foundation: "It is an (14) .... part of our diet but like everything else it should be taken in (15) ...."

3

	A	B	C	D
0	coloured	tested	(C) seasoned	perfumed
1	useful	valuable	normal	necessary
2	seldom	scarce	not	infrequent
3	everyday	current	habitual	common
4	led	brought	resulted	arrived
5	blamed	accused	condemned	faulted
6	improve	better	recover	benefit
7	direct	straight	missing	connecting
8	question	argue	investigate	enquire
9	absolutely	merely	totally	simply
10	agree	solve	discuss	treat
11	decrease	lessen	reduce	cut
12	achieved	done	given	won
13	phrase	sentence	statement	word
14	ordinary	influential	essential	avoidable
15	minimum	moderation	detail	control

Do not forget to put your answers on the answer sheet.

Example:

0   C

462

2 For questions **16–30**, complete the following article by writing each missing word on the answer sheet. **Use only one word for each space.** The exercise begins with an example (0).

The wells of Ethiopia

The Borana people are a semi-nomadic tribe living in south-west Ethiopia. One feature distinguishes (0) ... from all (16) ... East African societies. During dry seasons, they and (17) ... livestock become wholly dependent (18) ... a network of 40 or (19) ... groups of wells. New wells are constantly (20) ... dug, a process which takes a year, or (21) ... likely two, as all the work is (22) ... by hand. The men dig and the women carry (23) ... the earth in sacks. The water in a well (24) ... lie at a depth of 20 metres. To bring (25) ... water to the top, a chain of men is spaced (26) ... intervals of roughly two metres down the well. Standing on projections of rock or wooden supports, they rapidly and, (27) ... seems, tirelessly pass the water up from hand to hand in small leather buckets, chanting loudly and in rhythm to (28) ... another. At ground level the water is poured (29) ... low wooden troughs, from (30) ... up to a dozen camels, cattle or goats can drink.

Do not forget to put your answers on the answer sheet.

Example: | 0 | them |
|---|------|

SECTION B.

5

3 In **most** lines of the following text, there is **either** a spelling **or a** punctuation error. For each numbered line **31–43**, write the correctly spelled word(s) or show the correct punctuation in the spaces on your answer sheet. Some lines are correct. Indicate these lines with a tick (✓). The exercise begins with three examples (0).

GUIDE TO HEALTHY EATING OUT

0	Eating out is a wonderful treat; its a chance to enjoy those
0	complicated and delicious dishes that you never get round to
31	preparing at home. As long as you can eat healthily the rest
32	of the time, your body can stand a bit of luxury now and than.
33	However, if you eat out in restaurants more than once a week,
34	for business or pleasure, you need to keep a carefull eye on
35	the fat, sugar and alcohol you maybe unintentionally
36	taking in. If your can select a restaurant offering a good
37	range of healthy options so that eating sensibly doesn't
38	mean missing out on the tastiest dishes. Their are plenty
39	of exiting vegetarian and fish restaurants around where
40	there will be a good range of safe dishes to chose from as
41	long as you avoid anything in a rich source. Bear in mind,
42	too, that chinese and other foreign restaurants offer a lot
43	of good choices; as their cuisines are less rich and fatty
	than ours. Never be to shy to ask the waiter what is in a
	dish or how it is cooked.

Do not forget to put your answers on the answer sheet.

Example: | 0 | it's |
|---|------|
| 0 | delicious |
| 0 | ✓ |

6

4 For questions 44–58, read the following informal letter about a meeting and use the information to complete the numbered gaps in the formal version of the letter. Then write the new words in the correct spaces on your answer sheet. **Use no more than two words** for each gap. The exercise begins with an example (0). The words you need **do not occur** in the informal note.

INFORMAL LETTER

Dear Richard

Really pleased you can make the meeting on 14th. Sorry to let you know so late in the day. It couldn't be helped.

No problem about transport. I'll pick you up myself at the station. Your train gets in at 11.10. I've booked you into the Victoria Hotel – remember it was being done up last time you came down.

Just by chance our conference this year is at the same time as our local music festival, which is usually pretty good. I'll hang on till you come but I thought it might be nice to fit in one or two concerts while you're here. I know things are a bit tight but we should be able to get to something.

Anyway I'm really looking forward to seeing you. Say hello to Mary for me.

Best wishes

FORMAL LETTER

Dear Mr Downey

We are (0) ...... you are (44) .... to (45) .... the meeting on 14 September. We (46) .... apologise for the short (47) .... which unfortunately was (48) .... .

I have (49) .... arrangements to meet you myself. Your train is (50) .... to arrive at 11.10 a.m. A room has been (51) .... for you at the Victoria Hotel. If you remember, the hotel was being (52) .... when you were here last. Your visit (53) .... with the local music festival, which I can certainly (54) ...... Perhaps when you get here you (55) .... to select one or two events. Our programme is quite full but I feel (56) .... we could (57) .... at least one free evening.

We look forward very much to your visit. Please (58) .... our regards to Mrs Downey.

Yours sincerely

Do not forget to put your answers on the answer sheet.

Example:

| 0 | delighted |

7

SECTION C:

5 For questions 59–65, read through the following text and then choose from list A–L the best phrase or sentence to fill each of the blanks. Write one letter (A–L) in the correct box on your answer sheet. One answer has been given as an example.

DICTIONARY OF CONTEMPORARY ENGLISH IDIOMS

Everyday English conversation is bursting with the expressions and phrases that are so typical of the spoken language. It is amazing just how many of them there are. These phrases, which trip quite unconsciously off the native speaker's tongue, make life or her speech richly idiomatic.

(0) .... it can present something of a puzzle to many users and students of the spoken word.

(59) .... but generally these concentrate on colourful phrases, literary expressions, well-worn proverbs, or grammatical oddities. Few give even partial attention to speech idioms and until now there has been no complete guide to the large number of phrases peculiar to everyday conversation. It is very much to this book's credit (60) .... .

Any idiom, (61) .... , is misleading. Its real meaning is not quite what it appears to be on the surface. Only a second's thought is enough to make us wonder wh- to pull someone's leg should mean 'to make gentle fun of'. Most speech idioms do not provide such an unclear connection (62) .... as in this example – but they are perhaps all the more dangerous to handle correctly through being so innocent. Again, (63) .... . You will find in it the senses of each entry clearly defined, examples showing typical contexts of use, and notes on particular difficulties. (64) .... you have in your hands a dependable book of reference, a guide to conversational practice, and a feast for the curious and for those who enjoy just dipping into a book. (65) .... .

A this book is a reliable guide
B between the written and the spoken word
C whatever it is
D For that reason
E Dictionaries can be an expensive investment
F There already exist various dictionaries of idioms and their real meaning
G between the surface sense of the words and their real meaning

H that it is so reasonably priced
I know you will enjoy your reading
J In spite of this, it is worth having a copy
K that its entries are so extensive in their selection
L All in all

Do not forget to put your answers on the answer sheet.

Example:

| 0 | D |

1724

[Turn over

6

Use the following notes to write about the life of the writer, Alastair Maclean. Write in **complete sentences** *on the back of Answer Sheet Two for each numbered set of notes, using connecting words and phrases as appropriate. You may add words and change the form of the words given in the notes but do not add any extra information. The first point has been expanded for you as an example.*

Alastair Maclean (1922 - 1987)

0 Born Glasgow but spent childhood in small village where father a minister (Church of Scotland)

81 Educated Inverness Royal Academy - served Navy (1941-46)

82 English degree at Glasgow University (graduated 1953)

83 Became schoolteacher - wrote short stories in spare time - won short-story competition (1954)

84 First novel *HMS Ulysses* (1955), based on naval experience - outstanding documentary novel on war at sea - immediate best-seller

85 Strength of stories - plot, tension, exotic settings - not detailed characterisation or literary style

86 Author of over 30 novels - stories about war, industrial espionage, international crime, etc - many now successful films, e.g. *Guns of Navarone*, *Where Eagles Dare*

The space on page 9 can be used for your rough answers.

Do not forget to put your answers on the back of Answer Sheet Two.

Alastair Maclean (1922-1987)

0 Alastair Maclean was born in Glasgow but spent his childhood in a small village where his father was a minister in the Church of Scotland.

81

82

83

84

85

86

SECTION B

3

You will hear the organiser of a local festival announcing changes to the programme because of wet weather. For questions 9-15, make a note of where the events and activities will now take place.

Listen very carefully because you will hear the recording only ONCE.

EVENT	NEW VENUE
dancing display	9
refreshments	10 near entrance
wind band	11
cheese exhibition	12
honey exhibition	13
home-made produce	14
games & competitions	15

SECTION C

4

You will hear a radio programme in which two young people, Marilyn and Bob, are being interviewed about working abroad. During the interview they express various views.

For questions **16-23**, indicate which views are expressed by Marilyn and which are expressed by Bob, by writing **M** (for Marilyn) or **B** (for Bob) in the box provided.

You may write both initials, or one initial, or neither as an answer.
You will hear the piece twice.

You have no choice over where you join a project.   16

Unqualified volunteers may join a project.   17

The project involved environmental awareness.   18

Living conditions for volunteers are fairly basic.   19

It is difficult to build relationships.   20

The job can change once you arrive.   21

The work experience was valuable.   22

The job can turn out to be very boring.   23

UNIVERSITY OF CAMBRIDGE LOCAL EXAMINATIONS SYNDICATE
INTERNATIONAL EXAMINATIONS

CERTIFICATE IN ADVANCED ENGLISH
PAPER 5 SPEAKING

15 MINUTES

Note: the following sample materials are extracts from the CAE trialling. The material offered here is an example of the material for an oral interview. In a live examination the examiners will have a series of packs from which to chose one for each set of candidates interviewed.

Turn Over

5

SECTION D:

You will hear extracts of five different people commenting on their experiences at an international conference.
You will hear the series twice.

TASK ONE

Letters A–H list different people at the conference. As you listen, put them in order by completing the boxes numbered questions **24–28** with the appropriate letter.

A   the conference organiser
B   a guest speaker
C   the accommodation organiser
D   a regular delegate
E   a conference delegate
F   a chairperson of a talk
G   a newspaper reporter
H   a conference steward

24	25	26	27	28

TASK TWO

Letters I–P list the different opinions expressed by the people speaking in the five extracts. As you listen, put them in order by completing the boxes numbered questions **29–33** with the appropriate letter.

I   thinks this conference is badly organised
J   finds the conference very boring
K   worries about keeping a record of discussions
L   complains about a dull audience
M   feels their work is unappreciated
N   finds it difficult to keep order
O   is short of information about the speakers
P   complains about the lack of sleeping accommodation

29	30	31	32	33

Interlocutor — I'll ask your partner Cand B to describe a photograph to you. The photograph below is related to your partner's in some way.

At the end of one minute you should listen and ask short questions if you wish/if necessary. I'll then ask you to say what the relationship between the photographs is. You should then try to reach agreement with your partner.

PHASE B

1. **Man in videoshop** (Spot the difference)

Interlocutor — Cand A, I'd like you to describe your photograph (below) to Cand B, who has a photograph which is related to yours in some way.

At the end of one minute, I'll ask Cand B to say what the relationship between your pictures is. You should then try to reach agreement with your partner.

N.B. Task rubrics will be conveyed orally by the examiners.

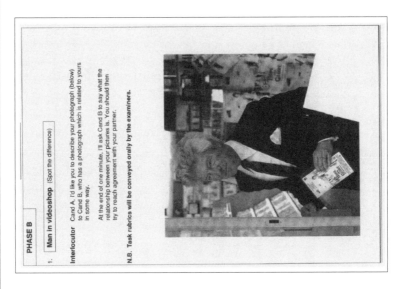

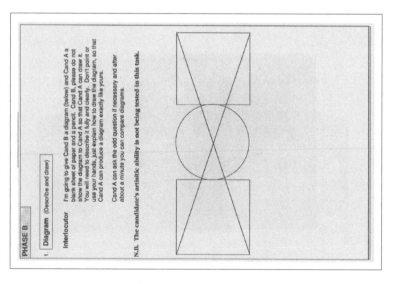

Appendix B

Case study: A quantitative analysis of the context validity of the CPE reading passages used in translation tasks (1913–88), summary tasks (1930–2010) and comprehension question (MCQ/SAQ) tasks (1940–2010)

Cyril J Weir

University of Bedfordshire

Introduction

The context validity of a reading test is concerned with the specific performance conditions under which the reading activities in a test are performed. It requires situational appropriateness in both the linguistic and content demands of the text to be processed, and the features of the task setting that impact on task completion. In Chapter 2 we relied on expert judgement to describe the contextual validity parameters of the passages employed in the CPE Reading papers 1913–2012. Views on the appropriateness of texts for the level and purpose of reading test were made on the basis of expert judgement alone (that of the individuals who wrote the tests and the author who evaluated them). In this case study we will examine the potential of recent automated procedures to supply us with empirical, contextual validity evidence concerning text complexity in these reading papers.

The literature on the potential sources of text complexity is extensive and so this survey is limited to those studies that considered a broad range of parameters of relevance to our study. Firstly a number of descriptive typologies of text characteristics have been designed for use in test development and validation studies (see, for example, Alderson, Figueras, Kuijper, Nold, Takala and Tardieu 2004, Bachman et al 1995, Enright, Grabe, Koda, Mosenthal, Mulcany-Ernt and Schedl 2000, Fortus, Coriat and Fund 1998, Freedle and Kostin 1993, Khalifa and Weir 2009, Masi 2002). Bachman et al's (1995) test comparability study identified textual properties such as the nature of the text, length, vocabulary, grammar, cohesion, distribution of new information, type of information, topic, genre, rhetorical organisation and illocutionary acts. Freedle and Kostin (1993), in a detailed analysis of reading comprehension item difficulty, took into consideration: referentials, rhetorical organisers, fronted structures, vocabulary, concreteness/abstractness, subject matter, coherence, length of various segments such as word, sentence, paragraphs, passage as text related variables. Fortus et al (1998) investigated: length, number of negations, number of referential markers, vocabulary, grammatical complexity, abstractness, topic, rhetorical structure as textual variables contributing to the level of difficulty of reading comprehension items. Enright et al (2000) identified three groups of salient textual features to operationalise in test texts: grammatical/discourse features, pragmatic/rhetorical features and linguistic variables. Alderson et al (2004) included: text source, authenticity, discourse type, domain, topic, nature of content, text length, vocabulary and grammar as relevant features for text analysis. There appears to be a measure of consensus in the subjective judgements of these different authors on the features to be addressed when considering text complexity. Additionally there is empirical evidence from studies such as Freedle and Kostin (1993) and Fortus et al (1998) that a subset of the listed characteristics do indeed impact on the difficulty of reading comprehension tests for learners.

Khalifa and Weir (2009) examined the contextual features proposed in the research literature and established a subset which, in the view of those involved in developing Cambridge ESOL reading tests, enabled the examining board to make criterial distinctions between levels of proficiency in their examinations. Khalifa and Weir (2009) suggest that linguistic demands of task input in reading tests can be explained in terms of lexical and structural resources, discourse mode, functional resources, content knowledge, topic familiarity, cultural knowledge, nature of the text, subject specificity of the text and text writer-reader relationships. Both individually and in combination these contextual parameters are thought likely to impact on the cognitive load imposed upon the reader and affect difficulty of processing.

Until relatively recently we lacked the quantitative tools necessary to compare automatically and accurately the various contextual characteristics of the range of written texts we use in our tests at different levels of ability (Biber, Conrad, Reppen, Byrd, Helt, Clark, Cortes, Csomay and Urzua 2004). However, recent advances in automated textual analysis, computational linguistics and the development of corpora have now made it feasible to provide more quantitative approaches focusing analytically on a wide range of individual characteristics (Crossley and McNamara 2008, Crossley, Louwerse, McCarthy and McNamara 2007, Graesser, McNamara and Kulikowich 2011, Graesser, McNamara, Louwerse and Cai 2004, Green 2012, Green, Ünaldi, and Weir 2010, Weir, Bax, Chan, Field, Green and Taylor 2012, Wu 2011). New technologies offer examination boards the potential of a more systematic, efficient way of describing a number of the contextual parameters in the texts they select for their language tests (see Green et al 2010).

Graesser et al (2011:223) make a strong case for using a system called Coh-Metrix:

> Recent advances in numerous disciplines have made it possible to computationally investigate various measures of text and language comprehension that supersede surface components of language and instead explore deeper, more global attributes of language. They have allowed the analysis of many deep-level factors of textual coherence and processing to be automated, permitting more accurate and detailed analyses of language to take place. A synthesis of the advances in these areas has been achieved in Coh-Metrix, a computational tool that measures cohesion and text difficulty at various levels of language, discourse, and conceptual analysis.

They argue that such 'automated analysis is unquestionably more reliable and objective than approaches that involve humans annotating and rating texts by hand' (op. cit. 2011:223–234). With one eye on the future development of reading tests at Cambridge and at other examining boards, this case study investigates the usefulness of automated techniques in establishing the comparability of texts used in Cambridge ESOL CPE Reading tests 1913–2012 and attempts to determine the potential value (or not) of the various parameters that the literature suggests are useful for this purpose. It was hoped that such analysis would provide us with an overview of the relative complexity of CPE Reading passages across a number of indices over the whole of the period under review.

However, we are aware that these quantifiable indices in themselves do not constitute a complete picture of the complexity of a text for readers. Graesser et al (2011:223) admit:

> First, computers obviously cannot identify and scale texts on all levels of language, discourse, and meaning . . . Some characteristics of texts require humans to provide informed, deep, critical analyses. Second, successful text comprehension involves much more than an analysis of text characteristics alone because prior knowledge, inference mechanisms, and skills of readers are also critically important.

Masi (2002) cautions that together with quantitative indicators, e.g. of word and sentence complexity, other less quantifiable factors such as text and genre type, and the reader's content and background knowledge, should be taken into account in estimating the suitability of a text for a given readership. Green, Ünaldi and Weir (2010) and (Wu 2011) investigated a number of these qualitative features and their work attests to their importance in establishing text complexity. The problem for the study described below was that these could not be measured automatically (some are not available through computational analyses and some that are, are not included in the publicly accessible version of Coh-Metrix). To establish these qualitative parameters retrospectively by pooled subjective judgement on all our 238 selected texts, in respect of each of these qualitative parameters, would be logistically challenging and require a huge investment of human resources. Unavoidably there is a pragmatic balance to be struck between comprehensiveness of description and viability of automatic application in test development and validation at the present time.

Accordingly a number of important contextual parameters:

- genre and rhetorical task (see also Barnett 1989, Carrell 1984, Goh 1990, Meyer and Freedle 1984, Koda 2005, Urquhart 1984)
- cultural knowledge (see also Al-Fallay 1994, Chihara, Sakurai and Oller 1989, Sasaki 2000, Steffenson, Joag-Dev and Anderson 1979)
- subject knowledge and topic familiarity (see also Alderson 2000, Clapham 1996, Khalifa 1997, Nuttall 1996, Tan 1990, Urquhart and Weir 1998)

had to be omitted from the study of text complexity reported here because they do not as yet lend themselves to *automatic* analysis or the relevant analyses in Coh-Metrix are not yet in the public domain (http://cohmetrix. memphis.edu), although their effect on text difficulty is well attested to in much of the research on contextual parameters referred to above.

The automated approach to text analysis is obviously still in its infancy and it will take some time to be able to say with full confidence that the parameters we select below for this initial study are the most efficacious. Nevertheless the indices chosen represent a principled attempt to establish a set of potentially useful parameters that have been made available by Coh-Metrix Version 2 and VocabProfile for use in the public domain.

We restricted our study to those text characteristics that could be measured *automatically* through publically available free software. The 20 parameters that we eventually used in our study were arrived at by an extensive programme of research to reduce them from our initial set of Coh-Metrix (Version 2) indices (54) (see Weir et al 2012 for a full listing of these and Coh-Metrix documentation at http://cohmetrix.memphis.edu/Coh-metrixWeb2/ HelpFile2.htm) and Web VocabProfile indices (7) at http://www.lextu- tor.ca/vp/eng/ (Cobb 2003). We adopted the following procedures to reach a decision on the most useful quantitative indices for predicting text complexity.

Firstly, the selection of parameters to establish whether CPE texts at C2 level were comparable from form to form, year on year, was informed by a survey of the Coh-Metrix related literature and of other literature on text difficulty to determine which indices had been found useful in the past for establishing the relative complexity of written texts at different levels such as school readers across the US grade range (see for example Crossley, Greenfield and McNamara 2008 and Graesser et al 2011). It also took into account the work done by Wu (2011) in her doctoral study which compared Cambridge Main Suite and GEPT Taiwan examinations in ESOL at the B1 and B2 levels in terms of contextual and cognitive parameters, the work by Green, Ünaldi and Weir (2010) in comparing IELTS and undergraduate texts at British universities and the investigation by Green (2012) of texts targeted at different levels of the Common European Framework of Reference for Languages (Council of Europe 2001).

Weir et al (2012) examined FCE (48), CAE (49) and CPE (69) texts to establish where criterial differences between them might be found in terms of quantifiable text complexity parameters. They sought to locate key indices which would facilitate the maintenance of distinctions of contextual complexity between Cambridge English language examination levels. Statistical analysis was carried out on a composite data set of text complexity parameters for Cambridge Reading texts at FCE, CAE and CPE obtained from previous studies to determine whether there were any significant differences between texts at different levels of proficiency. Multiple regression was then used to establish the best parameters for predicting which level a text belonged to. It must be remembered that the validity of such analysis is of course dependent on texts having been selected for FCE, CAE and CPE at appropriate levels of complexity in the first place. One might reasonably assume, however, that over such a wide time span the item writers perceptions of difficulty levels were comparable with those of other key stakeholders and any serious deviations would have been pounced upon.

We first eliminated the following 13 indices which did not exhibit any significant differences across 3 proficiency levels FCE/CAE and CPE in the study by Weir et al (2012). We had confirmed through focus group discussion of the data on CPE that they would not be useful in themselves for making year on year comparisons of the same examination in the study reported below:

- 8 Ratio of causal particles to causal verbs
- 13 Incidence of negative temporal connectives
- 19 Argument overlap all distances
- 24 Number of conditional expressions, incidence score
- 31 Mean hypernym value of nouns
- 36 average sentences per paragraph
- 45 Celex raw mean for content words
- 49 Concreteness mean for content words
- 50 Incidence of positive logical connectives
- 51 Incidence of negative logical connectives
- 52 Ratio of intentional particles to intentional content

- 54 Mean of tense and aspect repetition scores
- 59 Mean of location and motion ratio scores, average sentences per paragraph.

Further indices were eliminated after iterative focus group discussion of the results obtained from comparing CPE with other external measure of Academic English Proficiency (IELTS and a small corpus of extracts from undergraduate textbooks (Green, Ünaldi and Weir 2010), and with FCE and CAE (Weir et al 2012). The list of potential complexity indices was pruned where it was felt they:

- overlapped: e.g. Cohm 55 *sentence syntax similarity adjacent and 57 all within paragraphs (v 56 all, across paragraphs)*, as did *average characters (with 38 average syllables*)
- were redundant – other measures involved this already e.g. Cohm 40 *Flesch Kincaid and 39 Flesch Reading Ease* already covered by 38 *average syllables per word* and *37 average words per sentence. BNC 1000, 2000* already covered by Celex measures
- did not tell us anything useful: e.g. Cohm *17 stem overlap adjacent, 20 stem overlap all distances unweighted, 22 noun phrase incidence.*
- were difficult to interpret: e.g. Cohm 14 *incidence of negative causal connections, 12 negative additive connectives, 23 ratio of pronouns to noun phrase (affected by text type e.g. 1st person narrative at FCE)*
- would be difficult to use in selecting texts: e.g. Cohm 28 *LSA all sentences combination mean* rose according to level of text FCE/CAE/CPE
- showed unsatisfactory results on box plots i.e. not much difference between any two adjacent levels of proficiency or anomalous results
  - 7 Incidence of causal verbs, links and particles
  - 9 Incidence of positive additive connectives
  - 10 Incidence of positive temporal connectives
  - 11 Incidence of positive causal connectives
  - 15 Incidence of all connectives
  - 29 LSA Paragraph to paragraph mean
  - 30 Personal pronoun incidence score
  - 32 Mean hypernym value of verbs
  - 33 Number of paragraphs
  - 34 Number of sentences
  - 46 Celex logarithm minimum in sentence for content words
  - 47 Celex raw minimum in sentence for content words
  - 53 Incidence of intentional actions, events and particles

This eliminated a total of 28 further indices from our study.

Unlike the CAE study (Weir et al 2012) we decided to keep Cohm 35 *number of words* because, although not useful for comparisons between levels as length of passage varied considerably between levels and within a level, it was felt useful to monitor this index from year to year, from exam to exam to ensure comparability. *Lexical density* was omitted from the Weir et al (2012) CAE study because the texts had not been analysed in this respect in some of the original data sets (Green et al 2010) but it proved to be useful in our study of CPE below.

We ended up with a final total of 20 indices that were felt to be useful in establishing text complexity from year to year at the same level i.e. across the CPE texts 1913–2012 in our study. Confirming the links between these remaining indices and cognitive processing in our model for Reading (see Khalifa and Weir 2009 and Chapter 2) had been part of the iterative process of selection but was reviewed again formally by a focus group of 8 testing specialists in CRELLA as an important final consideration (these links are made for each contextual index in the discussion below). Where a clear relationship between an index and stage of cognitive processing can be established, we retained it even if did not feature strongly in the final multiple regression analyses carried out by Weir et al 2012 (see above) as contributing to the explanation of variance between levels.

Table 1 Final set of 20 indices for estimating text complexity

20 selected indices from Coh-Metrix Version 2 and Web VocabProfile
Cohm 16 Argument overlap, adjacent, unweighted
Cohm 18 Anaphor reference, adjacent, unweighted
Cohm 21 Anaphor reference, all distances
Cohm 25 number of negations incidence score
Cohm 26 Logical operator incidence score
Cohm 27 LSA, Sentence to sentence adjacent mean
Cohm 35 Number of words
Cohm 37 Average words per sentence
Cohm 38 Average syllables per word
Cohm 41 Mean number of modifiers per noun-phrase
Cohm 42 Higher level constituents per word
Cohm 43 Mean number of words before the main verb of main clause in sentences
Cohm 44 Type-token ratio for all content words
Cohm 46 Celex, logarithm, mean for content words (0–6)
Cohm 56 Sentence syntax similarity, all, across paragraphs
Cohm 58 Proportion of content words that overlap between adjacent sentences
Cohm 60 Concreteness, minimum in sentence for content words
AWL
words =>15K in BNC
Lexical density

Method

We carried out computerised analyses of reading passages used in Cambridge ESOL examinations in the translation tasks (1913–1988), text summary tasks (1936–2010), MCQ/SAQ comprehension tasks (1940–2010).The data sets are described in Table 2 below.

Each passage was retrieved from the Cambridge Assessment Archive bound test volumes and scanned; a pdf of each text was created and was then typed up into electronic format and made ready for analysis. In all we were able to analyse 84 passages that had been used for summary, 70 used with MCQ/SAQ and 85 used with translation over the period up to 2012 as outlined in Table 2 below. This represents one of the biggest data sets of Cambridge examinations analysed to date.

To frame our discussion, Table 3 below presents the complete data set for the analysis of CPE texts in the three different tasks Summary, MCQ/SAQ questions and Translation. The results are then discussed in detail below.

Analysis of results

Lexical complexity

First we examined the lexical complexity features listed in Table 4 below with the automated procedure indicated in the final column on the right. (Definitions in italics are from the Coh-Metrix website http://cohmetrix. memphis.edu/cohmetrixpr/index.html and relate to Coh-Metrix Version 2 which was the latest version when this study was carried out August 2011– July 2012).

Number of words

Weir et al (2012) note that what is perhaps more important than simple text length is the density and complexity of idea units within the text (Bachman 1990). That said, in a testing context, extending the length of a reading passage while keeping the number of items constant increases difficulty in that it provides a greater number of idea units between which a test taker has to choose when seeking a conceptual match for an item. In effect, it increases the size of the haystack within which the needles have to be found. The number of propositions contained in a text has an effect on text comprehension because of the strain multiple propositions can put on working memory (Kintsch and Keenan 1973).

Cohm 35 provides us with a way of quickly establishing total of number of words per passage and so we can compare the length of the passages used in the Cambridge tasks over our historical period. A quick inspection shows

Table 2 Overview of reading passages analysed

	Translation task 1913–75 Optional to 1988	Summary/Précis of text(s) 1936–2010	Passage plus SAQs/MCQs 1940–2010
1913	X		
1914	X		
1915	X		
1917	X		
1919	X		
1922	X		
1925	X		
1928	X		
1930	X		
1936	X	X	
1938	X	X	
1940	X	X	X
1945	X	X	X
1947	X	X	X
1950	X	X	X
1953	X	X	X
1955	X	X	X
1960	X	X	X
1966	X	X	X
1968	X	X	X
1970	X	X	X
1975	X	X	X (MCQ >>)
1978	X	X	X
1981	X	X	X
1984	X	X	X
1988	X	X	X
1992		X	X
1995		X	X
1998		X	X
2002		X_1	X
2005		X_1	X
2010		X_1	X

[1] *from 2002 two short passages for summary in CPE Use of English Paper 3 Question 5*
X = passages scanned for typing

Table 3 Kruskal-Wallis 1-way ANOVA for k samples among CPE Summary, SAQ/MCQ and Translation texts

Coh-Metrix Version 2 parameters + VocabProfile in Lexical tutor vocabulary parameters	CPE Summary (n=84)				CPE MCQ/SAQ (n=69)				CPE Translation (n=85)				Kruskal-Wallis 1-way ANOVA
	Mean	SD	Min	Max	Mean	SD	Min	Max	Mean	SD	Min	Max	Sig
Cohm 16 Argument overlap, adjacent, unweighted	0.61	0.23	0.17	1.00	0.37	0.24	0.00	1.00	0.50	0.26	0.00	1.00	0.000
Cohm 18 Anaphor reference, adjacent, unweighted	0.42	0.24	0.00	1.00	0.37	0.20	0.00	0.75	0.49	0.26	0.00	1.00	0.010
Cohm 21 Anaphor reference, all distances	0.22	0.18	0.00	0.90	0.18	0.13	0.00	0.56	0.30	0.22	0.00	1.00	0.000
Cohm 25 Number of negations incidence score	9.53	6.78	0.00	29.56	8.9	6.25	0.00	26.13	9.37	10.15	0.00	61.45	0.561
Cohm 26 Logical operator incidence score	47.60	14.49	15.87	76.19	44.87	15.11	9.80	77.82	50.02	18.80	12.58	96.77	0.205
Cohm 27 LSA, Sentence to sentence adjacent mean	0.23	0.08	0.08	0.48	0.18	0.07	0.06	0.43	0.19	0.09	0.04	0.52	0.000
Cohm 35 Number of words	343.08	120.21	129	640	405.71	152.95	179	849	212.46	53.82	104	390	0.000
Cohm 37 Average words per sentence	27.83	7.16	15.73	47.67	23.39	7.20	11.29	49.38	27.31	10.33	9.95	57.75	0.001
Cohm 38 Average syllables per word	1.55	0.13	1.86	2.57	1.55	0.13	1.30	1.92	1.46	0.12	1.23	1.74	0.000
Cohm 41 Mean number of modifiers per noun phrase	0.90	.166	0.58	1.21	0.90	0.16	0.55	1.28	0.89	0.19	0.47	1.41	0.713
Cohm 42 Higher level constituents per word	0.73	.036	0.65	0.81	0.72	0.03	0.66	.81	0.72	0.04	0.64	1.82	0.626
Cohm 43 Mean number of words before the main verb of main clause in sentences	5.72	2.35	1.63	14.86	5.26	2.15	2.07	11.57	5.73	3.40	1.00	19.50	0.365

Table 3 continued

Coh-Metrix Version 2 parameters + VocabProfile in Lexical tutor vocabulary parameters	CPE Summary (n=84)				CPE MCQ/SAQ (n=69)				CPE Translation (n=85)				Kruskal-Wallis 1-way ANOVA
	Mean	SD	Min	Max	Mean	SD	Min	Max	Mean	SD	Min	Max	Sig
Cohm 44 Standardised type-token ratio per word	0.79	0.06	0.46	0.70	0.80	0.07	0.40	0.70	0.88	0.06	0.50	0.76	0.000
Cohm 46 Celex, logarithm, mean for content words (0–6)	2.18	0.16	1.86	2.57	2.18	0.13	1.87	2.47	2.15	0.20	1.75	2.78	0.216
Cohm 56 Sentence syntax similarity, all, across paragraphs	0.07	0.02	0.03	0.14	0.08	0.02	0.04	0.12	0.07	0.03	0.012	0.13	0.137
Cohm 58 Proportion of content words that overlap between adjacent sentences	0.09	0.04	0.01	0.24	0.07	0.03	0.01	0.16	0.07	0.05	0.01	0.25	0.006
Cohm 60 Concreteness, minimum in sentence for content words	178.05	18.441	158.00	225.00	181.39	21.39	158.00	225.00	193.19	22.16	158.00	225.00	0.000
AWL level	4.83	2.64	0.58	12.13	5.02	2.82	0.93	12.96	2.25	1.81	0.00	7.48	0.000
Density	0.50	0.04	0.40	0.59	0.52	0.04	0.44	0.59	0.50	0.05	0.32	0.62	0.050
Words = >15k in BNC	1.16	1.06	0.00	3.94	1.61	1.64	0.00	7.68	1.67	1.47	0.00	6.91	0.017

Table 4 Lexical complexity parameters

	Contextual parameter	Definition	Instrument
	Number of words	*The average number of words per text.*	Coh-Metrix (Variable 35)
	Average syllables/ word	*The average number of syllables per word.*	Coh-Metrix (Variable 38)
	Standardised type-token ratio (standardised TTR basis: 100 words) for all content words	*Number of unique words (i.e. types) divided by tokens (i.e. word instances) per text. The STTR is calculated based on every 100 words in order to compare TTR on a common basis; as the text gets longer, the TTR falls so it is difficult to compare the TTR across texts.*	Coh-Metrix (Variable 44)
	Lexical density	*The ratio of the incidence of content words, to total number of words multiplied by 100.*	VocabProfile
Lexical Complexity	Celex, logarithm, mean for content words (0–6)	*The log frequency of all content words in the text. Taking the log of the frequencies rather than the raw scores is compatible with research on reading time (Haberlandt & Graesser 1985; Just & Carpenter 1980). A word with the lowest log frequency score is the most rare word in the sentence.*	Coh-Metrix (Variable 40)
	AWL frequency	*The ratio of words appearing in the Academic Wordlist (AWL; Coxhead 1998) to total number of words per text.*	VocabProfile
	BNC =>15K	*The ratio of words that do not appear in the BNC <15K wordlists to total number of words per text.*	VocabProfile

a good deal of variability in text length but interestingly few fall below the two hundred word level in any of the three task types. In the later years CPE introduced a number of short texts from different genres to test careful reading skills as well as retaining some longer texts to test expeditious reading skills. This resulted in a larger number of passages but the average length of some texts used in a paper was thereby reduced. This explains the large fluctuations between passages in later years in the SAQ/MCQ reading papers.

The bar charts in the data analyses below report the figure obtained on a particular index for a reading passage in each of the three task types for a CPE examination: translation tasks (1913–88), summary tasks (1930–2010) and comprehension question (MCQ/SAQ) tasks (1940–2010) in the named year. They provide us with a diachronic, empirical view of the exams over a period of time and show the variability from year to year in respect of a particular contextual parameter.

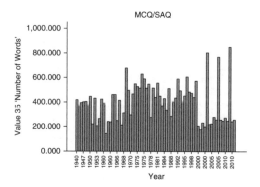

Across the three tasks we can see that some passages are noticeably longer in MCQ/SAQ and summary over the period but less so in translation where they were more similar. There is a good deal of variability in length in all task types.

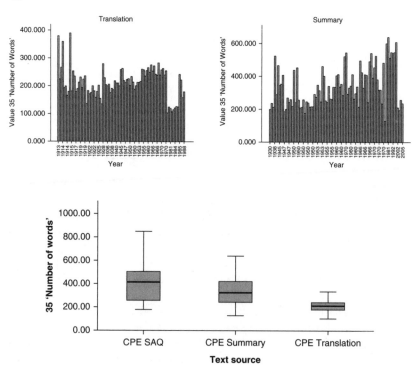

The box and whisker plots in the case study show the range of values for each index. The bottom and top of the box are always the 25th and 75th percentile (the lower and upper quartiles, respectively), and the band near the middle of the box is always the 50th percentile (the median). The top and bottom of the whisker shows the minimum and maximum of all the data. Extreme values which are between one and a half and three box lengths from either end of the box are entered as outliers by a small circle.

Cohm 35 Number of words	CPE summary (n=84)				CPE MCQ/ SAQ (n=69)				CPE Translation (n=85)				Kruskal-Wallis 1-way ANOVA
	Mean	SD	Min	Max	Mean	SD	Min	Max	Mean	SD	Min	Max	Sig
	343	120	129	640	406	153	179	849	213	54	104	390	0.000

The overall means show the differing lengths of text used in the three tasks from year to year and the variability in length within a task type. SAQ/ MCQ shows itself to be the most variable in terms of length of passage but this is in part explained by passages being used to test different skills/strategies. Summary and translation passages are comparatively more uniform.

Khalifa and Weir (2009) also compared the lengths of texts used in the various Cambridge Main Suite examinations over a 10-year period. Noticeably a number of longer texts have been used in some level tests (see overall number of words and number of texts and compare with maximum length) presumably in order to increase text difficulty or to encourage expeditious reading skills. There is a gradual growth in the lengths of texts used as one moves up the CEFR levels although there is no distinction between CAE and CPE as regards text length, presumably for practicality rather than validity reasons. There is however a fairly clear increase in the amount of text students are exposed to at the C1 and C2 levels as against the lower levels (A2-B2).

Examination	Overall number of words	Number of texts	Maximum for any single text
KET (A2)	Approximately 740–800 words	4	250
PET (B1)	Approximately 1450–1600 words	5	550
FCE (B2)	Approximately 2000 words	3	700
CAE (C1)	Approximately 3000 words	6	1100
CPE (C2)	Approximately 3000 words	9	1100

Average syllables per word

This is the mean number of syllables per content word, a ratio measure. (Definitions in *italics* are all from the Coh-Metrix website http://cohmetrix. memphis.edu/cohmetrixpr/index.html and refer to Version 2).

The notion that a skilled reader identifies a word purely by its shape has long been discredited according to Weir et al (2012). They argue that current models of lexical recognition (Rastle 2007) assume that a reader achieves lexical recognition by drawing upon a number of different cues in parallel. A word on the page is matched to an item in the reader's lexicon on the strength of: letter features, letters, digraphs, letter sequences, syllables and the word as a whole. Of these, the units most easily recognised by a computer program are the syllable and the whole word. Readers take longer to process a multisyllabic word than a monosyllabic one, allowing for frequency effects (Rayner and Pollatsek 1989). The demands of decoding a text at lexical level are thus better measured by counting syllables than by counting whole words.

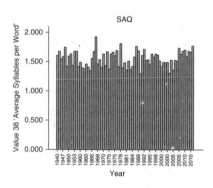

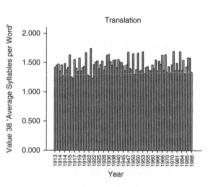

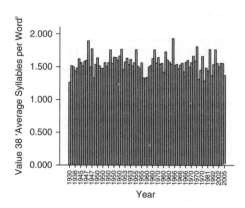

The small difference within and across tasks are shown below. The words in the summary task tended to have slightly higher syllable counts, those in translation the fewest on average. The differences between them are significant but slight.

Cohm 38 Average syllables per word	CPE Summary (n=84)				CPE MCQ/SAQ (n=69)				CPE Translation (n=85)				Kruskal-Wallis 1-way ANOVA
	Mean	SD	Min	Max	Mean	SD	Min	Max	Mean	SD	Min	Max	Sig
	1.55	0.13	1.86	2.57	1.55	0.13	1.30	1.92	1.46	0.12	1.23	1.74	0.000

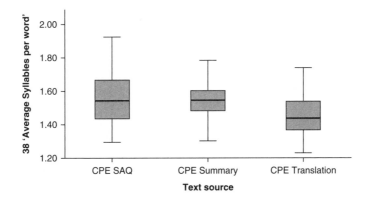

VocabProfile provides a very practical way of establishing the various facets of vocabulary used in reading passages. It offers a number of useful features:

- *lexical density* (number of content words as a proportion of the number of grammatical words) and word frequency levels in VP 3 programme

- *lexical frequency* the percentage of words in a text that occur among each 1000 of the most frequent words (from 1000 up to 20,000) in the British National Corpus (BNC) i.e., percentage of words in a text in the most frequent 1000 and the second and third most frequent 1000 right through to 20,000.

- *academic words* the percentage of words in a text also appearing on the AWL (sub-technical vocabulary). The academic word lists identify words used more commonly in academic than in other contexts, particularly the sub-technical vocabulary that occurs across disciplines (Campion and Elley 1971, Coxhead 2000).

Lexical density

Ratio of content to function words

Words can be defined as either content words or grammatical function words. A content or information carrying word is any verb, noun, adverb or adjective which has a stable and significant lexical meaning. Grammatical function words bind a text together by creating the relationships between the concepts in a sentence. Function words include: auxiliary verbs, numerals, determiners, pronouns, prepositions, and conjunctions.

Lexical density is an index in VocabProfile which measures the proportion of content words to total number of words in a text. Lexical density can be calculated as a percentage by the following formula:

Lexical density = (number of content words / total number of words) × 100

Weir et al (2012) argue that this measure relates to the processing differences between function words and content words. As the reader's eye moves across the page, it fixates the majority of content words, but only about 40% of function words (Rayner and Pollatsek 1989). The reader of English is able to anticipate and skip functors by detecting them in right parafoveal vision. They are readily recognisable because of their high frequency and short form. The higher the density of a text, the harder the text is to read since accessing the meaning of lexical items requires accessing the mental lexicon; function words can be dealt with directly by pattern matching

One might perhaps assume there would be an increase in the ratio of content words to function words as texts became more syntactically and lexically difficult (there might, for example, be more complex NPs). This could possibly slow down processing, in that the reader would need to fixate more. But it would be unlikely to add significantly to cognitive load, since at higher levels of proficiency automatic recognition routines should be in place for the more familiar content words.

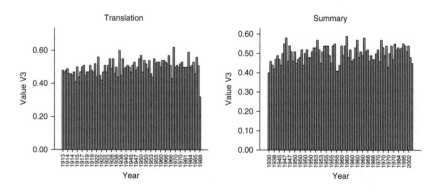

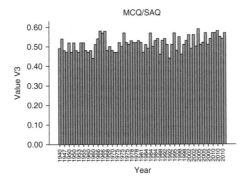

The data show a high degree of consistency in texts across the various tasks, over a wide historical span, providing an indication of the comparability of these texts in terms of lexical density over time. There was no significant difference in lexical density across all three tasks although there is a wider range for translation texts as can be seen from the data below.

Lexical density	CPE Summary (n=84)				CPE MCQ/SAQ (n=69)				CPE Translation (n=85)				Kruskal-Wallis 1-way ANOVA
	Mean	SD	Min	Max	Mean	SD	Min	Max	Mean	SD	Min	Max	Sig
	0.50	0.04	0.40	0.59	0.52	0.04	0.44	0.59	0.50	0.05	0.32	0.62	0.050

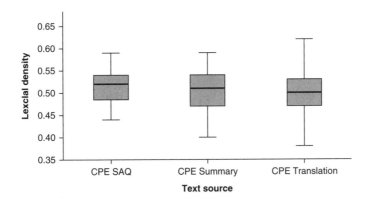

Word frequency

Crossley, Greenfield and McNamara (2008: 482, 488) point out that:

> Coh-Metrix calculates word frequency information through CELEX frequency scores. The CELEX database (Baayen, Piepenbrock,

& Gulikers, 1993) consists of frequencies taken from the early 1991 version of the COBUILD corpus, a 17.9 million-word corpus. For this study Celex logarithm mean for content words was selected as the lexical-level variable. This measure was selected because:

Frequency effects have been shown to facilitate decoding with frequent words being processed more quickly and understood better than infrequent ones (Haberlandt & Graesser, 1985; Just & Carpenter, 1980). Rapid or automatic decoding is a strong predictor of L2 reading performance (Koda, 2005). Texts which assist such decoding (e.g., by containing a greater proportion of high frequency words) can thus be regarded as easier to process. . . . The more frequent a word, the more likely it is to be processed with a fair degree of automaticity, thus increasing reading speed (even among lower level learners) and freeing working memory for higher level meaning building . . .

Celex logarithm mean for content words

This initially computes the lowest log frequency score among all of the content words in each sentence. A mean of these minimum log frequency scores is then computed . . . The word with the lowest log frequency score is the most rare word in the sentence. (Scores range from 0–6)

Low frequency can be used as a predictor of text difficulty. Weir et al (2012) report that a well-established frequency effect in reading results in slower decoding times for less frequent words (Garnham 1985). In addition, a high ratio of low-frequency content words increases the likelihood that a passage will contain a number of words that are unfamiliar to the test taker. However, too much should not be made of the contribution made by unfamiliar words to text difficulty. The fact is that many such words can be decoded by using analogy or derivational morphology; others can be ignored as not central to the main argument of the text. The true issue determining difficulty is the transparency of the words rather than necessarily their low frequency.

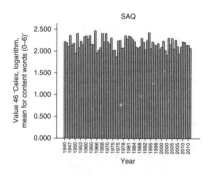

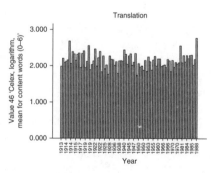

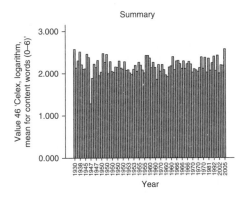

There was no significant difference in the Cohm 46 Celex, logarithm, mean for content words (0–6) across tasks indicating similar complexity of texts in all tasks for this index.

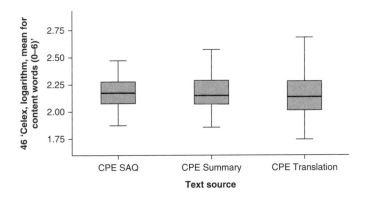

Cohm 46 Celex, logarithm, mean for content words (0–6)	CPE Summary (n=84)				CPE MCQ/SAQ (n=69)				CPE Translation (n=85)				Kruskal-Wallis 1-way ANOVA
	Mean	SD	Min	Max	Mean	SD	Min	Max	Mean	SD	Min	Max	Sig
	2.18	0.16	1.86	2.57	2.18	0.13	1.87	2.47	2.15	0.20	1.75	2.78	0.216

There is close similarity year on year within the texts used for a particular task type.

Percentage of words falling outside the 15,000 word frequency level in the British National Corpus (BNC)

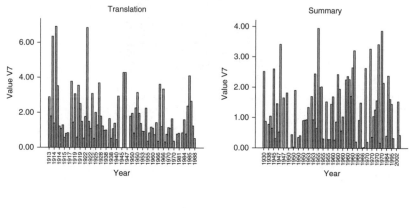

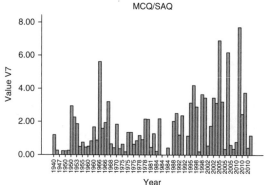

Few indices are above 4% in the translation tasks where examiners were probably more aware of the difficulty occasioned by less frequent vocabulary and none are more than 4% in the summary task. In MCQ/SAQ the most variable picture emerges with some quite high indices in a number of years and some very low in many others. Frequency of vocabulary is obviously an index that would benefit from closer attention in future reading test development. There was no significant difference in lexical frequency at the words = >15k across all three tasks over the period under review although there is some variability within tasks as can be seen from the range statistics. But this is not a large number of words per text and at CPE level candidates might be expected to deal comfortably with low frequency vocabulary.

	CPE Summary (n=84)				CPE MCQ/SAQ (n=69)				CPE Translation (n=85)				Kruskal-Wallis 1-way ANOVA
words >15k													
	Mean	SD	Min	Max	Mean	SD	Min	Max	Mean	SD	Min	Max	Sig
	1.16	1.06	0.00	3.94	1.61	1.64	0.00	7.68	1.67	1.47	0.00	6.91	0.017

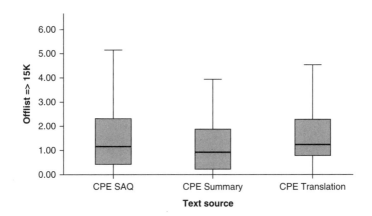

Khalifa and Weir (2009) provided an overview of lexical range across the Cambridge Main Suite examinations over the last decade. It is noticeable that CPE texts include lexis from right across the first 20k levels of the British National Corpus (BNC). The official BNC website describes the corpus as follows:

> BNC is a 100 million word collection of samples of written and spoken language from a wide range of sources, designed to represent a wide cross-section of British English from the later part of the 20th century, both spoken and written. The **written part** of the BNC (90%) includes, for example, extracts from regional and national newspapers, specialist periodicals and journals for all ages and interests, academic books and popular fiction, published and unpublished letters and memoranda, school and university essays, among many other kinds of text. The **spoken part** (10%) consists of orthographic transcriptions of unscripted informal conversations (recorded by volunteers selected from different age, region and social classes in a demographically balanced way) and spoken language collected in different contexts, ranging from formal business or government meetings to radio shows and phone-ins. (http://www.natcorp.ox.ac.uk/corpus/)

Lexical Characteristic	KET (A2)	PET (B1)	FCE (B2)	CAE (C1)	CPE (C2)
K1	89.30	84.73	84.17	78.67	78.95
K2	5.04	8.63	7.75	8.53	8.45
K3	0.69	2.32	2.57	3.30	3.71
K4	1.22	0.83	1.25	2.29	2.25
K5	0.69	0.43	0.82	1.26	1.13
K6	0.08	0.08	0.36	0.85	0.87
K7	0.15	0.05	0.18	0.67	0.54
K8	0	0.20	0.28	0.50	0.45
K9	0.08	0.20	0.09	0.34	0.36
K10	0	0.10	0.09	0.32	0.33
K11	0	0.15	0.05	0.24	0.31
K12	0	0	0.08	0.21	0.22
K13	0	0	0.07	0.16	0.21
K14	0	0	0	0.11	0.13
K15	0	0	0.01	0.04	0.06
K16	0	0	0	0.04	0.04
K17	0	0	0	0.01	0.03
K18	0	0	0.02	0.03	0.02
K19	0	0	0	0.01	0.05
K20	0	0	0.01	0	0.03
Off-list	2.75	2.27	2.19	2.42	1.88
Tokens per family (on-list)	3.54	4.66	8.42	7.45	6.65
Types per family (on-list)	1.28	1.37	1.59	1.56	1.53

There are some inconsistencies here and the indices are perhaps too close between PET/FCE and between CAE/CPE. To differentiate more clearly between these levels, this metric points to one aspect of the progression between levels that might be tightened up.

Percentage on Academic Word List

VocabProfile (Cobb 2003) enables us to identify the number of academic words in texts based on Coxhead (2000).

It is described on Victoria University's website as follows:

> The Academic Word List (AWL) was developed by Averil Coxhead as her MA thesis at the **School of Linguistics and Applied Language Studies** at Victoria University of Wellington, New Zealand. The list contains 570 word families which were selected according to principles. The list does not include words that are in the most frequent 2000 words of English. The AWL was primarily made so that it could be used by teachers as part of a programme preparing learners for tertiary level study or used by students working alone to learn the words most needed to study at tertiary institutions. The Academic Word List replaces the University Word List. (http://www.victoria.ac.nz/lals/resources/academicwordlist/information.aspx)

The incidence of academic words in a text proved to be a good predictor of level in the Weir et al (2012) study of FCE/CAE and CPE texts. CPE clearly exhibits a greater incidence of these semi-technical words.

	Mean	SD
FCE	1.61%	1.26%
CAE	1.63%	1.41%
CPE	5.82%	2.84%

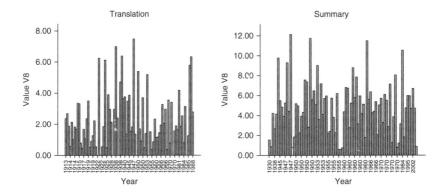

Lower indices of Academic Words are reported for the translation task than in any of the other with a number of texts having very few academic words. Given these texts tended to be based on literary texts this is perhaps to be expected.

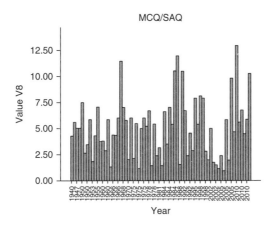

	CPE Summary (n=84)				CPE MCQ/SAQ (n=69)				CPE Translation (n=85)				Kruskal-Wallis 1-way ANOVA
AWL level	Mean	SD	Min	Max	Mean	SD	Min	Max	Mean	SD	Min	Max	Sig
	4.83	2.64	0.58	12.13	5.02	2.82	0.93	12.96	2.25	1.81	0.00	7.48	0.000

There is a significant difference in academic words across the three tasks. With an average of 4.83% in the summary tasks, 5.02% in the MCQ/SAQ tasks but only 2.25% in the translation task. The literary nature of many of the texts in the latter task may explain this.

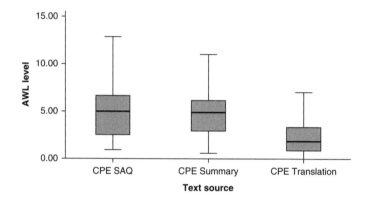

Such a wide variability in the percentage of academic words found in CPE texts is due in part to the mixture of text types used at this level. Narrative/ or literary texts are likely to produce quite different AWL indices than expository informational texts. Again this is an index that would bear closer scrutiny in the future as CPE (and CAE) is used for university entrance purposes and, as we can see in Tables 5 to 7 at the end of this appendix, the number of academic words is significantly fewer on average in CPE texts than it is in IELTS (7.9%) or undergraduate textbooks (10.51%). Coxhead (2000) found a c.10% coverage per passage in her original corpus of academic texts.

Type-token ratio

Coh-Metrix enables us to measure lexical diversity through Cohm 44 *Standardised type-token ratio* (TTR – the ratio of types or different words to tokens: the total number of words occurring in the text). Graesser, McNamara, Louwerse and Cai (2004) describe how TTR, expressed as a percentage, provides an indication of the number of different words the reader will need to know to understand a passage. The higher the TTR, the more demanding the passage is likely to be. Each unique word in a text is a word *type*. Each instance of a particular word is a *token*. The type-token ratio is the number of unique words divided by the number of tokens. When the type-token ratio is 1, each word occurs only once in the text; comprehension should be comparatively difficult because many unique words need to be encoded and integrated with the discourse context. A low type-token ratio indicates that words are repeated many times in the text, which should generally increase the ease and speed of text processing.

As the length of the reading passage increases, so does the likelihood of more than one occurrence of any given word. But the range of words also increases. This is particularly the case as (at higher levels) texts begin to approximate more closely to authentic writing style, where there are constraints against repeating a word in adjacent sentences. To avoid this kind of repetition, writers sometimes exercise a preference for a synonym rather than a pro-form – thus increasing the TTR. This trend can be seen in the presence of the criterion *range of vocabulary* applied in many advanced level English examinations in the writing section.

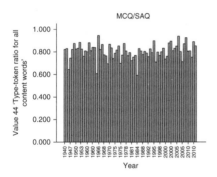

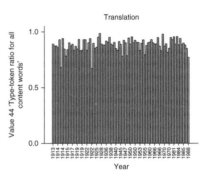

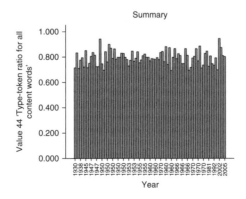

Cohm 44 Standardised type-token ratio per word	CPE Summary (n=84)				CPE MCQ/SAQ (n=69)				CPE Translation (n=85)				Kruskal-Wallis 1-way ANOVA
	Mean	SD	Min	Max	Mean	SD	Min	Max	Mean	SD	Min	Max	Sig
	0.79	0.06	0.46	0.70	0.80	0.07	0.40	0.70	0.88	0.06	0.50	0.96	0.000

It is noticeable that the TTR of the translation passages was much higher than those of either summary or MCQ/SAQ/MCQ indicating that these passages were quite demanding in terms of lexical access as one might expect given the focus of this particular test task. The mean for summary tasks was 0.79, for SAQ/MCQ 0.80 but for translation it was 0.88, evidence of significant differences in this index across tasks. Again the TTR's are fairly consistent over time across all three tasks though with a few exceptions as indicated by the range statistics.

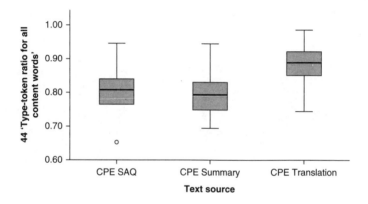

Syntactic complexity

Crossley, Greenfield and McNamara (2008:482) observe:

> [in careful reading] a reading text is processed linearly, with the reader decoding it word by word; but, as he or she reads, the reader also has to assemble decoded items into a larger scale syntactic structure (Just & Carpenter, 1987; Rayner & Pollatsek, 1994). Clearly, the cognitive demands imposed by this operation vary considerably according to how complex the structure is (Perfetti, Landi, & Oakhill, 2005).

Texts with less complex grammar tend on the whole to be easier than texts with more complex grammar. Berman (1984) investigated how opacity and heaviness of sentence structures could result in increased difficulty in processing. Again, this suggests that a valid test of reading should reflect the syntactic features likely to be encountered in target situation texts.

Work undertaken by Alderson and Clapham (1992) pointed to a very close relationship between a test of grammar and the IELTS reading component. Indeed the relationship was so close that a decision was taken to eliminate the grammar test from the IELTS battery. A similar result had been pointed out earlier by Weir (1983) and the grammar component had similarly been dropped from his TEAP battery despite showing itself to be the best single indicator of proficiency in academic English. Shiotsu (2003) explored components likely to affect reading test performance for Japanese undergraduates and found that syntactic knowledge played a central role. Shiotsu and Weir (2007), using structural equation modelling, demonstrated the relative importance of syntactic over lexical knowledge in accounting for variance in reading test scores with candidates from a variety of language backgrounds.

A considerable number of indices have been suggested in the literature for the estimation of grammatical complexity (see Ortega 2003, Wolfe-Quintero, Inagaki and Kim 1998). Based on the earlier review process we employed a range of the quantitative measures available through Coh-Metrix Version 2. The Coh-Metrix analysis suite includes:

- Cohm 37 *average number of words/ sentence* in general the longer the sentence the more processing time it takes up (ceteris paribus)
- Cohm 25 *number of negations incidence score*
- Cohm 36 *higher level constituents per word*
- Cohm 41 the *number of modifiers per noun phrase* concern the occurrence of complex noun phrases (these being a recognised feature of academic text)
- Cohm 43 the *mean number of words before the main verb* in sentences (structurally opaque texts tending to have proportionally more high order syntactic constituents and greater numbers of words before the main verb
- Cohm 50 *sentence syntax similarity, all, across paragraphs.*

(Definitions in italics below are from the Coh-Metrix website http://coh metrix.memphis.edu/cohmetrixpr/index.html)

Contextual parameter	Definition	Instrument
Average number of words/sentence	*The mean number of words per sentence.*	Word
Number of negations incidence score	*This is the incidence score for negation expressions.*	Coh-metrix (Variable 25)

Modifiers per noun phrase	*The mean number of modifiers per noun phrase. Modifiers per NP refer to adjectives, adverbs, or determiners that modify the head noun. Sentences with difficult syntactic compositions have a higher ratio of modifiers.*	Coh-Metrix (Variable 35)
Words before main verb of main clause	*The mean number of words before the main verb of the main clause per sentence. Sentences with a larger number of words before the main verb tend to be more difficult.*	Coh-Metrix (Variable 37)
Sentence syntax similarity, all, across paragraphs	*An index of syntactic similarity between two sentences is the proportion of nodes in the two syntactic tree structures that are intersecting nodes. The algorithms build an intersection tree between two syntactic trees, one for each of the two sentences being compared. The proportion of intersection tree nodes between all sentences and across paragraphs.*	Coh-Metrix (Variable 50)
Higher level constituents per (number of) word(s)	*The mean number of higher level constituents per number of words,. Sentences with difficult syntactic composition are structurally embedded and have a higher incidence of verb-phrases after controlling for number of words. Sentences with difficult syntactic compositions have a higher ratio of high-level constituents.*	Coh-Metrix (Variable 36)

Average sentence length

Weir et al (2012) claim that this index would appear to be a rough measure of both the syntactic complexity and the lexical density of a sentence. Clearly, the number of words in a sentence must often correlate loosely with the sentence's complexity in terms of number of clauses. Alternatively or in addition, a longer sentence might contain longer and more complex phrases – i.e. might be denser in lexical terms. This measure partly relates to processing at the level of structure building (Gernsbacher 1990) in that the more complex the sentence, the more elaborate is the structure that has to be assembled. If one assumes that longer sentences might also result from longer and more densely packed clauses, then the measure is also an indicator of difficulty of parsing. In parsing a reader has to hold a series of words in the mind until such time as he/she reaches the end of a clause and can trace a syntactic pattern in the string (Rayner and Pollatsek 1989). The longer the clause, the more words the reader has to hold in the mind. Lewis, Vasishth and Van Dyke (2006) suggest that processing items towards the end of longer sentences will be harder, since they usually have to be integrated with items that have occurred earlier on in the sentence. Graesser, Karnavat. Daniel, Cooper, Whitten and Louwerse (2001) also suggest that longer sentences tend to place more demands on working memory and are therefore more difficult

Khalifa and Weir (2009) describe how sentence length in Main Suite Reading examinations increases according to the level of the examination although again there seems to be considerable variation in the lengths of sentences featuring in the tests even at the same level. Again attention to this index might ensure greater homogeneity between the texts used at a particular level.

Main Suite Level	Average number of words per sentence	Range
KET (A2)	13.2	8–17
PET (B1)	14.9	10–20
FCE (B2)	18.4	11–25
CAE (C1)	18.6	13–27
CPE (C2)	19.6	13–30

In the figures below we can see great variety in sentence length in texts used from year to year at CPE which might be looked at more closely in future examinations.

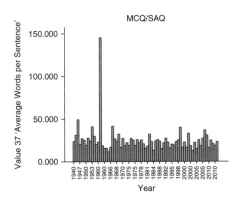

In the passage for 1960 there was one exceptionally long sentence: (145 words):

> Strangely enough there was not a sound in the house as having opened the street-door with his latchkey as he was in the habit of doing every evening at about this time, he walked into the lighted hall after shutting the door behind him with the customary click, noticing while his hands were occupied with the mechanical movements of hanging his hat and coat on the stand against the wall, that the light on the upper landing of the stairs was, for some reason, perhaps a perfectly trivial one, not on as it usually was, before moving, again habitually, to the door of the sitting-room at the foot of the stairs where, with his hand on the knob, he suddenly let the incipient feeling of alarm at the back of his mind take rigid hold of him with the discovery that the door was locked.

A Flesch reading ease of 0.0 and a Flesch-Kincaid Grade level of 57.5 hints at the difficulty this particular passage might have caused the reader. Given its status as an outlier it was removed from the calculations on average text lengths below.

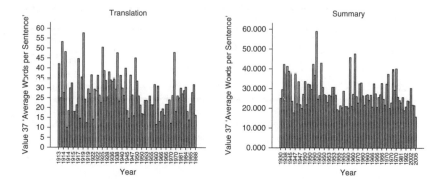

There seems to be considerable variability in sentence length within and across all three task types which needs more careful control in the future. The figures were:

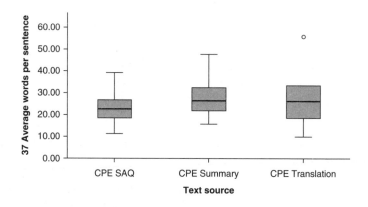

Cohm 37 Average words per sentence	CPE Summary (n=84)				CPE MCQ/SAQ (n=69)				CPE Translation (n=85)				Kruskal-Wallis 1-way ANOVA
	Mean	SD	Min	Max	Mean	SD	Min	Max	Mean	SD	Min	Max	Sig
	27.83	7.16	15.73	47.67	23.9	7.20	11.29	49.38	27.31	10.33	9.95	57.75	0.001

Additionally when the data are grouped into decades an interesting picture emerges as the average sentence lengths are much higher in the early period.

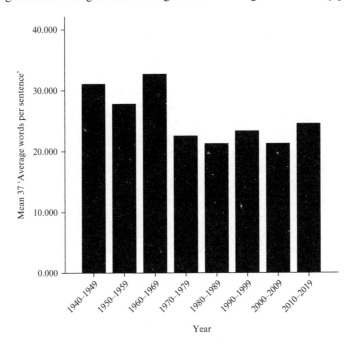

In the 1880s, Sherman had found that the English sentence was getting shorter. He describes how in Elizabethan times, the average sentence was 50 words long. In his time, it was 23 words long. Sherman wrote:

> Literary English, in short, will follow the forms of standard spoken English from which it comes. No man should talk worse than he writes, no man should write better than he should talk. . . . The oral sentence is clearest because it is the product of millions of daily efforts to be clear and strong. It represents the work of the race for thousands of years in perfecting an effective instrument of communication. (http://en.wikipedia. org/wiki/Plain_language)

One can only speculate on reasons for the fall in sentence length in the 1970s: maybe the appearance of graded readers in teaching and the graded objectives movement in general in the UK made people more aware of parameters such as sentence length, or perhaps it was the influence of advocates of 'Plain English' in official publications. The Plain English Campaign states on its website

> since 1979 . . . we have helped many government departments and other official organisations with their documents, reports and publications.

We believe that everyone should have access to clear and concise information.

Number of modifiers per noun phrase

The mean number of modifiers per noun phrase is an index of the complexity of referencing expressions. Barker (1998) argues that noun phrases carry much of the information in a text and computerised systems that attempt to acquire knowledge from text must first decompose complex noun phrases to get access to that information.

Graesser et al (2004) suggest that sentences with difficult syntactic composition have a higher ratio of constituents per noun phrase than do sentences with simple syntax. The presence of modifiers in the form of adjectives or prepositional phrases extends the length of a subject NP, and thus delays the point at which the verb is reached. However, the same argument would clearly not apply in the case of an object NP in an SVO sentence. Weir et al (2012) feel that a more satisfying explanation relates to the burden upon parsing: the inclusion of modifiers increases the length and complexity of the string of words that a reader has to hold in the mind while imposing a syntactic pattern upon it.

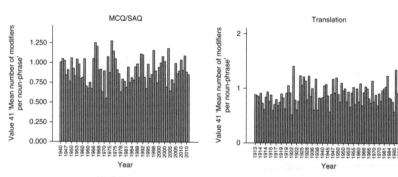

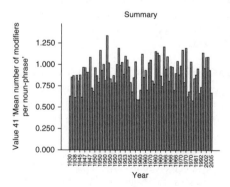

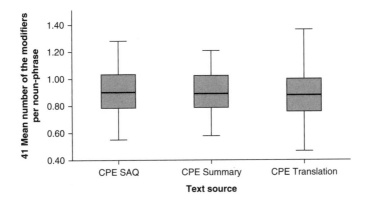

There was no significant difference in mean number of modifiers per noun phrase across all three tasks though some variation within texts from year to year.

Cohm 41 Mean number of modifiers per noun phrase	CPE Summary (n=84)				CPE MCQ/SAQ (n=69)				CPE Translation (n=85)				Kruskal-Wallis 1-way ANOVA
	Mean	SD	Min	Max	Mean	SD	Min	Max	Mean	SD	Min	Max	Sig
	0.90	0.17	0.58	1.21	0.90	0.16	0.55	1.28	0.89	0.19	0.47	1.41	0.713

Mean number of words before the main verb

Sentences that have many words before the main verb are taxing on working memory.

Weir et al (2012) maintain that the justification above from the Coh-Metrix specifications is not a convincing one; there the authors refer to working memory as a very general notion and do not specify at all how it operates in this case. The best explanation would seem to be a syntactic one associated with parsing. Critical to the parsing of a clause is the verb, which not only provides a predicator for the event being described but also signals the likely syntactic structure of the whole sentence through its valency (Trueswell, Tanenhaus and Kello 1993). The presence of modifiers in the form of adjectives or prepositional phrases extends the length of a subject NP, and thus delays the point at which the verb is reached. The words that occur before the verb are the first in a sentence to be analysed, and the longer the subject NP is, the greater the burden imposed at this early stage upon working memory.

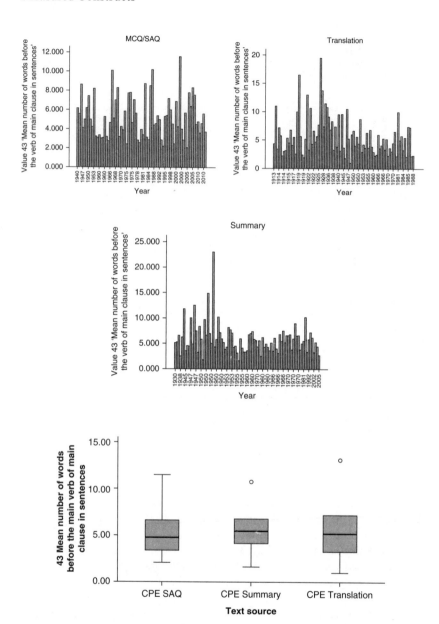

There was no significant difference in mean number of words before the main verb of the main clause in sentences across all three tasks although there is clearly a good deal of variability from one version to the next year on year with a number of clear outliers.

Cohm 43 Mean number of words before the main verb of main clause in sentences	CPE Summary (n=84)				CPE MCQ/SAQ (n=69)				CPE Translation (n=85)				Kruskal-Wallis 1-way ANOVA
	Mean	SD	Min	Max	Mean	SD	Min	Max	Mean	SD	Min	Max	Sig
	5.72	2.35	1.63	14.86	5.26	2.15	2.07	11.57	5.73	3.40	1.00	19.50	0.365

Sentence syntax similarity across all paragraphs

The sentence syntax similarity indices compare the syntactic tree structures of sentences. The algorithms build an intersection tree between two syntactic trees, one for each of the two sentences being compared. An index of syntactic similarity between two sentences is the proportion of nodes in the two tree structures that are intersecting nodes.

According to Weir et al (2012) what is at issue here is what is known as a syntactic priming effect. It is well attested in language production research (Pickering and Branigan 1998) that after a speaker has formulated a particular syntactic structure there is likelihood that he/she will employ a similar structure in the following utterance. The phenomenon is less clearly attested in reading comprehension. While syntactic priming appears to play a positive role in comprehension, it has been suggested that the effect may be partly or wholly due to the repetition of the verb. However, recent neurological evidence (Ledoux, Traxler and Saab 2007) suggests that syntactic parsing effects may be present even when the verb is not repeated.

There seems to be wide variation in syntactic similarity from year to year and this index would obviously be useful for item writers to apply in the future to try and ensure texts are closer in their syntactic complexity. However there was no significant difference between the means for the different tasks.

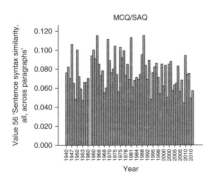

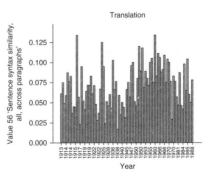

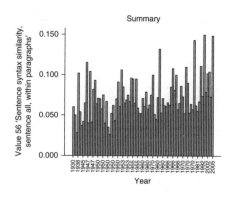

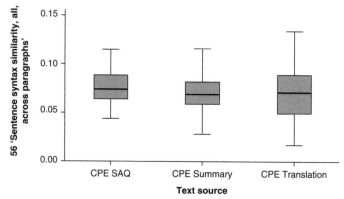

Cohm 56 Sentence syntax similarity, all, across para-graphs	CPE Summary (n=84)				CPE MCQ/SAQ (n=69)				CPE Translation (n=85)				Kruskal-Wallis 1-way ANOVA
	Mean	SD	Min	Max	Mean	SD	Min	Max	Mean	SD	Min	Max	Sig
	0.07	0.02	0.03	014	0.08	0.02	0.04	0.12	0.07	0.03	0.01	0.13	0.137

Higher-level constituents

Structurally dense sentences tend to have more high order syntactic constituents per word. . . . A second metric is mean number of higher level constituents per sentence, controlling for number of words. Sentences with difficult syntactic composition are structurally embedded and have a higher incidence of verb-phrases after controlling for number of words.

The term higher-level constituents is not adequately explained; however, it seems reasonable to assume that it refers to main and subordinate clauses. Weir et al (2012) feel that there appear to be two measures here: one relating to higher-level constituents per number of words (should this perhaps be reversed?) and one to higher-level constituents per sentence. If reversed, the first would indicate the mean length of the clauses in the text, whether main or subordinate. This has implications for the number of words that have to be held in mind during parsing since it is usually at clause boundaries that strings of words are 'made up' into propositions (Jarvella 1971).

The second provides an indication of the extent to which a text contains embedded clauses. Main verbs in a sentence are broadly indicative of the number of clauses. Sentences with complex syntactic composition have one or more clauses embedded in them and therefore have a higher incidence of verb phrases. Clearly, the higher the ratio of clauses to sentences, the higher the likelihood that a sentence will contain subordinate clauses. Subordinate clauses increase processing demands because, within the domain of a single sentence, a reader has to parse multiple groups of words into propositions and then to trace conceptual and logical links between the propositions that have been derived. This is clearly much more demanding than processing a series of simple sentences.

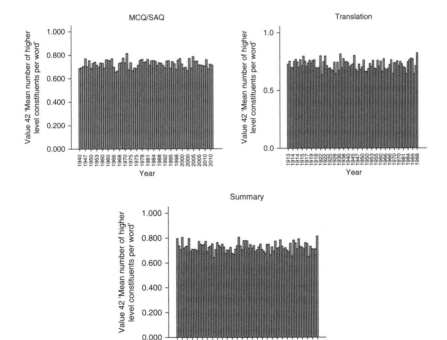

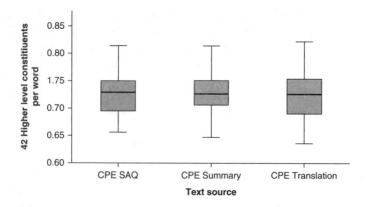

There was no significant difference in the mean number of higher-level con-stituents per word across the three tasks 0.73 for summary, 0.72 for SAQ/MCQ and 0.73 for translation. In addition there does not seem to be a great deal of variability within tasks over the period except perhaps in the texts used for translation.

Cohm 42 Higher level consti-tuents per word	CPE Summary (n=84)				CPE MCQ/SAQ (n=69)				CPE Translation (n=85)				Kruskal-Wallis 1-way ANOVA
	Mean	SD	Min	Max	Mean	SD	Min	Max	Mean	SD	Min	Max	Sig
	0.73	0.36	0.65	0.81	0.72	0.03	0.66	0.81	0.72	0.04	0.64	1.82	0.63

Number of negations incidence score

This is the incidence score for negation expressions.

Negative sentences have been shown to be more difficult to process than affirmative ones (Carpenter and Just 1975, MacDonald and Just 1989). The difficulty according to Weir et al (2012) does not appear to lie in the surface syntactic structure, as was once assumed (Fodor and Garrett 1967); but rather in the semantic difficulty of reversing a positive concept in order to construct a negative one. The most obvious example of negation is syntac-tic (The letter did not arrive); but lexically based negation surely has to be included. Most accounts of negation processing classify negatives as includ-ing positive verbs followed by a negative element (He agreed with nobody) and double negatives which cancel each other out (There was nobody who got nothing out of the new arrangements). There is clearly therefore a gra-dation of difficulty which cannot be represented in a simple measure. Some accounts also include morphological negation (friendless, untypical) and inherent negatives (absence, different) though these relate to processing at lexical rather than sentence level.

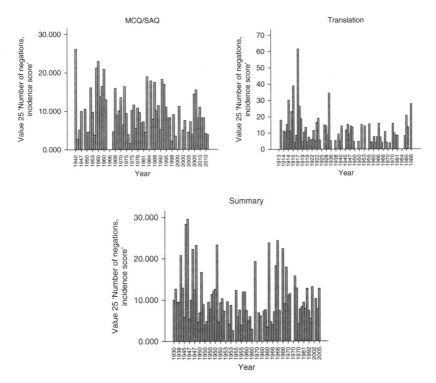

Though considerable variation is evident in number of negations incidence year on year within a task especially in translation, there were no significant differences between the means for each task.

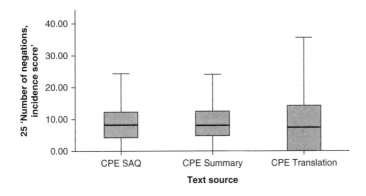

Cohm 25 Number of negations incidence score	CPE Summary (n=84)				CPE MCQ/SAQ (n=69)				CPE Translation (n=85)				Kruskal-Wallis 1-way ANOVA
	Mean	SD	Min	Max	Mean	SD	Min	Max	Mean	SD	Min	Max	Sig
	9.53	6.78	0.00	29.56	8.9	0.13	0.00	26.13	9.37	10.15	0.00	61.45	0.56

Cohesion

While Alderson (2000) notes that an absence of cohesive devices does not seriously damage comprehension when the topic is relatively familiar to readers, it has been argued that explicit cohesive devices help in establishing textual coherence (Goldman and Rakestraw 2000) and that their lack inhibits the recall of texts, being indicative of a less successful mental representation (Ehrlich 1991).

For the purposes of this study, we adopt the Graesser et al (2004:193) definition of cohesion as a property of a text that involves:

> explicit features, words, phrases or sentences that guide the reader in interpreting the substantive ideas in the text, in connecting ideas with other ideas and in connecting ideas to higher level global units (e.g. topics and themes).

McNamara, Graessar and Louwerse (in press) argue that:

> Cohesion arises from a variety of sources, including explicit argument overlap and causal relationships, and can operate between sentences, groups of sentences, paragraphs, and chapters (Givón, 1995; Graesser, McNamara, & Louwerse, 2003).

These cohesive devices cue the reader on how to form a coherent representation. The coherence relations are constructed in the mind of the reader and depend on the skills and knowledge that the reader brings to the situation. They argue that coherence is a psychological construct, whereas cohesion is a textual construct.

Two forms of textual cohesion are estimated by Coh-Metrix: referential cohesion (the extent to which words in the text co-refer) and conceptual cohesion (the degree of similarity between concepts in different parts of a text). In this analysis we employ three indices of referential cohesion and two of conceptual cohesion.

The public version of Coh-Metrix Version 2 offers three useful referential cohesion indices:

- Cohm 21 *Anaphor reference* is an indicator of referential cohesion. It is a measure of the proportion of anaphor references that refer back to a constituent up to five sentences earlier in the text.
- Cohm 16 *Argument overlap* (see Kintsch and van Djik 1978) is when a noun, pronoun, or noun-phrase in one sentence is a co-referent of a noun, pronoun, or noun-phrase in another sentence.
- Cohm 58 *Content word overlap* is the proportion of content words in the text that appear in adjacent sentences sharing common content words.

Contextual parameter		Definition	Instrument
Cohesion		**Anaphor reference adjacent unweighted**	*This is the proportion of anaphor references between adjacent sentences.*	*Coh-Metrix (Variable 18)*
		Anaphor reference, all distances, unweighted	*The proportion of unweighted anaphor references that refer back to a constituent up to 5 sentences earlier. A higher score indicates more cohesive and easier reading.*	*Coh-Metrix (Variable 21)*
	Referential cohesion	**Argument Overlap, all distances, unweighted**	*The proportion of all sentence pairs per paragraph that share one or more arguments (i.e. noun, pronoun, noun-phrase) or has a similar morphological stem. A higher score indicates more cohesive and easier reading.*	*Coh-Metrix (Variable 16*
		Proportion of content words that overlap between adjacent sentences	*The proportion of content words in adjacent sentences that share common content words. A higher score indicates more cohesive and easier reading.*	*Coh-Metrix (Variable 58)*
	Conceptual cohesion	**Logical operator incidence score**	*The incidence of logical operators, including and, or, not, if, then and a small number of other similar cognate terms. Texts with a high density of these logical operators tend to be more difficult.*	*Coh-Metrix (Variable 20)*
		LSA sentence to sentence adjacent mean	*Mean Latent Semantic Analysis (LSA) cosines for adjacent, sentence-to-sentence measure how conceptually similar each*	*Coh-Metrix (Variable 27)*

Contextual parameter		Definition	Instrument
		sentence is to the next sentence. Text cohesion is assumed to increase as a function of higher cosine scores between text constituents.	
Concreteness	**Minimum in sentence for content words**	*For each sentence in the text, a content word is identified that has the lowest concreteness rating. This score is the mean of these low-concreteness words across sentences.*	*Coh-Metrix (Variable 45)*

(Definitions in italics are all from the Coh-Metrix website http://cohmetrix. memphis.edu/cohmetrixpr/index.html)

Cohm 18 Anaphor reference adjacent unweighted

This is the proportion of anaphor references between adjacent sentences.

Weir et al (2012) point out that it is easier to resolve anaphoric reference where the anaphor occurs in a sentence that follows immediately after the one in which the referent occurs. The referent will remain foregrounded in the mind of the reader, and may have been tagged as a current topic focus. A potential weakness of a simple measure of proximity is that there are occasional cases of ambiguity where the first sentence contains more than one possible referent. In this case, the preferential choice would be made on the basis of parallel function (Arnold, Eisenband, Brown-Schmidt and Trueswell 2000, Sheldon 1974) with the anaphor matched by similarity of sentence function and position (a subject pronoun to a preceding NP subject, an object pronoun to a preceding NP object), rather than by closest proximity to the referent. It is not made explicit that Coh-Metrix excludes from consideration the first and second personal pronouns, which have referents outside the text. Nor is it made explicit that it includes referents such as this, that, the former, the latter.

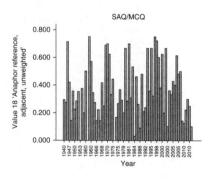

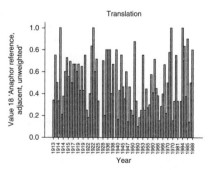

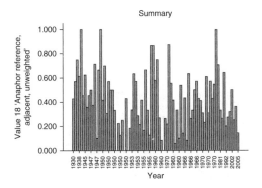

Cohm 21 Anaphor reference all distances

A measure of the proportion of anaphor references that refer back to a constituent up to 5 sentences earlier in the text.

This would appear to include instances already included under adjacent sentences. A more informative measure (with only an incremental effect on difficulty) might be of cases where an anaphoric referent occurs earlier than in the immediately preceding sentence. Where the referent is 'remote' from the anaphor, it is more difficult to process. Indeed, a major characteristic of children who are inexperienced readers is that they have problems in resolving this type of anaphor, but are often capable of resolving anaphoric reference where the referent is adjacent. (Yuill and Oakhill 1991). The difficulty lies in the need to carry forward one or more current topics, while at the same time, decoding and parsing written text.

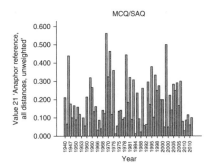

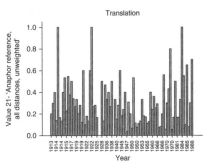

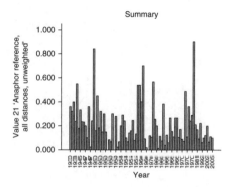

There is considerable variation from text to text from year to year in all tasks. Distance is a critical determinant. The greater the distance between the referent and the thing referred to the greater the difficulty in decoding the referent (Oakhill, Yuill and Parkin 1986:80–91).The differences between tasks are not significant for Cohm 18 Anaphor reference, adjacent, unweighted but are for Cohm 21 Anaphor reference, all distances, though not hugely different. Again translation is the most cohesive on this measure out of the three tasks.

Cohm 18 Anaphor reference, adjacent, un- weighted	CPE Summary (n=84)				CPE MCQ/SAQ (n=69)				CPE Translation (n=85)				Kruskal-Wallis 1-way ANOVA
	Mean	SD	Min	Max	Mean	SD	Min	Max	Mean	SD	Min	Max	Sig
	0.42	0.24	0.00	1.00	0.37	0.20	0.00	0.75	0.49	0.26	0.00	1.00	0.10
Cohm 21 Anaphor reference, all distances	0.22	0.18	0.00	0.90	0.18	0.13	0.00	0.56	0.30	0.22	0.00	1.00	0.00

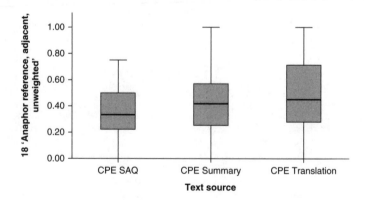

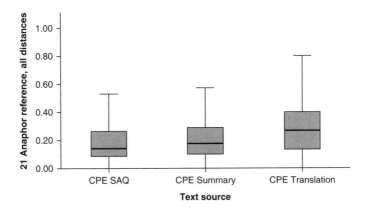

Argument overlap

When a noun, pronoun, or noun phrase in one sentence is a co-referent of a noun, pronoun, or noun phrase in another sentence.

The cognitive demands of storing information while reading are considerable. Weir et al (2012) describe how in addition to a) holding the surface language of the current sentence in the mind until it can be syntactically parsed and b) carrying forward a discourse representation of the text so far, a reader also has to carry forward an awareness of what constitutes the current topic or focus (Sanford and Garrod 1981). Items that have been mentioned in the immediately preceding text are said to be foregrounded and thus more easily matched to subsequent anaphors or incorporated into inferential processes. The value of the argument overlap measure is presumably that it indicates the extent to which the same entity is foregrounded in successive sentences, thus simplifying the process of identifying and carrying forward the topic focus.

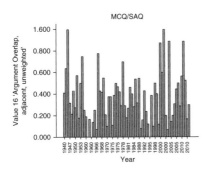
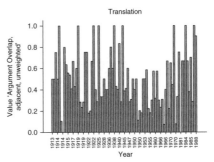

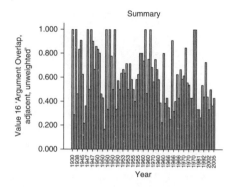

Cohm 16 Argument overlap, adjacent, un-weighted	CPE Summary (n=84)				CPE MCQ/SAQ (n=69)				CPE Translation (n=85)				Kruskal-Wallis 1-way ANOVA
	Mean	SD	Min	Max	Mean	SD	Min	Max	Mean	SD	Min	Max	Sig
	0.61	0.23	0.17	1.00	0.37	0.24	0.00	1.00	0.50	0.26	0.00	1.00	0.000

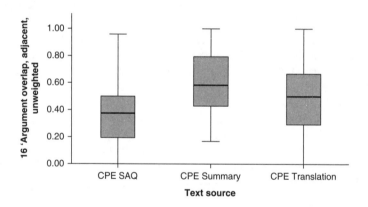

Summary texts showed themselves to be the most cohesive in this respect but there is a good deal of variability between texts in the same task type.

Content word overlap

The proportion of content words in the text that appear in adjacent sentences sharing common content words.

The occurrence of the same content word in adjacent sentences reduces text difficulty in two ways according to Weir et al (2012). At the level of decoding, a word is subject to a repetition priming effect (Scarborough, Cortese and Scarborough 1977, Stanners, Neiser, Hernin and Hall 1979), whereby a) it is recognised more readily on its second occurrence and b) lexical access is speeded up. At a discourse level, the repetition contributes to text cohesion, thus reinforcing current themes. Repetition priming is surprisingly long-lived and assists a reader in processing recurrent words throughout a text. On the other hand, as already mentioned, there are stylistic constraints which operate against the use of identical words in adjacent sentences, and foster the use of pro-forms and synonyms. This predictor seems likely to be based on relatively few examples.

Crossley, Greenfield and McNamara (2008:483) note:

> The Coh-Metrix index *content word overlap,* which measures how often content words overlap between two adjacent sentences, measures one of many factors that facilitate meaning construction . . . overlapping vocabulary has been found to be an important aspect in reading processing and can lead to gains in text comprehension and reading speed (Douglas, 1981; Kintsch & van Dijk, 1978; Rashotte & Torgesen, 1985).

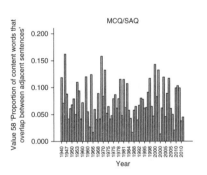

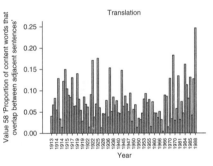

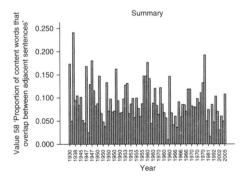

Cohm 58 Proportion of content words that	CPE Summary (n=84)				CPE MCQ/SAQ (n=69)				CPE Translation (n=85)				Kruskal-Wallis 1-way ANOVA
	Mean	SD	Min	Max	Mean	SD	Min	Max	Mean	SD	Min	Max	Sig
overlap between adjacent sentences	0.09	0.04	0.01	0.24	0.07	0.03	0.01	0.016	0.07	0.05	0.01	0.25	0.006

There are significant difference across the tasks in this index as well as variation from year to year within task though the proportions are quite close.

Summary is the most cohesive text type here, with translation and MCQ/SAQ texts fairly similar.

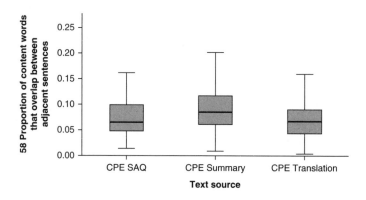

We established by our earlier investigations that two conceptual cohesion indices were worth investigating.

Logical operator incidence

This is the incidence of logical operators. Along with "and" and "or" , and negations, a number of conditionals are also included.

This criterion refers to logical connectives. A list of connectors is provided in the Coh-Metrix specifications, many of which do not appear to be logical in function. It is curious indeed that the examples above include 'negations' and counterfactuals, which known to be semantically difficult to process in their own right. Where there is no connective linking adjacent clauses or sentences, the reader has to rely upon inference (Brown and Yule 1983, Oakhill and Garnham 1988, Singer 1994) in order to trace a connection. If there is a logical connector, it marks the relationship between the two idea units unambiguously, and spares the reader the cognitive effort associated with having to infer the connection. Weir et al (2012) argue that this would suggest that the presence of connectives **reduces** difficulty rather than **increasing** it (as Coh-Metrix seems to postulate; for example McNamara et al 2005). An explanation for the assumption that this measure correlates with difficulty may be that the word incidence in the specification refers to types not to tokens. One would certainly expect a greater range of logical connectives in more advanced texts. Whilst question marks appeared against its usefulness for studies concerned with vertical scaling (as in the Weir et al 2012 study of FCE, CAE and CPE), it is obviously useful to try and maintain a similar level from year to year in the same examination such as CPE.

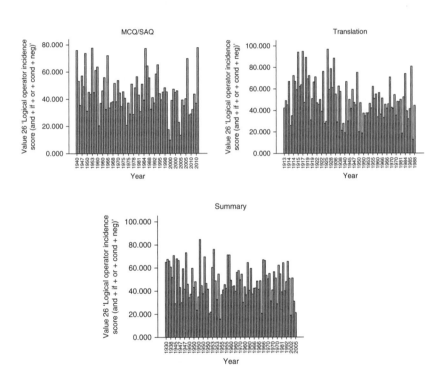

There was no significant difference in the logical operator incidence score across the three tasks 47.6 for summary 44.87 for SAQ/MCQ and 50.02 for translation though substantial differences on the index occur between texts. Range was 15.87–76.19 for summary, 9.80–77.82 for SAQ/MCQ and 14.89–88.79 for translation.

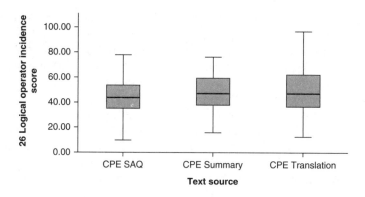

	CPE Summary (n=84)				CPE MCQ/SAQ (n=69)				CPE Translation (n=85)				Kruskal-Wallis 1-way ANOVA
Cohm 26 Logical operator incidence score	Mean	SD	Min	Max	Mean	SD	Min	Max	Mean	SD	Min	Max	Sig
	47.60	14.49	15.87	76.19	44.87	15.11	9.80	77.82	50.02	18.80	12.58	96.77	0.205

In addition there are indices that assess the extent to which the content of sentences or paragraphs are similar semantically or conceptually (semantic coreferentiality). Coherence is predicted to increase as a function of such similarity. LSA allows us to closely approximate human judgements of meaning similarity between words in a message. Latent Semantic Analysis (LSA) is a statistical method for representing the meaning of words based on large text corpora. Cohesion is held to increase as a function of higher LSA cosine scores between sentences.

Cohm 27 LSA mean sentence adjacent similarity

This appears to be a measure of the extent to which a particular theme extends across more than one sentence in the view of Weir et al (2012). It is partly calculated on the basis of words which share a particular lexical set and which contribute to representing a single, consistent topic. The logic is no doubt that this a) enables the reader to draw upon stored schematic knowledge relating to the theme in question (Bartlett 1932), and thus to provide a framework for better understanding of what follows; b) supports spreading activation (Hutchison 2003, Meyer and Schvanevelt 1971), whereby the occurrence of a particular word such as doctor primes related words such as nurse, hospital, etc. and ensures that they are more rapidly recognised; c) assists the reader in building up a coherent information structure for a text

(Gernsbacher 1990), since this type of pattern makes the thematic relationships in the text more transparent.

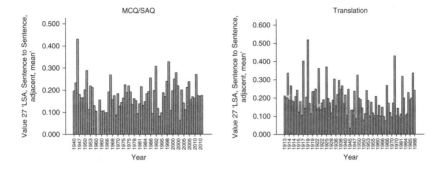

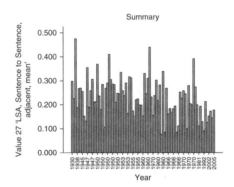

Cohm 27 LSA, Sentence to sentence adjacent mean	CPE Summary (n=84)				CPE MCQ/SAQ (n=69)				CPE Translation (n=85)				Kruskal-Wallis 1-way ANOVA
	Mean	SD	Min	Max	Mean	SD	Min	Max	Mean	SD	Min	Max	Sig
	0.23	0.08	0.08	0.48	0.18	007	0.06	0.43	0.19	0.09	0.04	0.52	0.000

The above figures show some quite wide variation in this index evidence that some texts are considerably more cohesive than others conceptually and therefore easier to process on this index at least. Though there are significant differences across and within tasks these do not appear to differ greatly in respect of this index. Again there is evidence from the range statistics that in this index some texts are far more conceptually cohesive than others.

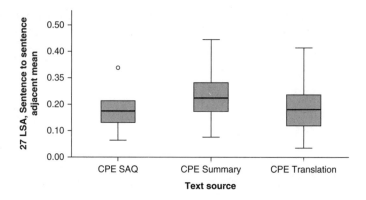

Cohesion did not prove to be that a useful indicator of level in the studies we considered in the literature, for example Graesser at al (2011:230) noted:

> ... conclusion is that different forms of cohesion are not always positively correlated with grade-level bands. Text cohesion has a small variation over grade level, with a slight decrease for referential cohesion within most text genres and a slight increase for causal cohesion

However, it is obviously the case that year on year tests at the same level should try to achieve similar degrees of cohesion

Concreteness/abstractness

Coh-Metrix 2.0 uses the MRC concreteness ratings for a large sample of content words. Concreteness measures how concrete a word is, based on human ratings. High numbers lean toward concrete and low numbers to abstract. Values vary between 100 and 700.

The concern here is with the extent to which the information in a text is concrete (i.e. concerning observable, concrete phenomena) or abstract (i.e. concerning unobservable phenomena such as social institutions) or, at a higher level of abstraction, meta-phenomenal (Moore and Morton 1999) (concerning theoretical treatment of abstract phenomena). Different levels of abstraction may, of course, be found within a single text. Alderson et al (2004:127) mark this as a useful feature to consider in estimating text difficulty in relation to the Common European Framework of Reference. Information that is more abstract may prove to be more difficult to process and so divert cognitive resources from language processing. At the same time abstract information often implies a linguistic complexity that may further stretch the L2 reader's resources. Much academic text, particularly in the humanities and social sciences, is concerned with abstract ideas.

Coh-Metrix Version 2 provides a number of indices that relate to degree of abstractness. *Concreteness* measures are based on a database of human judgements derived from psycholinguistic experiments representing a greater degree of concreteness. It offers Cohm 60:

> *Minimum concreteness of content words. For each sentence in the text, a content word is identified that has the lowest concreteness rating. This score is the mean of these low-concreteness words across sentences.*

This measure is based upon the well-established finding that abstract words are more difficult to process because they are not as imageable as concrete words (Weir et al 2012). There is some evidence (Bleasdale 1987) that there may be separate lexicons for the two types. However, it draws upon a Psycholinguistic Database which was quite small, compiled a long time ago (Coltheart 1981) and not very expertly assembled. The abstractness ratings of the words were partly based on a study by Paivio, Yuille and Madigan (1968) which featured only 925 items but was later expanded to 4000. Furthermore, the dataset does not deal adequately with a major area of controversy in relation to abstractness – the difference (Kintsch 1972) between abstract words which have been derived morphologically (happiness) and others which are unitary (truth). A word such as friendship would qualify semantically as abstract but can easily be deconstructed through a knowledge of derivational suffixation and is closely linked morphologically to its concrete stem.

The texts below, especially those used in MCQ/SAQ task types, show some variability from year to year but this is within a narrow range.

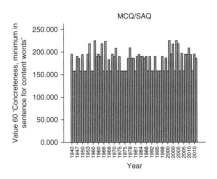

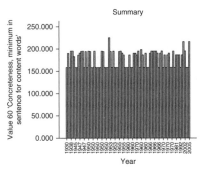

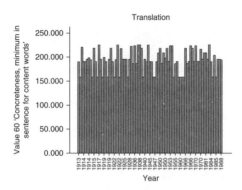

There are differences across the tasks with translation on average the least concrete and summary the most concrete texts although quite close to SAQ / MCQ.

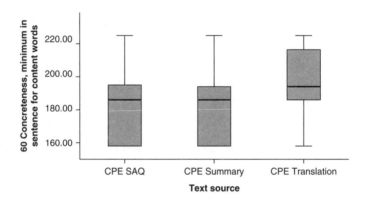

Cohm 60 Concreteness, minimum in sentence for content words	CPE summary (n=84)				CPE MCQ/SAQ (n=69)				CPE Translation (n=85)				Kruskal–Wallis 1-way ANOVA
	Mean	SD	Min	Max	Mean	SD	Min	Max	Mean	SD	Min	Max	Sig
	178.05	18.44	158.00	225.00	181.39	21.39	158.0	225.0	193.19	22.16	158.00	225.00	0.000

External points of reference: Comparison with IELTS and undergraduate texts.

As a final point of comparison we looked at the relative means of two other measures relevant to C2/CPE level reading tests namely 42 IELTS Reading texts and 42 key undergraduate texts from a British University (see Green et al

2010) and compared them with the findings from our analysis of the 3 CPE reading task types (Summary, MCQ/SAQ and Translation). This gave us two external reference points viz the complexity of texts students will face in their first year at university and texts to be found in the leading test of English for academic purposes used for gate-keeping functions in university admissions.

Looking at averages obviously simplifies a fairly complex picture but it does give us a general idea of the difficulty level of CPE texts as compared to IELTS which is used as a proficiency test for university admissions purposes and with core undergraduate texts in 15 key disciplines for overseas students (see Green et al 2010). CPE texts would appear to be:

1. More demanding than IELTS or UG texts in relation to the following indices:

   - standardised type-token ratio per word
   - mean number of higher level constituents (ns)
   - average words per sentence
   - anaphor reference, adjacent, unweighted
   - anaphor reference, all distances
   - argument overlap (ns)
   - LSA, Sentences adjacent mean
   - number of negations incidence score (ns)
   - logical operators incidence score
   - proportion of content words that overlap between sentences.

2. Less demanding in relation to:

   - lexical density (ns)
   - academic words
   - concreteness (ns)
   - average syllables per word (ns)
   - mean number of modifiers per noun phrase
   - off list words (< UG texts but > IELTS).

3. Very similar in respect of the remaining parameters:

   - higher-level constituents per word (ns)
   - sentence syntax similarity, all, across paragraphs (ns)
   - celex, logarithm, mean for content words (0–6) (ns).

The data suggest that CPE texts on the whole are likely to be at least as complex as IELTS or undergraduate texts which indicates that in this aspect of validity at least they are at an appropriate level of difficulty.

Table 5 Kruskal-Wallis one-way ANOVA among CPE Summary, IELTS and UG

	CPE Summary (n=84)				IELTS (n=42)				UG (n=42)				Kruskal-Wallis 1-way ANOVA
	Mean	SD	Min	Max	Mean	SD	Min	Max	Mean	SD	Min	Max	Sig
Cohm 16 Argument overlap, adjacent, unweighted	0.61	0.23	0.17	1.00	0.52	0.15	0.24	0.86	0.56	0.15	0.26	0.90	0.217
Cohm 18 Anaphor reference, adjacent, unweighted	0.42	0.24	0.00	1.00	0.25	0.11	0.05	0.59	0.24	0.13	0.00	0.62	0.000
Cohm 21 Anaphor reference, all distances	0.22	0.18	0.00	0.90	0.08	0.05	0.02	0.22	0.10	0.09	0.00	0.39	0.000
Cohm 25 Number of negations incidence score	9.53	6.78	0.00	29.56	6.56	3.57	0.00	16.20	5.88	4.11	0.00	15.96	0.002
Cohm 26 Logical operator incidence score	47.60	14.49	15.87	76.19	39.28	9.65	22.64	64.56	46.14	11.78	20.54	71.43	0.001
Cohm 27 LSA, Sentence to sentence adjacent mean	0.23	0.08	0.08	0.48	0.23	0.07	0.10	0.45	0.26	0.08	0.11	0.45	0.040
Cohm 35 Number of words	343.08	120.21	129	640	780.45	240.83	1.00	999.00	440.10	413.62	1.00	995.00	0.000
Cohm 37 Average words per sentence	27.83	7.16	15.73	47.67	21.89	3.73	16.11	34.71	21.47	4.26	13.76	30.30	0.000
Cohm 38 Average syllables per word	1.55	0.13	1.86	2.57	1.66	0.09	1.45	1.83	1.72	0.14	1.46	2.07	0.000
Cohm 41 Mean number of modifiers per noun phrase	0.90	0.166	0.58	1.21	0.98	0.09	0.71	1.13	0.95	0.15	0.64	1.24	0.010
Cohm 42 Higher level constituents per word	0.73	0.036	0.65	0.81	0.71	0.02	0.67	0.76	0.72	0.04	0.65	0.81	0.002
Cohm 43 Mean number of words before the main verb of main clause in sentences	5.72	2.35	1.63	14.86	5.48	1.35	3.32	10.08	4.59	1.39	1.86	7.97	0.005

Cohm 44 Standardised type-token ratio per word	0.79	0.06	0.46	0.70	0.68	0.04	0.60	0.77	0.65	0.08	0.51	0.90	0.000
Cohm 46 Celex, logarithm, mean for content words (0–6)	2.18	0.16	1.86	2.57	2.17	0.11	1.94	2.37	2.14	0.15	1.79	2.48	0.449
Cohm 56 Sentence syntax similarity, all, across paragraphs	0.07	0.02	0.03	0.14	0.08	0.01	0.06	0.10	0.07	0.01	0.05	0.10	0.002
Cohm 58 Proportion of content words that overlap between adjacent sentences	0.09	0.04	0.01	0.24	0.08	0.03	0.03	0.16	0.10	0.03	0.04	0.17	0.047
Cohm 60 Concreteness, minimum in sentence for content words	178.05	18.441	158.00	225.00	171.83	15.57	158.00	195.00	168.83	15.87	158.00	208.00	0.005
AWL level	4.83	2.64	0.58	12.13	7.90	2.33	2.20	14.03	10.51	3.47	4.33	22.22	0.000
Density	0.50	0.04	0.40	0.59	0.57	0.03	0.47	0.63	0.56	0.05	0.45	0.67	0.000
Offlist words = >15k	1.16	1.06	0.00	3.94	1.09	1.66	0.00	5.31	4.33	3.18	0.20	11.62	0.000

Table 6 Kruskal-Wallis 1-way ANOVA among CPE SAQ, MCQ, IELTS and UG

	CPE SAQ (n=69)				IELTS (n=42)				UG (n=42)				Kruskal-Wallis 1-way ANOVA
	Mean	SD	Min	Max	Mean	SD	Min	Max	Mean	SD	Min	Max	Sig
Cohm 16 Argument overlap, adjacent, unweighted	0.37	0.24	0.00	1.00	0.52	0.15	0.24	0.86	0.56	0.15	0.26	0.90	0.203
Cohm 18 Anaphor reference, adjacent, unweighted	0.37	0.20	0.00	0.75	0.25	0.11	0.05	0.59	0.24	0.13	0.00	0.62	0.234
Cohm 21 Anaphor reference, all distances	0.18	0.13	0.00	0.56	0.08	0.05	0.02	0.22	0.10	0.09	0.00	0.39	0.078
Cohm 25 Number of negations incidence score	8.9	6.25	0.00	26.13	6.56	3.57	0.00	16.20	5.88	4.11	0.00	15.96	0.529
Cohm 26 Logical operator incidence score	44.87	15.11	9.80	77.82	39.28	9.65	22.64	64.56	46.14	11.78	20.54	71.43	0.011
Cohm 27 LSA, Sentence to sentence adjacent mean	0.18	0.07	0.06	0.43	0.23	0.07	0.10	0.45	0.26	0.08	0.11	0.45	0.084
Cohm 35 Number of words	405.71	152.95	179	849	780.45	240.83	1.00	999.00	440.10	413.62	1.00	995.00	0.000
Cohm 37 Average words per sentence	23.39	7.20	11.29	49.38	21.89	3.73	16.11	34.71	21.47	4.26	13.76	30.30	0.737
Cohm 38 Average syllables per word	1.55	0.13	1.30	1.92	1.66	0.09	1.45	1.83	1.72	0.14	1.46	2.07	0.080
Cohm 41 Mean number of modifiers per noun phrase	0.90	0.16	0.55	1.28	0.98	0.09	0.71	1.13	0.95	0.15	0.64	1.24	0.409
Cohm 42 Higher level constituents per word	0.72	0.03	0.66	0.81	0.71	0.02	0.67	0.76	0.72	0.04	0.65	0.81	0.075
Cohm 43 Mean number of words before the main verb of main clause in sentences	5.26	2.15	2.07	11.57	5.48	1.35	3.32	10.08	4.59	1.39	1.86	7.97	0.003
Cohm 44 Standardised type-token ratio per word	0.80	0.07	0.40	0.70	0.68	0.04	0.60	0.77	0.65	0.08	0.51	0.90	0.002

Cohm 46 Celex, logarithm, mean for content words (0–6)	2.18	0.13	1.87	2.47	2.17	0.11	1.94	2.37	2.14	0.15	1.79	2.48	0.618
Cohm 56 Sentence syntax similarity, all, across paragraphs	0.08	0.02	0.04	0.12	0.08	0.01	0.06	0.10	0.07	0.01	0.05	0.10	0.002
Cohm 58 Proportion of content words that overlap between adjacent sentences	0.07	0.03	0.01	0.16	0.08	0.03	0.03	0.16	0.10	0.03	0.04	0.17	0.043
Cohm 60 Concreteness, minimum in sentence for content words	181.39	21.39	158.00	225.00	171.83	15.57	158.00	195.00	168.83	15.87	158.00	208.00	0.335
AWL level	5.02	2.82	0.93	12.96	7.90	2.33	2.20	14.03	10.51	3.47	4.33	22.22	0.000
Density	0.52	0.04	0.44	0.59	0.57	0.03	0.47	0.63	0.56	0.05	0.45	0.67	0.365
Offlist words = >15k	1.61	1.64	0.00	7.68	1.09	1.66	0.00	5.31	4.33	3.18	0.20	11.62	0.000

Table 7 Kruskal-Wallis 1-way ANOVA among CPE Translation, IELTS and UG

	CPE Translation (n=85)				IELTS (n=42)				UG (n=42)				Kruskal-Wallis 1-way ANOVA
	Mean	SD	Min	Max	Mean	SD	Min	Max	Mean	SD	Min	Max	Sig
Cohm 16 Argument overlap, adjacent, unweighted	0.50	0.26	0.00	1.00	0.52	0.15	0.24	0.86	0.56	0.15	0.26	0.90	0.133
Cohm 18 Anaphor reference, adjacent, unweighted	0.49	0.26	0.00	1.00	0.25	0.11	0.05	0.59	0.24	0.13	0.00	0.62	0.000
Cohm 21 Anaphor reference, all distances	0.30	0.22	0.00	1.00	0.08	0.05	0.02	0.22	0.10	0.09	0.00	0.39	0.000
Cohm 25 Number of negations incidence score	9.37	10.15	0.00	61.45	6.56	3.57	0.00	16.20	5.88	4.11	0.00	15.96	0.327
Cohm 26 Logical operator incidence score	50.02	18.80	12.58	96.77	39.28	9.65	22.64	64.56	46.14	11.78	20.54	71.43	0.001
Cohm 27 LSA, Sentence to sentence adjacent mean	0.19	0.09	0.04	0.52	0.23	0.07	0.10	0.45	0.26	0.08	0.11	0.45	0.000
Cohm 35 Number of words	212.46	53.82	104	390	780.45	240.83	1.00	999.00	440.10	413.62	1.00	995.00	0.000
Cohm 37 Average words per sentence	27.31	10.33	9.95	57.75	21.89	3.73	16.11	34.71	21.47	4.26	13.76	30.30	0.001
Cohm 38 Average syllables per word	1.46	0.12	1.23	1.74	1.66	0.09	1.45	1.83	1.72	0.14	1.46	2.07	0.000
Cohm 41 Mean number of modifiers per noun phrase	0.89	0.19	0.47	1.41	0.98	0.09	0.71	1.13	0.95	0.15	0.64	1.24	0.001
Cohm 42 Higher level constituents per word	0.72	0.04	0.64	1.82	0.71	0.02	0.67	0.76	0.72	0.04	0.65	0.81	0.108
Cohm 43 Mean number of words before the main verb of main clause in sentences	5.73	3.40	1.00	19.50	5.48	1.35	3.32	10.08	4.59	1.39	1.86	7.97	0.042

Cohm 46 Celex, logarithm, mean for content words (0–6)	2.15	0.20	1.75	2.78	2.17	0.11	1.94	2.37	2.14	0.15	1.79	2.48	0.542
Cohm 56 Sentence syntax similarity, all, across paragraphs	0.07	0.03	0.012	0.13	0.08	0.01	0.06	0.10	0.07	0.01	0.05	0.10	0.015
Cohm 58 Proportion of content words that overlap between adjacent sentences	0.07	0.05	0.01	0.25	0.08	0.03	0.03	0.16	0.10	0.03	0.04	0.17	0.000
Cohm 60 Concreteness, minimum in sentence for content words	193.19	22.16	158.00	225.00	171.83	15.57	158.00	195.00	168.83	15.87	158.00	208.00	0.000
AWL level	2.25	1.81	0.00	7.48	7.90	2.33	2.20	14.03	10.51	3.47	4.33	22.22	0.000
Density	0.50	0.05	0.32	0.62	0.57	0.03	0.47	0.63	0.56	0.05	0.45	0.67	0.000
Offlist words = >15k	1.67	1.47	0.00	6.91	1.09	1.66	0.00	5.31	4.33	3.18	0.20	11.62	0.000

CPE's place in the Cambridge Main Suite System: FCE versus CAE versus CPE

Finally, we analysed a set of FCE, CAE and CPE texts (Weir et al 2012) to allow a comparison between these different levels of Cambridge examinations. It is important for exams boards to know that that their examinations at C2, C1 and B2 are placing a different cognitive load on processing from each other. The results of this analysis are presented in Table 8 below. In nearly all our parameters CPE showed itself to be the most complex text and FCE the least complex. Significant differences between the three levels are present in 16/18 of our indices.

Results and discussion

Overall test developers seem to have done a reasonable job through connoisseurship in respect of many of the indices under consideration but more systematic procedures, as exemplified in this study, would help reduce variability in others where they have been less successful in selecting and editing comparable texts. This empirical case study of the context validity of the CPE examination 1913–2012 suggests that Coh-Metrix Version 2 and Web VocabProfile should prove useful in the future for English language reading test developers (and reading materials producers in general) in a variety of ways. Although most of the reading test passages investigated here were positively evaluated through a systematic, editorial process (see Khalifa and Weir (2009:197–201) for details of this at Cambridge), the study none the less identified certain texts with indices outside the normal range typically found in the examination task

Use of these automated tools in the future would ensure greater consistency in the characteristics of texts employed in a test. We need to ensure that the texts we use in an examination year on year are comparable in respect of as many of our contextual indices as possible. The case for this is clear. What remains is for examination boards to determine what is an acceptable range for each parameter, at each level of proficiency for which they offer examinations. An acceptance of collective responsibility amongst the examinations boards for this endeavour would guarantee the most dependable specifications for the different levels of proficiency which are, at best, vaguely and sparsely specified in the current CEFR (Council of Europe 2001).

Information derived from text analysis tools should also prove of considerable value in item writer training to help those involved better understand the characteristics of suitable texts and to help them to edit sources in ways that are compatible with the aims of the test and most crucially which do not impact adversely on the authenticity of the original texts (Green and Hawkey 2011).

Table 8 Results of one-way ANOVA among FCE, CAE and CPE texts

	FCE (n=48)				CAE (n=49)				CPE (n=69)				Kruskal-Wallis Test
	Min	Max	Mean	Std. Dev	Min	Max	Mean	Std. Dev	Min	Max	Mean	Std. Dev	
1 16 'Argument Overlap, adjacent, unweighted'	0.27	0.70	0.50	0.12	0.10	0.88	0.45	0.16	0.00	1.00	0.38	0.24	0.000
2 18 'Anaphor reference, adjacent, unweighted'	0.17	0.84	0.53	0.14	0.11	0.79	0.41	0.16	0.00	0.75	0.37	0.20	0.000
3 21 Anaphor reference, all distances	0.11	0.55	0.30	0.12	0.03	0.55	0.20	0.12	0.00	0.56	0.18	0.13	0.000
4 25 'Number of negations, incidence score'	0.00	16.39	5.83	3.70	0.00	19.92	6.44	4.72	0.00	26.13	8.90	6.25	0.015
5 26 Logical operator incidence score	18.77	53.25	35.72	8.31	16.71	66.27	38.58	11.42	9.80	77.82	44.87	15.22	0.001
6 27 LSA, Sentence to sentence adjacent mean	0.07	0.20	0.13	0.03	0.07	0.32	0.15	0.05	0.06	0.43	0.18	0.07	0.000
7 37 Average words per sentence	11.57	26.05	18.68	3.03	13.97	29.08	20.42	4.01	11.29	49.38	23.39	7.25	0.000
8 38 'Average Syllables per Word'	1.30	1.58	1.42	0.07	1.28	1.76	1.54	0.11	1.30	1.93	1.55	0.13	0.000
9 41 Mean number of modifiers per noun-phrase	0.42	1.13	0.75	0.16	0.54	1.37	0.92	0.20	0.55	1.28	0.90	0.16	0.000
10 42 Higher level constituents per word	0.68	0.84	0.76	0.04	0.61	0.80	0.72	0.04	0.66	0.81	0.72	0.03	0.000
11 43 Mean number of words before the main verb of main clause in sentences	1.89	6.63	4.07	1.12	2.09	7.41	4.40	1.30	2.07	11.57	5.23	2.15	0.014
12 44 'Type-token ratio for all content words'	0.64	0.83	0.75	0.04	0.59	0.95	0.75	0.08	0.59	0.95	0.80	0.07	0.000

Table 8 continued

	FCE (n=48)				CAE (n=49)				CPE (n=69)				Kruskal-Wallis Test
	Min	Max	Mean	Std. Dev	Min	Max	Mean	Std. Dev	Min	Max	Mean	Std. Dev	
13 46 'Celex, logarithm, mean for content words (0–6)'	2.15	2.65	2.35	0.11	1.94	2.48	2.21	0.15	1.87	2.47	2.18	0.13	0.000
14 56 'Sentence syntax similarity, all, across paragraphs'	0.05	0.11	0.09	0.02	0.05	0.12	0.08	0.02	0.04	0.12	0.08	0.02	0.003
15 58 Proportion of content words that overlap between adjacent sentences	0.03	0.15	0.08	0.03	0.01	0.14	0.07	0.03	0.01	0.16	0.07	0.03	0.007
16 60 Concreteness, minimum in sentence for content words	158.00	194.00	170.92	15.53	158.00	223.00	167.55	16.72	158.00	225.00	181.72	21.35	0.000
17 AWL	0.00	6.30	1.61	1.26	0.00	5.25	1.64	1.41	0.93	12.96	5.02	2.84	0.000
18 Offlist = >15k	0.00	2.48	0.67	0.59	0.00	3.89	1.05	0.91	0.00	7.68	1.61	1.64	0.001

Finally, more research is needed into the merits of both expert, pooled, subjective judgement and automated tools in text selection and adaptation. Such research might further ground which of the available contextual indices are of greatest value in establishing the validity of potential reading texts.

Appendix C

Some problems of oral examinations in modern languages: An experimental approach based on the Cambridge Examinations in English for Foreign Students (J O Roach 1945a)

SOME PROBLEMS OF ORAL EXAMINATIONS
IN MODERN LANGUAGES

An experimental approach
based on the
Cambridge Examinations in English
for Foreign Students

being a Report circulated to Oral Examiners and
Local Representatives for these Examinations

January, 1945

TABLE OF CONTENTS

INTRODUCTION

A. This is an account of some experiments made in order to discover (*a*) how far it is possible to coordinate the standards of oral examiners in modern languages by means of joint examining, and (*b*) whether standards could be defined, for examiners both near and far, by some more positive means than rather sketchy and abstract instructions. The kind of instruction with which we have had to content ourselves in the past may run as follows: "The minimum standard for spoken English for the Certificate of Proficiency is higher than the standard in the oral test for French as a Principal Subject of the Higher School Certificate examination; it approximates to the standard of an oral test in a modern language as part of an examination for an honours degree." Such definition by comparison *may* be helpful to an examiner, if the standards of the other examinations used for the comparison are recognizable constants and if he flatters himself that he knows them.

B. Our enquiry concerns itself with tests of foreign students of English, but the problems and the principles involved are much the same for tests of other modern languages, in England or elsewhere. The primary aim was the standardization of examiners within an existing system, rather than the improvement of oral examinations as such. Yet this secondary aim cannot fail to appear important in any experimental approach. The enquiry was chiefly concerned with tests of reading; it hardly touched the problems of conversation tests. The technique of such tests, with the standardization of the marking for them, offers a large field which has yet to be surveyed.

C. It might be held that tests of spoken French in England, or of spoken Afrikaans for the Syndicate's examinations in Southern Rhodesia, or even perhaps of spoken Hindi and Urdu for the Syndicate's examinations in India, are all susceptible of local adjustment by conferences of examiners. The problem will be seen to be more complex when, for instance, the same test of spoken French has to be applied in England, in India, and in the West Indies. The urgent case for guidance and control is clear from the outset in the oversea field.

D. The problem looms still larger when the examination is one which places in the foreground genuine ability to speak the language, and when it is taken by many different nationalities. Each nation brings its own typical errors and difficulties and local variations, while the examiners are dispersed over the face of the earth. At the moment of writing, the following countries appear in the list of centres for the Cambridge Certificate of Proficiency in English: Belgium, France, Gibraltar, Iceland, Italy, Portugal, Spain, Sweden, Switzerland; China, India, Iraq, Bahrain, Aden, Lebanon, Palestine, Persia; Egypt, Belgian Congo, Cyprus, Morocco, Northern Rhodesia; Argentina, Brazil, Chile, Colombia, Mexico, Peru, Uruguay, Venezuela. Centres have been held for the Royal Air Force, from Moose Jaw and Medicine Hat to S.E. Asia, and also for Allied military and naval forces. Mention may be made specially of Service centres for officers and men of Czechoslovakia, Greece, Holland, Norway, Poland and

4

Yugoslavia, which for the moment have no national centres for civilians in the list. Even before the war we had about fifty oversea centres and were setting papers in thirty different languages.

E. Since the experiments relate to tests within an existing system, it may be well to outline that system. For the Syndicate's School Certificate examination, 50 marks are allotted to an oral test in a modern language: Dictation 15, Reading 15, Conversation 20. The examiners are instructed to work with the following fixed standards: Pass 20, Credit 25, Very Good 36. Many teachers will agree that this last standard is poorly named. It results from the substitution by the Secondary School Examinations Council of one standard for two, Good and Very Good, which in the Syndicate's oral examinations were represented by 34 and 40 marks.

F. For the Cambridge Higher School Certificate, an oral test similarly carries 50 marks and there are three standards: Pass 25, Good 34, Very Good 40. There is no official standard lower than 25, but weakness in an oral test may be condoned by the Syndicate. The same system applies in the Cambridge Examinations in English, but here the condonation of even the slightest oral weakness is exceptional, and such weakness is recorded on the face of the certificate. As has been said above, oral competence is in the foreground of these examinations, and the examiners are specifically instructed not to relax standards in cases of doubt. Where a candidate who fails in oral is sufficiently good in written work, he may be set back to take the test again. In practice, if an oversea examiner rejects a candidate in the oral test, the Syndicate back the examiner. He is saved from too heavy a burden of responsibility, because he knows that the candidate will come up again for the oral test if the Syndicate so decide.

G. The various Cambridge oral tests may differ from the school examinations of certain other school examining bodies in England, in that dictation has hitherto been retained as part of the oral test. It will be seen that the enquiry calls in question the position, though not the importance, of dictation, and that it also suggests the experimental introduction of other semi-oral tests. In the allocation of marks to the component parts of the oral test, the Cambridge Examinations in English differ from the Syndicate's school examinations, 20 marks being allotted to reading and 15 to conversation, instead of the other way round. In recent years the twenty marks have been divided into two, ten for "reading" and ten for pronunciation and intonation, a division which was rejected at the outset of the first experiment. At the same time, by isolating the reading test, the experiment brought into relief the need to have clear standards in mind for "pass", "good" and "very good" in each test, as well as for the aggregate mark.

H. Of the Cambridge Examinations in English, the best known is that for the *Certificate of Proficiency in English*. Certificates are issued in three grades; the minimum standard of written work for the Third Grade is generally associated in our minds with School Certificate Credit work in English Language. The *Lower Certificate in English* is similarly comparable to Credit work in the Oversea Junior School Certificate examination. In March 1944 we started a more elementary examination at the request of

5

the Air Ministry, the *Preliminary Test in English for Allied Service Personnel.*
Very much at the other end of the scale, the University have authorized
us, on the recommendation of our Joint Committee with the British
Council, to institute a Cambridge *Diploma of English Studies.* A survey
of the history of these examinations is given at the end of this report.

J. Certain gramophone records were made in connection with these
experiments. Any teacher or examiner who is likely to hear these records
will be well advised to forget what is said in this report of the index-
numbers and standards of the candidates recorded, in order to keep his
mind free to "mark" the records experimentally himself. It remains to
thank the Education Officers and members of the Polish Initial Training
Wing, Royal Air Force, for making these first experiments possible, and
the Research Department of the Engineer-in-Chief, General Post Office,
for generous help in the preparation of the records. We must also thank
in advance those candidates of different nationalities who may lend
themselves as material for further experiment and recording, and all our
colleagues at home and overseas who may be led by this account to enlarge
our experience as well as their own, and thus to contribute to the efficiency
and usefulness of our joint enterprise. We still have much to learn and
none of the decisions and conclusions in this report need be taken as
final.

J. O. ROACH

SYNDICATE BUILDINGS
CAMBRIDGE.

December 1944

Part I

A TEST OF READING BEFORE A PANEL
OF EXAMINERS

POLISH INITIAL TRAINING WING, R.A.F.,
SEPTEMBER 1944

1. This experiment consisted in having twenty-four Polish officers and
men to read a passage of English in turns before a panel of three or four
examiners (see Table A). Examiners B and D were absent in turns
dictating to other groups. The candidates were taking the examination for
the Lower Certificate in English; the examiners had no idea of their
powers in dictation or other written or spoken English.

2. Certain British officers of the R.A.F. Education Staff listened to the
candidates, and to the discussions among the examiners when each
candidate had read and withdrawn. After the first four candidates, these
Education Officers were invited to record the marks that they would allot.
Some of them were absent in turns marshalling the candidates. By no
means all of them knew the work of this test batch; the unit presented
more than 200 candidates in the various grades on this one occasion.

6

3. The first point on which the examiners agreed was that they had little confidence in the allotment of separate marks on the existing mark-sheet, each out of a total of 10, one for fluency of reading and the other for pronunciation and intonation. This division was introduced as an experiment shortly before the war.

4. *Numerical Standards.* The examiners agreed to mark out of a maximum of 20 and to work to the following standards: Pass 8, Good 12, Very Good 16. The marks allotted to a candidate were all written down before any examiner or teacher called out his verdict.

5. *Abnormal features of the test.* (a) The teachers and examiners agreed in retrospect that the candidates did not do themselves full justice before an audience of several inquisitors, particularly when some of these were their officers. (b) The other abnormal feature was that the first seven candidates, while taking, in common with the others, the special September examination arranged for this unit for the Lower Certificate, were really prospective candidates for the Proficiency examination in December. They were being tested at both levels because, like so many Service candidates, they did not at all know where they might be by December.

6. The examiners were unaware that their first seven candidates were considered by the Education Officers to be of Proficiency calibre and that, moreover, these seven were more or less in order of merit according to the teacher's estimate. This probably contributed to give the examiners a wrong sense of standards; when they thought they were working to Lower Certificate standards they were probably nearer to Proficiency standards, particularly perhaps at the higher levels.

7. The examiners later decided to accept the marks for reading allotted in committee as part of the official Lower Certificate test, but only after increasing them by about ten per cent. Thus, the doubtful passes and near failures with 7 marks became passes with 8, and the two weak candidates assessed in committee at 6 remained failures at this stage; they had been deliberately included in the test batch to ensure a wide variety of standards.

8. It has occasionally been noticed in School Certificate modern language tests at a very few schools that a teacher will send candidates to the oral examiner in a particular order, apparently hoping to influence the marking for certain individuals by some policy of contrasts between good and bad. Setting aside interested motives, it certainly seems safer to let chance decide the order, or some consideration having nothing to do with the work in the subject under test. Alphabetical order is the obvious one; of course, it may be varied so as to take first, e.g., those candidates who have a train to catch or an appointment for a lesson in some other subject.

9. In much the same way that cold water may feel tepid by contrast with ice, it seems likely that an examiner's impression marking may fluctuate owing to contrasts between candidates, and it is at least possible that his standards may suffer a steady drift in one direction if the candidates are presented without his knowledge in order of ascending or descending merit. It is not certain that the drift, if any, will be in the same direction

7

for all examiners. Some examiners believe that, in marking such work as essays or history answers, fatigue makes them more generous; others say the contrary. Phoneticians may say that they are more generous when tired, because they become less alive to fine distinctions of sound.

10. It may be asked whether the examiners for this experiment had any clear idea of the standards which they were supposed to be applying, namely the standards for the Cambridge Lower Certificate in English. The examination was devised in 1938–9, primarily to meet the needs of certain oversea areas where Proficiency standards were clearly beyond attainment for the time being. There was also a desire to ensure that Proficiency standards should not be undermined by the presentation of substantial numbers of candidates of poor quality. A similar desire led to the requirement of a Second Grade Proficiency certificate as a qualification for admission to the Diploma examination. The Syndicate did not define standards of attainment to the examiners for the Lower Certificate in English when the examination was started in 1939. They suggested numerical standards and left the examiners and the candidates to do the rest. The statistics indicate that reasonable continuity has been achieved overseas, perhaps because the candidates in the mass have been of fairly consistent quality from year to year.

11. It is probably, at least to some extent, the candidates who tend to set the standard in any test which has no absolute criterion. In a hundred yard race, the runners might be placed in a clear order of merit, yet they might be allowed to score no points for their side if there were a standard time that they all exceeded. It is common ground that "Very Good" in the School Certificate examinations in Great Britain is merely a label attached, in accordance with the wishes of the Secondary School Examinations Council, to the work of approximately the top ten per cent of candidates in any main subject. The standard is relative, not absolute. If, by some secret arrangement among the schools, it were possible to withhold the best five per cent of School Certificate candidates in all subjects throughout England and Wales in a given year, the examining bodies might possibly adjust their statistics without being aware that they were tolerating a change of standard. There could be a similar shift in examinations which do not depend to that extent on the manipulation of statistics—even here the candidates tend to decide the standards.

12. As soon as the Lower Certificate examination was introduced into Great Britain for Allied Service personnel and others under wartime conditions, a new factor was brought in. These candidates were not like the oversea entry. In some respects they had had exceptional advantages, particularly for spoken English. In other respects they may have been handicapped by lack of time, of books, and even perhaps occasionally of a background of general education. The examination has not been running long enough and with sufficiently large numbers to justify firm conclusions. This much is certain of written examinations, even tests such as essays which are marked largely by impression: An examiner can watch his statistics as his marking proceeds, he may be guided by his statistics on previous occasions, he can look back at essays which he marked earlier,

8

or even at essays from a former examination, in order to stabilize his standard. That is not possible in an oral test marked by impression, particularly when in the nature of things each local examiner may have only a small number of candidates on each occasion. There is not time or sufficient evidence for the candidates to teach him the standard, nor can he go back and revise his earlier marking, since the "work" of the candidates vanishes as they speak.

13. During the war, in order to fill a gap, Examiner C made himself into an examiner in German for the School Certificate and Higher School Certificate, French being the language which he himself teaches at the university. At first he was fumbling for standards and relying on the opinion of the teachers. He had little idea how much spoken German ought to represent a "credit" achievement for the School Certificate, and he found his experience in French of less help than he might have hoped. After a year or two he began to get a genuine "feel" of the standard and to discuss results with teachers on more equal terms. He believes that the candidates taught him the standard; no doubt his general experience accelerated the process. In fact, as in French, he began to apply standards built up in him by a number of candidates in a wide variety of schools, whereas each teacher is guided chiefly by the standard of his own pupils. This has to be borne in mind when it is suggested that a teacher should test his own candidates. It is well known that a good teacher may sometimes be stiffer at the borderline than an examiner who is influenced also by the results at schools with less good teachers. On the other hand, experienced examiners have been known to wonder how they ever managed in the early days, when they were "let loose" on the schools with perhaps no conception of standards at all.

14. When the Preliminary Test for Allied Service personnel was started in March 1944 we could only hope that, there too, the candidates would teach us the standard. The test has been used by R.A.F. education officers to encourage relative beginners who are not yet ready for the Lower Certificate; the Polish I.T.W. presented about a hundred candidates on the occasion of the September experiment. In March 1944, Examiners B and C and Examiner No. 4, who appears in Table D, went to test a large number of candidates presented by the Czech Army. They hoped to learn their own standard. They had a delightful visit, but they learned nothing of the standard of that particular test. The Czechs had underrated themselves; virtually all their Preliminary candidates were fit to gain the Lower Certificate and some would have graced the Proficiency examination. What the examiners did perhaps gain was a certain confidence in the oral-cum-written side of the test as a standardizing element for the work of different examiners, if not as a guide to absolute standards.

15. The provisional conclusions at this point are: Standards of impression marking cannot be defined beforehand merely by written instructions; examiners probably learn standards of their own from the candidates as they go along, or they may bring standards with them that they have acquired in their teaching; there is no guarantee that standards learnt in this way by Examiner X in South America will correspond with those

9

learnt by Examiner Y in the Middle East; a travelling examiner may acquire valid standards by testing a large number of candidates, but this may not be possible for isolated examiners or teachers with relatively small numbers in one particular locality or service unit; impressions of oral work cannot be revised, since the work disappears as fast as it is created; the standards in an examiner's mind may be thrown out of the normal for a variety of reasons; and he has no fixed criterion by which to recapture and re-test his own standards.

16. An examiner with many candidates might perhaps test his own consistency on any one occasion by calling back certain of the earlier candidates and hearing them again. This may be possible in a Service unit, particularly when a batch of candidates are standing by for experimental purposes. It was done during the experiment under review. Given the necessary apparatus, an examiner might record the speech of particular candidates at various levels and refresh his mental standards periodically by this means. Permanent standards might be provided in this way on gramophone records, both as a means of securing uniformity between different parts of the world and as a guide by which the individual examiner might reset the standards in his mind at any time. The Syndicate's Art examiners similarly keep typical marked drawings or paintings by them, as a safeguard against a drift in standard. It may also be asked whether the provision of records would make it possible to plant standards in the minds of examiners so that they would not have to acquire standards—perhaps erroneous in any case and possibly based on too few candidates—in the course of their examining. Could a recorded batch of candidates be used time and again for the instruction of new examiners, including those at a distance?

17. The marking by examiners in committee may now be scrutinized in order to discover whether standards can be communicated from one examiner to another by joint testing of "live" candidates, not recorded, and joint discussion. The important thing here is not the validity of the absolute standards applied, but the possibility of reaching agreement among the examiners. The experiment furnished important and on the whole reassuring evidence. It seemed to confirm the impression of earlier and less ambitious experiments by Examiner C, as when in 1937 he and the Syndicate's resident examiner in Rome each tested the same batch of candidates. It encouraged the belief that a travelling examiner could transmit the Syndicate's central standards by joint examining with colleagues in different countries, particularly if they all had the touchstone of recorded standards. No doubt he would in the process himself acquire cosmopolitan standards, rather than standards based on experience in any one country.

18. Table A shows that Examiners A and C agreed exactly about the first candidate. As Examiner A said, he was a good "good", and they both placed him halfway between "good" and "very good". With the next candidate Examiner B came into line as regards category—"good"—and perhaps overshot the mark a little. With the third candidate there was agreement on category—sound pass—and virtual agreement on mark. With the fourth, Index No. 14, there was again agreement on category.

10

19. In the test as a whole, omitting the first candidate, there was agreement as to category among the examiners (sometimes four, sometimes three, and not always the same three) in 12 cases out of 23. In another case, Index No. 5, there was virtual agreement (8, 8 –, 7). In four more the divergence was not wide at the pass level, the passmark being straddled—No. 15, 7, 9, 9; No. 6, 7, 9, 9; No. 10, 9, 7 +, 8 –, 8; No. 21, 8, 9, 7, 8.

20. There were three cases showing a disagreement about category in which certain votes gave a bare "good" mark of 12. The candidate No. 79 had 12 from Examiner D and from one teacher. From the other examiners he had 10, 9, 8 + ; and from the other teachers 10, 8, 8, 10. Index No. 11 had 12 from Examiner B and 10 and 10 + from the others; the divergence was small. From the teachers he had 10, 11, 7 –, 11. Index No. 24 had 12 from Examiners B and D. From the others he had 9 and 10 and from the teachers 8 +, 8, 8, 7.

21. This leaves three cases showing a serious divergence. Examiner C excused his 12 – or doubtful "good" for Index No. 22 by saying that the candidate was nervous. From the others he had 8 –, 8 +, 7; and from the teachers 7 +, 8, 8, 10. Examiner A justified his mark of 15 for Index No. 8 on the ground that the intonation was excellent. It was agreed to hear the candidate again with the first two candidates if possible; in default of that, the candidate was given an "average" of 13, though for the other examiners he had 10 and 10 and for the teachers 9, 7, 8. The case of No. 17 was the most serious; one examiner was sure that he should fail, one placed him on the bare pass mark with a doubtful minus in a bracket, the third was sure he was good. A separate test the next day strengthened the conviction of the examiner who gave him the poor pass in committee that this candidate was neither good nor a failure; that view tallied with the verdict of the two teachers who heard him. In this separate test, for the official *Proficiency* examination, he received 9. When the gramophone record of this candidate's Proficiency reading was played to a committee of nine (not including the official Proficiency examiner) at the end of October he received 8, 12, 8, 9, 8, 8 +, 9, 9, 8. The examiner who had been sure that he should fail now gave 12 for the recorded reading.

22. Taken as a whole, the experiment showed that examiners could come together in the matter of standards in an astonishingly short time. No one would expect to mark such a test without a possible error of at least one mark in either direction. The occasional serious divergences pointed to the advantage of having two examiners, if only for this part of the oral examination. It was thought that, failing this, a teacher might sometimes assist in marking the reading. The test is as nearly objective as possible. The teacher would mark on what he heard, as does the examiner, and would be less influenced here than in the conversation by his personal knowledge of the pupils (see also paragraph 13).

23. It was indeed remarkable to see how the Education Officers adapted themselves to the standard of the examiners, the more so in that this standard was much stiffer than the standard they themselves would have applied, and indeed had applied when examining for the Syndicate on

11

earlier occasions (it has already been seen in paragraphs 6 and 7 that the standard of the examiners was too stiff). When the voting for Index No. 20 was announced, one of the officers commented: "We all know the bare passes now." The marks for that candidate were: 9, 8, 9 –, 8; 7, 9, 8, 8. The officers themselves felt that they profited greatly by the joint testing and the discussions.

24. This suggests a possible change in procedure. Instead of giving the dictation and then taking each candidate in turn for Reading and Conversation, the examiner might take all the candidates in turn for Reading alone after the dictation. There is something to be said for isolating this test from the conversation and for hearing all the candidates in succession handling identical material under identical conditions. Even for a large batch the reading test would not take very long, if one candidate was in the anteroom preparing the passage while another was reading. All the candidates could be held on the premises till the dictation and reading tests were ended, and it would thus be possible to call some of them in again if necessary. Furthermore, it should be easier to arrange for a second examiner or a teacher to assist in this part of the test if it could be concentrated into a relatively short period of time. Lastly, at certain large centres where the oral tests last for more than a day there is some possibility that the contents of the reading passage may become familiar and that the later candidates may practise it or even be coached in it. Concentration of this test would eliminate such a possibility. One objection raised to such a change is that candidates might protest at the extra time involved. Any such arrangement might have to be one of the conditions on which their application to be examined was accepted in the name of the Syndicate. An alternative proposal, to call candidates out for the purpose from one of the written papers, might perhaps be justified in an emergency, but in our experience it has grave disadvantages for nervous candidates and for those who find it difficult to switch their minds from one subject to another. Another possibility is that, at a large centre which has two examiners in view of the numbers, one might take the reading and the other the conversation. Candidates would pass from one examiner to the other and time would thus be saved for some of the candidates. When the reading was finished, the examiners would share the remaining candidates for conversation.

25. The use of an identical reading passage for all candidates standardizes the test for them, but it necessarily means that the examiner becomes progressively more familiar with its contents. He becomes increasingly less able to judge how far he would understand if he did not know the passage. We are planning to provide a substantial quantity of very short, numbered passages which examiners will be warned *not to read*. They will simply tell a candidate to read a given numbered passage and they will listen for *comprehensibility*. If the Reading test were isolated from the Conversation, this reading of a short passage unfamiliar to the examiner could take place when the candidate came for conversation. It could be a test of extempore reading of unprepared material and would afford some check on the mark allotted earlier for Reading. On the other hand, so long as the Reading and Conversation take place together, it will no doubt be

12

right for the examiner to hear the short, unfamiliar passage first, before he is accustomed to the candidate's voice.

26. The experiment therefore seems to justify the communication of standards from one examiner to another by joint examining. Standards may be acquired in this way, but they will not necessarily be the right standards. No individual judgement can be so consistent as to serve as an absolute measure. It may make for consistency in each individual, and for uniformity between examiners, if we provide gramophone records of certain candidates on whose standard agreement has been reached. Certain gramophone records were made in the course of the visit to the Polish I.T.W. The further experiment of having the recorded readings assessed in committee at Cambridge will be described later in this report. Readers of the report who themselves hear the records will, it is hoped, be able to assimilate the standards thus laid down by the Syndicate.

Part II

THE PROBLEM OF TESTING OUR STANDARDS

27. The second part of the experiment consisted in the independent testing by Examiner C, for the Proficiency oral examination, both reading and conversation, of the first seven candidates who had appeared for the reading test before the panel of examiners and Education Officers on the previous day. It would have been an interesting control, *pour rire*, if they had also been tested by one of the other examiners as Lower Certificate candidates for reading and conversation. Time was too short for examiners and candidates alike and, as has already been seen (paragraph 7), the examiners had agreed to accept the marks for reading before the panel as the Lower Certificate marks, but with a proportional addition; it was also agreed that Examiner C should make their one conversation test serve for the examination at both levels.

28. The general experience of examining bodies leads to the conclusion that an examiner as a member of a team on a written paper is doing what is required of him if he is *consistent* and if he places the candidates in the right order of merit. The chief examiner will report whether any member is out of step with the standards and methods imposed by him on all his team, and whether any examiner is erratic. The examination machine will then decide by statistics whether the standards to which the chief examiner and his team have worked are suitable in the light of past experience and general policy. It may here be noted from School Certificate practice that examiners in any one of the three papers of Mathematics, or the two papers of French, do not work with preconceived standards in mind. They simply follow an agreed mark scheme. In single paper subjects of literary character, such as English Language or History, examiners are much more likely to work with certain numerical standards in view, whether they are instructed to do so or not. In oral tests, as we have seen, the examining

13

body does not manipulate standards by the application of statistical methods, and each examiner attempts to apply absolute standards that he carries in him.

29. The testing by another examiner at supposedly Lower Certificate standards would have neither confirmed nor disproved the assessments of Examiner C at Proficiency standards. Nor would an independent Proficiency test by another examiner have proved whether or not Examiner C was applying the right absolute standards. The perhaps vain search for some yardstick by which to measure the probable validity of Examiner C's Proficiency standards led to some interesting discoveries. Examiner A, with British Council experience overseas, may be taken as likely to be a standard Oversea examiner. Education Officer I was recommended by the Senior Education Officer as knowing most about the standard of the Proficiency candidates. In Table B the marks of these two and of Examiner C are isolated for the *last twelve* candidates in the Reading test. The amount of divergence between them is also shown, the + or − sign being taken to have a value of half a mark.

30. If the plus or minus signs are taken, as was the intention of the examiners, to represent not half a mark but a slight element of doubt, there was only one serious difference as to category. This was the lapse of Examiner C in the case of No. 22, whom he thought a doubtful "good" while Examiner A thought him a doubtful "pass". Probably the teacher was right here, since he split the difference. In only two other cases was there a difference of category. Examiner C placed No. 21, with 7, one mark below the pass, while the others gave him 8 and 9; the teacher did the same with No. 24, the examiners allotting 9 and 10. Omitting No. 12, for whose reading this Education Officer was absent, and No. 22, for whom the marking was shaky, these are the total marks allotted to the other ten candidates: Examiner A, 87; Examiner C, 87½; Education Officer I, 90½. Whether or not they were working to the right standards, they seemed to be working with substantially the same general conception of standards.

31. Table C isolates the marks that Examiner C allotted for reading to the first seven candidates in the experimental test and the marks which he allotted to them when they read different material to him alone as Proficiency candidates on the following day. It shows—a fact of which he was quite unaware at the time—that he placed the seven candidates in descending order of merit during the experimental test, they having been entered on the list in order of merit by the Education Officers. It shows that he placed them in the identical order of merit in this part of their Proficiency test also, though all their marks ran consistently somewhat higher. This is the more interesting in that he did not examine them in the same order, but in a chance order; he did not know what mark they had gained the day before. They were preceded by a Proficiency candidate whom he had not seen earlier, and among them was another newcomer who spent the first four years of the war at an English public school. These are the reading marks of the nine candidates in the order in which they came for examination: [13], 12, [17], 11, 14, 15, 16, 9, 10. The marks in brackets are those of the two candidates not concerned in the experiment.

14

32. Next comes the teacher's estimate, in the shape of the opinion of Education Officer I, for the seven candidates in the experimental test.

Teacher's order of merit	Examiner's mark for reading and conversation (max. 35)
Index No. 1	$16^* + 12 = 28$
,, 3	$14 + 13 = 27$
,, 2	$15 + 13 = 28$
,, 14	$12 + 12 = 24$
,, 15	$11 + 13 = 24$
,, 16	$10 + 11 = 21$
,, 17	$9 + 12 = 21$

* Later reduced to 15.

At first sight it may seem that the examiner preferred slightly the order of merit—Nos. 1, 2, 3—in which the combined wisdom of the education staff had placed those three candidates the day before, although he knew neither their index-numbers nor the order in which they had come on the previous day. This is not quite certain, for another factor comes into play, the effect of the dictation mark on the total and its possible influence on the examiner's mark for reading and conversation.

33. Order of merit on the whole Proficiency oral test	Total mark (max. 50)	Mark for dictation
Index No. 1	42^*	15
,, 3	41	14
,, 14	39	15
,, 2	34	6
,, 15	34	10
,, 16	31	10
,, 17	21	0

* After reduction of reading mark from 16 to 15.

Allotment of marks:		Standards:	
Dictation	15	Pass	25
Reading, etc.	20	Good	34
Conversation	15	V. Good	40
Total	50		

34. It is clear enough that No. 2 fell from grace owing to his performance in the *dictation*. What is quite certain is that Examiner C manipulated the marks for reading and conversation in order to ensure that the candidate should have the minimum mark of 34 for the "good" standard on the whole test. It is doubtful whether, in this realm of uncertainties, the chance advantage of one mark which No. 2 had over No. 3 for reading and conversation had any other significance. This brings us to the part which the dictation at present plays in the result.

35. It may well be argued that Dictation is a semi-oral test having no rightful place in the oral examiner's personal assessment, particularly as

15

the standard of the passage set is beyond his control and may be a wrong standard, thus vitiating his results. Nevertheless, what matters to the candidate is the standard as determined by his total mark, and the examiner is responsible for that standard. That brings the question, whether the examiner should know the candidate's dictation mark before, or just after, he is assessing the oral work. This is apt to raise an argument of interest to all examiners and it may be well to let Examiner C speak from his experience of examining in modern languages for school examinations in England:

36. "I have developed fairly systematically the habit of checking my results with the teacher before leaving a school. What interests a teacher is the final category of each candidate and the general order of merit. Teachers will often produce an order of merit when they are unable or unwilling to assess the candidates in categories. They may say that the order of merit is within their competence, whereas the Syndicate's standards for pass, credit and so on are not. I generally start the post-mortem with them by asking, e.g., who is their best candidate. In order to discuss the results I *must* know the dictation result and the final mark before I meet the teacher. I could either mark the dictation just after or just before I see the candidate. Other examiners sometimes mark all the dictations in the evening or on their return home, claiming that it is not an oral test and has nothing to do with their judgement. I reply that, so long as the scheme of examination is what it is, they miss an opportunity of assessing the final standard while their memory of the candidate's oral work is really fresh in their mind, and while they can discuss borderline cases with the teacher. It is useless to discuss results which later prove not to be the genuine borderline cases when the dictation marks are added in.

37. "The Proficiency results quoted above show that I did not allow the dictation to determine my standards for me. I used my knowledge of the dictation result to pull up No. 2 to the 'good' standard in spite of it. I denied No. 16 the good standard, although he had the same dictation mark as No. 15. Furthermore, I deliberately denied No. 14 the 'very good' standard of 40, although he had full marks for dictation. The Education Officer agreed not only with my order of merit but with my placing of the candidates in the various categories. We both regretted the lapse of No. 2 in dictation.

38. "At the same time, a dictation that is too easy or too difficult may throw out of gear not only an examiner's numerical results but his notion of standards. It is true that the dictation may sometimes correct an examiner's assessment. No. 17 is a case in point. I apparently detected little difference between him and No. 16, yet he had $15\frac{1}{2}$ mistakes in dictation where No. 16 had 5, and he fails in the test, whereas No. 16 is an easy pass. Did the dictation save me from an erroneous decision? Did it perhaps prove a surer guardian of the Syndicate's standards? (See paragraph 69.)

39. "The answer is possibly that, if treated with not too much respect, the dictation does have a stabilizing influence on the examiner's mental

16

standards. It is not necessarily the best or the only guide for that purpose. An oral examiner in modern languages has just asked me how one can 'retune' one's standards when, for instance, after spending a day testing French at a really good school, one goes on to a really bad one, or vice versa. This is always a problem. At the bad school one may stretch one's conscience in order not to cause too much discouragement. At the good school one may reject pupils, with the cordial agreement of the teacher, who might pass if they were mixed in with the candidates at the bad school. Examiner B stated that towards the end of his oral work at the Polish I.T.W. he found himself testing alternately candidates for the Lower Certificate and for the Preliminary Test. This was due to the 'exigencies of the service' but, as he said, it set his standards adrift. It was such problems as these that led to the idea of oral-cum-written tests put forward in Circular No. 121 which the Syndicate sent to oversea centres for their examinations in English in July 1942."

40. What chiefly emerges from this part of the enquiry is that an examiner is not always free to allot the standard that he might desire for purely oral work because, under the existing regulations for the oral tests of this particular examining body, the total includes marks for dictation, and over the standard of this the examiner has little control. It is suggested that we should remove the dictation and place it with other semi-oral tests, which could then carry a separate symbol on the face of the certificate; we should thus be able to record a standard in purely oral work which would be fully under the control of the examiner. This would not diminish the need for central control and guidance of oral examiners. It would also leave open the question whether the examiner should make any use of the work in semi-oral tests as a check on the probable validity of his own standards.

Part III

GRAMOPHONE RECORDS AS A GUIDE TO EXAMINERS

41. It may be well first to repeat the warning given in the Introduction to this Report: Any teacher or examiner who has access to the gramophone records made in association with this experiment will be well advised to use the records for experimental marking *before* he studies the report; if that is not convenient, at least he should forget as far as possible the marks given and the numbers of the candidates. When the records are played, it will be preferable to hear the candidates in a chance order, not in the order of recording. *After* the records have been used experimentally, it may be well to hear the candidates in the official orders of merit given in paragraphs 56 and 58.

42. *The first and last readings of dictations.* We could not have defined hitherto our own phrase "an ordinary pace", and fairly evidently this pace will not be the same for Proficiency and for Lower Certificate candidates.

17

553

The first approach to this problem showed that there was no uniformity even between examiners associated with one another in England. Three examiners were timed in giving a first reading of the Proficiency dictation for June 1944, which was of 137 words. Their times were 52 seconds, 57 seconds, 62 seconds. The official reader for the Polish I.T.W. took 57 seconds. In reading the passage of 146 words for the I.T.W. he took 59 seconds. The same three examiners reading the Lower Certificate passage for June, of 133 words, took 54 seconds, 63 seconds, 71 seconds respectively. The official reader took 63 seconds. In reading the passage of 159 words for the I.T.W. he took 76 seconds. It has been suggested that the size of the examination room and the number of candidates may influence the rate of reading, but it may in any case be inadvisable to dictate to a batch of more than thirty at a time (see also paragraph 88).

43. The speeds indicated by the times given above are therefore to be taken as a standard guide by all who examine on behalf of the Syndicate. The time for reading being known, it should be possible for examiners to adopt the same speeds without hearing a gramophone record of the passages. At the same time, it may be desirable to provide records of model readings of dictations, because the manner and style of the reading may be important. As to speed, a uniform rate of so many words per minute, as used in the Syndicate's shorthand tests, may not suffice. In shorthand, the length of a symbol may bear no relation to the length of the word which it represents.

44. *Text of the Proficiency dictation for the Polish I.T.W.:*

A circle of light | from an electric torch | was moving slowly | on the wall. | The thieves | had obviously no idea | of the attack | that was being launched | against them. | As his eyes | grew accustomed | to the dim light, | the policeman made out | that one man | was holding the lamp | while the other | examined the books. | It was fascinating | to watch nothing | but a pair of hands | wandering | along the shelves. |
The men muttered | discontentedly. | Apparently the job | was proving harder | than they had bargained for. | Ancient authors | had a habit | of abbreviating the titles | on the backs | of their works, | or of leaving them | completely unnamed, | and this made things | extremely awkward. | The man with the torch | stretched his hand | to the light | with a piece of paper, | which they anxiously compared | with a book. | Then the volume | was replaced | and the tedious search | began again. [146 words.]

45. *Text of the Lower Certificate dictation for the I.T.W.:*

On Wednesday | we were taken away | again. | We were used | to obeying orders now. | A man | with thick black hair | was in charge of us. | He would not answer questions | or let us talk much | among ourselves. | We had a great way | to walk, | and it was twelve o'clock | when we came | to a long house | with a garden | shut in | by a high wall. | In it | grew apple | and plum trees. | There was no one | to be seen | and the soldier stopped, | sat down | on the lowest of the steps | that led up to the door | and ate bread and onions. | We lay on the ground | beside him | and waited. | The afternoon became hotter. | We were all very tired. | We had

18

had | nothing to eat | since early that morning, | and my brother | was complaining of his feet, | which were most painful. | We hoped | that our guard | would give us some food, | but we had to stay hungry. [159 words.]

46. A second, necessary warning concerns the quality of the reproduction of gramophone records. The records in the present experiment were made by courtesy of the Engineer-in-Chief, Post Office Research Station, London, who very kindly provided a mobile recording unit and the necessary expert staff. When the original steel discs were played at Cambridge through a high grade reproducing apparatus it was possible to obtain great fidelity, first by a visual device which can be used in association with electric light on a fifty-cycle supply to check the exact speed, and secondly through adjustment by ear, the examiner's voice being familiar to those concerned. It was found that a slight variation in speed, and hence in pitch, made the voice unfamiliar. At the same time, the records made on this occasion may be quite useful even with mediocre reproduction, but allowance will then have to be made for the fact that the original examiners, and the committee who sat in judgement at Cambridge, were hearing something better, and different. Similar considerations will always apply in the use of any gramophone records.

47. A further consideration is that the records do not give the authentic reading on which the original examiners based their marks, but a special reading of the same material before the microphone. Volunteers came to be recorded in the afternoon. The Proficiency candidates unexpectedly found themselves reading again parts of the passages on which they had been tested during the morning, while the Lower Certificate candidates read the piece that they had had the day before. It is impossible to say whether this slight additional familiarity with the reading matter offset the solemnity of the occasion. At the first reading they may have been nervous of the examiner, and at the second of the microphone.

48. It seems impracticable to record full-length conversation tests in any quantity, since each candidate might require a whole disc, part of which would be monopolized by the examiner. Shortened conversations might be both economical of recording time and useful as a guide. One or two full-length oral tests might also be useful for circulation as models, when the best technique for a conversation test has been investigated. A library of master copies of full-length conversations might be built up, for use at headquarters. The experiment was tried of recording the free speech of certain Proficiency candidates, to enable comparison with their reading. The weaker the candidate, the more likely he is to waste precious recording time and to require the intervention of the examiner. The Proficiency candidates had had their oral test in the morning, and their free speaking before the microphone covered much the same ground. They had not been warned of the nature of the test, but they were thinking along familiar channels and had no doubt prepared this material to some extent for the examination itself. Nevertheless, such records should give a clue to fluency and to degree of correctness in expression.

49. A fairly full conversation with one Lower Certificate candidate was recorded on the same disc as his reading. The question of his standard is

19

of interest, as will be seen later. At this point comment is only necessary on the recording itself. The candidate had read before the committee of Examiners and Education Officers the day before and had been tested in conversation that morning by some other examiner. When he came for recording, the examiner with the microphone first put a series of questions, writing them down as they occurred to him. The candidate answered each as it was put; they then immediately repeated the process before the microphone. The candidate's answers were thus completely "untouched" and no better than when he first gave them; the examiner interpolated certain questions which were not on his list. This method, based on the desire to avoid waste of recording time, explains the swiftness with which the examiner put the questions. He knew already that this particular candidate would have no difficulty in following him, and his speed is not to be taken as typical for the testing of Lower Certificate candidates.

50. An attempt was made, and abandoned, to record the conversation test of a Lower Certificate candidate who was considered a failure. The unfortunate who was invited rightly mistrusted his own powers and our motives, and the record would have been one of pauses and coaxing and hesitations. For the weak candidate reading seems the only test that can be successfully and economically recorded. It may be desirable to record at rock bottom, because we all need to learn where to draw the line. This experiment may reveal that we are applying higher standards in England than abroad, particularly for the Lower Certificate. A final note is needed concerning the limitations of any recording of this kind. These candidates were Poles. Their defects of intonation and their other errors would not be typical of candidates of other nationalities. The omission of the definite article in conversation may be paralleled in the Middle East, but not in France or South America. If we are to make use of records, we may need to build up a library showing different national characteristics of speech; we must also hope later for recordings of candidates at oversea centres who have not had the advantage of residence in an English-speaking country.

Part IV

EXPERIMENTAL MARKING OF RECORDED READINGS AT CAMBRIDGE

51. The results of this marking are given in Table D. The committee called for the purpose had not all had experience of oral examining. Nos. 1 and 9 had no knowledge of this field, though No. 9 is very closely acquainted with the written work for the Proficiency examination. Nos. 2, 3, and 4 were official examiners; two of them, including one who is a British Council teacher, had taken part in the original experiment nearly two months earlier. No. 5 was another British Council teacher with oversea experience. Nos. 6, 7 and 8 were linguists having had no previous contact with this particular field. Examiner C, whose official marks, for Proficiency

only, are given at the foot of the table, handled the records and noted the verdicts.

52. A first discovery is that this kind of competitive assessment can be quite enjoyable if each "examiner" will set aside undue diffidence. The meeting quickly began to get a "sense" of the standards, although the numbers to be assessed were far fewer than in the original experiment. The examiners were told that the first six were Proficiency candidates; there was a collective readjustment of ideas before the Lower Certificate recordings were played. The "candidates" were presented in a chance order, and the examiners were inadvertently tricked by a second playing of candidate No. 13.

53. Records may have certain advantages over "live" candidates for committee work. The "candidates" do not need time to prepare the reading passage; they do not tire or vary their standard when required to read a second time; excerpts from their reading can be heard again during discussion; they can be heard for comparison in various orders. They might be heard intermingled with a further batch of "live" candidates. There is little doubt that recorded conversations also can be useful for committee work; it may be possible to build up a wide selection, on the original coated steel discs, for use in training or comparing examiners in England, while not going to the expense of having all discs commercially reproduced for distribution. In peacetime a varied stock of discs, not reproduced in quantity, might be sent from one country to another, or be taken by a visiting examiner for demonstration purposes.

54. It will be seen from Table D that the aggregate marks allotted by the nine examiners at Cambridge placed the six Proficiency candidates in the same order of merit as Examiner C had placed them in the official test (it is noted on Table C that he lowered his mark for Candidate No. 1 from 16 to 15 after discussion with Examiner A). It will also be seen that there was agreement on category between his marks and the average struck at the meeting—two certain "goods", a bare "good", and three passes of varying merit. Examiner C is open to conviction that his marks of 15 for Nos. 1 and 2 would still be a little generous. If these are pulled down to 14 that sufficiently tallies with the 13 + of the October meeting; it also reverts to the mark which he and Examiner A originally allotted to No. 1 as a "good good", but in terms of Proficiency standards this time, not of Lower Certificate.

55. There is a certain "accent" and lack of clearness in these candidates which is not uncommon in those who have picked up English quickly by association with English people; they may compare unfavourably with oversea candidates who have been trained over a period of years. At the same time, No. 1 still deserves "very good" in the test as a whole, thanks to his fluency and his faultless dictation: 15/15 Dictation, 14/20 Reading, 12/15 Conversation, Total 41/50 ("very good" being 40). No. 14 does not quite deserve "very good" in his test as a whole, despite full marks for dictation; he was barely "good" in reading. No. 15, on the other hand, deserves the minimum for "good" in the test as a whole, though his reading

21

was not quite "good": 10/15 Dictation, 11/20 Reading, 13/15 Conversation, Total 34/50.

56. The final marks for the six recorded Proficiency readings are therefore:

Mark (out of 20)

Index No. 1 2	14
", 14	12
" 15	11
" 16	10
" 17	9

57. The recorded Lower Certificate readings led to a discussion of standards. It was felt that this is primarily an oversea examination and that we are in danger of expecting too much when basing standards on candidates in Great Britain. We also endeavoured to relate the standard to comparable standards for English schools in School Certificate French. It has, of course, to be remembered that Allied servicemen organized here in their own units do not necessarily find daily opportunities for talking English with the inhabitants. The averages of the marks allotted were not struck until after the meeting. They support the verdict reached in discussion, that No. 7 should be considered a "bare pass" in reading and that No. 13 should also have a pass. It is thought that this should correspond with standards overseas. Table A shows that Examiner C gave both these candidates a higher mark than did his colleagues in the original test. When he and some of the Education Officers heard the records immediately they had been made, they noted of No. 7 that he was "a safe pass for the Lower this time". They evidently did not think that the recorded reading of No. 13 was better than his reading the day before and they still rated him a failure.

58. The meeting at Cambridge considered that No. 10 was "good or just below good" in his reading, while No. 5 was to be considered "good" on his reading and conversation taken together (see paragraph 49). This tallies with the view reached by Examiner C and certain Education Officers when they first heard the records. The final classification of the recorded Lower Certificate readings is therefore as follows:

Index No. 10	11–12
" 5	11
" 7	8
" 13	8

59. This valuation of the recorded readings is a mark higher in each case than the final official mark for the "live" test of the Lower Certificate candidates in September. If we similarly add a mark to the official Lower Certificate mark of the six Proficiency candidates who are recorded we get the following comparison:

| Proficiency mark | 14 | 14 | 12 | 11 | 10 | 9 |
| Lower Certificate mark | 18 | 18 | 12 | 12 | 11 | 11 |

22

Little significance should be attached to this comparison, which is not the result of a controlled experiment. It should be possible to compare standards in the two examinations. A panel of examiners could hear a number of unidentified Proficiency candidates reading behind a screen. Later they would adjust their minds to easier standards and would hear a batch of Lower Certificate candidates, among whom some of the Proficiency candidates would be interspersed. A screen might perhaps be used in all experiments involving more than two examiners; one examiner would conduct the test in the ordinary way and the candidates might be less nervous when not confronted directly by several judges.

60. It has seemed advisable to set out the whole process of these experiments in detail as an encouragement to our Oversea and Service colleagues to attempt regional standardization of examiners along somewhat the same lines. It is well that they should know that we at headquarters, so far from feeling able to define and to justify absolute standards, are seeking a technique and methods of controlling it. They may be able to assist us in that search. It will no doubt be agreed that the exercise of individual and collective judgement upon a batch of candidates, whether live or recorded, is worth more than much discussion in the abstract. Oversea examiners and teachers may be able to provide their own "live" material for experiment and possibly, at a few centres, to record some of the results. If gramophone material is provided from Cambridge, it may be assumed that it will have passed through such a process of assessment as is here described before official standards are finally attached to it.

Part V

PROBLEMS INVOLVED IN JOINT EXAMINING
BY TWO EXAMINERS

61. The suggestion was made in paragraphs 22 and 24 that two examiners might jointly mark the reading test and that, if no second external examiner were available, some experienced teacher might on occasion collaborate with the official examiner for this purpose. Joint examining would be of greatest value where the examiners, by experimental marking of candidates or of gramophone records, or by collaboration on earlier occasions, had "come together" in the matter of standards. It would be of relatively less value to split the difference between two examiners who habitually disagreed. As has been seen, we are all liable to aberrations. On the other hand, there would be strong grounds for striking an average, possibly after hearing the candidate again, in a case where a substantial divergence occurred between two examiners who were generally in agreement. As was pointed out in the Syndicate's Circular No. 121 to Oversea centres, the use of two examiners should make for uniformity of standard at a particular centre or in a particular country. It will only make for uniformity between one country and another if one or both of the examiners have had

23

experience in other countries or if they have assimilated standards at headquarters and possess means of renewing contact with those standards, e.g. by gramophone records.

62. *Joint marking of the reading test in School Certificate oral examinations.* It may be useful to turn aside for a moment to consider whether joint marking could be introduced, e.g. for School Certificate Spoken French at schools in England. The problems of standardization are much the same for any language, but the material conditions are different in England, where School examinations are tending to become a joint undertaking of schools and universities. It is very unlikely that an examining body would impose on the schools the expense of two visiting examiners, even if the supply of examiners were sufficient. The teacher may therefore appear the obvious colleague. Where examiners are touring to a crowded time-table, it might be difficult for examiner and teacher to reach agreement on standards experimentally beforehand. Even so, joint marking of the reading test should make for the wider dissemination of uniform standards, particularly if we first ensure that the official examiners are adequately standardized. It would bring examiner and teacher closer together; it would give the teacher in small or remote centres a better idea of standards of pronunciation at which to aim; it would help to protect the candidates against erratic judgements, whether of an experienced examiner or of one who was relatively new to the work. Some teachers might prefer to test the candidates alone beforehand and to supply to the examiner, *after* his test, their own mark-list in order of merit. Where examiner and teacher diverged, the candidates might be heard again, possibly by both together. For the conversation, the presence of the teacher might be an embarrassment to the candidates rather than a help; any striking divergence between the mark for this and the agreed mark for reading could be discussed. Collaboration of this kind should give us more confidence in judgements on purely oral work, if it were decided to separate the dictation and to place its marks either with those for the written papers or with the marks for further semi-oral tests to be introduced. The time has gone by when the School Certificate oral examiner was an Olympian visitant. The experienced examiner can communicate standards to the young teacher; he has also learnt to respect the judgement of the experienced teacher. It would, of course, have to be borne in mind that a teacher dealing with a small group of pupils throughout the year will have less sense of general standards than an examiner whose experience is more varied (see paragraphs 13 and 36).

63. At centres for the Cambridge Examinations in English, particularly in foreign countries, public confidence in the tests is likely to depend for a long time on the extent to which they are felt to be directly controlled by the University and to represent worldwide standards. The ideal might be to have wherever possible one visiting examiner from headquarters and one local examiner. Even an occasional visit would be of great value if it afforded the opportunity of communicating central standards by joint examining and discussion. For this purpose joint examining of conversation also would clearly be desirable. It may on occasion be helpful to use as examiner a visitor from England who is chiefly travelling for other purposes.

24

Such a man could report firsthand impressions and discuss local difficulties. For the *propagation* of standards, however, it seems that we shall need men who have seriously assimilated standards beforehand and have proved their reliability. If, in the more spacious days of peace, the visiting examiner were able to travel with a mobile recording and reproducing unit, he could both demonstrate by means of records reproduced with high fidelity and also record further material.

64. For ordinary purposes, opinions may differ as to the value of having two examiners to test each candidate jointly in conversation. The examiners themselves may be somewhat constrained unless they are accustomed to working as a team. An examiner may be used to drawing people out and to letting one thing lead on to another, so that both he and the candidate forget they are in the middle of an examination. Alternate questions from two examiners might well break the thread. There is also the candidate to be considered. One examiner may make a friendly chat for him, whereas two may make an audience or a crowd. The sudden embarrassment of a candidate in the experimental test illustrated this when he was asked by Examiner C to talk to him again in the presence of another examiner and an officer.

65. If there were to be two examiners both playing an active part and both examining simultaneously, more time would clearly be needed owing to the inevitable delays and hesitations in a triangular conversation, and to the necessity for discussion. Would two separate oral tests be better? The first examiner might have a four or five minute conversation with the candidate, who would then pass on to the second examiner. Such a method *might* reduce itself to two conversations that hardly got started before they were ended. The second examiner might be saved from mere repetition of what the first had said by some agreement on the division of topics. Thus, the second might deal in specific tests such as dates, months, days of the week, the handling of numerals and perhaps weights and measures. One examiner might deal with books that candidates had read (wherever he found that candidates really wanted to talk about books), while the other kept off that topic, and so on. Two quite separate conversation tests may be of advantage when examiners are experimentally testing their independent conceptions of standard against one another at the outset, especially when one is a visiting examiner from headquarters. For general use this method may present certain drawbacks.

66. Even when two examiners test candidates jointly for conversation, it might be found profitable to divide the topics and to let each examiner have an "innings". One constraint we may always have to face in many foreign countries—the presence of a chaperon for girl candidates. This suggests the possible use of a "silent examiner". Examiner C once examined a batch of candidates in London in the presence of an eminent phonetician who took no active part but who marked the candidates independently. This did not seem to be disturbing either to the Examiner or to the candidates and it served excellently for the comparison of standards. There might well be embarrassment if the silent examiner were felt to be an inquisitor and not a fellow member of the jury. Another

25

suggestion that has been made is that the "silent examiner" alone should allot marks, while his colleague sustains the conversation. Oversea centres must feel free to experiment on such lines as these, but the supply of examiners must long remain a problem for many of them and it will mark a great advance if we can for the present urge simply that a second opinion—external examiner or teacher—be sought for the reading test. The whole problem of conversation tests needs fuller investigation.

Part VI

THE USE OF SEMI-ORAL TESTS

67. It may be argued that we are attempting the impossible when we invite examiners to allot numerical marks for purely oral work, and that they ought simply to place the candidates in categories—*a*, *b*, *c* or *d*. These experiments suggest that it is possible and desirable to work with both categories and numerical marks in view. When the awards for different tests have to be added, there may seem to be something more satisfying in adding, e.g. two elevens for one candidate in reading and conversation and two eights for another. If categories alone were allotted, in accordance with the scale of marks shown earlier in this Report, then those two candidates would be equal. Furthermore, it is a safeguard to require an aggregate for the test as a whole higher than the sum of the individual pass-marks. Otherwise, a candidate may "scrape home" when in each separate test the examiner has come very near to rejecting him outright. Thus, if 8/20 were the pass for conversation and for reading, a minimum of 18/40 might be required on the two together. This would be in keeping with the Syndicate's present practice (but see paragraph 83).

68. In paragraph 40 it was suggested that the dictation should be separated from the direct oral examination. It may be noted that, in evolving plans for the completely new Preliminary Test for Allied Service Personnel, we kept dictation and oral separate from the outset. The logical extension of this to the other examinations would place on examiners the full responsibility for the standard which they report to the Syndicate for each candidate—very good, good, pass, or fail. It would then for the first time be easily possible to make a comparison between the verdict of the local examiner for oral work and the standard of the candidate in the written papers. We should readily be able to see whether certain centres or areas were more optimistic than others concerning oral standards, on the basis of comparison with the written work.

69. It may be claimed that papers in English Composition, Literature and Translation, testing literacy, are too far removed from purely oral tests to give any valid correlation. Dictation obviously comes closer to oral work, in that it tests understanding of the spoken word as well as literacy. It was seen in paragraphs 33 and 38 that candidate No. 17 received the same total for reading and conversation as No. 16 and was ten marks behind in dictation, thus failing in the test as a whole, whereas No. 16

26

passed easily. This may have been the fault of the examiner. On the other hand, No. 17 may simply be less literate than No. 16. It may be noted in passing that the candidate who talks and reads well, but cannot spell or write English, is more likely to be found among service personnel stationed in Great Britain than among candidates abroad who acquire their knowledge more through books than orally.

70. If we standardize the speed of delivery of the dictation, and remove the responsibility for marking it from the local examiner, that should go a long way towards standardizing this particular test between the different centres. It will also make it possible to approach continuity of standard from one examination to the next. The mark distribution, and the report of a single examiner who has reviewed all the exercises, may lead us to seek uniformity by adjusting the pass-mark from one examination to the next—no two dictations are exactly equal in difficulty. Standardized marks for dictation, and for any similar tests which lend themselves to exact marking, might throw some light on the impression marks for oral tests, and on the marks for semi-oral tests which depend more on the examiner's judgement and impression than on an exact mark scheme. Such a test is mentioned in the following paragraph.

71. A natural development from the dictation would be a single reading of a short story, of about the same length as a dictation, which the candidates would be asked to reproduce in their own words. Powers are already taken by the Syndicate in the regulations to set tests of this kind, and it is possible that reproduction of a story will be an integral part of the examination in and after 1946. If so, the Syndicate will no doubt issue specimen tests in the meantime.

72. A further mixed test would be to put questions orally to the candidates concerning printed material laid before them, their answers being written. In School Certificate tests of French and other languages the Syndicate provide a comprehension test. Candidates answer in writing certain questions printed at the end of a passage which they are not required to translate. In the Preliminary Test in English for Allied Service Personnel, certain spoken questions are put to the candidates to which the clue lies in the dictation that they have just written down. Their answers also are written. In an oral test the examiner may often put questions orally, to be answered orally, concerning the reading passage which the candidate has before him. If the identical questions were put to all the candidates simultaneously under identical conditions, the answers being written, we should then have a test of which the evidence would remain and which could be readily standardized. The candidates would write what they would have said; the pronunciation which they would have revealed in the saying of it is tested elsewhere. True, literacy and spelling come into account, but these can nearly always be distinguished, in assessing written answers of this kind, from sheer comprehension and ability to give an intelligible answer.

73. The semi-oral test which is perhaps most satisfying, as coming nearest to direct oral examining or cross-examination, is a set of one-word

answers or short sentences to be written in reply to spoken questions. This has been tried with success in the Preliminary Test for Allied Service Personnel. It can be used to test a variety of things. It produces a most refreshing sense of alertness, partly perhaps because there is a time limit for each question and answer. Those who read Circular No. 121 may remember the report on the experimental tests of December 1941: "The candidates enjoyed the tests." The reader may picture to himself a hut at an operational aerodrome in Great Britain, and a class of Polish W.A.A.F.s and R.A.F. personnel. An R.A.F. Education Officer stands at the back of the room with an eye to the seconds-hand of his watch and signals the start for each question. The test on that occasion came so near to a "quiz" or a "Brains Trust", while being a legitimate test of English, that it seemed to be looked on as a pleasurable competition. On another occasion, testing Czech soldiers, Examiner C looked through the written answers to oral questions while each candidate was preparing his reading passage. Before the candidate opened his mouth the examiner was able to say to himself: "This man is well above the standard of the examination" or "This man obviously understands what is said to him. He could usefully be brought before a Court of Enquiry to give information in English." There might have been a lack of correlation between a candidate's written answers and his spoken answers in the conversation test; in fact none was detected. It is true that tests of this kind may be easier to devise at elementary levels than for advanced candidates.

74. In the last paragraph semi-oral tests were considered from the point of view of an oral examiner. A personal opinion that the correlation between semi-oral and oral tests is good offers no proof, but the matter lends itself to investigation. We might assess certain groups of candidates in oral work by means of controlled experiments, and then see how those candidates fared in a given set of semi-oral tests. We could tabulate their performance in the various types of test and send the results to oversea examiners; these would be asked in their turn to assess typical groups of students in oral work and then to set them the same semi-oral tests. If the relation between oral and semi-oral results differed substantially from one group of students or one country to another, we might all be encouraged to look further for some explanation. Tests of this kind might thus prove useful as a control, even if they were not an integral part of the examination. Each centre might set the same tests in successive years, in order to discover whether, apart from correlation with the Syndicate's central standards, a shift in average mark for oral results at the centre was accompanied by a corresponding shift in the semi-oral tests.

75. If such tests were a regular feature of the examination, could the examiner make use of them as a check on his oral standards in the course of the examination? The examiners for the Preliminary Test for Allied Service Personnel are authorized to look at the dictation exercises and written answers to oral questions, though they are not required to mark them; they are also invited to say whether there is a marked discrepancy between a candidate's oral standard and the written evidence of his work. Such tests being marked at Cambridge, the Syndicate might establish the correlation between oral and semi-oral results at various levels, both in

28

the examination as a whole and for each particular oral examiner. The resulting statistics might be of some guide to examiners for future occasions. In somewhat the same way, the Syndicate compile a table for School Certificate French showing what percentage of candidates each examiner in England places in each of the various categories, and also the average results for the whole. This interests and sometimes impresses examiners, but they are not instructed to make their results conform to the average on future occasions, because it is well known that the general quality of the schools or areas allotted to the examiners may vary. When an examiner is badly "out" in his results, we may compare them with results at the same schools in earlier years, and with the results of the same candidates in the written papers. When all is said and done, and when every allowance is made for exceptions, there is surely some general correlation between written and oral work at that level.

76. It has thus been seen that there is a whole field of tests of linguistic skills—comprehension of the spoken word, accurate listening and reporting, as well as knowledge of the language—in which the examiner speaks, but not the candidate, and which may offer the bridge to correlation of written and oral work. It may be found to offer a bridge also between the teacher and the examining body as regards standards, if the results of tests which lend themselves to exact marking can be communicated to, e.g., the staffs of British Institutes overseas, and if the general correlation can be established between such tests and purely written work on the one hand and purely oral work on the other. It seems desirable to experiment in the use of such tests and to invite the collaboration of oversea centres for the purpose.

Part VII

FURTHER EXPERIMENTS IN JOINT EXAMINING, DECEMBER 1944

77. In December 1944 a group of fifty-three Proficiency candidates of various nationalities were tested by three examiners. Two of these were Examiners B and D of the original enquiry (see Table A), Examiner B being also No. 3 on Table D for the marking of the Recorded readings. The third Examiner, No. 6 of Table D, was new to this work, apart from the marking of the records.

78. It may be interesting first to record the impression of examiners on first doing further examining after the experimental tests. Examiner C went in December to test a small group of Italian prisoners-of-war at the Lower Certificate level. He was haunted by the borderline candidates, Nos. 7 and 13, of the Polish experiment and felt himself setting the borderline Italian candidates against them. This was almost certainly not a mere illusion, although he had not heard the records again since the experiment at the end of October. Examiner B gave very similar testimony concerning his experience with the Proficiency candidates at the same time. It therefore seems that even examiners of long experience, with their own

29

legitimate ideas of standards, can be conditioned to certain standards, and that they will tend to retain those standards over a period without any examining. How long the standards will survive when overlaid with the impressions of further examining is another matter. Evidence might be brought to show that a sensitive reader of verse, having steeped himself in one style or one metre, may tend involuntarily to write his own verse in that style or that metre. He may be moulded to that pattern, as it were, and unable to free himself from it until the imprint on his nervous system fades, or until he has reconditioned himself with other reading.

79. *The Reading Test.* The examiners in London discussed their marks for the first three candidates and then marked independently, all hearing the candidates at the same time. They also announced their mark after each candidate had left; they thus had some cumulative effect upon one another's marking. Table E shows that, apart from the first three candidates, there was agreement on category in 40 out of 50 cases. Where they disagreed, two of the three allotted the same category; the third missed that category by one mark in seven cases, by two marks in another, and by three marks in the remaining two cases. In arriving at this interpretation of the figures, the plus and minus signs recorded by the examiners have been ignored. Italics have been used to isolate the ten candidates on whose category there was disagreement. This will help to show how near or how far the marks were, when the category differed; the majority of such cases, including all the serious ones, occurred early in the test.

80. *The Conversation Test.* The examiners did not see the dictation exercises and did not know what marks they or their colleagues had allotted for reading. Five candidates were taken by the three examiners jointly and received an agreed mark; the remainder were examined separately, though sometimes by two or even all three examiners in succession. In comparing the marks for reading and conversation, it must be borne in mind that on this occasion the total for conversation was 15, with Pass 6, Good 9, Very Good 12. Examiners B and D agreed on category for every one of the fifteen candidates whom they both tested separately; they gave the identical mark in twelve cases and only differed by one mark in the others. The new examiner agreed with them on category for six of the twelve candidates tested separately by all three; in four cases this examiner gave a higher, and in two a lower, category than did the other examiners.

81. *Correlation between Reading and Conversation.* Over the whole range of candidates, there was agreement in category between conversation and reading for 35 of the 53 candidates. Of the remaining 18, seventeen gained a higher category for conversation, that is, for fluency, than for pronunciation, intonation, skill in reading; this is what one might well expect of candidates in England, particularly those working in towns. The one candidate whose verdict went the other way failed in conversation and had the bare pass mark in reading.

82. It appeared from this more extensive experiment that, for continuity of standard, there was a substantial advantage in concentrating the reading test, instead of interlarding it with the conversation. The examiners became

30

painfully familiar with the passage to be read; it is the Syndicate's practice for School Certificate French to provide a selection of alternative passages. There appears to be no reason why, having got their standards well set with one passage, the examiners should not change to another passage provided by the Syndicate; this would be better than to set different passages to candidates alternately. It is also clear that, while all marks in this kind of work must in the last resort depend upon an impression, it is desirable to tell examiners what they should chiefly be listening for, and what they should try to leave out of account. Thus, in the new "unseen" reading test, what they will endeavour to assess is comprehensibility. The conversation tests fluency and correctness of speech, not the finer shades of pronunciation and intonation; indeed, errors of pronunciation ought perhaps only to affect the mark in so far as they make the candidate difficult to understand. Whether the examiner will succeed in isolating fluency from pronunciation is another matter. Pronunciation and intonation find their assessment in the mark for reading; yet this mark is inevitably affected by the candidate's skill—and perhaps his amount of practice—in the art of reading aloud.

83. The joint reading test gave reassuring confirmation of the experience at the Polish I.T.W., namely that examiners can come together remarkably in the matter of general standard in a very short time. The conversation test was only a joint test for five candidates; the independent testing of the other candidates by two or more examiners opens up interesting possibilities of testing the standard of a new and untried examiner against examiners of known or assumed standard and reliability. It also illustrates the possibility of reaching satisfactory correlation between conversation and reading tests which take place at different times and without any positive mark, for dictation or other semi-oral tests, to serve as a corrective. In this connection it was pointed out that, since no examiner controlled the assessment of a candidate's oral standard as a whole, it would be right on this occasion not to require any margin of marks above the sum of the bare passes in the different tests (see paragraph 67).

84. Another problem of oral examinations which came near the surface at times was the effect produced on the examiner by charm (or the reverse) of manner or voice or appearance in the candidate, or even simply by the candidate's good manners. These things may influence the atmosphere of the test, whether the candidate be a man or a woman; much may depend on the temperament of the examiner and on his ability to apply conscious correctives in his assessment. He will almost certainly enjoy testing some candidates more than others, though his own manner should conceal the fact; it is also unlikely that the reaction of a woman examiner to a given candidate will always be the same as that of a man examiner. Joint testing by two examiners will not necessarily provide a corrective if they both react in the same way, or if their reactions are unknown to themselves or denied. Indeed, the experience of Examiner B in university examinations might lead to the pessimistic conclusion that, where examiners are placed together of necessity rather than of choice to conduct a test, one of them may tend to impose his judgment while one has to give way.

31

85. In the meantime, Examiner C conducted a small experiment at an operational station of Bomber Command. This is of interest as an example of how the visiting examiner may communicate standards, or of how the examiner with a wide experience behind him can compare standards with the teacher who has experience only with his own pupils (paragraphs 13 and 63). There were four Proficiency candidates, Polish ground staff, and the Education Officer who had taught them played the role of "silent examiner" (paragraph 66). But for the visit of Examiner C, this officer might have had to examine his own pupils, as may sometimes happen at R.A.F. Stations. He perhaps learned something from a visit paid by Examiner C in September to conduct an informal test, and he presumably learned more from the preliminary talk concerning standards, but his experience of examining for the Syndicate was nil. After each candidate had been heard, the Education Officer announced his mark and Examiner C then announced his, explaining how he had arrived at it.

86. *Reading Test.* This was taken first separately, and the marks were as follows:

Candidate	A	B	C	D
Education Officer	5	9	11	10 −
Examiner C	7 −	9	10 −	9

Standards: Max. 20, V. Good, 16, Good 12, Pass 8.

Agreement on category was complete. For Candidate A the Education Officer's mark was probably right, and this pointed to certain factors in the mind of the visiting examiner. First, one does not wish to start by appearing harsh, especially when examining with the teacher. Then seniority. The first candidate was a sergeant and the senior of the four. The result of that—and there may be somewhat similar conditions in other walks of life—was not entirely negligible with this particular examiner. (He had found no pleasure earlier in the year in rejecting the gallant commander of the Recce Squadron of a certain Armoured Brigade, while private soldiers were distinguishing themselves.) Next, manner. The sergeant had a courteous, quiet manner—and was extremely nervous. The examiner instinctively wanted to help him. He therefore salved his conscience by rejecting the candidate firmly, but not ignominiously.

87. *Conversation Test.* The marks were as follows:

Candidate	A	B	C	D
Education Officer	6	10	11	9
Examiner C	7	9	10 +	8

Standards: Max. 15, V. Good 12, Good 9, Pass 6.

Here there was disagreement on category only for Candidate D, and that by the narrowest of margins. The examiner agreed that he was worth the "good" standard for general fluency, but denied it him on the specific ground that he showed a Polish lack of definite articles. Thus three of the candidates for Examiner C, and all four for the Education Officer, had a higher category in conversation than in reading. This seemed quite right in the circumstances (see also paragraph 81). It later appeared from the dictations that all four must fail in the test as a whole and would probably fail in the written papers. Candidate C, with the best oral result, was the weakest in dictation (see paragraphs 40 and 69).

88. The result of even such a brief piece of collaboration was that the Education Officer felt he had gained a real insight into the work. On his part, Examiner C left with the satisfying impression that the officer would apply reasonable standards when acting as examiner. One matter of general interest also came to light. The officer timed the examiner for the first and third readings of the dictation (134 words). The first reading took 70 seconds and the third 85 seconds. With the candidates anxiously making alterations during the third reading, the examiner found it impossible to keep the same "ordinary pace" of reading in accordance with the instructions (see paragraph 42). What is possibly needed here is to standardize what has been his own private practice—to read at the same pace for the third reading as for the first, but to make a substantial pause at each full stop or convenient point in order to give time for corrections.

89. *Dictation.* Further discussion of dictation has shown the need for some clearer definition of what it is intended to test. This may influence, not only the character of the passage to be set, but also the manner in which it is read and the principles on which it is marked. Investigation has shown that an examiner who puts much expression into the first reading is likely to reduce that expression greatly when speaking a few words at a time during the second reading, if only because the expression is difficult to sustain when the groups of words are spaced out. Should the passage be read at all *con espressione*, or indeed be presented in the first instance as a coherent whole? An expert in another field tells us that he does not give a preliminary reading of a dictation, but simply reads each group of words twice while the candidates write (whereas each group is read once according to the Syndicate's practice). He then reads the passage through as a whole when they have finished writing. That is a different technique, and one concerning which the opinions of teachers and examiners would be welcome, preferably after class experiment with both methods. The strong plea was made by Examiner A, on the eve of his departure for another hemisphere, that the dictation, when separated from the oral test, should nevertheless be marked as a written record of *spoken* English, not just as part of the written examination. We need to investigate and to define the relative importance of spelling mistakes and mistakes of understanding. Here, as in all these matters, we shall welcome the experience of our oversea colleagues and of teachers who have at heart the improvement of oral examinations, whether in English or in other modern languages. We are still only at the beginning.

33

THE CAMBRIDGE EXAMINATIONS IN ENGLISH

A SURVEY OF THEIR HISTORY

I. 1913–1939

The examination for the Certificate of Proficiency in English was instituted by the Local Examinations Syndicate in 1913. It was intended chiefly for foreign students who sought proof of their practical knowledge of the language "with a view to teaching it" in foreign schools. For a number of years it led a modest existence. It was held only at one centre, in London, and as lately as 1931 the total number of candidates was only 15.

The examination in its early period included a compulsory paper in Phonetics, and the literature test was a paper on a literary period as studied by advanced classes in English secondary schools. About 1926, Italian and Spanish were added to the original French and German as languages in which translation papers were set as a matter of course. In 1930 a special literature paper was for the first time provided for foreign students, and it was in that year that plans began to be laid to adapt the examination to the needs of a wider public.

The regulations for the year 1932 were published in May 1931. They showed two essential changes. The paper on Phonetics had disappeared as a formal test, and students no longer needed to go to London. Centres of examination were to be formed in England and also on the continent of Europe; at one or two places outside England the oral test could be conducted as well as the written examination. The oral test could be passed in London or Cambridge at any time. As a result, the numbers of candidates who completed the examination for the full certificate rose as follows:

1931	1932	1933	1934	1935	1936	1937	1938	1939
15	33	66	140	202	278	412	675	752

In 1935 the examination was for the first time held in December as well as in July; the regulations for that year, published in 1934, mentioned centres at Cambridge, London, Edinburgh and Rome. Two decisions of 1935 that took effect in 1936 were the inclusion of a syllabus in *Economic and Commercial Knowledge*, as an alternative to *Literature*, and the issue of the Certificate in three Grades: Special Mention, Good, Pass.

The regulations for 1936, published in June 1935, referred to arrangements at Rome, Naples, Hamburg, at the British Institute in Paris, and in Holland, Sweden and Switzerland. A second edition, dated December 1935, was notable for the announcement that the official approval of the Board of Education (the Ministry of Education of His Majesty's Government) had been given to the examination.

The regulations for 1937, published in 1936, gave information about Vacation Courses at Oxford, as well as at Cambridge, and showed that the Secretary of the Oxford Local Examinations Delegacy had consented to authorize examination centres both in Oxford and at certain schools taking

34

the Oxford school examinations. There now appeared also the first mention of the British Council, which had kindly undertaken to give information concerning the examination to cultural societies and to official representatives of other countries. The year was further notable for the establishment of collaboration with the University Colleges of Nottingham and Southampton, for the first mention of arrangements at German universities, and for the fact that the examination was held three times, in March, July and December.

The year 1937 brought a decision by the University of Cambridge to accept the Certificate of Proficiency as the equivalent of the standard in English required of all students, British or foreign, before entrance to the University; Oxford gave similar recognition in the following year. That summer, an official of the Syndicate visited several European countries in connection with this work. The regulations for 1938 mentioned centres at the following places outside Great Britain: Dublin, Paris, Berlin, Marburg, Hamburg, Florence, Rome, Naples, Milan, Hilversum, Lausanne, Basle, Malmö, Helsinki, Budapest, Belgrade, Zagreb, Ljubljana, Sarajevo, Vienna, Gdynia, Warsaw, Bucharest, Athens, Smyrna, Rabat, Beirut, Bagdad, Jerusalem, Shanghai, Oslo, Stockholm, Tallinn, Amiens, Bordeaux, Dakar.

By 1938 papers were being regularly set in Arabic, Chinese, Dutch, French, German, Greek, Hebrew, Italian, Serbo-Croat, .Spanish and Swedish; papers in other languages were available on request. In that year also a history alternative could be offered in lieu of literature, as an approach to the study of *English Life and Institutions*, a paper which was introduced under that title in the following year. Other alternative syllabuses were mentioned, the examination was held five times in the year, and the establishment of the Lower Certificate in English was announced for 1939. One of the five examinations was a special session arranged in August 1938 for the Oxford Vacation Course, in collaboration with the Oxford Delegacy for Extra-Mural Studies.

The regulations for 1939 showed collaboration with the Universities of Bristol and Reading, and with the University College of the South West at Exeter. Rumanian appeared as an addition to the list of regular languages and Bruges, Nice, Katowice, Sofia, Lisbon, Alexandria, Cairo, Yunnan, Hong Kong and Yokohama as additional centres. During 1938 and 1939 papers were set in the following eighteen languages, in addition to the twelve mentioned in the regulations: Czech, Bengali, Estonian, Bulgarian, Hungarian, Ganda, Latvian, Norwegian, Finnish, Polish, Turkish, Russian, Danish, Portuguese, Maltese, Lithuanian, Persian, and Slovene.

The most impressive regulations issued by the Syndicate so far were perhaps those prepared for 1940 before the war and published in September 1939. Germany still appeared in the list but, by a last minute alteration, the centres there were omitted. The list thus mentioned seventeen countries on the Continent of Europe, six in Asia, including India, three in Africa, and four in South America. New centres were Brussels, Strasbourg, Tours, The Hague, Luxembourg, Skoplje, Basra, Port Said, Suez, Casablanca, Buenos Aires, Rio de Janeiro, Valparaiso, Montevideo. There were also more than twenty regular centres in Great Britain. The British Association for the Advancement of Science had

35

offered through the Syndicate a number of presentation tickets for foreign students to attend the Annual Meeting of the Association in 1940.

The number of candidates for the Proficiency examination would have risen steeply in 1939 but for the outbreak of war, which brought a cruel but temporary check to a remarkable development. An official of the Syndicate paid visits to Belgium and Italy in the last months of 1939 to make new contacts, especially in a number of Institutes established by the British Council in Italy, and he also visited centres in France and Switzerland. Most of that work disappeared with much else in the summer of 1940, but little or no interruption was suffered in Switzerland.

II. 1939–1943

The following figures show the decline and the recovery in the Proficiency entries:

1938	1939	1940	1941	1942	1943
675	752	326	276	444	861

These figures are more significant if they are analysed into "Home" (Great Britain) and Oversea entries:

	1938	1939	1940	1941	1942	1943
Home	463	473	100	154	234	540
Overseas	212	279	226	122	210	321

The slump came at home in 1940. It continued overseas in 1941, owing to the loss of centres in Western Europe. For 1943 there was much the same balance of numbers as in 1938 or 1939, but the sources were very different. Of the 293 candidates examined outside Great Britain in the period from December 1938 to June 1939, 266 were at centres which for the time being no longer exist. The great bulk of the candidates in Great Britain in 1943 were members of the Allied Forces, while the Oversea entries were chiefly in South America, Portugal, Switzerland, Egypt and Palestine. The current regulations give a sufficient picture of the establishment of new centres since 1939.

With these figures must be considered the entries for the Lower Certificate in English, established on the eve of the war:

	1939	1940	1941	1942	1943	
Overseas	144	254	112	242	416⎫	846
Home	—	—	—	—	430⎭	

This Lower examination was originally intended for oversea centres only, but the response was considerable among the Allied Forces when it was made available in Great Britain and the year 1943 thus saw the record entry for the two examinations together of over 1700 (the total number of candidates for these examinations and for the Preliminary Test for Allied Service Personnel during 1944 is likely to be nearly 4000).

How far examinations of this kind may act as a stimulus and a focusing point for both teachers and taught, and thereby promote the expansion of the studies which they are designed to test, is a matter that does not lend itself to exact research. They are only part of a process. It is certain

36

that, in the revival and expansion of systematic English studies which is revealed by these statistics, the activity of the British Council bulks very large. Alike at home and abroad, the Council constantly sought new channels of service, responded to new requests, carried teaching and assistance wherever they were needed. Early in 1941 the Council and the Syndicate placed their collaboration upon a formal footing by the institution of a Joint Committee, and officers of the Council act increasingly as correspondents and advisers of the Syndicate.

Another important factor was the growing keenness of Service authorities to promote the study of English among Allied forces on British soil. Education officers and Liaison officers increasingly used the examinations, not merely as a test of progress made, but as an encouragement to regular study under conditions that were often difficult. For pupils of an Army Staff College or an R.A.F. Initial Training Wing, tuition in English might have to be fitted into a crowded time-table. A fighter squadron presented candidates ranging from Leading Aircraftman to Squadron Leader; in nearly every examination reports were received that certain candidates had come straight to the examination room from operations. Nor must one forget the allied civilians and friendly aliens who were learning English while working in war factories, as teachers and nurses, in commerce, or in the offices of Allied governments in London. Nor, finally, those British subjects who, having commonly spoken some other language, were improving their English while in prisoner-of-war or internment camps in Germany. One candidate, for lack of books, was prepared for the paper, *English Life and Institutions*, chiefly from the "combined memories" of several other members of the camp. But that is only a small part of the great work done by the Educational Books Section of the Red Cross and St John War Organization.

The story of these examinations during 1944 will be told elsewhere. It will give a picture of R.A.F. Stations and Allied military forces going from strength to strength, in spite of more pressing preoccupations. It will also record the reopening of examination centres in countries set free from German control; some of these centres may even be able to tell how they "carried on" throughout the occupation.

37

SUMMARY OF CONCLUSIONS

Note. While the lessons to be drawn from this enquiry may later lead to a review of the oral tests in modern languages for the Cambridge School Examinations, any changes here envisaged apply for the time being only to the Cambridge Examinations in English for foreign students.

Part I (page 6)

1. The separate allotment, in the Cambridge Examinations in English, of ten marks for reading and of ten for pronunciation and intonation should be abandoned (§ 3).

2. There should be marks for the various standards in each part of an oral test. With 20 marks for reading, 16 should be the minimum for Very Good, 12 for Good, and 8 for Pass (§ 4).

3. Candidates for an oral test should not be brought before the examiner in an order that is based in any way on their relative merit in the subject under test (§ 8).

4. There may be a drift in an examiner's mark towards either leniency or severity; this may be due to fatigue or to other causes (§ 9).

5. Standards of impression marking cannot well be defined beforehand merely by written instructions (§§ 10–12).

6. In any test which has no absolute criterion, no clear definition of pre-established standards, it is the candidates who tend to decide the standards (§ 11).

7. Examiners probably learn standards of their own from the candidates as they go along, or they may bring standards with them that they have acquired in their teaching (§ 13).

8. There is no guarantee that standards acquired by Examiner X through experience in South America will correspond with those learnt by Examiner Y in the Middle East (§ 15).

9. While a travelling examiner, through testing a large number of candidates, may acquire valid standards, this may not be possible for isolated examiners or teachers testing relatively small numbers in one particular locality (§ 15).

10. Impressions of oral work cannot be checked or revised, unless the examiner is able to recall candidates for a further test or is able to make sound recordings of the tests (§§ 15, 16).

11. The standards in an examiner's mind may be thrown out of the normal for a variety of reasons. He has no fixed criterion by which to recapture and re-test his own standards, unless he is aided by, e.g., sound recordings of candidates at known standards. The Syndicate's examiners in Art keep typical marked drawings or paintings by them as a guide (§§ 16, 39).

12. Competent examiners can quickly adapt themselves to common standards by joint assessment of a test of reading, but these will not

38

necessarily be the right standards and occasional serious divergencies may occur (§§ 22, 23). No individual judgement is likely to be so consistent as to serve as an absolute measure (§ 26).

13. Gramophone records of candidates at various levels should assist examiners, not only to reach agreement on standards among themselves, but to assimilate standards officially approved by the central examining body (§ 26).

14. There is something to be said for isolating the reading test from the conversation, where possible, so that examiners may hear all the candidates straight through in this test (§ 24).

15. The practice of calling out candidates from a written paper for their oral test has grave disadvantages, save in an emergency (§ 24).

16. The use of an identical reading passage for all candidates standardizes the difficulty of the test for them, but the examiners, through familiarity with the contents, become increasingly less able to use the test for an assessment of comprehensibility (§§ 25, 82). See also No. 57.

17. A second reading test, of material unseen by the examiner and quite unfamiliar to him, should provide him with an answer to the question, how readily he can understand what the candidate is saying (§ 25). *Note.* Such a test will be introduced by the Syndicate for the examinations of 1945, Certificate of Proficiency in English only.

18. If the main reading test is isolated from the conversation, it will be well to set the short, "unseen" test for each candidate immediately before his conversation. If reading and conversation are taken together, the unseen passage should come first, followed by the standard reading passage and then by the conversation (§ 25).

19. The possibility of occasional serious divergencies even between examiners who normally agree points to the value of having the reading test, if not conversation also, assessed by two examiners (§§ 22, 61, 62, 66).

Part II (page 13)

20. It is difficult to conceive any absolute means of assessing the validity of the judgement of a given examiner upon a given candidate. The opinion of a second examiner will not offer conclusive evidence, unless it is assumed that his judgement is right, not only in general, but in the particular instance (§§ 27–29).

21. One of the chief qualities in a good examiner is consistency (§ 28). This quality can be tested experimentally (§ 31).

22. Dictation is not an "oral" test, since the candidate does not speak. It is a test over which the individual examiner has not full control. Where it is included in the oral test, the examiner cannot always allot the standard which he would desire for a candidate's oral work as a whole (§§ 35–39).

23. Knowledge of a candidate's standard in dictation may possibly have a stabilizing influence on an examiner's mental standards; it is not necessarily the best or the only guide for that purpose (§ 39).

39

24. It is advisable to separate the dictation mark from the mark for oral work (§ 40). *Note.* This separation will be made in the examinations of 1945 for the Certificate of Proficiency and also for the Lower Certificate in English; all the dictation exercises will then be marked in England.

25. The separation of the dictation marks from the marks for oral work will not diminish the need for central control and guidance of oral examiners. It also leaves open the question, whether the results of dictation and other semi-oral tests can afford a clue to the probable validity of an oral examiner's standards (§ 40).

Part III (page 17)

26. In the absence of precise instructions there will be no uniformity in the interpretation of the "ordinary pace" for the first and third readings of a dictation (§ 42).

27. The speeds represented by the times taken by the official reader for Proficiency and Lower Certificate dictations should be taken as a standard guide by all who examine in Spoken English on behalf of the Syndicate (§§ 42, 43).

28. It may be desirable in future to stipulate the time to be taken for reading each dictation passage set by the Syndicate, and also to provide model readings of dictations (§ 43).

29. If the reproducing apparatus does not give great fidelity, those who use gramophone records of speech as a guide to examination standards will need to bear in mind that they may not be hearing what was heard by the examiners who assessed the standards at headquarters (§ 46).

30. The recording in quantity of full-length conversation tests would be uneconomical, though a library of master copies of records of this kind might well be built up for use at headquarters. One or two full-length conversations might be recorded later for circulation as models (§ 48).

31. Shortened conversations and free speech by candidates, with a minimum of intervention by the examiner, might usefully be recorded for circulation (§ 48).

32. It is difficult to record the conversation and free speech of really weak candidates; the reading test is a relatively simple matter. At the same time, we need as much guidance as possible at the weak pass level (§ 50).

33. If records are to be used for the standardization of marking, a library of them may be needed showing different national characteristics of speech (§ 50).

Part IV (page 20)

34. Reproduction of recorded speech can usefully be employed for experimental marking in committee (§§ 52, 53).

35. Records, reproduced with high fidelity, may even have certain advantages over "live" candidates for committee work (§ 53).

40

36. A varied stock of discs, not reproduced in quantity, might be sent from one country to another for demonstration purposes and committee work (§ 53).

37. It would be possible experimentally to compare the standards of the Proficiency and Lower Certificate examinations (§ 59).

38. Oversea examiners and teachers should be encouraged to attempt' regional standardization by experimental work in committee (§ 60).

Part V (page 23)

39. Joint examining would be of greatest value where the examiners, by experimental marking of candidates or of gramophone records, or by collaboration on earlier occasions, had "come together" in the matter of standards (§ 61).

40. The use of two examiners should make for uniformity at a particular centre or in a particular country; it will only make for uniformity between one country and another if one or both of the examiners have had experience elsewhere or have assimilated standards at headquarters and possess means of renewing contact with those standards, e.g. by gramophone records (§§ 61, 84).

41. Joint marking by examiner and teacher may offer useful possibilities for School Certificate oral examinations in England, but a teacher will probably have less sense of general standards than an examiner whose experience is more varied (§§ 13, 36, 62).

42. Public confidence in the Cambridge Examinations in English is likely to depend on the extent to which they are felt to be directly controlled by the University and to represent worldwide standards (§ 63).

43. For the Cambridge Examinations in English overseas visits by examiners from headquarters should be valuable, in order both to make firsthand contacts and to communicate standards by joint examining (§ 63).

44. For the propagation of standards by joint examining, examiners will be needed who have seriously assimilated standards beforehand and have proved their reliability (§ 63).

45. If a visiting examiner abroad were able to travel with a mobile recording and reproducing unit, he could both demonstrate by means of records reproduced with high fidelity and also record further material (§ 63).

46. The use of two examiners to test each candidate jointly in conversation presents certain problems (§§ 64, 65).

47. Where two examiners examine jointly in conversation, one might well be a "silent examiner", recording marks for a test conducted by his colleague (§ 66).

48. The whole problem of conversation tests needs fuller investigation (§§ 66, 84).

41

Part VI (page 26)

49. When dictation is separated from the purely oral work it should be readily possible to check the correlation of the marks for written work and the marks allotted by local examiners in the oral test (§ 68).

50. When the speed of delivery of the dictation is standardized, and all the exercises are marked by a single examiner, it should be possible by statistical methods to approach continuity of standard in this test from one examination to the next (§ 70). See also the Note to No. 24 above.

51. Written reproduction of a short story read once to the candidates might be added to the dictation in and after 1946. Powers for this are already taken in the regulations (§ 71).

52. As a further mixed or semi-oral test, questions might be put orally concerning printed matter laid before the candidates, who would be required to write their answers (§ 72).

53. A set of one-word answers or short sentences to be written in reply to spoken questions can be a very satisfying semi-oral test, particularly perhaps at elementary levels (§ 73).

54. The degree of correlation between oral and semi-oral tests could be investigated experimentally and might serve as a control of oral standards, both by the authorities at headquarters and by the local examiners (§ 74).

55. Semi-oral tests may on investigation show some correlation not only with purely oral work but also with purely written work. The experimental development of such tests is to be recommended (§ 76).

Part VII (page 29)

56. Examiners testify to the impression made upon them by hearing the reading, or recorded reading, of candidates of agreed standard. Such impressions may be effaced by subsequent examining and may need renewal (§ 78).

57. The advantage of keeping the main reading test separate from the conversation is confirmed by further experience (see 14 above). Alternative reading passages (see 16 above) should be provided when the number of candidates is substantial. Examiners should use one passage until they begin to tire of it, and then change to another (§ 82). *Note.* Alternative passages will be provided for the Proficiency examination in 1945.

58. Definition is needed of what the examiner should chiefly listen for in each test (§ 82).

59. Independent testing of a substantial number of candidates by a new examiner and two or more experienced examiners offers an opportunity of testing the reliability of the new examiner (§ 83). His reliability might similarly be tested by his marking of a substantial number of recorded readings of agreed standard (§ 53).

42

60. When the reading and conversation tests are separated, it is not quite certain that a higher pass mark should be required in the whole oral examination than the sum of the pass marks in the several parts, especially where different examiners are responsible for the various tests. Examiners should probably be allowed some latitude in this matter (§§ 67, 83).

61. The personal reaction of the particular examiner to the particular candidate is a factor in any oral examination or interview. While the successful elimination of this factor depends on the quality of the examiner, it may be well to put examiners on their guard by discussing its possible influence (§§ 84, 86).

62. A visiting examiner who conducts a joint test with a teacher may tend to leniency in a desire to save the teacher's feelings (§ 86).

63. The third reading of a dictation should be at the same pace as the first reading, but the examiner should pause at full stops or at convenient points, every two lines or so, in order to give time for corrections (§ 88).

64. Definition is needed of what a dictation is intended to test. This may influence the character of the passage to be set, the manner in which it is read, and the principles on which it is marked (§ 89).

43

TABLE A (see p. 6). *Experimental Lower Certificate Reading Test, Polish I.T.W., September* 1944

Index numbers of candidates / Examiners	1	2	3	14	15	16	17	4	5	6	7	8	10	79	11	12	13	18	19	20	22	21	23	24
A	14	13	10	8	7	8	6	9	8	7	5	15	9	10	10	9	6	8	9	9	8−	8	9	9
B	11	15	10	9	9	8−	12+	—	—	—	—	—	7+	9	12	8−	6	9	8	8	8+	9	8	12
C	14	13	11	10+	9	8+	8−	9+	8−	9	7	10	8−	8+	10+	9+	7	8+	11	9−	12−	7	10	10
D	—	—	—	—	—	—	—	10	7	9	6+	10	8	12	—	—	5	8	11	8	7	8	9	12
Provisional official mark	14	14	10	9	8	8	8	10	8−	8	6	13	8	10	11	9+	6	8	10	8+	9	8	9	10
Final official mark	17	17	12	11	11	10	10	12	10	10	7	16	10	10	13	11	7	10	12	10	11	10	11	12
Education Officers																								
E	—	—	—	—	—	—	—	—	—	?10	8	9	—	10	—	—	—	—	8	7	7+	8	12	8+
F	—	—	—	—	9	7−	11	11	7+	8−	7+	7	10	8	10	9	4	7	10	9	8	7	9	8
G	—	—	—	—	8	7	10	12	8+	8−	7	8	8	8	11	11	6	6	—	—	—	—	—	—
H	—	—	—	—	—	—	—	—	—	—	—	—	8	12	7−	10	4	6	12	8	8	8+	8	8
I	—	—	—	—	—	—	—	—	—	—	—	—	9	10	11	—	6	8	11+	8	10	9	11	7

Standards: Maximum 20 V. Good 16 Good 12 Pass 8

TABLE B (see p. 14). *Experimental Reading Test, Polish I.T.W., September* 1944

Marks of Examiners A and C, and of Education Officer I, for the last twelve of the twenty-four candidates

	Index numbers of candidates											
	10	79	11	12	13	18	19	20	22	21	23	24
Examiner A	9	10	10	9	6	8	9	9	8−	8	9	9
Examiner C	8−	8+	10+	9+	7	8+	11	9−	12−	7	10	10
Education Officer I	9	10	11	—	6	8	11+	8	10	9	11	7
Divergence between A and C	1½	1½	½	½	1	½	2	½	4	1	1	1
Divergence between C and I	1½	1½	½	—	1	½	½	½	1½	2	1	
Divergence between A and I	0	0	1	—	0	0	2½	1	2½	1	2	2

Standards: Maximum 20 V. Good 16 Good 12 Pass 8

TABLE C (see p. 14). *Marks allotted for reading to seven Proficiency candidates*

	Index numbers of candidates						
	1	2	3	14	15	16	17
By Examiner C in the joint experimental test	14	13	11	10+	9	8+	8−
By Examiner C next day in the Proficiency test	16*	15	14	12	11	10	9
Official Lower Certificate mark for the joint test after proportionate increase	17	17	12	11	10	10	10

* This mark was later reduced to 15, Examiner C agreeing with Examiner A that he had probably overmarked.

TABLE D (see p. 20). *Experimental marking of Recorded readings, Polish I.T.W., Cambridge, October 1944*

Index numbers	Proficiency candidates							Lower Certificate candidates				
Examiners	14	2	1	17	16	15	3	13	10	5	13	7
1. J. L.	10	16	18	8	6	12	8	8	10	12	—	7
2. R. K.	12	11	13	12	14	6	9	9	11	10	9	9
3. L. H.	13−	16	14	8	9−	11	8−	8−	11	11−	—	—
4. H. A.	10−	16	14	9	12	14	7	7	14	12	7	7
5. J. G.	12	14	10+	8	11	12	8	8	10+	9+	9	8+
6. B. G.	12	10	11	8+	8	11	10	10	12	12	8	7+
7. Mrs B.	11	13	13	9	7	10	8	8	12	11	8+	7
8. J. W.	11	12	15−	9	8	9+	8	8	10	11+	8+	8+
9. S. W.	12	10+	10+	8	6+	12+	8	—	—	—	7	—
Total mark	103	118	118	79	81	97	66	66	90	88	—	—
Average mark for the recording	11½	13+	13+	9−	9	11−	8+	8+	11+	11	8+	8
Official mark for the "live" test in September. See Table C	12	15	15	9	10	11	*7	*7	10*	10*	7*	7*

* Final official mark for the "live" test in September. See Table A.

Standards: Maximum 20 V. Good 16 Good 12 Pass 8

Table E (see pp. 29–30). Joint Oral Test of Proficiency candidates, December 1944

Reading

Index-nos. of candidates ...	464	465	466	467	468*	469	471	472	473*	474*	475	476	477	478*	479*	480	481	482
Examiners																		
L. H. (Examiner B)	10	16+	15−	14	11−	8−	8−	6−	7−	16−	10	17	8−	10−	13−	14	11	17−
W. W. (Examiner D)	10	16+	15	12	9	10	9	6	8	14	10	17	9	10	16−	14	11	17
B. G. (No. 6)	9	16	14+	12	7	10	9	5	8−	12+	10	16+	9	14−	14	14+	11	16+
Official mark	10[c]	16+[a]	15[b]	12[b]	9[c]	9[c]	9[c]	6[f]	8[c]	14[b]	10[c]	17[a]	9[c]	11[c]	14[b]	14[b]	11[c]	17[a]

Conversation

	464	465	466	467	468*	469	471	472	473*	474*	475	476	477	478*	479*	480	481	482
Examiners																		
L. H.	—	—	12	11	8	7+	12	—	↑7+	—	—	—	—	—	11	13	—	—
W. W.	9	14	12	11	—	7	8	—	—	12	12	14	6+	—	11	13	8	14
B. G.	—	—	9	—	—	—	—	8	—	9	—	14	—	9	13	13	—	—
Official mark	9[b]	14[a]	12[a]	11[b]	8[c]	7[c]	8[c]	8[c]	7[c]	12[b]	12[a]	14[a]	6[c]	9[c]	11[b]	13[a]	8[c]	14[b]

Reading

Index-nos. ...	484*	485*	486*	487	488	489	490	491	492	493	494	495	496	498	499	500	501	502
Examiners																		
L. H.	16	12−	14−	20	9−	9+	17−	18−	9−	17	8	12	9	15	8	8	16	12
W. W.	16	12−	11	20	10	9	16	18	9	17	8	15	9	15	8	8	16	12
B. G.	15+	11	10	19+	8−	9	16	18	8	16+	8	—	—	15	8	9	16	12
Official mark	16[a]	12[b]	11[c]	20[b]	9[c]	9[c]	16[a]	18[a]	9[c]	17[a]	8[c]	13[b]	9[c]	15[b]	8[c]	9[c]	16[a]	12[b]

Conversation

Examiners																		
L. H.	13·	13†	9·	—	—	8	—	15	15	15	—	11	10	—	—	12	13†
W. W.	13	—	—	—	7	—	15	15	15	9	11	9	13	10	—	—		
B. G.	11	—	15	10·	—	—	6	6	11—	12+	11—	—	—	6+	10	—		
Official mark	13^a	13^a	10^b	15^a	7^c	8^e	6^c	15^a	6^c	15^a	11^a	11^b	10^b	13^a	6^c	10^b	12^a	13^a

Reading

Index-nos. ...	503	505	506	507	508	509	510	511	512	513*	514	515	516	517	518*	68
Examiners																
L. H.	9+	12	10	11	11	13	9—	11	11	8	8—	8	8	8	13	14
W. W.	9	12	10	11	11	13	10	11	11	8	8	8	9	8	11	14
B. G.	9	14—	10	11	11	13	10	10	11	7+	8	9	9	11	11	14
Official mark	9^e	12^b	10^e	11^e	11^e	13^b	10^e	11^e	11^e	8^e	8^e	9^e	9^e	8^e	11^e	14^b

Conversation

Examiners																	
L. H.	8	12†	8	8	12—	—	7	8	—	5†	9	—	8	8	14·	—
W. W.	8	—	—	—	12—	11	8	8	7	—	9	7	—	—	13	12
B. G.	8	—	12	12	—	—	6	6—	—	6	9	—	6	—	14	14
Official mark	8^e	12^a	8^e	8^e	11^b	11^b	7^c	8^e	7^c	6^e	5^f	9^b	7^c	8^e	8^e	14^a	12^a

Standards—Reading: Maximum 20   V. Good 16   Good 12

Conversation: Maximum 15   V. Good 12   Good 9   Pass 8   Pass 6

^{a} = Very Good; ^{b} = Good; ^{e} = Good; ^{f} = Fail

* Candidates for whom there was disagreement on category (see paragraph 79).

† Mark agreed by three examiners.

Appendix D

Listening Comprehension papers and tapescripts

Appendix D

PASSAGE FOR QUESTIONS 1 to 5

Friday evenings were very special. / It was then that my hair was washed with green soap and rain water, and I would sit with a warm towel over my shoulders and watch Mrs. Penny do her weekly accounts. / First of all she would take out the pile of clean towels that looked as if they filled all the top left hand drawer of our kitchen cupboard; and there behind, in a tidy row, would be the purses, Mrs. Penny's house-keeping purses, each one a different shape, a different colour and used for a different purpose. /

She would take them all out and set one down on the table before us, together with a blue pencil and a red exercise book in which she wrote down every penny she spent. / And I would watch as she carefully counted into the green purse the cash to cover next week's meat supply. / Then into the long brown purse went the money for three pints of milk a day and four on Sunday from the milkman. / Into the silvery white one with a blue slip sailing on it went the money for the rent, and into the black one decorated with knaves went the money for all the other groceries. / At last we would come to the purse I loved best, the beautiful soft blue mother one. / Into this she only slipped a regular weekly sum, because she bought a real bargain, the very thing she wanted but far less than she had planned to spend on it, then into the blue purse went one half of the saving. / From this purse we not only bought presents for poor children in London but we also bought, for cash down, shoelaces, pastries of glass and matches from every beggar who came knocking at the door.

PASSAGE FOR QUESTIONS 6 to 10

I turned down the street by the bar entrance to the hotel. / There was no one in the doorway or in the entrance to the bar itself, nor had I expected to find anyone. / I made my way round to the hotel fire-escape, climbed up to the roof, and found the part that directly over-hung my own balcony. /

I looked over the edge. I could see nothing, but I could smell the burning tip of a cigarette. / I got to my feet carefully, and silently went down the fire-escape to the sixth floor. / Here I let myself in through the fire-escape door, and inched my way along to the door of my room, then listened. / I opened the door quietly, closing it as quickly as I could; even small draughts can affect cigarette smoke in a way to attract the attention of a smoker. /

As I had expected, it was the man who had been following me. / He was sitting comfortably in his armchair, his feet resting on the balcony, smoking a cigarette in his left hand; his right lay loosely on his knee and held a gun. /

I was behind him with my gun at his right ear and he still didn't know I was there. / I touched him on the right shoulder. / As he swung round and then cried out as his movement forced my gun against his right eye. / As he lifted both hands to his face I took the gun from him without difficulty, pocketed it, reached for his shoulder and twisted it hard. / He went right over, landing heavily on his back.

PASSAGE FOR QUESTIONS 11 to 15

I remember standing at the side of the stage when Mother's voice cracked and went into a whisper. / The audience began to laugh and whistle and to shout rude things. / It was all very confusing to a child of seven and I did not quite understand what was going on. / But the noise increased until Mother was obliged to walk off the stage. / When she came to the side she was very upset and argued with the manager who, having sent me perform before Mother's friends, said something about letting me go on in her place. / Finally she agreed, and ... /

Half-way through my song, a shower of money poured on to the stage. / Immediately I stopped and announced that I would pick up the money first and sing afterwards. / This caused much laughter. / The manager came on with a handkerchief and helped me to gather it up. / I thought he was going to keep it. / The audience realised this and laughed more, especially when he walked off with it and I anxiously following him. / Not until he handed it to Mother did I return and continue to sing. / I was quite at home. I talked to the audience, danced, and did several imitations, including ... Mother used to ... /

And in repeating the chorus, without any real reason I copied Mother's voice cracking and went into the effect it had on the audience. / There was laughter and cheers, then more money-throwing; and when Mother came on the stage to carry me off, her appearance was greeted with tremendous applause. / That night was my first appearance on the stage and Mother's last.

N.B. Any FOUR passages to be chosen for each complete test

[TURN OVER]

PASSAGE FOR QUESTIONS 16 to 20

The village school at that time provided all the teaching we were likely to ask for. / It has been replaced for many years now by a building with properly separated classrooms. / When I was a child, however, it was just a small stone building divided by a high wooden screen into two rooms—for the small children and the older ones. / There was one woman teacher, and perhaps a young girl assistant. / Every child in the valley came crowding there, remained till he was fourteen years old, and then was sent to work in the fields or factory with nothing more in his head than a few tricks for remembering things, a confused list of wars, and a rough idea of the world's geography. / It seemed enough to manage with, in any case; and was more than our grandparents had learned. /

This school, when I came to it, was very busy. / Universal education and unusually large families had pushed it to the walls with pupils. / Wild boys and girls from miles around—from the distant farms and half-hidden cottages way up at the ends of the valley—swept down each day to add to our numbers, bringing with them strange oaths and swords, unusual clothes and customs habits. / They were my first sight of any world outside the womanly warmth of my family. / I didn't expect to survive it for long, and I faced it at the age of four.

PASSAGE FOR QUESTIONS 21 to 25

We stopped the car at the house and I led Elizabeth through the half-light of the passage. / She felt suddenly over a parcel. / I began climbing the stairs, when it was even darker. / Mrs. Davies, the landlady, could be heard calling out:

"Who's up there? Who is it? Who's in my house?"

"Only me, Mrs. Davies," I made myself call.

"Oh it's you, Mr. Lewis," the voice called. / "Is Mrs. Lewis with you?"

"No, I have a visitor," I said.

"I don't want any noise, Mr. Lewis."

"Neither do I, Mrs. Davies."

"All right then, Mr. Lewis." /

In one room we found the whole of my family. / The baby was sitting in his chair, crying steadily. / Mary, our daughter, was sitting on Jean's knee, sleeping. / Jean, my wife, wearing only a house coat, was drying the child's hair with a towel. / They had clearly all been having a bath together, a favourite entertainment of theirs. / Around them was a collection of objects. There was a half-eaten apple, a doll, some children's books. /

"Well, hello," Jean said.

"I see your husband is home," said Elizabeth, waving to her.

"The thing is, a few of us are going out for a few drinks tonight and I was wondering whether you'd care to join us." /

"Jerry, just a minute." Jean said to her, then to me: "See to the baby, will you, John? I can't think with all that noise." / Quite pleased to leave things to the two women, I went up to the baby. / After I'd made several noises and faces he stopped crying and began to smile and chatter.

N.B. Any FOUR passages to be chosen for each complete test

FCE

UNIVERSITY OF CAMBRIDGE LOCAL EXAMINATIONS SYNDICATE

First Certificate in English

JUNE 1975

LISTENING COMPREHENSION TEST (PAPER 4)

Instructions for this test are on the answer sheet already given out, and the examiner will give you further instructions. You will hear four passages, each of them twice over, and you will be given time to choose your answer to the questions on each passage. The examiner will tell you which set of questions to answer, and which set you will not be answering.

REMEMBER TO MARK YOUR CHOICE OF ANSWER ON THE ANSWER SHEET

1 The first thing done on Friday evening was that
A the towels were taken out of the drawer
B a towel was placed on the child's shoulder
C the housekeeping person put on the table
D the child's hair was washed

2 Where did Miss Penny keep the purse?
A Behind the kitchen cupboard
B In a drawer behind some towels
C On top of the kitchen cupboard
D On the kitchen table

3 The child's favourite purse was
A a blue one
B a silvery white one
C a black one
D a brown one

4 How careful was Mrs. Penny with money?
A She really occasional attention to her accounts
B She sometimes forgot what she had spent
C She was very exact over her accounts
D She did not remember which purse was which

5 When Mrs. Penny bought a bargain, she would
A pay for it from her special purse
B put some money in her special purse
C give all the had saved to the poor
D give a present to the child

6 The writer entered the hotel
A through the bar
B by the fire-escape
C over the balcony
D by the roof

7 When did the writer first suspect that somebody was in his room?
A When he heard a small noise
B When he saw someone's shoes
C When he could smell cigarette smoke
D When he saw a lighted cigarette

8 The writer took the man's gun and then
A shot him in the shoulder
B hit him on the back of the head
C kicked him onto the floor
D threw him onto the floor

9 Why was the person in the room sitting in the armchair smoking?
A Because he wasn't expecting the writer then
B Because he was to know that the writer had entered
C Because he was just about to shoot the writer
D Because he was trying to attract somebody's attention

10 The writer closed the door of his room quickly so that the person in the room wouldn't
A hear any sound
B see any light
C small grey smoke
D notice any change

REMEMBER TO MARK YOUR CHOICE OF ANSWER ON THE ANSWER SHEET

11 When the boy's mother was singing the audience was very noisy because
A the song was very amusing
B it was really waiting for her son
C she had lost her voice
D she walked off the stage angrily

12 Why did the manager invite the boy to go on stage?
A The boy was well known to the audience
B He already knew what he could do
C The manager wanted to frighten the boy
D The boy asked if he could go

13 Why did the audience laugh so much at the boy?
A His singing was so bad
B He stopped singing to pick up the money
C He dropped his money on the stage
D He looked so small on the stage

14 Why did the manager come on the stage during the boy's performance?
A To ask the audience to keep quiet
B To tell the boy to sing more loudly
C To pick up the money
D To give the boy a handkerchief

15 When Mother came on the stage for the last time, the audience
A shouted at her madly
B cheered wildly
C demanded another song
D was surprised

16 In the writer's childhood, the village school was
A one building with several classrooms
B one building with two classrooms
C two buildings with two classrooms in each
D two buildings with one classroom in each

17 At school, the writer says, the children learnt
A nothing of any use
B enough for their lives
C more than they needed
D the same as their grandparents had done

18 After leaving school, some children
A worked in industry
B went to university
C helped their grandparents
D became soldiers

19 One reason for the school being half full was that
A all children now had to go to school
B fewer children were having school to go to work
C there were only two schools in the village
D more families had come to live in the village

20 The wild boys and girls came from
A factories
B other countries
C farms
D the next village

21 When the writer and Elizabeth entered the house
A they brought a parcel with them
B they couldn't see very clearly
C she had to guide him
D the lamps were lit

22 Mrs. Davies, the landlady, was anxious because
A Mr. Lewis was a visitor
B she had never met Mr. Lewis
C she didn't know who had entered the house
D she was expecting a visitor

23 When the writer and Elizabeth went into the sitting-room, his wife was
A having a bath
B washing clothes
C doing her hair
D busy with her daughter

24 Elizabeth invited them
A to a party at her house
B to spend an evening with friends
C to go out for dinner that evening
D to meet her husband that evening

25 What were John's feelings when asked to deal with this baby?
A He would have preferred to leave it to the women
B He was happy to do this
C He was annoyed at being asked to do this
D He could not face it

REMEMBER TO MARK YOUR CHOICE OF ANSWER ON THE ANSWER SHEET

1975 CPE Listening comprehension test

CONFIDENTIAL.—FOR THE ORAL EXAMINER'S USE ONLY

CPE

UNIVERSITY OF CAMBRIDGE LOCAL EXAMINATIONS SYNDICATE

Certificate of Proficiency in English

JUNE 1975

LISTENING COMPREHENSION TEST (PAPER 4)

To be given exactly as directed, to groups of not more than 30 candidates at a time. Each test takes 20–30 minutes. This booklet should be looked through before the day of the examination, together with the specimen copies of the question paper and candidate's answer sheet provided, so that the procedure for the test is fully understood. The reading of the passages should be rehearsed, with particular attention to timings.

Please note in particular:

(i) Each complete test consists of twenty questions only, based on any four of the five passages given in this booklet. The arrangement gives a series of alternative tests for use at centres with more than one group of candidates.

(ii) No group should be allowed to start the test unless it is established that each candidate has an answer sheet printed with his name and examination index number, or an emergency answer sheet supplied by the Supervisor.

(iii) Overleaf is a fully detailed procedure for beginning and ending the test, and for the reading of the first passage and the three subsequent passages. The wording of the instructions to candidates, given in plain type, may be verbal and repeated at the examiner's discretion, in the interest of ensuring that all candidates understand what is required. All reports and pauses, with other notes for the examiner, are given in italics. The pauses indicated must not be reduced unless all the candidates in a group are very obviously ready.

(iv) No other assistance of any kind must be given, except for reminders, at discretion, about the method of recording answers or about passing on to the next question. Extra repetition of phrases must only take place as an exceptional matter because of sudden traffic noise etc.

(v) This booklet is confidential until 23 June 1975, together with corresponding question papers for candidates. These must be collected up with the answer sheets at the end of each test and kept secure in one of the envelopes provided, either by the oral examiner or the Supervisor according to the arrangements for each centre.

PROCEDURE FOR THE TEST

You have an answer sheet for the listening comprehension test which I am going to give you. Check first that this sheet shows your name and examination index number marked correctly. Sign your name if so. *Pause for check; one note (G), on first page.* Before the test begins, make sure you understand how to show your answers. This is explained on the sheet. Ask any questions now, as you will not be allowed to speak during the test. *Pause for up to one minute.*

Now the test begins. You are warned that any attempt to copy or allow copying, or any kind of communication between candidates during the test, will be reported and may lead to rejection from the examination. I shall give out the question papers, and leave you time to read through questions ☐ * to ☐ * * *Repeat numbers, which are on the first passage I shall read.* There will be four passages altogether in the test, and you will hear each one twice.

* *At this point you should already have decided, in consultation where necessary with the examiner in charge and the Supervisor, which four passages are to be read to each group of candidates. The numbers of the set of five questions for the first passage read should now be given accordingly. Repeat the numbers as necessary; these may also be written up on a blackboard. Allow about one minute after giving out the question papers, and continue when the group is ready.*

Now be ready with your pencil and answer sheet to answer these questions when you have heard the passage. Here is the first reading.

First reading of the first passage chosen.
This should take approximately 2½ minutes.
Do not make the marked pauses (I) in this reading.

This is the end of the first passage. Now there will be a pause for you to choose your answers to questions ☐ to ☐. *Repeat numbers.* Remember you need not answer the questions in order, and you may leave any that you are not sure of until the second reading. *Pause one to two minutes or needed.*

Here is the passage for a second time. You are answering questions ☐ to ☐. Remember that your choice of answer must be shown on the answer sheet.

Second reading of first passage chosen.
Slower, with pauses of 5 seconds where indicated.
Pause after the reading for one to two minutes or needed.

For the next passage, look at questions ☐ * * to ☐. ** *Repeat numbers, and pause about one minute.* **Give in each case the numbers of the set of five questions appropriate to the passage chosen.* Now be ready to answer these questions when you have heard the passage. Here is the first reading.

First reading. Approximately 2½ minutes, no marked pauses (I)

This is the end of the passage. Now there will be a pause for you to choose your answers to questions ☐ to ☐. *Repeat, and pause one to two minutes as needed.*

Here is the passage for a second time. You are answering questions ☐ to ☐.

Second reading. Pauses of 5 seconds where indicated.
Pause after the reading of one to two minutes as needed.

After the two-minute pause following the fourth passage chosen. That is the end of the test. Make sure you have shown all answers on the answer sheet, in the way required, before I collect them. You must also mark off, in the way explained on the answer sheet, the numbers of the set of ten questions which you have not answered in this test. Specify these. This is necessary for the correct reading of your own answer. Short further pause as necessary.

Collect the answer sheets, and ALL COPIES OF THE QUESTION PAPER

REPEAT THIS THREE TIMES

PASSAGE FOR QUESTIONS 1 to 5

When, at eight o'clock, the School House butler walked down the dormitories ringing a horribly cracked bell, no one paid any attention. There was tons of time. Ordinarily no one ever got up till a quarter past, and to-day—well, twenty-past would be magic to prepare for the day of the Confirmation. [...]

PASSAGE FOR QUESTIONS 6 to 10

Most drivers get quite a fright when a police car, siren blaring, blue light flashing, cuts in ahead and orders them to stop. They are so unaccustomed to think out tactics for handling the questions that will follow. [...]

PASSAGE FOR QUESTIONS 11 to 15

She found herself in a corridor which was unfamiliar, but after trying one or two doors discovered her way back to the entrance hall. [...]

N.B. Any FOUR passages to be chosen for each complete text

[TURN OVER]

PASSAGE FOR QUESTIONS 16 to 20

As late as the eighteenth century to brew your own beer was the rule rather than the exception. Cobbett's opinion, writing in 1821, was that to persuade Englishmen, every year to have them to brew their own beer would have been unnecessary. [...]

PASSAGE FOR QUESTIONS 21 to 25

At a station in southern Poland, the porter who watched me struggling along the platform with all my heavy luggage said he'd carry the biggest case to the hotel himself, rather than have me wait in a taxi queue at 10 p.m. on a drizzly evening. [...]

N.B. Any FOUR passages to be chosen for each complete text

CPE

UNIVERSITY OF CAMBRIDGE LOCAL EXAMINATIONS SYNDICATE

Certificate of Proficiency in English

JUNE 1975

LISTENING COMPREHENSION TEST (PAPER 4)

Instructions for this test are on the answer sheet already given out, and the examiner will give you further instructions. You will hear four passages, each of them twice over, and you will be given time to choose your answers to the questions on each passage. The examiner will tell you which set of questions to answer, and which set you will not be answering.

REMEMBER TO MARK YOUR CHOICE OF ANSWER ON THE ANSWER SHEET

1 When the butler rang the bell at eight o'clock the boys
   A wondered what all the noise was about.
   B knew they had very little time.
   C knew they must get up before a quarter past
   D were in no hurry to get up.

2 After the bell rang, what was Gordon's immediate reaction?
   A He muttered sleepily: "Damn that bell"
   B He woke the others up for fear they should all be late.
   C He thought that as the new boy he should waken the others.
   D He thought everyone would get up at once

3 Why was Gordon terrified when he touched the other boy's arm?
   A Because the boy woke up and shouted at him
   B Because the boy did not wake
   C Because he heard someone moving next door
   D Because it was so unlike home

4 What happened to reassure Gordon?
   A The boy next to him explained that they would not be punished
   B The other boys at last started getting up
   C He realised he would not be late
   D Another boy who was fairly new began to get up

5 The room where the boys had to wash
   A was not properly fitted up as a bathroom
   B was too small for the purpose
   C had a floor designed to carry away the water
   D had showers which drained directly to the floor

6 Why are motorists at a disadvantage when told to stop by a mobile policeman?
   A They know that they were committing an offence
   B It can usually stop just in front of them
   C The police are cable enough to think what to say
   D They don't know the answers to the questions the policeman will ask

7 When stopped by the police, how is the motorist advised to behave?
   A He should say nothing until he has seen his lawyer
   B He should give only what additional information the law requires
   C He should say only what the law requires
   D He should in no circumstances say anything

8 Why is it suggested that it is best to be an eye-to-eye level with the policeman?
   A It gives you confidence in dealing with the situation
   B It gives you the opportunity to speak first
   C It does not suggest that you are guilty
   D It shows that you are not afraid to get out of the car

9 What is the risk involved in giving an angry reply?
   A It shows that you think you have been provoked
   B It can be used in evidence against you
   C It may give away information which your insulting it
   D It may cause the policeman to lose his temper

10 The writer warns that if the motorist is not carrying his driving documents, he
   A will be asked to give his name and address
   B may have to go to court
   C will be allowed to produce the documents later
   D will be taken to the nearest police station

REMEMBER TO MARK YOUR CHOICE OF ANSWER ON THE ANSWER SHEET

No. 16572

11 What were Dora's reactions on finding herself in the corridor?
   A She felt frightened because she was alone
   B She realised she had temporarily lost her way
   C She tried to find out if she was being followed
   D She waited a moment because her feet were aching

12 From the description of the hall, we learn that
   A it was very artistically decorated
   B a fire was burning cheerfully in the grate
   C only the fireplace had any kind of decoration
   D a broom had been left in the fireplace

13 One of the effects produced by the setting out was to
   A illuminate the lake brightly
   B make the Abbey tower seem taller
   C reveal some white birds' feathers
   D show up the outline of a row of trees

14 What did Dora do after reaching the bottom of the second flight of steps?
   A She ran on immediately towards the lake
   B She set down to rest because she was tired
   C She stumbled and hurt her foot
   D She waited a moment because her feet were aching

15 The way to the lake led from dry stone steps to
   A long, wet grass
   B short grass just becoming wet
   C short grass still wet from the day's rain
   D long grass dried by the sun

16 In eighteenth century England, brewing beer at home was
   A common
   B exceptional
   C compulsory
   D necessary

17 At the time of the second world war, there was
   A more brewing of beer at home than in Cobbett's time
   B hardly any brewing of beer at home
   C more brewing of beer at home than there is today
   D much frustration because of legal restrictions on brewing at home

18 At present the commercial brewers fear
   A direct competition on the export market
   B direct competition on the home market
   C loss of sales through people drinking their own beer
   D loss of sales through high taxation

19 Brewing beer at home appeals, according to the passage, to people who want to
   A evade the legal restrictions on drinking
   B develop it as an industry
   C use the special kits which are available
   D take up an interesting but challenging hobby

20 A recent conference supported the idea of
   A less brewing of beer at home
   B more brewing of beer at home
   C higher taxes on beer
   D higher taxes on beer-making kits

21 The author must have been glad when the porter offered to carry his case because
   A the handle was broken
   B there was no taxis running at that time of night
   C it would not have been very pleasant waiting for a taxi
   D he was extremely tired

22 After the author had tipped him, the porter said that
   A the author was immediately generous
   B the author would certainly be able to buy some straps
   C he could not accept payment for only doing his duty
   D he would try to get the author some straps

23 In his instructions the author first went into
   A he couldn't make them understand what he wanted
   B they told him they would have some straps later
   C they suggested that he should try elsewhere for the straps
   D they suggested that he have some straps made

24 When he returned to the store the next day, the woman in charge of the leather goods section
   A asked one of her colleagues to serve him
   B was in the store room
   C told him that the straps had not arrived
   D was not available

25 When the author offered the saleslady a tip, she
   A rudely refused to accept it
   B accepted it gracefully
   C gracefully refused to accept it
   D accepted it without comment

REMEMBER TO MARK YOUR CHOICE OF ANSWER ON THE ANSWER SHEET

589

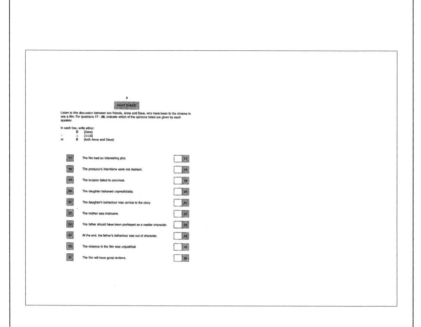

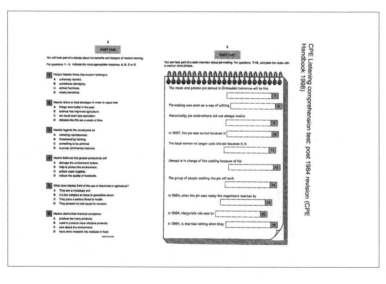

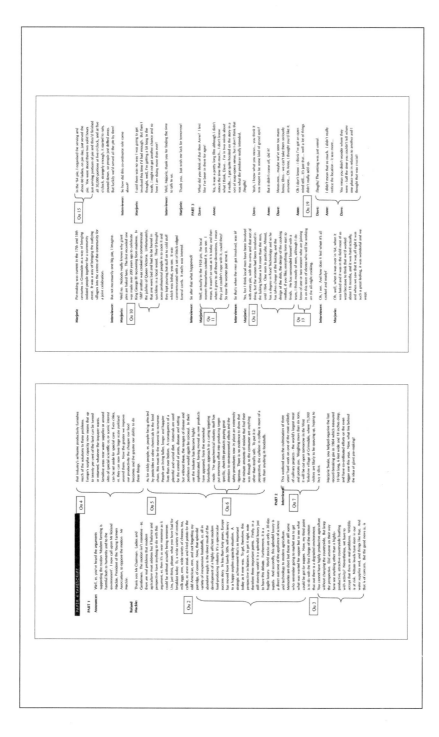

Measured Constructs

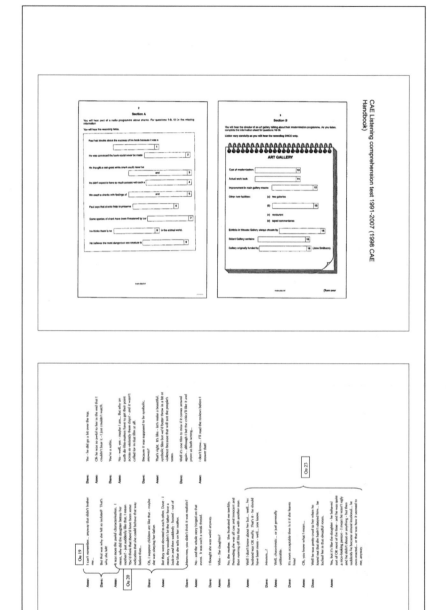

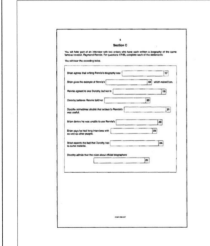

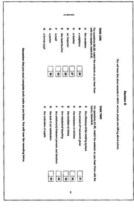

Section C

Interviewer: Well, I have with me today two people whose written books about the same man, the novelist Raymond Bronte: his official biographer, Dorothy Heseman, and his unofficial biographer, Brian Feltham. Now, Brian, you're the person who is writing a biography of me, how complicated they are going to find it, how misled they are going to be... Brian, we're talking...

Brian: Very much so. An unofficial biographer is especially vulnerable, but part of the fun of the chase is discovering all the false leads. Bronte's still superbly difficult to follow. Here was a man who kept two diaries, either or both of which might have misled, but who couldn't resist telling his fiction with real names and biographical facts.

Interviewer: Well, Dorothy, you were the official biographer, your project had Bronte's official blessing, what help did you get from him when he was alive?

Dorothy: Not a great deal. What he did for me was this, he said, 'Dorothy, if you want to see me, you can see me. If you want to see my papers, you can see mine. I will see you when you want to see me.' And he also went on and said that, 'I will not tell you everything.' Dorothy, but if you ask me a question, I will tell you the truth.' And I believe he did just that.

Interviewer: And, of course, you had an enormous amount of help by having access to his letters. Help? Since I've you got something like two and a half tons of them, it doesn't always seem like help. Sometimes, I feel as though I'm drowning.

Dorothy: Well, Brian doesn't have that problem, not having access to any private papers. You had to, shall we say, marauding from what is in the fictional and what is in the public domain. How much of your work in this area, do you think, is accurate and how much is just surmise, which you would like to be truthful because it makes good reading?

Brian: No, it's incorrect to say I haven't had access to Bronte's private papers. In fact, both of these biographies are based on the same major collections of papers, most of which are open to scholars. Over a thousand letters and a huge collection of various other documents are available. When I make allegations, I make them on the basis of many of the same documents as Dorothy has used, as well as, of course, interviews with hundreds of people who knew Bronte, including his wife, who spoke to me at great length.

Interviewer: And did you feel that you were getting at one truth, that there was one Raymond Bronte, or were you on the track of a number of Brontes?

Brian: Well, my job was made more difficult by Dorothy, in fact. It seems to me officially wrong to have an official biographer who has exclusive access to some of the material. I think that's a real problem for people who see biography as history. It's not one person's province to have a culturally important figure as her sole preserve. It should be open to other people in order to get at a good healthy debate on the subject. If Bronte's important enough, several people should be working on him.

Interviewer: Umm — what do you say to that, Dorothy?

Dorothy: The fact remains that this is always done, you have official biographies and the same rules have always applied. I see why this should be changed, but it hasn't happened yet. Brian's book, however, doesn't tell me anything about Bronte that I didn't already know, it's just that he's selected different data on which to build his biography. It's a matter of what, amongst all this material, you regard as relevant, as adding to our understanding of the man.

Brian: And that's exactly my point. That's why we shouldn't have an official biographies, it shouldn't just be one person's view.

Interviewer: And then, I'm afraid, we'll have to leave it for the moment. Brian, Dorothy, thank you both very much indeed.

Section D

1. Well, it was very different when I was at school. Oh no. When I went, we were always taught to keep ourselves neat and tidy, not like these youngsters nowadays. I mean, you should see the effort who live in our street walking past each day. Long greasy hair, shirts hanging out, kicking tin cans along the pavement... oh dear, oh dear. More discipline at home and school, that's what they need.

2. I tell you, it's a dog's life. Up and down to the boiler room, turning the heating on and off. I wish they'd make their minds up! And then it's time to move a few hundred chairs for some exam or other. You'd think these young rascals could move the odd chair themselves, wouldn't you? And do I get a word of thanks? Not likely! Ah well, no rest for the wicked, I suppose. Just off to replace a broken window. The little...

3. It'd be alright if we didn't have so much extra work. I mean, the lessons are quite interesting. Sometimes. Well, not very boring anyway. But the assignments and projects just go on and on. You never seem to get to the end of them. I think it's seriously affecting my football.

4. You see, it all boils down to one thing. These days, people have a choice. All my staff do their best in the classroom and I have every confidence in them, but at the end of the day it's up to the individual pupil to decide whether he or she is going to do the homework, or revise for the exams, or learn anything at all! We can't force them. It simply doesn't work. No, what we have to do is much more difficult. We have to make them want to learn, his easy task. Believe you me! I just hope they're going to push her enough. You know what I mean, at that age they're in a dozen half the time, thinking about make-up or boys or something. At her last school they said she needed to spend more time on her homework. What's more, her report didn't look all that good to me. I'll have to speak to her form teacher about it next time I see her — I don't get the impression she's particularly concerned.

References

Abbs, B, Cook, V J and Underwood, M (1968) *Realistic English Dialogues* Oxford: Oxford University Press.

Adams, M L (1978) Measuring foreign language speaking proficiency: A study of agreement among raters, in Clark, J L D (Ed.) *Direct Testing of Speaking Proficiency: Theory and Application*, Princeton, NJ: Educational Testing Service, 129–151.

Adams, R (1981) *The Reliability of Marking of Five June 1980 Examinations*, Mimeo. Associated Examining Board, Guildford.

Adamson, J W (1919) *A Short History of Education*, Cambridge: Cambridge University Press.

Alderson, J C (1978) A study of the cloze procedure with native and non-native speakers of English, unpublished PhD thesis, University of Edinburgh.

Alderson, J C (1981) Report of the discussion on Testing English for Specific Purposes, in Alderson, J C and Hughes, A (Eds) *Issues in Language Testing*, The British Council, 123–135.

Alderson, J C (1991) Bands and scores, in Alderson, C J and North, B (Eds) *Language Testing in the 1990s: The Communicative Legacy*, London: Macmillan, 71–86.

Alderson, J C (1993) The relationship between grammar and reading in a test of English for Academic Purposes, in Douglas, D and Chapelle, C (Eds) *A New Decade in Language Testing Research*, Alexandra, VA: TESOL.

Alderson, J C (2000) *Assessing Reading*, Cambridge: Cambridge University Press.

Alderson, J C (2001) *Is translation a good testing technique? The lift is being fixed. You will be unbearable today*, plenary address to the Magyar Macmillan Conference, Hungary, April 8 2001, available online: www.lancs.ac.uk/fass/projects/examreform/Media/Article01.pdf

Alderson, J C (2002) *Common European Framework of Reference for Languages: Learning, Teaching, Assessment: Case Studies*, Strasbourg: Council of Europe.

Alderson, J C and Bachman, L (2006) Series editors' preface, in Chappelle, A and Douglas, D (Eds) *Assessing Language Through Computer Technology*, Cambridge: Cambridge University Press, ix–xi.

Alderson, J C and Clapham, C M (1992) Applied linguistics and language testing: a case study of the ELTS Test, *Applied Linguistics* 13 (2), 149–167.

Alderson, J C, Clapham, C M and Wall, D (1995) *Language Test Construction and Evaluation*, Cambridge: Cambridge University Press.

Alderson, J C, Figueras, N, Kuijper, H, Nold, G, Takala, S and Tardieu, C (2004) *Specification for item development and classification within the CEF: the Dutch CEFR construct project*, paper presented at workshop on research into and with the CEFR, University of Amsterdam, Feb 2004.

Alderson, J C and Hughes, A (1981) *Issues in Language Testing*, ELT Documents 111, London: The British Council.

Alderson, J C and Wall, D (1996) Special Issue: Washback, *Language Testing* 13 (3).

Alexander, L G (1967) *New Concept English: First Things First; Practice and Progress; Developing Skills; Fluency in English*, Harlow, England: Longman.

Al-Fallay, I (1994) *Limiting bias in the assessment of English as a foreign language: the impact of background knowledge on the proficiency of Saudi Arabian students learning English as a foreign language*, unpublished doctoral dissertation, University of New Mexico, Albuquerque.

Allington, R L (1984) Oral reading, in Pearson, P D (Ed.) *Handbook of Reading Research*, New York: Longman, 829–864.

Altick, R D (1957) *The English Common Reader*, Chicago: University of Chicago Press.

American Educational Research Association, American Psychological Association and National Council on Measurement in Education (1999) *Standards for Educational and Psychological Testing*, Washington, DC.

Anastasi, A (1988) *Psychological Testing* (6ᵗʰ edition), New York: Macmillan.

Anderson, J R (2000) *Cognitive Psychology and its Implications* (5ᵗʰ edition), New York: W.H. Freeman.

Anderson, A and Lynch, T (1988) *Listening*, Oxford: Oxford University Press.

Applebee, A N (1974) *Tradition and Reform in the Teaching of English: A History.* Urbana: NCTE.

Aravind, M and Chung, K C (2010) Evidence-based medicine and hospital reform: tracing origins back to Florence Nightingale, *Plastic & Reconstructive Surgery* 125 (1), 403–409.

Armytage, W H G (1965) *Four Hundred Years of English Education*, Cambridge: Cambridge University Press.

Arnold, J E, Eisenband, J, Brown-Schmidt, S and Trueswell, J C (2000) The rapid use of gender information: Evidence of the time course of pronoun resolution from eyetracking, *Cognition* 76, B13–B26.

Attia, A (2002) *Developing listening comprehension strategies among prospective teachers of English in Egypt*, unpublished PhD thesis, University of Warwick.

Bachman, L F (1990) *Fundamental Considerations in Language Testing*, Oxford: Oxford University Press.

Bachman, L F (2007) What is construct? The dialectic of abilities and contexts in defining constructs in language assessment, in Fox, J, Wesch, M, Bayliss, D, Cheng, L, Turner, C E and Doe, C (Eds) *Language Testing Reconsidered*, Ontario: University of Ottawa Press, 41–71.

Bachman, L F and Davidson, F (1990) The Cambridge-TOEFL comparability study: an example of the cross-notional comparison of language tests, in de Jong, H A L (Ed.) *Standardization in Language Testing*, AILA Review, Amsterdam, 24–45.

Bachman, L F, Davidson, F, Ryan, K and Choi, I C (1995) *An Investigation into the Comparability of Two Tests of English as a Foreign Language*, Studies in Language Testing volume 1, Cambridge: UCLES/Cambridge University Press.

Bachman, L F and Palmer, A S (1981) The construct validation of the FSI oral interview, *Language Learning* 31 (1), 67–86.

Bachman, L F and Palmer, A S (1996) *Language Testing in Practice*, Oxford: Oxford University Press.

Bae, J and Bachman, L F (1998) A latent variable approach to listening and reading: Testing factorial invariance across two groups of children in the Korean/English Two-Way Immersion Program, *Language Testing* 15 (3), 380–414.

Balfour, A J (1905) *Essays and addresses*, Edinburgh: D Douglas.

Ballard, P B (1923) *The New Examiner*, London: Hodder & Stoughton.

Bardell, G S, Forrest, G M and Shoesmith, D J (1978) *Comparability in GCE: A Review of the Boards' Studies, 1964–1977*, Manchester: Joint Matriculation Board on behalf of the GCE Examining Boards.

Barker, K (1998) A trainable bracketer for noun modifiers, in *Proceedings of the Twelfth Canadian Conference on Artificial Intelligence (LNAI 1418)*, Vancouver, 196–210.

Barnett, M (1986) Syntactic and lexical/semantic skills in foreign language reading: importance and interaction, *Modern Language Journal* 70, 343–349.

Barnett, M (1989) *More Than Meets the Eye*, Englewood Cliffs, NJ: Prentice Hall Regents.

Barnwell, D P (1996) *A History of Foreign Language Testing in the United States*, Temple, Arizona: Bilingual Press.

Barry, A L (2008) Reading the past: Historical antecedents to contemporary reading methods and materials, *Reading Horizons* 49 (1), 31–52.

Bartlett, F C (1932) *Remembering*, Cambridge: Cambridge University Press.

Bax, S (2011) *Discourse and Genre*, Palgrave Macmillan.

Bax, S and Weir, C J (2012) Investigating learners' cognitive processes during a computer-based CAE reading test, *Research Notes* 47, 3–14.

Beak, G B (1908) *Indexing and Précis Writing*, London: Macmillan.

Beard, R (1972) *Teaching and Learning in Higher Education*, Harmondsworth: Penguin Books.

Beebe, L M (1980) Sociolinguistic variation and style shifting in second language acquisition, *Language Learning* 30 (2), 433–445.

Beebe, L M and Zuengler, J (1983) Accommodation theory: An explanation for style shifting in second-language dialects, in Wolfson, N and Judd, E (Eds) *Sociolinguistics and second language acquisition*, Rowley, Mass: Newbury House.

Bensoussan, M and Kreindler, I (1990) Improving advanced reading comprehension in a foreign language: summaries vs. short-answer questions, *Journal of Research in Reading* 13 (1), 55–68.

Bensoussan, M and Ramraz, R (1984) Testing EFL Reading Comprehension using a multiple choice rational cloze, *Modern Language Journal*, 68, 230–239.

Bereiter, C and Scardamalia, M (1987a) *The Psychology of Written Composition*, Hillsdale, New Jersey: Lawrence Erlbaum.

Bereiter, C and Scardamalia, M (1987b) Knowledge telling and knowledge transforming in written composition, in Rosenberg, S (Ed.) *Advances in Applied Psycholinguistics, Volume 2: Reading, Writing and Language Learning*, Cambridge: Cambridge University Press.

Berggren, O (1966) Is translation a good language test? *ELT Journal* 20 (3), 206–213.

Berman, R (1984) Syntactic components of the foreign language reading process, in Alderson, J C and Urquhart, A (Eds) *Reading in a Foreign Language*, London: Longman, 139–159.

Berne, J E (1998) Examining the relationship between L2 listening research, pedagogical theory and practice, *Foreign Language Annals* 31, 169–190.

Bernstein, J, Van Moere, A and Cheng, J (2010) Validating automated speaking tests, *Language Testing* 27 (3), 355–377.

Berry, V (1993) Personality characteristics as a potential source of language test bias, in Huhta, A, Sajavaara, K and Takala, S (Eds) *Language Testing: New Openings*, Jyvaskyla, Finland: University of Jyvaskyla, 115–124.

Berry, V (2004) *A study of the interaction between individual personality differences and oral performance test facets*, unpublished PhD dissertation, King's College, The University of London.

Berwick, R and Ross, S (1996) Cross-cultural pragmatics in oral proficiency strategies, in Milanovic, M and Saville, N (Eds) *Performance testing, cognition and assessment. Selected papers from the 15th language testing research colloquium, Cambridge and Arnhem*, Cambridge: UCLES/Cambridge University Press, 34–54.

Bhatia, V (1993) *Analysing Genre: Language Use in Professional Settings*, London: Longman.

Biber, D, Conrad, S, Reppen, R, Byrd, P, Helt, M, Clark, V, Cortes, V, Csomay, E and Urzua, A (2004) *Representing Language Use in the University: Analysis of the TOEFL 2000 Spoken and Written Academic Language Corpus*, ETS TOEFL Monograph Series 25, Princeton, NJ: Educational Testing Service.

Billows, F L (1961) *The Techniques of Language Teaching*, London: Longmans, Green.

Black, E L (1954) *Comprehension Tests for College Education Students*, Slough: National Foundation for Educational Research.

Bleasdale, F A (1987) Concreteness-dependent associative priming, *Journal of Experimental Psychology: Learning, Memory and Cognition* 13, 582–594.

Bloomfield, L (1926) A set of postulates for the science of language, *Language* 2, 153–164.

Bloomfield, L (1933) *Language*, New York: Henry Holt.

Blum-Kulka, S and House, J (1989) Cross-cultural and situational variation in requesting behavior, in Blum-Kulka, S and Kasper, G (Eds) *Cross-cultural pragmatics: Requests and apologies*, Norwood, NJ: Ablex, 123–154.

Bond, O F (1953) *The Reading Method: An Experiment in College French*, Chicago: University of Chicago Press.

Bond, T G and Fox, C M (2001) *Applying the Rasch Model*, NJ: Lawrence Erlbaum Associates.

Boroughs, R (2003) *The change process at paper level. Paper 4, Listening*, in Weir, C J and Milanovic, M (Eds) *Continuity and Innovation: Revising the Cambridge Proficiency in English Examination 1913–2002*, Studies in Language Testing volume 15, Cambridge: UCLES/Cambridge University Press, 315–366.

Bossers, B (1992) *Reading in Two Languages: A Study of Reading Comprehension in Dutch as A Second Language and in Turkish as a First Language*, Rotterdam: Drukkerij Van Driel.

Boyle, J P (1986) Testing language with students of literature in ESL situations, in Brumfit, C and Carter, R (Eds), *Literature and language teaching*, Oxford: Oxford University Press, 199–207.

Boyle, J P and Suen, D L K (1994) Communicative considerations in a large-scale listening test, in Boyle, J P and Falvey, P (Eds) *English Language Testing in Hong Kong*, Hong Kong: The Chinese University Press, 32–55.

Brereton, J L (1944) *The Case for Examinations*, Cambridge: Cambridge University Press.

Bridges, G (2010) Demonstrating cognitive validity of IELTS Academic Writing Task 1, *Research Notes* 42, 24–33.

Brindley, G (1998) Assessing listening abilities, *Annual Review of Applied Linguistics* 18, 171–191.

Brindley, G and Nunan, D (1992) *Draft Bandscales for listening, IELTS Research Project No. 1*, Sydney: National Centre for English Language Teaching and Research.

Brindley, G and Slatyer, H (2002) Exploring task difficulty in ESL listening assessment, *Language Testing* 19 (4), 369–394.

Britton, J N (1963) Experimental marking of English compositions written by fifteen year olds, *Educational Review* 16 (1), 17–23.

Britton, J N, Martin, N C and Rosen, H (1966). Multiple marking of English compositions: an account of an experiment, *Schools Council Examinations Bulletin* 12.

Britton, J N, Burgess, T, Martin, N C, McLeod, A and Rosen, H (1975) *The Development of Writing Abilities (11–18)*, Illinois: Mcmillan.

Brooks, R (2009) Interacting in pairs in a test of oral proficiency: Co-constructing a better performance, *Language Testing* 26 (3), 341–366.

Brooks, N (1960) *Language and Language Learning; Theory and Practice*, New York: Harcourt, Brace.

Brooks, V (1980) *Improving the reliability of essay marking. A survey of the literature with particular reference to the English language composition*, unpublished PhD thesis, University of Leicester.

Brown, A L (1992) Design experiments: Theoretical and methodological challenges in creating complex interventions in classroom settings, *The Journal of the Learning Sciences* 2 (2), 141–178.

Brown, A L (1995) The effect of rater variables in the development of an occupation-specific language performance test, *Language Testing* 12 (1), 1–15.

Brown, A L (2003) Interviewer variation in the co-construction of speaking proficiency, *Language Testing* 20 (1), 1–25.

Brown, A L and Day, J D (1983) Macrorules for summarizing texts: The development of expertise, *Journal of Verbal Learning and Verbal Behaviour* 22 (1), 1–14.

Brown, A L and McNamara, T (2004) The devil is in the detail: Researching gender issues in language assessment, *TESOL Quarterly* 38 (3), 524–538.

Brown, G T L (1987) 25 years of teaching listening comprehension, *English Teaching Forum* 25 (1), 11–15.

Brown, G T L (1990/1996) *Listening to Spoken English* (2nd edition), Harrow: Longman.

Brown, G T L and Yule, G (1983) *Teaching the Spoken Language: An Approach Based on the Analysis of Conversational English*, Cambridge: Cambridge University Press.

Brown, J D and Hudson, T (1998) The Alternatives in Language Assessment, *TESOL Quarterly* 32 (4), 653–675.

Brown, P and Levinson, S C (1987) *Politeness. Some Universals in Language Usage,* Cambridge: Cambridge University Press.

Brumfit, C J and Johnson, K (Eds) (1979) *The Communicative Approach to Language Teaching*, Oxford: Oxford University Press.

Brutt-Griffler, J (2002) *World English: A Study in its Development*, Clevedon: Multilingual Matters.

Buck, G (1989) Written tests of pronunciation: Do they work?, *ELT Journal* 43, 50–56.

Buck, G (1990) *The testing of second language listening comprehension*, unpublished PhD thesis, Lancaster University.

Buck, G (1991) The testing of listening comprehension: An introspective study, *Language Testing* 8 (1), 67–91.

Buck, G (1992a) Listening comprehension: Construct validity and trait characteristics, *Language Learning* 42 (3), 313–357.

Buck, G (1992b) Translation as a language testing procedure: does it work? *Language Testing* 9 (2), 123–148.

Buck, G (1995) How to become a good listening teacher, in Mendelson, D and Rubin, J (Eds) *A Guide for the Teaching of Second Language Listening*, San Diego, CA: Dominie Press.

Buck, G (2001) *Assessing Listening*, Cambridge: Cambridge University Press.

Buck, G and Tatsuoka, K (1998) Application of rule-space methodology to listening test data, *Language Testing* 15, 119–157.

Bung, K (1973) *The Foreign Language Needs of Hotel Waiters and Staff, CCC/ EES 16*, Strasbourg: Council of Europe.

Buros, O K (1978) *The Eighth Mental Measurements Yearbook*, University of Nebraska Press.

Burt, C L (1921) *Mental and Scholastic Tests*, London: London County Council.

Bygate, M (1987) *Speaking*, Oxford: Oxford University Press.

Calfee, R and Hiebert, E (1991) Classroom assessment of reading, in Barr, R, Kamil, R M L, Mosenthal, P B and Pearson, P D (Eds) *Handbook of Reading Research, volume 2*, New Jersey: Lawrence Erlbaum Associates, 281–309.

Call, M E (1985) Auditory short-term memory, listening comprehension and the input hypothesis, *TESOL Quarterly* 19 (4), 765–781.

Calver, L and Bell, C (2010) *CAE Annual Speaking Report 2009*, Cambridge ESOL internal publication.

Campbell, R and Wales, R (1970) The study of language acquisition, in Lyons, J (Ed.) *New Horizons in Linguistics*, Harmondsworth: Penguin, 242–260.

Campion, M and Elley, W (1971) *An Academic Vocabulary List*, NZCER: Wellington.

Canale, M (1983) From communicative competence to communicative language pedagogy, in Richards, J C and Schmidt, R W (Eds) *Language and Communication*, London: Longman, 2–27.

Canale, M and Swain, M (1980) Theoretical bases of communicative approaches to second language teaching and testing, *Applied Linguistics* 1 (1), 1–47.

Candlin, C (Ed.) (1981) *The Communicative Teaching of English: Principles and an exercise typology*, Harlow: Longman.

Candlin, C (1986) Explaining communicative competence limits of testability, in Stanfield, C W (Ed.) *Toward Communicative Competence Testing: Proceedings of the Second TOEFL Invitational Conference*, Princeton, New Jersey: ETS, 38–57.

Carpenter, P A and Just, M A (1975) Sentence comprehension: a psycholinguistic processing model of verification, *Psychological Review* 82, 45–73.

Carrell, P (1984) The effects of rhetorical organisation on ESL readers, *TESOL Quarterly* 18 (3), 441–469.

Carrell, P, Devine, J and Eskey, D (1988) *Interactive Approaches to Second Language Reading*, New York: Cambridge University Press.

Carroll, B J (1961) *Research on Teaching Foreign Languages*, Ann Arbor: University of Michigan Press.

Carroll, B J (1980) *Testing Communicative Performance: An Interim Study*, Oxford: Pergamon.

Carroll, J B (1981) Twenty-five years of research on foreign language aptitude, in Diller, K C (Ed.) *Individual Differences and Universals in Language Learning Aptitude*, Rowley, MA: Newbury House, 83–118.

Carroll, J B (1990) Cognitive abilities in foreign language aptitude: Then and now, in Parry, T S and Stansfield, C W (Eds) *Language Aptitude Reconsidered*, Englewood Cliffs, NJ: Prentice Hall, 11–29.

Carroll, J B and Sapon, S (1959) *Modern Language Aptitude Test—Form A*, New York: Psychological Corporation.

Carroll, J B and Sapon, S (1967) *Elementary Modern Language Aptitude Test*, San Antonio, TX: Psychological Corporation.

Carter, R and Long, M (1991) *Teaching Literature*, Harlow: Longman.

Carter R and McCarthy M (1997) *Exploring Spoken English*, Cambridge: Cambridge University Press.

Cartledge, H A (1954) Conversation Groups, *English Language Teaching Journal* 8 (3), 90–97.

Carver, R P (1992) Reading rate: Theory, research and practical implications, *Journal of Reading* 36, 84–95.

Cast, B M D (1939) The efficiency of different methods of marking English composition. Part I, *British Journal of Educational Psychology* 9 (1), 257–69.

Chalhoub-Deville, M (1997) Theoretical models, assessment frameworks and test construction, *Language Testing* 14, 3–22.

Chalhoub-Deville, M (2003) Second language interaction: Current perspectives and future trends, *Language Testing* 20 (4), 369–383.

Chalhoub-Deville, M and Deville, C (2005) A look back at and forward to what language testers measure, in Hinkel, E (Ed.) *Handbook of Research in Second Language Teaching and Learning*, Mahwah, NJ: Lawrence Erlbaum, 815–831.

Chalhoub-Deville, M and Turner, C (2000) What to look for in ESL admission tests: Cambridge certificate exams, IELTS, and TOEFL, *System* 28, 523–539.

Chambers, L, Galaczi, E D and Gilbert, S (2012) Test-taker familiarity in speaking tests: Does it make a difference? *Research Notes* 49, 33–40.

Chamot, A U and El-Dinary, P B (1999) Children's learning strategies in language immersion classrooms, *Modern Language Journal* 83 (3), 319–338.

Chamot, A U and O'Malley, J M (1994) *The CALLA Handbook: Implementing the Cognitive Academic Language Learning Approach*, Reading, MA: Addison-Wesley.

Chaplen, E F (1970) *The identification of non-native speakers of English likely to under-achieve in university courses through inadequate command of the language*, unpublished PhD thesis, University of Manchester.

Chaplen, E F (1971) *An appraisal of the Syndicate's written examinations in English as a Foreign Language together with some suggested modifications*, internal UCLES report.

Charge, N and Taylor, L B (1997) Recent developments in IELTS, *ELT Journal* 51 (4), 374–380.

Chaytor, H J (1945) *From Script to Print: An Introduction to Medieval Vernacular Literature*, Cambridge: Heffer & Sons.

Cheng, L (2008) The key to success: English language testing in China, *Language Testing* 25 (1), 15–37.

Chihara, T, Sakurai, T and Oller, J (1989) Background and culture as factors in EFL reading comprehension, *Language Testing* 6 (2), 143–151.

Cipolla, C M (1969) *Literacy and Development in the West*, Hamondsworth: Penguin Books.

Clapham, C (1996) *The Development of IELTS: A Study of the Effect of Background on Reading Comprehension*, Studies in Language Testing volume 4, Cambridge: UCLES/Cambridge University Press.

Clark, J L D (1978a) *Direct Testing of Speaking Proficiency: Theory and Application*, Princeton, NJ: Educational Testing Service.

Clark, J L D (1978b) Interview Testing Research at Educational Testing Service, in Clark, J L D (Ed.) *Direct Testing of Speaking Proficiency: Theory and Application*, Princeton, NJ: Educational Testing Service, 211–229.

Clark, J L D (1979) Direct vs. Semi-direct tests of speaking ability, in Briere, E J and Hinofotis, F B (Eds) *Concepts in Language Testing: Some Recent Studies*, Washington DC: TESOL, 35–49.

Clark, J L D (1983) Language Testing: Past and Current Status – Directions for the Future, *The Modern Language Journal* 67 (4), 431–443.

Clark, J L D and Clifford R T (1988) The FSI/ILR/ACTFL proficiency scales and testing techniques, *Studies in Second Language Acquisition* 10, 129–147.

Clark, J L D and Swinton, S S (1979) *An Exploration of Speaking Proficiency Measures in the TOEFL Context, TOEFL Research Reports*, Princeton: Educational Testing Service.

Clifford, R T (1978) Reliability and validity of language aspects contributing to oral proficiency of prospective teachers of German, in Clark, J L D (Ed.) *Direct Testing of Speaking Proficiency: Theory and Application*, Princeton, NJ: Educational Testing Service, 191–211.

Cobb, T (2003) *VocabProfile. The Compleat Lexical Tutor*, available online: www.lextutor.ca

Cohen, A (1984) On taking language tests: what the students report, *Language Testing* 1 (1), 70–82.

Collie, J and Slater, S (1987) *Literature in the Language Classroom*, Cambridge: Cambridge University Press.

Coltheart, M (1981) The MRC Psycholinguistic Database, *Quarterly Journal of Experimental Psychology* 33, 497–505.

Committee on Resolutions and Investigations (CORI) (1917) Report of Committee on Resolutions and Investigations Appointed by the Association of Modern Language Teachers of the Middle States and Maryland, *The Modern Language Journal* 1 (7), 250–261.

Committee to enquire into the position of modern languages in the educational system of Great Britain (Committee GB) (1918) *Report of the committee appointed by the Prime Minister to enquire into the position of modern languages in the educational system of Great Britain*, London: His Majesty's Stationery Office.

Conant, J B (1934) Notes and News: President Conant speaks again, *Modern Language Journal* 19: 465–6.

Council of Europe (2001) *Common European Framework of Reference for Languages: Learning, Teaching, Assessment*, Cambridge: Cambridge University Press.

Council of Europe (2008) *Relating Language Examinations to the Common European Framework of Reference for Languages: Learning, Teaching, Assessment*, available online: www.coe.int/t/dg4/portfolio/documents/exampleswriting.pdf

Coupland, N, Coupland, J and Giles, H (1991) *Language, society and the elderly*, Oxford: Blackwell.

Courchene, R J and de Bagheera, J (1985) A theoretical framework for the development of performance tests, in Hauptman, P C, Le Blanc, R and Wesche, M B (Eds) *Second Language Performance Testing*, Ottawa: University of Ottawa Press, 45–58.

Courtis, S A (1914) Standard tests in English, *The Elementary School Teacher* 14 (8), 374–392.

Courtis, S A (1917) The problem of measuring ability in silent reading, *School Board Journal* 54, 17–18; 81.

Coxhead, A (2000) A new academic word list, *TESOL Quarterly* 34 (2), 213–238.

Cranney, A G and Miller, J S (1987) History of reading: Status and sources of a growing field, *Journal of Reading* 30 (5), 388–398.

Criper, C and Davies, A (1988) *Research Report 1: ELTS Validation Project Report*, the British Council and the University of Cambridge Local Examinations Syndicate.

Crofts, J M and Caradog Jones, D (1928) *Secondary School Examination Statistics*, London: Longmans.

Crossley, S A and McNamara, D S (2008) Assessing L2 reading texts at the intermediate level: An approximate replication of Crossley, Louwerse, McCarthy & McNamara (2007), *Language Teaching* 41(3), 409–429.

Crossley, S A Greenfield, J and McNamara, D S (2008) Assessing text readability using cognitively based indices, *TESOL Quarterly* 42 (3), 475–493.

Crossley, S A, Louwerse, M M, McCarthy, P M and McNamara, D S (2007) A linguistic analysis of simplified and authentic texts, *Modern Language Journal* 91(2), 15–30.

Crystal, D (1997) *English as a Global Language*, Cambridge: Cambridge University Press.

Cumming, A, Grant, L, Mulcahy-Ernt, P and Powers, D (2004) A teacher-verification study of speaking and writing prototype tasks for a new TOEFL, *Language Testing* 21(2), 107–145.

Cumming, A, Kantor, R, Baba, K, Eedosy, U, Eouanzoui, K and James, M (2005) Differences in written discourse in independent and integrated prototype tasks for next generation TOEFL, *Assessing Writing* 10, 5–43.

Danziger, K (1990) *Constructing the subject: Historical Origins of Psychological Research.* Cambridge: Cambridge University Press.

Darian, S G (1969) Backgrounds of modern language teaching: Sweet, Jespersen and Palmer, *Modern Language Journal* 53 (8), 545–550.

Davey, B and Lasasso, C (1984) The interaction of reader and task factors in the assessment of reading comprehension, *Experimental Education* 52 (4), 199–206.

Davies, A (1978) Language testing. Survey article Part I and II, *Language Teaching and Linguistics Abstracts* 113 (4), 145–59, 215–31.

Davies, A (1981) Reaction to the Palmer and Bachman and the Vollmer Papers (2) in Alderson, J C and Hughes, A (Eds), *Issues in language testing, ELT Documents* 111, 182–186.

Davies, A (1984) Validating three tests of English language proficiency, *Language Testing* 1 (1), 50–69.

Davies, A (1987) Certificate of Proficiency in English, in Alderson, J C, Krahnke, K J and Stansfield, C W (Eds) *Reviews of English Language Proficiency Tests*, Washington, DC: TESOL, 20–21.

Davies, A (2003) *The Native Speaker: Myth or Reality*, London: Multilingual Matters Ltd.

Davies, A (2008a) Textbook trends in teaching language testing, *Language Testing* 25 (3), 327–347.

Davies, A (2008b) *Assessing Academic English: Testing English Proficiency 1950–1989 – the IELTS Solution,* Studies in Language Testing volume 23, Cambridge: UCLES/Cambridge University Press.

Davies, A (2012) Kane, validity and soundness, *Language Testing* 29 (1), 37–42.

Davis, L (2009) The influence of interlocutor proficiency in paired oral assessment, *Language Testing* 26 (3), 367–396.

de Cervantes, M (1605) *The Ingenious Hidalgo Don Quixote of La Mancha (El ingenioso hidalgo don Quijote de la Mancha)*.

Decker, W C (1925) Oral and Aural Tests as Integral Parts of the Regents' Examination, *The Modern Language Journal* 9 (5), 369–371.

De Swaan, A (2001) *Words of the World* Cambridge: Polity.

Diederich, P, French, S and Carlton, S (1961) *Factors in Judgments of Writing Ability*, Research Bulletin 61–15, Princeton, N.J.: Educational Testing Service.

Douglas, D (2000) *Assessing Language for Specific Purposes*, Cambridge: Cambridge University Press.

Drew, E (1935) The Essay, in Drew, E (Ed.) *The Enjoyment of Literature*, W W Norton & Company Inc, 38–61.

Ducasse, A M and Brown, A (2009) Assessing paired orals: Raters' orientation to interaction, *Language Testing* 26 (3), 423–443.

Dunkel, P A (1991) Listening in the native and second/foreign language: Toward an integration of research and practice, *TESOL Quarterly* 25, 431–457.

Ebel, R L and Frisbie, D A (1986) *Essentials of Educational Measurement* (4th edition), Englewood Cliffs, NJ: Prentice-Hall, Inc.

Eckersley, C E (1938–42) *Essential English for Foreign Students*, Volumes 1–4, London: Longmans, Green.

Ede, L and Lunsford, A (1985) Let them write-together, *English Quarterly* 18, 119–127.

Edgeworth, F Y (1888) *The Statistics of Examinations*, Journal of the Royal Statistical Society, LI, 599–635.

Edgeworth, F Y (1890) The element of chance in competitive examinations, *Journal of the Royal Statistical Society* 53, 460–75 and 644–63.

Editorial (1980) Why comprehension? *Reading Research Quarterly* 15 (2), 181–182.

Educational Testing Service (2004) *Mapping Test Scores onto the Common European Framework (CEF)*, available online: www.ets.org/ell/cef.html

Educational Testing Service (1997) *TOEFL Test and Score Manual*, Princeton, NJ: Educational Testing Service.

Eger, N, Ball, L J, Stevens, R and Dodd, J (2007) Cueing retrospective verbal reports in usability testing through eye-movement replay, in Ball, L J, Sasse, M A, Sas, C, Ormerod, T C, Dix, A, Bagnall, P and McEwan, T (Eds) *People and Computers XXI – HCI . . . but not as we know it: Proceedings of HCI 2007*, Swindon: The British Computer Society.

Együd, G and Glover, P (2001) Oral testing in pairs – a secondary school perspective, *English Language Teaching Journal* 55 (1), 70–76.

Ehrlich, M (1991) The processing of cohesion devices in text comprehension, *Psychological Research* 53 (2), 169–174.

Elbow, P (1973) *Writing without Teachers*, New York: Oxford University Press.

Elliott, M and Wilson, J (2013) Context validity, in Geranpayeh, A and Taylor, L (Eds) *Examining Listening: Research and Practice in Assessing Second Language Listening*, Studies in Language Testing volume 35, Cambridge: UCLES/Cambridge University Press, 152–241.

Ellis, R and Yuan, F (2004) The effects of planning on fluency, complexity and accuracy in second language narrative writing, *Studies in Second Language Acquisition* 26 (1), 59–84.

Emig, J (1971) *The Composing Processes of Twelfth Graders*, Urbana: NCTE.

Enright, M, Grabe, W, Koda, K, Mosenthal, P, Mulcany-Ernt, P and Schedl, M (2000) TOEFL 2000 Reading Framework: A Working Paper, *TOEFL Monograph Series 17*, Princeton, NJ: ETS.

Eom, M (2006) *An investigation of operationalized constructs of second language listening tests*, unpublished PhD thesis, University of Iowa.

Ericsson, K A, Charness, N, Feltovich, P J and Hoffman, R R (Eds) (2006) *The Cambridge Handbook of Expertise and Expert Performance*, Cambridge: Cambridge University Press.

Ewing, N R (1949) Trends in modern language teaching, *Educational Review 1*, 147–57.

Falvey, P (2008) English language examinations, in Raban, S (Ed.) *Examining the World*, Cambridge: Cambridge University Press, 131–157.

Falvey, P and Shaw, S D (2005) IELTS Writing: revising assessment criteria and scales (Phase 5), *Research Notes 23*, 7–13.

Farr, R, Carey, R, and Tone, B (1986) Recent theory and research into the reading process: implications for reading assessment, in Orasanu, J (Ed.) *Reading Comprehension: from Research to Practice*, New Jersey: Lawrence Erlbaum Associates, 135–149.

Farr, R, Pritchard, R and Smitten, B (1990) A description of what happens when an examinee takes a multiple-choice reading comprehension test, *Journal of Educational Measurement 27* (3), 209–226.

Faucett, L W (1933–1934) *The Oxford English Course. 4 vols*. London: Oxford University Press.

Faucett, L W, Palmer, H E, Thorndike, E L and West, M P (1936) *Interim Report on Vocabulary Selection for the Teaching of English as a Foreign Language*, London: King.

Ferreira-Buckley, L and Horner, W B (2001) Writing instruction in Great Britain: The eighteenth and nineteenth centuries, in Murphy, J J (Ed.) *A Short History of Writing Instruction from Ancient Greece to Modern America*, NJ: Lawrence Erlbaum, 173–212.

ffrench, A (2001) *Revised Certificate of Proficiency Speaking Test Assessment Criteria Validation Study*, internal UCLES report.

ffrench, A (2003) The change process at the paper level. Paper 5, Speaking, in Weir, C and Milanovic, M (Eds) *Continuity and Innovation: Revising the Cambridge Proficiency in English Examination 1913–2002*, Studies in Language Testing volume 15, Cambridge: UCLES/Cambridge University Press, 367–473.

ffrench, A and Gutch, A (2006) *FCE/CAE Modifications: Building the validity argument: Application of Weir's socio-cognitive framework to FCE & CAE*, Cambridge ESOL internal report.

Fick, J C (1793) *Praktische englische Sprachlehre für Deutsche beyderley Geschlechts. Nach der in Meidingers französischen Grammatik befolgten Methode. ["Practical English Language Textbook for Germans of Both Sexes. Following the Method Used in Meidinger"s French Grammar"]* Erlangen: Walther.

Field, J (1998) Skills and strategies: Towards a new methodology for listening, *English Language Teaching Journal 52* (2), 110–118.

Field J (2001) *Lexical segmentation in first and foreign language listening*, unpublished PhD thesis, University of Cambridge.

Field, J (2004) *Psycholinguistics. The key concepts*, London: Routledge.

Field, J (2008) *Listening in the Language Classroom*, Cambridge: Cambridge University Press.

Field, J (2009) T*he cognitive validity of the lecture-based question in the IELTS Listening paper*, IELTS Jointly Funded and Published Research Volume 9, University of Cambridge ESOL Examinations, available online: www.ielts. org/PDF/Vol9_Report1.pdf

Field, J (2011) Cognitive validity, in Taylor, L (Ed.) *Examining Speaking: Research and practice in assessing second language speaking*, Studies in Language Testing volume 30, Cambridge: UCLES/Cambridge University Press, 65–110.

Field, J (2013) Cognitive validity, in Geranpayeh, A and Taylor, L (Eds) *Examining Listening: Research and Practice in Assessing Second Language Listening*, Studies in Language Testing volume 35, Cambridge: UCLES/ Cambridge University Press, 77–151.

Finlayson, D L (1951) The reliability of the marking of essays, *British Journal of Educational Psychology* 21 (2), 126–34.

Flower, L and Hayes, J R (1981) A cognitve process theory of writing, *College Composition and Communication* 32, 365–387.

Foden, F (1989) *The Examiner. James Booth and the Origins of Common Examinations*, Leeds: Studies in Adult and Continuing Education.

Fodor, J A and Garrett, M (1967) Some syntactic determinants of sentential complexity *Perception and Psychophysics* 2, 289–296.

Folland, D and Robertson, D (1976) Towards objectivity in group oral testing, *English Language Teaching Journal* 30, 156–167.

Fortus, R, Coriat, R and Fund, S (1998) Prediction of item difficulty in the English subtest of Israel's inter-university psychometric entrance test, in Kunnan, A (Ed.) *Validation in Language Assessment: Selected Papers from the 17th Language Research Colloquium*, Long Beach, Mahwah, New Jersey: Lawrence Erlbaum, 61–87.

Foucault, M (1979) *Discipline and Punish: The Birth of Prison*, New York: Vintage.

Fox, J (2004) Biasing for the best in language testing and learning: An interview with Merrill Swain, *Language Assessment Quarterly* 1 (4), 235–251.

Francis, J C (1978) *An Investigation into the Reliability of Impression and Analytic Marking Methods in the Oral Test in Italian at Ordinary Level*, MS, Aldershot: Associated Examining Board.

Freedle, R and Kostin, I (1993) The Prediction of TOEFL Reading Comprehension Item Difficulty for Expository Prose Passages for Three Item Types: Main Idea, Inference, and Supporting Idea Items, *TOEFL Research Reports*, RR-93-44, Princeton, NJ: Educational Testing Service.

Freedle, R and Kostin, I (1994) Can multiple choice reading tests be construct valid?, *Psychological Science* 5, 107–110.

Freedle, R and Kostin, I (1999) Does the text matter in a multiple-choice test of comprehension? The case for the construct validity of TOEFL's minitalks, *Language Testing* 16 (1), 2–35.

Fries, C (1945) *Teaching and Learning English as a Foreign Language*, Michigan: Michigan University Press.

Fries, C C and Lado, R (1962) *English Sentence Patterns, Understanding and Producing Grammatical Structures*, Ann Arbor: University of Michigan Press.

Fulcher, G (1987) Tests of oral performance: the need for data-based criteria, *English Language Teaching Journal* 41 (4), 287–291.

Fulcher, G (1996a) Does thick description lead to smart tests? A data-based approach to rating scale construction, *Language Testing* 13 (2), 208–238.

Fulcher, G (1996b) Testing tasks: issues in task design and the group oral, *Language Testing* 13 (1), 23–53.

Fulcher, G (1999) Review of Barnwell, D. P. 1996: A History of Foreign Language Testing in the United States: from its beginnings to the present. Tempe, Arizona: Bilingual Press, *Language Testing* 16 (3), 389–394.

Fulcher, G (2000) The 'communicative' legacy in language testing, *System* 28, 483–497.

Fulcher, G (2003) *Testing Second Language Speaking*, London: Longman Pearson Education.

Fulcher, G, Davidson, F and Kemp, J (2011) Effective rating scale development for speaking tests: Performance decision trees, *Language Testing* 28 (5), 5–29.

Furneaux, C and Rignall, M (2000) *The effect of standardisation-training on rater-judgements for the IELTS Writing Module*, Reading: University of Reading.

Galaczi, E D (2003) Interaction in a paired speaking test: the case of the First Certificate in English, *Research Notes* 14, 19–23.

Galaczi, E D (2008) Peer-peer interaction in a speaking test: The case of the First Certificate in English examination, *Language Assessment Quarterly* 5 (2), 89–119.

Galaczi, E D (2010a) Face-to-face and computer-based assessment of speaking: Challenges and opportunities, in Araújo, L (Ed.) *Computer-based assessment of foreign language speaking skills*, Luxemburg: Publications Office of the European Union, 29–51.

Galaczi, E D (2010b) *Interactional competence across proficiency levels*, Oral presentation at the 32nd Language Testing Research Colloquium, University of Cambridge, UK, April 2010.

Galaczi, E D and ffrench, A (2007) Developing revised assessment scales for Main Suite and BEC Speaking tests, *Research Notes* 30, 28–31.

Galaczi, E D and ffrench, A (2011) Context validity, in Taylor, L (Ed.) *Examining Speaking: Research and practice in assessing second language speaking*, Studies in Language Testing volume 30, Cambridge: UCLES/ Cambridge University Press, 112–170.

Galaczi, E D, ffrench, A, Hubbard, C and Green, A (2011) Developing assessment scales for large-scale speaking tests: A multiple-method approach, *Assessment in Education* 18 (3), 217–237.

Gan, Z, Davison, C and Hamp-Lyons, L (2008) Topic Negotiation in Peer Group Oral Assessment Situations: A Conversation Analytic Approach, *Applied Linguistics* 30 (3), 315–334.

Garnham, A (1985) *Psycholinguistics: Central Topics*, London: Routledge.

George, H V (1962) Testing – Another Point of View, *English Language Teaching Journal* 16 (2), 72–77.

Geranpayeh, A (2000) *Language Proficiency Testing: A comparative analysis of IELTS and TOEFL*, unpublished PhD thesis, University of Edinburgh.

Geranpayeh, A (2005) *Building the construct model for the CAE examinations*, Cambridge ESOL internal report.

Geranpayeh, A (2007) Using Structural Equation Modelling to facilitate the revision of high stakes testing: the case of CAE, *Research Notes* 30, 8–12.

Geranpayeh, A and Kunnan, A J (2007) Differential item functioning in terms of age in the Certificate of Academic English Exam, *Language Assessment Quarterly* 4, 190–222.

Geranpayeh, A and Somers, A (2006a). *Building the construct model for the FCE examinations*, Cambridge ESOL internal report.

Geranpayeh, A and Somers, A (2006b) *Testing the construct model for the CAE examinations*, Cambridge ESOL internal report.

Geranpayeh, A and Somers, A (2006c) *Testing the construct model for the FCE examinations*, Cambridge ESOL internal report.

Geranpayeh, A and Taylor, L (Eds) (2013) *Examining Listening: Research and practice in assessing second language listening*, Studies in Language Testing volume 35, Cambridge: UCLES/Cambridge University Press.

Gernsbacher, M A (1990) *Language Comprehension as Structure Building*, Mahwah, NJ: Erlbaum.

Gilbert, M (1953) The origins of the reform movement in modern language teaching in England (Part 1), *Durham Research Review* 4, 1–9.

Gillard, D (2011) *Education in England: a Brief History*, availalable online: www.educationengland.org.uk/

Glaser, R (1991) Expertise and assessment, in Wittrock, M C and Baker, E L (Eds) *Testing and Cognition*, Englewood Cliffs: Prentice Hall, 17–30.

Godshalk, F I, Swineford, F and Coffman, W E (1966) *The Measurement of Writing Ability*. New York: College Entrance Examination Board.

Goh, S (1990) The effects of rhetorical organisation in expository prose on ESL readers in Singapore, *RELC Journal* 21 (2), 1–13.

Goldman, S and Rakestraw, J (2000) Structural aspects of constructing meaning from text, in Kamil, M, Rosenthal, P, Pearson, P and Barr, R (Eds) *Handbook of Reading Research*, Mahwah, NJ: Lawrence Erlbaum, 331–335.

Grabe W (2009) Teaching and testing reading, in Long, M H and Doughty, C J (Eds), *The Handbook of Language Teaching*, Chichester: Wiley-Blackwell, 441–462.

Grabe, W and Stoller, F L (2002) *Teaching and Researching Reading*, London: Longman.

Graddol, D (1997) *The Future of English?* London: British Council.

Graddol, D (2006) *English Next: Why Global English May Mean the End of English as a Foreign Language*, London: The British Council.

Graesser, A C, Karnavat, A B, Daniel, F K, Cooper, E, Whitten, S N and Louwerse, M (2001) A computer tool to improve questionnaire design, in *Statistical Policy Working Paper 33, Federal Committee on Statistical Methodology*, Washington, DC: Bureau of Labor Statistics, 36–48.

Graesser, A C, McNamara, D S and Kulikowich, J M (2011) Coh-Metrix: Providing multilevel analyses of text characteristics, *Educational Researcher* 40 (5), 223–234.

Graesser, A McNamara, D, Louwerse, M and Cai, Z (2004) Coh-Metrix: Analysis of text on cohesion and language, *Behavioral Research Methods, Instruments, and Computers* 36, 193–202.

Graham, S (2006) Writing, in Alexander, P and Winne, P (Eds), *Handbook of Educational Psychology*, Mahwah, NJ: Erlbaum, 457–477.

Gray, W S (1915) *Standardized Oral Reading Paragraphs Test*, Bloomington, IL: Public School Publishing Co.

Gray, W S (1917) *Studies of elementary school reading through standardized tests (Supplemental Educational Monographs No. 1)*, Chicago: University of Chicago Press.

Green, A (2007) *IELTS Washback in Context: Preparation for Academic Writing in Higher Education*, Studies in Language Testing volume 25, Cambridge: UCLES/Cambridge University Press.

Green, A (2012) *Language Functions Revisited: Theoretical and Empirical Bases for Language Construct Definition Across the Ability Range*, English Profile Studies volume 2, Cambridge: UCLES/Cambridge University Press.

Green, A and Hawkey, R (2011) An empirical investigation of the process of writing Academic Reading test items for the International English Language Testing System, *IELTS Research Report* 11, 269–372.

Green, A, Unaldi, A and Weir, C J (2010) Empiricism versus Connoisseurship: Establishing the Appropriacy of Texts for Testing Reading for Academic Purposes, *Language Testing* 27 (3), 1–21.

Grellet, F (1981) *Developing Reading Skills*, Cambridge: Cambridge University Press.

Gruba, P A (1999) *The role of digital video media in second language listening comprehension*, unpublished PhD thesis, University of Melbourne.

Gude, K and Duckworth, M (2002) *Proficiency Masterclass: Students Book*, Oxford: Oxford University Press.

Hall, G (2005) *Literature in Language Education*, Hampshire, New York: Palgrave Macmillan.

Halliday, M A K (1970) The form of a functional grammar, in Kress, G. (Ed.) (1976) *Halliday: System and Function in Language*, Oxford: Oxford University Press.

Halliday, M A K (1975) *Learning how to mean,* London: Edward Arnold.

Hamilton, J, Reddel, S and Spratt, M (2001) Teachers' perceptions of on-line rater training and monitoring, *System* 29, 505–520.

Hamp-Lyons, L (1984) *Assessment Guide for M2 Writing*, London: The British Council.

Hamp-Lyons, L (1987) Cambridge First Certificate in English, in Alderson, J C, Krahnke, K J and Stansfield, C W (Eds) *Reviews of English Language Proficiency Tests*, Washington, DC, TESOL, 18–20.

Hamp-Lyons, L (1990) Second language writing: Assessment issues, in Kroll, B (Ed.) *Second Language Writing: Research Insights for the Classroom*, Cambridge: Cambridge University Press, 69–87.

Hamp-Lyons, L (1991) Basic concepts, in Hamp-Lyons, L (Ed.) *Assessing Second Language Writing in Academic Contexts*, Norwood, NJ: Ablex Publishing Corporation, 5–15.

Hamp-Lyons, L (2000) Social, professional and individual responsibility in language testing, *System* 28, 579–591.

Hamp-Lyons, L (2001) Fourth generation writing assessment, in Silva, T and Matsuda, P K (Eds) *On Second Language Writing*, Mahwah, NJ: Lawrence Erlbaum, 117–128.

Hamp-Lyons, L (2002) The scope of writing assessment, *Assessing Writing* 8 (1), 5–16.

Hamp-Lyons, L and Condon, W (2000) *Assessing the Portfolio: Principles for Practice, Theory and Research*, Cresskill, NJ: Hampton Press.

Hansen, C and Jensen, C (1994) Evaluating lecture comprehension, in Flowerdew, J (Ed.) *Academic Listening: Research Perspectives*, Cambridge: Cambridge University Press, 241–268.

Harding, L W (2008) *The use of speakers with L2 accents in academic English listening assessment: A validation study*, unpublished PhD thesis, University of Melbourne.

Harris, D (1969) *Testing English as a Second Language*, New York: McGraw Hill.

Hartog, P J (1918) *Examinations and Their Relation to Culture and Efficiency*, London: Constable.

Hartog P and Rhodes E C (1935) *An Examination of Examinations*, London: Macmillan.

Hartog, P J, Rhodes, E C and Burt, C (1936) *The Marks of Examiners*, London: Macmillan.

Haswell, R H (2004) Post-secondary entry writing placement: A brief synopsis of research, available online: comppile.org/profresources/writingplacement research.htm

Hawkey, R (1982) *An investigation of inter-relationships between cognitive/ affective and social factors and language learning. A longitudinal study of 27 overseas students using English in connection with their training in the United Kingdom*, PhD thesis, University of London.

Hawkey, R (2004) *Specifications describing the construct of both FCE and CAE, making reference where necessary to the FCE revised internal specifications (1994), the CPE revised internal specifications (2000) and Bachman's communicative competence model*, Cambridge ESOL internal document.

Hawkey, R (2005) *A Modular Approach to Testing English Language Skills: The Development of the Certificates in English Language Skills (CELS) Examinations*, Studies in Language Testing Series volume 16, Cambridge: UCLES/Cambridge University Press.

Hawkey, R (2006) *Impact theory and practice: studies of the IELTS test and Progetto Lingue 2000*, Studies in Language Testing volume 24, Cambridge: UCLES/Cambridge University Press.

Hawkey, R (2009) *Examining FCE and CAE: Key Issues and Recurring Themes in Developing the First Certificate in English and Certificate in Advanced English Exams*, Studies in Language Testing volume 28, Cambridge: UCLES/ Cambridge University Press.

Hawkey, R (2011) Consequential validity, in Taylor, (Ed), *Examining Speaking: Research and Practice in Assessing Second Language Speaking*, Studies in Language Testing volume 30, Cambridge: UCLES/Cambridge University Press, 234–258.

Hawkey, R (2013) Consequential validity, in Geranpayeh, A and Taylor, L (Eds) *Examining Listening: Research and Practice in Assessing Second Language Listening*, Studies in Language Testing volume 35, Cambridge: UCLES/ Cambridge University Press, 273–302.

Hawkey, R (n.d.) *A study of the impact of IELTS especially on candidates and teachers*, available online: www.britishcouncil.org/goingglobal-session-21225thursday-elt-roger-hawkey-paper.pdf

Hawkey, R and Milanovic, M (2013) *Cambridge English Exams – The First Hundred Years. A History of English Language Assessment from the University of Cambridge 1913–2013*, Studies in Language Testing volume 38, Cambridge: UCLES/Cambridge University Press.

Hayes, J and Flower, L (1983) Uncovering cognitive process in writing: An introduction to protocol analysis, in Mosenthal, P, Tamor, L and Walmsley, S A (Eds) *Research on Writing: Principles and Methods*, New York: Longman, 207–220.

Haynes, M and Carr, T H (1990) Writing system background and second language reading: a component skills analysis of English reading by native speakers of Chinese, in Carr, T H and Levy, B A (Eds) *Reading and its Development: Component Skills Aapproaches*, San Diego, CA: Academic Press, 375–421.

Head, J J (1966) Multiple marking of an essay item in experimental "0" level Nuffield biology examinations, *Educational Review* 19 (1), 65–71.

Heaton, J B (1975) *Writing English Language Tests*, London: Longman.

Hedge, T (1988) *Writing*, Oxford: Oxford University Press.

Hedge, T (2000) *Teaching and Learning in the Language Classroom*, Oxford: Oxford University Press.

Herzog, M (n.d.) *How did the Language Proficiency Scale Get Started*, retrieved on 15 July 2011 from: <http://www.govtilr.org/Skills/IRL%20Scale%20 History.htm>

Hillegas, M B (1912) *A Scale for the Measurement of Quality in English Composition By Young People*, New York: Teachers College.

Hillocks, G (2008) Writing in secondary schools, in Bazerman, C (Ed.) *Handbook of Research on Writing: History, Society, School, Individual, Text*, NY, London: Lawrence Erlbaum, 311–329.

Hinds, J (1987) Reader versus writer responsibility: a new typology, in Connor, U and Kaplan, R (Eds) *Writing across Languages: Analysis of L2 Text*. Mass: Addison-Wesley, 141–152.

Hobbs, C L and Berlin, J A (2001) *A Century of Writing Instruction in School and College English*. J.J. Murphy, Epilogue.

Hoejke, B and Linnell, K (1994) Authenticity in language testing: Evaluating spoken language tests for international teaching assistants, *TESOL Quarterly* 28 (1), 103–126.

Hoffman, B (1961) *The Tyranny of Testing*, New York: Penguin.

Holmes, J (1989) Sex differences and apologies: One aspect of communicative competence, *Applied Linguistics* 10, 194–213.

Hoover, W and Tunmer, W E (1993) The components of reading, in Thompson, G B, Tunmer, W E and Nicholson, T (Eds) *Reading Acquisition Processes*, Clevedon, England: Multilingual Matters, 1–19.

Hornby, A S (1946a) *First issue of English Language Teaching*, London: Oxford University Press.

Hornby, A S (1946b) Linguistic Pedagogy: I. The Doctrines of de Saussure, *English Language Teaching* 1(1), 7–11.

Hornby, A S (1946c) Linguistic Pedagogy: II. The Beginning Stage, *English Language Teaching* 1 (2), 36–39.

Hornby, A S (1950) The situational approach in language teaching, *ELT Journal* IV (4), 98–103.

Hornby, A S (1954–56) *Oxford Progressive English for Adult Learners*, London: Oxford University Press.

Hornby, A S, Gatenby, E V and Wakefield, H (1948) *A Learner's Dictionary of Current English, [Photographically reprinted from Hornby, Gatenby and Wakefield 1942; subsequently (in 1952) retitled The Advanced Learner's Dictionary of Current English]*, London: Oxford University Press.

Horner, W B (1990) The roots of modern writing instruction: eighteenth- and nineteenth-century Britain, *Rhetoric Review* 8 (2), 322–345.

Hosenfeld, C (1977) A preliminary investigation of the reading strategies of successful and nonsuccessful second language learners, *System* 5 (2), 110–123.

Howatt, A P R (1984) *A History of English Language Teaching*, Oxford: Oxford University Press.

Howatt, A P R (1997) Talking shop: transformation and change in ELT, *English Language Teaching Journal* 51 (3), 263–268.

Howatt, A P R and Widdowson, H G (2004) *A History of English Language Teaching* (second edition), Oxford: Oxford University Press.

Hudson, R (1991) *English Word Grammar*, Cambridge, Mass: Blackwell.

Hudson, T (1996) *Assessing second language academic reading from a communicative competence perspective: Relevance for TOEFL 2000*, TOEFL Monograph Series MS-4, Princeton, NJ: Educational Testing Service.

Hughes, A (1981) Reaction to the Palmer and Bachman and the Vollmer Papers (I), in Alderson, J C and Hughes, A (Eds) *Issues in language testing, ELT Documents*, 111, 152–174. London: The British Council.

Hughes, A (1989) *Testing for Language Teachers*, Cambridge: Cambridge University Press.

Hughes, A (2003) *Testing for Language Teachers* (2nd edition), Cambridge: Cambridge University Press.

Huot, B, O'Neill, P and Moore, C (2010) A usable past for writing assessment, *College English* 72 (5), 495–517.

Hutchison, K A (2003) Is semantic priming due to association strength or to feature overlap? A micro-analytic review, *Psychonomic bulletin and review* 10, 785–813.

Huxley, A (1958) *Collected Essays*, Chatto & Windus: London.

Hyland, K (2002) *Teaching and Researching Writing, Applied Linguistics in Action Series*, London: Longman.

Hymes, D (1972) On communicative competence, in Pride, J B and Holmes, J (Eds) *Sociolinguistics*, Harmondsworth: Penguin.

Hymes, D (1974) *Foundations in Sociolinguistics: An Ethnographic Approach*, Philadelphia: University of Pennsylvania Press.

In'nami, Yo (2007) *The effects of task types on listening test performance: a quantitative and qualitative study*, unpublished PhD thesis, University of Tsukuba, Japan.

Interagency Language Roundtable, *Descriptions of Proficiency Levels*, available online: www.govtilr.org/Skills/ILRscale1.htm

International Phonetics Association (1878) *Articles*, London: International Phonetics Association.

International Reading Association (2004) *Standards for Reading Professionals— Revised 2003 : A Reference for the Preparation of Educators in the United States*. Developed by the Professional Standards and Ethics Committee of the International Reading Association located at http://www.reading.org/downloads/resources/545standards2003/index.html

Iwashita, N (1998) The validity of the paired interview format in oral performance assessment, *Melbourne Papers in Language Testing* 5 (2), 51–65.

Iwashita, N, Brown, A, McNamara, T and O'Hagan, S (2008) Assessed levels of second language speaking proficiency: How distinct?, *Applied Linguistics* 29 (1), 24–49.

Iwashita, N, McNamara, T and Elder, C (2001) Can we predict task difficulty in an oral proficiency test? Exploring the potential of an information-processing approach to test design, *Language Learning* 51 (3), 401–436.

Jacobs, H L, Zinkgraf, D R, Wormuth, V F, Hartfiel, V F and Hughey, J B (1981) *Testing ESL Composition: A Practical Approach*, Rowley, MA: Newbury House.

Jacoby, S and McNamara, T (1999) Locating Competence, *English for Specific Purposes* 18 (3), 213–241.

James, G C A (1988) *Considerations in the design of an oral test in English for Academic Purposes*, unpublished doctoral thesis, University of Exeter, available online: /ethos.bl.uk/OrderDetails.do?did=5&uin=uk.bl.ethos.534676

Jarvella, R J (1971) Syntactic processing of connected speech, *Journal of Verbal Learning and Verbal Behaviour* 10, 409–416.

Jespersen, O (1904) *How to Teach a Foreign Language*, London: G. Allen & Unwin.

Johnson, K (1982) *Communicative Syllabus Design and Methodology*, Oxford: Pergamon.

Johnson, M (2001) *The art of non-conversation*, New Haven: Yale University Press.

Johnson, M and Tyler, A (1998) Re-analyzing the OPI: How much does it look like natural conversation?, in Young, R and He, A (Eds) *Talking and testing: Discourse approaches to the assessment of oral proficiency*, Amsterdam: John Benjamins.

Johnston, P H (1984) Assessment in reading, in Pearson, P D (Ed.) *Handbook of Reading Research*, New York: Longman, 147–182.

Jones, D (1909) *The Pronunciation of English*, Cambridge: Cambridge University Press.

Jones, D (1917) *An English Pronouncing Dictionary*, London: Dent.

Jones, D (1922) *Outline of English Phonetics* (second edition), Leipzig and Berlin.

Jones, L C (2008) Listening comprehension technology: building the bridge from analog to digital, *CALICO Journal* 25 (3), 400–419.

Jones, N (2000) Background to the validation of the ALTE Can Do Project and the revised Common European Framework, *Research Notes* 2, 11–13.

Jones, N (2001) The ALTE Can Do Project and the role of measurement in constructing a proficiency framework, *Research Notes* 5, 5–8.

Jones, N (2002) Relating the ALTE Framework to the Common European Framework of Reference, in Alderson, J C (Ed.) *Common European Framework of Reference for Languages: Learning, Teaching, Assessment: Case Studies*, Strasbourg: Council of Europe, 167–183.

Jones, N and Hirtzel, M (2001) The ALTE Can Do Project, English Version: Articles and Can Do statements produced by the members of ALTE 1992–2002, in Council of Europe, *Common European Framework of Reference for Languages: Learning, Teaching and Assessment*, Cambridge: Cambridge University Press, 244–257.

Jones N and Shaw S D (2003) Task difficulty in the assessment of writing: Comparing performance across three levels of CELS, *Research Notes* 11, 11–15.

Jones, R L (1984) Testing the receptive skills: Some basic considerations, *Foreign Language Annals* 17 (4), 365–367.

Jones, R L and Spolsky, B (1975) (Eds) *Testing Language Proficiency*, Washington DC: Center for Applied Linguistics.

Joyce, P (2008) *Componentiality in Tests of Listening Comprehension*, unpublished PhD thesis, University of Surrey, Roehampton.

Just, M A and Carpenter, P A (1980) A theory of reading: from eye fixations to comprehension, *Psychological Review* 87 (4), 329–54.

Katona, L (1998) Meaning negotiation in the Hungarian oral proficiency examination of English, in Young, R and He, A (Eds) *Talking and testing: Discourse approaches to the assessment of oral proficiency*, Amsterdam/ Philadelphia: John Benjamins, 239–267.

Kaulfers, W V (1944) Wartime development in modern-language achievement testing, *The Modern Language Journal* 28 (2), 136–150.

Kellogg, R T (1996) A model of working memory in writing, in Levy, C M and Ransdell, S E (Eds), *The Science of Writing*, Mahwah, NJ: Lawrence Erlbaum, 57–71.

Kelly, F J (1916) The Kansas silent reading tests, *Journal of Educational Psychology* 7, 63–80.

Kelly, L G (1969) *Twenty-five Centuries of Language Teaching*, Rowley, MA: Newbury House.

Kelly, L G (1976) *Twenty-five Centuries of Language Teaching*, 2nd edition, Rowley, MA: Newbury House.

Kelly, R (1978) *On the construct validation of comprehension tests: an exercise in applied linguistics*, unpublished PhD thesis, University of Queensland.

Kenyon, D and Malone, M (2010) Investigating examinee autonomy in a computerized test of oral proficiency, in Araujo, L (Ed.) *Computer-based assessment of foreign language speaking skills*, Luxembourg: European Union, 1–28.

Khalifa, H (1997) *A study in the Construct Validation of the Reading Module of an EAP Proficiency Test Battery: Validation from a variety of perspectives*, unpublished PhD Thesis, University of Reading.

Khalifa, H and Weir, C J (2009) *Examining reading: Research and practice in assessing second language reading*, Studies in Language Testing volume 29, Cambridge: UCLES/Cambridge University Press.

Kijak, A (2009) *How stressful is L2 stress? A cross-linguistic study of L2 perception and production of metrical systems*, unpublished PhD thesis, University of Utrecht.

Kintsch, W (1972) Abstract nouns: Imagery versus lexical complexity, *Journal of Verbal Learning and Verbal Behaviour* 11, 59–65.

Kintsch, W and Keenan, J M (1973) Reading rate and retention as a function of the number of propositions in the base structure of sentences, *Cognitive Psychology* 5, 257–279.

Kintsch, W and Van Dijk, T A (1978) Toward a model of text comprehension and production, *Psychological Review* 85 (5), 363–394.

Kintsch, W and Yarborough, J C (1982) Role of rhetorical structure in text comprehension, *Journal of Educational Psychology* 74 (6), 828–834.

Kobayashi, M (1995) *Effect of text organisation and test format on reading comprehension test performance*, unpublished PhD thesis, Thames Valley University.

Koda, K (2005) *Insights into Second Language Reading: A Cross-Linguistic Approach*, New York: Cambridge University Press.

Kormos, J (1999) Simulating conversations in oral proficiency assessment: A conversation analysis of role plays and non-scripted interviews in language exams, *Language Testing* 16 (2), 163–188.

Kramsch, C (1986) From language proficiency to international competence, *Modern Language Journal* 70 (4), 366–372.

Kramsch, C (1998) *Language and Culture*, Oxford: Oxford University Press.

Kunnan, A J (1998) Approaches to validation in language assessment, in Kunnan, A (Ed.) *Validation in Language Assessment*, Mahwah, NJ: Lawrence Erlbaum.

Kunnan, A J (2008) Large scale language assessments, in Shohamy, E and Hornberger, N H (Eds) *Encyclopedia of Language and Education* (2nd edition) Volume 7: Language Testing and Assessment, Amsterdam: Springer, 135–155.

Lado, R (1960) English language testing: Problems of validity and administration, *ELT Journal* 14 (4), 153–161.

Lado, R (1961) *Language Testing: the Construction and use of Foreign Language Tests*, London: Longman.

Lado, R (1964) *Language Teaching: A Scientific Approach*, New York: McGraw Hill.

Lantolf, J P and Frawley, W (1985) Oral-Proficiency Testing: A Critical Analysis, *The Modern Language Journal* 69 (4), 337–345.

Lantolf, J P and Frawley, W (1988) Proficiency: Understanding the Construct, *Studies in Second Language Acquisition* 10, 181–195.

Latham, H (1877) *On the Action of Examinations Considered as A Means of Selection*, Cambridge: Deighton, Bell.

Lazaraton, A (1992) The structural organisation of a language interview: A conversation analytic perspective, *System* 20 (3), 373–386.

Lazaraton, A (1994) *An analysis of examiner behaviour in CAE Paper 5, based on audiotaped transcriptions*, report prepared for the EFL Division, University of Cambridge Local Examinations Syndicate, Cambridge.

Lazaraton, A (1996) Interlocutor support in oral proficiency interviews: the case of CASE, *Language Testing* 13 (2), 151–172.

Lazaraton, A (1997) *An analysis of differences between task features and candidate output for the Revised FCE Speaking Examination: 1996 Standardization video*, report prepared for the EFL Division, University of Cambridge Local Examinations Syndicate, Cambridge.

Lazaraton, A (2002) *A Qualitative Approach to the Validation of Oral Language Tests*, Studies in Language Testing volume 14, Cambridge: UCLES/ Cambridge University Press.

Lazaraton, A and Frantz, R (1997) *An analysis of differences between task features and candidate output for the Revised FCE Speaking Examination*, report prepared for the EFL Division, University of Cambridge Local Examinations Syndicate, Cambridge.

Ledoux, K, Traxler, M J and Saab, T Y (2007) Syntactic priming in comprehension: evidence from event-related potentials, *Psychological Science* 18, 135–143.

Lewkowicz, J (1997) *Investigating authenticity in language testing*, unpublished PhD thesis, University of Lancaster.

Levelt, W J M (1989) *Speaking*, Cambridge, MA: MIT Press.

Lewis, E G and Massad, C E (1975) *The Teaching of English as a Foreign Language in Ten Countries*, Stockholm: Almqvist and Wiksell, and New York: Wiley.

Lewis, L R, Vasishth, S and Van Dyke, J (2006) Computational principles of working memory in sentence comprehension, *Trends in Cognitive Science* 10, 447–454.

Liao, Y F (2009) *A construct validation study of the GEPT reading and listening sections: re-examining the models of L2 reading and listening abilities and their relations to lexico-grammatical knowledge*, unpublished PhD thesis, Teachers College, Columbia University.

Liberman, A M, Cooper, F S, Shankweiler, D P, and Studdert-Kennedy, M (1967) Perception of the speech code, *Psychological review* 74 (6), 431–461.

Littau, K (2006) *Theories of Reading: Books, Bodies, and Bibliomania*, Cambridge: Polity Press.

Littlewood, W T (1986) Literature in the school foreign-language course, in Brumfit, C and Carter, R (Eds) *Literature and language teaching*, Oxford: Oxford University Press, 177–183.

Lombardo, L (1984) Oral testing: Getting a sample of the real language, *English Teaching Forum* 22 (1), 2–6.

Londe, Z (2008) *Working Memory and English as a Second Language Listening Comprehension Tests: A Latent Variable Approach*, unpublished PhD thesis, University of California, Los Angeles.

Long, D R (1989) Second language listening comprehension: a schema-theoretic perspective, *Modern Language Journal* 73, 34–40.

Long, D R (1990) What you don't know can't help you, *Studies in Second Language Acquisition* 12, 65–80.

Lott, B (1964) Conversation practice, *English Language Teaching* 19 (1), 18–23.

Lowe, P (1988) The unassimilated history, in Lowe, P and Stansfield, C W (Eds) *Second Language Proficiency Assessment: Current Issues*, Englewood Cliffs NJ: Prentice Hall Regents, 11–51.

Lowe, P and Clifford, R T (1980) Developing an indirect measure of overall oral proficiency, in Frith, J R (Ed.) *Measuring spoken language proficiency*, Washington D.C.: Georgetown University Press, 31–39.

Lumley, T (2002) Assessment criteria in a large-scale writing test: what do they really mean to raters? *Language Testing* 19 (3), 246–276.

Lundeberg, O K (1929) Recent Developments in Audition-Speech Tests, *The Modern Language Journal* 14 (3), 193–202.

Lunsford, A A (1986) The past – and future – of writing assessment, in Greenberg, K L, Wiener, H S and Donovan, R A (Eds) *Writing assessment: Issues and Strategies*, NY, London: Longman, 1–12.

Luoma, S (1997) *Comparability of a tape-mediated and a face-to-face test of speaking: A triangulation study*, University of Jyvaskyla, Jyvaskyla.

MacDonald, M C and Just, M A (1989) Changes in activation levels with negation, *Journal of Experimental Psychology: Learning, Memory, and Cognition* 15, 633–642.

Mackey, W F (1965) *Language Teaching Analysis*, London: Longman.

Mackey, W F (1966) Applied Linguistics: Its meaning and use, *ELT Journal* 20 (3), 197–206.

Malarkey, J, Bell, C and Somers, A (2010) *PET Annual Speaking report 2009*, Cambridge ESOL internal report.

Malinowski, B (1923) The problem of meaning in primitive languages, in Ogden, C K and Richards, I A (Eds) *The Meaning of Meaning*, London: Routledge, 146–152,

Manguel, A (1997) *A History of Reading*, London: Harper Collins.

Markham, P (1985) The rationale deletion cloze and global comprehension in German, *Language Learning* 35 (3), 423–430.

Marshall, E G and Schaap, E (1955) *A Concise Manual of English for Foreign Students*, London: Hachette.

Mathieson, M (1975) *The Preachers of Culture*, London: Allen and Unwin.

Masi, S (2002) The literature on complexity, in Merlini Barbesi, L (Ed.) *Complexity in Language and Text*, Pisa: PLUS-University of Pisa, 197–228.

May, L (2009) Co-constructed interaction in a paired speaking test: The rater's perspective, *Language Testing* 26 (3), 397–421.

McCarthy, M (2010) Spoken fluency revisited, *English Profile Journal* 1 (1), 1–15.

McNamara, D S, Graesser, A C and Louwerse, M M (in press). Sources of text difficulty: Across the ages and genres, in Sabatini, J P and Albro, E (Eds), *Assessing Reading in the 21st century: Aligning and Applying Advances in the Reading and Measurement Sciences*, Lanham, MD: R&L Education.

McNamara, T (1996) *Measuring Second Language Performance*, Longman: London and New York.

McNamara, T (1997) Interaction in second language performance assessment: Whose performance?, *Applied Linguistics* 16 (2), 159–179.

McNamara, T (2003) Looking back, looking forward: rethinking Bachman, *Language Testing* 20 (4), 466–473.

McNamara, T (2007) Language assessment in foreign language education: The struggle over constructs, *Modern Language Journal* 91 (2), 280–282.

McNamara, T (2009) Australia: The Dictation Test redux? *Language Assessment Quarterly* 6 (1), 106–111.

McNamara, T and Roever, C (2006) *Language testing: The social dimension,* Malden, MA & Oxford: Blackwell.

McNamara, T, Hill, K and May, L (2002) Discourse and assessment, in McGroarty, M (Ed.) *Annual review of applied linguistics,* 221–242.

Mehnert, U (1998) The effects of different lengths of time for planning on second language performance, *Studies in Second Language Acquisition* 20, 83–108.

Meidinger, J V (1783) *Praktische französische Grammatik ["Practical French Grammar"],* Frankfurt.

Mendelsohn, D J (1994) *Learning to Listen: A Strategy-based Approach for the Second Language Learner,* San Diego, CA: Dominie Press.

Messick, S A (1989) Validity, in Linn, R L (Ed) *Educational Measurement* (3rd edition), New York: Macmillan, 13–103.

Messick, S A (1994) The interplay of evidence and consequences in the validation of performance assessments, *Educational Researcher* 23 (2), 13–23.

Meyer, B and Freedle, R (1984) Effects of discourse type on recall, *American Educational Research Journal* 21 (1), 121–143.

Meyer, D and Schvanevelt, R (1971) Facilitation in recognising pairs of words: evidence of dependence between retrieval operations, *Journal of Experimental Psychology* 90, 237–244.

Midwinter, E (1970) *19th Century Education,* London: Longman.

Milanovic, M (2003) Series Editor's note, in Weir, C and Milanovic, M (Eds) *Continuity and Innovation: Revising the Cambridge Proficiency Examination in English Examination 1913–2002,* Studies in Language Testing volume 15, Cambridge: UCLES/Cambridge University Press, xiii–xx.

Milanovic, M and Saville, N (1994) *An Investigation of Marking Strategies Using Verbal Protocols,* Cambridge: University of Cambridge Local Examination Syndicate.

Milanovic, M and Saville, N (1996) *Considering the impact of Cambridge EFL examinations,* Cambridge: UCLES internal report

Milanovic, M, Saville, N, Pollitt, A and Cook, A (1996) Developing Rating Scales for CASE: Theoretical Concerns and Analyses, in Cumming, A H and Berwick, R (Eds) *Validation in Language Testing,* Clevedon: Multilingual Matters, 15–34.

Milanovic, M, Saville, N and Shen, S (1991) *An investigation of the inter-rater and intra-rater reliability of FCE Oral interviews,* UCLES internal report.

Milanovic, M, Saville, N and Shen, S (1996) A study of the decision-making behaviour of composition markers, in Milanovic, M and Saville, N (Eds) *Performance Testing, Cognition and Assessment: Selected Papers from the 15th Language Testing Research Colloquium, Cambridge and Arnhem,* Studies in Language Testing volume 3, Cambridge: UCLES/Cambridge University Press, 92–114.

Miyazaki, I (1976) *China's Examination Hell: The Civil Service Examinations of Imperial China,* New York and Tokyo: Weatherhill.

Moller, A D (1981) Reaction to the Morrow paper (2), in Alderson, J C and Hughes, A (Eds), *Issues in language testing ELT Documents 111*, London: The British Council, 38–44.

Moller, A D (1982) A *study in the validation of proficiency tests of English as a foreign language*, unpublished PhD thesis, University of Edinburgh.

Monahan, T (1998) *The Rise of Standardized Educational Testing in the U.S.: A Bibliographic Overview*, Troy, NY: Rensselaer Polytechnic Institute.

Monroe, W S (1918) Monroe's standardized silent reading tests, *Journal of Educational Psychology* 9, 303–312.

Montaigne, M (1575) *Essays*, available online: wpscms.pearsoncmg.com/long_longman_mhlw_0/0,11868,31260

Montgomery, R J (1965) *The Rise of Examinations as Administrative Devices*, London: Longman.

Moody, H L B (1983) Teaching literature overseas: language-based approaches, in Brumfit, C J (Ed.) *ELT Documents 115*, Oxford: Pergamon in association with the British Council, 17–36.

Moore, T and Morton, J (1999) Authenticity in the IELTS academic module writing test: a comparative study of Task 2 items and university assignments, in Tulloh, R (Ed.) *IELTS Research Reports, Volume 2*, Canberra: IELTS Australia, 64–106.

Moore, T, Morton, J and Price, S (2010) *Construct validity in the IELTS academic reading test: A comparison of reading requirements in IELTS test items and in university study*, unpublished IELTS Research Report, British Council/IDP Australia.

Moore, C, O'Neill, P and Huot, B (2009) Creating a Culture of Assessment in Writing Programs and Beyond, *College Composition and Communication* 61 (1), 107–132.

Morley, J (1991) Listening Comprehension in Second/Foreign Language Instruction, in Celce-Murcia, M (Ed.) *Teaching English as a Second Foreign Language*, Boston, MA: Heinle & Heinle Publishers, 81–106.

Morris, N (1961) An historian's view of examinations, in Wiseman, S (Ed.) *Examinations and English education*, Manchester: Manchester University Press, 1–43.

Morris, S (1978) How good a test of English is the First Certificate in English? *ARELS Journal*, 1–2.

Morrison, R B (1968) *English language 'O' Level–June 1967 marking experiment*, mimeo, Guildford: AEB.

Morrison, R B (1969) *English language 'O' Level–June 1968 marking experiment*, mimeo, Guildford: AEB.

Morrow, K E (1977) *Techniques of Evaluation for a Notional Syllabus*, London: Royal Society of Arts.

Morrow, K E (1979) Communicative language testing: revolution or evolution? in Brumfit, C J and Johnson, K (Eds) *The Communicative Approach to Language Teaching*, Oxford: Oxford University Press, 143–158.

Munby, J L (1978) *Communicative Syllabus Design*, Cambridge: Cambridge University Press.

Murphy, R J L (1978) *Sex Differences in Objective Test Performance*, mimeo, Associated Examining Board Research Report RAC/56.

Murphy, R J L (1982) A further report of investigations into the reliability of marking of GCE examinations, *British Journal of Education Psychology* 52 (1), 58–63.

Murphy, S and Yancy, K B (2008) Construct and Consequence: Validity in writing assessment, in Bazerman, C (Ed.) *Handbook of Research on Writing: History, Society, School, Individual, Text*, New York, London: Lawrence Erlbaum, 365–385.

Murray, L (2007). Blog writing integration for academic language learning purposes: towards an assessment framework, *IBÉRICA* 14, 9–32.

Murray, S (2007) Reviewing the CAE Listening Test, *Research Notes* 30, 19–23.

Nakatsuhara, F (2009) *Conversational styles in group oral tests: How is the conversation co-constructed?* unpublished PhD thesis, University of Essex.

Nakatsuhara, F (2012) The relationship between test-takers' listening proficiency and their performance on the IELTS Speaking Test, in Taylor, L and Weir, C J (Eds) *IELTS Collected Papers 2: Research in Reading and Listening Assessment*, Studies in Language Testing volume 34, Cambridge: UCLES/ Cambridge University Press, 519–573.

Nevo, N (1989) Test-taking strategies on a MC test of reading comprehension, *Language Testing* 6 (2), 199–217.

Nguyen, T N H (2008) *An investigation into the validity of two EFL (English as a Foreign Language) listening tests: IELTS and TOEFL iBT*, unpublished PhD thesis, Department of Linguistics and Applied Linguistics, University of Melbourne.

North, B (2000) *The Development of a Common Framework Scale of Language Proficiency*, New York: Peter Lang Publishing.

North, B (2002) Developing descriptor scales of language proficiency for the CEF Common Reference Levels, in Alderson, J C (Ed.) *Common European Framework of Reference for Languages: Learning, Teaching, Assessment: Case Studies*, Strasbourg: Council of Europe, 87–105.

Northcote, S H and Trevelyan, C E (1854) *Report on the organisation of the Permanent Civil Service*, paper presented to both Houses of Parliament in February, 1854, available online: www.civilservant.org.uk/northcotetrevelyan. pdf

Nunan, D (1989) *Designing Tasks for the Communicative Classroom*, Cambridge: Cambridge University Press.

Nuttall, C (1982) *Teaching Reading Skills in a Foreign Language*, London: Heinemann Educational Books.

Nuttall, C (1996) *Teaching Reading Skills in a Foreign Language*, London: Heinemann.

Nystrand, M (2006) The social and historical context for writing research, in MacArthur, C A, Graham, S and Fitzgerald, J (Eds) *Handbook of Writing Research*, NY, London: Guilford Press, 11–27.

Oakeshott-Taylor, J (1979) Cloze procedure and foreign language listening skills, *International Review of Applied Linguistics* 17 (2), 150–158.

Oakhill, J V and Garnham, A (1988) *Becoming a Skilled Reader*, Oxford: Basil Blackwell.

Oakhill, J V, Yuill, N M, and Parkin, A J (1986) On the nature of the difference between skilled and less-skilled comprehenders, *Journal of Research in Reading* 9, 80–91.

Ockey, G J (2009) The effects of group members' personalities on a test taker's L2 group oral discussion test scores, *Language Testing* 161–186.

O'Keefe, A (2006a) *First certificate in English. Evaluation of modifications to speaking test,* internal report: University of Cambridge ESOL Examinations.

O'Keefe, A (2006b) *Certificate in advanced English. Evaluation of modifications to speaking test*, internal report: University of Cambridge ESOL Examinations.

Oller, J W (1971) Dictation as a device for testing foreign language proficiency, *ELT Journal* 25 (3), 254–259.

Oller, J W (1973) Pragmatic language testing, *Language Science* 28, 7–12.

Oller, J W (1976) Evidence for a general language proficiency factor: an expectancy grammar, *Die Neueren Sprachen* 75, 165–174.

Oller, J W (1979) *Language Tests at School*, London: Longman.

O'Loughlin, K (2001) *The equivalence of direct and semi-direct speaking tests*, Cambridge: Cambridge University Press.

O'Loughlin, K (2002) The impact of gender in oral proficiency testing, *Language Testing* 19 (2), 169–192.

O'Malley, J M and Valdez Pierce, L (1996).*Authentic Assessment for English Language Learners: Practical Approaches for Teachers*, New York: Addison Wesley.

O'Neil, R (1970) *English in Situations*, Oxford: Oxford University Press.

Ortega, L (2003) Syntactic complexity measures and their relationship to L2 proficiency: A research synthesis of college-level L2 writing, *Applied Linguistics* 24 (4), 492–518.

Osada, N (2002) *The effects of silent pause on listening comprehension: a case of Japanese learners of English as a foreign language*, unpublished PhD thesis, Waseda University.

Osada, N (2004) Listening comprehension research: a brief review of the past thirty years, *Dialogue* 3, 53–66.

O'Sullivan, B (2000) *Towards a model of performance in oral language testing*, unpublished PhD thesis, University of Reading.

O'Sullivan, B (2002) Learner acquaintanceship and oral proficiency test pair-task performance, *Language Testing* 19 (3), 277–295.

O'Sullivan, B (2006) *Issues in Testing Business English: The BEC Revision Project*, Studies in Language Testing volume 17, Cambridge: UCLES/Cambridge University Press.

O'Sullivan, B and Rignal, M (2002) *Effect on Rater Performance of Systematic Feedback During the Rating Procedure – the IELTS General Training Writing*, Cambridge ESOL/The British Council/ IDA Australia: IELTS Research Report.

O'Sullivan, B, Weir, C J and Saville, N (2002) Using observation checklists to validate speaking-test tasks, *Language Testing* 19 (1), 33–56.

Paivio, A (1986) *Mental Representations*, Oxford: Oxford University Press.

Paivio, A, Yuille, J C and Madigan, S A (1968) Concreteness, imagery and meaningfulness values for 925 nouns, *Journal of Experimental Psychology Monograph Supplement* 76 (1), 1–25.

Palmer, H E (1917/1968) *The Scientific Study and Teaching of Languages*, London: Harrap.

Palmer, H E (1921a) *The Oral Method of Teaching Languages*, Cambridge: Heffers.

Palmer, H E (1921b) *The Principles of Language-Study*, London: Harrap.

Palmer, H E (1924) *A Grammar of Spoken English on a Strictly Phonetic Basis*, Cambridge: Heffer.

Palmer, H E (1925) *English Through Actions*, Tokyo: The Institute for Research in English Teaching.

Palmer, H (1940) The Teaching of Oral English, reprinted in Smith, R C (Ed.) (2005) *Teaching English as a Foreign Language, 1936–1961: Foundations of ELT*, Volume 1 Selected Papers, 89–185.

Palmer, H E and Redman, H V (1932) *This Language Learning Business*, London: Harrap.

Palmer, H E and Redman, H V (1969) *This Language Learning Business,* Language and Learning, Oxford: Oxford University Press.

Pashler, H and Johnston, J C (1998) Attentional limitations in dual-task performance, in Pashler, H (Ed.) *Attention,* England: Psychology Press/ Erlbaum (UK) Taylor & Francis, Hove, 155–189.

Passy, P (1899) *De la méthode directe dans l'enseignement des langues vivantes,* Paris: Colin.

Patrick, H J (2008) Home examinations after 1945, in Raban, S (Ed.) *Examining the World: A History of the University of Cambridge Local Examinations Syndicate,* 71–106.

Pemberton, R (2003) *Spoken word recognition and L2 listening performance: an investigation of the ability of Hong Kong learners to recognise the most frequent words of English when listening to news broadcasts,* unpublished PhD thesis, University of Wales, Swansea.

Penfold, E D M (1956) Essay marking experiments: shorter and longer essays, *British Journal of Educational Psychology* 26 (2).

Pennycook, A (1994) *The Cultural Politics of English as a Foreign Language,* Harlow: Longman.

Perfetti, C A (1985) *Reading Ability,* New York: Oxford University Press.

Perrin, G (2000) *The effect of multiple-choice foreign language tests of listening and reading on teacher behaviour and student attitudes,* unpublished PhD thesis, University of Lancaster.

Pickering, M J and Branigan, H P (1998) The representation of verbs: evidence from syntactic priming in language production, *Journal of Memory and Language* 39, 633–651.

Pike, L W (1979) *An Evaluation of Alternative Item Formats for Testing English as a Foreign Language,* TOEFL Research Reports 2, Princeton, NJ: Educational Testing Service.

Phillipson, R (1992) *Linguistic Imperialism,* Oxford: Oxford University Press.

Pimsleur, P (1966) *Pimsleur Language Aptitude Battery (PLAB),* New York: Harcourt Brace Jovanovich.

Plakans, L (2008) Comparing composing processes in writing-only and reading-to-write test tasks, *Assessing Writing* 13 (2), 111–129.

Pocock, G N (1917) *Précis Writing for Beginners,* London: Blackie and Son.

Poelmans, P (2003) *Developing second-language listening comprehension: Effects of training lower-order skills versus higher-order strategy,* unpublished PhD thesis, University van Amsterdam.

Pollitt, A and Murray, N L (1996) What raters really pay attention to, in M Milanovic and N Saville (Eds) *Performance Testing, Cognition and Assessment: Selected Papers from the 15th Language Testing Research Colloquium, Cambridge and Arnhem,* Studies in Language Testing volume 3, Cambridge: UCLES/Cambridge University Press, 74–91.

Pollitt, A and Taylor, L (2006) Cognitive psychology and reading assessment, in Sainsbury, M, Harrison, C and Watts, A (Eds) *Assessing Reading: from theories to classrooms,* Slough: NFER, 38–49.

Porter, D (1983) Assessing communicative proficiency: the search for validity, in Johnson, K Porter, D (Eds) *Perspectives in communicative language teaching,* London: Academic Press, 189–203.

Porter, D and O'Sullivan, B (1999) The effect of audience age on measured written performance, *System* 27, 65–77.

Porter, D and Roberts, J (1981) Authentic Listening Activities, *ELT Journal* 36 (1), 37–47.

Porter, T M (1995) *Trust in numbers: The Pursuit of Objectivity in Science and Public Life*, Princeton, New Jersey: Princeton University Press.

Prabhu, N S (1987) *Second Language Pedagogy*, Oxford: Oxford University Press.

Prokosch, E (1922) The Direct Method in College Examinations, *The Modern Language Journal* 6 (4), 181–189.

Pugh, A K (1978) *Silent Reading: An Introduction to its Study and Teaching*, London: Heinemann Educational Books.

Pumfrey, P D (1976) *Reading: Tests and Assessment Techniques*, London: Hodder and Stoughton Educational.

Purpura, J (1999) *Strategy Use and Second Language Test Performance: A Structural Equation Modelling Approach*, Cambridge: Cambridge University Press.

Purpura, J (2004) *Assessing Grammar*, Cambridge: Cambridge University Press.

Purves, A (1992) Reflections on research and assessment in written composition, *Research in the Teaching of English* 26 (1), 108–122.

Raimes, A (1985) What unskilled ESL students do as they write: A classroom study of composing, *TESOL Quarterly* 19, 229–258.

Raimes, A (1990) The TOEFL Test of Written English: causes for concern, *TESOL Quarterly* 24 (3), 427–442.

Rastle, K (2007) Visual word recognition, in Gaskell, M G *The Oxford Handbook of Psycholinguistics*, Oxford: Oxford University Press, 71–87.

Rayner, K and Pollatsek, A (1989) *The Psychology of Reading*, Englewood Cliffs, NJ: Prentice Hall.

Rea, P M (1978) Assessing language as communication, *MALS Journal* 3.

Read, J (1990) Providing relevant content in an EAP Writing Test, *English for Specific Purposes* 9, 109–121.

Read, J (1997) Vocabulary and testing, in Schmitt, N and McCarthy, M (Eds) *Vocabulary: Description, Acquisition, and Pedagogy*, Cambridge: Cambridge University Press, 303–320.

Read, J (2000) *Assessing Vocabulary*, Cambridge: Cambridge University Press.

Reves, T (1981) The group oral examination: A field experiment, *World Language English* 1–2 (4), 259–262.

Resnick, D (1982) History of educational testing, in Wigdor, A K and Garner, W R (Eds) *Ability testing: Uses, consequences, and controversies, Part II*, Washington, D C: National Academy Press, 173–194.

Richards, I A (1947) English language teaching films and their use in teacher training, *English Language Teaching* 2 (1), 1–8.

Richards, J C (1983) Listening comprehension: Approach, design, procedure, *TESOL Quarterly* 17, 219–240.

Richards, J C and Rodgers, T S (1986) *Approaches and Methods in Language Teaching: A Description and Analysis*, Cambridge: Cambridge University Press.

Richards, J C and Rogers, T S (2001) *Approaches and methods in language teaching* (second edition), Cambridge: Cambridge University Press.

Richterich, R (1973a) Definition of language needs and types of adults, in Council of Europe (Eds) *Systems Development in Adult Language Learning: A European Unit/credit system for Modern Language Learning by Adults*, Strasbourg: Council for Cultural Cooperation of the Council of Europe, 31–88.

Richterich, R (1973b) *A Model for the Definition of Adult Language Needs in Systems Development in Adult Language Learning*, Strasbourg: Council of Europe.

Richterich, R and Chancerel, J L (1978) *Identifying the Needs of Adults Learning a Foreign Language*, Strasbourg: Council of Europe.

Riggenbach, H (1998) Evaluating learner interactional skills: Conversation at the micro level, in Young, R and He, A (Eds) *Talking and testing: Discourse approaches to the assessment of oral proficiency*, Amsterdam: John Benjamins.

Rivers, W M (1968) *Teaching Foreign Language Skills*, Chicago: University of Chicago Press.

Rixon, S (1986) *Developing Listening Skills*, London: Macmillan.

Roach, J O (1929) '*Memorandum of Reform*', 1/1d i.

Roach, J O (1931a) *Certificates of Proficiency*.

Roach, J O (1931b) *Proposal to eliminate phonetics from the CPE syllabus.*

Roach, J O (1935) *Modern languages and international relations*, PP JOR

Roach, J O (1936) The reliability of school certificate results, *Overseas Education: a Journal of Educational Experiment and Research in Tropical and Subtropical Areas* 7, 113–118.

Roach, J O (1937) *Report on visit to Central Europe.*

Roach, J O (1939) *Diary of official visits to Europe.*

Roach, J O (1944a) *The Cambridge Exams in English relating to Basic English.*

Roach, J O (1944b) *The Cambridge Examinations in English: A survey of their history.*

Roach, J O (1945a) *Some problems of oral examinations in modern languages: An experimental approach based on the Cambridge Examinations in English for foreign students*, UCLES report circulated to oral examiners and local examiners.

Roach, J O (1945b) *Report on policy and future development.*

Roach, J O (1956a) *Examinations as an instrument of cultural policy.*

Roach, J O (1956b) *Examinations in English as a Foreign Language II.*

Roach, J O (1971) *Public Examinations in England 1850–1900*, Cambridge: Cambridge University Press.

Roach, J O (1984) *"My work" with the Local Examinations Syndicate, 1925–1945.*

Robeson, F E (1913) *A progressive course of precis writing*, London, New York: Henry Frowde, Oxford University Press.

Robertson, K, Hohmann, J and Stewart, I (2005) Dictating to one of 'us': The migration of Mrs Freer, *Macquarie Law Journal* 5, 241–275.

Robinson, P (1971) Oral Expression Tests: 2, *English Language Teaching Journal* 25 (3), 260–266.

Roemmele, J A (1966) The Language Laboratory as an Aid in Oral Tests Overseas, *English Language Teaching Journal* 21 (1), 50–55.

Ross, S and Berwick, R (1992) The discourse of accommodation in oral proficiency interviews, *Studies in Second Language Acquisition* 14, 159–176.

Rost, M (1990) *Listening in Language Learning*, Cambridge: Cambridge University Press.

Rost, M (2002) *Teaching and Researching Listening*, Harlow: Pearson Education.

Rupp, A A, Ferne, T and Choi, H (2006) How assessing reading comprehension with multiple-choice questions shapes the construct: a cognitive processing perspective, *Language Testing* 23 (4), 441–474.

Russell, D R (2002) *Writing in the Academic Disciplines: A Curricular History* (2nd edition), Carbondale: Southern Illinois University Press.

Salisbury, K (2005) *The edge of expertise? Towards an understanding of listening test item writing as professional practice*, unpublished PhD thesis, King's College, University of London.

Sanderson, M (1975) *The Universities in the 19th Century*, London: Routledge.

Sanford, A J and Garrod, S C (1981) *Understanding Written Language: Explorations of Comprehension Beyond the Sentence*, Chichester: John Wiley.

Sasaki, M (2000) Effects of cultural schemata on students' test-taking processes for cloze tests: a multiple data source approach, *Language Testing* 17, 85–114.

Savignon, S J (1985) Evaluation of communicative competence: The ACTFL Provisional Proficiency Guidelines, *The Modern Language Journal* 69 (2), 129–134.

Saville, N (2003) The process of test development and revision within UCLES EFL, in Weir, C J and Milanovic, M (Eds) *Continuity and Innovation: Revising the Cambridge Proficiency in English Examination 1913–2002*, Studies in Language Testing volume 15, Cambridge: UCLES/Cambridge University Press, 57–120.

Saville, N (2009) *Developing a model for investigating the impact of language assessment within educational contexts by a public examination provider*, unpublished PhD thesis, University of Bedfordshire.

Saville, N and Hargreaves, P (1999) Assessing speaking in the revised FCE, *English Language Teaching Journal* 53 (1), 42–51.

Scarborough, D L, Cortese, C and Scarborough, H S (1977) Frequency and repetition effects in lexical memory, *Journal of experimental psychology: human perception and performance* 3, 1–17.

Schmidt-Rinehart, B B (1994) The effects of topic familiarity on second language listening comprehension, *Modern Language Journal* 78 (2), 179–198.

Schmitt, N (1999) The relationship between TOEFL vocabulary items and meaning, association, collocation and word-class knowledge, *Language Testing* 16 (2), 189–216.

Schmitt, N (2009) Lexical analysis of input prompts and examinee output of Cambridge ESOL Main Suite speaking tests, internal report, Cambridge: UCLES.

Severinson Eklundh, K and Kollberg, P (2003) Emerging discourse structure: computer-assisted episode analysis as a window to global revision in university students' writing, *Journal of Pragmatics* 35, 869–891.

Shaw, S D (2003a) Electronic Script Management: Towards on-screen assessment of scanned paper scripts, *Research Notes* 12, 4–8.

Shaw, S D (2003b) *IELTS Writing Assessment Revision Project (Phase 3): Validating the Revised Rating Scale – A Quantitative Analysis*, Cambridge: UCLES internal report.

Shaw, S D (2003c) IELTS Writing: revising assessment criteria and scales (Phase 3), *Research Notes* 16, 3–7.

Shaw, S D (2004) IELTS Writing: revising assessment criteria and scales (concluding Phase 2), *Research Notes* 15, 9–11.

Shaw, S D (2005a) *Examining CAE Writing Examiner Behaviour (Phase 2): a multi-faceted Rasch measurement approach*, Internal Report No. 676, Cambridge: UCLES internal report.

Shaw, S D (2005b) *IELTS Writing Assessment Revision Working Group: Summary of Progress (June 2001 – October 2005)*, Cambridge: UCLES internal report.

Shaw, S D (2005c) *The impact of word processed text on rater behaviour: a review of the literature*, Internal Validation Report No 670, Cambridge: UCLES internal report.

Shaw, S D and Falvey, P (2006) *The IELTS Writing Assessment Revision Project: towards a revised rating scale*, Cambridge ESOL Web-Based Research Report No. 1.

Shaw, S D and Geranpayeh, A (2005) *Examining CAE Writing Examiner Behaviour: a multifaceted Rasch measurement approach*, Internal Report No. 614, Cambridge: UCLES internal report.

Shaw, S and Weir, C J (2007) *Examining Writing: Research and Practice in Assessing Second Language Writing*, Studies in Language Testing volume 26, Cambridge: UCLES/Cambridge University Press.

Shayer, D (1972) *The teaching of English in schools, 1900–1970*, London: Routledge and Kegan Paul.

Sheldon, A (1974) The Role of Parallel Function in the Acquisition of Relative Clauses in English, *Journal of Verbal Learning and Verbal Behavior*, 272–281.

Sherman, J (1997) The effect of question preview in listening comprehension tests, *Language Testing* 14, 185–213.

Sherman, L A (1893) *Analytics of Literature: A Manual for the Objective Study of English Prose and Poetry*, Boston: Ginn and Co.

Shi, L (2004) Textual borrowing in second language writing, *Written Communication* 21 (2), 171–200.

Shin, Dong-il (1999) *Construct validation of a diagnostic L2 Listening test: An operational model utilizd and multidimensionality issues revisited*, unpublished PhD thesis, University of Illinois at Urbana-Champaign.

Shin, Sun-young (2007) *Examining the construct validity of a web-based academic listening test: an investigation of the effects of response formats in a web-based listening test*, unpublished PhD thesis, University of California, Los Angeles.

Shiotsu, T (2003) *Linguistic knowledge and processing efficiency as predictors of L2 reading ability: a component skills analysis*, unpublished PhD dissertation, University of Reading.

Shiotsu, T and Weir, C J (2007) The relative significance of syntactic knowledge and vocabulary breadth in the prediction of second language reading comprehension test performance, *Language Testing* 23 (4), 99–128.

Shohamy, E (1994) The validity of direct versus semi-direct oral tests, *Language Testing* 11, 99–123.

Shohamy, E (2001) *The Power of Tests: A Critical Perspective on the Uses of Language Tests*, Harlow: Pearson Education.

Shohamy, E (2008) Introduction, in Shohamy, E and Hornberger, N (Eds) *Encyclopedia of language and education* (2nd edition), Language testing and assessment volume 7, New York: Springer, xiii-xxii.

Shohamy, E, Reves, T and Bejarano, Y (1986) Introducing a new comprehensive test of oral proficiency, *English Language Teaching Journal* 40 (3), 212–220.

Simmonds, P (1985) A survey of English language examinations, *English Language Teaching Journal* 39 (1), 33–42.

Singer, M (1994) Discourse inference processes, in Gernsbacher, M A (Ed.) *Handbook of Psycholinguistics*, San Diego, CA: Academic Press, 479–516.

Skehan, P (1989) State-of-the-Art article: Language testing, Part 2, *Language Teaching* 22 (1), 1–13.

Skehan, P (1996) A framework for the implementation of task based instruction, *Applied Linguistics* 17, 38–62.

Skehan, P (1998) *A cognitive approach to language learning*, Oxford: Oxford University Press.

Skehan, P (2001) Tasks and language performance assessment, in Bygate, M, Skehan, P and Swain, M (Eds) *Researching Pedagogic Tasks*, London: Longman, 167–185.

Skehan, P and Foster, P (1997) The influence of planning and post-task activities on accuracy and complexity in task based learning, *Language Teaching Research* 1 (3), 185–211.

Skehan, P and Foster, P (1999) The influence of task structure and processing conditions on narrative retellings, *Language Learning* 49 (1), 93–120.

Smagorinsky, P (1994) Think-aloud protocol analysis: Beyond the black box. In Smagorinsky, P (Ed.) *Speaking about writing*, USA: Sage Publications, 3–19.

Smith R C (1999) *The Writings of Harold E. Palmer: An Overview*, Hon-no-Tomosha: Tokyo: Japan.

Smith, R C (2004) *An Investigation into the Roots of ELT, with a Particular Focus on the Career and Legacy of Harold E. Palmer (1877–1949)*, unpublished PhD thesis, University of Edinburgh.

Sokal, M M (1987) *Psychological Testing and American Society: 1890–1930*, London: Rutgers University Press.

Sollenberger, H E (1978) Development and current use of the FSI Oral Interview test, in Clark, J L D (Ed.) *Direct Testing of Speaking Proficiency: Theory and Application*, Princeton, NJ: Educational Testing Service, 89–103.

Song, M (2008) *The Effect of the Notetaking Format on the Quality of Second Language Test Takers' Notes and The Performance on an Academic Listening Test*, unpublished PhD thesis, University of California, Los Angeles.

Spack, R (1984) Invention strategies and the ESL college composition student, *TESOL Quarterly* 18, 649–670.

Spolsky, B (1968) Language testing: The problem of validation, *TESOL Quarterly* 2, 88–94.

Spolsky, B (1978) Introduction: Linguists and language testers, in Spolsky, B (Ed.) *Approaches to language testing: Advances in Language testing series 2*, Virginia: Center for Applied Linguistics, 5–10.

Spolsky, B (1990a) Oral examination: an historical note, *Language Testing* 7 (2), 158–173.

Spolsky, B (1990b) The prehistory of TOEFL, *Language Testing* 7, 98–118.

Spolsky, B (1995a) *Measured Words*, Oxford: Oxford University Press.

Spolsky, B (1995b) Prognostication and language aptitude testing, 1925–62, *Language Testing* 12 (3), 321–340.

Spolsky, B (1998) *Sociolinguistics*, Oxford: Oxford University Press.

Spolsky, B (2000) Language Testing, *The Modern Language Journal* 84 (4), 536–552.

Spolsky, B (2004) Review: Continuity and Innovation: Revising the Cambridge Proficiency in English Examination 1913–2002, *ELT Journal* 58 (3), 305–309.

Spolsky, B (2008a) Introduction – Language testing at 25: Maturity and responsibility? *Language Testing* 25 (3), 297–305.

Spolsky, B (2008b) Language assessment in historical and future perspective, in Shohamy, E and Hornberger, H (Eds) *Encyclopedia of language and education* (2nd edition), volume 7: Language Testing and Assessment, New York: Springer, 445–454.

Spufford, M (1981) *Small Books and Pleasant Histories*, London: Methuen.

Stabb, M S (1955) An experiment in oral testing, *The Modern Language Journal* 39 (5), 232–236.

Stanners, R F, Neiser, J J, Hernin, W P and Hall, R (1979) Memory representation for morphologically related words, *Journal of Verbal Learning and Verbal Behaviour* 18, 399–412.

Stansfield, C W (1985) A history of dictation in foreign language teaching and testing, *The Modern Language Journal* 69 (2), 121–128.

Stansfield, C W (1991) A comparative analysis of simulated and direct oral proficiency interviews, in Anivan, S (Ed.) *Current developments in language testing*, Singapore: RELC.

Stansfield, C W and Kenyon, D (1988) *Development of the Portuguese speaking test*, Washington, DC: Center for Applied Linguistics.

Stansfield, C W and Kenyon, D (1992) Research on the comparability of the oral proficiency interview and the simulated oral proficiency interview, *System* 20 (3), 347–364.

Steffensen, M, Joag-Dev, C and Anderson, R (1979) A cross-cultural perspective on reading comprehension, *Reading Research Quarterly* 15, 10–29.

Stern, H H (1983) *Fundamental Concepts of Language Teaching*, Oxford: Oxford University Press.

Stevenson, D K (1985) Authenticity, validity and a tea party, *Language Testing* 2 (1), 41–47.

Stone, M H (1974) Bonehead English, *Time*, 11 November, 106.

Storch, N (2002) Patterns of interaction in ESL pair work, *Language Learning* 52 (1), 119–158.

Stray, C (2001) The shift from oral to written examination: Cambridge and Oxford 1700–1900, *Assessment in Education: Principles, Policy & Practice* 8 (1), 33–50.

Stray, C (2005) From oral to written examinations: Cambridge, Oxford and Dublin 1700–1914, *History of Universities* 20 (2), 76–130.

Strevens, P (1960) The Development of an Oral English Test for West Africa, *English Language Teaching Journal* 15 (1), 17–24.

Strevens, P (1965) Recent British Developments in Language Teaching, in Kreidler, C E (Ed.) *Monograph Series on Languages and Linguistics 18*, Washington D.C.: Georgetown University Press, 171–179.

Sutherland, G R (2001) Examinations and the construction of professional identity: A case study of England 1800–1950, *Assessment in Education: Principles, Policy & Practice* 8 (1), 51–64.

Suvorov, R (2011) The effects of context visuals on L2 listening comprehension, *Research Notes* 45, 2–8.

Swain, M (2001) Examining dialogue: Another approach to content specification and to validating inferences drawn from test scores, *Language Testing* 18 (3), 275–302.

Sweet, H (1899) *The Practical Study of Languages*, London: Dent.

Tan, S (1990) The role of prior knowledge and language proficiency as predictors of reading comprehension among undergraduates, in de Jong, J and Stevenson, D (Eds) *Individualising the Assessment of Language Abilities*, Clevedon, PA: Multilingual Matters, 214–224.

Tao, H (2003) Turn initiators in spoken English: A corpus-based approach to interaction and grammar, in Leistyna, P and Meyer, C F (Eds) *Corpus analysis: Language structure and language Use,* Amsterdam: Rodopi, 187–207.

Tattersall, K (2007) A brief history of policies, practices and issues relating to comparability, in Tattersall, K, Newton, P, Baird, J A, Patrick, H and P. Tymms, P (Eds) *Techniques for Monitoring the Comparability of Examination Standards,* London QCA, 43–96.

Taylor, K K (1986) Summary writing by young children, *Reading Research Quarterly* 21 (2), 193–208.

Taylor, L (1992) *Report on the PET Review Project 1991–1992: A review of the administrative infrastructure for the Preliminary English Test,* internal UCLES document.

Taylor, L (2003) The Cambridge approach to speaking assessment, *Research Notes* 13, 2–4.

Taylor, L (2009) Assessment Literacy, *Annual Review of Applied Linguistics* 29, 21–36.

Taylor, L (2011a) Introduction, in Taylor, L (Ed.) *Examining Speaking: Research and Practice in Assessing Second Language Speaking,* Studies in Language Testing volume 30, Cambridge: UCLES/Cambridge University Press, 1–35.

Taylor, L (Ed.) (2011b) *Examining Speaking: Research and Practice in Assessing Second Language Speaking,* Studies in Language Testing volume 30, Cambridge: UCLES/Cambridge University Press.

Taylor, L and Falvey, P (Eds) (2006) *IELTS collected papers: Research in speaking and writing assessment,* Cambridge: Cambridge University Press.

Taylor, L and Galaczi, E (2011) Scoring validity, in Taylor, L (Ed.) *Examining Speaking: Research and Practice in Assessing Second Language Speaking,* Studies in Language Testing volume 30, Cambridge: UCLES/Cambridge University Press, 171–233.

Taylor, L and Geranpayeh, A (2011) Assessing listening for academic purposes: Defining and operationalising the test construct, *Journal of English for Academic Purposes* 10, 89–101.

Taylor, L and Jones, N (2006) Cambridge ESOL exams and the Common European Framework of Reference (CEFR), *Research Notes* 24 (2–5).

Taylor, L and Wigglesworth, G (2009) Are two heads better than one? Pair work in L2 assessment contexts, *Language Testing* 26 (3), 325–339.

Taylor, L, Barker, F, Geranpayeh, A, Green, A, Khalifa, H and Shaw, S (2006) *Defining the construct(s) underpinning the Cambridge ESOL UMS tests: a socio-cognitive perspective on overall language proficiency and the four language skills,* Cambridge ESOL internal report.

Templin, M C (1957) *Certain Language Skills in Children,* Minneapolis: University of Minnesota Press.

Thighe, D (2006) Placing the International Legal English Certificate on the CEFR, *Research Notes* 24, 5–7.

Thorndike, E L (1904) *An Introduction to the Theory of Mental and Social Measurements,* New York: The Science Press.

Thorndike, E L (1911) A scale for measuring the merit of English writing, *Science* 33, 935–938.

Thorndike, E L (1912) *Education: A First Book,* New York: Macmillan.

Thorndike, E L (1914) The measurement of ability in reading, *Teachers College Record* 15, 207–227.

Thorndike, E L (1917a) Reading as reasoning: A study of mistakes in paragraph reading, *Journal of Educational Psychology* 8, 323–332.

Thorndike, E L (1917b) The psychology of thinking in the case of reading, *Psychological Review* 24, 220–234.

Tickoo, M L (1964) Structural approach in India: Fact, fiction or fallacy, *English Language Teaching Journal* 18 (4), 178–180.

Tinajero, A (2010) *El Lector: A History of the Cigar Factory Reader*, TX: University of Texas Press.

Travis, J E (1947) The use of the film in language teaching and learning, *English Language Teaching Journal* 1 (6), 145–149.

Trim, J (1970) Definition of language contents on modern language courses at the university level – introduction to discussion, and appendix, Skepparholmen Symposium, *CC/ESR/LV*, 71 (19), Strasbourg: Council of Europe.

Trim, J (1980) *Developing a Unit/credit Scheme of Adult Language Learning*, Oxford: Pergamon.

Trimbur, J (2008) The Dartmouth Conference and the geohistory of the native speaker, *College English* 71 (2), 142–169.

Trueswell, J C, Tanenhaus, M K and Kello, C (1993) Verb-specific constraints in sentence processing: Separating effects of lexical preference from garden-paths, *Journal of Experimental Psychology: Learning, Memory and Cognition* 19 (3), 528–553.

Underhill, N (1994) *Testing Spoken Language: A Handbook of Oral Testing Techniques*, Cambridge: Cambridge University Press.

Underwood, M (1971) *Listen to This!* Oxford: Oxford University Press.

Underwood, M (1976) *What a Story!* Oxford: Oxford University Press.

Underwood, M (1989) *Teaching Listening*, London: Longman.

Upshur, J A and Turner, C E (1995) Constructing rating scales for second language tests, *English Language Teaching Journal* 49 (1), 3–12.

Ur, P (1984) *Teaching Listening Comprehension*, Cambridge: Cambridge University Press.

Urquhart, A (1984) The effect of rhetorical ordering on readability, in Alderson, J C and Urquhart, A (Eds) *Reading in a Foreign Language*, London: Longman, 160–181.

Urquhart, A and Weir, C J (1998) *Reading in a Second Language: Process, Product and Practice*, Harlow: Pearson Education Ltd.

Valentine C W and Emmett, W G (1932) *The Reliability of Examinations*, London: University of London Press.

Van Dijk, T A (1977) *Text and Context. Explorations in the Semantics and Pragmatics of Discourse*, London: Longman.

Van Dijk, T A and Kintsch, W (1983) The notion of macrostructure, in Van Dijk, T A and Kintsch, W *Strategies of Discourse Comprehension*, New York: Academic Press, 189–223.

Van Ek, J (1975) *Systems development in adult language learning: the Threshold Level; with an appendix by L Alexander*, Strasbourg: Council of Europe.

Van Ek, J and Trim, J L (1998a) *Threshold 1990*, Cambridge: Cambridge University Press.

Van Ek, J and Trim, J L (1998b) *Waystage 1990*, Cambridge: Cambridge University Press.

Van Ek, J and Trim, J L (2001) *Vantage*, Cambridge: Cambridge University Press.

van Lier, L (1989) Reeling, writhing, drawling, stretching and fainting in coils: Oral proficiency interviews as conversations, *TESOL Quarterly* 23, 480–508.

Van Moere, A (2006) Validity evidence in a university group oral test, *Language Testing* 23 (4), 411–440.

Van Moere, A (2012) A psycholinguistic approach to oral language assessment, *Language Testing* 29 (3), 325–344.

Van Moere, A and Kobayashi, M (2004) *Group oral testing: Does amount of output affect scores?*, paper presented at the Language Testing Forum.

Venezky, R L (1984) The history of reading research, in Pearson, P D (Ed.) *Handbook of Reading Research*, New York: Longman, 3–38.

Venezky, R L (1996) The development of literacy in the industrialized nations of the west, in Barr, R, Kamil, R M L, Mosenthal, P B and Pearson, P D (Eds), *Handbook of Reading Research*, volume 2, New Jersey: Lawrence Erlbaum, 46–67.

Vernon, M D (1931) *The Experimental Study of Reading*, Cambridge: Cambridge University Press.

Vernon, P E and Milligan, G D (1954) A further study of the reliability of English essays, *British Journal of Statistical Psychology* 7 (2), 65–74.

Viëtor, W (1882) *Der Sprachunterricht muss umkehren! Ein Beitrag zur Überbürdungsfrage. ["Language teaching must turn round! A Contribution to the Overloading Question"]*, Heilbronn: Henninger.

Vollmer, H J (1979) Why aren't we interested in general language proficiency?, in Klein-Braley, C and Stevenson, K D (Eds) *Practical and Problems in Language Testing*, Duisburg: Verlag Peter D. Lang, 96–123.

Vollmer, H J (1981) Why aren't we interested in general language proficiency?, in Alderson, J C and Hughes, A (Eds) *Issues in language testing, ELT Documents 111*, London: The British Council, 152–174.

Wagner, E (2010) The effect of the use of video texts on ESL listening test-taker performance, *Language Testing* 27 (4), 493–513.

Wagner, M (2006) *Utilizing the Visual Channel: An Investigation of the Ise of Videotexts on Tests of Second Language Listening Ability*, unpublished PhD thesis, Teachers College: Columbia University.

Wainer, H, Dorans, N, Eignor, D, Flaugher, R, Green, B, Mislevy, R, Steinberg, L and Thissen, D (2000) *Computer adaptive testing: A primer*, Mahwah, NJ: Erlbaum.

Wall, D (1997) Test impact and washback, in Clapham, C and Corson, P (Eds) *Encyclopaedia of Language Education*, Language Testing and Assessment Volume 7, Dordrecht: Kluwer, 291–302.

Wall, D and Alderson, J C (1993) Examining washback: the Sri Lankan impact study, *Language Testing* 10 (1) 41–69.

Wallace, M (1980) *English for Academic Study Series: Study Skills for Academic Writing*, London: Prentice Hall.

Watts, A (2008a) Cambridge Local Examinations 1858–1945, in Raban, S (Ed.) *Examining the World: A History of the University of Cambridge Local Examinations Syndicate*, 36–71.

Watts, A (2008b) Independent examination boards and the start of a national assessment system. Cambridge Assessment Network, *Research Matters* 5, 2–6.

Weedon, A (2003) *Victorian Publishing: The Economics of Book Publishing for a Mass Market 1836–1916*, Ashgate.

Weigle, S C (1998) Using FACETS to model rater training effects, *Language Testing* 15 (2), 264–288.

Weigle, S C (2002) *Assessing Writing*, Cambridge: Cambridge University Press.

Weigle, S C (2004) Integrating reading and writing in a competency test for non-native speakers of English, *Assessing Writing* 9, 27–55.

Weigle, S C (2010) Validation of automated scores of TOEFL ibt tasks against non-test indicators of writing ability, *Language Testing* 27 (3), 335–353.

Weir, C J (1983) *Identifying the language problems of the overseas students in tertiary education in the United Kingdom.* unpublished PhD thesis, University of London.

Weir, C J (1988) *Communicative Language Testing with Special Reference to English as a Foreign Language*, Exeter: A. Wheaton & Co. Ltd.

Weir, C J (1990) *Communicative Language Testing*, Englewood Cliffs, NJ: Prentice Hall.

Weir, C J (1993) *Understanding and Developing Language Tests*, London: Prentice Hall.

Weir, C J (2003) A survey of the history of the Certificate of Proficiency, in English (CPE) in the twentieth century, in Weir, C J andMilanovic, M (Eds) *Continuity and Innovation: The History of the CPE 1913–2002*, Studies in Language Testing volume 15, Cambridge: Cambridge University Press, 1–56.

Weir, C J (2005a) *Language Testing and Validation: An Evidence-Based Approach*, Basingstoke: Palgrave Macmillan.

Weir, C J (2005b) Limitations of the Council of Europe's Framework of Reference (CEFR) in developing comparable examinations and tests, *Language Testing* 22 (3), 281–300.

Weir C J, Bax. S, Chan S, Field J, Green A and Taylor, L (2012) unpublished Project Report for Cambridge ESOL UK on the contextual parameters of CAE Examinations.

Weir, C J, Hawkey, R, Green, A and Devi, S (2009) The cognitive processes underlying the academic reading construct as measured by IELTS, in Thompson, P (Ed.) *Research Reports Volume 9*, British Council/IDP Australia, 157–189.

Weir, C J, Hawkey, R, Green, A Unaldi, A and Devi, S (2009) The relationship between the academic reading construct as measured by IELTS and the reading experiences of students in their first year of study at a British University, in Thompson, P (Ed.) *Research Reports Volume 9*, British Council/ IDP Australia, 97–156.

Weir, C J and Milanovic, M (2003) *Continuity and innovation: A History of the CPE examination 1913–2002*, Studies in Language Testing volume 15, Cambridge: UCLES/Cambridge University Press.

Weir, C J and O'Sullivan (2011) Language testing = validation, in O'Sullivan, B (Ed.) *Language Testing: Theories and Practices*, Basingstoke: Palgrave, 13–32.

Weir, C J and Wu, J R W (2006) Establishing test form and individual task comparability: a case study of a semi-direct speaking test, *Language Testing* 23 (2), 167–197.

Weir, C J, Yang, H and Jin, Y (2000) *An Empirical Investigation of the Componentiality of L2 Reading in English for Academic Purposes*, Studies in Language Testing volume 12, Cambridge: UCLES/Cambridge University Press.

West, M (1926a) *Bilingualism (with special reference to Bengal)*, Calcutta: Government of India.

West, M (1926b) *Learning to Read a Foreign Language: An Experimental Study*, New York: Longmans, Green.

West, M (1932) *Language in Education*, London: Longmans, Green.

West, M (1953) *A General Service List of English Words*, London: Longmans, Green.

White, E M (1995) An apologia for the timed impromptu essay test, *College Composition and Communication* 46 (1), 30–45.

White, G (1998) *Listening*, Cambridge: Cambridge University Press.

White, R and Arndt, V (1991) *Process Writing*, London: Longman.

Wicker, C D (1984) Processing resources in attention, in Parasuraman, R and Davies, D R (Eds) *Varieties of Attention*, Orlando, FL: Academic Press.

Widdowson, H G (1968) The teaching of English through science, in Dakin, J, Tuffen, B and Widdowson, H G, *Language In Education: The Problem In Commonwealth Africa And The Indo-Pakistan Sub-Continent*, London: Oxford University Press, 115–175.

Widdowson, H G (1972) The Teaching of English as Communication, *English Language Teaching Journal* 27 (1), 15–19.

Widdowson, H G (1978) *Teaching Language as Communication*, Oxford: Oxford University Press.

Widdowson, H G (1983) *Language Purpose and Language Use*, Oxford: Oxford University Press.

Widdowson, H G (2003) *Defining Issues in English Language Teaching*, Oxford: Oxford University Press.

Wigglesworth, G (1997) An investigation of planning time and proficiency level on oral test discourse, *Language Testing* 14, 85–106.

Wigglesworth, G (2000) Issues in the development of oral tasks for competency-based assessments of second language performance, in Brindley, G (Ed.) *Studies in Immigrant English Language Assessment*, Macquarie University, Sydney: National Centre for English Language Teaching and Research.

Wigglesworth, G and O'Loughlin, K (1993) An investigation into the comparability of direct and semi-direct versions of an oral interaction test in English, *Melbourne Papers in Language Testing* 2, 56–67.

Wilkins, D A (1973a) *Grammatical, situational and notional syllabuses*, ELT *Documents* 6.

Wilkins, D A (1973b) An investigation into the linguistics and situational common core in unit/credit system, in Trim, J L M, Richterich, R, van Ek, J A and Wilkins, D A (Eds) *Systems Development in Adult Language Learning*, Strasbourg: Council of Europe, 129–145.

Wilkins, D A (1976) *Notional Syllabuses*, London: Oxford University Press.

Williams, R (1961) *The Long Revolution*, London: Chatto and Windus.

Wilmott, A S and Nuttal, D L (1975) *The Reliability of Examinations at 16+*, London: Macmillan.

Wiseman, S (1949) The marking of English composition in grammar school selection, *British Journal of Education Psychology* 19 (3), 200–209.

Wiseman, S and Wrigley, J (1959) *Manchester Reading Comprehension Test (senior)* 1, London: University of London Press.

Wolfe-Quintero, K, Inagaki, S and Kim, H-Y (1998) *Second Language Development in Writing: Measures of Fluency, Accuracy, and Complexity*, Honolulu, HI: University of Hawaii Press.

Wolfson, N (1989) *Perspectives: Sociolinguistics and TESOL*, Boston, MA: Heinle & Heinle.

Wood, B D (1927) *New York Experiments with New-type Modern Language Tests*, New York: Macmillan.

Wood, R and Quinn, B (1976) Double impression marking of English language essay and summary questions, *Educational Review* 28 (3), 229–245.

Wood, R and Wilson, D (1974) Evidence for differential marking discrimination among examiners of English, *The Irish Journal of Education* 8 (1), 36–48.

Wright, B D and Stone, M H (1979) *Best Test Design*, Chicago: MESA Press.

Wu, R Y F (2011) *Establishing the validity of the General English Proficiency Test Reading Component through a critical evaluation on alignment with the Common European Framework of Reference*, unpublished PhD thesis, University of Bedfordshire.

Wu, Y (1998) What do tests of listening comprehension test? – A retrospection study of EFL test-takers performing a multiple-choice task, *Language Testing* 15 (1), 21–44.

Wyatt, T S (1956) *University of Cambridge Local Examinations Syndicate Report on Mr Wyatt's Visit to Examination Centres in France*, UCLES internal report.

Wyatt, T S (1966) *Report by the Secretary on his visit to New York and Princeton, USA, October/November 1966*, UCLES internal report.

Wyatt, T S and Hudson (1951) *Examinations in English*, UCLES internal report.

Wyatt, T S and Roach, J O (1947) The examinations in English of the Cambridge University Local Syndicate, *ELT Journal* 1 (5), 125–130.

Xi, X (2010) Automated scoring and feedback systems: Where are we and where are we heading?, *Language Testing* 27 (3), 291–300.

Yamashita, J (1999) *Reading in a first and a foreign language: a study of reading comprehension in Japanese (the L1) and English (the L2)*, unpublished PhD thesis, Lancaster University.

Yancey, K B (1999) Looking back as we look forward: historicizing writing assessment, *College Composition and Communication* 50 (3), 483–503.

Young, R and Halleck, G B (1998) 'Let them eat cake!': Or how to avoid losing your head in cross-cultural conversations, in Young, R and He, A (Eds) *Talking and testing: Discourse approaches to the assessment of oral proficiency*, Amsterdam/Philadelphia: John Benjamins, 359–388.

Young, R and Milanovic, M (1992) Discourse variation in oral proficiency interviews, *Studies in Second Language Acquisition* 14, 403–424.

Yu, G (2008) Reading to summarize in English and Chinese: A tale of two languages? *Language Testing* 25 (4), 521–551.

Yuill, N and Oakhill, J (1991) *Children's Problems in Text Comprehension*, Cambridge: Cambridge University Press.

Zamel, V (1983) The composing processes of advanced ESL students: Six case studies, *TESOL Quarterly* 17 (2), 165–187.

Zhou, S, Weir, C J and Green, R (1998) *The Test for English Majors Validation Project*, Shanghai: Foreign Language Education Press.

From Cambridge Assessment Archives

The following official UCLES/Cambridge ESOL documents were consulted in the writing of this book (in the alphabetical order):

Annual Reports

UCLES (1859) *Annual Report.*
UCLES (1913) *Annual Report.*
UCLES (1914) *Annual Report.*
UCLES (1915) *Annual Report.*
UCLES (1921) *Annual Report.*
UCLES (1923) *Annual Report.*
UCLES (1924) *Annual Report.*

UCLES (1925) *Annual Report.*
UCLES (1926) *Annual Report.*
UCLES (1927) *Annual Report.*
UCLES (1994) *Annual Report.*
UCLES (1957) *Annual Report.*

Exam-related Committee Minutes

English Examinations – Research and Development Sub-Committee Minutes October 1958.

Executive Committee for the Syndicate's Examinations in English for foreign students: Draft minutes from: November 1957, October 1960, October 1961, May 1965, October 1965, October 1963, October 1967, 1968, October 1970, October 1971, May, November 1972, May 1973, October, November, 1975, May, November 1978, November 1979, November 1980, May 1981, November 1981, October 1984, May 1986, November 1986, May 1987, May 1988.

Joint Committee of the Cambridge Local Examinations Syndicate and the British Council: Draft minutes from: October, December 1941, June 1944, November 1945, 1947, July, November 1950, July 1951, May 1952, July 1958, June 1959, 1960, 1961, 1962, July 1964, 1967, July 1968, July, November 1971, 1972, June 1974, 1977, 1978, 1980, December 1985, July 1989.

Report on the "Cambridge Workshop" held at the British Institute, Madrid on 22 and 23 October 1975 (for the meeting of the Executive Committee 29 October 1975).

UCLES (1944) *26 October 1944. For Agendum 10.*

Exam Handbooks

Certificate in Advanced English (CAE): Handbook for Teachers 1991, 1995, 1998, 2001a, 2001b, 2005a, 2005b, 2007a, 2008.

Certificate of Proficiency in English (CPE): 1938, 1949, 1975, 1977, 1995, 1998, 2003, 2008.

English as a Foreign Language: General Handbook: 1987.

First Certificate in English (FCE): 1975, 1976, 2001.

First Certificate in English (FCE): Handbook for Teachers 1994 (up to June 1966 included), 1995, 1996, 2001, 2003a, 2003b, 2007.

Key English Test (KET): Handbook for Teachers 1994, 2004, 2009.

Preliminary English Test: Handbook for Teachers 1984, 2009.

Exam Papers

Cambridge Locals: Dec 1858.

Certificate of Advanced English (CAE): 1991.

Certificate of Advanced English (CAE): Oral Examiners' Materials for CAE 1991, 1999.

Certificate of Proficiency in English (CPE): June 1913, 1914, 1924, 1925, 1926, 1927, 1931, July, December, 1936, March, July, 1938, 1939, 1940, 1942, July, December 1945, June 1949, 1953, June 1955, June, 1966, 1975, 1976 March, June 1975, June 1977, 2002, June 2005.

Certificate of Proficiency in English (CPE): (1986): Examiners' Materials for CPE Interview.

Certificate of Proficiency in English (CPE) sample paper.

Fifty Reading Passages 1944.

First Certificate in English (FCE): June 1975, June 1976, December 1977, 1984, 1990, 1993, 1996.

First Certificate in English (FCE): (1985) Examiners' Materials for FCE Interview.

Lower Certificate in English (LCE): June 1939, June 1945. *Preliminary Test in English* 1945, Listening Comprehension question paper December 1972 (with Oral Examiners' Materials).

Exam Regulations

UCLES (1923) *Regulations*, University of Cambridge Local Examinations Syndicate.

UCLES (1927) *Examination for the Certificate of Proficiency in English July, 1927*, University of Cambridge Local Examinations Syndicate.

UCLES (1932) *Regulations*, University of Cambridge Local Examinations Syndicate.

UCLES (1933) *Examination for the Certificate of Proficiency in English July, 1933*, University of Cambridge Local Examinations Syndicate.

UCLES (1933) *Regulations*, University of Cambridge Local Examinations Syndicate.

UCLES (1939) *Regulations*, University of Cambridge Local Examinations Syndicate.

UCLES (1947) *Regulations*, University of Cambridge Local Examinations Syndicate.

UCLES (1951) *Regulations for the Certificate of Proficiency in English and Lower Certificate in English 1951*, University of Cambridge Local Examinations Syndicate.

UCLES (1956) *Regulations*, University of Cambridge Local Examinations Syndicate.

UCLES (1969) *Regulations for the Certificate of Proficiency in English and Lower Certificate in English 1969*, University of Cambridge Local Examinations Syndicate.

UCLES (1974) *Regulations for the Certificate of Proficiency in English and Lower Certificate in English*, University of Cambridge Local Examinations Syndicate.

UCLES (1975) *Examinations in English for Foreign Students: Regulations for 1975*, University of Cambridge Local Examinations Syndicate.

UCLES (1982) *Cambridge Examinations in English: Changes of Syllabus in 1984*, University of Cambridge Local Examinations Syndicate.

UCLES (1983) *Amendment to the Regulations*, University of Cambridge Local Examinations Syndicate.

UCLES (1984) *Examinations in English as a Foreign Language: Regulations for 1984*, University of Cambridge Local Examinations Syndicate.

UCLES (1986) *Examinations in English as a Foreign Language, Amendment to the Regulations for 1986*, University of Cambridge Local Examinations Syndicate.

UCLES (1987) *Examinations in English as a Foreign Language: Regulations for 1987*, University of Cambridge Local Examinations Syndicate.

Measured Constructs

Exam Reports

UCLES (1938) *Regulations for the Lower Certificate in English*, University of Cambridge Local Examinations Syndicate..

UCLES (1945) *Headings for Reports on Oral Examinations*, University of Cambridge Local Examinations Syndicate.

UCLES (1954) *Extracts from the reports of Chief Examiners*, University of Cambridge Local Examinations Syndicate.

UCLES (1957) *Report on the Work of Candidates in the English Language paper*, University of Cambridge Local Examinations Syndicate.

UCLES (1958) *CPE Examination Report June*, University of Cambridge Local Examinations Syndicate.

UCLES (1961) *LCE Examination Report June*, University of Cambridge Local Examinations Syndicate.

UCLES (1969) *General Report on the work of candidates in the English Language Paper*, University of Cambridge Local Examinations Syndicate.

UCLES (1975) *CPE Examination Report June and December*, University of Cambridge Local Examinations Syndicate.

UCLES (1979) *CPE Examination Report*, University of Cambridge Local Examinations Syndicate.

UCLES (1979b) *Examiners Report*, University of Cambridge Local Examinations Syndicate.

UCLES (1991) *Cambridge Assessment of Spoken English CASE: CASE Report*, internal UCLES report.

UCLES (2003b) *FCE Examination Report December*, University of Cambridge Local Examinations Syndicate.

UCLES (2003c) *CPE Examination Report December*, University of Cambridge Local Examinations Syndicate.

Exam Surveys

Joint Committee of the Local Examinations Syndicate and the British Council (1942) *Cambridge Examinations in English for Foreign Students: Survey for 1941*, Cambridge: University of Cambridge Local Examinations Syndicate.

Joint Committee of the Local Examinations Syndicate and the British Council (1943) *Cambridge Examinations in English for Foreign Students: Survey for 1942*, University of Cambridge Local Examinations Syndicate.

Joint Committee of the Local Examinations Syndicate and the British Council (1945) *Cambridge Examinations in English for Foreign Students: Survey for 1944*, Cambridge: University of Cambridge Local Examinations Syndicate.

Joint Committee of the Local Examinations Syndicate and the British Council (1946) *Cambridge Examinations in English for Foreign Students: Survey for 1945*, Cambridge: University of Cambridge Local Examinations Syndicate.

Joint Committee of the Local Examinations Syndicate and the British Council (1952) *Cambridge Examinations in English for Foreign Students: Survey for 1951*, Cambridge: University of Cambridge Local Examinations Syndicate.

Joint Committee of the Local Examinations Syndicate and the British Council (1972) *Cambridge Examinations in English for Foreign Students: Survey for 1971*, Cambridge: University of Cambridge Local Examinations Syndicate.

Joint Committee of the Local Examinations Syndicate and the British Council (1973) *Cambridge Examinations in English for Foreign Students: Survey for 1972*, Cambridge: University of Cambridge Local Examinations Syndicate.

Exam Syllabuses (specifications and sample papers)

UCLES (1973) *Cambridge Examinations in English: Changes of Syllabus in 1975*, University of Cambridge Local Examinations Syndicate.
UCLES (1975) *The Cambridge Examinations in English: Changes of Syllabus in 1975*, University of Cambridge Local Examinations Syndicate.
UCLES (1982) *Cambridge Examinations in English: Changes of Syllabus in 1984*, University of Cambridge Local Examinations Syndicate.
UCLES (1982a) *Changes of Syllabus booklet*, University of Cambridge Local Examinations Syndicate.
UCLES (1982b) *FCE information booklet*, University of Cambridge Local Examinations Syndicate.
UCLES (1985) *FCE Sample Material*, University of Cambridge Local Examinations Syndicate.
UCLES (1989) *Specifications*, University of Cambridge Local Examinations Syndicate.
UCLES (1991) *Certificate in Advanced English (CAE) Specifications*, University of Cambridge Local Examinations Syndicate.
UCLES (1994) *CPE Revision Specifications*, University of Cambridge Local Examinations Syndicate.
UCLES (1994) *FCE: Specifications for the Revised Examination for the December 1996 and subsequent examinations*, University of Cambridge Local Examinations Syndicate.
UCLES (1994) *Revised FCE internal specifications November 1994*, University of Cambridge Local Examinations Syndicate.
UCLES (1995) *FCE: Specifications and Sample Papers for the Revised FCE Examination*, University of Cambridge Local Examinations Syndicate.
UCLES (1996) *FCE Specifications*, University of Cambridge Local Examinations Syndicate.
UCLES (2007) *Reviewing FCE and CAE, Bulletin 9*, University of Cambridge Local Examinations Syndicate.
UCLES (2008) *CAE sample paper*, University of Cambridge Local Examinations Syndicate.

Instructions to Oral Examiners

UCLES (1945) *Cambridge Examinations in English for Foreign Students: Instructions to Oral Examiners, 1945*, University of Cambridge Local Examinations Syndicate.
UCLES (1947, 1958, 1963, 1970, 1971) *Certificate of Proficiency and Lower Certificate in English: Instructions to Oral Examiners*, University of Cambridge Local Examinations Syndicate.
UCLES (1958) *Instructions to Oral Examiners*, University of Cambridge Local Examinations Syndicate.
UCLES (1958) *Oral Examinations in English Standards Sheet*, University of Cambridge Local Examinations Syndicate.

UCLES (1963) *Certificate of Proficiency and Lower Certificate in English: Instructions to Oral Examiners*, University of Cambridge Local Examinations Syndicate.

UCLES (1970) *Certificate of Proficiency and Lower Certificate in English: Instructions to Oral Examiners*, University of Cambridge Local Examinations Syndicate.

UCLES (1971) *Certificate of Proficiency and Lower Certificate in English: Instructions to Oral Examiners*, University of Cambridge Local Examinations Syndicate.

UCLES (1975) *First Certificate and Certificate of Proficiency in English: Instructions to Oral Examiners*, University of Cambridge Local Examinations Syndicate.

UCLES (1976, 1984, 1986, 1995) *First Certificate and Certificate of Proficiency in English: Instructions to Oral Examiners*, University of Cambridge Local Examinations Syndicate.

UCLES (1992) *Proposed TLC Scheme for Overseas Centres FCE/CPE/CAE/PET*, University of Cambridge Local Examinations Syndicate.

UCLES (1993–1994) *Certificate of Advanced English: Instructions to Oral Examiners*, University of Cambridge Local Examinations Syndicate.

UCLES (1999) *FCE, CAE and CPE Instructions to Oral Examiners*, University of Cambridge Local Examinations Syndicate.

UCLES (2003) *Minimum Professional Requirements for ESOL Speaking Tests*, University of Cambridge Local Examinations Syndicate.

UCLES (2004/05) *Guidelines for Oral Examiner Training*, University of Cambridge Local Examinations Syndicate.

UCLES (2008) *Instructions to Oral Examiners (for ICFE)*, University of Cambridge Local Examinations Syndicate.

1944/5 CPE and LCE Gramophone recordings

M-GR-1, M-GR-2, M-GR-4

Author index

Subject index

Measured Constructs